Value Added Tax

This book integrates legal, economic, and administrative materials about value added tax. Its principal purpose is to provide comprehensive teaching tools – laws, cases, analytical exercises, and questions drawn from the experience of countries and organizations around the world. It also serves as a resource for tax practitioners and government officials that must grapple with issues under their VAT or their prospective VAT. The comparative presentation of this volume offers an analysis of policy issues relating to tax structure and tax base as well as insights into how cases arising out of VAT disputes have been resolved. In the new edition, the authors have expanded the coverage to include new VAT-related developments in Europe, Asia, Africa, and Australia. A new chapter on financial services has been added as well as an analysis of significant new cases.

Alan Schenk teaches VAT at Wayne State University and has taught VAT at other universities such as Harvard University, the University of Michigan, and the University of San Diego. For the past eight years, Professor Schenk has served as Technical Advisor for the International Monetary Fund, drafting and reviewing legislative proposals for sales and value added tax for several countries in Africa and for emerging economies of Eastern Europe. He is the author of four books and has published many articles on VAT including several involving the taxation of financial services.

Oliver Oldman is Learned Hand Professor of Law, Emeritus, at the Harvard Law School. For twenty-five years until July 1989, he was the Director of the School's International Tax Program. He has been a member of the Law School Faculty since 1955 when he began directing the Tax Program's training activities and was appointed Professor of Law in 1961. He began teaching about value added taxes in his Comparative Tax Policy course in the 1960s and offered his first separate course on the value added tax in 1979. He has taught the course continuously at Harvard Law School since then. Professor Schenk has been a frequent guest lecturer.

Value Added Tax

A COMPARATIVE APPROACH

Alan Schenk
Wayne State University

Oliver Oldman
Harvard Law School

CAMBRIDGE
UNIVERSITY PRESS

CAMBRIDGE UNIVERSITY PRESS
Cambridge, New York, Melbourne, Madrid, Cape Town, Singapore, São Paulo

Cambridge University Press
32 Avenue of the Americas, New York, NY 10013-2473, USA

www.cambridge.org
Information on this title: www.cambridge.org/9780521851121

First published 2007

Printed in the United States of America

A catalog record for this publication is available from the British Library.

Library of Congress Cataloging in Publication Data

Schenk, Alan.
Value added tax : a comparative approach / Alan Schenk, Oliver Oldman. – [Rev. ed.].
   p.   cm.
Includes bibliographical references and index.
ISBN-13: 978-0-521-85112-1 (hardback)
ISBN-10: 0-521-85112-2 (hardback)
ISBN-13: 978-0-521-61656-0 (pbk.)
ISBN-10: 0-521-61656-5 (pbk.)
1. Value-added tax – Law and legislation.   2. Spending tax – Law and legislation.   3.
Taxation of articles of consumption – Law and legislation.   I. Oldman, Oliver.   II. Title.
K4573.S337   2006
343.05′5 – dc22   2006008216

ISBN-13   978-0-521-85112-1 hardback
ISBN-10   0-521-85112-2 hardback

ISBN-13   978-0-521-61656-0 paperback
ISBN-10   0-521-61656-5 paperback

To
Jared, Ethan, Daniel, Jordan & Rae
AS

Sumi & Robyn
OO

Contents

List of Tables, Figures, and Charts

List of Cases

Cases listed by name of the taxpayer or, for action by the European Commission, the country. Highlighted cases are main textual cases.

Preface to the Revised Edition

Thanks to our students at Wayne State, Harvard, and Michigan law schools for their contributions to the revision of this book. Thanks to Dean Frank Wu and Wayne State University Law School, and to Georgia Clark, Director of the Wayne Law Library, and her staff for the support that made this revision possible. Thanks to our colleague Richard Ainsworth and the two anonymous readers who made helpful suggestions on how we could improve our first attempt at comparative value added tax. Thanks to Karen Kissinger for her very helpful research assistance. Thanks to our faculty assistants, Olive Hyman and Lise Berg, for their assistance with various aspects of the manuscript. Thanks to John Berger, our editor at Cambridge University Press, and Peggy Rote, Laura Lawrie, and Dianne Scent for their help in the process of converting our manuscript to final text.

The cutoff date for this book generally was March 31, 2006, although we have included some material published after that date. In particular, we included some European Court of Justice cases, including those covering the Italian subnational tax (IRAP) and some VAT-abusive transactions. This book is not intended to be exhaustive. It therefore does not include all significant cases in all countries or even all English-speaking countries. It is designed to illustrate, analyze, and explain the principal theoretical and operating features of value added taxes, including their adoption and implementation.

The European Union is in the process of revising its Sixth Directive that includes the principles that all member countries must adopt as part of their value added taxes. The Recast of the Sixth Directive, to enter into force, must be adopted by the EU Council of Ministers by unanimity. That action was not taken by this date. In some parts of the book, we included references not only to the Sixth Directive in its present form but also to the Recast.

Alan Schenk, Detroit, Michigan
Oliver Oldman, Cambridge, Massachusetts
June 1, 2006

Value Added Tax

1

Survey of Taxes on Consumption and Income, and Introduction to Value Added Tax

I. INTRODUCTION

The VAT has spread around the world more quickly than any other new tax in modern history.[1] According to Alan Tait, the value added tax "may be thought of as the Mata Hari of the tax world – many are tempted, many succumb, some tremble on the brink, while others leave only to return, eventually the attraction appears irresistible."[2] The extreme of a country that left, only to return, is Japan. It enacted a VAT in 1950, delayed its effective date for several years, repealed it in 1954, and then enacted a different version of VAT in 1988.[3]

This book covers value added tax and, in some parts, other consumption taxes in use or proposed in developing and developed countries. A valuable resource in electronic form that assists in locating tax legislation around the world is http://www.itdweb.com, developed jointly by the International Monetary Fund, the Organization for Economic Co-operation and Development, and the World Bank.

Tax on consumption generally refers to a tax on goods and services that are acquired by individuals for their personal use or satisfaction. It generally does not include goods and services that are physically used or incorporated by business in the production or distribution of goods or in the rendition of services (business inputs).

It is difficult for a business to operate internationally without considering the implications of sales tax or value added tax on international trade, whether or not the company's country of residence has a broad-based tax on consumption. For example, the United States does not have a sales tax or value added tax, except at the state and local levels of government. Nevertheless, a U.S. business operating in or shipping goods or transferring services to developed or developing countries with VATs must consider the VAT implications of exports to or imports from those countries.

---

[1] See Appendix A, listing the countries with VATs and sales taxes.

[2] TAIT, VALUE ADDED TAX: INTERNATIONAL PRACTICE AND PROBLEMS 3 (IMF 1988) [hereinafter Tait, VAT].

[3] See Schenk, Japanese Consumption Tax: The Japanese Brand VAT, 42 *Tax Notes* 1625 (Mar. 27, 1989).

This book explores value added and other consumption tax principles from a comparative perspective in the hope that this scrutiny may lead to suggestions for improving existing VAT systems and designing new ones. We will discuss VAT systems in the member states of the European Union (EU), as well as examine the implications of the EU VAT directives on domestic law in the member states. We will explain major departures from the EU model in non-European countries (especially in New Zealand, Japan, and South Africa), and highlight the wide variety of consumption tax proposals in the United States, ranging from proposals to adopt a federal VAT as an additional revenue source to proposals to replace some or most existing federal taxes with some form of consumption tax. In a later chapter, we will discuss several of these U.S. proposals. None of the U.S. proposals has been subjected to serious congressional debate. Appendix B is a theoretical VAT Act for the Commonwealth of New Vatopia that can be used as a starting point for a country interested in adopting a VAT or revising an existing VAT. It is used in this book as a reference and a source to compare VAT rules in effect in a variety of countries.[4] This chapter provides background for the study of consumption taxation. It discusses direct and indirect taxes, and explores tax structures in developing and developed economies. The impetus for improvement in the taxation of goods and services is highlighted, and the basic concepts and terms used in the VAT literature are detailed.

II. Development of Taxes on Consumption – A Brief Review of History

Most early forms of taxation were levies on land[5] or on the produce from land. The following is only a thumbnail sketch of how the produce of land and goods have been the subject of taxation throughout recorded history. The tax on land in early civilizations was payable in kind with the produce from the land.[6] The tithe in Egyptian kingdoms was imposed as a proportion of agricultural produce.[7] In the days of the city-states of Athens and Rome, although there were taxes in the form of rents from state-owned land (including taxes on natural resources extracted from these lands), the rulers supplemented revenue from land with indirect taxes.[8] Customs duties were imposed at the ports and taxes were extracted at the markets for goods that arrived by land.[9] In the third century A.D., Diocletion imposed fees (or taxes) from the monopolies that he granted for the production and sales of goods.[10]

---

[4] This VAT is on the IMF website. See www.imf.org/external/np/leg. Go to Tax Law Drafting Samples: VAT.

[5] Land, as a representation of wealth, was a favorite subject of taxation because it was visible and the tax was collectible.

[6] C. Webber & A. Wildavsky, A History of Taxation and Expenditure in the Western World 44 (Simon & Schuster 1986). In the early civilizations of the Sumer city-states, tax payable in grain was transported to the ruler's storehouses. *Id.* at 43.

[7] *Id.* at 71.

[8] *Id.* at 107.

[9] *Id.*

[10] *Id.* at 112.

During the late thirteenth century, England imposed taxes on its wool exported by the Italian merchants who were granted the monopoly on this export. This "Ancient Custom," as it was known, later was expanded to cover all exports of goods from England.[11] In the late Middle Ages, in Italy and elsewhere, goods produced by artisans were taxed by taxing the guilds. The guilds raised the needed funds by taxing their members.[12]

The taxation of goods changed as firms were organized to produce goods and sell them through distributors to retailers. It became common, especially in Europe, to impose tax on business turnover (gross receipts). Thus, a cascading turnover tax was imposed every time that goods were transferred in the process of production and distribution to the final consumer. "Cascading taxes cannot be reclaimed by the purchaser, so that the tax component of the price of goods becomes larger and larger the more stages there are between producer and consumer – with obvious distortionary effects as between highly integrated enterprises and other enterprises."[13] For example, assume that a lumber mill sold lumber to a carpenter for a pretax price of $1,000. With a 1 percent turnover tax, the mill added $10 tax and charged a tax-inclusive price of $1,010. The carpenter fashioned the lumber into tables and sold the tables to a retailer. To its $5,010 pre-turnover-tax price (including the $10 tax on the lumber), the carpenter added $50 tax, for a tax-inclusive price of $5,060 (the numbers are rounded to dollars). The retailer sold the tables to consumers for a pretax price of $10,060. The retailer added $101 tax, for a tax-inclusive price of $10,161. The government collected total tax of $161 (10 + 50 + 101).

To take an extreme comparison, assume that the carpenter operated his own mill and sold his crafted tables directly to consumers. If there were no turnover tax on the mill's purchase of trees, and if the carpenter sold the tables to consumers for pretax prices of $10,000 (because he would not bear the $60 tax imposed by the multiple turnovers), the carpenter would add turnover tax of $100, for tax-inclusive prices totaling $10,100. This comparison made in Table 1.1 illustrates some of the deficiencies of the turnover tax – the cascading of taxes and the incentive to integrate a business vertically.

Businesses must pay turnover tax on all purchases, that is, on all business inputs. At each subsequent turnover of goods (i.e., sale), the taxes previously paid and the values previously taxed are again subjected to tax in a process often referred to as pyramiding or cascading, or just as "tax-on-a-tax." In the example just described, the carpenter charges $50 tax on his $5,010 sales price that includes the $10 tax buried in his $1,010 cost for the milled lumber (or, to put it differently, he collects a total of $60 of tax from the retailer, of which the $50 tax charged on the sale is paid to the government and $10 buried in the pre-tax $5,010 price is paid to his lumber supplier).

As indicated, the cascading tax element in retail sales is reduced if the carpenter vertically integrates his operations. The classic example of a vertically

---

[11] *Id.* at 197.

[12] *Id.* at 149.

[13] See Owens, *The Move to VAT*, 1996/2 Intertax [hereinafter Owens, The Move to VAT], p. 45.

Table 1.1. Turnover tax nonintegrated and vertically integrated business

	Nonintegrated	Vertically integrated
Mill sale to carpenter $1,000 × 1%	$10	
Carpenter sale to retailer $5,010 × 1%	50	
Retailer sale to consumers $10,060 × 1%	<u>101</u>	
Carpenter sales directly to consumers $10,000 × 1%		<u>$100</u>
Total tax imposed & collected	$161	$100

integrated American business was the Ford Motor Company's River Rouge complex (in Dearborn, Michigan) that processed the steel and glass and other parts for the cars that were assembled on its assembly line. A more recent example is the Benneton company that operates its own retail shops to sell the apparel that the company manufactures.

In Germany, Dr. Wilhelm von Siemens recognized the problems with turnover taxes and developed what he referred to as the "improved turnover tax" or "the refined turnover tax."[14] Adams discussed a value added concept in the United States in 1921.[15] The principle was to reduce the tax on sales by the tax already paid on business inputs in order to avoid the tax-on-a-tax effect and to remove the incentive to vertically integrate a business. The effect of this "improved" turnover tax for a nonintegrated series of businesses and a vertically integrated business is illustrated in Table 1.2.

This "improved" turnover tax is imposed and collected at each stage of the production and distribution of goods and services whenever there is a transaction, but the net tax liability represents only the tax on the value that has been added by the selling business at that stage. By granting a reduction in tax liability for the tax imposed on taxable purchases (the input tax credit), the tax base at each stage basically is limited to the value added by the employment of labor and capital. The various methods of calculating net VAT liability will be discussed in Chapter 2.

Before the widespread use of multistage VATs, some countries imposed single stage consumption taxes. Single stage taxes at the retail level still are used by almost all states in the United States and by several provinces in Canada (and formerly in Sweden). More commonly, a single stage tax is imposed at the manufacturer's (Canada formerly) or wholesaler's level (Australia before its GST).

---

[14] C. SULLIVAN, THE TAX ON VALUE ADDED, Col. U. Press 1965 [hereinafter Sullivan, Tax on Value Added], p. 12, citing Gerhard Colm, "Methods of Financing Unemployment Compensation," *Social Research*, II (May, 1935), 161.

[15] Sullivan, Tax on Value Added, *supra* note 14, at 41, citing Adams, "Fundamental Problems of Federal Income Taxation," *Quarterly Journal of Economics*, XXV (1921), 553. Adams referred to his proposal as a tax on "approximate net income" or "modified gross income," and recommended it to replace the direct personal income tax. *Id.*

Table 1.2. Improved turnover tax nonintegrated and vertically integrated business

	Nonintegrated	Vertically integrated
Mill sale to carpenter		
Taxable sale of $1,000 × 1%	$10	
Carpenter sale to retailer		
Taxable sale- $5,000[16] × 1%	50	
Credit for tax on purchases	(10)	
Retailer sales to consumers		
Taxable sale- $10,000[17] × 1%	100	
Credit for tax on purchases	(50)	
Carpenter sales directly to consumers		
Taxable sales- $10,000 × 1%		$100
Total tax imposed and collected	$100	$100

III. DIRECT AND INDIRECT TAXES ON AN INCOME OR CONSUMPTION BASE

A. DIRECT AND INDIRECT TAXES

Direct and indirect taxes can be imposed on an income base or consumption base. But what is the distinction between a direct and indirect tax?

Taxes customarily have been classified either as direct or indirect taxes. "A *direct tax* is one that is assessed upon the property, business or income of the individual who is to pay the tax. Conversely *indirect taxes* are taxes that are levied upon commodities before they reach the consumer who ultimately pay[s] the taxes as part of the market price of the commodity."[18] This distinction, based on the incidence of the tax, has been criticized because "modern economic theory" points out that income taxes (considered a direct tax) may be shifted.[19]

According to J. S. Mill's classic economic principles, the distinction between direct and indirect taxes relates to "whether the person who actually pays the money over to the tax collecting authority suffers a corresponding reduction in his income. If he does, then – in the traditional language – impact and incidence are on the same person and the tax is direct; if not and the burden is shifted and the real income of someone else is affected (i.e., impact and incidence are on different people) then the tax is indirect."[20]

---

[16] The price would be $5,000 instead of $5,010 because the carpenter recovers the $10 tax on his taxable purchases.

[17] The sales prices would total $10,000 instead of $10,060 because the retailer would only be charged a pre-tax price of $5,000 and he would recover the $50 tax charged on the purchase of the tables.

[18] *The Guide to American Law*, vol. 10:25 (1984) (defined by Schenk).

[19] See, for example, V. THURONYI, COMPARATIVE TAX LAW, pp. 54–55 (Kluwer 2003).

[20] Walker, "The Direct-Indirect Tax Problem: Fifteen Years of Controversy," 10 *public Finance* 153, 154 (1955), citing J. S. MILL, PRINCIPLES OF POLITICAL ECONOMY, Book V, ch. III.

In the field of international trade, an Annex to the World Trade Organization agreement defines "direct taxes" as "taxes on wages, profits, interests, rents, royalties, and all other forms of income, and taxes on the ownership of real property" and "indirect taxes" as "sales, excise, turnover, value added, franchise, stamp, transfer, inventory and equipment taxes, border taxes and all taxes other than direct taxes and import charges."[21]

The direct versus indirect tax distinction has legal significance in countries subject to the World Trade Organization rules.[22] Under the SCM Agreement,[23] which is Annex 1 to the WTO, a contracting party is restricted in its ability to grant subsidies to exports or to impose more burdensome taxes on imports than apply to domestic goods.[24]

According to the WTO rules, border tax adjustments for indirect taxes do not constitute subsidies of exports or disadvantages to imports.[25] This WTO direct–indirect tax distinction apparently does not depend on who bears

---

[21] Agreement on Subsidies and Countervailing Measures (SCM), Annex I (Illustrative List of Export Subsidies), item (e), footnote 58. The SCM is Annex 1A to the WTO. Item (e) treats as an export subsidy (t)he full or partial exemption, remission, or deferral specifically related to exports, of direct taxes or social welfare charges paid or payable by industrial or commercial enterprises, and footnote 58 to the term "direct taxes" includes the definitions in the text.

[22] This direct–indirect distinction has a special role in Canada. "In Canada, both the federal and provincial governments have the constitutional authority to levy sales taxes." N. Brooks, *The Canadian Goods and Services Tax: History, Policy, and Politics* 141 (Australian Tax Foundation 1993). The federal government has broad power to raise revenue with any mode or system of taxation, but the provincial governments are authorized to impose only direct taxes. Although a sales tax typically is considered an indirect tax, a 1943 Canadian Privy Council case held that a provincial retail sales tax was a direct tax for constitutional purposes. *Id.* at note 304. Professor Brooks quoted from the case: "when the purchase is made by an agent acting for his principal the tax nevertheless remains 'direct,' being paid by the agent for and on behalf of his principal who really bears it." *Atlantic Smoke Shops, Ltd. v. Conlon*, [1943] A.C. 550, at 551.

[23] The Agreement on Subsidies and Countervailing Measures [hereinafter SCM Agreement], supplementing GATT, Articles VI & XVI.

[24] The WTO, incorporating Article XVI of the original 1994 GATT agreement, provides: "(C)ontracting parties shall cease to grant either directly or indirectly any form of subsidy on the export of any product other than a primary product which subsidy results in the sale of such product for export at a price lower than the comparable price charged for the like product to buyers in the domestic market." Uruguay Round of Multilateral Trade Negotiations General Agreement on Tariffs and Trade, Apr. 15, 1994 [World Trade Organization, or WTO], encompasses, among other agreements, the General Agreement on Tariffs and Trade (GATT) 1994,. The quote is from GATT 1994, Ad Art. XVI(4). The Results of the Uruguay Round of Multilateral Trade Negotiations: The Legal Texts (GATT Secretariat 1994) [hereinafter GATT], p. 509. If a contracting party grants or maintains any subsidy to increase exports or reduce imports, it is obligated to notify the other contracting parties "in writing of the extent and nature of the subsidization of the estimated effects . . . and of the circumstances making the subsidization necessary." *Id.* at Art. XVI.

[25] Whereas if "government revenue that is otherwise due is foregone or not collected (e.g. fiscal incentives such as tax credits)" is a subsidy under SCM, *supra* note 23, Article 1.1(a)(1)(ii), a footnote to that item provides that "the exemption of an exported product from duties or taxes borne by the like product when destined for domestic consumption, or the remission of such duties or taxes in amounts not in excess of those which have accrued, shall not be deemed to be a subsidy."

the tax.[26] The prohibition against export subsidies may affect the border adjustability of some of the federal taxes proposed in the United States to replace or supplement the federal income taxes, especially proposals for a sales-subtraction VAT that allows a deduction for wages paid.[27]

In some countries, the imposition of a value added or other tax on consumption raise constitutional issues.[28] For example, the province of Alberta, Canada challenged the constitutionality of the Canadian Goods and Services Tax (GST), a European-style VAT.[29] The Canadian Supreme Court upheld the GST.[30] The Australian High Court struck down a tobacco franchise license fee imposed by a state because Parliament[31] had the exclusive power "to impose duties of customs and of excise, and to grant bounties on the production or export of goods...." In that case, New South Wales imposed this tax on duty-free shops that sold retail tobacco to members of the public.[32] In contrast, the Federal Court of Australia upheld the constitutionality of the Australian GST.[33]

In the Philippines, the Supreme Court upheld against a constitutional attack, congressional changes in the VAT that included the grant of authority to the President to raise the VAT rate under special circumstances.[34] In some cases, the nation's constitution must be amended to give a level of government power to impose a tax previously the province of another level of government.[35]

---

[26] It is not clear if the direct/indirect tax distinction applies to imports. See letter from Leslie B. Samuels, Assistant Secretary for Tax Policy, U.S. Dept. of Treasury, to Senator Sam Nunn, February 1995.

[27] See the discussion of these proposals in Chapter 14 *infra*.

[28] In 2002, the Supreme Court of Papua New Guinea held that the national VAT was unconstitutional because it violated the Organic Law on Provincial and Local Level Governments that granted to the provinces exclusive power to levy sales taxes. *VAT Monitor*, Nov./Dec., 2002, p. 519. The national government apparently sought constitutional and legislative changes to address the constitutional challenge. The authors do not have information on the outcome.

[29] Alberta claimed that the GST represented an unconstitutional attempt by the national government to interfere with Alberta's jurisdiction over property and civil rights under Head 3 of section 91 of the *Constitution Act, 1867*.

[30] *Reference re Goods and Services Tax*, [1992] 2 W.W.R. 673; 2 Alta. L.R. (3d) 289; 138 N.R. 247; 2 S.C.R. 445, affirming in part and reversing in part [1991] 82 Alta. L.R. (2d) 289. The Court of Appeals of Alberta upheld the constitutionality of the tax, but "found that the federal government was required to reimburse suppliers for the costs of withholding and remitting GST, and that the obligation imposed on a province, as supplier, to collect and remit GST violated the *Constitution Act, 1867*." A. SCHENK, GOODS AND SERVICES TAX: THE CANADIAN APPROACH TO VALUE-ADDED TAX, p. 1, note 2 (1993). The Supreme Court reversed this part of the holding of the Alberta court.

[31] The Australian Constitution, section 90.

[32] *Ha and anor v State of New South Wales* & ors; *Walter Hammond & Associates v State of New South Wales & ors*, 189 CLR 465 (High Ct. Australia 1997).

[33] *O'Meara v. Commissioner of Taxation*, [2003] FCA 217.

[34] See Gutierrez, "Philippines' Arroyo Scores Victory in Supreme Court on VAT Measure," *BNA Daily Tax Report*, Sept. 2, 2005, p. G-2.

[35] The Indian Constitution, Art. 268A was added in 2003 to empower the Union government to impose the Service Tax. See http://www.servicetax.gov.in/servicetax/overview/ovw.

The United States does not have a federal sales tax or VAT. Nevertheless, there have been academic discussions about the constitutionality of a federal VAT or other consumption-based tax to replace or supplement existing federal income and payroll taxes.[36] The issue under the U.S. Constitution is whether any proposed consumption tax is a "direct tax" that must be apportioned among the states on the basis of population.[37] There is no significant argument that a European, New Zealand, or Japanese VAT discussed in this book would constitute an unconstitutional direct tax if it were enacted by the United States Congress.[38] Even if some of the VAT, due to competitive pressures, were borne by the seller, the indirect VAT would not thereby be transformed into an unconstitutional direct tax.[39]

B. Income and Consumption Base for Tax

Thomas Hobbes, in his *Leviathan*, advocated consumption as an appropriate base for taxation. In his view, people should pay tax based on what they consume (withdraw from society's limited resources) rather than on what they earn in income (contribute to those resources through their labor). Both receive the protection from the government.[40]

Income and consumption can be viewed as different aspects of "consumption" in a broad sense. In this respect, income represents the potential power to consume and consumption represents the exercise of the power by consuming goods and services. An annual tax on individuals can be imposed on an income base (the hybrid income-consumption base is used to impose the individual income tax in the United States) or on a consumption base.

Consumption-based taxes can be imposed on or collected by business, its workers, and individuals.[41] If the tax is imposed on business, it can be measured by sales or by the value added by business firms at each stage of production and distribution. The tax (like the flat tax discussed later in this book) can be imposed both on business and its workers. Under this form of tax, the base for business is sales less both tax-paid purchases and tax-paid wages. The wage portion of the value added base then is taxed to the wage earners and reported on returns filed by them. If a consumption-based tax is imposed only on individuals, the tax base is income less savings.

---

[36] See discussion *infra* Chapter 14.

[37] U.S. Const., art. I, sec. 2, cl. 3, and art. I, sec. 9, cl. 4.

[38] For an in-depth discussion of this issue, see Johnson, "Apportionment of Direct Taxes: The Foul-Up in the Core of the Constitution," 7 William & Mary Bill of Rights Journal 1 (1998); Jensen, "The Apportionment of 'Direct Taxes': Are Consumption Taxes Constitutional?," 97 *Colum. L. Rev.* 2334 (1997) [hereinafter Jensen, Are Consumption Taxes Constitutional?].

[39] Jensen, Are Consumption Taxes Constitutional?, *supra* note 38, at 2405.

[40] "What reason is there, that he which laboureth much, and sparing the fruits of his labor, consumeth little, should be charged more, than he that living idlely, getteth little, and spendeth all he gets: Seeing that one hath no more protection from the commonwealth thatn the other?" T. Hobbes, Leviathan 184 (Dutton ed. 1914).

[41] See Toder, "Comments on Proposals for Fundamental Tax Reform," 66 *Tax Notes* 2003 (1995).

As discussed earlier, taxes can be classified as direct or indirect taxes. Direct taxes imposed on an income base include the familiar individual and corporate income tax and the payroll taxes. A direct tax like the income tax imposed on individuals can be imposed on a consumption base by removing returns to capital (such as interest, dividends, and capital gains) from the tax base.[42] For example, a personal expenditure tax was used briefly in India and Sri Lanka and was proposed in the United States in 1995.[43] Many forms of indirect taxes can be levied on a consumption base, including selective excise taxes, a turnover tax, a single stage sales tax (such as a manufacturer or a retail sales tax), or a multistage sales tax like a value added tax.[44]

Unlike the individual income tax imposed on an income or hybrid income-consumption base, consumption-based taxes imposed on transactions (like the VAT) cannot be tailored to individual circumstances. As a result, comparing the individual income tax with a European-style VAT, the individual income tax is more flexible as a tool to achieve progressive taxation.

This book does not discuss the politics of raising revenue with an income-based tax or a consumption-based tax, or both, but includes the following thoughts on the importance of considering spending as well as taxation as part of fiscal policy.

One complaint about a VAT is that it is a regressive tax – the tax represents a larger percentage of the income of a low-income household than a high-income household. One response to this argument comes from the noted economist John Kenneth Galbraith, who focuses not only on the incidence of the tax but the combined effect of the tax and how its revenue is spent:[45]

> The relation of the sales tax to the problem of social balance is admirably direct. The community is affluent in privately produced goods. It is poor in public services. The obvious solution is to tax the former to provide the latter – by making private goods more expensive, public goods are made more abundant. Motion pictures, electronic entertainment and cigarettes are made more costly so that schools can be more handsomely supported. We pay more for soap, detergents and vacuum cleaners in order that we may have cleaner cities and less occasion to use them. We have more expensive cars and gasoline so that we may have more agreeable highways and streets on which to drive them. Food being relatively cheap, we tax it in order to have better medical services and better health in which to enjoy it.

It is proper that a portion of the revenue obtained from a VAT be set aside for the design and implementation of the spending measures, whether they

---

[42] See Lessons of Tax Reform, at Box 2 on pp. 24–25 (World Bank 1991). On consumption tax, see the in-depth discussion in Fried, "Fairness and the Consumption Tax," 44 *Stanford L.Rev.* 961 (1992).

[43] See S.722, USA Tax Act of 1995, 104th Cong., 1st Sess., 141 *Cong. Rec.* S.5664 (Apr. 24, 1995).

[44] See discussion of Direct and Indirect Tax in Section IV.

[45] John Kenneth Galbraith, The Affluent Society 238 (4th ed. Houghton Mifflin Co. 1984).

be food stamps, subsidized rents, or other social welfare measures. Thus, to the extent that a value added tax increases prices of goods that poor people buy, it is proper for public policy to provide relief through public spending measures tailored to the needs of those targeted for relief. The best modern brief statement of this policy comes from the Fiscal Affairs Department of the International Monetary Fund:

> Fiscal policy – taxation and spending – is a government's most direct tool for redistributing income, in both the short and the long run. However, the effect of redistributive tax policies, especially in the face of globalization, has been small. Policymakers should focus on developing a broadly based, efficient, and easily administered tax system with moderate marginal rates. Although the primary goal of the tax system should be to promote efficiency, policymakers also need to consider how to distribute the burden of taxation so the system is seen as fair and just.
>
> The expenditure side of the budget offers better opportunities than the tax side for redistributing income. The link between income redistribution and social spending – especially spending on health and education, through which governments can influence the formation and distribution of human capital – is particularly strong, and public investment in the human capital of the poor can be an efficient way to reduce income inequality over the long run.[46]

Advocates of consumption-based taxes claim that income-based taxes discourage savings by double taxing it. Richard Goode disagrees:[47]

> Saving is an individual decision about the use of income that does not diminish the saver's capacity to bear taxation. Saving itself does not attract tax. What an income tax does strike is the additional economic resources that a saver gains by lending or investing. In this respect, the return on savings is treated exactly like wages or any other accretion to one's command over economic resources.[48]

> Goode concedes that consumption taxes encourage savings, "which is especially desirable in developing countries. Under a consumption tax, the net return that can be obtained on income that is saved and invested is higher (in relation to the amount of immediate consumption foregone) than it is under an income tax. With comparable tax rates, the difference is due solely to the fact that postponement of consumption also postpones payment of a consumption tax but does not postpone payment of an income tax."[49]

Figure 1.1 illustrates the income and product flows for income and consumption tax bases. Table 1.3 and its acccompanying notes show the

---

[46] Excerpt from *"Should Equity Be a Goal of Economic Policy?"* by staff of IMF's Fiscal Affairs Department, 35 Financial Development #3, Sept. 1998, p. 4.

[47] Goode was the first director of the IMF's Fiscal Affairs Department, serving from 1965–1981.

[48] R. Goode, Government Finance in Developing Countries (Brookings Instit. 1984) [hereinafter Goode, Government Finance in Developing Countries], pp. 141–142.

[49] *Id.* at 142.

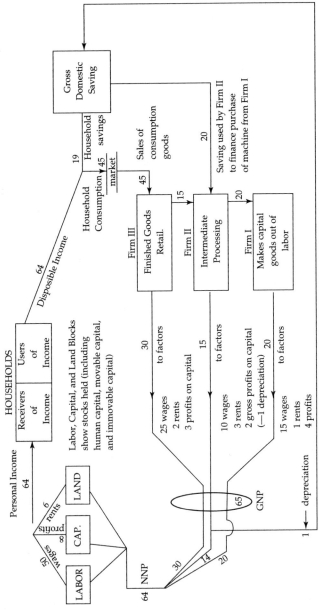

NOTES: 1. Government Sector omitted 2. Foreign Trade Sector omitted 3. Assumed that depreciation held as savings, not paid to factors of production 4. Assumed that all firm earnings paid out as profits, with no retained earnings 5. Interest is omitted.

Figure 1.1. Income and product flows in relation to income and consumption bases

11

Table 1.3. Flows of factor payments to households and tax bases of firms

	Tax bases of households					Tax bases of firms					
	Income (factor payments from firms to households)					Sales price – goods		Value-added by firms			
	Total	Wages paid	Pfts paid out	Rent paid	Expenditures	Retail sales of consumer good & services	Sales consumer & cap goods	C-type	Income type	GDP type	Turnover
Firm I	*	15	4	1				20	20	20	20
Firm II		10	(2-1)	3				−5	14	15	15
Firm III	*	25	3	2		45	45	30	30	30	45
Households-inc.side	64	wages recd 50	Pft recd 8	rent recd 6							
Households-expend.side					45						
Total	64	50	8	6	45	45	65	45	64	65	80

* Assumes all firm earnings paid out as profits, with no retained earnings: the base for an "income tax" on firms would be 8 (pft to households), which is gross (65) less the sum of depreciation (1), wages (50), and rent (6).

Notes to Table 1.3 and Figure 1.1

1 The taxes on households, whether on income or expenditure, can be readily personalized and made progressive; this is not so for the taxes on sales.

2 The value added taxes are not a separate category of taxes for most purposes; they are different ways of doing what is now done through other sales taxes. Thus, the consumption-type VA tax may be regarded as an administrative alternative to a retail sales tax and should be judged on administrative grounds. The income-type VA tax may be regarded as an administrative alternative to a proportional income tax on all factor shares, or as an alternate to a sales tax that covers capital as well as consumer goods with an allowance for depreciation.

3 Tax concessions to capital (to spur economic development) may be examined under both income and sales taxes. If an income tax covers wages only, instead of both wages and profits, there is an obvious concession or favor to capital. Similarly, if a sales tax covers only consumer goods and not both consumer and capital goods, there is a favor to capital. Which concession is greater, other aspects being equal? In the long run a tax concession to savings is analogous to or the same as one to capital goods. Both sales taxes and income taxes can be designed, in effect, to exempt savings, one by providing exemptions to certain income and the other by providing exemptions to certain expenditures.

factor payments by firms to households and the varying tax bases of firms under retail sales, value added, and turnover taxes.

IV. Tax Structures in Developed and Developing Economies

This section includes some comparative data on the composition of tax regimes in developed countries. Many developing countries find it difficult to collect personal income tax in agricultural economies with a dispersed population. "As a result, the personal tax base [in developing countries] is often limited to public employees and employees of large firms, particularly multinational firms.... Taxes on the income of large companies – including taxes levied on the profits of large mining operations and agricultural estates – present fewer administrative difficulties."[50]

In many developing countries, sales taxes at the retail or manufacturer level, complicated with numerous exemptions on imports and domestic sales, are being replaced by broad-based retail sales taxes or value added taxes.[51]

Developing countries must import a significant portion of the goods sold in the domestic market and raw materials and supplies used in domestic production. Taxes on imports (Customs duties and VAT) may represent a much larger percentage of revenue than taxes on domestic sales. The majority of VAT revenue will be collected by Customs and Excise personnel at the border. The remainder of VAT will be collected by the agency (if separate from Customs) responsible for the VAT.

Compared with developing countries, developed (or industrial) countries impose higher taxes as a percentage of gross domestic product (GDP) and tend to rely more heavily on direct personal income and payroll taxes.

Table 1.4, covering selected members of the Organization for Economic Cooperation and Development (OECD), lists 2002 total tax revenue as a percentage of GDP, and details the percentage of total revenue from various kinds of taxes.

Table 1.5 compares the sources of federal revenue within one developed country – the United States – for 1960, 1980, and 2004. The total U.S. federal tax as a percentage of GDP has actually increased and then declined during this period. The individual income tax has decreased from about 8 percent to 7 percent of GDP, the corporate income tax has declined dramatically from 4.1 to 1.6 percent of GDP, and payroll taxes have increased almost 2.5-fold.

To put the overall United States tax structure (federal, state, and local taxes) in a broader perspective, Table 1.6 compares the U.S. taxes as a percentage of GDP with the taxes in selected member countries of the OECD. For this

---

[50] See Lessons of Tax Reform, *supra* note 42, at 16. Note that the phrase "trade taxes" in the final paragraph refers to customs duties, tariffs, and export taxes, that is, taxes on internationally traded goods.

[51] See, for example, the Sales Tax Act, 1995, replaced by the Value Added Tax Act 2001, Act No. 7 of 2001 (Lesotho).

Table 1.4. Select OECD Countries – 2002

	Canada	France	Germany	Japan	U.K.	U.S.	OECD unweighted avg.
Rev. as % of GDP*	33.9	44.0	36.0	25.8	35.8	26.4	36.3
Rev. composition							
As % of total rev.**							
Direct taxes							
Company & personal income	46.2	23.9	28.0	30.6	37.8	44.4	35.3
Soc.sec. & Payroll	17.2	39.5	40.3	38.3	17.0	26.1	26.3
Property	9.8	7.5	2.3	10.8	12.0	11.9	5.5
Indirect taxes							
Goods & services	26.3	25.4	29.2	20.1	32.7	17.6	31.9
Other tax	0.5	3.6	–	0.3	–	–	0.9

* Organization for Economic Cooperation and Development, Revenue Statistics 1965–2003, Table 3 (2004). [These data include federal, state, and local taxes in the United States and other federal countries.
** *Id.* at Table 1.6.

Table 1.5. U.S. federal tax receipts as percentage of GDP*

	1960	1980	2004
Indiv. income tax	7.8	8.9	7.0
Corp. income tax	4.1	2.4	1.6
Payroll taxes	2.8	5.8	6.3
Excise taxes	2.3	0.9	0.6
Other	0.8	1.0	0.7
Totals	17.8	18.9	16.3

* Office of Management & Budget, Historical Tables: Budget of the United States Government, Fiscal Year 2006, Table 2.3, Receipts by Source as Percentages of GDP: 1934–2010. Amounts are rounded, so they may not add to the totals listed.

Table 1.6. Total taxes as percentage of GDP*

	1980	2002
Canada	30.9	33.9
France	40.6	44.0
Germany	34.6	36.0
Japan	25.1	25.8
New Zealand	31.8	34.9
Sweden	46.1	50.2
United Kingdom	35.2	35.8
United States	27.0	26.4
OECD Unweighted Avg.	32.0	36.3

* Organization for Economic Cooperation & Development, Revenue Statistics 1965–2003, Table 3, Total tax revenue as percentage of GDP (2004).

Table 1.7. Total tax on goods and services as % of GDP* (the date in parentheses is the date VAT was introduced or became effective)[52]

	1980	2002
Canada (1991)	10.1	8.9
France (1968)[53]	12.4	11.2
Germany (1968)	9.4	10.5
Japan (1989)	4.1	5.2
New Zealand (1986)	7.1	12.3
Sweden (1969)	11.1	13.3
United Kingdom (1973)	10.3	11.7
United States (no VAT)	4.8	4.6
OECD Unweighted Avg.	10.0	11.4

* Organization for Economic Cooperation and Development, Revenue Statistics 1965–2002, Table 24 (2004). Goods and services taxes include sales and value added taxes, excises and customs duties, taxes on the use of goods such as motor vehicle taxes, and others.

purpose, the taxes are compared for 1980 and 2002. Note the spread for 2002 from about 26 percent of GDP at the low end (Japan and the United States) to over 50 percent at the high end (Sweden).

In this book, we will concentrate on taxes imposed on goods and services. Table 1.7 lists the tax on goods and services in the countries selected in Table 1.6. The data compare 1980 and 2002. Again, Japan and the United States imposed the lowest tax on goods and services, as a percentage of GDP, in 2002.

Table 1.6 reveals that total taxes as a percentage of GDP increased in all of the compared countries, except the United States, between 1980 and 2002. As a percentage of GDP, Table 1.7 shows that New Zealand and to a lesser extent, Sweden, Germany, the United Kingdom, and Japan increased their reliance on goods and services taxes, whereas Canada, France, and the United States reduced their reliance on these taxes.[54] Although many assume that once enacted, the VAT rate only increases and many have, in fact the tax rate in some countries has declined.[55]

---

[52] The data in parentheses were taken in large part from Tait, VAT, *supra* note 2, at 40–41.

[53] France introduced a form of VAT in 1954, but it did not become broadly based and imposed down to the retail stage until 1968.

[54] "It is apparent that, over the longer term, the OECD member countries have relied increasingly on taxes on general consumption to provide their tax revenue." OECD CONSUMPTION TAX TRENDS, OECD 2004 [hereinafter OECD Consumption Tax Trends] at 20. In part, this resulted from a "substitution of VAT/GST for [excises and] other consumption taxes." *Id.* at 23.

[55] Venezuela reduced its VAT rate from 15 to 14 percent, effective October 1, 2005. Official Gazette No. 38,263 dated Sept. 1, 2005, discussed in IBFD Tax News Service Headlines, Sept. 6, 2005. The Canadian Prime Minister is proposing to reduce the GST rate from 7 percent to 6 percent. Governor General Michaelle Jean's speech from the Throne, April 4, 2006, in which she said in part: "[T]he Government will reduce the Goods and Services Tax by one percent. Cutting the GST will help all Canadians deal with the rising cost of living,

V. Broadening the Base of a Tax System

A country's tax revenue can be expanded by adding new taxes or by expanding the base of existing taxes. A nation without an individual or business income tax, without payroll, sales, or property taxes could add one or more of these revenue sources. More commonly, a nation may expand the base of an existing tax. "Defining the base of a tax is critical. The narrower the base, the higher the rate that is required to generate a given amount of revenue. The higher the tax rate, the greater the benefits of avoiding or evading the tax. Tax evasion erodes the tax base and hence the amount of public revenue that is generated."[56]

In the context of the material in this book, a nation (typically a developing nation) with a single stage sales tax imposed only at the manufacturer or retail level that is riddled with exemptions may expand its sales tax base by extending the tax to all levels of production and distribution with a value added tax. Alternatively, it could reduce the number of exemptions on particular sales or imports. It also could impose tax on entities or sectors that previously were excluded from the sales tax base because sellers lacked adequate record keeping or tax collection personnel were not adequately trained or their departments were understaffed.

A new or existing VAT may be designed with a tax base that includes entity or item exemptions in order to achieve nonrevenue economic, social, or political goals. For example, small businesses may be exempt for administrative reasons because they operate without adequate record keeping or have low sales turnover. Nonprofit organizations and units of government may be exempt because they provide services normally provided by government or because taxing them merely shifts tax from one part of government to general revenue. Food, housing, and medical care may be exempt in order to reduce the tax burden on necessities for the lowest income households. Some services, such as financial services, may be exempt because of the administrative difficulty taxing intermediation services that are not rendered for explicit fees. The taxation of nonprofits and government is discussed in detail in Chapter 9, and the texation of financial services in Chapter 10.

VI. The Value Added Tax

According to the European Commission, the pioneering organization in developing a common system of VAT, a "Value Added Tax (VAT) is a general

---

put money back in people's pockets and help stimulate the economy. Cutting the GST is the best way to lower taxes for all Canadians, including low-income Canadians who need it most. The Government will continue with a responsible approach to lowering taxes for the benefit of Canadians and the Canadian economy, including a further reduction of the GST to five percent." The EU extended the period during which Member States may maintain a reduced 5 percent rate on labor-intensive services such as hair dressing and repairs on bikes, clothing and houses. See "EU Ministers Clear Hard Fought Agreement on Reduced VAT Rates," Feb. 15, 2006, p. G-4. On the other hand, Sri Lanka increased its VAT rate on luxuries from 18 percent to 20 percent and on financial services to 20 percent. See IBFD Tax News Service, May 1, 2006.

[56] See *Lessons of Tax Reform, supra* note 42, at 30.

consumption tax"[57] designed to be imposed on all commercial activities involved in the process of producting goods or rendering services (a general tax) and a tax to be borne by consumers (a consumption tax). The First VAT Directive of the European Commission attempts a detailed definition of a VAT. It provides:[58]

> The principle of the common system of value added tax involves the application to goods and services of a general tax on consumption exactly proportional to the price of the goods and services, whatever the number of transactions which take place in the production and distribution process before the stage at which tax is charged.
>
> On each transaction, value added tax, calculated on the price of the goods or services at the rate applicable to such goods or services, shall be chargeable after deduction of the amount of value added tax borne directly by the various cost components.

In recent years, developing countries searching for additional revenue or pressured by business to modernize their sales taxes have enacted value added taxes. In some countries, such as Lesotho in southern Africa, the government modernized its sales tax law and improved its sales tax administration as a first step toward the eventual replacement of the sales tax with a VAT.[59]

> Ultimately, the effectiveness of a value-added tax, like that of an income tax, depends upon efficient administrative audit to ensure taxpayer honesty.... To administer a full-fledged value-added tax properly is also not an easy task. Even a poorly-administered broad-based sales tax, however, can produce a lot of revenue with relatively few complaints from taxpayers. The revenue productivity of value-added taxes, even when relatively poorly administered, is undoubtedly one of their most attractive features to governments all over the world, in developing and developed countries alike.[60]

VII. THE PROLIFERATION OF VATs

There are several reasons why VAT has become such a popular source of revenue. France adopted a primitive version of a VAT after World War II. In the Treaty of Rome (1957),[61] France and the other member countries agreed to share some of their national revenue (including revenue from VAT) to finance the operation of the European Economic Community, now the European

---

[57] See European Union in the U.S., EU Law + Policy Overview, Value Added Tax – Practical Aspects, http://www.eurunion.org/legislat/VATweb.htm, p. 1.

[58] First Council Directive of 11 April 1967 on the harmonization of legislation of member states concerning turnover taxes (67/227/EEC)(OJ P 71, 14.4.1967, p. 1301), Art. 2.

[59] See Lesotho, *supra* note 51.

[60] R. Bird & O. Oldman, *Taxation in Developing Countries* (4th ed. 1990) [hereinafter Bird & Oldman], p. 368.

[61] See Treaty Establishing the European Economic Community, March 25, 1957, art. 99, 298 U.N.T.S. 11, 76.

Union (EU). The Treaty required member states to convert their turnover taxes (described earlier) to a harmonized VAT. All newly admitted members are likewise required to adopt the harmonized VAT.[62]

After World War II, many of the major industrialized countries became signatories to the General Agreement on Tariffs and Trade (GATT), now the World Trade Organization (WTO). They could not subsidize exports, or tax imports more than domestically produced goods. When GATT was being negotiated, most of the European countries relied heavily on indirect taxes for their revenue. For many, international trade also represented a significant factor in their economies. In addition, it was easier to identify the indirect tax component in the price of exports, and difficult if not almost impossible to identify any direct tax buried in product prices. It thus is not surprising that GATT permitted signatory countries (contracting parties) to rebate indirect, but not direct, taxes on exports. Contracting Parties assumed that they could rebate sales tax or VAT but not income or payroll taxes included in export prices.[63] The United States (a nation without a border-adjustable, federal broad-based consumption tax) did not object to this provision. Thus, countries that relied on turnover or value added tax had border-adjustable taxes; that is, they were able to rebate these taxes on exports and impose them on imports.

The International Monetary Fund (IMF) provides technical assistance in the area of finance to member countries. Over the past couple decades, the IMF has assisted developing countries and emerging economies of Eastern Europe to convert their turnover taxes, manufacturer's tax, retail sales tax, and other indirect taxes to VATs.

In 1985, New Zealand adopted a European-style invoice VAT with a much broader base than had been adopted elsewhere. For example, N.Z. taxes certain government services and nonlife insurance. The N.Z. approach has been copied, with modifications, in the Republic of South Africa[64] and elsewhere.

In 1989, Japan introduced its Consumption Tax, a VAT that differs from the European-style VAT in its calculation of net VAT liability and its use of

---

[62] The major EU document on the harmonization of the VATs in the Community is the Sixth Council Directive in 1977. Sixth Council Directive of May 17, 1977, On the Harmonization of the Laws of the Member States Relating to Turnover Taxes – Common System of Value Added Tax: Uniform Basis of Assessment, Official Journal No. L145, 20 J.O. Comm. Eur. (1977).

[63] GATT, *supra* note 24, at Annex I, Ad. Art. XVI, 8 U.S.T. at 1798–99, T.I.A.S. No. 3930, at 33, 278 U.N.T.S. at 218. This kind of tax on domestic consumption is acceptable under an annex to Art. XVI(4), which provides: "The exemption of an exported product from duties on taxes borne by the like product when destined for domestic consumption, or the remission of such duties or taxes in amounts not in excess of those which have accrued.…" It is considered impractical to identify the income or payroll tax included in the price of domestically sold products. The GATT rules reflect prevailing views that sales taxes like VAT are shifted forward and are borne by consumers, whereas income and payroll taxes are borne by owners and shareholders and employees.

[64] Value-Added Tax Act. No. 89 of 1991, as amended, effective Sept. 30, 1991 (Republic of South Africa).

invoices.[65] Canada's Goods and Services Tax became effective on January 1, 1991.[66] Canada has an unusual tax structure to accommodate the special status of an Indian or Indian band on certain First Nation (Indian band) land. The national GST does not apply to taxable supplies made on a reserve (land over which an Indian band exercises governmental powers) to an Indian.[67] Several band councils or other governing bodies of a First Nation adopted the First Nation GST (FNGST). The FNGST is comparable to the Canadian GST and GST/HST. Where enacted, the FNGST, not the Canadian GST, applies to taxable supplies on First Nations lands.[68]

The Australian Goods and Services Tax became effective July 1, 2000.[69] The United States, of the major industrialized countries, remains one of the only countries without a VAT.[70] Although political leaders in some countries proposed to repeal the VAT, rarely does that threat become a reality.[71]

VIII. GLOSSARY OF VAT TERMS[72]

Accounts-based VAT. In an accounts-based VAT, the taxpayer computes his tax liability from data for each tax period taken from books of account. An accounts-based VAT typically will be an *addition* or *sales-subtraction VAT*. The alternative to this type of VAT is a transaction-based VAT like the *credit-subtraction* VAT that relies on invoices (credit-invoice VAT). The **Japanese Consumption Tax** has features of a transactions- and accounts-based VAT.

Addition-method VAT. In an addition-method VAT, a taxpayer calculates her value added by summing the value of the factors of production (typically labor, rent, interest, and profits calculated for VAT purposes) that it

---

[65] After World War II, the Allied Mission to Japan recommended that Japan adopt a value added tax as a revenue source for the prefectures. The Diet enacted a national VAT with a delayed effective date. The effective date was postponed several times and the VAT was repealed in 1954, without ever taking effect. The CT is Law No. 108, part IV (1988) (Shohizei-ho). The English Translation is published in *Japan – National Consumption Tax Law: An English Translation* (CCH Int'l 1989).

[66] The Canadian GST is Part IX (and some Schedules to that part) of the Excise Tax Act, An Act to Amend the Excise Tax Act, the Criminal Code, the Customs Act, the Customs Tariff, the Excise Act, the Income Tax Act, the Statistics Act and the Tax Court of Canada Act, S.C. 1990, c. 45. It received Royal Assent on December 17, 1990.

[67] See RC 4365 First Nation Goods and Services tax, p. 4.

[68] *Id.* at 5. The FNGST does not apply if the First Nation Tax applies to the sale (alcoholic beverages, fuel, and tobacco products).

[69] A New Tax System (Goods and Services Tax) Act 1999, No. 55 of 1999, assented to on July 8, 1999.

[70] The United States is the only OECD country without a VAT. OECD Consumption Tax Trends, *supra* note 54, at 11.

[71] See Philippine President Arroyo's plea to replace VAT with a tax simpler to administer and comply with. Gutierrez, "Philippine President in Collision Course With Country's Congress Over Tax Package," *BNA Daily Tax Report*, Aug. 27, 2004, p. G-4.

[72] Some portions of this glossary were adapted from the glossary in Schenk, "Policy Issues in the Design of a Value-Added Tax: Some Recent Developments in OECD Countries," 1 *Tax Notes Intl 111*, 124–125 (July 1989). The glossary in that article was prepared with the assistance of Michael J. McIntyre.

uses in the production of taxable goods and services. For example, assume that, a taxpayer hires employees at a cost of $400 to process wool purchased in the marketplace, pays rent for her business premises of $100, and sells the processed wool at a profit for VAT purposes of $50. The value added by this firm, and thus the amount subject to the VAT, would be $550 ($400 + $100 + $50). Note that items included in value added do not include purchases that were taxed to prior suppliers, that is, VAT-paid inputs. It therefore assumes that interest and rent expenses are not subject to VAT. An alternative to an addition-method VAT is a **subtraction-method VAT**.

Consumption VAT. The tax base of a consumption-type VAT is the value of goods and services sold or transferred for personal consumption. For example, in a consumption, credit-subtraction VAT, a taxpayer typically claims an **input credit** for VAT paid on purchases of capital goods, as well as on inventory, and **intermediate goods and services** used in his business. Almost all existing VATs are consumption VATs. The alternatives are a **gross-domestic-product VAT** and an **income VAT**.

Credit-method VAT. See **Credit-subtraction VAT**.

Credit-subtraction VAT. In a credit-subtraction VAT, the taxpayer determines his tax liability by subtracting his **input credit** from his **output tax.** For example, assume that T, the taxpayer, sells taxable garden tools for $100,000 during a taxable period. The VAT rate is 10 percent of sales, exclusive of the VAT. T makes taxable purchases of inventory and supplies of $65,000, and a VAT of $6,500 is paid by the seller on those purchases. T would pay net VAT liability of $3,500 ($10,000 output tax on sales less $6,500 input credit on purchases). The two credit-subtraction forms of VAT are the **credit-invoice VAT** and the **credit-subtraction VAT without invoices**. Most VATs are credit-subtraction VATs that rely on invoices. The Japanese Consumption Tax is a credit-subtraction VAT that does not rely on invoices in the same way.

Credit-invoice VAT. A credit-invoice VAT is a **credit-subtraction VAT**, like the European VATs, that relies on invoices to verify tax reported on taxable sales by sellers and input credit claimed by purchasers on allowable taxable purchases.

Credit-subtraction VAT without invoices. The Japanese Consumption Tax (CT) is the only major **credit-subtraction VAT** in use that does not rely on invoices like the credit-invoice VAT does. The taxpayer determines his **output tax** by multiplying taxable sales by the tax rate. In contrast to the treatment under the **credit-invoice VAT**, the **input credit** is usually calculated from company records for taxed purchases (at tax-inclusive prices) by multiplying the purchases by a fraction, the numerator of which is the tax rate and the denominator is 100 + the tax rate. To prevent the claim for unwarranted input credits, Japan requires CT taxpayers to retain documentation to substantiate claimed input credits.

Destination principle. In a VAT that defines its tax jurisdictional reach on the destination principle, the tax is imposed in the country of consumption – generally where the goods and services are delivered for personal consumption. Imports are subject to VAT and exports are free of VAT. Most nations with destination principle VATs tax only some imported services and zero rate only some exported services. The alternative to the destination principle is the **origin principle**.

Exempt sale. An exempt sale is a sale that is not subject to VAT. The seller is not entitled to an **input credit** (or other adjustment) for VAT imposed on purchases allocated to the exempt sale. The alternatives to an exempt sale are a **taxable sale**, a **zero-rated sale**, and a **nontaxable transaction**.

Gross-domestic-product (GDP) VAT. The tax base of a gross-domestic-product VAT is goods and services included in gross domestic product, which includes personal consumption and capital goods (GDP also takes into account government consumption and gross investment, as well as the net of exports over imports). Taxpayers are not allowed an **input credit** (or other adjustment) for the VAT that they have paid on capital goods used in their business.

Income-style VAT. The tax base of an income VAT is the tax jurisdiction's net national income. Taxpayers are allowed an **input credit** (or other adjustment) for the VAT that they have paid on inputs, including capital goods used in connection with their taxable business activity, but they must spread the credit on capital goods over their useful lives through a depreciation-like allowance.

Input credit. An input credit is a credit that the taxpayer may take against output tax for the VAT that was paid (or is deemed to have been paid) on the purchases that qualify for credit under that type of VAT. In a **consumption VAT**, the taxpayer is typically allowed a credit for VAT paid on purchases of capital goods, inventory, and **intermediate goods and services** used in his taxable activities. An input credit is a feature of a **credit-subtraction VAT**. In an **invoice-based, credit-subtraction VAT**, the taxpayer determines the amount of the input credit by taking the sum of the VAT that appears on his purchase invoices. In a **credit-subtraction VAT** that does not rely on invoices (the **Japanese Consumption Tax**), the taxpayer typically determines the amount of the credit by multiplying his allowable purchases (deemed inclusive of VAT), as they appear in the books of account, by a fraction. The numerator of that fraction is the tax rate and the denominator is 100 plus the tax rate. The input credit is also referred to as the input tax credit.

Intermediate goods and services. Intermediate goods and services are goods and services that are purchased to produce other goods and services and are not used for personal consumption. Examples would be diesel fuel and accounting services purchased by a trucking firm as part of its business operations.

Invoice-based VAT. In an invoice-based VAT, the taxpayer computes his tax liability from the VAT shown on the invoices he receives on his allowable taxable purchases and the invoices he issues on his taxable sales. In practice, every invoice-based VAT is a **credit-subtraction VAT**. The alternatives to this type of VAT are a credit-subtraction VAT that does not rely on invoices (the Japanese Consumption Tax) and an **accounts-based VAT**.

Japanese Consumption Tax. See **Credit-subtraction VAT without invoices**.

Nontaxable transaction. A nontaxable transaction (or a transaction that is not a sale for VAT purposes) is a transaction that does not come within the scope of the tax. For example, a transfer of an asset to a creditor as security for a loan is a nontaxable transaction. Tax on purchases allocable to the transaction may or may not qualify for the **input credit**. The alternative to a nontaxable transaction is either a taxable sale (at a positive or zero rate) or an **exempt sale**.

Origin principle. In a VAT that defines its tax jurisdictional reach on the origin principle, the tax is imposed in the country where goods are produced and services are rendered – where the value is added to those goods and services. To achieve a pure origin principle VAT, imports are not taxed and exports bear tax. The alternative to the origin principle is the **destination principle**.

Output tax. The output tax is the amount chargeable on a taxable sale and collected by the seller from the buyer. It constitutes the first step in computing the amount to be remitted by the seller to the government. Typically, the taxpayer (seller) calculates it by multiplying the price of his taxable sales, exclusive of VAT, by the applicable tax rate. With a VAT imposed at a single positive rate, the output tax also may be computed by multiplying taxable sales, inclusive of VAT, by a fraction, the numerator of which is the tax rate and the denominator of which is 100 plus the tax rate.

Sales-subtraction VAT. In a sales-subtraction VAT, the taxpayer pays tax at the applicable VAT rate on the difference between taxable sales and allowable (generally previously taxed) purchases, both inclusive of tax. For example, assume that T, a taxpayer, purchases wool in the marketplace for $1,000. That price includes the VAT collected by the seller of the wool. T processes the wool, and then sells the processed wool to customers for a final price, after VAT, of $1,550. T would be subject to VAT on $550 ($1,550 minus $1,000). At a VAT rate of 10 percent applied to a **tax-inclusive** base, the VAT due would be $55 ($550 x 10%). This VAT is one type of **subtraction-method VAT**.

Subtraction-method VAT. In a subtraction-method VAT, a taxpayer pays tax either on the difference between taxable sales and allowable taxable purchases, or on the difference between the tax on taxable sales less the tax on taxable purchases. There are thus two types of subtraction-method VATs: the first is a **sales-subtraction VAT** and the second is a **credit-subtraction VAT**. The alternative to a subtraction-method VAT is an **addition-method VAT**.

Tax-deduction-method VAT. See **Credit-subtraction VAT**.

Tax-inclusive base (TIB) and tax-exclusive base (TEB). To raise equivalent revenue, the rate applied to a tax-inclusive base (a base that includes the tax itself) is lower than the rate applied to a tax-exclusive base (a base that omits the tax itself). For example, a 10 percent rate on a TEB is equal to a 9.0909 percent rate on a TIB, calculated by the formula: rate on TIB = $1/(1+$ rate on TEB). Thus, if the rate on a TEB is 10 percent, the comparable rate on a TIB is 9.0909 percent, calculated as follows: TIB rate $= 1/(1+10)$, or $1/11 = 9.0909\%$.

Value added tax (VAT). There are many forms of tax that can be classified as a VAT. In this book, value added tax (VAT) is used to describe a type of multistage sales tax imposed on goods and services that is collected in chunks at each stage of production and distribution of goods or the rendition of services in proportion to the value added by each taxpaying firm.

Zero-rated sale. A zero-rated sale is a taxable sale that is subject to a zero tax rate. The taxpayer does not report VAT on the sale and is entitled to an **input credit** for VAT imposed on purchases allocable to the sale. The goods or services sold are therefore free of tax.

IX. Outline of Issues Pertaining to Consumption Taxes

(Consider after Discussion Questions below and over the next several chapters.)

1. Role of a general sales tax in a tax system
   a. Revenue generated with relatively little distortion in the economy
   b. Broad participation in financing government
   c. Cover costs of publicly financed human services (such as health, education, and welfare) by taxing privately financed personal consumption
2. Regressivity aspects
   a. Consumption pattern studies showing that taxing all income or all consumption of poor people is equivalent[73]
   b. Luxuries
   c. Incentive goods, such as bicycles
   d. Subsidized prices
   e. Goods subject to excise taxes
   f. Ad valorem versus specific excises: response to inflation or quality differences
3. Business versus personal consumption, such as food[74] or bicycles
4. Services versus goods: differences and similarities
5. Structural points
   a. Definitions, such as a taxable firm, a taxable transaction, and a small business
   b. Tax rate applied to tax-inclusive or tax-exclusive prices (prices before tax or after tax)
   c. Enforcement mechanism

---

[73] See Aaron, "The Political Economy of a Value-Added Tax in the United States," 38 *Tax Notes 1111*, 1113 (1988), stating that "(a)lthough the ratio of consumption to income declines with respect to *annual* income, it declines little with respect to *long-term average* income."

[74] Live to eat or eat to live.

     i. Suspension (ring) system that relies on resale exemption certifi-
cates[75]

     ii. Credit (deduction) system of fractional payments (now archaic
language for describing a VAT)

     iii. Forfait assessment estimating tax from payroll, rent, and such
other available information as utility bills)

  d. Cascade of tax and pyramiding of base (now used interchangeably) –
The base at each stage makes no allowance either for the part of the
base, namely the cost, previously taxed or for the tax paid on that cost.
The new tax at each stage is on the full price and may be collected as
a tax-inclusive percentage of a firm's gross receipts.

  e. Self-deliveries (self-supplies) – when should these transactions be
treated as taxable transactions?

6. Producers goods (physical and financial "consumption" by business
firms). How should the following be handled under a retail sales tax
or a value added tax?

  a. Physical ingredients

  b. Industrial consumables

  c. Financial ingredients

  d. Capital goods

7. Stages or levels of tax collections – manufacture, wholesale, retail, and
"hybrid"

8. International and interjurisdictional issues

  a. Jurisdictional reach of the tax – origin versus destination principle

  b. Import and selective export taxes

  c. Interstate transactions in federal countries, such as the United States,
Canada, India, Brazil, and Switzerland

  d. Common market tax harmonization

  e. Exchange rate aspects

X. DISCUSSION QUESTIONS

1. A popular argument against sales and excise taxes is that they are not
progressive as to income, that is, they are not based on the taxpayer's ability
to pay. Can sales and excise taxes be made progressive? How? Does having
a higher rate of tax on luxury items make the sales tax progressive?

2. What does it mean to say that a sales tax distorts the pattern of consumption? Can a sales tax be neutral with respect to the pattern of consumption?
How would you go about measuring distortion in the context of sales taxation? Why would you or should you do it?

3. Is a system of selective excise taxes preferable to a general sales tax in a
developing country? In a developed country? Is it a question of having either
excise taxes or a general sales tax, or is it a question of emphasis? Explain.

---

[75] See Zimbabwe and Connecticut experience with the misuse of exemption certificates.
With respect to Connecticut, see Pomp and Oldman, *State and Local Taxation*, Fifth Edition
2005, Volume 1, pp. 7–1, 7–4, 7–19, 7–20, 7–57, 7–59.

4. Assume that a country has chosen a system of *selective* excise taxes for administrative convenience but wants to design the tax system so that it will have a redistributive impact. Which goods and services should be tax exempt? Which should be subject to the normal rate of tax ? Which should be subject to a high rate of tax?

5. Should capital goods be subject to sales taxation? Are there reasons why both developing and developed countries might wish to include capital goods in the base of a comprehensive value added tax? Might it be rational for a developing country to tax capital goods while at the same time selectively awarding extensive tax incentives for investment? See Goode, *Government Finance in Developing Countries* (1984), p. 254. Would the regressivity of a VAT be reduced by applying it to capital goods? See C. Sullivan, *The Tax on Value Added* (1965), ch. 5.

6. A major problem of sales taxation is how to treat "small" firms – artisans, producers, independent contractors, itinerant vendors, small shops, owners of two- or three-family homes, family farms, and so on. Can they be "exempt" from filing tax returns without destroying or seriously distorting the tax base? What possible practical solutions can you identify?

7. What are the advantages and disadvantages of the various "national accounts" type bases (e.g., turnover or total transactions, gross domestic product, net product or income, or consumption)? If you assume both a comprehensive base and a single rate of tax, what are the implications of each of these bases for each of the following often mentioned goals of tax policy: revenue, computational simplicity, economic neutrality, income distribution, stabilization of prices, promotion of exports, and the supply of cross-checking information for administrative purposes?

8. If, during an accounting period (1 year), a firm pays $100 for rent, $50 for interest, $500 for materials, $1,000 for wages, and $300 for salaries to managers and if the firm realizes a profit of $600, what is the firm's value added? To put the question another way, who adds value in each of these accounts to the economic output of the country? Who should be the taxpayer with respect to each item of value added?

Appendix A: Development Taxation

I. Introduction

The following material from Bird and Oldman's *Taxation in Developing Countries* also is relevant for developed countries:[76]

> The relation between taxation and economic growth has long been a matter of concern to policy makers and students of public policy alike. The classical economists devoted substantial efforts to analyzing the effects of taxation on growth and the related question of the distribution of factor incomes, as

---

[76] Bird & Oldman, *supra* note 60, at 1–3.

witnessed by the full title of Ricardo's famous treatise, *Principles of Political Economy and Taxation*. With the rise of Keynesian economics in the postwar era, the effects of taxation on the stability of the economy also became an important subject of analysis. These classical and Keynesian concerns constituted prominent themes in early analyses of taxation in developing countries....Subsequently, the range of concerns widened to include the effects of taxation not just on the rate of growth of national income but also on the distribution of that income by income size class,...on employment,...and on other objectives of policy. [The]...objectives of fiscal policy [are]...the promotion of economic growth, the reduction of income disparities between households and regions, the promotion of economic stability and economic efficiency, and the increasing of host-country returns from natural resource endowments.

As the range of policy concerns widened, the nature of the analysis applied to development taxation altered. [By 1980],...both the content and the appearance of normative taxation theory had altered drastically, bringing it more into line with the increased level of mathematical sophistication and theoretical rigor of economics in general....This new approach has just begun to be applied to taxation in developing countries....

[T]he accumulated experience of the last few decades with tax reform in a wide variety of developing countries has undoubtedly played an important role in shaping the way development taxation is now approached. In particular, there is now much more recognition of the vital importance of tax administration in shaping the tax systems of developing countries, as well as of the incredible variety found in these countries and the difficulty of making meaningful policy generalizations in the absence of close and careful attention to local institutional detail....The sort of generalized and idealized prescription of what a "perfect" tax system might look like that was once all too characteristic of much writing on tax reform in developing countries has increasingly been replaced by more pragmatic and eclectic attempts to develop better systems than those that now exist, in the face of substantial and continuing political and administrative obstacles to reform.

The best approach to reforming taxes in a developing country – indeed in any country – is one that takes into account taxation theory, empirical evidence, and political and administrative realities and blends them with a good dose of local knowledge and a sound appraisal of the current macroeconomic and international situation to produce a feasible set of proposals sufficiently attractive to be implemented and sufficiently robust to withstand changing times, within reason, and still produce beneficial results. This modest prescription is, alas, still often beyond our reach, owing to deficiencies on all sides, ranging from such theoretical and empirical conundrums as the incidence of the corporate income tax and the effects of income taxes on work effort to such political puzzles as the acceptability of the (usually implicitly) postulated social weights on incomes and the willingness of the powerful to tax themselves (perhaps in the interests of their long-term survival?). Nonetheless,...much progress has been made since the days when the main question seemed to be "Will the Underdeveloped Countries Learn to Tax?" (Kaldor, 1963), and it was presumed to be simply a matter of time and progress before every country ended up with a global progressive personal income tax as its main source of revenue.

II. The Reform of Indirect Taxation[77]

Indirect taxes on foreign trade and consumption have long been the mainstay of taxation in developing countries. Such taxes provide two-thirds or more of tax revenues in many countries, with taxes on foreign trade (especially imports) more important in the poorest countries and domestic taxes on goods and services more important in the others.... Few tax questions are more important in developing countries than the appropriate mix and design of indirect taxes....

The fact is that indirect taxes have not only retained their share of revenues in most countries, they have even increased it. This surprising outcome reflects both the recent widespread move to value-added taxes and, more importantly, the greater buoyancy (responsiveness to income changes) of indirect than direct taxes in most countries – a development, quite contrary to the experience of developed countries, which demonstrates clearly the importance of the administrative constraint on taxation in developing countries....

The great attention now paid to such general sales taxes as the value-added tax, however, should not be allowed to obscure the fact that, as already noted, in many developing countries taxes on foreign trade – on imports and exports – are more important in revenue terms than domestic consumption taxes. The treatment of these revenue sources has, on the whole, been less satisfactory in the tax than in the trade context. Perhaps the main impression one gains from the literature... with respect to import taxes, for instance, is that if they must exist they should be, on the one hand, uniform (to provide any desired protection in as nondistorting a fashion as possible) and, on the other, equal to domestic consumption taxes on the same products (essentially for the same reason). This balancing act is strictly tenable only if a uniform tax is levied on all domestic consumption of tradeable goods – but then, of course, tariffs would afford no protection at all to domestic production.

Similarly, the usual view of export taxes is that they are always and unequivocally bad. Yet many countries not only rely on such taxes to some extent but must continue to do so if they wish to tax their agricultural sectors effectively... or simply to raise enough revenue to meet the minimal needs of government.... (T)he appropriate taxation of exports, even more than that of imports, is clearly related as much or more to trade or agricultural policy as to tax policy.

III. Taxing Imports

As discussed earlier, in developing countries, taxes on imports constitute a significant if not the most significant source of tax revenue. Although the taxation of imports is easy to administer, some countries have acceded to the demands of importers and allowed this tax to be paid at a later date. Some have learned that deferring the tax on imports merely provides opportunities for evasion of the tax because revenue officers are not able to identify all such

---

[77] The material in this section is from *id.* at 311–312.

imports and verify that tax has been paid. In some countries, the communication is inadequate between Customs that verifies imports at the border and the VAT department that audits the deferred tax payments. Import duties may be used to protect domestic industry from foreign competition.

A clear distinction between excises and import duties, nevertheless, would have the important advantage of avoiding unintended protection for local production of items that are taxed for revenue or regulatory purposes. For countries that have not gone far in industrialization and that import most of the consumer goods suitable for taxation, customs duties have seemed the obvious means of taxing consumption. Especially when duty rates are high, an incentive is offered for the establishment of domestic production, even if the country enjoys no comparative advantage in the process. When the import duties are much higher on finished goods than on components or ingredients, the local production may be essentially an assembly or repackaging activity, with little value added, that contributes nothing to the acquisition of skills and improved technology. If excises apply to both imports and domestic production, the unintended inducement to establish local production is avoided. It is advisable to rely on excises even when there is no local production because it will be politically difficult to withdraw protection after domestic production begins.[78]

IV. Taxing Exports[79]

A well-established proposition in international trade is that a uniform tax on imports is essentially the same as a uniform tax on exports.... The fiscal treatment of exports and that of imports are thus, in principle, two sides of the same coin. In practice, however, export and import taxes are usually designed and implemented largely in isolation from each other. In some countries, exports – usually of manufactured goods – are [subsidized, for others, exports – usually of natural resources – are] taxed, sometimes, explicitly, sometimes through the operations of state marketing boards, and sometimes through multiple exchange rates.... In still others, both export subsidies and export taxes may simultaneously exist in different sectors. Moreover, the precise significance and effects of these various arrangements may differ greatly, depending on how such other policy levers as exchange rates are set.... The following selection... [explains] briefly the economic rationale for taxing exports.

Traditional arguments for export taxes are that they may serve as a means of stabilization policy..., as a substitute for income or other taxes on farmers..., as a means of offsetting restrictions on importers, or as a means of reaping monopoly benefits.... Each of these arguments may have merit in particular circumstances. Nevertheless, with respect to export taxation as to most other areas of development taxation, the apparently strong and clear conclusions emerging from simple economic analysis need to be

---

[78] Goode, *Government Finance in Developing Countries, supra* note 48, at 149–150.
[79] Bird & Oldman, *supra* note 60, at 331–332.

carefully considered, and often modified, before they can serve as the basis of sound policy recommendations for any particular country....

(M)any countries levy heavier implicit taxes than explicit taxes on exports.... "Implicit" or "quasi" taxes reduce the income accruing to exports but do not produce any revenue for the government: instead, the proceeds are generally used, one way or another, to subsidize imports....

If an import tariff, for example, succeeds in discouraging all imports of a product, it effectively levies a "tax" on all consumers of the (domestically-produced) product and pays a subsidy to the factors of production engaged in the protected sector.

2

Forms of Consumption-Based Taxes and Altering the Tax Base

I. FORMS OF CONSUMPTION-BASED TAXES

A. INTRODUCTION

In this section of the chapter, there is a discussion of a direct tax on individuals that is measured by their level of consumption rather than their income. This tax is commonly referred to as a cash-flow or consumption-based income tax. Most taxes on consumption are indirect taxes. These taxes, also discussed in this chapter, are collected by sellers of taxable goods and services and are expected to be borne by final consumers of those goods and services. The indirect tax on consumption may take the form of a single-stage tax like the retail sales tax or a multistage tax like a value added tax.

A value added tax is a generic name associated with a multistage tax that is levied on the value added by each business firm at every stage of production and distribution of goods and services. In part, the description of a VAT depends on the method used in calculating tax liability. In this chapter, there is a discussion of the addition, sales-subtraction, and credit-subtraction methods of calculating VAT liability.

The legislature may alter a VAT base by removing some sellers or some goods and services. This alteration of tax base is accomplished by providing an exemption for designated businesses (such as small businesses) or entities, such as units of government or nonprofit organizations. The legislature also can alter the tax base by granting exemption or altering the rate for particular goods and services, regardless of the nature of the seller. In this chapter, there is a discussion of these various methods of providing special treatment under a value added tax.

B. CONSUMPTION-BASED DIRECT TAX ON INDIVIDUALS

A consumption-based income tax (or direct expenditure tax) was discussed by the British economist Nicholas Kaldor in his 1955 book, *An Expenditure Tax*.[1] Kaldor wrote that a progressive tax can be imposed on an expenditure

---

[1] N. KALDOR, AN EXPENDITURE TAX (George Allen & Unwin Ltd 1955). Kaldor notes that the principle of taxing individuals on the basis of their expenditure rather than income

base and still "advance towards an egalitarian society whilst improving the efficiency of operation and rate of progress of the economy."[2] In effect, Kaldor proposed an annual tax on personal expenditures at graduated rates.

Under another approach to taxing consumption that relies on Irving Fisher's ideas, the tax base could be calculated by adding to income "monies received from the sale of capital assets, depletion of bank balances, etc., and *deducting* sums spent on the purchase of capital assets and on 'non-personal' or 'non-chargeable' expenditure."[3] Kaldor criticizes this approach that relies on income as the legal basis of the tax.[4]

Kaldor would rely on personal expenditures as the legal basis of the tax – the approach that satisfies "the requirements of equity and efficient administration."[5] Under Kaldor's approach, taxpayers would be required to declare their personal expenditures annually and pay tax directly to the government rather than pay tax to the sellers of goods and services as part of each sale, the so-called indirect consumption tax. In effect, the taxpayer is required to report all income and receipts for the year and then deduct all investment (carefully defined), the difference being consumption. Kaldor acknowledges that this approach to taxing annual consumption raises many difficult problems, such as the distinction between personal consumption and capital wealth (or investment), the treatment of gifts and bequests, and the need to set an annual exemption threshold for lower-income taxpayers, to name a few.

Kaldor also recognized that there were significant transition problems in moving from an individual income tax measured by annual income (an accretion-type tax) to one measured by annual consumption. He therefore recommended a two-stage process. The expenditure tax could be introduced to operate alongside the individual income tax and to apply only to those taxpayers in the top income groups. If successful, the legislature could expand the scope of the expenditure tax and reduce the scope of the individual income tax.[6]

There were a series of articles and monographs by noted tax scholars and government agencies, discussing the feasibility and desirability of a cashflow or consumption-based income tax. This debate was stimulated in large part by Professor Andrew's extraordinary 1974 article on this topic[7] and expanded on by others.[8]

originated more than three hundred years ago in a book by Thomas Hobbes in *Leviathan*, chapter XXX, and has been urged since then by John Stuart Mill, Marshall, and Pigou in England and Irving Fisher in the United States. *Id.* at intro. Kaldor notes in his book that Treasury Secretary Morgenthau proposed a form of expenditure tax in 1942 as an addition to the income tax. *Id.* at 16. He refers to *New York Times* reports on this tax proposal in the September 4–8, 1942, issues.

[2] *Id.* at 15.

[3] *Id.* at 192.

[4] *Id.* at 193.

[5] *Id.*

[6] *Id.* at 223. A personal expenditure tax was used for a brief period in Sri Lanka and India.

[7] Andrews, "A Consumption-Type or Cash Flow Personal Income Tax," 87 *Harv. L. Rev.* 1113 (1974) [hereinafter Andrews, Consumption-Type or Cash Flow Personal Income Tax].

[8] See, for example, Graetz, "Implementing a Progressive Consumption Tax," 92 *Harv. L. Rev.* 1575 (1979); Andrews, "Fairness and the Personal Income Tax: A Reply to Professor

Professor Andrews suggested that an ideal for a tax on individuals may be a tax calculated on a cash-flow basis that would tax personal consumption, but not the accumulations of business and investment assets.[9] He criticizes the assumption in tax policy debate that the ideal tax system is a system that taxes "total personal gain or accretion, without distinctions as to source or use" – what he calls "an accretion-type personal income tax."[10] He claims that the individual income tax in the United States is inconsistent in its treatment of accumulations. According to Andrews, a cash-flow tax (a consumption-type tax) would produce net simplification in the income tax, and result in a tax that is fairer and one that more efficiently distributes the tax burdens.[11] The tax is reported on tax returns designed for this purpose and is paid directly to the government by consumers.

The U.S. Treasury's 1977 Blueprints for Basic Tax Reform[12] considered, as one option, the conversion of the individual income tax into a consumption-based income tax.[13] Blueprints concluded that a cash-flow, consumption-based income tax was simpler than a comprehensive income tax (the latter merely broadened the income tax base). By including "*all* monetary receipts in the tax base, including the entire proceeds of sales of assets and gifts received, and allowing deductions for purchases of assets and gifts given, the annual consumption of a household could be measured without directly monitoring the purchases of goods and services."[14]

In 1995, U.S. Senators Nunn and Domenici proposed the USA Tax System to replace the existing federal income taxes. One portion of this proposal

---

Warren," 88 *Harv. L. Rev.* 947 (1975); Warren, "Fairness and a Consumption-Type or Cash Flow Personal Income Tax," 88 *Harv. L. Rev.* 931 (1975); Bradford, The Case for a Personal Expenditure Tax, in WHAT SHOULD BE TAXED: INCOME OR EXPENDITURE (J. Pechman ed. 1979); Advisory Comm. on Intergovernmental Relations, The Expenditure Tax (Information Report M-84 1974); and Institute for Fiscal Studies, The Structure and Reform of Direct Taxation (1978)(The Meade Commission Report). For a discussion of some of the problems during a transition from the individual income tax to a cash-flow, consumption-based income tax, see Andrews, Consumption-Type or Cash Flow Personal Income Tax, *supra* note 7; Graetz, noted above, and Shachar, "From Income to Consumption Tax: Criteria for Rules of Transition," 97 *Harv. L. Rev.* 1581 (1984).

[9] Andrews, Consumption-Type or Cash Flow Personal Income Tax, *supra* note 7, at 1113.

[10] *Id.*

[11] *Id.*

[12] U.S. Dep't of the Treasury, Blueprints for Basic Tax Reform, Second Edition, 1984 [hereinafter Blueprints]. Information for a sample tax form is included *id.* at pp. 99–100. The primary work on Blueprints was done by Deputy Assistant Secretary of the Treasury David F. Bradford. The first edition of Blueprints was issued on January 17, 1977, by outgoing Treasury Secretary William E. Simon a few days before the Carter administration took office. See also, DAVID F. BRADFORD, THE X TAX IN THE WORLD ECONOMY: GOING GLOBAL WITH A SIMPLE, PROGRESSIVE TAX, The AEI Press (2004). Bradford's X Tax is patterned after the Hall-Rabushka Flat Tax, discussed later in the book.

[13] A few years earlier, in 1974, Congress enacted the Individual Retirement Account, which represented a very modest movement toward a consumption base for the individual income tax. See IRC section 219, enacted by the Pension Reform Act of 1974, P.L. 93-406, section 2002(a), effective for tax years beginning after 1974, and subsequently limited to taxpayers with modest income who did not have certain other qualified pension plans.

[14] Blueprints, *supra* note 12, at 102.

was to replace the individual income tax with a direct, personal, progressive tax on consumption (a consumption-based income tax) that would not tax savings and investment.[15] This tax, proposed by Congressman English in 2003 as The Simplified USA Tax, is discussed later in this book.[16]

C. Single and Multistage Sales Taxes

An indirect tax on consumption like a sales tax (or tax on goods and services) can be imposed at a single or at multiple stages of production or distribution. Single stage sales taxes include retail sales taxes like those imposed by most of the states in the United States or by some of the provinces in Canada. A single stage tax can be imposed at the manufacturing level, such as the prior Canadian Manufacturer's Tax that was replaced by the Canadian Goods and Services Tax (a VAT), or at the wholesale level, such as the prior British Purchase Tax that was replaced by a VAT. A sales tax also can be imposed at more than one but less than all levels of production or distribution. For example, the Louisiana sales tax is imposed at the wholesale and retail levels, with relief provided to retailers for the tax they paid on purchases from wholesalers.[17] The modern sales tax imposed at all levels of production and distribution is the VAT.

II. Overview of the Value Added Tax[18]

A. In General

The Value Added Tax is intended to tax personal consumption comprehensively, neutrally, and efficiently. The VAT has been the most pervasive tax reform throughout the world during the second half of the twentieth century and into the twenty-first century, and has proved to be a major source of government revenue. The VAT is widely used in both developed and developing countries and is used at local, subnational, national, and even supra-national (e.g., the European Union) levels of government. An occasional voice is even heard suggesting its use to finance a world infrastructure development fund or an international humanitarian relief fund.[19]

---

[15] S.722, USA Tax Act of 1995, 104th Cong., 1st Sess., 141 *Cong. Rec.* S.5664 (Apr. 24, 1995) [hereinafter USA Tax Act], at Title II – USA Tax for Individuals, Ch. 1 – Unlimited Savings Allowance Tax for Individuals, §1. See also, Pepperell, "Thoughts on the Progressive Consumption Tax," 85 *Tax Notes* 529 (Oct. 25, 1999).

[16] H.R. 269, Simplified USA Tax Act of 2003, 108th Cong., 1st Sess. (Jan. 8, 2003).

[17] J. Due & J. Mikesell, *Sales Taxation: State and Local Structure and Administration* (The Johns Hopkins Univ. Press 1983), p. 6.

[18] For the European Commission definition of a VAT, see *supra* Chapter 1 Section VI.

[19] See Speer, "French President Writes World Leaders Seeking Support for Global Development Tax," *BNA Daily Tax Report*, June 4, 2004, p. G-5, suggesting an international tax to finance human development. President Chirac suggested that the tax might be imposed on "international arms trade, cross-border financial transactions, or environmental emissions...." France has been studying a global tax system to fund development projects. Professor Kaneko proposed an international humanitarian tax – a consumption

The base of the VAT – predominantly the personal consumption of individuals,[20] as measured by the price paid for goods and services – historically has been in one form or another an important source of government revenues. If, as is true in a growing number of jurisdictions, the rate of tax is uniform and the base is broad, the VAT will not interfere with patterns of consumption (that is, how consumers decide to divide their purchases among available choices), except for the choice between untaxed consumption (e.g., leisure) and taxed consumption. One of the most fundamental questions relating to Value Added Tax is the use of a uniform rate applied to a comprehensive base that excludes only items too difficult to reach. Nonuniform rates and extensive exemptions destroy neutrality and affect patterns of consumption, as well as patterns of production and distribution, while greatly increasing administrative and compliance costs.

There are several different kinds of multistage consumption taxes that can be described as VATs. A VAT can be described on the basis of the mechanical method used to calculate net tax liability for each tax period. The methods are the addition method and three forms of the subtraction method. The addition method (the Michigan Single Business Tax and the New Hampshire Business Enterprise Tax rely on variations of the addition method for a state level tax)[21] adds the components of value added by the firm for each tax period.[22] The subtraction methods are the sales-subtraction VAT (proposed in the United States and Canada but not in use), and two forms of credit-subtraction VATs. One credit-subtraction VAT relies on invoices (the almost universally used "credit-invoice" or "invoice" VAT) and the other does not rely on invoices (the originally enacted Japanese Consumption Tax). These methods are described in the next section of this chapter.

The definition of the tax base depends, in part, on the treatment of international transactions (origin versus destination principle tax), the treatment of the VAT itself (a tax-inclusive or tax-exclusive base), and the treatment of capital purchases (a gross domestic product, income, or consumption tax base). Each of these elements is briefly explained next, followed by a more detailed explanation of various methods of calculating VAT liability.[23]

---

tax on international travel to provide relief funds. Kaneko, "Proposal for International Humanitarian Tax – A Consumption Tax on International Air Travel," 17 *Tax Notes Int'l* 1911 (Dec. 14, 1998), discussed *infra* at Chapter 8.

[20] Some VAT is borne by nonprofit organizations, units of government, small businesses, and others that purchase taxable goods and services and sell goods or services exempt from VAT.

[21] See discussion later in this book.

[22] If landlords and banks are included among the firms paying tax, the addition method is simply the sum of payroll plus profits. If landlords and banks are not taxpayers, the addition method is the sum of wages, profits, rent, and interest.

[23] A. Schenk, Value Added Tax – A Model Statute and Commentary: A Report of the Committee on Value Added Tax of the American Bar Association Section of Taxation 1–2 (1989) [hereinafter ABA Model VAT]. For an excellent reference on VAT, including administration issues, see V. Thuronyi, ed., Tax Law Design and Drafting, 2 vol's, IMF. For an extensive discussion of the elements of a VAT, see C. Shoup, Public Finance 250–266 (1969) [hereinafter Shoup, Public Finance]; C. Sullivan, The Tax on

B. Jurisdictional Reach of the Tax

Except for taxes levied on a global basis, tax legislation must define the extent to which a tax is imposed on cross-border transactions or activities. The same applies to the VAT. In a shrinking world marked by cross-border activities, it becomes critical to decide whether the VAT should exempt exports and tax imports, or tax exports and exempt imports. Virtually all VATs use the so-called destination principle[24] under which personal consumption is taxed in the country of destination, which is assumed to be the country of consumption.[25] There are some examples, however, of origin-based VATs, under which exports are taxed. Tax reform proposals in the United States sometimes have features of origin-based VATs.[26]

Under the destination principle, any VAT paid by the exporter on its purchases is refunded. In the terminology of a VAT, exports are zero-rated, that is, not only is the sale for export not taxed, but also a refund is given of VAT paid on inputs included in the exports.[27] Imports are taxed under the destination principle.

Most countries have detailed rules to identify the location of a transaction as a domestic sale, an import, an export, or a foreign sale. These rules tend to limit a country's VAT jurisdiction under the destination principle to sales within the country, imports, and exports, although exports are free of tax.

New Zealand expanded its VAT jurisdiction beyond these conventional parameters. It also does not rely on the traditional detailed location of supply rules. South Africa and some other countries in southern Africa adopted the New Zealand approach. The jurisdictional reach of the N.Z. GST and South African VAT will be discussed more fully in Chapter 7.

C. Inclusion of VAT in Tax Base

A VAT can be imposed on a base that includes or excludes the tax itself. For example, assume that under a credit-invoice VAT, an umbrella sells for a pretax price of $10. If the 10 percent VAT is imposed on a tax-exclusive base, the tax is 10 percent of $10, or $1, and the price to the consumer is $11. If the

---

Value Added, ch. 1 and 5 (1965); C. McLure, Jr., The Value-Added Tax: Key to Deficit Reduction? [hereinafter McLure, VAT], 71–102 (1987). See also Shoup, *Choosing Among Types of VATs*, in Value Added Tax in Developing Countries (M. Gillis, C. Shoup, and G. Sicat, eds., World Bank, 1990) [hereinafter Shoup, Choosing Among VATs]; Schenk, "Value Added Tax: Does This Consumption Tax Have a Place in the Federal Tax System?" 7 *Va. Tax Rev.* 207 (1987).

[24] See New Vatopia VAT, appendix B, §§9(1) and 17, and Sch. I, ¶2.

[25] The destination principle also has been adopted by the American states for their retail sales taxes, although the policy has not been articulated or debated the way it has in a VAT. The states typically have provisions that exempt from the sales tax goods shipped in interstate commerce, thus ceding taxation over "exports." The destination state will assert a use tax on the consumer. This pattern tends to assign the sales tax to the jurisdiction in which consumption is likely to occur.

[26] See, for example, the Flat Tax discussed in Chapter 14.

[27] For a discussion of the origin and destination principles applied to international transactions in the context of GATT, see Messere, "Consumption Tax Rules," *IBFD Bulletin*, Dec. 1994, p. 665. See also Chapter 7 *infra*.

10 percent tax is imposed on a tax-inclusive base and the merchant is to get the same $10 after remitting the tax imposed on the sale, the merchant will charge the consumer $11.11 and the tax is 10 percent of that price, or $1.11. Note that a 10 percent tax imposed on a tax-exclusive base yields exactly the same amount of tax revenue, namely $1 in the example, as a rate of 9.0909 percent does on a tax-inclusive base (.090909 × 11 = 1). A transactional VAT such as the European invoice VAT can be imposed on either base. In contrast, an accounts-based VAT calculated under the sales-subtraction or addition method is imposed on the results of operations for a tax period, not on each sales transaction. The accounts can be adjusted to reflect a base that is tax-inclusive or tax-exclusive.[28]

D. Inclusion of Capital Goods in Tax Base

Looking at the VAT through concepts used in national income analysis aids thinking about how the tax works in practice. According to U.S. government data, gross domestic product is the sum of personal consumption expenditures, gross private domestic investment, net of exports over imports, and government consumption expenditures and gross investment. The modern VAT, as practiced, reaches only value added reflected in personal consumption (although it could, and some so advocate, reach further by seeking to tax net national product by including depreciation or to tax gross domestic product by including capital goods). To reach only personal consumption, those who draft the legislative structure of the VAT have to consider carefully the way in which value added reflected in inventory and in capital goods is treated in constructing the tax base and collecting the tax.

To put this range from gross domestic product to consumption into perspective, Table 2.1 illustrates the makeup of GDP for the United States for 2004, including a breakdown of personal consumption expenditures into categories of goods and services. A succinct but complex matrix and examples of bases and methods presented in Table 2.7 shows the calculation of tax under consumption, income, and GDP bases along with addition, subtraction, and credit methods of calculating tax liability.

The following material discusses the treatment of capital goods under a credit-invoice VAT. The same treatment can be provided under a sales-subtraction[29] or additional method VAT. "The items that a firm purchases from other firms consist of raw materials, semi-manufactured goods, supplies used up in the process of manufacture or handling, services (e.g., banking, insurance, advertising), finished goods ready for resale to consumers (in the case of retailers), and finally machinery, equipment, and other capital goods. The treatment accorded to capital goods differs, however, depending on the type of value-added tax employed."[30]

---

[28] See EC Directive 98/6 of 16 Feb. 1998, requiring sellers to show "selling price" and "unit price," both of which include VAT.

[29] C. Shoup, Public Finance, *supra* note 23, at ch. 9, General Sales Taxes: Retail Sales Tax, Value Added Tax, p. 258 (1969).

[30] *Id.* at 251.

Table 2.1. Gross domestic product and personal consumption data for 2004 (in billions)[31]

Gross Domestic Product 2004		11,735.0
Less:		
Gross private domestic investmetnt	1,927.3	
Net exports of goods and services	(606.2)*	
Government consumption expenditure & gross investment	2,183.9	3,505.0
Personal Consumption Expenditures		8,230.0**
Categories of 2004 Personal Consumption Expenditures		
Durable goods		
Motor vehcles & parts	447.8	
Furniture & household equipment	351.3	
Other	194.9	
	994.0	
Nondurable goods		
Food	1150.3	
Clothing & shoes	326.5	
Gasoline, fuel oil, & other energy	244.9	
Other	655.3	
	2377.0	
Services		
Housing	1239.0	
Household operation (including utilities)	452.0	
Transportation	301.7	
Medical care	1391.7	
Recreation	335.1	
Other	1139.5	
	4859.0	
Personal Consumption Expenditure	8230.0	

* Do you understand the meaning of a negative figure on this line? (Hint: think about the relationship among imports, exports, and personal consumption.
** Rounding difference. The table shows 8,229.9.

Under a Gross Domestic Product (GDP) VAT, VAT on capital purchases is not recoverable as an input tax credit. This VAT is borne by the capital goods purchaser and, depending on competitive forces, may be shifted as a cost of doing business to its customers in the form of higher prices.

A National Income (Income) VAT allows the capital goods purchaser to recover the VAT on capital purchases, through a depreciation-like allowance, over the lives of the capital goods.

A Consumption VAT allows the capital goods purchaser to claim input credits for VAT on capital purchases immediately and in full in the period in which the capital goods are purchased. VAT on capital goods is treated the

---

[31] Bureau of Economic Analysis, U.S. Dept. of Commerce, Survey of Current Business, National Data, Tables 1.1.5 & 1.5.5 (July, 2005).

same as VAT on purchases of inventory, supplies, and other business inputs. Some countries (particularly developing countries), in order to reduce the cash drain from refunds of excess input credits on capital purchases, require VAT-registered persons to carry forward excess input credits to a number of future tax periods and to use these credits to offset future VAT liabilities before any remaining credits are eligible for refund. "A carryforward to reduce a future year's positive value-added will not suffice, unless it is enlarged by an interest factor, since delay in tax relief is equivalent to reduction in tax relief....."[32] Although most VATs today are consumption-style VATs, China is still in the process of converting its VAT to a consumption VAT.[33]

As discussed earlier, a multistage value added tax is described in part by the method employed to calculate tax liability. The next section provides a detailed discussion of the major methods of calculating VAT liability for each tax period.

III. METHODS OF CALCULATING VAT LIABILITY[34]

The special feature of the modern value added tax is the mode of collection. This section discusses the widely used European-style, credit-invoice VAT, the Japanese-style credit-subtraction VAT that does not rely on invoices, the sales-subtraction VAT proposed but not enacted, and the addition-method VAT not used at the national level.

A. CREDIT-INVOICE VAT

The most prevalent method of calculating VAT worldwide is the credit-invoice VAT (or invoice VAT) that relies on a tax-against-a-tax methodology. This form of VAT was established after World War II in Western European countries (countries now members of the EU).[35] Including the other elements

---

[32] C. Shoup, Public Finance, *supra* note 23, at 254.

[33] See Zhongha [2003] No. 11, authorizing input tax credits for certain industries operating in the old industrial areas of northeastern China. Zhang, "New VAT system in north-eastern China," *VAT Monitor*, Sept/Oct. 2004, p. 366. On the consequences of the GDP or production-based VAT in China, see Ahmad, Singh, & Lockwood, "Taxation Reforms and Changes in Revenue Assignments in China," IMF Working Paper 04/125 (July 2004).

[34] For a thorough analysis of the advantage of the invoice VAT over the sales-subtraction VAT, see McLure, VAT, *supra* note 23. For another discussion of the various methods of calculating VAT liability, see Schenk, "The Plethora of Consumption Tax Proposals: Putting the Value Added Tax, Flat Tax, Retail Sales Tax, and USA Tax Into Perspective," 33 *San Diego L. Rev.* 1281, 1305–1309 (1996) [hereinafter Schenk, The Plethora of Consumption Tax Proposals]. See New Vatopia VAT, appendix B, §36.

[35] Before it reformed its VAT, Russia combined a credit-invoice VAT for producers before the wholesale stage, with a "gross margins" tax for wholesalers, retailers, and some services. See Summers & Sunley, *An Analysis of Value-Added Taxes in Russia and Other Countries of the Former Soviet Union*, IMF Working Paper (1995)..., p. 20. "(T)he margin used is not the actual difference between the amount paid for the goods and the price at which

in the description of the credit-invoice VAT, the EU-style VAT reaches international transactions under the destination principle, imposes tax on a consumption base, and typically calculates output tax on tax-exclusive prices.[36]

With the almost universally used invoice method (used in the illustration here and in the New Vatopia VAT in Appendix B), the taxable firm calculates net tax liability for each tax reporting period (typically one month) as the difference between the tax charged on taxable sales (output tax) and the tax paid on imports and domestic purchases from other firms (input tax credits).[37]

Output tax (tax on taxable sales)
Less Input tax credits (tax on taxable imports and taxable domestic purchases)
Net tax liability for the period

In this calculation, output tax = taxable sales multiplied by the tax rate, and input credits consist of both VAT on taxable imports listed on import documents and VAT on taxable domestic purchases listed on VAT invoices. Input credits for tax on imports and purchases are allowed only to the extent that the business inputs are used in making taxable sales.[38] In some countries, such as sales within the EU, imports of goods are not taxed at the border but are reported and paid as output tax in the tax period in which the goods are imported, generally with an offsetting input credit.

they are sold. Rather, the 'margin' as derived under Russian accounting is a percentage defined in advance, sometimes also including so-called 'trade discounts' or 'increments' as well. This margin is calculated on a tax inclusive basis, and the tax liability is the margin multiplied by the tax-inclusive rate of VAT. *Id.* at 20–21. [This system is derived from the old turnover tax in use in the Soviet system and other planned economies. Since all prices were set in the plan, margins were contrived and prices and margins bore no relation to supply and demand, let alone value added by any particular level of production. The turnover tax was applied at whatever rate was required to leave the planned amount of 'profit' in each enterprise. . . .] The authors discuss the significant problems created by this complex gross margins method, especially when it must operate within a system that also uses the credit-invoice method. For example, "the margin is derived by deducting from sales not all purchased inputs, but only those removed from inventory. Those items remaining in inventory are therefore held on a tax-paid basis. . . . Because the planned margin, on which the tax is imposed, is not affected by inflation, the increased selling price of the goods as a result of inflation does not affect the firm's liability for value added tax when they are withdrawn from inventory." *Id.* at 21. [Edited by the authors].

[36] The tax credit method can be especially useful if it is desired to reduce the rate of the value added tax at some stage in the productive and distributive process, say the raw materials or farm products stage, for administrative reasons, without reducing the total tax paid on total value added. The reduced tax at the earlier stage simply gives rise to an equally increased tax at a later stage. The determinative tax rate on the entire value of any commodity will be the tax rate applicable at the last stage, typically the retail stage. This result cannot be achieved under the addition or subtraction method. Shoup, *Public Finance, supra* note 23, at 259.

[37] The European Union's Sixth Directive, which lays down the fundamental structure and rules for member countries of the EU, describes the credit as a deduction from the tax collected on a firm's sales.

[38] For example, purchases from exempt small traders do not qualify for the input tax credit.

Table 2.2.

Output tax	
Taxable sales $100,000 × 10% rate	$10,000
Input credits	
Purchases from exempt small businesses $5,300	(00)
Taxable domestic purchases $60,000 × 10%	(6,000)
Taxable imports $10,000 × 10%	(1,000)
Net VAT liability for the period	$ 3,000

For example, if the final product is novelty shirts for sports teams, the final shirt passes through many different firms and processes, starting with the production of the cotton and ending with the sale by the retailer. At each step in the process, the shirt becomes more valuable. Each firm adds additional value to the shirt.

To illustrate just one stage of the VAT collection process, assume that a VAT-registered retailer sold thousands of these shirts (taxable sales) in a tax period for $100,000, makes taxable purchases of $60,000, and taxable imports of $10,000 (all at tax-exclusive prices). The imports and domestic purchases are all used in making the taxable sales. The VAT rate is 10 percent, applied to tax-exclusive prices. As shown in Table 2.2, the retailer's net VAT liability for the period is $3,000, calculated as follows:

The total VAT received by the government from all stages of production and distribution with respect to these shirts is $10,300, of which the dealer paid $4,000 ($3,000 with the VAT return and $1,000 on taxable imports), the retailer's suppliers other than the exempt small business paid $6,000, and it is assumed that the exempt small business paid $300 of noncreditable VAT on its purchases. In short, except for the exempt small business, the share of the total tax that is paid by each firm is in proportion to the value each firm added to its taxable inputs.

A modern 10 percent VAT collects 10 percent of the value added at each stage in the process. In essence, the VAT can be looked at as a way of collecting in stages a retail sales tax. Readers are familiar with the use of withholding in the context of the income tax; the VAT can be looked at as a form of withholding in the context of a retail sales tax. At each stage in the production and distribution process, part of the ultimate amount of the VAT is collected, just like part of the ultimate amount of the income tax is collected over the year through withholding. This collection mechanism has proven to be effective in raising revenue while keeping the costs of tax administration and compliance low.

The credit-invoice method used almost universally is a tax imposed on transactions. The credit-invoice method, which relies on invoices and links reported sales to the prices charged in market transactions, does not easily handle some industries and transactions, such as secondhand goods acquired by a registered person from consumers for resale, financial intermediation services (including casualty insurance), and gambling.

Table 2.3.

Output tax		
Taxable sales $100,000 \times 10\%$		$10,000
Input credits[39]		
Purchases from exempt small businesses	$5,300	(482)
Taxable domestic purchases	$66,000	(6,000)
Taxable imports	$11,000	(1,000)
Net VAT liability for the period		$ 2,518

The prompt recovery of tax by VAT-registered persons on business inputs is designed to remove VAT as a business cost and thereby remove VAT as an element in the tax-exclusive prices of taxable goods and services. To fully remove VAT as a business cost, a VAT-registered business should receive a prompt refund of any excess input credits for a tax period.

B. Credit-Subtraction VAT That Does Not Rely on VAT Invoices

The credit-subtraction VAT without invoices is illustrated by the unique Japanese Consumption tax, effective in 1989.[40] Under that tax, tax on taxable sales (output tax) is calculated the same as under the credit-invoice VAT. Output tax is equal to total taxable sales for the period (exclusive of tax), multiplied by the tax rate. The CT did not require registered businesses to issue VAT invoices on taxable sales. The CT also allowed registered businesses to claim credits for CT on purchases from exempt small businesses as well as from registered suppliers. As a result, a registered business did not have any incentive to prefer a registered supplier. Input credits are denied for CT on purchases of exempt goods and services. Input credits are calculated from the tax-inclusive costs recorded in purchase records, except for the cost of purchases exempt from CT. Input credit is equal to the tax-inclusive cost of allowable purchases and imports, multiplied by the tax fraction. The tax fraction is the tax rate divided by 100 plus the tax rate. The retail firm in this example, if subject to the CT, has net CT liability for the period of $2,518, calculated as shown in Table 2.3.

---

[39] Since imports and purchases are recorded at CT-inclusive prices, the input credits = the CT-inclusive prices multiplied by the fraction, the numerator of which is the tax rate (10%) and the denominator is 100 + the tax rate (110), even for purchases of otherwise taxable items from exempt small businesses. The actual Japanese CT rate is 5 percent, but 10 percent was used to make the various calculations comparable.

[40] Shohizei – ho [Consumption Tax Law], Law No. 108 of 1988, pt. IV [hereinafter Japanese CT Law]. The original Japanese VAT, adopted in 1950 but never implemented, calculated the tax by levying the tax rate on the difference between a firm's sales and its purchases. The evolving CT increased the substantiation requirements for input tax credits. The result is the movement of the CT closer to the European model that relies on invoices to verify output tax on taxable sales and input credit on domestic taxable purchases.

C. Sales-Subtraction VAT

The sales-subtraction method calculates net VAT liability by multiplying the tax rate by the base. The base is the difference between total taxable sales less total taxable purchases from other firms.[41] This information may be available from modified company sales and purchase records. Like an addition VAT, the sales-subtraction VAT is a period tax based on cumulative data for each tax period, not a tax imposed on individual transactions. The seller must price taxable goods and services inclusive of VAT. This VAT-inclusive data is used to calculate periodic VAT liability.[42]

The VAT liability for each period is the product of the tax base multiplied by the VAT rate. This method of calculating tax liability makes it difficult to impose more than one rate of VAT on taxable goods or services. Although it is possible to deny deductions for VAT on purchases from exempt small businesses, for administrative reasons, these purchases may be deductible, in which case this VAT has been described as the "naïve" sales-subtraction VAT.[43]

To make the illustration comparable to the tables earlier in this chapter, for taxable sales and taxable purchases, Table 2.4 uses a 9.0909 percent rate on VAT-inclusive prices instead of the 10 percent rate applied to tax-exclusive prices. The retailer's net VAT liability for the period is the same $2,518 as under the Japanese-style, credit-subtraction VAT that does not rely on invoices. If it is administratively feasible to deny deductions for purchases from exempt small businesses, the net VAT liability would be the same $3,000 payable under the credit-invoice VAT.

D. Addition-Method VAT

The addition-method VAT requires a taxable firm to calculate tax liability for each tax period by adding the firm's economic factors of production for the period (wages, rent and interest expense, and profit for VAT purposes) and

---

[41] Finland relied on a sales-subtraction VAT, enacted in 1978, that had a base analogous to national income. See Shoup, Choosing Among VATs, *supra* note 23, at 14. Under existing value added taxes (although some modern American proposals are different), wages and salaries are not treated as a taxable purchase; that is, wage earners are not VAT taxpayers. If landlords and banks are subject to value added taxes (a number of countries tax the former but not the latter), then payment for those rental and financial services would also be subtracted from sales in computing a business firm's value added tax base.

[42] "[The legislature] . . . could require disclosure of tax at the cash register or by a sign posted in retail stores indicating the tax rate that is included in the prices." Oldman & Schenk, "The Business Activities Tax: Have Senators Danforth & Boren Created à Better Value Added Tax?" [hereinafter Oldman & Schenk, Business Activities Tax], 65 *Tax Notes* 1547, 1551 (Dec. 19, 1994).

[43] Dr. McLure refers to this kind of sales-subtraction VAT that allows deductions for purchases from exempt small businesses as the naïve sales-subtraction VAT. See McLure, VAT, *supra* note 23, at 71–79.

Table 2.4.

Taxable sales		$110,000
Purchases allowable as deductions		
Purchases from exempt small businesses	5,300	
Taxable domestic purchases	66,000	
Taxable imports	11,000	
		$82,300
Tax base		27,700
Tax rate		9.0909%
Net VAT liability for the period		$2,518

Table 2.5.

Taxable sales		$110,000
Expenses for VAT purposes		
Wages	$17,000	
Interest and rent expenses	2,000	
Purchases	82,300	
Total expenses		101,300
Profit for VAT purposes		$8,700

multiplying the total by the tax rate. The Michigan Single Business Tax is a modified version of an addition-method VAT.[44]

The addition method has not been adopted as a national tax, except for Israel's taxation of financial institutions and insurance companies under a tax measured by the sum of the firm's wages and profits. This tax is administered by the income tax department, outside the VAT system.

Like the accounts-based sales-subtraction VAT (also a period tax), an addition VAT must be imposed at one rate because "company accounts do not usually divide sales by different product categories coinciding with different sales tax rates, and . . . they certainly never divide inputs by differential tax liabilities. . . . "[45]

If the "profit" portion of the addition-method VAT base is taken from data prepared for income tax purposes, this method of calculating VAT liability may be expected to be an income-based, not consumption-based, tax.[46] Because the tax base includes only the value added as measured by the economic factors of production employed at each stage, revenue lost at a prior stage is not recovered (as under the invoice VAT) at the next stage of production or distribution of goods or rendition of services. "As a period tax, an addition method VAT probably will be treated as a cost of production and

[44] See also New Hampshire Business Enterprise Tax, discussed later in this book.
[45] A. TAIT, VALUE ADDED TAX: INTERNATIONAL PRACTICE AND PROBLEMS (IMF 1988) [hereinafter Tait, VAT], p. 5.
[46] McLure, VAT, *supra* note 23, at 95. See also Shoup, Public Finance, *supra* note 23, ch. 9.

Table 2.6.

Wages	$17,000
Interest and rent expenses	2,000
Profit for VAT purposes	8,700
Tax base	$27,700
Tax rate	9.0909%
Net VAT liability for the period	$2,518

included in the pricing structure of taxable goods and services. Since the VAT liability is not based on the . . . sales price [of] . . . goods, it is unlikely that the exact VAT, no more and no less, will be shifted to consumers."[47]

To make the calculation of net VAT liability for a tax period consistent with the above example, it is necessary to add some assumptions. Sales and purchases listed in Tables 2.5 and 2.6 are at tax-inclusive prices and the tax rate in Table 2.6 is 9.0909 percent. Assume that the retailer, in addition to the total purchases of $82,300 (including purchases from exempt small businesses), pays $17,000 in wages and $2,000 in interest and rent expense. The profit for VAT purposes is $8,700, calculated as follows:

Applying this data, the net VAT liability for the period is $2,518, the same as under the "naïve" sales-subtraction VAT.

Table 2.7 is a matrix presentation of the basic differences among these different kinds of VAT (addition, subtraction, and credit methods), combined with the three methods of handling purchases of capital goods (gross product, income, and consumption types, using national income account concepts).[48] For this purpose, the following data set for the firm are used.

Data set for Table 2.7

Current purchases	300	Computation of profit:		
Depreciation	40	Sales		1000
Wages	400	Less Costs:		
Rent	100	Purchases	300	
Profit	180	Depreciation	40	
Beginning inventory	100	Wages	400	
Investment in fixed		Rent	100	
assets	50		840	
Sales	1,000	Change in invty	(20)	
Closing inventory	120			820
		Profit		180

The addition method included in the first column of numbers in Table 2.7 is calculated under the gross product, income, and consumption treatment for capital goods. Rent and interest are accounted for in each block as part of the computation of value added by each firm. The assumption is that the provider of the leased premises or the loan is not a firm included in the VAT

---

[47] ABA Model VAT, *supra* note 23, at 6.
[48] This table is based on Shoup, Public Finance, *supra* note 23, at 257–260.

Table 2.7. Calculation of base under gross product, income, and consumption VAT

Base	Addition		Subtraction		Credit	
Gross Product	+Profit	180	+Sales	1,000	+Tax on sales	100
	+Depr.	40	−Purchases (current)	(300)	−Credit on purchases	(30)
	+Wages	400	+Increase in inventory	20	+Tax on invty increase	2
	+Rent pd	100				
	+Int. pd	0				
	VAT Base	720	VAT Base	720		
	Tax (10%)	72	Tax	72	Tax	72
Income	+Profit	180	+Sales	1,000	+Tax on sales	100
	+Wages	400	−Purchases (current)	(300)	−Credit on purchases	(30)
	+Rent pd	100	+Increase in inventory	20	+Tax on invty increase	2
	+Int. pd	0	−Depr.	(40)	−Tax on depreciable part of property	(4)
	VAT Base	680	VAT Base	680		
	Tax (10%)	68	Tax	68	Tax	68
Consumption	+Profit	180	+Sales	1,000	+Tax on sales	100
	+Wages	400	−Purchases (current)	(300)	−Credit on current & investment purchases	(35)
	− Increase in inventory	(20)	−Investment	(50)		
	+Depr.	40				
	−Investment	(50)				
	+Int. pd	0				
	+Rent pd	100				
	VAT Base	650	VAT Base	650		
	Tax (10%)	65	Tax	65	Tax	65

Assumptions: 1. General comprehensive VAT at single uniform 10% rate. 2. Profit is net income after depreciation and adjustment for inventory.

base. Hence, the value added by rent and interest as factors of production is included in the accounts of the firm paying the rent or interest (just as they would be imputed, or would increase "profit" if the firm used its own property or money).

Table 2.8. Illustration of car rental firm renting only for personal consumption

Outlays		Receipts	
Purchase of car, Jan 1	5,000	Rentals (20/day for 300 days/yr)	6,000
Labor – auto service & clerical	1,500		
Interest, office rent & insurance	1,000	Sale of used auto at year end, Dec. 31	2,000
	7,500		8,000

Notes: Interest, office rent, and insurance paid by firm are part of firm's value added tax base. Capital goods transactions (office furniture, etc.) are omitted. Cars are inventory, not capital goods.

In the Subtraction and Credit methods columns of Table 2.7, there is no mention of rent and interest. Do you see how they are nevertheless accounted for? They must be, of course, since all columns are based on the same data set preceding Table 2.7. Hint – look at the "spread" between sales (or tax on sales) and purchases (or tax on purchases) after adjustments for capital.

Tables 2.8 and 2.9 take a different approach. They illustrate how assumed tax-exclusive data from a firm that provides leasing services to consumers (Table 2.8) can be used to construct tax bases under a single stage retail sales tax and under credit, addition, and subtraction method VATs (Table 2.9).

IV. Methods of Altering the Tax Base

In drafting an administrable VAT, tax policy makers must try to satisfy "the deep, widespread feelings of the people as to what is fair."[49]

A normative base for a tax on consumption like the VAT is one that taxes final consumption of all goods and services. If the jurisdictional reach of the VAT is defined by the destination principle, the tax should be imposed on all imported goods and services and returned (by credit, or refund in the case of excess input credits) on all exported goods and services. In its pure state, the tax base would include services rendered by government, an isolated sale to a neighbor of a used refrigerator, toys, or an automobile, or the sale of a personal residence. For administrative as well as political or social reasons, no nation employs a VAT with this base.

As a tax generally imposed on domestic consumption, a seller's quarterly or annual total sales activities should not be relevant. However, for administrative and compliance reasons, it is impractical to impose a collection and

---

[49] Gen. Headquarters, Supreme Commander for Allied Powers, Tokyo, 1 *Report on Japanese Taxation* 17 (1949) (four-volume report).

Table 2.9. Possible sales tax bases and tax payments (10% rate)

Base		Tax	Description
			Retail taxes
a. Purchase of car	5,000 @ 10%	500	On goods
b. Rentals	6,000 @ 10%	600	On services
c. a + b		1,100	Double tax on goods and services
d. Sale of used car	2,000 @ 10%	200	On used goods
e. a + b + d		1,300	On goods & services & used goods
f. b + d	8,000 @ 10%	800	Retail sales tax (consumption base)
g. Tax on annual receipts	8,000 @ 10%	800	CREDIT-METHOD VAT
Tax on purchase of car	5,000 @ 10%	500	
Tax due		300	
h. Labor		1,500	ADDITION-METHOD VAT
Interest, etc.		1,000	
Profit	8,000		
	−1,500		
	−1,000		
	−5,000	500	
Tax base		3,000	
Tax rate		10%	
Tax due		300	
i. Annual receipts		8,000	SUBTRACTION-METHOD VAT
Tax paid purchases		5,000	
Net value added		3,000	
Tax rate		10%	
Tax due		300	

Note: Total tax collected in (f) is same as in (g),(h) & (i), but in VAT, there is 500 tax collected before retail stage.

reporting requirement on every seller of any product or service. Every wage earner provides services and could be regarded as a taxable supplier of them. No existing VAT does this.[50] The quantum and nature of the sales activity therefore is used in most countries to define the persons or entities that are subject to VAT.[51]

---

[50] [A flat tax proposal in the United States imposes part of the tax on business, but business can deduct compensation paid to workers. The workers are taxed separately under a wage tax that allows generous deductions and exemptions to provide some progressivity to the tax. See the Shelby bill, Freedom and Fairness Restoration Act of 1995, S. 1050, 104th Cong. 1st Sess. *Added by authors.*]

[51] Some of the material in this section is taken from Oldman & Schenk, Business Activities Tax, *supra* note 42.

Most VATs apply to firms engaged in regular and continuous business activity, removing from the VAT base isolated sales by an individual. A small business exemption may remove a significant number of firms but a small percentage of value added from the tax base. Government services and, in some countries, government purchases are not in the tax base.[52] Other exemptions, based on the nature of the seller, may be provided for charities and other nonprofits.

Multiple rates may be used to increase tax on luxuries or reduce the VAT burden on goods and services deemed necessities. Special treatment may be granted by exempting or zero-rating particular categories of goods or services.[53] Some may be based on treaties or international agreements, such as diplomatic exemptions.[54] Finally, a transaction may be removed from the VAT base because it is easy to identify, typically is for a large consideration, and will not result in any net revenue loss to the government. A sale of a going business between two VAT-registered firms falls in this category.[55] "Lower VAT rates on labour intensive services has been suggested as a means to promote employment."[56] The Michigan Single Business Tax (a state-level addition-method VAT) includes a tax concession to labor-intensive businesses.[57]

As the VAT base is narrowed, especially by multiple rates and grants of exemptions and zero-rating, the costs increase for business to comply with and for the tax authorities to administer the tax. These methods of altering the VAT base are discussed in this section.

A. Entity Exemptions

There are two different kinds of entity exemptions granted under VAT regimes. The first is the small business exemption that does not depend upon the kind of goods or services provided by the seller. The second is

---

[52] "For example, some registered charities are exempt from [the Canadian] GST on their sales of property or services and they also can claim rebate for a portion of their non-creditable input tax on purchases attributable to their charitable activities." A. Schenk, Goods and Services Tax: The Canadian Approach to Value-Added Tax [hereinafter Schenk, Canadian GST], p. 10, citing Canadian GST, Sch. V, Part VI, Public Sector Bodies.

[53] "In some cases, special treatment may be linked both to the nature of the seller and the nature of the sale. For example, under the [Canadian] GST, if a business qualifies as a financial institution, it is exempt from tax on its rendition of specified financial services, but it is subject to tax on its other sales." Schenk, Canadian GST, *supra* note 52, at 10.

[54] New Vatopia VAT, appendix B, §38, provides for a refund instead of exemption or zero-rating for diplomats and organizations covered by a technical assistance or humanitarian assistance agreement.

[55] *Id.* at appendix B, Sch. I zero rates these sales.

[56] Consumption Tax Trends, OECD 1995 [hereinafter 1995 OECD Consumption Tax Trends], p. 20.

[57] Single Business Tax Act, P.A. 1975, No. 228, MCL §208.1 et seq.

the exemption provided for all sales or particular sales made by an entity because of the nature of the entity. For example, the national government may be exempt from VAT or only essential governmental services rendered by a unit of government may be exempt.

Typically, countries with VATs remove from the tax base firms with annual sales at or below the small business exemption threshold. The small business exemption threshold varies among countries. For example, for complete exemption from tax, the threshold in Canada is Can.$30,000,[58] in the United Kingdom is £45,000,[59] and in Japan is ¥30 million.[60] Businesses exempt from tax do not report taxable sales and do not claim credit for tax on taxable purchases, and their customers generally are denied any VAT benefit from the cost of purchases from these exempt sellers.

A business making only sales that are exempt from tax would be treated the same as an exempt small business. In contrast, a business making both taxable and exempt sales would come within the VAT system for its taxable business activity and fall outside the VAT system for its exempt business activity.

There is a notable difference between the European-style VATs and the Japanese Consumption Tax (CT) but that difference is not inherent in the Japanese credit-subtraction VAT that does not rely on invoices. A business subject to the CT can claim credit for implicit tax in the cost of purchases from exempt sellers such as exempt small businesses.[61] Thus, if a business subject to a 5 percent CT purchases supplies for $1,030 from an exempt small business, the business can claim an input credit for the full 5/105 of $1,030, or $49.05, even though it is unlikely that the purchase price contains that much CT. Under a European VAT, a credit cannot be claimed with respect to a purchase from an exempt supplier.[62]

An exemption, based on the nature of the seller, may be provided for units of government and nonprofit organizations. These entities, even if outside the VAT registration system because all of their services are exempt, still must pay tax on their inputs and imports. Others may be taxable on services that compete with services rendered by the private sector.[63]

---

[58] Canadian GST, subsection 148(1). The threshold for public service bodies is Can$50,000. There is no threshold for taxi and limousine operators and nonresident performers.

[59] VATA 1994, §3 and Sch. 1, ¶1(1) (United Kingdom).

[60] Japanese CT Law, *supra* note 40, at Art. 9.

[61] The Japanese CT denies input tax deductions for purchases exempt from tax, such as exempt medical supplies.

[62] The material in this subsection is taken in part from Oldman & Schenk, Business Activities Tax, *supra* note 42, at 1556–1557.

[63] Under the VAT in the United Kingdom, tax applies "to taxable supplies by the Crown as it applies in relation to taxable supplies by taxable persons." VATA 1983, section 27(1) (United Kingdom). Sales by government departments are not treated as sales made in the course of business (and therefore are not taxable) unless the Treasury so directs. *Id.* at section 27(2). In Japan, the complex provisions governing units of government and their eligibility for refunds of input tax are covered in Article 60 of the CT. See Japanese CT Law, *supra* note 40.

New Zealand treats activities of a public authority or local authority[64] as taxable activities.[65] In fact, New Zealand subjects "rates" to VAT as a surrogate for the taxation of services rendered with the revenue from the rates. New Zealand exempts sales by a nonprofit body of donated goods and services.[66]

An exempt entity that is denied credit for VAT on inputs used in its exempt business activities (and for competitive or other reasons it cannot pass this cost on to its customers) may attempt to avoid tax on some purchased services by providing them in-house rather than purchasing them from outside taxable suppliers. To prevent this incentive toward vertical integration, some countries treat certain self-supplies by exempt entities or organizations as taxable sales to themselves, reportable on VAT returns, notwithstanding their general exemption from VAT.[67]

B. ZERO RATING[68]

Zero rating is the mechanism under a VAT system by which the tax can be completely removed from a particular product or service or from a particular transaction. Under a credit-invoice VAT, a seller of a zero-rated item does not charge VAT on the sale. The sale is classified as a taxable sale subject to a zero rate. As such, the seller is entitled to recover as input credit the tax included in the cost of taxable purchases attributable to that sale.[69]

Under a sales-subtraction VAT, zero rating is accomplished by excluding the designated sales from gross receipts and allowing the business to deduct taxed purchases attributable to these zero-rated sales.

Countries that rely on the destination principle to tax international transactions typically zero rate exports of goods (regardless of the nature of the

---

[64] See NZ Goods & Services Tax Act 1985, No. 141, as amended, at section 6(1)(b). A public authority is any agency of government, including departments, but is not the Governor-General, ministers, members of Parliament, or members of the Executive Council. *Id.* at section 2 definition of "public authority." A local authority is an authority included in section 2(1) of the Rating Powers Act 1988. *Id.* at section 2 definition of "local authority." Any payment by the Crown to the public authority is treated as a sale by the public authority that may be subject to GST. *Id.* at section 5(6).

[65] The New Zealand GST imposes tax on sales by a registered person in connection with a taxable activity. *Id.* at section 8(1).

[66] *Id.* at section 14(1)(b). A nonprofit body is an organization that is not conducted for profit or gain of a proprietor, member, or shareholder, and that is prohibited from making distributions to any such person. *Id.* at section 2 definition of "non-profit body."

[67] Value Added Tax Act 1994, §5(4)–(6) (United Kingdom).

[68] The material in subsections B–D is taken largely from Oldman & Schenk, Business Activities Tax, *supra* note 42, at 1557–1560, but it has been edited. The footnotes are renumbered, some footnotes are omitted, and the table numbers have been changed. In OECD countries, "(z)ero rating is only practised to any significant extent in Canada, Ireland and the United Kingdom (and, to some extent, Mexico), where the role of zero-rating is analogous to the use of reduced rates elsewhere. In other countries where zero-rating is not extensively employed, zero-rating is often applied to books and newspapers, reflecting a belief that 'knowledge' should not be taxed." 1995 OECD Consumption Tax Trends, *supra* note 56, at 19.

[69] If a sale may be exempt and zero-rated, the legislation may give priority to the zero-rating. See New Vatopia VAT, appendix B, §16(2).

goods exported) and specified services because those exports will be consumed outside the taxing country. This zero rating is not a preference. The export sales are merely beyond the jurisdictional reach of the tax.[70] The destination principle reflects the near universal understanding that in geographically assigning sales tax or VAT burdens and revenues, the country of consumption gets both; the country of production gets neither. Consistently, most countries do not tax sales of goods located abroad for delivery abroad because these sales are beyond the scope of the VAT.[71]

Some countries include item or transactional zero rating of particular goods or services for social or political reasons (such as sales of food). Some countries with credit-invoice VATs zero rate a long list of goods and services.[72] For example, the United Kingdom zero rates, among other items, exports, certain food, water, books and other printed matter, recording aids for the blind and disabled, newspaper advertisements, news services, fuel and power, gold, and drugs and medicines.[73] The newer VATs (outside the EU) tend to restrict zero rating to exports of goods and services related to the exported goods.

Many VAT systems zero rate certain otherwise taxable domestic transactions between registered businesses both for administrative convenience and to avoid cash flow burdens on the parties to the transactions.[74] The most common transaction in this group is the sale of a going business. This kind of transaction usually involves no net change in revenue to the government because the tax otherwise reportable by the seller is offset by an input credit or deduction to the purchaser or transferee.[75]

Some transactions are not subject to VAT because legal ownership to property is not transferred.[76] Although they are not specifically zero rated,

---

[70] The zero rating typically extends to transportation and other services directly attributable to the exported products. The zero rating also may extend to the export of some other services.

[71] Under the EC's Sixth Directive, transactions conducted outside the taxing jurisdiction (such as foreign sales of goods located outside the country), exports, export-related services, and international transport are zero rated. Sixth VAT Directive of May 17, 1977, On the Harmonization of the Laws of the Member States Relating to Turnover Taxes – Common System of Value Added Tax: Uniform Basis of Assessment, Official Journal No. L145 [hereinafter Sixth VAT Directive], at Articles 15 & 17(3). For a discussion of these zero-rated transactions, see Terra & Kajus, *A Guide to the European VAT Directives: Introduction to European VAT and other indirect taxes 2005* [hereinafter Terra & Kajus], 17.3 & 19.1 et seq. See discussion of Recast Sixth Directive *infra* Chapter 3. New Zealand zero rates exports of goods and allied services performed outside New Zealand, foreign sales of goods not located in New Zealand, services on property located outside the country, and services related to intellectual property to be used outside New Zealand. New Zealand Goods and Services Tax Act 1985, No. 141, §11 (other than §11(c)). The Japanese CT zero rates only export sales, including international transportation and telecommunications. See Japanese CT Law, *supra* note 40, at Articles 7 & 8.

[72] See New Vatopia VAT, appendix B, §17 and Sch. I, ¶2.

[73] See Value Added Tax Act 1994, Sch. 5, as amended (United Kingdom).

[74] New Vatopia VAT, appendix B, §17 and Sch. I, ¶2(o).

[75] A purchaser of a zero-rated sale of a going business may be required to report tax on the purchase to the extent that the acquired assets are used in exempt activities. See Vatopia, appendix B, §4(18) & (19).

[76] New Vatopia VAT, appendix B, §4(16).

the transactions receive treatment comparable to zero rating. For example, Canada removes from the tax base transactions involving property seized or repossessed by a creditor to satisfy a debtor's obligation,[77] or transactions involving property transferred to an insurer in satisfaction of an insurance claim.[78] No tax is imposed on the repossession or transfer.

C. Transaction Exemption

If a sale of a particular good or service is exempt under a credit-invoice VAT or the Japanese CT variant, the sale is not taxed and the seller is denied an input credit for the tax paid on purchases used in that exempt activity. The grant of exemption for domestic sales substantially increases the administrative and compliance costs of a VAT,[79] especially if a business makes both taxable and exempt sales. In the latter situation, the business must allocate credits between taxable and exempt activities because it is denied credit for input tax on purchases attributable to this exempt activity. The EU Sixth Directive sanctions exemptions for a long list of services,[80] and Japan also exempts many categories of sales.[81] The New Vatopia VAT, consistent with the recent trend, contains limited exemptions of domestic sales[82] and imports.[83]

---

[77] These transactions are deemed to have been made for no consideration and therefore are not includible in the GST base. Canadian GST, Part IX of the *Excise Tax Act*, S.C. 1993, c. 27, at section 183(1)(a),(b). These transactions nevertheless are treated as supplies. If the recipient has any purchases associated with this seizure or repossession, input tax on such purchases qualify for input credit.

[78] These transactions also are deemed to have been made for no consideration. *Id.* at section 184(1)(a),(b).

[79] See *US General Accounting Office, Value-Added Tax: Administrative Costs Vary With Complexity and Number of Businesses, Report to the Joint Committee on Taxation, US Congress,* May, 1993, p. 7. Some countries are attempting to reduce the number of item exemptions under their VAT regimes. See, for example, the Philippine Expanded Value Added tax Act of 2005, Republic Act No. 9337), which dropped the exemptions for power and electricity, and air and sea transport. See Gutierrez, "Philippine Leader Signs Law to Increase Corporate Tax Rate, Modify VAT Regime," *BNA Daily Tax Report,* May 25, 2005, p. G-5.

[80] Under the Sixth Directive, there are exemptions for postal services, hospital and medical care, human organs, dental technicians and dental prostheses, welfare and social security, protection of children, education, religious organizations, trade unions, culture, public radio and television, insurance, banking, certain other financial services, and certain imports. Sixth VAT Directive, *supra* note 71, at Articles 13–16, discussed in detail in Terra & Kajus, *supra* note 71.

[81] The Japanese refer to exemptions as nontaxable transactions. The Japanese CT exempts sales and leases of land and interests in land, rentals for residential purposes, sales of interest in partnerships and cooperatives, certain financial and insurance services, government-run lotteries, horse and bicycle races, postal stamps, certain public services for which fees are charged, certain medical services, certain educational fees charged by some schools, books for educational purposes, social welfare services, certain burial services, and sales and leases of certain goods for the physically handicapped. Japanese CT, *supra* note 40, Art. 6, as amended.

[82] New Vatopia VAT, appendix B, §18 and Sch. II, ¶2.

[83] *Id.* at §21 and Sch. III.

Table 2.10. Adapted[84] from "The Value-Added Tax in Developing Countries"[85]

	Purchases	VA at each stage	Sales (incl. VAT)	Sales (before VAT)	Gross tax	10% VAT Credit on purchases	Net tax paid	If Miller's sales exempt – VAT net
Farmer	250[86]	1,000	1,100	1,000	100	(00)	100	100
Miller	1,100	500	1,650	1,500	150	(100)	50	00
Baker	1,650	1,000	2,750	2,500	250	(150)	100	250
Retailer	2,750	1,500	4,400	4,000	400	(250)	150	150
		4,000					400	500

An exemption granted under the invoice VAT at an intermediate stage of production or distribution may increase the price paid by the final consumer and increase revenue to the fisc over the situations where this exemption is not provided.[87] A retail stage exemption reduces revenue and, to the extent the tax saving is passed on to consumers, reduces retail prices as well.

Under a sales-subtraction VAT, transactions are exempted by removing the sales from taxable gross receipts and by denying the deduction for the cost of purchases attributable to those exempt sales. Of course, the prices charged by sellers on exempt transactions may include tax paid by them on purchases used in that exempt sales activity.

Table 2.10 provides a graphic illustration of the effect of a midstream exemption under a credit-invoice VAT. The workings of a VAT may be illustrated by this simplified example based on the various stages involved in the production and sale of bread produced from, say, five hundred bushels of wheat. The figures shown are in U.S. dollars.

---

[84] Adapted by O. Oldman.

[85] G. E. Lent, M. Casanegra, and M. Guerard, IMF STAFF PAPERS, July 1973, p. 321.

[86] Assume no tax paid on purchases made by farmer. The value added represented by those purchases (250) is included in the farmer's value added of 1,000.

[87] "If ... one or more of the earlier stages of value added are completely exempt, the tax-credit method fails to record the correct amount of cumulated tax paid unless either (a) the stage so exempted is the very first stage, typically the raw materials stage, or (b) either (1) at the exempt stage there is a refund of prior tax paid or (2) a shadow tentative tax is computed that can be shown on the invoice issued by the exempt seller and claimed as a credit by the one who purchases from him. If, no tax at all being due at the stage in question, no tax credit is taken by the exempt seller, all record of earlier tax paid is lost, and no account can be taken of it at later stages where taxation resumes. . . . Under the subtraction or addition method, exemption of the small firm at an intermediate stage does not give rise to over-taxation. On the other hand, revenue is always lost by the exemption; there is no catching up at a later stage, as there is under the tax credit for an earlier-stage exemption. On balance, this failure to regain the revenue, equal to the tax rate times the value added by the exempt firm, seems less serious than the injustices that can occur under the tax-credit system. Apart from adding administrative complications, an exemption at any point along the cycle (except at the very beginning or at the ultimate stage) normally results in a break in the tax-credit chain, leading to an element of double taxation." C. S. Shoup, General Sales Taxes: Retail Sales Tax, Value Added Tax, in PUBLIC FINANCE, pp. 259–260 (1969) [hereinafter Shoup, General Sales Taxes, Retail Sales Tax, Value Added Tax].

It can be seen that a 10 percent tax is assessed at each stage of the process on the amount of sale, excluding the VAT, but that credit is taken for tax paid on purchases, leaving a net amount of tax chargeable on the value added at each stage. The cumulative tax – $400 – is equivalent to a rate of 10 percent on the $4,000 tax-exclusive retail sale of the product to consumers.

D. Alteration of Base by Granting or Denying Credits

The tax base of a credit-invoice VAT or a credit-subtraction VAT without invoices (the Japanese CT) can be altered by granting extra input credits or denying otherwise available credits to promote some social, economic, or other nonrevenue goal. Foreign VAT systems make only limited use of this device to alter the VAT base.

The Sixth Directive provides that a Member may disallow otherwise allowable input credits on purchases for luxuries, amusement, or entertainment.[88] The Japanese CT, by contrast, grants more input credit than can be accounted for (or was paid) with respect to some purchases. For example, the CT allows taxable businesses to claim input credit imputed from the full cost of purchases from exempt small businesses.

E. Multiple Rates

To achieve political or other nonrevenue goals, a nation may employ multiple VAT rates rather than grant exemption or zero rating to particular categories of goods or services. A higher rate may be employed to discourage the consumption of particular goods (alcohol and tobacco) or to attempt to make the tax more progressive (luxuries). Many European countries impose lower positive rates on a variety of goods and services.[89] For example, France imposes a lower 5.5 percent rate on chocolate.[90] The EU may make permanent a scheme under which a reduced VAT rate may be imposed by member states on some labor-intensive services.[91] Argentina imposes a lower rate on the sale of camels and goats.[92]

> The tax credit method can be especially useful if it is desired to reduce the rate of the value-added tax at some stage in the productive and distributive

---

[88] Sixth VAT Directive, *supra* note 71, at Article 17(6) [Art. 170 in the Recast Sixth Directive]. The disallowance of the input credits has the effect of taxing these expenditures as final consumption by those business firms (or the employees or customers who enjoy these purchases), but the tax-inclusive cost of these purchases will be included in the firm's pricing of its taxable output. The result is, of course, additional tax borne by the firm's customers.

[89] See "Practical Information on VAT," *VAT Monitor*, Jan/Feb 2003, p. 2.

[90] See Cotessat, "Chocolate," VAT Monitor, Mar./Apr. 2005, p. 133.

[91] See Directive 2004/15/EC, extending the interim scheme until December 31, 2005. The European Parliament has supported the proposal, but it requires the approval of the EU Council of Ministers. *BNA Daily Tax Report*, Dec. 15, 2004, p. G-3.

[92] Law No. 25,951, effective Nov. 30, 2004, discussed in Calzetta, "VAT rate on camels and goats," *VAT Monitor*, Jan./Feb. 2005, p. 37.

process, say the raw materials or farm products stage, for administrative reasons, without reducing the total tax paid on total value added. The reduced tax at the earlier stage simply gives rise to an equally increased tax at a later stage. The determinative tax rate on the entire value of any commodity will be the tax rate applicable at the last stage, typically the retail stage. This result cannot be achieved under the addition or subtraction method.[93]

V. Discussion Questions

1. If the goal of a VAT is computational simplicity, which method of calculating tax liability (addition or one of the subtraction methods) is preferable for a consumption-type VAT?

2. Assuming that the credit-subtraction method of calculating tax liability is used, is the GDP, Income, or Consumption VAT most compatible with the "simplified bookkeeping" used by some small firms? Why?

3. Is an Income VAT using the addition method easier to administer than an Income VAT using the sales-subtraction method?

4. If the tax base is to be measured by market sales transactions, rather than by the receipt of factor incomes or production during a given period, is a consumption-style VAT the logical choice?

5. If a firm builds a plant with its own labor force, how is the price (i.e., the value added) of this labor taken into account in the consumption-style VAT? In an Income VAT? In a GDP VAT?

6. Under a single rate consumption-style VAT, which method of calculating tax liability is the best if a nation wants to exempt specific commodities, such as unprocessed food or medical drugs? Does the same reasoning apply if a higher rate is desired for luxury items?

7. What are the best ways to ease the compliance burden on farmers? On small retailers? On artisans who sell primarily to businesses?

8. How does zero rating differ from exemption? Is the concept of zero rating appropriate for any method of calculating tax liability other than the credit-invoice method? How would you describe the equivalent concept under the other methods, for example, the addition method?

9. Does adoption of the credit-subtraction method require the use of invoices for each transaction?

10. Reread footnote 87, an excerpt from Dr. Shoup's book on public finance. Do you agree with Dr. Shoup's last sentence in that footnote? Try to construct examples or point to examples in the reading. How does this analysis mesh with the effect of exemptions (especially the small business exemption) under the Japanese Consumption Tax?

---

[93] Shoup, General Sales Taxes, Retail Sales Tax, Value Added Tax, *supra* note 87, at 259–260 (footnotes omitted).

11. A nation is considering the possible adoption of a national sales tax. Before it proposes specific legislation, it would like you to consider some of the basic issues that may affect the structure of the tax on consumption. The following are a few facts about the nation's economy and preliminary comments about the new tax.

About twenty thousand businesses account for about two-thirds of all production and distribution of goods and services in the country. There are a very large number of small retailers that sell goods and render services to final consumers. The remaining third is provided by more than 150,000 retailers and traders. Most of these, including street vendors and small shopkeepers, do not maintain detailed records of their operations.

The strength of the nation's economy comes, in large part, from the export both of agricultural products and consumer goods. Its manufacturers also import significant amounts of raw materials and parts for goods that are consumed domestically and that are exported. The government wants the tax to be paid by consumers, but it is concerned about the effects that this new tax may have on the economy. The government also wants to encourage increased investment in new ventures and wants existing firms to modernize in order to remain competitive in the international markets.

    a. Should the government rely on a retail sales tax or a multistage VAT?
    b. Should the government adopt an origin or destination principle consumption tax?
    c. Politically, the government cannot set the tax rate above 5 percent. What difference does it make if it includes or excludes the new tax from the tax base?
    d. Should the government propose a gross national product, national income, or consumption-style tax?

12. Country X has a consumption-style, destination principle 10 percent European-style, credit-invoice method VAT levied on the tax-exclusive sales price of taxable goods and services and on imports. It provides a "small trader" exemption for businesses that have total taxable receipts below $50,000 annually. In the current period, a distributor imports goods for $30,000 (before VAT), and pays $2,050 for services from a small trader exempt from VAT. This price includes $50 that the small trader paid in VAT on its purchases. The distributor sells to retailers all of its goods for $65,000 (before VAT). These retailers do not make any other purchases, and they sell these goods for $100,000 (before VAT). How much VAT does the government collect from the above transactions?

13. Nation A wants to provide special treatment for some suppliers of goods and services and for some specific goods and services. In the following questions, you should decide if the special treatment should take the form of zero rating or exemption of the supplier and/or the particular goods and services.

a. Nation A wants to provide that charities and units of government shall not charge VAT on their sales of goods or their rendition of services, but they shall not obtain a refund for VAT paid on their purchases.
b. Same as (a), except that the charities and units of government shall obtain a refund for VAT paid on their purchases.
c. Nation A wants to provide that consumers of food sold at retail shall not bear any VAT on food.
d. Nation A wants to provide that insurance companies shall not charge VAT on insurance premiums, but they shall bear VAT paid on their purchases.

14. Why do most nations that impose VAT zero rate all exports of goods, but zero rate only limited categories of services?

3

Varieties of VAT in Use

I. Introduction

Excluding VATs that are covered only tangentially in this book, such as those in effect in China, Russia, and excluding those in civil law, non-English-speaking countries outside the European Union (EU), most VATs imposed at the national level can be classified in four groups. The most prevalent form of VAT is the harmonized VAT in the EU member states. The EU model has the most extensive case law on VAT issues. More recent entrants to the VAT family have expanded the VAT base and made other significant changes. Other customs or common market communities may move to harmonize their indirect taxes in order to provide for the free movement of goods, services, and capital within the community.[1]

New Zealand departed from the EU model in a number of significant ways, including the expansion of the tax base for its Goods and Services Tax (GST) by limiting exemptions and zero rating and by taxing many government services. South Africa modeled its VAT after the New Zealand GST, but included some of its own unique features. For example, South Africa taxes all fee-based financial services.

Canada has a national VAT (its GST) and several provinces have harmonized VATs. The combined Quebec-national GSTs are administered by Quebec. The combined national and maritime provinces GSTs (the Harmonized Sales Tax) are administered at the national level. The Canadian GST is discussed elsewhere in the book.

Japan departed from the EU model by requiring registered firms to calculate periodic tax liability in a different fashion. Under the Japanese Consumption Tax (CT), taxable firms are not required to issue VAT invoices that represent a central feature of other VAT regimes. This chapter describes these four VAT variants.

---

[1] See Decision No. 599 on VAT of the Commission of the Andean Community of Bolivia, Columbia, Ecuador, Peru, and Venezuela pursuant to the Cartegena Agreement establishing this community.

The final section of the chapter briefly notes some differences between VATs in commonlaw and civil law countries.

II. European Union: A Mature VAT Resistant to Change

A. VAT in the European Community

The European Union's (EU) credit-invoice VAT is the most prevalent form of VAT in use today. The EU, formerly the European Economic Community, was created by the Treaty of Rome in 1957.[2] Article 93 of that treaty, as revised, requires the Council, *"acting unanimously on a proposal from the Commission and after consulting the European Parliament and the Economic and Social Committee,"* to adopt provisions for the harmonization of turnover taxes within the Community.[3] Although there have been many attempts to change the rules governing approval of tax changes, VAT directives still can be modified only with the unanimous consent of all member states. This unanimity requirement has stifled the modernization of the EU VAT.

As part of the Treaty of Rome, member states are required to harmonize their value added taxes, although rates among members can vary.[4] A convenient byproduct of this harmonization was the decision to use a portion of the VAT revenue to help finance Community operations. The VAT component is calculated by applying a rate (fluctuating between 1 and 1.4 percent) to an assessment basis that is capped at 50 percent of a Member State's GDP.[5]

The VATs in place in member states define the jurisdictional reach of the tax on international transactions (outside the EU) under the destination principle. As a result, imports of goods from outside the Community are subject

---

[2] The treaty establishing the European Economic Community (EEC) (later changed to the "European Community") was signed in Rome March 25, 1957, and came into force January 1, 1958. This treaty, commonly referred to as the Treaty of Rome, was revised many times, including the Treaty on European Union, signed in Maastricht February 7, 1992, entered into force on November 1, 1993, when the name was changed to the European Union. The Treaty of Amsterdam, signed on October 2, 1997, in force May 1, 1999, amended and renumbered the EU and EC treaties. The Treaty of Nice, entered into force February 1, 2003, merged the Treaty of the European Union and the Treaty of the European Community. See http://europa.eu.int/abc/treaties_en.htm. See the consolidated version of the Treaty on European Union and the Treaty establishing the European Community, 2002 (Official Journal of the European Communities, 2002/C 325/01) [hereinafter Consolidated EU Treaties or Treaty of Nice].

[3] *Id.*

[4] See Directive 2001/4/EC, establishing a minimum standard rate of 15 percent until 12/31/05. See also First VAT Directive of April 11, 1967 (67/227/EEC), requiring all Member States to replace their indirect taxes with a common system of VAT.

[5] See Council Decision 70/243 of April 21, 1970, OJ 1970, English Spec. Ed. (I), 224, discussed in P. Farmer & R. Lyal, EC Tax Law (1994), p. 87. See also B. Terra & P. Wattel, European Tax Law, 2d ed. (1997). One proposal is to finance the EU with a 1 percent VAT imposed on a specified range of goods and services in all member countries. See Kirwin, "European Parliament, States Fail to Agree on Tax to Finance Budget," BNA Daily Tax Report, May 11, 2006, p. G-5.

to VAT in the country of import. Exports to recipients outside the Community are zero-rated. The jurisdictional rules for transactions with individuals and businesses within the Community are governed by a "transitional arrangement" that was to be replaced by 1997 but is still in place. The transitional arrangement is a hybrid origin-destination system. Sales to individuals resident in the Community generally are taxed in the country of sale (origin) regardless of the residence of the buyer.[6] During this transitional period, intra-Union business-to-business sales remain zero-rated, the same as sales outside the Community, and are taxed by the importing member state.

The Member States are required to harmonize their VATs in accordance with a series of VAT Directives issued by the Commission of the Community, most importantly the Sixth Directive. The harmonization mandate applies not only to the adoption of specified exemptions but also to the scope of the exemptions. For example, a Member State that exempts gambling (this exemption is optional) cannot discriminate among various gambling operators. If gambling at licensed public casinos is exempt, so also must be gambling conducted at restaurants and clubs.[7]

The influence of the Sixth Directive extends beyond the EU. For example, the Eastern European countries that recently became members or hope to become part of the EU adopted Sixth Directive concepts in their VAT systems.[8]

Member States must adopt national legislation to implement the Sixth and other VAT directives. The directives bind "the Member States to achieve specific goals, leaving it up to the states to choose the form and the means for achieving them in national law."[9] The national courts interpret these national statutes in conformity with the VAT directives.[10] National VAT laws can be challenged if they are inconsistent with the Community directives. A national judge can refer a case involving the interpretation of a VAT Directive to the European Court of Justice (ECJ).[11] For example, a British court (such as a VAT Tribunal) may refer a VAT question to the ECJ in order to resolve an issue under the Sixth Directive or a possible conflict between domestic law and the Sixth Directive. A VAT decision by the ECJ is binding on national courts of the Member States. The following case illustrates the interplay between domestic VAT law and the Sixth Directive.

---

[6] A resident of the Community that purchases goods in another member state generally is not subject to VAT on the purchases upon his return home. There are exceptions covering (1) transport vehicles such as automobiles, and (2) mail order sales within the Community. See http://www.eurunion.org/legislat/VATweb.htm.

[7] Combined cases – Case C-453/02, *Finanzamt Gladbeck v. Edith Linneweber*; and Case C-462/02, *Finanzamt Herne-West v. Savvas Akritidis* (Judgment of the ECJ 2005).

[8] See Kronbergs, "Survey of Latvia's VAT Legislation," 6 *VAT Monitor* 350 (Nov./Dec. 1995).

[9] Mastrapasqua, *Current Status in Italy of EC Directives Regarding Taxation,* 26 Intertax 413 (1998) [hereinafter Mastrapasque].

[10] On the EU legal system, see A. J. EASSON, TAXATION IN THE EUROPEAN COMMUNITY (1993), pp. 89–95.

[11] *Id.* at 90.

W. G. Haydon-Baillie v. Commissioners of Customs and Excise[12]

The taxpayer, registered for VAT as a consultant, engaged as a sideline in the acquisition and restoration of a small number of ex-naval patrol boats of the 'Vosper Brave' class. He did this because they were a superb example of marine engineering and an important part of the British heritage. He sank some £750,00 into the work. He claimed that those costs should be treated as input tax and therefore VAT-deductible.

DECISION. This is the appeal of Mr. Wensley Grosvenor Haydon-Baillie against decisions of the Commissioners of Customs and Excise covering 1 July 1980 to 31 March 1984. The Commissioners claimed that the taxpayer was not entitled to credit for input tax because the relevant goods or services were not 'used or to be used for the purpose of any business carried on or to be carried on by him' within the meaning of the Value Added Tax Act 1983, section 14(3). The taxpayer claims that he is entitled to input credits under the test contained in Article 17 of the Sixth EEC Directive.

The taxpayer referred to the Value Added Tax Act 1983, section 14(3), and to the Sixth Council Directive of 17 May 1977, Title IV Article 4(1) and (2) and Title XI Article 17(1). The taxpayer's representative also referred the Value Added Tax Act 1983, section 47(1), which states:

"In this Act 'business' includes any trade, profession or vocation."

He contends, and we accept, that 'business' has a wider connotation than trade, profession or vocation and that an activity may be a 'business' even though it would not for income tax purposes constitute a 'trade'. He contends that the future use of the craft for exhibition purposes and for chartering etc. will constitute the carrying on of a business by the appellant. He further makes the point that the preparation of the craft, from the period when it was acquired until the time when it will be ready for use, a period which includes the employment of many people for restoration, the sale of the engines from the boat, and the accumulation and in many cases the sale of spares and equipment, also constitute the carrying on of a business.

[The Sixth Directive provides for deductions for input tax.... The] taxpayer claims that he meets the Sixth Council Directive's description [in Article 4] of 'any person who independently carries on in any place any economic activity specified in paragraph 2 whatever the purpose or results of that activity', bearing in mind that paragraph 2 states that 'the economic activities referred to in paragraph 1 shall comprise all activities of producers, traders and persons supplying services.... The

---

[12] 1986 VATTR 79 (United Kingdom) [edited by the authors].

exploitation of tangible or intangible property for the purpose of obtaining income therefrom on a continuing basis shall also be considered an economic activity.'

The Commissioners submit that the taxpayer had not demonstrated that his future 'museum' activities constituted a 'business' within the meaning of the Value Added Tax Act 1983, section 14(4). Those activities would be no more than a pleasant hobby. Alternatively any intention to turn the craft to pecuniary account in future is at present too vague to satisfy the words in section 14(4) 'business . . . to be carried on.' The present activities should not be considered separately; they were merely preparatory to the future, non-business, activity. As respects the Sixth Directive, it is, in the present respect at least, superseded by the Value Added Tax Act 1983. This case depends on the meaning of section 14(4).

We deal first with the Sixth Council Directive. We have considered the decision of the Court of Justice of the European Communities in *Rompelman v. Minister Van Financien.*[13] All that *Rompelman* really shows, in our view, is that a present input for a future economic activity may be a proper input. It leaves open the question whether the appellant's activities present or future are truly 'economic activities'.

Generally, had we to decide this matter by reference to the Sixth Directive and not to the Value Added Tax Act 1983, we should reach the same conclusion that we do reach by reference to the Value Added Tax Act 1983. However, we accept that the Sixth Directive was binding upon the United Kingdom legislature, who complied with it by making extensive amendments that are now incorporated in the consolidating statute, the Value Added Tax Act 1983. Consequently in our view, there is no further room for reliance on the Sixth Directive. The statute supersedes it.

[The Tribunal went on to consider whether the taxpayer's activities with respect to the restoration action was a business for purposes of the Value Added Tax Act 1983].

The work of restoration in itself is, we find, aimed at covering financial outgoings by receipts, so far as practical; and once restoration is complete, the uses to which the craft is likely to be put clearly differentiate it in character from a pleasure craft. This is a business, irrespective of whether the appellant hopes to, or eventually does, make an overall profit in income tax terms. The present activities constitute a business carried on by the appellant; and if we were wrong in that conclusion, we would nevertheless hold that the purpose of the present activities is to provide in the future a restored craft, which will then be the subject matter of a business 'to be carried on by' the taxpayer.

Held that since the relevant rule in the Value Added Tax Act 1983 [the VAT in the United Kingdom] echoed the intent of the Sixth VAT Directive there was no need to pay any further attention to the directive

---

[13] See *infra* Ch. 4(IV)(C).

> and the case should be decided on a construction of the English statute
> following English precedents, *that* the taxpayer's intention was to cover
> his financial outgoings by receipts from hiring out, exhibitions etc. *and
> that* this constituted a business under section 14 of the Act. Therefore the
> expenses were deductible as VAT input.
>   We therefore allow the appeal.

B. EUROPEAN COURT OF JUSTICE

The European Commission or a Member State may bring to the ECJ a claim
"that a Member State has failed to fulfill an obligation under" the Treaty.[14] If
a national court hearing a tax dispute involving EU legislation (Community
law) is not certain about the interpretation or validity of the Community law,
the court may refer the issue to the European "Court of Justice."[15]

Most VAT cases come to the ECJ as a request for a preliminary ruling under
Article 234 of the Treaty.[16] "The Court is not qualified to interpret domestic
law."[17]

Advocates-General prepare nonbinding "opinions"[18] on cases brought
before the ECJ, and present them "with complete impartiality and independence."[19] The ECJ may sit to hear a case in a panel ranging from three to four,
in a Grand Chamber, or the full court.[20]

The court issues "judgments" decided by a majority of the panel, with no
dissenting opinions. Once the ECJ rules on the meaning of a word or term in
the Sixth Directive, the national court decides the individual cases applying
the ruling of the ECJ.[21]

---

[14] Treaty of Nice, Art's. 226 & 227.

[15] See Consolidated EU Treaties, *supra* note 2, at Art's. 220–245. The Court of First Instance
was created in 1989 under the Single European Act to handle certain cases that are within
the province of the ECJ (*id*. at Art. 225a of the Treaty of Nice).

[16] The ECJ has jurisdiction to give preliminary rulings on "(a) the interpretation of this
Treaty; (b) the validity and interpretation of acts of the institutions of the Community
and of the ECB; (c) the interpretation of the statutes of bodies established by an act of the
Council, where those statutes so provide." *Id*. at Art. 234. The national court may bring
the matter to the ECJ "if it considers that a decision on the question is necessary to enable
it to give judgment" or where a question that the court can address by a preliminary
ruling is raised in a court or tribunal of a Member State and "there is no judicial remedy
under national law" against a decision by that national court or tribunal. *Id*.

[17] Mastrapasque, *supra* note 9, at 414.

[18] Advocate-General "opinions" are published separately and may be incorporated as part
of the court's "judgment." According to Art. 222 of the Treaty of Nice, the Advocate-
General shall "make, in open court, reasoned submissions on cases which, in accordance
with the Statute of the Court of Justice, require his involvement."

[19] *Id*. See http://europa.eu.int/institutions/court/index_en.htm.

[20] The size of the panels may change as a result of the admission of ten new members. For
example, until the change, the Grand Chamber consisted of thirteen judges, and the full
court consisted of fifteen judges.

[21] See Case C-320/88, *Staatssecretaris van Financien v. Shipping and Forwarding Enterprise Safe
BV* (Judgment of the ECJ 1990).

C. Application of the EU Sixth VAT Directive

1. History and Proposal for Recodification

The Council of the European Union (the "Council") issues directives (approved by all member states) that bind "the Member States to achieve specific goals, leaving it up to the states to choose the form and the means for achieving them in national law."[22] The directives usually require implementing legislation in the member states, although in some cases they may become directly effective.[23] There have been many directives dealing with VAT. The most significant is the Sixth Directive, originally issued in 1977.[24] The Sixth Directive expanded over the years, and has become an unwieldy document that is difficult to work with. As a result, the EU embarked on a project to recodify the Sixth Directive, renumbering and reorganizing its provisions. To date, the recodification of the Sixth Directive remains a Proposal for a Council Directive on the common system of value added tax (Recast) presented by the Commission of the European Communities.[25] Some references in this book to the Sixth Directive include references both to the Sixth Directive and the 2004 Recast Sixth Directive. The Recast likely will be amended before it is formally adopted.

Despite the mandate from the EU to harmonize the rules regarding VAT, the VAT rules of the Member States diverge on a number of topics. As a result, the EU issued a Regulation to implement measures relating to the interpretation of some aspects of VAT, such as the place of a supply of goods and services, the scope of some exemptions, a valuation rule, and the definition of electronically supplied services.[26] They are designed to bring more consistency in the areas covered.

2. When Is a Tax on Consumption Not a Turnover Tax or VAT in Violation of the Sixth Directive?

A VAT by any other name is still a VAT.[27] Member States of the European Union are subject to the Sixth VAT Directive harmonization rules for any VAT

---

[22] Mastrapasque, *supra* note 9, at 424.

[23] A directive may be directly effective if the directive is unconditional or a member failed to comply with the implementation deadline, and other conditions are satisfied. *Id.* at 414.

[24] Sixth Council Directive 77/388/EEC of May 17, 1977 on the harmonization of the laws of the Member States relating to turnover taxes – Common system of value added tax: uniform basis of assessment (OJ 1977 L145), p. 1.

[25] COM (2004) 246 final, 2004/0079 (CNS). A compromise text of the Recast (FISC 14) was presented by the Austrian presidency to the Working Party on Tax Question – indirect Taxation (VAT) on Feb. 15, 2006 and released in April, 2006 (8547/06).

[26] The Regulations become effective July 1, 2006. See Council Regulation (EC) No. 1777/2005 of October 17, 2005, OJ L288 of October 29, 2005. The end of the Regulation provides that it is "binding in its entirety and directly applicable in all Member States." The Regulation is not covered in detail.

[27] Adapted from Shakespeare, Romeo and Juliet, II, ii, 43. "What's in a name? That which we call a rose / By any other name would smell as sweet."

they impose and they are prohibited from imposing any other cumulative multistage tax like the EU-VAT.[28] The First VAT Directive defines the common system of value added tax as a tax that "involves the application to goods and services of a general tax on consumption exactly proportional to the price of the goods and services, whatever the number of transactions which take place in the production and distribution process before the stage at which tax is charged."[29] A deduction (input tax credit) against that tax liability is available for tax borne "directly by the various cost components."[30]

Article 33 of the Sixth Directive "prohibit(s) both internal taxes charged on transactions between Member States and taxes charged at a stage preceding the retail sale and that would not be repaid in the case of export to the territory of another Member State."[31] Article 33 of the Sixth VAT Directive allowed Members to adopt or continue "any taxes, duties, or charges which cannot be characterized as turnover taxes," but they are prohibited from imposing a tax comparable to VAT.[32] In *Fazenda Publica and Solisnor-Estaleiros Navais SA*, the Portuguese government imposed a stamp duty on "all the documents, books, papers, acts and products specified in the TGIS" (General Scale of Stamp Duties). Under Article 91 of the stamp duty, the tax is imposed on "works contracts and contracts for the supply of materials or any kind of consumer article" and is imposed at various rates applied "to the value of the act." When VAT became effective in Portugal, the government started phasing out the stamp duty by excluding various categories of economic transactions from the tax. Article 91 and some other articles of the stamp duty were repealed in 1991 as "incompatibility with the general tax on consumption covered by value added tax." According to the European Court of Justice in the *Solisnor-Estaleiros Navais SA* case,[33] Member States were free to maintain indirect taxes without violating Article 33 of the Sixth Directive so long as the tax could not be characterized as a turnover tax. The ECJ listed as the characteristics of a VAT:

1. "VAT applies generally to transactions relating to goods and services;"
2. "it is proportional to the price of those goods or services, irrespective of the number of transactions which take place;"
3. "it is charged at each stage of the production and distribution process;" and

---

[28] The background and rationale for the prohibition of cumulative multistage taxes other than VAT under EU law is well documented in Philippart, " Cumulative Multi-Stage Taxes under Community Law," *VAT Monitor*, March/April 2003 [hereinafter Philippart], p. 83.

[29] First Council Directive of April 11, 1967 on the harmonization of legislation of Member States concerning turnover taxes (67/227/EEC) (OJ P71, 14.4.1967, p. 1301), Art. 2.

[30] *Id*.

[31] Philippart, *supra* note 28, at 88.

[32] Article 33 of the Sixth Directive was modified by Article 1(23) of Directive 91/680/EEC of 16 December 1991, providing "that those taxes, duties or charges do not, in trade between Member States, give rise to formalities connected with the crossing of frontiers."

[33] *Solisnor-Estaleiros Navais SA*, Case 130/96, [1997] ECR I-5053.

4. "it is imposed on the added value of goods and services, since the tax payable on a transaction is calculated after deducting the tax paid on the previous transaction."

The ECJ found that the Portuguese stamp tax did not violate Article 33 of the Sixth Directive. It was not a general tax since it did not apply to all economic transactions in the Member State.[34] The same issue under Article 33 arises if the tax is levied at a subnational or regional level of government in a Member State. The dispute relating to the Italian Regional Tax on Productive Activities (IRAP) will be discussed in detail in Chapter 12.

The following case illustrates the continuing dispute within the EU as to whether a domestic national tax is a turnover tax like the VAT and therefore prohibited.[35]

GIL Insurance Ltd and Others v. Commissioners of Customs and Excise[36]

Starting in the 1960s, the durable household appliance market in the United Kingdom was dominated by firms renting these appliances to consumers. The rental price included the agreement by the rental company to service the appliances during the term of the rental. With the expansion of consumer credit and the availability of more durable televisions, washing machines, and other major household appliances, consumers increasingly purchased these appliances, along with service contracts. The service contracts, independent of the sales agreements, were subject to the 17.5 percent VAT.

The United Kingdom enacted a VAT, effective April 1, 1973. Insurance services were exempt from the U.K. VAT, as mandated under Article 13B(a) of the Sixth Directive.[37] To take advantage of this exemption, many large suppliers of the major household appliances offered service contracts as insurance contracts.

In 1994, the United Kingdom introduced an insurance premium tax (IPT), independent of the VAT. The initial 2.5 percent rate was increased over the years to 5 percent. The major suppliers of these appliances established their own insurance companies. They received commissions from their insurance companies on the sale of the insurance

---

[34] In a judgment by the ECJ in *Wisselink and others v Staatssecretaris van Financien*, Case 94/88 [1988] ECR 2671, I-5053, the court found that a consumption tax in The Netherlands did not violate the First and Sixth Directive because it was levied only at delivery or on import of passenger cars (not a cumulative multi-stage tax).

[35] See Mauritzen, "What Is a Turnover Tax in the Sense of Article 33 of the Sixth VAT Directive?" 8 *VAT Monitor* 3 (Jan/Feb 1997).

[36] Case C-308/01, [2004] ECR I-4777 (Judgment of the ECJ 2004) [hereinafter GIL Insurance].

[37] The exemption is in VATA 1994, §31 and Sch. 9, Group 2 (United Kingdom).

contracts (extended warranties) covering their appliances. A small amount was sold directly by insurance companies to consumers.

In 1997, the United Kingdom introduced a higher IPT rate equal to the standard 17.5 percent VAT rate. The higher rate applied only to premiums for insurance coverage on domestic appliances, motor cars, and certain travel.[38] The insurance companies challenged this tax as violative of the Sixth Directive.

Citing the Advocate-General's opinion that the higher-rate IPT has the appearance of a regulatory charge to prevent this form of tax avoidance, according to the ECJ, the higher rate IPT is compatible with the Sixth Directive. "The introduction of a higher rate of IPT on certain contracts was not intended to confer an advantage on all operators who offer contracts of insurance subject to the standard rate of IPT, in application of the general system of taxation of insurance."[39] In addition, the court ruled that "the application of the higher rate of IPT to a specific part of the insurance contracts previously subject to the standard rate must be regarded as justified by the nature and the general scheme of the national system of taxation of insurance. The IPT scheme cannot therefore be regarded as constituting an aid measure...."[40]

III. Japanese Consumption Tax

1. Credit-Subtraction VAT without Invoices

Japan's first experience with VAT was unique. The Japanese Diet enacted a sales-subtraction VAT in 1950, but deferred the effective date and modified its terms. In 1953, the Diet converted the method of calculating periodic VAT liability to the addition procedure.[41] In 1954, the Diet repealed the VAT before it ever became effective.

In the 1980s, succeeding governments unsuccessfully tried to enact a VAT. A VAT (the Consumption Tax (CT)) ultimately was adopted in December 1988, effective April 1, 1989.[42] To accommodate political opposition from small businesses and others, the CT included an atypical method of calculating periodic tax liability. The CT did not require CT-registered firms to issue VAT invoices relied on in other VAT countries

---

[38] Initially, only travel insurance sold through travel agents was subject to the higher rate. As a result of litigation, starting in August 1998, the higher rate was imposed on all travel insurance.

[39] GIL Insurance, *supra* note 36, at ¶75.

[40] *Id.* at ¶78.

[41] This tax was recommended by the Shoup Mission after World War II as a revenue source for the subnational prefectures. See Schenk, "Japanese Consumption Tax: The Japanese Brand VAT," 42 *Tax Notes* 1625 (Mar. 27, 1989); C. K. Sullivan, The Tax on Value Added, 1965, pp. 134–139.

[42] Law No. 108, part IV (1988) (Shohizei-ho).

to verify output tax to registered sellers and input credit to registered purchasers.

Whereas the CT was enacted as a tax-against-a-tax credit-subtraction VAT, the data for output tax and input credits are taken from accounting records for each tax period rather than from VAT invoices. The calculation of output tax liability mirrors the EU-style VAT. A registered seller multiplies taxable sales by the CT rate to arrive at output tax liability. If the taxable sales are recorded at CT-inclusive prices, the seller first calculates the CT-exclusive prices by multiplying CT-inclusive prices by the tax fraction. The tax fraction is the tax rate (originally 3 percent and now 5 percent) divided by 100 + the tax rate. For example, if CT-inclusive taxable sales are ¥1,050,000 and the tax rate is 5 percent, the CT-exclusive taxable sales are ¥1,000,000. The seller multiplies this amount by the 5 percent rate to arrive at ¥50,000 output tax liability.

The CT departs from the EU model VAT in calculating input credits. Data on taxable purchases are taken from the firm's purchase records. Assume that the CT-inclusive cost of purchases qualifying for the credit are deductible, ¥630,000. The allowable input credit is ¥30,000 (630,000 × the tax fraction 5/105).

The Japanese CT departs from the European model in another way. To prevent discrimination against unregistered small businesses, registered sellers may claim input credits for CT on purchases of taxable goods and services, whether acquired from registered or unregistered suppliers. Input credit therefore is denied only for CT on purchases that are exempt from tax, such as postage stamps and certain medical services.[43]

Japan has special schemes for smaller businesses to calculate periodic CT liability. These schemes will be discussed later in this book.[44]

Japan segregates one percentage point of its CT as prefecture (subnational) revenue. Under a revenue-sharing arrangement, the prefectures also receive a portion of the national government's CT revenue.[45]

2. Movement Toward Invoice-Method VAT

As the Japanese CT matured, the government increased the substantiation requirements for registered firms to claim input credits. Although, formally, a registered seller is not required to issue a VAT invoice (central to the EU-style credit-invoice VAT), as a practical matter, registered sellers are required to retain documentation to substantiate their claims for input credits, such as bills, receipts, statements of delivery, or other kinds of invoices that show the details of the transaction.[46] This documentation requirement allows the

---

[43] *Id.* at §6.

[44] See Chapter 6 (Section VII).

[45] Schenk, "Japanese Consumption Tax after Six Years: A Unique VAT Matures," 69 *Tax Notes* 899, 911 (Nov. 13, 1995).

[46] *Id.* at 906.

tax authority to deny credits if the taxpayer lacks adequate documentation, similar to the denial of credits without required VAT invoices under the European-style, credit-invoice VATs.

IV. New Zealand Goods and Services Tax

New Zealand's Goods and Services Tax (a VAT) was adopted on December 3, 1985, and became effective on October 1, 1986. The N.Z. GST has four features that distinguish it from earlier VATs, especially the harmonized EU VAT governed by the Sixth Directive:

1. The GST has a broader tax base with fewer categories of goods and services exempt from tax;
2. The GST is imposed on a broad category of services rendered by units of government;
3. The GST is imposed on casualty and other nonlife insurance; and
4. The jurisdiction to tax is based on the residence of the supplier, not the location of the supply.

Each of these features is discussed in this section.

A. Broad Tax Base

New Zealand exempts only limited categories of goods and services. It exempts financial services, the rental and some sales of a residential dwelling, fine metal, certain fringe benefits, and supplies of donated goods and services by a nonprofit body.[47] Absent from the list of exempt items are goods and services commonly viewed as necessities and exempt elsewhere, such as food, medical care, and education.

B. Taxation of Government Services

New Zealand indirectly taxes many services rendered by local units of government (local authorities). A local authority is deemed to make a taxable supply of goods and services to a person for consideration equal to rates (property taxes) the person pays to the local authority.[48] Many other charges the government imposes, such as road user charges, are specifically taxed under the GST.[49]

---

[47] See New Zealand Goods and Services Tax Act 1985, No. 141 [hereinafter NZ GST], §§14(1) and 21(I)(2).

[48] *Id.* at §5(7)(a). The same rule applies to council dues payable to the Chatham Islands Council. *Id.* at §5(7)(b).

[49] *Id.* at §5(6)–(6E).

C. TAXATION OF CASUALTY AND OTHER NONLIFE INSURANCE

New Zealand imposes GST on premiums charged by providers of casualty and other nonlife insurance.[50] In addition to input credits for GST on business inputs, these providers can claim input credits for the GST component in claims paid. Registered businesses that purchase taxable insurance contracts can claim credit for GST paid on the insurance premiums. If an insured business receives payment on an insurance claim, the claim received is treated as consideration for a supply of services.[51]

D. GLOBAL REACH OF THE NEW ZEALAND GST

Most countries impose VAT only on imports into the country and domestic sales within the country. These countries have place or location of supply rules to determine if a supply falls within the scope of the tax. If a supply takes place outside the country, the supply is not subject to tax. It is the place where the supply occurs, not the residence of the supplier, that determines if a supply comes within the scope of the tax. In these countries, foreign sales are beyond the scope of the tax. In order to relieve exports of tax (a zero-rated transaction), exports are treated as supplied within the taxing jurisdiction. Although the place of supply rules are relatively clear with respect to tangible goods, they are complex with respect to services.[52] It therefore is quite easy for a business to negotiate a contract for services in order to "place" the services outside a country and beyond the reach of the VAT.

New Zealand has different rules defining the scope of the tax. N.Z. imposes GST based on the residence of the supplier, not the place where the supply takes place. In theory, a supplier resident in New Zealand is subject to GST on its worldwide supplies. The Act, however, narrows the scope of the tax considerably. The GST is imposed on a supply *in New Zealand* by a registered person in the course or furtherance of a taxable activity conducted by that person.[53] Goods and services are deemed supplied *in New Zealand* if the supplier is resident in New Zealand and is deemed supplied outside New Zealand if the supplier is not a resident in New Zealand.[54] There are special rules treating certain supplies by nonresidents as supplied in New Zealand and treating certain supplies by nonresidents to registered persons (otherwise treated as supplied in N.Z.) as supplied outside New Zealand.[55] Certain

---

[50] Premiums on life insurance contracts or reinsurance of life contracts are exempt financial services under §3. Other insurance is taxable under the definition of insurance under §2(1) that defines insurance as insurance that is not exempt under §3. Insurance is defined as "insurance or guarantee against loss, damage, injury, or risk of any kind whatever, whether pursuant to any contract or any enactment; and includes reinsurance."

[51] See generally *id*. at §5(13).

[52] See discussion *infra* at Chapter 7 (Section V).

[53] NZ GST, *supra* note 47, at §8(1).

[54] *Id*. at §8(2).

[55] *Id*. at §8(3) and (4). A supplier may elect not to have the §8(4) rules apply.

exports of goods are zero-rated, even when made by residents. Special rules apply to telecoms.

V. African Experience Expanding Base to Tax Financial Services

South Africa apparently used the New Zealand GST as the model for its VAT. South African adopted the New Zealand approach of taxing many government services. If a local authority imposes charges for electricity, gas, water, sewerage, and a few others, then the charges are subject to VAT. If the local authority does not charge for these services, then the rates on real property are taxable.[56]

South Africa expanded its VAT base beyond the New Zealand GST's broad base by taxing many financial services commonly exempt under most other VATs. South Africa taxes all fee-based financial services other than those services zero-rated as exports. Financial intermediation services for which there are no specific charges remain exempt from tax. In consultation with the banking industry, the South African Revenue Service developed a list of all banking services and classified them for VAT purposes as taxable, exempt, or zero-rated. This experimental system seems to be working well. Namibia and Botswana, South Africa's neighbors, adopted the South African approach that taxes fee-based financial services.[57]

VI. Commonlaw and Civil Law Approaches

The early development of the VAT occurred in France and other members of the European Union. France, Germany, and twelve other early members of the EU are civil law countries. The United Kingdom is a commonlaw country. As discussed earlier, most of the English-speaking countries that departed significantly from the EU model were basically commonlaw countries such as New Zealand and South Africa.

In civil law countries, the "classical sources of law are laws, treatises, regulations, jurisprudence [caselaw], and doctrine [writings]."[58] Civil law legal systems reflect "attitudes about the nature of law, the role of law in society, organization and operation of legal system, and the way law is or should be made."[59] The principles that serve as the basis for various VAT rules are

---

[56] Value-Added Tax Act No. 89 of 1991, §10(15) (Republic of South Africa). Levies imposed by regional services councils, joint services boards, and transitional metropolitan councils are taxable. *Id.* at 8(6)(b) and 10(15), discussed in C. Beneke, ed., Deloitte & Touche VAT Handbook, 6th ed. (2003), pp. 55–57.

[57] In recent years, Singapore and Australia adopted rules permitting financial institutions to recover some VAT on business inputs attributable to otherwise exempt intermediation services. These approaches are discussed in a later chapter of the book.

[58] V. Thuronyi, Comparative Tax Law [hereinafter Thuronyi, Comparative Tax], at 62.

[59] Merryman, The Civil Law Tradition (2d ed. 1985), p. 2.

important in civil law countries. As a generalization, civil law countries favor "less detailed drafting style."[60]

The importance of the precedential value of caselaw in common law countries results in a different emphasis in the development of the law.[61] Courts in the commonlaw countries influence the development of tax law, like the VAT.[62] The European Court of Justice, with its effect on EU member countries has to balance these two different legal traditions.

---

[60] Thuronyi, Comparative Tax, *supra* note 58, at 18.

[61] *Id.* at 63.

[62] *Id.* at 25.

4

Registration, Taxpayer, and Taxable Business Activity

I. INTRODUCTION

Most VAT regimes require registered (or taxable) persons to file returns (and remit tax). In most cases, a firm is required to register if it makes or expects to make at least the statutory minimum level of annual taxable sales in connection with its business or economic activity.

Not all sales by a person come within the scope of a VAT. For example, in most countries, an individual's casual sales do not constitute taxable business activity and are not taxed. Hobbies and similar activities that do not rise to the level of a "business" generally are not taxed. An employee could be treated as a person rendering taxable services to her employer and therefore a VAT taxpayer, but no country has done this.[1] This chapter discusses registration (including some required registration by nonresidents), who is liable for tax, and what economic activity subjects a seller to tax under various VAT regimes. In a significant case decided by the European Court of Justice, the court ruled that a person who, without his knowledge, participated in a carousel fraud was engaged in economic activity and was entitled to claim input tax credits.[2]

II. REGISTRATION

A. IN GENERAL

Registration is part of a self-assessment VAT system that typically is reinforced with harsh civil and criminal penalties for noncompliance. Many VAT systems define a taxable person subject to the VAT rules as a person who is

---

[1] The flat tax proposed, but not enacted, in the United States requires employees to file returns and pay tax on their wages and allows employers a flat tax deduction for the compensation paid to employees. See discussion *infra*, Chapter 14.

[2] Joined cases C-354/03, C-355/03, and C-484/03, *Optigen Ltd, Fulcrum Electronics Ltd and Bond House Systems Ltd v Commissioners of Customs & Excise*, [2003] ECR I-»»; OJ C 74, 25.03. 2006, p. 1 [hereinafter *Optigen, Fulcrum, and Bond*].

registered (a registrant) or is required to register. Nonresidents without a fixed location in the country may be subject to a different set of rules. The registration requirement generally is imposed on a person or firm that makes at least a threshold amount of taxable sales.[3] The government may maintain a list of registered persons. The requirement to file returns then is imposed only on those who must register.

An alternative, designed to provide government with information on all firms engaged in business activity, is to require all businesses to register and to permit small firms with sales below a threshold amount to affirmatively request exemption from registration. This system does not assure the tax authority that it has a record of all potential taxpayers, and imposes substantial costs both on the requesting small business and on the government that must process these requests for exemption. For these reasons, this alternative generally has not been adopted.

B. Mandatory Registration

1. General Rules

Most VAT systems require persons engaged in regular business activity to register if their taxable sales (sales and leases of goods and services) in a given period (usually a year) exceed a threshold level.[4] The calculation of total taxable sales generally is based on the value of sales determined under the nation's valuation rules for VAT purposes.[5] Businesses with low turnover may temporarily have taxable sales above the threshold due to sales out of the ordinary course of business. For example, a business may replace its worn out equipment or may sell in bulk some inventory as part of a program to terminate a product line. The tax authority may be authorized to ignore those sales in determining if the business has taxable sales above the threshold.[6]

---

[3] In the EU and in several other European countries with VATs, there are thresholds for distance selling and retail export schemes. See "Practical Information on VAT," *VAT Monitor*, Jan./Feb. 2003, p. 2.

[4] New Vatopia VAT, Appendix B, at §20. Canadian Goods and Services Tax, Part IX of the Excise Tax Act, An Act to amend the Excise Tax Act, the Criminal Code, the Customs Act, the Customs Tariff, the Excise Act, the Income Tax Act, the Statistics Act and the Tax Court of Canada Act [hereinafter Canadian GST], §240(1). The Canadian GST is reproduced (with annotations) in D. M. Sherman, The Practitioner's Goods and Services Tax Annotated, with Harmonized Sales Tax (HST), 13th ed. 2003. See also *CCH Canadian Goods & Services Tax Reporter* (2004). A person must apply for registration in a prescribed form and manner, and the application must include the information required by the Minister. §240(5). There is no specific penalty for failure to register. But see the §329(2) offence for failure to comply with any provision of the GST (such as §240) for which no other penalty is provided.

[5] New Vatopia VAT, Appendix B, at §11(3). The Vatopia valuation rules are covered in §16.

[6] See, for example, Value Added Tax Act, No. 1 of 2001 [hereinafter Botswana VAT], §16(3) (Botswana).

Benefits as well as VAT obligations may be limited to registered persons. For example, registered persons can recover VAT paid on business inputs (input tax credits) used in making taxable sales, and registered persons with excess input credits may be entitled to refunds of the excess credits.[7]

The level of taxable sales may be calculated by looking back or looking forward, such as the past or the following twelve months. To prevent a person from dividing up a single business into small parts in order to fall below the threshold required for registration, the VAT legislation may authorize the tax authority to aggregate sales by businesses owned by related persons.[8]

Failure to register and collect tax from customers does not relieve a person of the obligations imposed on registered persons to collect and remit tax.[9] In fact, the tax authority may unilaterally register persons who fail to register.[10] Likewise, under some VAT regimes, the VAT authorities may refuse to register an applicant if the authorities determine that the person does not meet the registration requirements or, for persons who register voluntarily, if the authorities determine that the applicant will not maintain adequate records or comply with other obligations imposed on registered persons.[11]

Some nations require registered persons to publicly post their certificates of registration[12] in locations where they make taxable sales. To reduce the opportunity for VAT fraud, including unwarranted use of certificates of registration, registered persons generally must notify the VAT authorities of any change in the name, location, or nature of the business activities they conduct.[13]

2. Promoters of Public Entertainment

Music concerts, isolated athletic events such as boxing matches, circuses, and other shows to which the public is invited may be promoted by a sponsor operating within the country or by a nonresident who comes into the country for a single show or event. Unless the person regularly promotes events within the country, it may be extremely difficult for the tax authorities to

---

[7] The Vatopia VAT grants these rights to taxable persons – persons registered or required to register. See New Vatopia VAT, Appendix B, at §26.

[8] See the discussion *infra* subsection (C)(3) on splitting a business and the related party rules.

[9] Under the Canadian GST, the seller may not be able to recover tax from its customers when, after the sale, his liability to register and to pay tax on prior sales is established. On the recovery of GST from recipients, see Canadian GST, *supra* note 4, at §§223 and 224.

[10] New Vatopia VAT, Appendix B, at §21(4).

[11] *Id.* at §21(3).

[12] *Id.* at §21(10).

[13] *Id.* at §21(11).

locate the promoter and collect VAT chargeable on the sale of tickets for the event. Even if the promoter is a nonresident who promotes only one event in a twelve-month period, the grant of a small business exemption for this promoter may raise significant competitive inequities.

Some countries address this problem by requiring all promoters of public entertainment to register for VAT before they start selling tickets to an event, even if they do not expect to make annual taxable sales above the small business exemption threshold. To avoid unfair competition and to prevent tax avoidance by nonresidents who make taxable sales while in a country for a short time, Canada[14] requires nonresidents to register before selling tickets to such events.[15] Canada imposes another obligation on these non-residents in order to safeguard the revenue. A nonresident who is registered or required to register and who does not have a permanent establishment in Canada must provide adequate security for its tax liability.[16] Barbados (and the New Vatopia VAT)[17] impose similar obligations on promoters of public entertainment.[18] Barbados has a strict rule on remittance of tax before the event. Before the scheduled event in Barbados, the promoter must remit 5 percent (the regular VAT rate is 15 percent) of the value of tickets printed for the event.[19] If tickets have not been printed, the promoter must remit an amount determined by the comptroller.[20]

3. Registration Regardless of Turnover

To prevent unfair competition or for other reasons, a nation with a small business exemption may require some sellers with low turnover to register. The promoters of public entertainment, discussed earlier, is one example.

In some countries, the state, state agencies, and local units of government are exempt from registration, regardless of turnover.[21] In other countries, the opposite is true. They must register if they conduct certain activities (typically in competition with the private sector) even if their taxable turnover is below the threshold.[22] Some countries treat auctioneers as the sellers of

---

[14] This includes a place of amusement, a seminar, an activity, or an event.

[15] Canadian GST, *supra* note 4, at §240(2).

[16] Canadian GST, *supra* note 4, at §240(6). The security must be provided in the amount and form acceptable to the Minister. *Id*.

[17] See New Vatopia VAT, Appendix B, §2 definition of "public entertainment" and "promoter of public entertainment"; and §§20(8); 21(5)(b); and 22(9).

[18] The Value Added Tax Act, Cap. 87, 1996, §34(6), (8)–(9) (Barbados).

[19] *Id*. at §34(8).

[20] *Id*.

[21] See A New Tax System (Goods and Services tax) Act 1999 [hereinafter Australian GST] §§149–10.

[22] The United Kingdom subjects the State to VAT, and local authorities making taxable sales must register, regardless of taxable turnover. Value Added Tax Act 1994, §§41(1) & 42 (United Kingdom). See Value-Added Tax Act No. 89 of 1991 [hereinafter RSA VAT], §1 definitions of "enterprise" (including public and local authorities) and

auctioned property and require auctioneers to register regardless of taxable turnover.[23]

To prevent unfair competition between registered and unregistered taxi owners, Canada and Australia require all persons who conduct a taxi business to register the taxi business for GST purposes, regardless of the level of taxable turnover from the operation of the taxis.[24]

C. REGISTRATION THRESHOLD AND THE SMALL BUSINESS EXEMPTION

1. In General

A VAT could be imposed on all persons making sales of taxable goods and services, regardless of the dollar volume of sales. This definition of a person required to collect and remit tax would catch every casual sale by a consumer, and all sales by street vendors and other occasional sellers. Such a broad definition that caught sales of used toys to a neighbor or sales of used clothing at a lawn sale would impose an undue burden on both casual sellers and the government and would not raise any significant net revenue. "The quantum of business activity therefore is used in most countries to define the persons or entities that are subject to VAT."[25]

Countries typically include special VAT rules for small businesses. Certain small businesses may not be required to register and pay VAT, may be eligible for reduced tax liability, may be entitled to use simplified procedures to calculate tax liability, or may be subject to reduced record keeping requirements.[26]

"vendor" (persons registered or required to register), §23 requiring registration of persons engaged in enterprises, and §7(1)(a) imposing tax on taxable supplies by vendors in connection with enterprises (Republic of South Africa). See also New Vatopia VAT, Appendix B, §20(6).

[23] See Canadian GST, *supra* note 4, at §177(1.2). See also New Vatopia VAT, Appendix B, §§20(7) and 86(7).

[24] Canadian GST, *supra* note 4, at §240(1.1). If the operator of the taxi has other commercial activity but the person's total taxable supplies are below the threshold for registration, the nontaxi activity is not covered by the taxi registration. *Id.* at §§171.1 and 241(2). Australian GST, *supra* note 21, at §144–145.

[25] Oldman & Schenk, "The Business Activities Tax, Have Senators Danforth & Boren Created a Better Value Added Tax?" 65 *Tax Notes* 1547, at 1556.

[26] Professor Turnier suggests ways to accommodate small businesses. "There are five major ways to accommodate small business' special problems. First, small businesses either can be exempted or can be subject to taxation under special schemes. Second, the government may tax small businesses but may allow them to retain a percentage of the tax collected to compensate them for their substantially higher compliance costs. Third, rather than requiring small businesses to account for taxes under a variation of the accrual method typically used to calculate VAT liability, they can be allowed to employ the cash method. Fourth, one need not assign to the invoice the same critical weight that it has for larger taxpayers. Last, instead of requiring frequent periodic reporting of taxes (e.g., quarterly or bimonthly), small businesses can be permitted to report their taxes annually, with periodic payment of estimated taxes." Turnier, "Accommodating to the Small Business

Some countries reduce the compliance burden on small businesses by lengthening the accounting period (reducing the number of returns required each year) or permitting them to report on the cash or payments basis of accounting.[27] Others impose a turnover tax (at a rate lower than the standard rate, but without any input credits) on very small businesses.[28]

As discussed earlier, some countries require some persons with sales below the exemption threshold to register, or exempt others with taxable turnover above the threshold. As an example of the latter, in Canada, a person is not required to register for GST if the person's commercial activity is limited to real property sales not in the ordinary course of business.[29]

Businesses exempt from tax on sales because of their low taxable turnover may be given the option to register and be taxable on their taxable sales.[30] Given the option, most small businesses making domestic retail sales to consumers will remain exempt.

"Opting for registration may be a more rational choice for traders who contribute a smaller proportion of value-added to their supplies and either supply to registered traders, [export goods, or sell other zero-rated or lower-rated goods or services].... Registration effectively allows the supplier to pass on the value-added tax without an increase in the cost to the registered customer (who gets a credit for the tax charged and invoiced). In the case of zero-rated goods, the trader will, by registering, be able to obtain refunds of any tax paid on purchases."[31] It has been reported that some smaller firms register because they are embarrassed to admit to their customers (by not posting a certificate of registration) that their sales are below the registration threshold.

Small business exemption thresholds vary greatly.[32] At one extreme, Taiwan taxes even the smallest vendors.[33] In the middle are countries like New

---

Under a VAT," 47 *Tax Law.* 963, 969 (1994) [hereinafter Turnier, Accommodating the Small Business].

[27] See *Treatment of small businesses under VAT systems*, in Consumption Tax Trends 44 (OECD (1995) [hereinafter OECD].

[28] See, for example, the Republic of China, discussed *infra* note 33.

[29] Canadian GST, *supra* note 4, at §240(1)(b). A nonresident who does not conduct business in Canada also is not required to register. *Id.* at §240(1)(c). A nonresident may be deemed to conduct business in Canada if the person solicits orders for prescribed property to be sent to an address in Canada by mail or courier. *Id.* at §240(4).

[30] See Turnier, Accommodating the Small Business, *supra* note 26, suggesting value added as a standard instead of sales turnover. Vatopia VAT, Appendix B, §20(5).

[31] *Id.* at 44.

[32] For an analysis of the VAT registration threshold in Europe, see Annacondia & van der Corput, "VAT Registration Thresholds in Europe," *VAT Monitor*, Nov./Dec. 2005, p. 434. For thresholds in OECD countries, see *OECD Consumption Tax Trends: VAT/GST and Excise Rates, Trends and Administrative Issues*, 2004 ed., Table 3.6 (OECD 2005).

[33] These small vendors are assessed by the tax authority. Value-added and Non-value-added Business Tax Act, amended June 25, 2003, Art. 13 (Republic of China).

Zealand with a $40,000 local currency exemption (US$25,300)[34] and Canada with $30,000 (US$27,300).[35] At the other extreme, Japan grants exemption for businesses with annual sales during the base period of ¥10 million (about US$87,700),[36] and Singapore exempts businesses with annual taxable supplies of $1 million or less (about US$629,000).[37]

Smaller firms tend to be less efficient than their larger competitors. A low exemption threshold therefore may not give those firms any competitive

---

[34] *Id.* New Zealand, in essence, has a small business exemption because it requires registration only by persons with taxable sales exceeding NZ$40,000. See New Zealand Goods and Services Tax Act 1985, No. 141 [hereinafter NZ GST], §51(a), as amended. *CCH New Zealand Goods and Services Tax Guide,* paragraph 21-200 (2004). The exchange rate on the New Zealand dollar was about $1.58 to the U.S. dollar in June 2006. See *New York Times,* June 13, 2006, C12.

[35] See Canadian GST, *supra* note 4, at §148(1). The exchange rate on Canadian dollars was about $1.10 to the U.S. dollar in June, 2006. *New York Times,* June 13, 2006, C12. The small business exemption is Can.$50,000 for a public service body. In Australia, the threshold for most persons engaged in an enterprise is Aus.$50,000, but is Aus.$100,000 for a nonprofit body. Australian GST, *supra* note 21, at §23-15.

[36] The turnover threshold was reduced from ¥30 to ¥10 million, effective April 1, 2003. See VAT Monitor, Jan./Feb. 2003, p. 50. In June, 2006, the exchange rate on Japanese yen was about 114 to the U.S. dollar. See *New York Times,* June 13, 2006, C12. See also V. Beyer, Translation of Japan's Consumption Tax Law, Law No. 108, 1988, as amended, art. 9(1). The base period is the tax year two years preceding the current taxable period. This base period rule does not apply in certain specified situations. For example, the base period rule does not apply if a business subject to CT is transferred to another corporation upon merger or transferred to an heir upon death. The Consumption Tax Law enacted on December 24, 1988, Law No. 108, part IV, was translated in *Japan – National Consumption Tax Law: An English Translation* (CCH Intl. 1989), at Art. 10.

For taxable years beginning on or after April 1, 1997, a newly organized corporation with paid-in capital of 10 million yen or more is not eligible for this base period rule that permits exemption for a business' first two years. [Beyer, unofficial translation of the 1994 amendments [1994(partial) Amendment Act of the Income Tax Law and the Consumption Tax Law], Art. 12(2) amendment, and Appendix, Art. 9. A business that qualifies for this complete exemption can elect to be subject to the consumption tax. An exporter or other business that expects to have input tax credits exceeding its tax liability on sales may elect to be taxable in order to claim refunds for its excess input tax credits. Adapted from Schenk, "Japanese Consumption Tax After Six Years: A Unique VAT Matures," 69 *Tax Notes* 899, 904–905 (Nov. 13, 1995). A previous partial, but complicated, exemption system available for businesses with taxable sales of between 30 and 50 million was eliminated, effective April 1, 1997.

The government estimated that in 1992 (when complete exemption was turnover of less than ¥30 million), about 60 percent of all businesses were exempt from tax, yet sales by these businesses accounted for only 2–3 percent of total domestic taxable sales. In the BAT proposed in the United States, the small business exemption applies to businesses with annual gross receipts of $100,000 or less. The Comprehensive Tax Restructuring and Simplification Act of 1994, 140 cong. Rec. S. 6527, adding ch. 100 of new Subtitle K to the Internal Revenue Code of 1986, §10042(a),(d).

[37] Goods and Services tax Act, Cap. 117A, 2001 ed., First Sch., §1(1). The exchange rate on Singapore dollars was about 1.59 to the U.S. dollar in June 2006. *New York Times,* June, 13, 2006, C12.

advantage of their registered competitors.[38] By contrast, a high threshold may create some competitive inequities. If the exemption extends to efficient retailers, they "may obtain a competitive advantage over their taxable counterparts by selling at a lower tax-inclusive price to consumers who cannot claim input credits for the VAT element in their purchases."[39]

The following chart shows, based on the assumptions stated, the VAT advantage to a consumer who buys from an exempt small business rather than a taxable business, and the VAT disadvantage to a taxable business that buys from an exempt rather than a taxable supplier.

Illustration of the Problem of Small Business Under a Credit-Method VAT

Exempt small business (SB) selling to consumer[40]		Taxable (registered) small business (SB) selling to consumer	
Purchases	100	Purchases	100
input tax	100	input tax	10
Margin or value added	50	Margin or value added	50
Sales (exempt)	160	Sales (before tax)	150
		output tax	15
		Tax-inclusive sales price	165
		Small bus. pays to govt. after getting input credit	5
Total VAT to govt = 10*		Total VAT to govt = 5*	

If customer from exempt SB is BB, then:		*If customer from taxable SB is BB, then:*	
BB		BB	
Purchases	160	Purchases	150
input tax	0	input tax	15
Margin or value added	240	Margin or value added	240
Sales (before tax)	400	Sales (before tax)	390
output tax	40	output tax	39
		BB pays govt.	24
Total VAT to govt = 40 + 10 = 50**		Total VAT paid to govt = 10 + 5 + 24, or 39**	

SB = Small business, trader, or farmer
C = Consumer who buyers from SB for personal consumption
BB = Big business (big enough to be required to register under VAT)
* Note that C saves 5 by buying from an exempt small trader (retailer) rather than from a taxable trader (retailer). Exemption of the small business does not save the consumer the full tax of 15.
** BB pays more by buying from exempt small business, government receives more, and consumer pays more if competitive considerations allow SB to shift tax.

---

[38] One alternative is to limit the small trader exemption to retailers, especially if the exemption has a high threshold. McLure, Jr., THE VALUE-ADDED TAX: KEY TO DEFICIT REDUCTION, at 115–117.
[39] A. Schenk, Value Added Tax – A Model Statute and Commentary: A Report of the Committee on Value Added Tax of the American Bar Association Section of Taxation 86–89 (1989) [hereinafter ABA Model VAT].

2. What Is the Business?

Under VAT regimes, it may be important to determine if multiple businesses owned by a single person or members of a family must register and file separately or must file as a single VAT taxpayer. The question is whether each operation can be treated as a separate business for VAT purposes. This issue is significant if a person files multiple registrations in order to claim exemption under the small business exemption.

The classification of an activity as a separate business may depend on a number of criteria, such as the following:

- *Premises*
The person carrying on the business should own or rent the premises and equipment.

- *Records and Accounts*
These should be maintained for the separate business.

- *Invoices (Both Purchase and Sale)*
All invoices must be in the name of the person carrying on the business, and the arrangements for the supply must be directly between the taxable person and the customer.

- *Legal*
Legal responsibility must be with the taxable person.

- *Bank Accounts*
These should be in the taxable person's name.

- *Wages and Social Security Contributions*
Such contributions should be paid by the taxable person.

- *Income Tax Benefits*
These should be identified separately for the business.

If these criteria are met, the business might be considered separate for VAT purposes, but even so, in some countries, if it could be proved that the intent was to evade VAT, then tax might still be claimed.[41]

3. Splitting a Business and the Related Person Rules

The owner of a business may claim the benefits of the small business exemption by splitting up the business into separate parts or separate entities (usually by splitting ownership among members of a family) and treat each as a separate seller. To prevent this tax avoidance, some VAT statutes give the tax authorities power to aggregate the sales of businesses owned by related

---

[40] With exemption, there is no tax on output and the small business must pay tax on business inputs.

[41] A. Tait, Value Added Tax: International Practice and Problems, pp. 369–370 (IMF 1988).

parties. The concept of a "related person" raises difficult definitional issues, especially in countries where it is common practice for extended families to participate in the ownership and operation of retail shops.[42] The split of a single business into smaller parts owned by family members is illustrated by the British *Marner and Marner* case.

[42] See New Vatopia VAT, Appendix B, definition of "related person" in §2. An example of broad definitions of a "related person" and "relative" is the Botswana VAT, *supra* note 6, Article 2, which provides:

"related persons" means –
(a) an individual and –
    (i) any relative of that natural person; or
    (ii) a trust in respect of which such relative is or may be a beneficiary; or
(b) a trust and a person who is or may be a beneficiary in respect of that trust; or
(c) a partnership, or unincorporated association or body or private company and –
    (i) any member thereof; or
    (ii) any other person where that person and a member of such partnership, or unincorporated association or body, or private company as the case may be, are related persons in terms of this definition; or
(d) an incorporated company, other than a close corporation and –
    (i) a person, other than an incorporated company, where that person or that person and a person related to the first mentioned person in terms of this definition controls 10 percent or more of –
      (A) the voting power in the company;
      (B) the rights to distributions of capital or profits of the company, either directly or through one or more interposed companies, partnerships, or trusts; or
    (ii) any other incorporated company in which the first mentioned person referred to in sub-paragraph (i) or that person and a person related to that first mentioned person in terms of this definition controls 10 percent or more of –
      (A) the voting power in the first-mentioned company; or
      (B) the rights to distributions of capital or profits of the first-mentioned company, either directly or through one or more interposed companies, partnerships, or trusts; or
    (iii) any person where that person and the person referred to in subparagraph (i) or the other incorporated company referred to in subparagraph (ii) are related persons in terms of this definition; or
    (iv) any person related to the person referred to in sub-paragraph (iii) in terms of this definition; or
(e) a registered person and a branch or division of that registered person which is separately registered under section 46(3) as a registered person; or
(f) any branches or divisions of a registered person which are separately registered under section 46(3) as registered persons;
    "relative", in relation to an individual, means –
    (a) the spouse of the individual;
    (b) an ancestor, lineal descendant, brother, sister, uncle, aunt, nephew, niece, stepfather, stepmother, stepchild, or adopted child of that person or her spouse, and in the case of an adopted child her adoptive parent; or
    (c) the spouse of any person referred to in paragraph (b),
    and for the purposes of this definition, any adopted child is treated as related to her adoptive parent within the first degree of consanguinity. Value Added Tax Act 2000, No. 1 of 2001 (Botswana).

Commissioners of Customs and Excise v. Marner and Marner[43]

The appellants, a married couple, ran a public house in partnership. In addition the wife provided catering services at the public house as a separate venture, keeping the profits for herself, as she had done when the public house had been run by her father-in-law. The partnership was registered for value added tax purposes. The wife's catering services were not included with the taxable bar takings of the public house partnership nor was the catering business separately registered. The receipts from catering were below the registration threshold. The Commissioners decided that the catering services were taxable services rendered by the partnership. The appellants maintained that the catering was a separate business run by the wife alone and accordingly not taxable.

DECISION. Clearly in our view the catering element was a matter of assistance to the bar side of the premises, in that the probabilities and expectations would normally be that it would attract customers. This was a somewhat loose arrangement, such as one frequently finds where husband and wife are together concerned in business activities.

As a matter of law, if the catering is a separate enterprise by Mrs. Marner, the enterprise was neither registrable for the purposes of VAT nor would it be taxable.[44] On the other hand if it was part of the general activities of the partnership then the catering receipts would be taxable activities and would be liable to be aggregated with the bar takings for the purposes of computation of VAT.

Again as a matter of law we regard it as perfectly feasible for a partner to indulge in business activities outside the partnership enterprise. Mr. Marner was perfectly well aware, as he could hardly fail to have been, of her activities and of the way in which she dealt with the financial aspect of payment for supplies and retention of profits for herself.

Referring to *Lindley on Partnership*, where a partnership agreement is not in writing, the intention must be derived from the words and conduct of the parties. It is, in our judgment, significant that in this case the catering activities had been carried on by Mrs. Marner prior to the formation of the partnership.

While the cost of utilities increased by the catering activities to an appreciable extent, it was substantially offset by the benefit to the bar trade by the catering activities. This was an activity in a rather loose business relationship between husband and wife, and we do not consider that this particular aspect carries sufficient weight to displace the general

---

[43] 1 BVC 1060 (1977)(VATTR Manchester). *CCH British Value Added Tax Cases (1973–1983)* (edited by the authors).

[44] The receipts were below the threshold amount required for registration. *Added by authors.*

view which we have formed regarding the independence of the catering activities.

Had a receipt been asked for in respect of the bar sales it would by law have been required to carry the VAT registration number of the partnership. On the other hand Mrs. Marner said that she had been asked for catering receipts and that she issued these without a VAT registration number on them. That is, in our view, an indication in favour of severance.

The menus and bills were in the partnership name but that, in our view, is a rather loose way of putting it. We think that any customer consuming a snack or a meal would naturally assume that it was being supplied by the public house and would not be concerned to delve in any great detail into the question whether or not it was being supplied by one or other of the partners as a separate enterprise if, indeed, he was even conscious that the bar enterprise was being run in partnership.

A more serious item is however the consolidation of the trading and profit and loss accounts and balance sheet; this shows the catering purchases and sales consolidated with those of the bar takings and sales and it shows drawings in a composite sum which, as these were consolidated accounts, included also the drawings made by Mrs. Marner on her own account from the catering side of her enterprise.

It is perhaps unfortunate that separate accounts were not prepared for the two businesses but, having regard to the separation which has been achieved in the books of account and the working papers and in the dealings with the catering receipts, we do not consider that this is a factor which is sufficient to displace the conclusion which we have reached that the catering enterprise was a separate enterprise carried on by Mrs. Marner on her own account and that it was an entirely separate enterprise from the enterprise carried on by appellants in partnership; in respect of bar sales.

Held, allowing the taxpayers' appeal:

In *Commissioners of Customs and Excise v Glassborow and Another*,[45] a husband and wife engaged in two distinct economic activities through two separate partnerships. One partnership engaged in business as an estate agent and the other as a land developer. In that case, the Queen's Bench held that the structure of the British VAT is to register "persons," not the businesses that persons engage in. As a result, the court held that two partnerships consisting of the same partners are entitled to only one registration.

4. Severing Value from the Business

To reduce the firm's taxable sales in order to come within a small business exemption, the owner of a business attempted to treat the firm's employees

---

[45] [1975] QB 465, [1974] 1 ALL ER 1041, [1974] 2 WLR 851 (Queen's Bench Division) (edited by the authors).

as independent contractors. In that way, the owner expected to remove the value of the employees' services from the employer's taxable sales. This approach was attempted in the following *Jane Montgomery (Hair Stylists) Ltd* case, in which a hair salon claimed that its stylists were self-employed so that the stylists' receipts from their customers were not reportable as receipts of the salon.

Customs and Excise Commissioners v. Jane Montgomery (Hair Stylists) Ltd[46]

HEADNOTE. Jane Montgomery (Hair Stylists) Ltd (the company) operated a hairdressing salon. Its three hair stylists were first treated as employed by the company and payments received for the services they supplied were included in the company's turnover. In 1985 the stylists entered into franchise agreements with the company and thereafter they were treated as self-employed, their receipts were separated from those of the company. The commissioners issued a notice of compulsory registration for value added tax (VAT) and a penalty for late registration against the company on the basis that the receipts of the stylists fell to be aggregated with the receipts of the company with the result that the company's turnover had exceeded the VAT registration threshold. The company appealed contending that the hair stylists were self-employed and their receipts did not form part of the company's turnover. The tribunal considered that, although the degree of risk undertaken by the stylists was low, there were many factors which were incompatible with an employer/employee relationship and allowed the company's appeal. The commissioners appealed.

LORD MCCLUSKEY. The court is satisfied that this appeal raises no general question of law. The only issue is whether the supplies referred to in the appeal were made by the company and so constituted part of its turnover. If the turnover of the stylists must be added to that of the company's business then the turnover of the company's business becomes such that the business should be registered for VAT purposes.

In determining that question we must look at the substance of what has been established here rather than at mere matters of form. What is happening in these premises ... is substantially the same as what was happening before the agreement took effect. [I]t cannot be said that on balance there has been any material and substantial change in the nature of the business carried on and the way in which it has been carried on. They have all engaged the same accountant; he was and is the accountant to the company and it was he who was responsible for preparing the agreement and setting up the scheme which lies at the heart of this particular case. When the agreement was entered into blanks were left in it; and it was left to the accountant to fill in the blanks.

---

[46] [1994] STC 256 (Court of Exchequer – Scotland) [edited by the authors].

By doing so he effectively determined the stylists' income from their work. That circumstance seems to us to yield the clear inference that the persons who had been employees were effectively ceding control over their remuneration, as well as many other things, to the accountant. The fact that they all employed the same accountant who was the accountant to the company clearly indicates that no one supposed that any conflict of interest could arise between the company's business and the work of the stylists. We also think it is significant that there is no finding at all that the stylists acted in ways that independent contractors would be expected to act in, for example, in relation to advertising their business or otherwise acting independently.

The correct inference from the established facts is that, just as before the agreement was entered into, there was only one business which was being carried in the hairdressing salon. That was the company's business; and it follows that it was the company who made the taxable supplies provided by the stylists.

Although there is no ground of appeal couched in quite the correct terms, we are satisfied that the proper course is to allow the appeal.

D. Voluntary Registration

A business exempt from registration because its taxable sales are below the registration threshold can voluntarily register under many VAT regimes.[47] A person may voluntarily register, for example, if the person's customers are registered traders who prefer to purchase from registered sellers so that these customers can claim credit for tax paid on purchases. A new or expanding business also may voluntarily register in order to claim credit for VAT on its purchases of business inputs, including capital goods and inventory.[48] A person who registers voluntarily generally must remain registered for a minimum period, such as two years, and must recapture input credits claimed on goods that are on hand on the date the registration is canceled.

---

[47] Australia GST, *supra* note 21, at §23–10. Canadian GST, *supra* note 4, at §240(3)(a). "[A] non-resident person who in the ordinary course of carrying on business outside Canada regularly solicits orders for the supply by the person of tangible personal property for export to, or delivery in, Canada" may register voluntarily. *Id*. at §240(3)(b). A listed financial institution that is resident in Canada (exempt from GST on many financial services) may register voluntarily. *Id*. at §240(3)(c). A resident holding company (or company organized to acquire other corporations) that does not engage in commercial activity may voluntarily register if certain conditions are met. *Id*. at §240(3)(d). Schenk, *Goods and Services Tax: The Canadian Approach to Value-Added Tax* [hereinafter Schenk, Canadian GST], p. 17. See New Vatopia VAT, Appendix B, §20(5).

[48] "A person who registers voluntarily must recapture some previously-claimed input credits attributable to assets on hand when de-registering. Under the British VAT, in *Marshall v. C & E Commissioners*, 1975 VATTR 98, a taxpayer who voluntarily registered his yacht charter business was taxed when he later sold the yachts and ceased to conduct business." Schenk, Canadian GST, *supra* note 47, at 17 and note 34.

E. CANCELLATION OF REGISTRATION

A registered person may cease to be registered if the person no longer meets the registration requirements or if the tax authority cancels the person's registration.[49] When registration is canceled some or all of the input credits claimed on property held at that time must be repaid.[50]

A nation may provide a small business exemption because small businesses tend not to maintain adequate record keeping. If this is the rationale for the exemption, then once a business exceeds the threshold, and must register and keep required records, registration should be maintained even if that business' sales slip below the threshold. Australia adopted this principle.[51] A VAT proposed in the United States is comparable.[52]

Another rationale for the small business exemption is that the compliance costs for a business with low turnover and the administrative costs for the government outweigh the tax liability payable by such businesses with low levels of value added. Countries such as Canada, favoring this rationale for the exemption, typically deregister the businesses whose taxable sales drop below the threshold.[53] A business' sales could drop below the threshold because its total sales (and taxable sales) decline or because the firm shifts its activities from taxable to exempt sales, with its taxable sales falling below the threshold.

Even if a business qualifies for deregistration because its turnover falls below the threshold, the person remains registered until the person completes the de-registration process.[54] A business that registers voluntarily may be required to maintain registration for a minimum period such as two years.[55]

Registration may be canceled at the government's initiative. The government may cancel a person's registration if the business closes or no longer engages in taxable activity.[56] The cancellation prevents the person from

---

[49] The New Vatopia VAT provides that the government may cancel a person's registration or a taxable person may request cancellation. New Vatopia VAT, Appendix B, §22.

[50] See discussion in the next section of this chapter.

[51] See Australia GST, *supra* note 21, at §25–50.

[52] Revenue Restoration Act of 1996, H.R. 4050, 104th Cong., 2d Sess., 142 CONG. REC. E1572 (1996) (Congressman Gibbons's bill was not enacted).

[53] Canadian GST, *supra* note 4, at §§148(1) & 242. There are special rules governing a person engaged in a business involving games of chance. §148(1)(c) and 148(2)(c). Some sales are not included in calculating the $30,000 threshold. See §148(1)(a) and 148(2)(a) on sales of capital property and on financial services.

[54] See New Zealand Case R29 (1994), 16 NZTC 6,155.

[55] Canadian GST, *supra* note 4, at §242(2) has a one-year period. Unless the person ceases to engage in economic activity, Australia requires all registrants (whether mandatory or voluntary) to be registered for at least twelve months before deregistering. Australia GST, *supra* note 21, at §25–55. See New Vatopia VAT, Appendix B, at §13(8), providing for cancellation of registration for mandatory or voluntary registrants only after the expiration of two years from the effective date of the registration.

[56] See, for example, Explanatory Notes to Bill C-62 as passed by the House of Commons on April 10, 1990, Department of Finance, May 1990 [hereinafter 1990 Explanatory Notes], at 115.

issuing tax invoices and forces the person to recapture tax credits claimed on purchases of goods and sometimes services still on hand.

F. Transition to Registration and Cancellation of Registration

A previously unregistered person who is required to register or voluntarily registers may be eligible to claim input credits for VAT paid on goods on hand when it becomes a registered person. The input credits generally are available for tax paid on purchases made within a short period before registration, but only for goods that (1) are on hand when registration becomes effective, and (2) will be used in connection with taxable activity.[57] It is less common for a VAT law to provide input credits for tax on services, rent and capital goods on hand when registration becomes effective, even if these items are used by the newly registered person in making taxable sales.[58] It is costly, in lost revenue, to expand the credit to cover these items. In addition, it is difficult administratively to verify that the business had unused services on hand when registration becomes effective.

When a registrant deregisters, it must repay tax benefits claimed while registered.[59] Otherwise, the deregistering person would obtain a tax advantage over its competition. In Canada, a deregistering business generally must report as taxable sales the goods on hand immediately before it ceases to be registered.[60] In New Zealand, the recapture rules cover both goods and services.[61]

G. Registration of Branches and Group of Companies

There are significant nontax reasons for VAT-registered businesses to file VAT returns (a) by branch or division of the company, or (b) by consolidating

---

[57] See Canadian GST, *supra* note 4, at §171(1) and (2). Canada does not have a time limit. The input credit is not available with respect to assets on which GST was not paid, such as assets acquired before January 1, 1991, the date the GST became effective. See 1990 Explanatory Notes, *supra* note 56, at 60.

[58] Canada allows credits for tax on some services on hand when registration becomes effective. See Canadian GST, *supra* note 4, at §171(2)(a). Such input tax is not creditable if it is attributable to services provided before he becomes a registrant or to rents, royalties, or similar payments attributable to the preregistration period. *Id.* at §171(2)(b).

[59] Under the British VAT, in *Marshall v. C & E Commissioners*, *supra* note 48, a taxpayer who voluntarily registered his yacht charter business was taxed when he later sold the yachts and ceased to conduct business.

[60] The assets include property acquired for consumption, use, or supply in the course of commercial activities. Canadian GST, *supra* note 4, at §171(3)(a)(i). §171(3)(a) does not apply to a direct seller's independent sales contractor's sales aids if the contractor ceases to be a registrant and such contractor received the sales aids from the direct seller or one of the direct seller's other independent sales contractors after March 1993, while an approval to use the alternate collection method under §178.2(3) was in effect. §178.5(11).

[61] New Zealand requires the deregistering business to report the lesser of the cost or the market value of goods and services that are part of the assets of a taxable activity conducted by the person ceasing to be registered. NZ GST, *supra* note 34, at §5(3).

operations for a group of related companies. For example, in a developing country with inadequate roads, postal services, and telecommunications, a company with branches in remote areas may find it almost impossible to collect branch data and file a single VAT return by the due date. By contrast, filing by branch or division may increase VAT compliance costs. If related companies engage in significant intercompany transactions, the filing of consolidated returns that disregard those transactions may significantly reduce VAT reporting obligations.

There also may be tax-motivated reasons for businesses to file by branch or by consolidating operations of related companies. Filing by branch does not (or should not) enable a business to come within the small business exemption. The calculation of taxable sales is made for the entire company. Consolidated reporting may allow a group of companies to ignore intercompany transactions and gain some cash-flow benefits. In addition, if one company has excess input credits that must be carried forward and a related company has net VAT liability that must be remitted to the tax authorities, consolidated reporting may allow the group to offset the excess credits against the net tax in order to reduce the tax payable in that tax period. Consolidated reporting gives the group a quicker recovery of excess credits than would be available if they reported separately because there generally is a delay (in some countries a significant time delay) in recovering refunds for excess credits.

H. ELECTRONIC COMMERCE

Electronic commerce has been defined "as business transactions taking place through the electronic transmission of data over communications networks such as the Internet."[62] It may be goods, and services, including software, that can be downloaded (digital products) or provided in physical form. Some other VAT issues related to electronic commerce are covered elsewhere in the book.[63] This section is limited to the registration issues related to providers of electronic commerce.

A ministerial level conference organized by the OECD Committee on Fiscal Affairs, entitled "A Borderless World Releasing the Potential of Global Electronic Commerce," was held in Ottawa in October 1998.[64] The conference participants identified problems and discussed possible solutions.

As a follow-up to this OECD conference, the Commission of the European Communities proposed a directive covering certain legal aspects of electronic commerce within the EU.[65] In addition, a 1999 European Commission

---

[62] Jenkins, "VAT and Electronic Commerce: The Challenges and Opportunities," 10 *VAT Monitor* 3 (Jan./Feb. 199), at 3.

[63] See the discussion of the person liable for VAT on electronic commerce *infra* this chapter; and the place of supply of electronic commerce *infra* Chapter 7.

[64] See Lambert, "VAT & Electronic Commerce: European Union Insights into the Challenges Ahead," 17 *Tax Notes Int'l* 1645 (Nov. 23, 1998).

[65] Proposal for a European Parliament and Council Directive on certain legal aspects of electronic commerce in the internal market, COM/98/0586, 1999 OJ C 030 (Feb. 5, 1999). The proposed directive seeks to ensure "the free movement of Information Society services

working paper suggested legislative changes in order to provide "an efficient, simple and non-distorting application of the VAT legislation" to e-commerce.[66] In developing the working paper, the Commission assumed that the solution would not involve any new or additional taxes, that digital products would be treated as supplies of services for VAT purposes, and that services consumed in the EU would be taxed, but not services consumed outside the EU.[67] Assuming that suppliers can distinguish between supplies to business and supplies to consumers, the Commission suggested "a reverse charge mechanism for cross-border business-to-business transactions and a VAT registration obligation for non EU suppliers."[68] Sales to private consumers should be taxed in the country of consumption, so information must be collected that identifies the customer's tax jurisdiction.[69] Three options were considered:

1. A non-EU seller could register by setting up an establishment in the European Union.
2. A non-EU seller could be required to register in each Member State in which it conducts business.
3. The EU could establish a single Community registration and the non-EU seller could report all electronic supplies within the Community in a return filed under a registration number.[70]

In May 2002, the Council of the European Union issued a Council Directive amending the Sixth Directive as it applied to radio and television broadcasting services and some electronically-supplied services.[71] This directive adopted a combination of options 2 and 3. Nonresident suppliers of covered services must register in each Member State in which they render those services. These services are deemed supplied where the services are consumed.

---

between the Member States." *Id*. at Art. 1(1). Information Society services are services provided for a fee at the recipient's request, when provided at a distance by electronic means. *Id*. at Art. 2(a).

[66] Lejeune, Cambien, & Joostens, "E-commerce – The European Commission," 10 *VAT Monitor* 156 (July/Aug. 1999) [hereinafter Lejeune, Cambien, & Joostens, E-commerce]. The working paper is DG XXI, Working Paper on Indirect Taxes and e-commerce, XXI/99/1201, June 8, 1999.

[67] See *id*. at 156.

[68] *Id*.

[69] *Id*. at 157.

[70] *Id*.

[71] Council Directive 2002/38/EC of May 7, 2002. The Council of the European Union adopted Directive 2006/58/EC, extending this Directive until the end of 2006. IBFD Tax News Service 28 June 2006. The following illustrative list of electronically supplied services is included as Annex I to the Directive:

1. "Website supply, web-hosting, distance maintenance of programmes and equipment.
2. Supply of software and updating thereof.
3. Supply of images, text and information, and making databases available.
4. Supply of music, films and games, including games of change and gambling games, and of political, cultural, artistic, sporting, scientific and entertainment broadcasts and events.
5. Supply of distance teaching."

"Non-established taxable persons"[72] may use a special scheme to report and pay VAT on covered services to person in Member States. Under the special scheme, this nonestablished person may register in one Member State and report and remit tax on taxable services rendered to persons in all Member States. The Council issued rules governing transactions covered in this Directive.[73]

In the United States, there has been a moratorium on the imposition of state taxes (retail sales taxes) on certain Internet-provided services such as Internet access. Legislation extending the moratorium on taxes on Internet access until November 2007 was enacted in 2004.[74]

The EU, in taking the opposite approach, taxes Internet-provided goods and services, including those provided by nonresidents who do not otherwise operate in the EU. A firm engaged in electronic commerce that does not have a fixed establishment in the EU is required to register in an EU member state.

I. Telecommunication Services

As discussed above, the EU requires nonresident suppliers of electronically supplied services to EU customers to register in an EU country, file returns, and pay VAT on those services within the EU. The EU rules designed to tax telecommunication services provided by non-EU suppliers do not focus on registration by the nonresident suppliers. Rather, the EU rules focus on the place where these services are deemed to be rendered. They provide that the telecom services are rendered at the customer's location (the user of the services). The user is taxable on these services, but the nonresident may be jointly and severally liable for the tax.

Before these rules mandated by the 1999 Council Directive on telecom services were enacted into the domestic law of a Member State, a telecom company established in that EU country was at a competitive disadvantage in attracting customers outside the EU. Under Article 9(1) of the Sixth Directive,

---

[72] "Non-established taxable person" means a taxable person who has neither established his business nor has a fixed establishment within the territory of the Community and who is not otherwise required to be identified for tax purposes under Article 22. *Id.* at Art. 1, adding A(a) definition in new Art. 26c of the Sixth Directive.

[73] See Council Regulation (EC) No. 792/2002 of May 7, 2002, amending temporarily Regulation (EEC) No. 218/92, OJ L 128/1, May 15, 2002. See also Desmeytere, "VAT Registration in the EU," *VAT Monitor*, May/June 2003, p. 197, discussing the mechanism by which foreign businesses may register in various EU countries.

[74] The Internet Tax Nondiscrimination Act, P.L. 108-435, 150 Cong. Rec. D 1124 (Dec. 3, 2004). The moratorium was for four years, but was retroactive to November 3, 2003. The legislation also bans new, multiple, and discriminatory taxes on electronic commerce. Some existing state taxes on digital subscriber line (DSL) service and telephone calls made over the Internet were not affected. For an economic analysis of the taxation of electronic commerce under a commodity tax that supports the taxation of electronic commerce at a rate comparable to the rate imposed on other goods and services, see Zodrow, "Optimal Commodity Taxation of Traditional and Electronic Commerce," LIX *National Tax Journal* 7 (Mar. 2006).

a service takes place where the supplier established its business or has a fixed establishment. As a result, an EU vendor of telecom services in that country was required to charge VAT on services to customers outside the EU. Those potential customers could obtain telecom services from suppliers outside the EU free of VAT.[75]

The EU response was to issue Council Directive 1999/59/EC of June 17, 1999,[76] amending the Article 9 place of supply rules for telecom services. The Sixth Directive, Article 9(2)(e) was amended and Article 9(4) was added. At the end of Article 9(2)(e), the following was added:

> Telecommunication services shall be deemed to be services relating to the transmission, emission or reception of signals, writing, images and sounds or information of any nature by wire, radio, optical or other electromagnetic systems, including the related transfer or assignment of the right to use capacity for such transmission, emission or reception. Telecommunications services within the meaning of this provision shall also include provision of access to global information networks.

The revised Article 9(2)(e) removes the competitive disadvantage for an EU telecom company that provides services outside the Member State in which it established its business or that provides services to customers outside the EU. These services now take place at the customer's (not the supplier's) place of business or fixed establishment if the customer is established in an EU country that is not the telecom supplier's country.[77]

New Article 9(4) provides:

> In the case of telecommunications services referred to in paragraph 2(e) supplied by a taxable person established outside the Community to non-taxable persons established inside the Community, Member States shall make use of . . . [Article 9(3)(b)][78]

---

[75] See Lejeune & Cambrien, "Telecommunications Services – The New Regime as From 1 January 2000," 10 *VAT Monitor* 150 (July/Aug. 1999) [hereinafter Lejeune & Cambien, Telecom].

[76] OJ L 162, June 17, 1999.

[77] Lejeune & Cambien, Telecom, *supra* note 75, at 151. For services covered by Art. 9(2)(e), the tax is payable by the recipient of the services. Sixth Directive, *infra* note 78, at Art. 21(1)(b), as amended by Council Directive 1999/59/EC.. According to amended Art. 21(1)(b): "taxable persons to whom services covered by Article 9(2)(e) are supplied or persons who are identified for value added tax purposes within the territory of the country to whom services covered by Article 28b(C), (D), (E) and (F) are supplied, if the services are carried out by a taxable person established abroad; however, Member States may require that the supplier of services shall be held jointly and severally liable for payment of the tax."

[78] Sixth Council Directive of May 17, 1977, on the harmonization of the laws of the Member States relating to turnover taxes – Common system of value added tax: uniform basis of assessment (77/388/EEC), Art. 9(3)(b), [hereinafter Sixth Directive], provides that a Member State may consider "the place of supply of services, which under this Article would be situated outside the Community, as being within the territory of the country where the effective use and enjoyment of the services take place within the territory of the country." Article 58(b) of the Recast Sixth Directive is comparable. It provides that Member States may treat, as the place of supply of services situated outside the

The new Article 9(4) prevents EU consumers and unregistered EU public bodies from avoiding VAT by purchasing telecom services from suppliers outside the EU. For these purchasers, with the combination of Article 9(4) and Article 9(3)(b) of the Sixth Directive, telecom services take place where the effective use and enjoyment of the services occur.[79] The services therefore are taxed uniformly in the EU and, under revised Article 21(1)(b), a foreign supplier to an EU customer may be held jointly and severally liable for the payment of the tax.

III. Person Liable for Tax

A. General Principles

VAT generally is imposed on taxable domestic supplies of goods and services and on imports of goods and imports of some services. The person treated as the importer of taxable goods and the recipient of taxable imported services generally is liable for tax on those imports.[80] The liability for tax on imports is not discussed in this section.

On taxable domestic supplies of goods and services, the tax is imposed upon, or must be accounted for, by the taxable (or registered) person making the supply.

Some countries rely both on the concepts of a registered person and a taxable person in defining transactions that are taxable and persons who are required to file returns and account for tax on taxable sales.

In Australia, the liability to pay tax is imposed on the person who makes taxable supplies – the supplier.[81] It is only a person who is registered or required to register that can make a taxable supply; that is, a supply for consideration in connection with a supply connected with Australia and made in the course of the person's enterprise. As a result, "registration" is the key concept in Australia.[82]

The EU Sixth Directive imposes VAT on taxable supplies by a taxable person. In the United Kingdom, South Africa, and in other countries that are consistent with of the New Vatopia approach, the concepts of a taxable

---

Community that are rendered to non-taxable persons within the Community as being "within their territory, if he effective use or enjoyment of the services takes place within their territory" Proposal for a Council Directive on the common system of value added tax (Recast), COM (2004) 246 final, 2004/0079 (CNS) April 15, 2004.

[79] Lejeune & Cambien, Telecom, *supra* note 75, at 151. The vendor is responsible to pay the VAT. See Sixth Directive, *supra* note 78, at Art. 21(1)(b).

[80] See, for example, New Vatopia VAT, §9(2)(b) and (c).

[81] Australian GST, *supra* note 21, at §9–40. Botswana imposes tax on registered persons, who also are required to file returns and pay tax. See Botswana VAT, *supra* note 6, at §§7(1)(a), 19(1), and 26(1).

[82] *Id*. at §23-15. Botswana imposes tax on registered persons, who also are required to file returns and pay tax. See Botswana VAT, *supra* note 6, at §§7(1)(a), 19(1), and 26(1).

person (or vendor) and a registered person both have significance.[83] In the United Kingdom, subject to the Sixth Directive rules, a taxable person is a person registered or required to register.[84] Tax is imposed on a taxable person, and it is only a person registered or required to register who may be a taxable person.[85] In many countries, a person is not a taxable person unless he makes sufficient taxable sales in connection with an "economic activity" (as required in some countries) or in connection with a "business" (as required in other countries). The concept of business or business activity is discussed in a later section of this chapter.

Under the EU's Sixth VAT Directive, a taxable person is defined as "any person who independently carries out in any place any economic activity specified…, whatever the purpose or results of that activity."[86] Member States may "treat as a taxable person anyone who carries out, on a occasional basis, a transaction relating to" the specified activities.[87] According to the Sixth Directive, governmental authorities and bodies governed by public law are not taxable persons if they engage in activities as public authorities.[88] In some cases, the question is whether a person engages in activity as an employee of a public authority (the sales are not sales by a taxable person) or as an independent contractor (the sales are sales by a taxable person). For example, in a case from the Netherlands, where notaries and bailiffs are independent officers (not public employees), the European Court of Justice decided that the services provided by notaries and bailiffs to individuals constituted economic activity of a taxable person subject to VAT. The exemption for their services provided by the Netherlands therefore violated the Sixth VAT Directive.[89]

B. Person Treated as Seller

1. In General

Ordinarily, the person conducting business and making sales is the one who is subject to the registration rules and is liable for VAT. The identity of the seller may affect who must register for VAT purposes – who is a taxable person with sales above the registration threshold. The question is who is the seller arises with sales over the Internet, auction sales, consignment sales, sales by

---

[83] RSA VAT, *supra* note 22, §§1 definition of "vendor," 7(1) imposition of tax on vendors, 23 liability to register, and 28 liability of vendor to file returns and pay tax (Republic of South Africa). See also New Vatopia VAT, Appendix B, §§6, 9, 23, and 24.

[84] Value-Added Tax Act 1994, §3(1) (United Kingdom).

[85] *Id*. at §4(1).

[86] Sixth Directive, *supra* note 78, at Art. 4(2). "The [ABA] Model Act, section 4005(a), defines a taxable person as a person who engages in a taxable or nontaxable transaction in connection with a business, and a person who engages in a taxable casual sale under section 4003(a)(3); but the latter is a taxable person only with respect to the taxable casual sale." ABA Model VAT, *supra* note 39, at 31.

[87] Sixth Directive, *supra* note 78, at Art. 4(3).

[88] *Id*. at Art. 4(5).

[89] *Re Notaries and Bailiffs: EC Commission v. Netherlands*, [1988] 2 CMLR 921 (ECJ 1987).

representatives of the owner of property, and local government services. Many of these transactions are discussed in this section.

If sales are made by a seller who operates as a partnership, as a club, or in some other form, who must register? The following edited excerpt discusses this issue:

> *Partnerships.* In the United Kingdom, it has been accepted for VAT that a partnership can be registered in the name of a firm. However, in most civil law countries, most partnerships are not legal entities; they are usually registered in the managing partner's name. Generally, all partnerships can be sued, but if there is a "sleeping partner" (who provides capital), he can only be sued up to the amount of capital he has provided. . . .
>
> *Clubs.* To reduce the administrative hassle of preregistration each time the "taxable person" of, say, a club changes (this could be annually if it were the elected treasurer), it might be acceptable to make the firm or club, as a legal entity, the taxable person, while retaining the usual requirement for most cases that an individual must be named the taxable person. Similarly, tax tribunals or courts must be able to look behind the firm as necessary to establish if the taxable persons are responsible for more than one firm or club.[90]

For administrative or other practical reasons, for some transactions, a person other than the legal owner of property or other than the person rendering services may be treated as the supplier charged with the responsibility to account for VAT on goods sold or services rendered. Some of those special situations are discussed in the following subsections.

2. Electronic Commerce and Telecommunication Services Rendered by Nonresidents

It is customary for nations to tax imported services only by persons who are not eligible to recover the tax on the import through the input tax credit. The recipient of the taxable imported services is the person liable for the tax on these services. The tax generally must be reported and paid by the recipient of the services under a reverse charge system. Although the imposition of the tax liability on the recipient of the services under this self-assessment system may work when the recipient is a nonprofit organization, a unit of government, or business making exempt domestic sales, it is not effective when the recipient is an individual consumer.

When the EU developed a system to tax electronically supplied services by a nonestablished (nonresident) operator, the Council Directive imposed the obligation to report and remit the tax on the nonresident operator and required that supplier to register in at least one EU member state.[91] In contrast, EU rules applicable to telecommunication services rendered by nonresidents of the EU provide that the user of the services is the person liable

---

[90] Tait, *supra* not 41, at 366–367.
[91] Council Directive 2002/38/EC of May 7, 2002. See discussion of the registration requirements applicable to electronic commerce *supra* II(H), this chapter.

for the tax, but the nonresident supplier may be jointly and severally liable for the tax.[92]

3. Auctions

There are several different kinds of auctions. Some are private auctions of goods in which the auction company serves as agent for the owner selling the property being auctioned. The owners may be private individuals, registered businesses, or charitable or governmental organizations that are selling property owned by them. Others involve auctions by a unit of government of goods confiscated from persons under authority of law (such as illegal contraband or goods seized or distrained to recover taxes or other obligations to the government). Goods repossessed on default by a debtor may be auctioned pursuant to a mortgage or other credit agreement.

In most or all of these situations, the "seller" at auction in the person who owns or is treated as the person with legal authority to sell and the auction house serves as agent of the seller, receiving a commission for its services. Under the general rules in many VAT systems, the person making the taxable supply or sale is liable for VAT if the person is VAT-registered.[93] Generally, when an agent makes a sale on behalf of a principal, the supply is considered a supply by the principal.[94] As a result, without special rules governing auction sales, these sales would be treated under most VATs as sales by the principal (usually the owner of the goods). Auction sales by private consumers would escape tax, while sales of used goods by used goods dealers would be taxed. To remove this inconsistency, some VATs treat the auction house as the seller of the auctioned goods in connection with its taxable activity.[95] Under those regimes, the auction house must include the auction sales as part of its taxable sales.[96]

4. Other Sales by Nonowners

When a registered person is other than a natural person, it is important to designate a person or categories of persons within the registrant's organization who is charged with the responsibility to comply with the VAT obligations and can be held liable for noncompliance. The registrant and not the responsible officer or employee is the person making taxable sales or importing taxable goods or services, but the responsible officer may be liable for VAT compliance. For example, any partner in a partnership or a treasurer in a

---

[92] See discussion of the registration requirements applicable to telecommunication services *supra* II(I), this chapter.

[93] See, as an example, New Vatopia VAT, Appendix B, §9(2)(a) and the §2 definition of supplier.

[94] See New Vatopia VAT, Appendix B, §5(1)(a).

[95] See New Vatopia VAT, Appendix B, §5(3).

[96] If the VAT law gives registered sellers of used goods input credits attributable to used goods acquired in a transaction not subject to VAT, the auction house should be entitled to comparable credits when the auctioned goods are presumed to be acquired for auction in a transaction not subject to tax.

corporation can be designated in the VAT law as the person responsible for reporting, collecting, and paying the VAT.[97]

Representatives of the owners include such persons as a mortgagee in possession of mortgaged property, an executor of a deceased person's estate (including a business of the decedent operated as a sole proprietorship), a conservator of a legally incompetent person's assets, and a custodian of the assets of a person (such as a minor) under a legal disability.

It is not clear that a single rule should determine who is the seller for each of these persons serving in a representative capacity who does not own but legally has the authority to manage assets of another. When the representative manages a business (a taxable activity) of the owners and thereby has all of the data necessary to file returns and comply with other VAT obligations, the representative should be treated as the seller or importer with respect to sales and imports made on behalf of the owner. If the representative engages in economic activity for more than one owner, then consistent with customary rules governing trustees, the representative should be treated as a separate person with respect to each such owner.[98]

5. Local Government Services

Common practice is to exempt local services rendered by local units of government.[99] Occasionally, services rendered by local (or even national) governments that compete with the private sector, such as electrical services, are taxed. When they are taxed, the local government or parastatel that renders the services is the seller or taxpayer with respect to the services. Some countries have expanded the list of government services subject to tax, and again it is the provider of the services that is the taxpayer making the sale.

New Zealand adopted a GST which at the time (1989) had the broadest tax base of any value added tax in the world. New Zealand decided to include services financed with real property taxes (local rates) in its GST base. New Zealand in effect treats rates as payments for the local public services provided with revenue from those local rates. Local government is rendering taxable services to real property owners equal to the rates payable by each owner. Local government is the taxpayer and adds the GST rate to the charges for rates. South Africa adopted a similar approach, but it taxes supplies of some specific goods and services even if provided by a local government, including electricity, gas, water, sewerage, parking grounds, cement making, nurseries, brick yards, and liquor sales for which charges are imposed.[100]

---

[97] See New Vatopia VAT, Appendix B, §54, especially §54(5).

[98] See New Vatopia VAT, Appendix B, §59.

[99] See discussion *infra*, Chapter 9.

[100] RSA VAT, *supra* note 22, at §1 definition of "enterprise" and Government Notice No. 2570: Determination of category of businesses, October 21, 1991 (Republic of South Africa).

C. Tax Collectible from Third Persons

Some countries authorize the tax authorities to recover unpaid tax from third parties that owe money to, hold money for, or have possession of property belonging to the person who owes the unpaid tax.[101] Typically, the tax authorities must notify the third party of the name of the taxpayer and the amount of the taxpayer's assets in that party's possession that should be remitted to the tax authorities to satisfy the tax in default. A third party making payment under this notice is treated as having made payment under the authority of the taxpayer in default. The third party making payment pursuant to that notice is indemnified against liability for making such payment.

IV. Business Activity Subject to VAT

A. Taxable Activity

As discussed earlier in this chapter, a person is a taxable person (or in some countries a registered person) if he makes taxable sales above a threshold amount and such sales are made in connection with certain economic or taxable activity. This section examines the kind of activity that gives rise to sales subject to tax. A taxable activity for VAT purposes generally is broader than the concept of trade for income tax purposes.[102]

---

[101] See, for example, Value Added tax Act 2005, Act No. 7 of 2005, §50 (Dominica). In South Africa, a court upheld this authority to demand payment from third persons even before the tax authorities assessed the taxpayer for the unpaid tax. *National Educare Forum v. Commissioner, South African Revenue Service,* 2002 (4) JTLR 119 (High Ct. Transkei 2002), reported by Botes, VAT Monitor, July/Aug 2002, p. 332.

[102] The tests include:

•*Continuity*
Supplies should be made regularly and fairly frequently as part of a continuing activity. Isolated or single transactions will not usually be liable to VAT.

•*Value*
The supplies should be for a significant amount; trivial, even if repeated, transactions would not usually count.

•*Profit (in the Accounting Sense)*
Not necessary; after all, large concerns can create substantial value added and pay large sums in wages, yet make no profit (many publicly owned firms do precisely this). Such firms should certainly pay VAT.

•*Active Control*
Control should be in the hands of the supplier. He should be actively engaged in the "control or management of the assets concerned" (including operation through an agent). The proprietor should be independent and, hence, should be excluded from coverage.

•*Intra- Versus Intertrade*
Supplies should be to members outside the organization and not just between members of the organization.

The U.K. VAT limits taxable sales to those made in furtherance of a business.[103] A U.K. court, interpreting the concept of business, held that a business "must amount to a continuing activity which is predominantly concerned with the making of supplies to others for a consideration. There are, in effect, two parts to the test. First, for there to be an 'activity' there must be sufficiency of scale to the supplies and they must be continued over a period of time. Second, the predominant concern of the person conducting the activity must be the making of supplies."[104]

New Zealand relies on the concept of taxable activity that is based on factors such as continuity and frequency of activity. The New Zealand GST taxes a broad range of economic activity by defining taxable activity to include activities of governmental entities and activity conducted "continuously or regularly by any person, whether or not for a pecuniary profit.... "[105] New Zealand removes activities conducted "essentially as a private recreational pursuit or hobby" and activities conducted in an employment relationship, in a judicial capacity, or in a public administrative capacity.[106]

The EU Sixth VAT Directive imposes obligations to collect and remit tax on a "taxable person"; that is, on a person who engages in economic activity. Economic activity is broadly defined to include "all activities of producers, traders and persons supplying services including mining and agricultural activities and activities of the professions. The exploitation of tangible or intangible property for the purpose of obtaining income therefrom on a continuing basis shall also be considered an economic activity."[107] Economic activity under the Sixth Directive is very expansive, yet relies on an objective test.[108]

In a U.K. case, the tax authority claimed that tax avoidance transactions did not constitute economic activity under the EU's Sixth Directive[109] and, as a result, denied the seller input credits for VAT on acquisitions used in engaging in those transactions. The European Court of Justice ruled that

---

• *Appearance of Business*
The activities should have the characteristics of a normal commercial undertaking with some acceptable method of record keeping in place. Tait, VAT, *supra* note 38, at 368–369.

---

[103] See Value Added Tax Act 1994, §4 (United Kingdom); Sixth Directive, *supra* note 78, at Art's. 2(1) and 4(1).

[104] *The National Society for the Prevention of Cruelty to Children v. Customs and Excise Commissioners* [1992] VATTR 417, at 422.

[105] NZ GST, *supra* note 34, at §6(1).

[106] *Id.* at §6(3).

[107] Sixth Directive, *supra* note 78, at Art. 4(2). Member States may also treat as a taxable person anyone who carries out, on an occasional basis, a transaction relating to the activities referred to in paragraph 2. *Id.* at Art. 4(3). See Warburton, *Value Added Tax: Business and the Predominant Concern Test*, 1995 Brit. Tax Rev. 534 (1995) [hereinafter Warburton].

[108] See Warburton, *supra* note 107, at 539. *Notaries & Bailiffs*, *supra* note 89, found that activities of notaries and bailiffs constituted economic activity. Qualification as economic activity should turn "on the nature and scale of the activities and not the reasons why those activities are being carried out." Warburton, *supra* note 107, at 539.

[109] Sixth Directive, *supra* note 78, at Art. 4(2).

transactions can constitute economic activity even if engaged in solely to obtain a tax advantage. It is for the national court to determine the substance and significance of any such transactions, and can recast the transactions as if the abusive transaction was not undertaken.[110]

The United Kingdom also claimed that "a circular carousel fraud" (transactions, for example, going from to Bob to Carl and back to Abel.) is not economic activity; thus, the input credits are denied with respect to the sale.[111]

In *The Scottish Solicitors' Discipline Tribunal* case,[112] it was the taxpayer that sought registration as a body engaged in business, presumably to claim input credits for tax on its purchases. In that case, the solicitors who served on the disciplinary tribunal received only expenses and the lay members received expenses plus a fee. The disciplinary tribunal ruled on complaints of professional misconduct, and was empowered to impose sanctions or fines, as well as costs. If the disciplinary tribunal's expenses exceeded its receipts, the Law Society made up the balance. Distinguishing arbitration from this activity, the VAT Tribunal held that the activities of the disciplinary tribunal did "not amount to the carrying on of a business, having no element of commerciality, nor of economic activity."[113]

The following United Kingdom VAT case raises the issue of what constitutes a business for VAT purposes.

Atlas Marketing v. Commissioners of Customs and Excise[114]

[Atlas Marketing was listed as a dealer in precious metals in its VAT registration form. It operated as a proprietorship owned by Mr. Steele. Mr. Steele, a former amateur race car driver in New Zealand, decided to start a separate race car business, Steele Competition, with him serving as the professional race car driver. Mr. Steele also applied for registration for Steele Competition for those activities. The latter registration was refused because he already was registered.

---

[110] See *Halifax plc, Leeds Permanent Development Services Ltd, County Wide Property Investments Ltd v Commissioners of Customs & Excise*, Case C-255/02, Judgment on Feb. 21, 2006, [2006] ECR I-..., [2006] All ER (D) 283. In the *Optigen, Fulcrum, and Bond* joined cases, *supra* note 2, the ECJ ruled that an innocent person who is involved in a carousel fraud still is engaged in economic activity and his supplies remain supplies of goods and supplies of services.

[111] See *VAT Monitor*, July/Aug. 2003, p. 356. The United Kingdom amended the Value Added Tax Act 1994 (c. 23) to add §77A, imposing joint and several liability on traders in a supply chain involving telephone and telecommunications equipment and computer and equipment connected with computers or computer systems, where VAT was not paid on a supply within the chain. Finance Act 2003, Ch. 14, §18.

[112] *The Scottish Solicitors' Discipline Tribunal v The Commissioners of Customs & Excise* [1989] 4 BVC 636 (Edinburgh VAT Tribunal).

[113] *Id.* at 638. See Discussion Question 7 at the end of this chapter.

[114] [1986] 1 C.M.L.R. 71 (VATTR London 1985) (edited and summarized by the authors).

Mr. Steele employed a first class team to maintain his car and participate in races. Mr. Steele advertised for sponsors for his racing activities with a "Steele Competition" brochure that showed the car with the names Atlas Marketing and British Bullion Buyers painted on the side. Mr. Steele obtained one sponsorship from a carpet company for 6,000 pounds Sterling. He also received 500 pounds Sterling in prize money. In an October 1981 accident, he suffered injuries that prevented him from racing his car for about six months. In January 1982, Mr. Steele went into partnership with Mr. Hellyar and transferred his precious metals business to the partnership but not his motor racing business. Mr. Hellyar withdrew in June 1983. In 1983, Steele decided that he could not raise the needed funds and abandoned the racing activity, at least for the time being. From November 20, 1980, to January 31, 1983, Atlas Marketing's expenses "on telephones, on printing and on legal matters were no less than, 75,000, excluding expenses of, 27,000 incurred on motor racing." Its net profits were about 5,000. Mr. Steele believed that his racing activities increased his precious metals business.]

Mr. Conlon, for the Commissioners, claimed that Steele's racing activities were a hobby, relying on *Customs and Excise Commissioners v Lord Fisher*.[115] He also submitted that the advertising of "Atlas Marketing" on the cars could not be expected to have any real effect on Atlas Marketing's scrap jewellery business.

[The issue is whether the race car activities constituted a hobby of Mr. Steele or were part of Atlas Marketing's business. Only if the latter can Atlas Marketing claim credit for input tax on purchases related to the race car activities].

Section 14(3) provided in part: "input tax," in relation to a taxable person, means the following tax, that is to say –

(a) tax on the supply to him of any goods or services; and
(b) tax paid or payable by him on the importation of any goods,

being (in either case) goods or services used or to be used for the purpose of any business carried on or to be carried on by him.

It was contended by Mr. Conlon that Mr. Steele was not carrying on any business in relation to his motor racing activities, that the test to be applied in relation to the words 'any business carried on or to be carried on by him' was whether he was making taxable supplies or would make taxable supplies in the immediate future. Mr. Conlon contended that Mr. Steele's activities in motor racing were not those of a business being carried on, since there was no proximate likelihood of taxable supplies being made.

Mr. Steele submitted that his activities in both fields were exclusively professional and everything was directed to establishing his professional career as a motor racing driver.

[115] [1981] S.T.C. 238.

We accept Mr. Steele's evidence as to his intentions to run his motor racing as a business rather than a hobby. We also accept that he genuinely intended to carry out these intentions by obtaining sponsorships from individuals and companies.

Registration for value added tax is by reference to a person and not to a trade or business, although such particulars are required. Once a person is registered he is taxable in respect of all taxable supplies made in the course of any business carried on by him. In our judgement, during 1982 Mr. Steele was holding himself out as a professional motor racing driver with particular reference to obtaining sponsorship, and we consider that the sponsorship from Fineweave was a receipt obtained from such holding out and that it was received in the course of a business carried on by Mr. Steele. As such it was a taxable supply made in the course of this business.

In our judgement Mr. Steele's sole intention in incurring the expenses of running and maintaining a racing car was to establish himself as a top grade professional motor racing driver and thereby to make taxable supplies at the earliest possible date. When he realised this was not likely to happen in the proximate future, he abandoned the venture. Against this background we conclude that Mr. Steele's motor racing activities were not carried on as a hobby and were not in the words of the *Lord Fisher* case, "activities for pleasure or social enjoyment."

Held for the appellant Atlas Marketing.

B. Personal Sales

Taxable sales generally are limited to sales made in connection with a business or economic activity. In some cases, the question is whether the person is engaged in activities that are extensive enough to be characterized as a business, rather than just a hobby or other "nonbusiness" activity. In the United Kingdom, a person is entitled to claim input credits for tax only on purchases of "goods or services used or to be used for the purpose of any business carried on or to be carried on by him."[116] If a person is engaged in business, the person is taxable only on sales made incident to that business, not personal sales made by the same person. See New Vatopia VAT, Section 6, incorporating the principles used in many VATs.

If a taxable person can establish that some sales are personal sales independent of his trade or business, those sales are not subject to VAT. For example, where a farmer grew cannabis in a remote and inaccessible area of his farm, the New Zealand Taxation Review Authority held that it did not constitute part of the taxable farming activity and therefore was not

---

[116] Value Added Tax Act 1994, §24(1)(United Kingdom). For a Canadian case holding that a sale of an asset on which an input credit was denied is not a sale in the course of a commercial activity and therefore not taxable, see *Aubrett Holdings Ltd. v H.M. The Queen*, 1998 Can. Tax Ct. LEXIS 509.

subject to the GST.[117] This principle also is illustrated by the following *Stirling* case.

Stirling v. The Commissioners of Customs and Excise[118]

The Appellant was registered for value added tax, and carries on the business of mixed farming, forestry, and the leasing of property and sporting rights, under his own name at Fairburn Estate. The Commissioners' assessment relates to the sale by the Appellant of part of a stamp collection and of furniture and other valuables contained in Fairburn House, which is part of the appellant's estate. [They claim] that these sales were made "in furtherance of" the businesses carried on by him.

The said estate, including Fairburn House, had been in the hands of the Appellant's family for nearly 100 years. He received it from his father in 1963. In 1979 the Appellant decided, in order to improve the profitability of his farming enterprise, to build a new dairy unit. The cost of the new dairy unit, due to unforeseeable causes, escalated to such an extent that by 1981 it reached £316,835. The financial problems were further aggravated by the sharp rise in bank rate. In 1977, Fairburn House (which had been empty since his father's death) was leased furnished for a period of 5 years in order to reduce the burden of rates [local real property taxes] and maintenance and in the hope that financially matters would improve. The most valuable portable items, including a number of paintings, were locked away in 2 storerooms. The remaining articles were large items such as paintings which could not be so stored and were therefore left for the Appellant's convenience in the tenanted rooms. During the currency of the lease the Appellant sold part of an inherited collection of valuable stamps, with the object of reducing the farm overdraft. In 1982, on the expiry of the lease, the Appellant could not service the interest payable on the farm overdraft from either branch of his business. He decided to sell Fairburn House and its contents, as well as other parts of the estate. The House was sold for a net price of £124,133, and the contents were sold by auction on 10 November 1982 for £280,000. The latter sum was paid into the farm's bank account and entered in the farm's account as capital injections into the business. The money was applied to reduce the overdraft to a manageable level. The Respondents' assessment relates to the said sales of stamps and the contents of the House.

Section 2(2) of the Finance Act 1972 provided that:

'Tax on the supply of goods or services shall be charged only where

(a) the supply is a taxable supply; and
(b) the goods or services are supplied by a taxable person in the course of a business carried on by him.'

---

[117] Case T2 (1997) 18 NZTC 8,007, digested in *CCH New Zealand Goods and Services Tax Guide*, ¶96–145 (1997).

[118] [1985] VATTR 232, [1986] 2 CMLR 117 (Edinburgh VAT Tribunal) (edited by the authors).

The Finance Act 1977, with effect from 1 January 1978, substituted the following provision (which is now section 2(1) of the Value Added Tax Act 1983):

'Tax shall be charged on any supply of goods or services made in the United Kingdom, where it is a taxable supply made by a taxable person in the course or furtherance of any business carried on by him.'

The principal argument for the Respondents turned upon the meaning of the words "furtherance of any business" introduced by the 1977 Act. The supply was a taxable supply, not being an exempt supply. The Appellant was a taxable person. The sale of any goods by the Appellant, whether or not they were connected in any way with his business, were taxable if made in furtherance of that business. It was not disputed that the purpose of the sales in question was to keep the Appellant's farming business from possible collapse by applying the proceeds of sale to a substantial reduction in the farm overdraft. The word "furtherance" could not be restricted to the disposal of assets belonging to the business, because section 45(6) of the 1977 Act (section 47(6) of the Value Added Tax Act 1983) provides that the disposition of assets of a business is a supply made in the course or furtherance of the business. Section 2(1) of the 1983 Act cast the net more widely than the wording of the original section 2(2) of the 1972 Act. The Respondents relied on *Alan Ridley v. Commissioners of Custom and Excise....* In that case the Appellant, who had acquired 1,600 acres of land on which he carried on the business of farming, later sold the sporting rights over the land in order to reduce his substantial bank overdraft....

[The Tribunal found that]...the sale of the shooting rights in this case for the purpose of reducing the bank overdraft incurred in respect of the farming business assisted the finances of that business. In our judgment it follows from this that such sale was in furtherance of that business.

Counsel for the Appellant submitted that "furtherance" of any business meant that the assets sold had to be linked with the business activities of the taxpayer. In the present case the proceeds of sale had been entered as contributions to the capital accounts of the business; no input tax had been claimed on the commission paid for carrying out the sales; there had been no change in the structure of the farming business (apart from modernisation); and there was no reference in the accounts to the stamps and furniture as capital assets or stock in trade of the business. Further, the sales in question were an isolated transaction and not part of a continuing business.

No reference was made in the argument for either side to the provisions of the Sixth Council directive (VAT) of the European Economic Community (77/388)..., but we are able to gain some assistance from its terms. Article 2 of the Sixth Directive charges the tax as follows:

'The following shall be subject to value added tax:

(1) the supply of goods or services effected for consideration within the territory of the country by a taxable person acting as such.'

Article 4 provides:

(1) 'Taxable person' shall mean any person who independently carries out in any place any economic activity specified in paragraph 2, whatever the purpose or results of that activity.
(2) The economic activities referred to in paragraph 1 shall comprise all activities of producers, traders and persons supplying services including mining and agricultural activities and activities of the professions. . . . '

The said Act of 1977 was passed *inter alia* to give effect to the provisions of that Directive. The crucial phrase in the above-quoted Articles is the phrase 'acting as such' in Article 2(1). The supply of goods according to the Directive must exclude the supply by a taxable person who is acting in a personal capacity, and this is consistent with the description of a taxable person as a person who carries out the economic activities referred to in Article 4. In our opinion, the 1977 Act when it added the words 'or furtherance of' any business to section 2(2) of the Finance Act 1972 did not intend, in defiance of the Sixth Directive, to extend the ambit of value added tax to supplies made by a taxable person who was not acting as such and was not carrying out an economic activity in terms of Article 4. In our opinion the purpose of the 1977 Act in adding the words 'or furtherance' was to ensure that all business activities were caught by the section, for example, fringe activities carried on separately from a main business; or transactions related in some way to the main business but which are different in character from the general run of the business, as where a retailer sells a delivery van. In the present case we reach the conclusion that the amended subsection does not result in the imposition of value added tax as the assets sold were not linked with the Appellant's business activities. The Appellant was merely selling personal assets which were in no way connected with his business. The leasing of the property, albeit at a low rent, was a business operation and the assets falling under the tenancy were business assets for the purposes of value added tax under section 47(6) of the 1983 Act, being a disposition of assets of the business in the course of the business. But such assets did not in the opinion of the tribunal include the stamps or the valuable items which were locked away in the house. Nor, in our opinion, were the valuable paintings and articles of virtu in the let rooms included in the lease, whose terms made no reference to such items and whose rent was much lower than it would have been if the inclusion of these items had been a matter of contract. On the other hand, the basic furniture supplied in the let rooms was an asset of the business, and on the evidence (as the parties agreed) this represented 15 per cent of the total proceeds of sale, resulting in a reduction of the Appellant's assessed liability to £4,761.

We accordingly allow the appeal to the extent of reducing the Appellant's liability to the said figure.

C. When Does a Business Begin?

Persons who are organizing a business may incur preorganization expenses or purchase immovable property to be used in the business to be conducted in the future. In this situation, tax authorities may be concerned that the persons will be claiming input credits on assets that ultimately are not used in business because the persons decide not to enter business. For preopening or organizational expenses, the tax authority may challenge the input credit to force the persons to prove that the expenditures were indeed made in connection with the subsequent business activity. There is a case that allows credits even for input VAT on purchases made before a VAT-registered person engages in any taxable sales. In INZO, the business engaged in feasibility studies before conducting commercial transactions, and subsequently decided to liquidate instead of engage in business. According to the court in INZO, once a business has the status of a VAT taxpayer, VAT paid on preparatory activities is deemed to relate to the business's economic activity and therefore is creditable.[119]

Once a person is registered for VAT purposes, the person is entitled to claim credits for tax on inputs related to taxable sales made in connection with business. Tax authorities have challenged claims for input credits by registered persons that relate to activities preliminary to making taxable sales. They claim that the business inputs do not relate to the registered person's business unless they are satisfied that taxable activity will be conducted. For this purpose, when does economic activity or a business begin? In the following widely cited case involving the EU Sixth Directive, the European Court of Justice examined the question of whether an investor's intent must be established by objective evidence before preliminary activities are considered economic activity.

Rompelman & Another v. Minister van Financiën[120]

The taxpayers, a husband and wife, acquired the right to future title to two units under construction that were expected to be used as showrooms, together with a usufructuary interest in the land. The taxpayers

---

[119] *Intercommunale voor zeewaterontzilting (Inzo), in liquidation v. Belgian State*, c-110/94, [1996] ECR I-857.

[120] *Rompelman and Another v. Minister van Financiën* (judgment in Case No. 268/83), 1985 ECR 655, (ECJ 1985) (edited and summarized in part by the authors).

informed the inspector of taxes that the showrooms would be let to traders, and that the lessor and lessee would apply to be taxable on the leasing of the showrooms. They also applied under the Netherlands VAT to deduct the input tax on the instalments of the sale price payable by the taxpayers as building progressed.

On 18 October 1979 the taxpayers made a return claiming a refund of input tax, although title was not transferred until 31 October so the premises had not been let at the time the return was made.

The Supreme Court of the Netherlands sought a preliminary ruling on the question of whether "exploitation" within the meaning of the second sentence of Art. 4(2) of the Sixth Directive commenced as soon as a person purchased future property with a view to letting that property in due course and whether the purchase of such a right in future property might be regarded as an economic activity within Art. 4(1) of the Sixth Directive.

Before: Due (President of Chamber), Pescatore and Bahlmann JJ.

DECISION. The Rompelmans take the view that property is exploited as from the time of the acquisition of title to it. Such a preparatory act must be treated as part of the commercial activity since it is necessary in order to make that activity possible.

The Netherlands Government maintains that the moment at which an economic activity must be considered as having commenced precedes the date on which the property begins to yield regular income. In the present case, that means that a person who lets immovable property began to exploit it at the time when he bought it as future property. However, since an investment may, but does not necessarily, lead to the exploitation of property, exploitation must not be considered to exist until there is more objective evidence of the investor's intention. A declaration of intention must be confirmed by other facts and circumstances.

According to the Commission, it follows from Art. 17(1) of the Sixth Directive that the exploitation of immovable property will generally begin with the first preparatory act, that is to say with the first transaction on which input tax may be charged. The first transaction completed in the course of an economic activity consists in the acquisition of assets and therefore in the purchase of property. Any other view would be contrary to the purpose of the VAT system since in the period between the payment of the VAT which is payable on the first transaction and the refund of that VAT a financial charge on the property will arise; however, under the VAT system, the intention is precisely to relieve the trader entirely of that burden.

The question submitted by the national court is in substance designed to ascertain whether the acquisition of a right to the future transfer of ownership of part of a building yet to be constructed with a view to letting such premises in due course may be regarded as an economic activity within the meaning of Art. 4(1) of the Sixth Directive....

[The court described the issue as follows in slightly different language]. Having regard to those elements of the common VAT system it is necessary to consider the question whether the acquisition of a right to the transfer of the future ownership of a building which is still to be constructed in return for the payment of the purchase price in instalments as building progresses must in itself be regarded as the commencement of exploitation of tangible property and therefore as goods or as a service used for the purposes of taxable transactions, in this case for letting.

As regards the letting of immovable property, Art. 13B.(b) of the Sixth Directive provides that it is in principle exempt from VAT. However, since the Rompelmans apparently exercised the option provided for in Art. 13(c) to be taxed on lettings of immovable property, the letting in this case must be treated as a taxable transaction.

The preparatory acts, such as the acquisition of assets and therefore the purchase of immovable property, which form part of those transactions must themselves be treated as constituting economic activity.

The principle that VAT should be neutral as regards the tax burden on a business requires that the first investment expenditure incurred for the purposes of and with the view to commencing a business must be regarded as an economic activity. It would be contrary to that principle if such an activity did not commence until the property began to yield taxable income. Any other interpretation of Art. 4 of the Sixth Directive would burden the trader with the cost of VAT in the course of his economic activity without allowing him to deduct it in accordance with Art. 17 and would create an arbitrary distinction between investment expenditure incurred before actual exploitation of immovable property and expenditure incurred during exploitation.

THE COURT hereby rules:

The acquisition of a right to the future transfer of property rights in part of a building yet to be constructed with a view to letting such premises in due course may be regarded as an economic activity within the meaning of Art. 4(1) of the Sixth Directive. However, that provision does not preclude the tax administration from requiring the declared intention to be supported by objective evidence such as proof that the premises which it is proposed to construct are specifically suited to commercial exploitation.

D. Employee Not Engaged in Taxable Activity

Services provided by an employee to an employer are not taxable services under VAT regimes in use today. Individuals therefore are not, by virtue of their positions as employees, taxable persons subject to VAT. In some situations, there are disputes about the status of a person as an employee whose services are not taxable or an independent contractor whose services are taxable. For example, in The Netherlands, a managing director owning more than 50 percent of his company's stock was held to be independent under the Sixth Directive.[121] As a result, the director's compensation was subject to VAT.

Typically, employers purchase tools and all other equipment used by employees and therefore get credit for tax paid on these items. Employees sent out to do work elsewhere, for example, plumbers, often furnish their own tools as a matter of efficient management practice.

"An employee may suffer a VAT disadvantage by not being treated as a taxable person. For example, if a musician must purchase her own expensive cello, a carpenter must purchase his own tools, or a guard must purchase his own uniform, the employee must bear VAT that cannot be offset by an input credit.... One alternative would be to enable the employee to claim credit for VAT charged on the purchases. An employee could be granted the option to file a VAT return and claim refund for VAT on an employment-related purchase. Alternatively, employers could be eligible to claim input credits for VAT on an employment-related purchase by employees. Each alternative presents administrative problems for taxable persons and for the ... [government]."[122]

V. Discussion Questions

1. Taxpayer A is a building contractor. In order to help his son to start his own business, he gives him two used trucks and a crane. What will be the tax consequences? Would the situation be different if taxpayer B ceased his business and gave all the assets to his daughter?
2. In order to characterize the "taxable person," how do New Vatopia and the EU Sixth Directive take into account:
   - The nature of the activity performed
   - The place where this activity is performed
   - The aims of the activity
   - The legal status of the person carrying on the activity?
3. Can a person carrying on only exempt activities be a "taxable person" under the EU Sixth Directive? How does New Vatopia handle the ideas of exempt persons and exempt activities?
4. How are occasional transactions treated in the New Vatopia VAT and the EU Sixth Directive?
5. Under which circumstances are governments and other public law organizations deemed to be "taxable persons" under the EU Sixth Directive and the New Vatopia VAT?

---

[121] The Sixth Directive, *supra* note 78, at Art. 4(1) defines a taxable person as one who independently conducts economic activity, whatever the purpose or results of that activity. See Ravensberger & Heezen, "Managing directors/major shareholders are taxable persons," VAT Monitor, Sept/Oct 2002, p. 429 (Netherlands); Gurtner, *VAT Symposium 2003, VAT Monitor*, Nov/Dec 2003, p. 474 (Austria).

[122] ABA Model VAT, *supra* note 39, at 32–33.

6. Does either the receipt of rents from movable (personal) or immovable (real) property, or the receipt of wages lead to the status of "taxable person" under either the EU Sixth Directive or the New Vatopia VAT?

7. Does either the New Vatopia VAT or the EU Sixth Directive provide a special treatment for nonprofit organizations? Explain. See the summary of the Scottish Discipline Tribunal case in the text accompanying at note 112. Do you agree with the result? Is the tribunal a nonprofit organization? How would you treat a trade association?

8. Suppose you are drafting VAT legislation for your country. In defining the "taxable person" or "registered person," would you rely on:
   a. The definition of business for income tax purposes.
   b. The definition of industrial and commercial activities, as this definition may be found in your private law.
   c. A completely independent definition for VAT purposes?
   d. Or do you think you can do without the concept of "taxable person" and define the scope of the tax only by reference to the "taxable transactions"?

9. Is a merger between two companies a taxable transaction for VAT purposes? Is a special treatment provided in this case by the New Vatopia VAT and the EU Sixth Directive? Why?

5

Taxable Supplies of Goods and Services, and Tax Invoices

I. Introduction

Most VAT regimes impose VAT only on sales for consideration, and the sale is taxable if there is a clear connection between the sale and that consideration.[1] This chapter examines the required link between a sale and the consideration received by the seller that is a prerequisite to a taxable sale.

The classification of a sale as a sale of goods or a sale of services may be significant for tax purposes. For example, in most countries, imports of most goods are taxed but imports of only specified services are taxed. A sale for a single price may incorporate elements of multiple supplies that are taxed differently. For example, a portion of the sale, if supplied independently, would be taxable at a positive rate, and another portion, if supplied independently, may be exempt from tax. It therefore is significant for VAT purposes if the transaction is respected as a single supply or is treated as multiple supplies. In some cases, a transaction that includes elements that are both taxable and exempt, the VAT legislation and case law may draw a distinction between mixed supplies (with main and incidental elements) that are classified as a single supply of the main element, and composite supplies that can be disaggregated and classified as multiple independent supplies. This chapter explores the question – "what is 'the supply' for VAT purposes?"

A VAT invoice containing required information and issuable only by registered persons is considered central to a European-style invoice VAT. Some aspects of the VAT invoice are discussed in this chapter.

II. Sales of Goods and Services

A VAT generally is considered a method of collecting in chunks a tax on the consumption of goods and services by final consumers, but the VAT bases are not constructed in a way that taxes all supplies for final consumption and removes from the base purchases in the nature of investments. Thus, the purchase of a work of art as an investment may be VAT-able.

---

[1] See Amand, "When Is a Link Direct?" 7 *VAT Monitor* 3 (Jan/Feb. 1996) [hereinafter Amand, When Is the Link Direct?].

A. What Is a Sale or Supply?

The domestic supply of taxable goods or services for consideration by a registered person, the import of taxable goods by anyone, and the import of taxable services by designed persons. are subject to transactional VATs like those in force in over 125 countries.[2] The domestic supply of goods and services generally includes sales, leases, and other transfers of rights.[3] The concept of a supply as broader than a sale is illustrated by the British case involving the taxpayer's sale of a known stolen car at auction. Although the sale may be void as a matter of local law, the Queen's Bench held that a supply "is the passing of possession in goods pursuant to an agreement whereunder the supplier agrees to part with and the recipient agrees to take possession" of the goods, even if, as in this case, the innocent purchaser at auction may have to give up the car.[4] Another British case held that serving a member a drink for a consideration in a nonprofit member's club was a supply for VAT purposes.[5] Selling is not a necessary prerequisite for a supply. "Supply," the term commonly used in VAT Acts, is generally used in this chapter, but occasionally "sale" and "supply" are used interchangeably.

In some cases, the dispute is whether a transaction constitutes "a supply" within the VAT system and, if so, if it is a "supply of services" or a "supply of goods." For example, is the borrower of funds engaging in a supply of services? in connection with the negotiation and execution of the loan transaction and the receipt of the loan proceeds? Is a company issuing its own shares engaging in a supply of services? In both cases, if the transaction were a supply of services, it would be an exempt financial service and input tax on the legal and other expenses associated with the exempt loan or share transaction would be disallowed.

In the *Trinity Mirror* case,[6] the company issued its own shares, with the proceeds to be used to finance business expenses. It incurred and claimed input credits for tax on legal, financial, and other fees related to the stock issue. The Commissioners allowed the credits attributable to the stock sold to non-EU residents as zero-rated exports of services.[7] They denied the credits attributable to the stock issued to residents of the EU, claiming these

---

[2] See, for example, Sixth Council Directive of May 17, 1977 on the harmonization of the laws of the Members States relating to turnover taxes – Common system of value added tax: uniform basis of assessment (77/388/EEC), Art. 2 [hereinafter Sixth Directive]. See New Vatopia VAT, Appendix B, §9.

[3] *Id.* at Art's. 5 and 6. In an unusual decision involving the Australian GST, the New South Wales Supreme Court, relying in part on the analysis of the Australian Tax Office, held that there was not a taxable supply if a registered business received compensation for expropriated property. See *CSR Ltd. v. Hornsby Shire Council*, [2004] NSWSC 946, discussed in Krever, "Involuntary and Statutory Supplies – The Australian GST Base Narrows," *VAT Monitor*, Jan./Feb. 2005, p. 19.

[4] *Customs and Excise Commissioners v Oliver*, [1980] 1 All ER 353.

[5] *Carlton Lodge Club v Customs and Excise Commissioners*, [1974] 3 All ER 798.

[6] *Trinity Mirror plc (formerly Mirror Group Newspapers Ltd) v Customs and Excise Commissioners*, [2001] STC 192 (Ct. App. 2001)(UK).

[7] Sixth Directive, *supra* note 2, at Art. 17(3)(c).

were supplies of exempt financial services. The court held that a company's issuance of its shares is a supply of services for consideration. The case extends a prior ECJ decision that the disposition of shares a company holds in another company is a supply of services. In *BLP Group plc v Customs and Excise Commissioners*,[8] the ECJ denied the deduction for VAT on costs associated with the disposal of such shares as an exempt supply of services – a transaction in shares.[9]

When a company borrows funds from a bank or other lending institution instead of issuing its bonds to investing bondholders, the company is the recipient of services from the bank. It is not supplying services. In this case, the VAT on the costs associated with the loan is creditable if the loan is used in connection with taxable transactions.

1. Nonsupplies or Supplies Other Than in the Course of Taxable Activity

The VAT systems are not uniform in their classification of transactions as "nonsupplies" and therefore not subject to VAT. If a VAT-registered business is denied an input credit for tax on the acquisition of an asset and the business sells that asset, the sale typically is not subject to VAT. For example, if a firm purchases an automobile for use in its business and is denied credit for tax on the automobile (as some VATs do), the sale of the automobile is not a supply under some VAT regimes.[10] The same applies if the tax on a purchased asset was not eligible for the input credit because the asset is used in connection with activities exempt from tax.[11] For example, if a bank purchases furniture for use in providing exempt financial services under those regimes, the sale of that used furniture by the bank is not subject to VAT.

In some transactions, there is no transfer of legal title. In others, the transfer of an asset may be to a person who holds the asset in a representative capacity. These transactions, varied by country, may not be treated as supplies and therefore fall outside the scope of the VAT. For example, VATs in some countries provide that a consignment of goods is not a supply.[12] Others

---

[8] Case C-4/94, [1995] All ER 401, [1995] STC 424 (ECJ 1995).

[9] See Sixth Directive, *supra* note 2, at Art. 13B(d)(5). In a curious opinion, the Canadian Tax Court held that the failure to issue shares in return for a capital contribution turned what might otherwise have been a supply (a taxable supply) into a transaction that was not a taxable supply. *Sutter Salmon Club Ltd. v. Her Majesty The Queen*, 2004 Can. Tax Ct. LEXIS 1015 1015.

[10] See Value Added Tax Act 1994, c. 23, Sch. 9, group 14 (United Kingdom) [hereinafter VATA 1994]; New Vatopia VAT, Appendix B, §4(17), treats this kind of sale as a supply "otherwise than in the course or furtherance of a taxable activity," and therefore is not within the scope of the VAT.

[11] See Canadian Goods and Services Tax, Part IX of the Excise Tax Act, §141.1(1) and (2), treating them as supplies "otherwise than in the course of commercial activities" [hereinafter Canadian GST].

[12] In the United Kingdom, if goods are provided on approval, the supply occurs when it is certain that the supply has taken place, but not more than twelve months after they are removed. VATA 1994, *supra* note 10, at §6(2)(c). However, in transactions not covered by

provide the opposite – consignments must be reported as supplies. Technically, the consignment of goods should not be treated as a supply of goods for VAT purposes because there is no transfer of ownership to the consignee. Nevertheless, it may be treated as a supply in order to keep account of the asset that is not longer at the seller's location.

A transfer of assets (or an entire business) to a legal representative generally is not treated as a supply subject to tax. For example, transfers of assets of a business to a receiver in bankruptcy commonly are not supplies and therefore do not attract tax.[13] Likewise, tax may not be imposed when the business assets of an incompetent person are transferrred to a representative who then operates the ongoing business.[14]

There are a range of transactions that may be treated as beyond the scope of VAT for policy or other reasons. These transactions could be removed from the tax base by classifying them as exempt or zero-rated supplies, or as nontaxable transactions or "non" supplies.

The "nontaxable" status has the effect of zero rating the transaction if input credit is available for tax on purchases attributable to these transactions. A nontaxable transaction is taxed like an exempt transaction if the statute denies credit for tax on purchases attributable to it. The following additional categories of transactions involve goods or services that may be removed from the VAT base.

Asset Transfers to Creditors. If a debtor, as a result of an agreement or court order, transfers physical possession of an asset (or merely a security interest in an asset that is not physically transferred), there typically is no transfer of ownership of the asset, no discharge of an obligation using the asset as payment, nor an exchange for consideration. As a result, there is no supply subject to VAT. In addition, as illustrated earlier, the same principle applies if an asset of a person under a legal disability is transferred to the person's legal representative.[15] If the transfer merely defers the point at which a taxable supply occurs, a VAT-registered transferor should be entitled to claim input credits for tax on purchases attributable to these transfers.

Business-to-Business Sales of a Going Concern. When a going concern is sold, the sale is not part of the process of production and distribution

§6(2)(c), if the supplier retains the property in goods until the goods are appropriated by the buyer, the supply generally occurs at the earliest of the date appropriated by the buyer, when the supplier issues an invoice, or the supplier receives a payment. SI 1995/2518, reg. 88. Under an exception, if an invoice is issued within fourteen days after the buyer appropriates the goods, the invoice date may govern. *Id.* & §6(5).

[13] See VATA 1994, *supra* note 10, at §46, and SI 1995/2518, reg. 9 (United Kingdom). See New Vatopia VAT, Appendix B, §4(16).

[14] VATA 1994, *supra* note 10, at §46(4), and SI 1995/2518, reg. 9 (United Kingdom).

[15] See A. Schenk, Value Added Tax – A Model Statute And Commentary: A Report of the Committee on Value Added Tax of The American Bar Association Section of Taxation, p. 28 [hereinafter ABA Model VAT].

commonly included in a consumption tax base. The sale nevertheless is a taxable supply unless the law provides otherwise. When the sale is between VAT-registered businesses that make taxable sales, if it were taxable, the tax payable by the buyer would be recoverable by the buyer as an input credit. Aside from any cash flow benefit, the government would not receive any net revenue from the transaction. Nevertheless, the buyer's cost to finance the tax until it is recovered may be significant, especially if excess credits must be carried forward for a period of months before they are eligible for refund. Many VAT systems therefore address this problem by zero-rating the sale of a going concern.[16] By zero-rating the transaction, the seller is entitled to claim credit for tax on purchases used in connection with the negotiation and sale of the business. Unless the seller is required to transfer VAT records to the buyer, the audit chain is broken. The buyer will not have invoices covering all of the transferred goods and services. If the documents confirming the sale do not specify that the sale is zero-rated, the seller and the buyer may take inconsistent VAT positions with respect to the sale. The seller might claim that the sale is zero-rated (so that the seller does not have to report and remit VAT on the sale), and the buyer may claim that the purchase was taxable (so that the buyer can claim credit for the VAT component in the purchase price). To avoid this potential conflict, some statutes that zero-rate a sale of a going concern impose conditions on the grant of zero-rating.[17] The seller and the buyer may be required to file a form signed by both, specifying that the sale is being treated as a zero-rated sale of a going concern. The supplier of a zero-rated sale of a going business must issue a tax invoice and therefore must describe the goods transferred.[18]

The EU Sixth Directive gives Member States the option to provide that no supply occurs on the transfer of a going concern but may include rules to prevent the distortion of competition if the recipient is not subject to tax on all of its supplies.[19] Applying this rule, the Treasury in the United Kingdom has authority to issue an order removing transactions from the scope of the

---

[16] See New Zealand Goods and Services Tax, 1985, No. 141, §11(1)(m) [hereinafter N.Z. GST], discussed *infra*; New Vatopia VAT, Appendix B, §4(2), and Sch. I, ¶2(o). Although many VATs zero rate both a sale of an entire business as a going concern or a sale of a portion of a business capable of separate operation, Azerbaijan amended its VAT law to remove zero-rating for the transfer of an independent division of a business. See Bati, "Azerbaijan: Transfer of assets," *VAT Monitor*, Mar./Apr. 2005, p. 122.

[17] N.Z. GST, *supra* note 16, at §11(1)(m); Value Added Tax Act No. 89 of 1991, §11(1)(e) (South Africa) [hereinafter RSA VAT]. In South Africa, the requirements for zero-rating are discussed in practice No. 14, discussed in C. BENEKE, ED., *Deloitte & Touche VAT HANDBOOK*, ¶7.43 (2003).

[18] N.Z. GST, *supra* note 16, at §24(1).

[19] See Sixth Directive, *supra* note 2, at Art. 5(8). If an EU member state adopts this option, it cannot then restrict the "no supply" rule to certain transactions only. For example, a member state cannot restrict the rule only to transfers to persons authorized by national law to conduct the transferred activity. Case C-497/01, *Zita Modes SARL v. Administration de l-enregistrement et des domains*, [2003] ECR I-14, 393.

tax by treating them as neither supplies of goods nor supplies of services. Under this authority, the Treasury ruled that the transfer of a business as a going concern is neither a supply of goods nor a supply of services.[20]

2. Sales for Consideration

A sale is subject to VAT in most countries only if the sale is a taxable sale made for consideration by a taxable person (or registered person) in connection with business.[21] Implicit in this basic rule is the requirement that there must be a sufficient link or connection between the sale and the consideration.[22] This subsection examines this requirement that there be a direct connection between the sale and the consideration. In some cases, the exchange of consideration for only a right to purchase goods or services is not a taxable supply at that time. For example, the purchase of a gift certificate or voucher may or may not be taxable until the certificate or voucher is redeemed.[23]

The EU Sixth Directive is permissive in allowing member states to treat a number of transactions as supplies for consideration. This includes self-supplies of goods where the VAT on the purchase of such goods would not be eligible for the input tax credit; and the retention of goods with respect to which an input tax credit was claimed when a registered person ceases to conduct a taxable activity and registration is cancelled.[24]

For some transactions, the VAT law may specifically provide that the transaction is a supply of goods or services for consideration. For example, in New Zealand, the local authority rates (local real property taxes) are treated as consideration for supplies of goods and services by a registered local authority.[25]

In the following case involving the rendition of services without any required monetary payment, the European Court of Justice held that the activity was not a supply of services taxable under the VAT Directives due to the lack of consideration.

---

[20] SI 1995/1268, art. 5. VATA 1994, *supra* note 10, at §49(1), generally requiring the transferor's records to be preserved by the transferee.

[21] See, for example, Sixth Directive, *supra* note 2, at Art. 2(1).

[22] See Amand, *When is a Link Direct?*, *supra* note 1. Personal gifts generally are not VAT-able, because they are not sales (they are not transferred for consideration) and they do not arise in connection with a business. Gratuitous transfers inter vivos to an individual or into trust thus would not attract VAT. Likewise, gratuitous transfers of personal articles, furniture, and other assets on death to an executor or administrator or directly to a beneficiary (or transfers by an executor or administrator to a beneficiary) would not be VAT-able. These transfers are not sales and they do not arise in connection with a business. ABA Model VAT, *supra* note 15, at 26.

[23] See discussion of vouchers *infra* this chapter. The treatment varies dramatically. For example, in New Zealand, the original issuance of a voucher is a supply of goods or services. N.Z. GST, *supra* note 16, at §5(11E).

[24] Penalties for the late payment of rates are not consideration for the taxable goods and services provided by local authorities. Sixth Directive, *supra* note 2, at Art. 5(7). A third category is the application of goods to a nontaxable transaction when VAT on the acquisition of the goods was creditable.

[25] N.Z. GST, *supra* note 16, at §5(7). See Marie Pallot, "Local authorities," *VAT Monitor*, Nov./Dec. 2003, p. 496.

Staatssecretaris van Financiën v. Cooperatieve Aadappelenbewarplaats G.A.[26]

[Reference from the Netherlands Supreme Court. A co-operative association operated a cold storage warehouse for members to store their potatoes. Each member with shares in the co-op was entitled to store one thousand kilograms of potatoes a year per share and the co-op ordinarily imposed charges for the storage at the end of the season. In the years in issue, "pending the sale of the cold-store," the co-op decided not to charge members for potatoes stored in the warehouse. As a result, the value of the shares held by the members declined as the co-op incurred expenses to operate the warehouse.]

FACTS. Article 2 (a) of the Second Directive.[27] on harmonization of turnover taxes provides that:

'The following shall be subject to the value added tax:
(a) The supply of goods and the provision of services within the territory of the country by a taxable person against payment';

and Article 8 provides:

'The basis of assessment shall be:
(a) in the case of supply of goods and the provision of services, everything which makes up the consideration for the supply of the goods or the provision of services, including all expenses and taxes except the value added tax itself.'

Finally Annex A point 13 regarding Article 8 (a) provides that:

'The expression "consideration" means everything received in return for the supply of goods or the provision of services, including incidental expenses (packing, transport, insurance, etc.) that is to say not only the cash amounts charged, but also, for example, the value of the goods received in exchange or, in the case of goods or services supplied by order of a public authority, the amount of the compensation received' . . .

But the Inspector thought that the co-operative had nevertheless charged its members something in return owing to the reduction in value of their shares owing to the non-collection of their storage charges and he therefore assessed what was received in return to be the storage charge ordinarily charged, namely 2 cents per kilogram of potatoes, . . .

[The Netherlands Supreme Court referred the case to the Court of Justice to determine if there was . . . "consideration" within Article 8(a) of the Second Directive.]

---

[26] Case 154/80, [1981] ECR 445, [1981] 3 CMLR 337 (ECJ 1980) (edited by the authors). See New Vatopia VAT, Appendix B, §5(5).
[27] Second Council Directive, 67/228 of April 11, 1967.

JUDGMENT. The co-operative claimed that it provided its services for no consideration because it had not required anything in return. The court held that VAT community law does not refer to the law of the Member States for its meaning, so the definition of terms may not be left to the discretion of each Member-State.

Services are taxable, within the meaning of the Second Directive, when the service is provided against payment and the basis of assessment for such a service is everything which makes up the consideration for the service; there must therefore be a direct link between the service provided and the consideration received which does not occur in a case where the consideration consists of an unascertained reduction in the value of the shares possessed by the members of the co-operative and such a loss of value may not be regarded as a payment received by the co-operative providing the services.

The consideration for services must be capable of being expressed in money. Such consideration is a subjective value since the basis of assessment for the provision of services is the consideration actually received and not a value assessed according to objective criteria.

Consequently a provision of services for which no definite subjective consideration is received does not constitute a provision of services "against payment" and is therefore not taxable within [Article 8(a)] ... of the Second Directive.

As discussed earlier, a sale is not taxable unless the sale is for consideration. Under the EU Sixth VAT Directive, the taxable amount is the entire consideration payable for the goods or services, including any "subsidies directly linked to the price...."[28] Ambiguity occurs if the consideration (whether or not it includes a subsidy) received by the person is not directly linked to the product sold or service rendered.

The relationship between the service and the consideration, as well as the existence of reciprocal obligations, is important, if not determinative.[29] Except where specifically included in the tax base,[30] a forced exaction in the nature of a tax presumably is not subject to VAT, even if the party making the payment receives some benefit from the services provided with his funds. Likewise, gratuitous receipts are not taxable, even if the person making the payment receives, as a result, some psychic or other indirect benefits. In some cases, the issue is to determine whether the payment is gratuitous or is in fact for services expected or actually received.

The issue arises in the case of grants made for research work. For example, under the Singapore GST, there is no supply if the grantor does not receive

---

[28] Sixth Directive, *supra* note 2, at Art. 11(1)(b).
[29] Amand, When Is a Link Direct?, *supra* note 1, at 10. According to Amand, the core of the direct link requirement is the "principle of reciprocal obligation." *Id.*
[30] See RSA VAT *supra* note 17, at §8(6)(a).

rights or other value from the research work done with the grant. The grant is a supply for GST purposes if the grantor obtains intellectual property rights or other benefits that arise from the work undertaken with the grant.[31]

Commonly, a supply of goods does not occur until the delivery of the goods takes place. If a supplier of land requires the buyer to make progress payments on the purchase price before the land is transferred (delivered), and requires the buyer to make a payment (denominated as interest) if the required progress payments are deferred beyond their due dates, the European Court of Justice held that the amounts paid on these deferred payments were part of the consideration for the supply of the land until the transfer of the land – the supply – occurs.[32] These payments were not respected as interest on a supply of credit that is exempt from VAT.

In the United Kingdom, a VAT tribunal held that if a restaurant automatically added a service charge to its bills (and notified the customers of this fact on the menus), the service charge was part of the consideration for the meal and therefore taxable.[33] However, if customers were not informed on the menus or otherwise that a service charge would be added, a VAT tribunal held, in the *NDP Co.* case, that payments by customers for service were not part of the consideration for the meals and therefore not taxable,[34] even though the staff as a matter of routine added a service charge to customers' bills.[35]

Within a month of the decision in *NDP Co.*, the European Court of Justice decided the *Apple and Pear Development Council* case.[36] In that case, the Council (a body governed by public law) claimed that its activities funded with mandatory fees paid by its members[37] were services provided for consideration, so that the input tax on its purchases were recoverable. The court held that a direct link was necessary between the service provided and the consideration received in order for a sale to be for consideration, a prerequisite for taxation under the VAT Sixth Directive.[38] The fees paid by each grower only indirectly benefitted him, and there was no relationship between the fees paid and the level of benefits received from the Council's promotional efforts. The ECJ therefore concluded that the Council's exercise of its functions with the funds provided by its members was not a supply of services for consideration within Article 2(1) of the Sixth Directive.

---

[31] See e-Tax Guide No. 1994/GST/2 (Singapore), discussed in *CCH Singappore Goods & Services Tax Guide*, ¶ 3-180 (2005).

[32] *Muys' en DeWinter's Bouw – en Aannemingsbedrijf BV v Staatssecretaris van Financien*, Case C-281/91 (Judgment of the ECJ 1993).

[33] *Potters Lodge Restaurant Ltd v. Commissioners of Customs and Excise*, LON/79/286.

[34] *NDP Co. Ltd v. The Commissioners of Customs and Excise*, [1988] VATTR 40.

[35] Customers were not legally obligated to pay the service charge, and some refused to pay or paid only a portion of the listed service charge.

[36] *Apple and Pear Development Council v. Commissioners of Customs and Excise*, [1988] ECR 1443, [1988] 2 CMLR 394.

[37] By statute, the Council was authorized to impose and did impose mandatory annual fees on growers. The fees were used mainly for publicity and research.

[38] See Sixth Directive, *supra* note 2, at Art. 2(1).

The ECJ also relied on the "direct link" requirement to find that a street musician Tolsma who solicited funds from pedestrians did not make sales for consideration under the Sixth Directive[39] and therefore was not subject to VAT on his receipts. According to the court in *Tolsma*, the musician played his barrel organ voluntarily and those who deposited money in his tin did not necessarily make payment in any relationship to the benefits that they may obtain.[40] "The court [in *Tolsma*] considered that there was no agreement in that case between the parties, since the passers-by voluntarily made a donation, whose amount they determined as they wished. In addition, the court found that there was no necessary link between the musical service and the payments to which it gave rise, since the passers-by did not request music to be played for them. Moreover, they paid sums which depended not on the musical service but on subjective motives which might bring feelings of sympathy into play."[41]

Is the *Tolsma* decision correct for the reasons stated? Should the courts in cases like *Tolsma* decide if the payments made to the performer are for services or merely gratuitous payments made for altruistic or other reasons?

A European-style VAT is a transactions-based tax, with VAT imposed on the consideration received for each transaction. The tax for each accounting period is measured by the difference between the tax imposed on the consideration received for each taxable supply and the tax paid on purchases from registered suppliers attributable to those taxable supplies. In some cases, that formulation does not work, especially when a substantial portion of the business inputs are acquired from unregistered persons, not registered suppliers. One example is a dealer in used goods who purchases from consumers the goods that are refurbished and resold. Another example is a casino that pays winnings to gamblers who are not registered for VAT. In these cases, to fit these businesses into a European-style, transactions form of VAT, the calculation of the consideration received in taxable supplies may be adjusted to take payments to unregistered persons into account. These transactions are discussed elsewhere in the book.

A transactional VAT also does not fit well in a business in which the actual charge for a service is buried in prices. This occurs most frequently in financial services. For example, in the *First National Bank* case,[42] the bank served as a market maker in certain foreign currencies. The spread between the bid and the offer prices for a currency represented the bank's gross profit over a period of time on the purchases and sales of the currency. The British Commissioners of Customs and Excise claimed that each foreign exchange transaction was not a supply for consideration but merely an exchange of one means of payment for another. As a result, the Commissioners claimed

---

[39] *Id.*

[40] *Tolsma v. Inspecteur der Omzetbelasting Leeuwarden*, (Case C-16/93), [1994] STC 509. The musician also knocked on doors of homes and shops to ask for funds.

[41] *Id.* at 516, cited in *Customs and Excise Commissioners v First National Bank of Chicago*, Case C-172/96, [1998], [1998] All ER (EC) 744, STC 850 (ECJ) [hereinafter *First National Bank*].

[42] *First National Bank*, *supra* note 41.

that the bank was not entitled to include these transactions in the formula used to calculate allowable input tax credits. The High Court referred to the European Court of Justice the questions of whether foreign exchange transactions are supplies for consideration and, if so, what are the taxable amounts of these supplies.

The currency transactions in the *First National* case typically are exempt financial services, but the issue of "what is the consideration for the supply" arises in the context of the bank's allocation of input tax between its taxable and exempt services. The ECJ, in an attempt to fit these currency transactions within the framework of a transactions-based VAT, held that the consideration for the currency transactions was equal to the net result of all of those transactions involving the purchases and sales of the currencies over a period of time. The following excerpts are from Advocate General Lenz's Opinion and from the Judgment of the court:

> It is the customer who approaches the bank and asks for a service, namely the exchange of a foreign currency. According to the bank, the customer is aware that that service will not be performed free of charge. This, moreover, is contested only by the United Kingdom, which considers that the spread between the bid and offer price does not constitute consideration for the service. On the other hand, the United Kingdom also states that customers generally inquire at the bank about the two rates, that is to say also about the spread. Customers therefore know by how much the selling price of foreign currencies exceeds the purchase price. Consequently, customers know that they are paying for the service and are aware of how much they are paying.

> It is also absolutely clear to the bank itself, which constitutes the other party to the reciprocal relationship, that its payment for the service of exchanging currencies results from its spread. This means that there is no doubt as between the supplier and the recipient of the service that the service is effected for consideration and that the consideration relates to the transaction in question. It remains to be noted therefore that, in the case of the rates at which the bank is prepared to purchase currencies from customers and to sell currencies to customers, the spread resulting from the difference in rates constitutes the payment for the service supplied by the bank. . . .

> From the mere fact that no [explicit] fees or commission are charged by the bank upon a specific foreign exchange transaction it does not follow that no consideration is given. Moreover, any technical difficulties which exist in determining the amount of consideration cannot by themselves justify the conclusion that no consideration exists. . . .

> To hold that currency transactions are taxable only when effected in return for payment of a commission or specific fees, which would thus allow a trader to avoid taxation if he sought to be remunerated for his services by providing for a spread between the proposed transaction rates rather than by charging such sums, would be a solution incompatible with the system put in place by the Sixth Directive and would be liable to place traders on an unequal footing for purposes of taxation.

> It must therefore be held that foreign exchange transactions, performed even without commission or direct fees, are supplies of services provided in return

for consideration, that is to say supplies of services effected for consideration within the meaning of art 2(1) of the Sixth Directive....

So, the consideration, that is to say the amount which the bank can actually apply to its own use, must be regarded as consisting of the net result of its transactions over a given period of time....[43]

There are some transactions that do not involve the transfer of an asset for consideration. If tax is imposed only on supplies for consideration, these transactions would not be taxable. To avoid this result, the VAT legislation may treat some transactions without consideration as supplies for consideration. These transactions are discussed next.

3. Transactions or Transfers Deemed to Be Supplies for VAT Purposes

In some situations, in order to prevent loss of revenue, transactions conducted without the transfer of monetary consideration are treated as sales made for consideration. When a registered business deregisters but stays in operation, the deregistration can be treated as a supply of the goods (and possibly the services) on hand on the day the person ceases to be a registered person. The diversion of business assets by a taxable person to the personal use of the owner or employees, or the use of a taxable person's business assets for nonbusiness purposes (generally a service), may be treated as a sale for consideration.[44] If an asset used in making taxable supplies is converted to use in making exempt supplies, the change in use may be treated as a supply for VAT purposes. If a seller repossesses goods previously sold in a taxable sale, the repossession may be treated as a supply by the defaulting buyer. These transactions are discussed in this subsection.

a. *Cease to Conduct Taxable Transactions*
A registered person claims input credits for tax on purchases of inventory, supplies, and other assets to be used in making taxable supplies. If that person deregisters (such as because the person's taxable sales fall below the registration threshold), the person will be holding goods and services free of VAT. Subsequent sales by the deregistered person will not attract VAT. As a result, in the absence of a rule that requires the clawback of previously claimed credits, the deregistered person will obtain a competitive advantage

---

[43] *Id.* at ¶¶43–45 of the Opinion, and ¶¶30–34 and 47 of the Judgment.

[44] Sixth Directive, [*supra* note 2], at Art's. 5(6) and 6(2). Member States may change the rules with respect to services if it does not result in the distortion of competition. *Id.* at Art. 6(2). Self-supplies may also be treated as a sale for consideration in some circumstances. *Id.* at Art. 5(7). The self-supply rule may be "needed to treat a transaction as a taxable transaction in order to prevent the distortion of competition or VAT abuse in cases where persons engaging in exempt transactions can avoid VAT by vertically integrating their operations instead of purchasing property or services from outside vendors.... Section 4037 treats certain self-consumption of property and services by a government entity or exempt organization as a deemed sale of property and services by it in a taxable transaction." ABA Model Act, *supra* note 15, at 38. See New Vatopia VAT, Appendix B, §4(6).

over registered or never registered competitors. Many VATs provide that a deregistering person is deemed to have supplied goods (and sometimes services) on hand on the last day that the person is registered.[45] The person may be required to report as output tax the fair market value of the goods or services on hand.[46] Under some VATs, the value of the deemed supply is the lesser of the cost to the deregistering person to acquire the assets on hand or the open market value (fair market value) of the goods or services on hand.[47] The justification for the former valuation rule is that the person should be placed in the same position as if he did not claim credit for VAT on those goods and services on hand. There are at least two justifications for the later rule requiring the deregistering person to report the lesser of cost or the current fair market value of the goods and services on hand as taxable supplies in the last accounting period in which the person was registered. One is that it is administratively easier to impose a fair market value rule, rather than requiring the deregistering person to locate the original cost of items that may have been purchased long ago. The second justification is that the fair market value rule puts the deregistering person in the same position as if he began business and purchased the goods or services in taxable acquisitions immediately before deregistering.

b. *Diversion of Business Assets to Personal or Employee Use*

If a VAT-registered business transfers goods or services acquired for use in the business to an owner, officer, or employee without charge, the transfer may represent compensation or a fringe benefit. The transfer may be an appropriate business expenditure, deductible for income tax purposes, but it provides the opportunity for VAT abuse. When the asset was purchased, the business claimed credit for tax on the acquisition. The business therefore holds the asset free of VAT. If the transfer to the employee or other is not VAT-able, the goods or services would be acquired by the owner, officer, or employee free of VAT. To avoid this result, these transfers without charge may be treated as supplies for consideration subject to VAT.[48]

---

[45] See, for example, NZ GST, *supra* note 16, at §5(3), where the deemed supply occurs immediately before the person ceases to be a registered person, unless the business is continued by another registered person, such as on the zero-rated sale of a going concern; New Vatopia VAT, Appendix B, §4(21).

[46] In New Zealand, the value of the deemed supply is the open market value. NZ GST, *supra* note 16, at §10(7A). See Singapore Goods and Services Tax Act, Cap. 117A, 2001 ed., Sch. 3, ¶8(2)(a) [hereinafter Singapore GST]. The deregistering person must account for output tax on goods on hand that are part of the business assets. See form GST F8, entitled Final Goods and Services Tax return, reproduced in *CCH Singapore Goods and Services Tax Guide*, ¶31-225. See also IRAS Circular, 2003/GST/4, cited *id.* at ¶3-455. The value is the open market value equal to the price payable if the deregistering person purchased identical goods at that time. If that value is not ascertainable, the value for similar goods may be used. If the value for similar goods is not available, then the value is the cost to produce the goods. Singapore GST, Sch. 3, ¶8(2)(b) and (c).

[47] RSA VAT, *supra* note 17, at §§8(2) and 10(5).

[48] Sixth Directive, *supra* note 2, at art. 5, ¶6, and art. 6, ¶2(a). The New Zealand GST, *supra* note 16, at §21I(1) generally imposes tax on a registered employer's provision of a fringe benefit (goods or services) to an employee. It is treated as a supply in the course of a taxable

c. *Change in the Use of Goods or Services*

If a VAT-registered business acquires assets for use in making taxable supplies, the business can claim as input credit the tax on the acquisition of the asset. If the business acquires assets for use in making exempt supplies, the business cannot claim as input credit the tax on the acquisition of the asset. If the business acquires an asset for use in making taxable supplies and then decides to use the asset in connection with its exempt activities, the VAT consequences should be the same as if the asset were acquired at that point for use in making exempt supplies. To accomplish that purpose, many VATs include change-of-use rules rules that require the VAT-registered business to treat the change-in-use as a supply of the asset to itself in a taxable transaction.[49] The change-in-use rules can be quite complex, especially in a country such as Canada that has different rules for capital goods than for other assets.[50] To simplify the change-in-use rules, they could be limited to changes for assets above a threshold value.

d. *Repossession of Goods Sold in a Taxable Transaction*

If a registered person makes a taxable sale, the sale is reportable in full at the point of sale, even if the sale is on credit. The seller is required to remit the VAT on the sale without regard to the portion of the sale that is paid at that time. A registered buyer likewise can claim credit in the accounting period in which the asset is acquired, even if the buyer has not paid the purchase price and the tax imposed on the sale. If the buyer defaults and the seller repossesses the goods, the buyer should be required to report the repossession as a taxable supply of goods, and repay some or all of the VAT claimed on the asset repossessed. This treatment generally is provided with respect to repossessions of taxable goods from a registered buyer.[51] If the buyer was not entitled to claim credit for VAT on the asset when acquired, the buyer should not be required to report the repossession as a taxable supply of goods.

B. Goods or Services

In the next subsections of this chapter, it is assumed that there is a supply and that it is a supply of goods or a supply of services. In most cases, it is apparent and clear. Shoes are goods and having a lawyer prepare a will is a service. Nevertheless, for some transactions, there is ambiguity as to whether the supply involves goods or services. The distinction may be significant if there

activity. The value of the supply is the value of the fringe benefit under the Income Tax Act 1994. See also *id*.at§§20(3A) and 23A. See Vatopia VAT, Appendix B, §4(6).

[49] The change in use rules generally do not apply if a VAT-registered person was not entitled to claim credit on the acquisition of the asset. For example, the change in use rule would not apply to an automobile if the registered person were denied an input credit on the acquisition of the automobile, even if used in connection with taxable supplies.

[50] See, for example, Canadian GST, *supra* note 11, at §206(3)–(5); NZ GST, *supra* note 16, at §21(1) et seq.

[51] See NZ GST, *supra* note 16, at §5(2); New Vatopia VAT, Appendix B, §4(7).

are different rules on the time and place of a supply of goods or a supply of services,[52] or if imported goods are taxed but not most imported services.

The classification of a supply as one involving goods or involving services may be difficult if the supply is a composite or multiple supply. These problems are discussed later in this chapter. In this section, attention is focused on transactions that are classified as goods or services for policy reasons; that is, the classification is made in order to have the rules governing goods or services apply for timing, place of supply, or other VAT purposes. There also are transactions that appear to be services but the service is provided in the form of a tangible product, such as a compact disc.

If a person provides to another the use of tangible personal property or real property, retaining legal title and ownership, the transaction is a lease.[53] There is no uniformity of treatment of true leases in VATs around the world. Consistent with the EU's Sixth Directive, the British VAT treats the transfer of possession of goods (use of goods) as a supply of services.[54] The Canadian GST[55] and the South African VAT[56] treat leases as supplies of goods.

Some countries do not merely classify a lease as a good or as a service. Rather, they identify the timing or other rules that apply to lease transactions. For example, the Australian GST treats leases as supplies on a progressive or periodic basis; that is, they are treated as separate supplies.[57] As a result, leases may be taxed (under the timing rules) as each progressive or periodic payment becomes due or is paid.

C. Supply of Goods

The advantage of most VATs over selective excise taxes is that the VATs are imposed on broad bases; that is, achieving more economic neutrality or less economic distortion. Some countries, typically developing countries, define their sales tax bases by listing items that are subject to tax. Items not included in the list are not taxed. This approach is more common for services than for goods. Ideally, VAT should be imposed on sales (in a broad

---

[52] For example, while installment sales are taxable when the contract is entered into, rental or lease agreements become subject to VAT upon the earlier of receipt of payment or payment becoming due. N.Z. GST, *supra* note 16, at §9(3).

[53] There also are classification issues when what in form is a lease in substance is a sale. Transactions respected as operating leases are treated as leases for VAT purposes. Installment sales or finance leases are considered sales for VAT purposes. VAT laws may provide statutory guidance to determine if the supply is a sale or lease. For example, the definition of a "rental agreement" and an "instalment credit agreement" in RSA VAT, *supra* note 17, at §1.

[54] VATA 1994, *supra* note 10, at §5 and Sch. 4(1).

[55] Canadian GST, *supra* note 11, at §136(1) treats a "lease, licence or similar arrangement . . . [for]the use or right to use real property or tangible personal property" as a supply of the real or tangible personal property.

[56] RSA VAT, *supra* note 17, §8(11). See Vatopia VAT, Appendix B, §4(1).

[57] See A New Tax System (Goods and Services Tax) Act 1999, §156-22 (Australia) [hereinafter Australia GST]. There are special rules for leases of fifty years or more. *Id.* at §40-35, §40-70, and Division 75.

sense to include leases) of all goods and services. If some items must receive special treatment, such as exemption or zero-rating, this treatment should be provided as exceptions to the general rule that all are taxed.

A "supply of goods" is not defined in a uniform manner in VAT statutes, but the Sixth Directive is representative of the principles that define a supply of goods adopted in many countries. According to the EU Sixth Directive,[58] the supply of goods is the transfer of the right to dispose of tangible property as owner. Utilities, such as electricity, heat, gas and air conditioning, may be classified as goods or as services.[59] They are considered tangible property for purposes of the Sixth Directive.[60] Member states can treat transactions such as transfers of shares that give rights to immovable property as tangible property.[61] If a business claims input credit for tax paid on goods that then are diverted to the personal use of the owner of the business or his staff, as discussed earlier in this chapter, the diversion may be treated as a taxable supply of goods for consideration.[62] By contrast, EU member states can treat a transfer of a going business as though it were not a supply of goods and therefore not taxable.[63]

D. SUPPLY OF SERVICES

Services pose special problems under a VAT. First, some personal services tend to be provided by small businesses. Second, many services may be used by the purchaser either for business or personal use. Third, services such as banking, insurance, and real estate are complex to tax under any VAT. The taxation of hard-to-tax services is covered in more detail in subsequent chapters.

Many American states with retail sales taxes list the specific services that are taxable under the sales rather than tax all services except those specifically exempt. In contrast, most VAT statutes define the supply of services as any supply that is not a supply of goods. This catch-all definition is designed to prevent sales from escaping tax by not falling within either the definition of goods or services.[64]

---

[58] Sixth Directive, *supra* note 2, at Art. 5(1).
[59] For the Swiss treatment of electricity transactions under VAT, see Derks, "VAT Treatment of Electricity Transactions Under Swiss Law," *VAT Monitor*, July/Aug. 2002, p. 267. Although the Swiss VAT treats electricity as a good, many transactions involving the international flows of electricity, such as the physical import of electricity, are treated as imported services. See New Vatopia VAT, Appendix B, §4(1)(a)(iii).
[60] Sixth Directive, *supra* note 2, at Art. 5(2).
[61] *Id.* at Art. 5(3).
[62] *Id.* at Art. 5(6).
[63] *Id.* at Art. 5(8). They may adopt measures to prevent possible distortions of competition resulting from such a rule.
[64] See A. TAIT, VALUE ADDED TAX: INTERNATIONAL PRACTICE AND PROBLEMS, IMF 1988 [hereinafter Tait, VAT], at 387. "For instance, the sale of a racehorse is a supply of a taxable good, but the sale of a share in a syndicated racehorse would be the supply of a service. If all the shares were sold then, in essence, the horse is sold and that becomes a supply

There are at least four powerful reasons to ensure that the VAT includes services from the start. First, the contribution of the sector to gross national product is sizable and grows as the economy grows. Consequently, it may have a fairly large revenue potential. Second, failure to tax services distorts consumer choices, encouraging spending on services at the expense of goods and saving. Third, untaxed services mean traders are unable to claim VAT on their service inputs. This causes cascading, distorts choice, and encourages business to develop in-house services, creating further distortions. Fourth, as most of the services that are likely to become taxable are positively correlated with the expenditure of high-income households, subjecting them to taxation may improve equity.[65]

The principles in the Sixth Directive are representative of principles incorporated into the definition of a supply of services under many VAT statutes. The Sixth Directive[66] provides a catch-all classification rule that defines a sale of services as any transaction that does not constitute a sale of goods. The British VAT, incorporating this concept, defines a supply of services as "anything which is not a supply of goods but is done for a consideration."[67] The New Zealand VAT, adopting the EU approach, defines services as "anything which is not goods or money."[68] As discussed later in this chapter, the diversion of the *use* of business assets to the private use of the owner or employee is a taxable supply of services for consideration.[69] Services provided to the owner or his staff without charge likewise can be treated as taxable supplies of services.[70]

Under the Sixth Directive, supplies of services may include transfers of intangible property and obligations to refrain from an act, such as under covenants not to compete.[71] If consideration received for an agreement to refrain from an act is a supply of services, then is a payment to a dairy farmer to discontinue milk production under a European Council Regulation[72] designed to reduce guaranteed global quantities of milk a supply of services for consideration taxable under the Sixth Directive? The following excerpted case decides this issue within the EU.

---

of goods. Either way, VAT is payable." *Id.* at 387–88. See New Vatopia VAT, Appendix B, §4(1)(b).

[65] Tait, VAT, *supra* note 64, at 388. "The question remains, however, whether it is better to include services under a VAT or to use selective taxation (special excises) instead. Both approaches have been used. It has been argued that inclusion of services under the VAT is greatly preferable to the use of a separate tax or taxes on services to avoid multiple taxation, which arises from the nondeductibility of service taxes on purchases by business firms and, at the same time, the application of VAT to purchases by service firms" *Id.* Tait adds that this advantage does not apply as strongly when the services are rendered to final consumers.

[66] Sixth Directive, *supra* note 2, at Art. 6(1).

[67] VATA 1994, *supra* note 10, at §5(2)(b).

[68] N.Z. GST, *supra* note 16, at §2.

[69] On the New Zealand treatment of fringe benefits, see *supra* note 48.

[70] *Id.*

[71] Sixth Directive, *supra* note 2, at Art. 6(1).

[72] Council Regulation (EEC) 1336/86 of May 6, 1986.

Jurgen Mohr v. Finanzamt Bad Segeberg[73]

JUDGMENT. Mr Mohr was the owner of an agricultural holding on which he kept dairy cattle. In March 1987 he applied to the Bundesamt fuer Ernaehrung und Forstwirtschaft (Federal Office for Food and Forestry) for a grant under Council Regulation (EEC) No 1336/86 of 6 May 1986 fixing compensation for the definitive discontinuation of milk production (OJ 1986 L 119, p. 21). In his application he undertook definitively to discontinue milk production and not to make any claim for a milk reference quantity under the common organization of the market.

On 23 September 1987 the Bundesamt upheld his application and granted him a single payment of DM 385 980. Subsequently, Mr Mohr sold his cattle and converted the business into a horse-riding centre, thus ceasing all milk production during that same year.

In his turnover tax declaration for 1987 Mr Mohr did not mention the amount received by way of compensation for discontinuation of milk production. The Finanzamt decided to treat such compensation as consideration for a taxable supply, namely the discontinuation of milk production, and to make it subject to turnover tax.

Mr Mohr unsuccessfully challenged the Finanzamt' s decision before the Finanzgericht. He then brought the matter before the Bundesfinanzhof. The Bundesfinanzhof decided to stay the proceedings and referred the following questions to the Court of Justice for a preliminary ruling:

"1. Does a farmer who is a taxable person and definitively discontinues milk production thereby make a supply of services within the meaning of Article 6(1) of Council Directive 77/388/EEC of 17 May 1977 on the harmonization of the laws of the Member States relating to turnover taxes (the Sixth Directive)? and

2. Is the compensation received for such discontinuation under Council Regulation (EEC) No 1336/86 of 6 May 1986 a monetary payment which is taxable under Article 11(A)(1)(a) of the Sixth Directive?"

By those two questions the national court essentially seeks to ascertain whether Articles 6(1) and 11(A)(1)(a) of the Directive are to be interpreted as meaning that an undertaking to discontinue milk production constitutes a supply of services so that the compensation received for that purpose is subject to turnover tax.

According to Article 2(1) of the Directive, "the supply of goods or services effected for consideration within the territory of the country by a taxable person acting as such" is to be subject to value added tax.

---

[73] Case C-215/94, *1996 ECJ CELEX LEXIS 10783;* 1996 ECR I-959 (ECJ Judgment 1996) (edited by the authors).

Article 6(1) provides:

"Supply of services" shall mean any transaction which does not constitute a supply of goods within the meaning of Article 5. Such transactions may include inter alia: obligations to refrain from an act or to tolerate an act or situation

Article 11(A)(1)(a) provides that the taxable amount is to be, "in respect of supplies of goods and services..., everything which constitutes the consideration which has been or is to be obtained by the supplier from the purchaser, the customer or a third party for such supplies including subsidies directly linked to the price of such supplies".

Regulation No 1336/86 is part of a series of measures adopted by the Community with a view to limiting milk production. According to the third recital of the preamble to that regulation, in order to facilitate the reduction of deliveries and direct sales involved in reducing guaranteed global quantities, a Community system should be established to finance the discontinuation of milk production by granting any producer, at the latter's request and provided that he fulfils certain eligibility requirements, compensation in return for his undertaking to discontinue definitively all milk production.

The first paragraph of Article 1(1) of the regulation thus provides that: "At the request of the party concerned and subject to the conditions defined in this Regulation... compensation shall be granted to any producer... who undertakes to discontinue milk production definitively." Article 2(2) provides that, within the limits of the amounts referred to in Annex II, "Member States are authorized to pay maximum compensation of 4 ECU per year and per 100 kilograms of milk or milk equivalent..." According to Article 2(3), Member States may contribute to the financing of the measure by increasing the level of compensation.

The German and Italian Governments submit that a milk producer who undertakes definitively to discontinue his production supplies a service for consideration within the meaning of Articles 2 and 6(1) of the Directive. Both Governments state in this regard that payment of compensation and an undertaking to discontinue milk production are mutually dependent, thus establishing the direct link between the service provided and consideration for it, as required by the case-law of the Court (Case 154/80 Staatsecretaris van Financien v Cooeperatieve Aardappelenbewaarplaats 1981 ECR 445 and Case C-16/93 Tolsma v Inspecteur der Omzetbelasting 1994 ECR I-743). The service consists in an obligation to refrain from an act, within the meaning of the second indent of Article 6(1) of the Directive, namely to refrain from continuing milk production, and the compensation paid is in the nature of consideration for that undertaking, thus constituting a taxable amount within the meaning of Article 11(A)(1)(a) of the Directive.

That interpretation of the Directive cannot be accepted. According to Article 2(1) of the First Council Directive (67/227/EEC) of 11 April 1967 on the harmonization of legislation of Member States concerning turnover taxes (OJ, English Special Edition 1967 (I), p. 14), VAT is a general tax on the consumption of goods and services. In a case such as the present one, there is no consumption as envisaged in the Community VAT system.

As the Advocate General [Jacobs] notes at point 27 of his Opinion, by compensating farmers who undertake to cease their milk production, the Community does not acquire goods or services for its own use but acts in the common interest of promoting the proper functioning of the Community milk market.

In those circumstances, the undertaking given by a farmer that he will discontinue his milk production does not entail either for the Community or for the competent national authorities any benefit which would enable them to be considered consumers of a service. The undertaking in question does not therefore constitute a supply of services within the meaning of Article 6(1) of the Directive.

The answer to the questions referred to the Court for a preliminary ruling should therefore be that Articles 6(1) and 11(A)(1)(a) of the [Sixth] Directive must be interpreted as meaning that an undertaking to discontinue milk production given by a farmer under Regulation No 1336/86 does not constitute a supply of services. Consequently, any compensation received for that purpose is not subject to turnover tax.

E. What Is "the" Supply for VAT Purposes? – Single, Mixed, and Composite Supplies

When a VAT system taxes some transactions at a positive rate, some at a zero rate, and still others are exempt from tax, there may be an incentive for a supplier to bundle several independent supplies together as a single supply or disaggregate a single supply into separate component supplies in order to reduce the VAT borne by the purchaser on the transaction. The VAT incentive is greatest if the buyer, such as a consumer, cannot claim credit for VAT on the purchase. In part, the controversies in this area arise because many VATs classify a transaction as a supply of goods or a supply of services by the nature of the major elements in the transaction. The issue in these cases relates to "what is the supply?"

As discussed earlier, the distinction between a supply of goods or a supply of services is important in the typical VAT regime that contains different timing and place of supply rules for supplies of goods and supplies of services. As a result, there also may be some incentive to combine or disaggregate elements of a transaction into supplies of goods and supplies of services in order to obtain the desired timing or place of supply rules for the various elements.

Some VAT systems, in an attempt to simplify the administration of the VAT, contain rules to classify a supply that contains major and incidental elements based on the nature of the major elements.[74] If a seller sells a machine for a price that includes installation of the machine in the buyer's premises, the entire transaction may be treated as a supply of goods (the machine) if the installation services are merely incidental to the sale of the goods, or as a supply of services if the installation services represent most of the value of the installed machine.

The identification of "the supply" goes beyond the distinction between a supply of goods or a supply of services. Most VAT systems tax, exempt, or zero rate a variety of transactions. In many cases, the differences in tax treatment depend on the nature of the item sold, prompting an aggregation or disaggregation mentioned above. Although most of the disputes discussed in this section involve the taxable or exempt status of elements of a transaction, the same analysis could apply to resolve the place of supply or time of supply for elements of a transaction.

For transactions that involve issues of taxation, exemption, or zero-rating, the analysis tends to focus on the distinction between single and composite supplies. In the latter cases, the issue is whether there are multiple major elements that can be disaggregated. The challenge in this area is to determine if the transaction should be analyzed as one containing major and incidental elements or as one containing multiple major elements.

The European Court of Justice decided a case involving multiple and composite supplies that is widely cited within and outside the EU. In *Card Protection Plan Ltd v Customs and Excise Commissioners*,[75] the company sold customers a credit card protection plan that indemnified them against financial loss and inconvenience if their cards were lost or stolen.[76] The company assisted customers by notifying the credit card issuers of the lost or stolen cards and providing their customers other services. The company purchased a block policy from an insurance company and listed its customers with the insurance company as the assured. The Commissioners claimed that the company provided a basket of taxable services,[77] not exempt insurance, because there was no direct contractual relationship between the company's customers and the insurance company. The company claimed that its services constituted an arrangement for insurance services and that there was a sufficient direct relationship between the customers and the insurance company to constitute exempt insurance services. Each side argued that there was a single supply, either of exempt insurance or taxable card registration services. In the request for a preliminary ruling, the ECJ was asked about

---

[74] New Vatopia VAT, Appendix B, §4(10)–(12).

[75] Case C-349/96, [1999] STC 270, [1999] All ER (EC) 339 [hereinafter Card Protection Plan].

[76] In some cases, the company covered car keys, passports, and insurance documents.

[77] The array of services provided by the company includes payment of indemnity for losses associated with the fraudulent use of cards, costs to find lost luggage or other items with the company's label previously attached, telephone advice on access to medical and other services, and repayable benefits such as cash advances and replacement of air tickets. *Id.* at paragraph 9 of the Judgment.

"the proper test to be applied in deciding whether a transaction consists for VAT purposes of a single composite supply or of two or more independent supplies."[78] Applying the principles of the Sixth Directive,[79] the court held:

> Every supply of a service must normally be regarded as distinct and independent and ... a supply which comprises a single service from an economic point of view should not be artificially split. So as not to distort the functioning of the VAT system, the essential features of the transaction must be ascertained in order tò determine whether the taxable person is supplying the customer, being a typical consumer, with several distinct principal services or with a single service.

> There is a single supply in particular in cases where one or more elements are to be regarded as constituting the principal service, whilst one or more elements are to be regarded, by contrast, as ancillary services which share the tax treatment of the principal service. A service must be regarded as ancillary to a principal service if it does not constitute for customers an aim in itself, but a means of better enjoying the principal service supplied.[80]

According to the European Court of Justice, the national court must determine, in light of the criteria set by the ECJ, whether transactions such as those in Card Protection Plan constitute two independent supplies or whether there is a principal supply to which the other is ancillary, so that both are taxed like the principal supply.

In one such case in which retail customers acknowledged on their sales receipts that 2.5 percent of the sales price represented a card handling charge when customers paid by debit or credit card, the British Court of Appeal held that there was a single supply of goods to the retail customers.[81] As a result, no part of the sales price was an exempt financial service. In contrast, the British Court of Appeal held that a cable television fee could be separated from a zero-rated supply of a magazine to the cable subscribers, in part because there were two separate suppliers, even though the subscribers paid a single fee to the cable company for both and all subscribers received the magazine.[82]

Assume that a seller of machinery regularly sells its machinery for a single price that includes delivery of the machinery to the buyer's premises. If a newly introduced VAT taxes machinery but exempts domestic freight charges and the sale is made to a buyer that cannot claim credit for VAT on purchases (such as a university providing exempt education services), the

---

[78] *Id.* at paragraph 12 of the Judgment.

[79] Sixth Directive, *supra* note 2, at Art. 2(1) imposes tax on "the supply of goods or services ... by a table person acting as such."

[80] Card Protection Plan, *supra* note 75, at paragraphs 30 and 31 of the Judgment.

[81] *Debenhams Retail plc v. Revenue and Customs*, [2005] EWCA Civ. 892; [2005] All ER (D) 233 (Ct. App. Civil Div).

[82] *Telewest Communications plc and Another v. Customs & Excise Commissioners*, [2005] EWCA Civ. 102; [2005] STC 481 (Ct. App. Civil Div.) hereinafter Telewest.

seller may disaggregate the price of the merchandise to separately charge for freight in order to claim that this portion of the selling price is exempt from the VAT.

In a British case, the court held that the purchase of automobiles with delivery charged separately was a single supply, not an independent sale of a car (on which no input credit was allowable) and separate delivery services (on which input credit was allowable).[83] The delivery services were ancillary to the main supply of the car. If one element of a supply dominates the other elements, according to another U.K. case, the dominant element may be the one and only supply.[84]

In contrast, when a day train trip was coupled with "fine wine and dining," and the supplier emphasized the food, wine, and service in advertising for the trips, a British court held that the transaction was a mixed supply of transport and catering – the catering was an aim in itself.[85] A distance learning college that provided books and face-to-face teaching for a single fee for a course was allowed to treat the transaction as two supplies – a zero-rated supply of books and an exempt educational service. The court noted that the goods were physically dissociable from the education service.[86] The connection of a cable in a customer's premises was held to be a supply independent of the supply of cable television services.[87] Likewise as discussed above, a Cable Guide magazine received as part of the cable subscription was held to be a separate zero-rated supply of a magazine.[88]

In some cases, such as *Canadian Airlines* excerpted next, the determination of when a transaction begins and ends can be critical.

---

[83] *Commissioners of Customs and Excise v British Telecommunications plc*, [1999] 3 All ER 961.

[84] *Customs and Excise Commissioners v Wellington Private Hospital Ltd*, [1997] BVC 251 (United Kingdom), cited in Goods and Services Tax Ruling, GSTR 2001/8, Goods and services tax: apportioning the consideration for a supply that includes taxable and nontaxable parts, §51 (Australia) [hereinafter GSTR 2001/8]. See also *Dr. Beynon and Partners v Customs and Excise Commissioners*, [2005] STC 55 (House of Lords 2004)(United Kingdom), holding that the administration of a drug by a doctor to a patient is a single supply of exempt medical care, not separate zero-rated drugs and exempt medical care. The case involved doctors able under National Health regulations to provide pharmacy services if there was no pharmacy nearby.

[85] *Sea Containers Ltd v Customs and Excise Commissioners*, [2000] BVC 60 (United Kingdom). In an earlier British case, *Customs and Excise Commissioners v Professional Footballers' Association (Enterprises) Ltd*, [1992] STC 294, the Court of Appeal held that the presentation of trophies at an awards dinner was part of a single supply of the dinner function because of the link between the trophies presented and the price paid for the ticket to the dinner.

[86] *College of Estate Management v Customs and Excise Commissioners*, [2004] STC 1471 (Ct. App. United Kingdom).

[87] *DA Mac Carthaigh, Inspector of Taxes v Cablelink Limited, Cablelink Waterford Limited and Galway Cable Vision*, [SC No 155 of 2003], [2003] 4 IR 510. Ireland Sup. Ct. The installation of the cable connection was a supply on immovable property that qualified for a lower VAT rate than the supply of the cable television services.

[88] Telewest, *supra* note 82.

Canadian Airlines International Ltd v. The Commissioners of Customs and Excise[89]

JUDGMENT. This is an appeal against assessments... that limousine services supplied to full fare business class passengers on Trans Atlantic flights formed a separate supply from the zero-rated supply of the flights.

[T]he question [is] whether there were single composite supplies of the flights to which the limousine element was incidental or separate supplies.

[The zero-rating applies to:]

"Transport of Passengers – . . .

(c) on any scheduled flight; or
(d) from a place within to a place without the United Kingdom or vice versa, to the extent that those services are supplied in the United Kingdom". This provision does not reflect an exemption under the Sixth Directive but is a derogation under Article 28(3)(b) during the transitional period.

The Appellant is a scheduled airline, transporting passengers between (inter alia) Canada and the UK. At the relevant time flights were from Gatwick and Manchester and from eight (later nine) airports in Canada.

During the period covered by the assessments the Appellant offered its business class passengers paying full fare a limousine service consisting of chauffeur driven limousine transport of them and their baggage between their home, hotel or office and Gatwick or Manchester [airport].

The business class fare schedules contained the words, "Free limousine service available within 80 mile radius of Gatwick or Manchester Airport."

There was no written contract with the passenger regarding the limousine service.

The reservations clerk would ask business passengers whether they wanted the limousine service and if they did would record the necessary details. Most passengers requiring a limousine booked then, but they could do so up to 24 hours before departure. On occasion a limousine could be booked at shorter notice.

Limousines could only be utilised directly before or after the flight. The limousines and chauffeurs were actually provided by Tristar who contacted passengers 24 hours in advance to confirm. Passengers travelling more than the free radius were told to pay the chauffeur. It is unclear whether passengers were told of the identity of the limousine operating company. . . .

[89] LON/93/587A (1994) [edited by the authors].

Business fares were the same whether or not the limousine service was taken up. There was a single undivided fare. If at the last minute a passenger decided not to use Canadian Airlines, he could get a refund on the ticket; if he had already used a limousine he would be charged for it.

The take-up rate was very small, being mainly passengers arriving from Canada.

[T]he business class full fares were not increased on introduction of the limousine service or reduced on its cessation in September 1992.

Since the question where there is one supply or two is a question of law in each case, it would seem to follow that there must be legal principles on which this is to be decided. While the incidental/integral test is the basic test, in many cases it does not provide an answer, since the question remains whether or not one supply is in law an integral part of the other or incidental to it.

In our judgment the consideration was obtained by the Appellants in return for supplying two elements, the flight and the transfer option.

At the time of the contract between the Appellant and a passenger, there was no certainty as to whether or not the transfer option would be utilised.

[T]he transfer available under the option was not contemporaneous with the flight. Although closely linked in point of time it only applied either before or after the flight and the unavoidable ground formalities.

Furthermore since the take-up rate was so low it is less clear that the passenger was paying for the limousine option as well as the flight. Most did not use it.

It does not seem to us that the transfer options can be said to be integral to the supply of the flights in any normal sense of the word. The fact that they were linked by a contract does not make them integral. We ask ourselves whether they can be regarded as incidental. It does not seem to us that they cannot be practically separated in an economic sense. The fact that they were discontinued in September 1992 shows that the Appellants felt that the option did not have to be provided. We also consider it to be important that the limousines were not capable of being used at the same time as the flight. It seems to us that when an element is not contemporaneous with the main supply it is less likely to be incidental.

We hold that the right to the limousine element was a separate supply.

Canada addressed the single versus multiple supply issue with principles taken from jurisprudence. The Canadian policy is designed to provide guidance on whether a transaction with several elements constitutes a single or multiple independent supplies for VAT purposes. According to this proposed policy, each supply should be considered distinct and independent, an "economically" single supply should not be artificially split for tax purposes, and a supply is a single supply "where one or more elements constitute the supply and any remaining elements serve only to enhance the supply."[90] The thrust of the policy is that "two or more elements are part of a single supply when the elements are integral components; the elements are inextricably bound up with each other; the elements are so intertwined and interdependent that they must be supplied together; or one element of the transaction is so dominated by another element that the first element has lost any identity for fiscal purposes."[91]

The Australian approach is to distinguish between mixed supplies that contain taxable and nontaxable parts and composite "supplies that appear to have more than one part but that are essentially supplies of one thing."[92] The focus is on elements of a transaction that may be combined or disaggregated in order to change the nature of the supply from taxable to nontaxable or vice versa. The Australian Tax Office (ATO) takes the position that the consideration for a mixed supply (with taxable and exempt parts that produce different tax consequences) must be apportioned, but not the consideration for a composite supply. "A mixed supply is a supply that has to be separated or unbundled as it contains separately identifiable taxable and non-taxable parts that need to be individually recognized.... "[93] In contrast, "a supply that contains a dominant part and the supply includes something that is integral, ancillary or incidental to that part, then the supply is composite."[94] According to the ATO, the distinction between separately identifiable and integral is a question of fact and degree that should be resolved by adopting a commonsense approach.[95] Expanding upon the differences, the ATO position is that "a supply has separately identifiable parts where the parts require individual recognition and retention as separate parts, due to their relative significance in the supply."[96] In contrast, "a part of a supply will be integral, ancillary or incidental where it is insignificant in value or function, or merely contributes to or complements the use or enjoyment of the dominant part of the supply."[97]

---

[90] Policy P-077R2, entitled "Single and Multiple Supplies" (April 26, 2004) (Canada), at "Decision."

[91] *Id.* at "Discussion, General Comments."

[92] GSTR 2001/8, *supra* note 84. For a lengthy discussion of the ATO approach to mixed and composite supplies, see Stacey & Brown, "A Unifying Composite Supply Doctrine? An Australian View," *VAT Monitor*, May/June 2003, p. 178. Additional articles by these authors explore the applicability of the composite supply doctrine in debt and equity streams. See Stacey & Brown, "GST Treatment of Debt & Equity Income Streams: An Australian View," VAT Monitor, July/Aug. 2003, p. 295; *GST analyzing income streams – Part II*, 3 AGSTJ 41 (2003).

[93] GSTR 2001/8, *supra* note 84, at ¶16.

[94] *Id* .at ¶17.

[95] *Id.* at ¶20.

[96] *Id* at ¶52.

[97] *Id.* at ¶59. Although South Africa does not have the same definition distinction between mixed and composite supplies, the Tax Court held that "passenger service charges" (airport charges) separately stated on airline tickets were part of the fare for international transport of passengers and therefore a single zero-rated supply. Income Tax Case No. 1775, discussed in Botes, "South Africa: Single supply?" *VAT Monitor*, Nov./Dec. 2004, p. 470.

F. Vouchers

The use of vouchers such as gift certificates and transportation tickets raises a number of VAT issues. The issuance of a voucher by a taxable person may be treated as a supply when issued of goods or services that can be obtained with the use of the voucher, or the voucher may not result in any VAT consequences until the voucher is exchanged for taxable goods or services. The rules governing the time when a supply takes place also may influence the taxation of vouchers. The range of transactions involving the use of vouchers is so broad that it is difficult to treat all vouchers alike. If the issuance of any voucher is taxable when issued, vouchers cannot be used to delay the reporting of VAT attributable to the voucher until it is redeemed. Some countries, however, encourage the use of vouchers by not taxing the consideration received on the issuance of a voucher until it is redeemed, notwithstanding the customary timing rule that taxes a supply at the earliest of the time the supply occurs, the invoice is issued, or any payment is received.[98]

Vouchers have been the subject of extensive review and analysis in Australia.[99] In Australia, "(a) voucher evidences a right or entitlement to receive supplies in the future, and the obligation to make supplies, on the exercise or redemption of that right or entitlement."[100] The issuance of a voucher under the Australian GST generally is a taxable supply as a supply connected with Australia for a consideration in the course of an enterprise conducted by a registered person.[101] However, the supply of a voucher may not be taxed until the voucher is redeemed if the voucher satisfies a series of conditions.[102] Conditions are imposed because taxing a voucher only on redemption provides opportunities to defer the reporting of tax on supplies acquired with the redemption of the voucher.

A voucher that qualifies as a "face value voucher" (FVV) is not subject to the Australian GST until the voucher is redeemed. To obtain this deferral of the point when a voucher is subject to VAT, the voucher must satisfy the conditions in both sections 100–25 and 100–5.

A voucher meets section 100–25 if the redemption of the voucher "entitles the holder to receive supplies in accordance with its terms." In addition, the voucher must have a single function or purpose (such as a bus ticket),[103] the voucher (such as a gift certificate) must be presented when it is redeemed for supplies, and the voucher must give the holder the right to supplies on

---

[98] See New Vatopia VAT, Appendix B, §4(19).

[99] Goods and Services Tax Ruling 2003/5 (Australia) [hereinafter GSTR 2003/5]. For an extensive examination of the taxation of telephone cards and its relationship to the taxation of vouchers, see Millar, "The Australian GST Treatment of Telephone Cards," *VAT Monitor*, Sept./Oct. 2003, p. 365.

[100] GSTR 2003/5, *supra* note 99, at ¶7.

[101] See Australian GST, *supra* note 57, at §9-5.

[102] GSTR 2003/5, *supra* note 99, at ¶¶8 and 9. Even if the supply of a voucher is not subject to GST until it is redeemed, the supply of the voucher is taxed on issuance to the extent that the consideration received for the voucher exceeds its face value. *Id.* at ¶9.

[103] *Id.* at ¶26. On redemption, the holder's right to receive supplies with the use of the voucher must terminate. *Id.* at ¶27.

redemption.[104] The supply of a voucher is not a taxable supply, even if it meets section 100–25, unless it also meets section 100–5. The supply of a voucher must otherwise be a taxable supply (e.g., it is supplied for consideration), and upon redemption, the holder must be entitled to "a reasonable choice and flexibility of supplies"[105] with a value up to the monetary value stated on the voucher. For example, a voucher entitling the holder to a car wash and other services up to a $50 value (a choice of services) is a FVV that is not reportable for tax purposes until it is redeemed.[106] A voucher that entitles the holder only to a particular kind of supply (such as a particular kind of car wash) priced at $30 is taxable when the voucher is supplied because there is no choice.[107]

Vouchers may influence the value of a supply for VAT purposes. In a dispute between Germany and the Commission of the European Communities, the ECJ held that Germany failed to comply with the Sixth Directive by failing to allow a manufacturer to reduce the taxable amount of its supply for the vouchers it issued that were used by retail customers to reduce the price paid for the goods purchased from retailers and subsequently were submitted by retailers for reimbursement.[108] Germany unsuccessfully claimed that the vouchers reduced the taxable amount of the supply only when the manufacturer supplied the goods directly to the trader, and then only if the manufacturer issued a corrected invoice that resulted in a reduction in the input tax deducted by the trader.[109] The taxable amount of the sale by the retailer is the actual retail price paid by the final consumer plus the amount reimbursed to the retailer by the manufacturer.[110]

III. THE TAX OR VAT INVOICE

A. ROLE OF VAT INVOICE

The tax or VAT invoice is a central feature of a European-style, credit-invoice VAT system. A registered person is allowed to claim credit against output tax liability for VAT imposed on acquisitions used in making taxable supplies. As a tax credit, the registered person reduces tax liability one dollar for each one dollar of VAT qualifying for the input credit. It is only a registered person who can issue a VAT invoice, and severe penalties generally are provided for anyone who improperly issues a VAT invoice.[111]

---

[104] *Id.* at ¶26.

[105] *Id.* at ¶55.

[106] *Id.* at ¶77.

[107] *Id.* at ¶78.

[108] *Commission of the European Communities v Federal Republic of Germany*, Case C-427/98 of October 15, 2002.

[109] *Id.* at ¶20 of the Judgment.

[110] *Id.* at ¶59 of the Judgment.

[111] Goods and Services Tax (General) Regulations, Cap. 117A, Rg 10(1) (1993); and Singapore GST, *supra* note 46, at §64(2) imposing a civil penalty. See New Vatopia VAT, Appendix B, §32(1).

B. Who Receives VAT Invoices?

In many VAT systems, a registered person must issue a VAT invoice for all taxable sales. In other systems, in order to reduce the opportunity for trading in VAT invoices, VAT invoices can be issued only on sales to other registered persons.

C. Contents of Required VAT Invoices

In taxable transactions before the retail stage, the VAT listed on the seller's tax invoice can be used to verify that the sale was reported on the seller's VAT return and then can be cross-matched against the buyer's claimed input credit on the same transaction.[112] The centrality of the VAT invoice results in elaborate rules in VAT Acts and regulations on the requirement to issue invoices and what information they should contain.

In the EU, VAT invoices generally are issued in transactions between registered persons. Sellers ordinarily do not issue tax invoices on retail sales.[113]

New Zealand has particularly detailed rules governing tax invoices.[114] A registered person who sells to a registered purchaser must, if the purchaser requests it, issue a tax invoice containing the following information:[115]

1. "tax invoice" is placed in a prominent place
2. seller's name and registration number
3. recipient's name and address
4. date invoice is issued
5. description of items sold, including quantity or volume
6. list tax-exclusive and tax-inclusive prices and amount of tax, or statement of consideration and that it includes tax

A tax invoice may contain less information if the consideration is below a certain threshold.[116] In limited situations, New Zealand allows the recipient to create a tax invoice for a taxable supply that it receives.[117] If a consumer sells secondhand goods to a registered recipient, the recipient will not receive

---

[112] There is scant data that this cross-matching in fact occurs with any degree of consistency. Korea and Taiwan relied upon an elaborate computer system of cross-matching copies of tax invoices sent to the government by the seller and the buyer. Korea greatly curtailed this practice by the early 1990s. The follow-up of mismatches has been difficult and spotty in both Korea and Taiwan.

[113] See Sixth Directive, *supra* note 2, at art. 22(3)(a). In the United Kingdom, the Commissioners by regulations may require taxable persons to issue VAT invoices that include particular information, such as whether VAT is chargeable on the supply, the amount of VAT chargeable, and the identification of the seller and the buyer. U.K. VATA 1994, *supra* note 10, *supra* note, at Sch. 11, ¶2A(1) and (2).

[114] N.Z. GST, *supra* note 16, at §24. See New Vatopia VAT, Appendix B, Sch. IV.

[115] *Id.* at §24(1) and (3). The seller ordinarily can issue only one tax invoice for each taxable supply. If the original invoice is lost, the seller can issue a copy if it is clearly marked as such. *Id.* at §24(1)(a) and (b).

[116] *Id.* at §24(4).

[117] *Id.* at §24(2). The statute provides that if the seller issues a tax invoice governing the same sale, the recipient's invoice is deemed to be the tax invoice.

a VAT invoice and must maintain records of the transaction, including much of the same information required on a tax invoice.[118]

D. Waiver of Required VAT Invoices

> Under some foreign statutes, the tax authority is authorized to waive the seller's obligation to issue a tax invoice. This waiver pertains to the issuance of a tax invoice and is not a waiver . . . of some of the data required to be included in a tax invoice. This waiver . . . would be particularly important if . . . sellers [were required] to issue tax invoice in all taxable sales, including sales to consumers.[119]

In New Zealand, some registrants are not obligated to issue tax invoice or may be obligated to provide only limited information on tax invoice. A supplier is not required to issue tax invoices if the consideration is below a stated threshold.[120] If the Commissioner is satisfied that sufficient records are available on certain supplies or that requiring all of the particulars on tax invoices would be impractical, the Commissioner may waive certain particulars or may waive the requirement to issue tax invoices, subject to conditions the Commissioner imposes.[121]

IV. Discussion Questions

1. In the cases discussed in this chapter, can you identify the value added or the item that can be regarded as adding value to the personal consumption being taxed at the end of the line, that is, the final retail sale?
2. Mr. Brown is a lawyer who has always kept the deepest attachment to the university where he graduated and gladly helps it on many instances with his legal advice given free of charge. Is there any provision in the EU Sixth Directive relating to this situation? Should there be such a provision in a "model" VAT?
3. In defining taxable transactions, do the EU Sixth Directive and the ABA Model take into account the onerous or gratuitous nature of the operation, or the contractual nature of the operation?
4. What are the main purposes of the distinction drawn by the EU Sixth Directive between goods and services? Could you draft a VAT Code without using this distinction?
5. Do the Vatopia VAT and the EU Sixth Directive provide comparable VAT treatment for fringe benefits provided by employers to employees? See EU Sixth Directive, Art 5(6). Is denial of employer's credit for inputs used in providing fringe benefits a technically sound solution to the problem or a compromise? What do you recommend and why?

---

[118] *Id.* at §24(7).
[119] ABA Model Act, *supra* note 15, at 124.
[120] N.Z. GST, *supra* note 16, at §24(5).
[121] *Id.* at §24(6).

6

The Tax Credit Mechanism

I. TAX CREDIT FOR PURCHASES

A. BASIC INPUT TAX CREDIT RULES

1. Allowance of Credit – General Rules

Under the credit or invoice VAT used almost universally, tax liability for each period is calculated as the difference between the tax imposed or collected on taxable sales (output tax) and tax paid or incurred both on taxable purchases and on taxable imports (input tax credit). Some credit-invoice VATs are worded so that the input tax is deducted from tax on taxable sales (output tax). In this book, input tax credit and input tax deduction are used interchangeably to mean subtraction of input tax from output tax.

Unlike an income tax imposed on an income base that requires capital goods to be capitalized and depreciated and requires beginning and ending inventories to be taken into account in determining gross income from sales, VATs typically are consumption-based taxes that allow an immediate input credit for tax imposed on purchases of capital goods and inventory items. There are some exceptions discussed in this chapter.

Nations with VATs provide varying input credit rules. For example, in Mexico, there is a threshold condition. Only VAT on goods or services deductible for income tax purposes can qualify for input credits. The qualifying input VAT still may be disallowed, such as input VAT attributable to exempt supplies.[1]

The EU Sixth VAT Directive contains extensive rules on the availability of input tax credits (or what under the Directive is referred to as deductions).[2] An input credit is available for tax on purchases of goods or services,

---

[1] Salas, "Focus on Mexico," *VAT Monitor*, Mar./Apr. 2003, pp. 102, 107–108.

[2] See Sixth Council Directive of May 17, 1977, on the harmonization of the laws of the Member States relating to turnover taxes – Common system of value added tax: uniform basis of assessment (77/388/EEC), Art's. 17–20 [hereinafter Sixth Directive]. Member States are authorized, after consultation, to disallow some input credits "for cyclical economic reasons." *Id.* at Art. 17(7). For a discussion of some input tax credit issues under EU VATs, see Jenkins, "The Right to Recover Input Tax and Its Enemies," 6 *VAT Monitor* 164 (May/June 1995).

imports of goods, or on certain taxable self-supplies if these items are used for purposes of taxable transactions.[3] Taxpayers may engage in tax-motivated transactions in an attempt to convert assets used in making exempt supplies into assets used in making taxable supplies.[4]

In order to claim credits for tax on goods acquired, the goods must exist. Although it seems self evident, there are situations in which the existence of the goods may be in doubt. For example, a business enters agreements to buy containers to ship mud to oil rigs, immediately leases the containers without physically inspecting them, and receives rent on some but not all of the containers. There apparently was fraud and some of the alleged containers listed on VAT invoices did not exist. The ECJ held that if goods listed on invoices do not exist when the goods are to be transferred under the sale agreement, there is no supply unless the goods later come into existence, and therefore no input VAT is creditable.[5]

There are other cases of VAT fraud involving VAT invoices too numerous to discuss in the book. In a Canadian case involving vehicles, *R v. Prokofiew*,[6] the accused engaged in schemes involving purported sales to status Indians and resales by them (the purchases and sales were not subject to the Canadian GST) under circumstances in which the Indians were not intended to be the owners of the vehicles.[7] In South Africa, false export documents have been used to claim zero-rating for goods that are not exported, a seller and buyer conspire to falsify invoices, and input VAT is claimed on falsified invoices covering services that cannot be physically investigated.[8] In another case, the ECJ ruled that an innocent person who was an unknowing participant in a carousel fraud still is engaged in economic activity and is making supplies of goods and supplies of services and therefore is able to claim input tax credits with respect to those transactions. In the joined cases of *Optigen, Fulcrum, and Bond*, the court ruled: "The right to deduct input value added tax of a taxable person who carries out such transactions cannot be affected by the fact that in the chain of supply of which those transactions form part another prior or subsequent transaction is vitiated by value added tax fraud, without that taxable person knowing or having any means of knowing."[9]

---

[3] Sixth Directive, *supra* not 2, at Art. 17(2).

[4] See Case C-223/03, *University of Huddersfield Higher Education Corporation v. Commissioners of Customs and Excise*, (ECJ Opinion 7 April 2005).

[5] *Howard v. The Commissioners of Customs and Excise*, LON/80/457 (VATTR 1981)(United Kingdom).

[6] *R. v. Prokofiew (No. 1)*, [2004] GSTC 103 (Canada).

[7] See Sherman, "Five of nine accused convicted in huge GST vehicle fraud," *VAT Monitor*, Jan./Feb. 2005, p. 76.

[8] See Botes & Botes, "Money-Laundering in South Africa," *VAT Monitor*, July/Aug. 2002, p. 258.

[9] Joined Cases C-354/03, C-355/03, and C-484/03, *Optigen Ltd, Fulcrum Electronics Ltd and Bond House Systems Ltd v Commissioners of Customs & Excise*, [2006] ECR I->>>>, OJ C 251 of 18.10.2003 OJ C 35 of 07.02.2004. The European Commission issued a proposal for a Council Directive on a number of issues, including evasion of VAT. 2005 – COM (89), Countering tax evasion and avoidance. It has been estimated by the British Office for National Statistics that VAT fraud accounts for about 10% of U.K. exports. Seager, *Fraud could account for 10% of UK's exports*, The Guardian, May 11, 2006.

If tax is paid on purchases used both for transactions qualifying for the input credit and those that do not qualify, the input credit is available under the Sixth Directive and most other VATs only for the portion attributable to the former.[10] For example, if in a tax period, a registered business has $60,000 in taxable purchases directly attributable to taxable sales and $30,000 in taxable purchases directly attributable to exempt sales, the person can claim credit only for VAT on the $60,000 of purchases attributable to taxable sales.

2. Credit for Input VAT on Capital Goods

Chapter 2 discusses the classification of a value added tax as a Gross Domestic Product, Income, or Consumption VAT. The difference is the treatment of the input VAT on capital purchases. The overwhelming choice among countries with VATs is the Consumption-style VAT that provides an immediate credit for input VAT on capital purchases. There are a few exceptions. Some countries start with a GDP or Income VAT only as a transition to a Consumption-style VAT.[11]

China is one of the last holdouts in denying full credit for input VAT on capital purchases but is in the process of joining the Consumption VAT club. China does not grant credits for input VAT on purchases of fixed assets – a broad concept of capital goods. The switch for China apparently will occur in several stages.[12]

Some countries have elaborate rules covering the input credit on capital goods, especially on the acquisition of such property, on the change in the

---

[10] Sixth Directive, *supra* note 2, at Art. 17(5). See also Art. 19(1) for the formula to calculate allowable credits. For this purpose, member states may make some adjustment for tax on capital purchases. *Id.* at Art. 19(2).

[11] For example, Belarus went from a system providing for the recovery of input VAT on capital goods over a twelve-month period to a system allowing full input VAT credit at the time that capital (fixed) goods are put into operation. See Belarus Presidential Decree No. 1 of January 13, 2005, discussed in Strachuk, Belarus, IBFD Tax News Service, March 22, 2005. As part of its program to encourage industrial investment, Argentina is providing VAT refunds on capital purchases made during the period between November 2000 and November 2004, if the authorities are satisfied that the rebated VAT is reinvested into business expansion. Decree 379/2005, discussed in *BNA Daily Tax Report*, April 29, 2005, p. G-5.

[12] See Fay, "The P.R.C.'s New Consumption-Oriented VAT," 35 *Tax Notes Int'l* 727 (Aug. 23, 2004). According to the report, the credit for input VAT on fixed assets applies in a portion of northeastern China to equipment manufacturing, petrochemicals, metallurgy, shipbuilding, auto manufacturing, military product processing, and high-tech industries. The experimental input VAT deductions were authorized in Caishui [2004] No. 156, cited in Lixic Zhang, "VAT reform in north-eastern China," *VAT Monitor*, Nov./Dec. 2004, p. 428. "Fixed assets," according to this report, includes "machines, equipment, transport vehicles and other equipment, tools and apparatus, to be used for more than one year for the enterprise's production and management; and other goods, provided that the unit price exceeds CHY 2,000, and the goods will be used for more than two years." Some input VAT is disallowed. See also Ahmad, Singh, & Lockwood, *Taxation Reforms and Changes in Revenue Assignments in China*, IMF Working Paper, WP/04/125 (July 2004), at p. 4.

use of capital goods from taxable to exempt activities, and on the disposition of capital goods.[13]

3. Conditions to Claim Credit for Input VAT

Generally, a registered (or taxable) person can claim credit for input VAT on acquisitions (imports and domestic purchases) of goods and services used in connection with taxable supplies. The underlying principle is that a registered person reporting taxable supplies is entitled to claim input VAT on these acquisitions in order to prevent the cascading of tax attributable to business inputs. As will be discussed later, a registered person may be denied credit on acquisitions used for a mixed purpose – to use in making taxable transactions and for personal or other purposes. For example, credit for input VAT may be denied on purchases of automobiles that can be used both for business and for the personal use of officers, employees, or others.

In the EU and in many countries, an input VAT is deductible in the tax period in which goods are delivered or services are rendered, but only if the registered person holds a document covering the goods or services that serves as an invoice.[14] Thus, a registered person who acquired services in year one and the invoice was not received until year two (although mailed in year one), cannot claim credit for the input VAT until the invoice was received.[15]

"A buyer [generally] is entitled to the input credit even if the seller does not remit the tax charged on its tax invoices. In this situation, the government's recourse is an action against the defaulting seller, not denial of the credit to the buyer who relied on the tax invoice and who either paid the seller in good faith or is liable to the seller."[16] This principle does not apply if the sale on which VAT was charged was a fraudulent sale, even if the purchaser was not aware of the fact that the sale was fraudulent.[17]

The input tax credit generally is available only to the taxpayer who is charged VAT on purchases that it makes for use in connection with its taxable activities. Some courts interpret this requirement strictly. For example, in *Turner v. Commissioners of Customs and Excise*,[18] a taxpayer, as unsuccessful plaintiff in litigation, was required to pay the defendant's costs, including some taxable services provided to the defendant. The tribunal held that the

---

[13] See Canadian Goods and Services Tax, S.C. 1990, c. 45, as amended [hereinafter Canadian GST], §§195–211.

[14] *Terra Baubedarf-Handel GmbH v Finanzamt Osterholz-Scharmbeck*, Case C-152/02, [2004] ECR I-0000, OJ C 118, 30.04.2004, p. 21 [hereinafter *Terra Baubedarf-Handel GmbH*], interpreting the Sixth Directive, *supra* note 2, at Arts. 17(2)(a), 18(2), and 22(3).

[15] *Terra Baubedarf-Handel GmbH*, *supra* note 14, at ¶¶37 and 38.

[16] A. Schenk, reporter, Value Added Tax – A Model Statute And Commentary: A Report Of The Committee On Value Added Tax Of The American Bar Association Section Of Taxation 96 (1989) [hereinafter ABA Model Act].

[17] See *Customs & Excise Commissioners v. Pennystar Ltd*, [1996] BVC 125. But see *Greenall*, (1987) 3 BVC 1,320.

[18] [1992] BVC 82.

services paid for by the taxpayer were the defendant's expenses, not that of the taxpayer, and therefore denied input credits for VAT imposed on those services. In contrast, when an airline paid airport restaurants to feed delayed passengers, the input VAT was creditable even though the service was not provided directly to the airline.[19]

In some situations, the question is whether the person who pays VAT is entitled to claim the input credit. This issue may arise when acquired items are transferred to another person in a non-taxable or zero-rated transaction. As discussed earlier, the input VAT generally is creditable only by the person who acquires the taxable goods or services and pays the tax. In *Faxworld*,[20] a partnership was established to assist in the creation of a capital company. The partnership purchased goods and services to be transferred to the newly created capital company. The issue in *Faxworld* was whether the input VAT was creditable to the partnership or to the transferee capital company. The transfer of the assets was a "nonsupply" under the Sixth Directive.[21] According to the Opinion by the Advocate General in this case, the tax was deductible by the person who bore the burden of the tax (the partnership). In the Judgment by the ECJ in the same case, the court held that the partnership was entitled to claim input VAT on its acquisitions "where its only output transaction . . . was to effect . . . the transfer for consideration" that was not a supply of goods or services.[22]

New Zealand limits the credit on purchases acquired by the person claiming the credit. Thus, if a person imports components, pays GST on the imports, and does not charge for these components when it provides them free of charge as agent or bailee of the foreign company obligated to provide warranty service in New Zealand, the importer is not eligible to claim credit for the GST on imports.[23] In that case, the taxpayer paid tax on the import of components that it stored and provided to the foreign manufacturer's New Zealand customers, even though it did not take legal title to the components. The taxpayer was paid by the foreign company for the storage and transfer of these components to the manufacturer's customers. The Tax Review Authority held that there was no taxable sale by the taxpayer for consideration, so the taxpayer did not acquire the components to make taxable sales.

The input tax credit reduces tax liability. It therefore is not surprising that VAT statutes impose substantiation requirements to support claims for the input credit. The Sixth Directive requires input credits to be supported by

---

[19] *British Airways plc v Commissioners of Customs and Excise*, [2000] VAT and Duties Tribunal No. 16,446.

[20] *Finanzamt Offenback am Main-Land v Faxworld Worgrundungsgesellschaft Peter Hunninghausen und Wolfgang Klein Gbr*, Case C-137/02, [2004] ECR I-5547 [hereinafter Faxworld].

[21] See Sixth Directive, *supra* note 2, at Arts. 5(8) and 6(5).

[22] *Faxworld, supra* note 20, at ¶43.

[23] Case T35, (Tax Review Authority 1996), 18 NZTC 8,235, digested in *CCH NZ GST Guide*, ¶96–162 (1998).

invoices, import documents, or other documentation required by Member States.[24]

What if a supplier fails to charge VAT in the honest belief that VAT is not chargeable and a court subsequently holds that the supply is taxable? The ECJ held that highway tolls are fees for services, not user taxes, and therefore are subject to VAT under the EU Sixth Directive.[25] Although France's highway operators started charging VAT on tolls, the trucking firms sought refunds for presumed VAT in tolls paid during 1996–2000. The highest French court for administrative decisions held that the ECJ decision had retroactive application, so the toll road operators could issue retroactive VAT invoices.[26]

The N.Z. GST requires registered persons to have an invoice or other supporting document in its possession in order to claim the credit.[27] In one case under this N.Z. statute, the taxpayer was denied input credits due to lack of invoices to support its claimed credits. The Tax Review Authority found that the taxpayer was in the position to obtain and retain invoices as documentary evidence to support its claimed input credits.

In the following British case, the taxpayer was denied input credits for estimates of tax on petrol purchased for a vehicle that the taxpayer claimed was used for business reasons.

Pelleted Casehardening Salts Ltd v. The Commissioners of Customs and Excise[28]

The Appellant Company carries on business as a manufacturer of general chemicals and has since 1st April 1973 been registered for the purposes of the [VAT]. Except in one area, which the tribunal will hereinafter consider in detail, its record in value added tax accounting and payment appears to have been immaculate.

The disputed portion of the assessment thus amounts to £405, being, £45 in respect of each quarterly accounting period. All of such quarterly claims to deduct input tax of, £45 made by the Appellant Company were in respect of value added tax charged by suppliers of petrol which Mr Lindley alleges were supplied for the purposes of the business which was carried on by the Appellant Company. The Commissioners . . . contend

---

[24] Sixth Directive, *supra* note 2, at Art. 18(1). Effective July 1, 2006, according to Council Regulation (EC) No. 1777/2005 of October 17, 2005, if an importing member state adopted an electronic system for customs, an "import document" covers "electronic versions of such documents, provided that they allow for the exercise of the right of deduction to be checked." Art. 18.

[25] Case C-260/98, *Commission of the European Communities v. Heleinic Republic*, [2000] ECR I-06537.

[26] *SA Etablissements Louis Mazet et autres v. Ministere d'Economie, Finances, et de l'Industrie*, Counseil d'Etat, No. 268681 (June 29, 2005), reported in Speer, "French Trucking Firms Demand VAT Refund from Highway Tolls," *BNA Daily Tax Report*, Oct. 7, 2005, p. G-4.

[27] New Zealand Goods and Services Tax, 1985, No. 141 [hereinafter NZ GST], at §20(2). The registered person also must retain the required documents as required by §75.

[28] VATTR (MAN/84/287), (1985) 2 BVC 205,192 (United Kingdom).

that such deduction of input tax was incorrect in that the entitlement was claimed in respect of supplies which were not supported by the requisite documentation in the form of invoices.

[According to the VAT in effect at that time, a taxable person can claim input credits if] the goods or services supplied are used or to be used for the purpose of any business carried on or to be carried on by the taxable person making the claim.[29] I find it unnecessary to decide in this appeal whether or not the supplies of petrol in issue were for the purpose of a business carried on by the Appellant Company. I am prepared for the purposes of this appeal to assume that they were because, in my judgment, the only relevant issue herein is the sufficiency of the evidence whereby such supplies and the payment therefor are sought to be proved by the Appellant Company.

[R]egulations may provide, inter alia, for tax on the supply of goods or services to a taxable person . . . to be treated as his input tax only if and to the extent that the charge to tax is evidenced and quantified by reference to such documents as may be specified in the regulations or as the Commissioners may direct either generally or in particular cases or classes of cases. Regulation 55 provides, so far as relevant to be here stated:

'55(1) Save as the Commissioners may otherwise allow or direct either generally or in particular cases or classes of cases, a person claiming deduction of input tax under section 3(2) of the Act shall do so on the return furnished by him for the prescribed accounting period in which the tax became chargeable and, before so doing, shall if the claim is in respect of –

(a) a supply from another registered person, hold the document which is required to be provided under regulation 8. . . .

Such Regulation 8(1) provides that save as otherwise provided in those Regulations, or as the Commissioners may otherwise allow, a registered taxable person making a taxable supply to a taxable person shall provide him with a tax invoice. The particulars required in a tax invoice are contained in Regulation 9, but the stringency of those is controlled by Regulation 10 which provides:

10(1) Subject to paragraph (2) of this regulation, a registered taxable person who is a retailer shall not be required to provide a tax invoice, except that he shall provide such an invoice at the request of a customer who is a taxable person in respect of any supply to him: but in that event, if, but only if, the value of the supply, including tax, does not exceed £50, the tax invoice need contain only the following particulars: –

(a) the name, address and registration number of the retailer;
(b) the date of the supply;

---

[29] A comparable rule is provided in Value Added Tax Act 1994, ch. 23 (United Kingdom) [hereinafter VATA 1994], §24(1). [Added by authors].

(c) a description sufficient to identify the goods or services supplied;

(d) the total amount payable including tax; and

(e) the rate of tax in force at the time of the supply.

(2) [which is not relevant to this appeal].

The modified form of tax invoice specified in Regulation 10 may be demanded by the taxable recipient of a supply from a retailer and, in my judgment, upon the true construction of Regulation 55 he must demand such modified tax invoice if he is to comply with Regulations 55 and 8(1). The Appellant Company did not obtain any such tax invoices from its petrol suppliers and Mr Lindley now submits that such evidence was not required by law. I do not agree with this submission for the reasons hereinbefore stated. It must be a matter of common – if not judicial – knowledge that petrol stations automatically issue modified tax invoices on any sales of petrol and in the event that they do not do so Regulation 10 enables a customer to demand such an invoice.

The only alleviation of the strict requirements of Regulations 55 and 8(1) seems to me to lie in the discretion of the Commissioners otherwise to allow or direct contained in the opening words of Regulation 55(1). I think that this is the submission which is inherently put forward in the argument of Mr Lindley. He says that in 1981 the Appellant Company was in precisely the same position of being assessed in respect of unvouched supplies of petrol and that the Commissioners then reduced that assessment by allowing input tax deduction of some £49 per quarter. He says that upon that precedent the Commissioners ought now to exercise a similar discretion in respect of an even greater sum of input tax than the sum of £45 per quarter which the Appellant Company claimed to deduct in its returns. In reply to this submission Mr CJM Peters, representing the Commissioners, referred the tribunal to a letter dated 5th May 1981 addressed to Mr Lindley on the occasion of the reduction of that assessment. Such letter states:

> As a result of a review of the circumstances regarding the assessment for £442.41 notified on 26th January 1981 the Commissioners of Customs and Excise now reduce it to £63.00.
>
> However I should like to point out that future claims of input tax may not be allowed unless some supporting evidence is provided e.g. a tax invoice. In relation to this matter I would like to draw your attention specifically to the paragraph entitled "Evidence required to support claims to input tax" on page 7 of VAT News. No 13 and also Para 32 and Section IV of Public Notice No 700.
>
> I enclose copies of the relevant notices for your purposes.

On production of this letter Mr Lindley drew the attention of the tribunal to the use of the word 'may' in the second paragraph thereof and said that in order to justify the instant assessment it should have read 'will'. That submission, in my judgment, does not require any comment from me. I regard it as a fair warning which could readily have been complied with by the requirement by the Appellant Company of a modified tax invoice from its petrol suppliers. It did not see fit so to require. I am unable to find, having regard to the warning contained in their letter dated 5th May 1981, that the Commissioners improperly exercised their discretion not to allow any evidence other than that required by [the Regulations].

DISPOSITION. Appeal dismissed.

4. Credit Denied on Purchases for Exempt and Other Nontaxable Transactions

Some acquisitions are treated as personal consumption or represent such an inseparable aggregate of personal and business use that they are treated as nonbusiness and therefore, in order to reduce the opportunities for tax abuse, VAT on those acquisitions is not creditable. In some countries, registered persons are categorically denied credit for input VAT on these acquisitions, whether or not the registered person can show that they were used partially or exclusively in making taxable supplies. Most commonly, especially in developing countries, these disallowance rules apply to passenger vehicles, entertainment expenses, and membership in country clubs and comparable facilities.[30] Canada denies 20 percent of the input credit on purchases of food, beverages, and entertainment, consistent with the 20 percent disallowance rule under the income tax for the cost of these items.[31] A registrant also may be denied any credit for tax on purchases of passenger vehicles or on purchases of certain travel and entertainment expenses.

In the EU, the Sixth Directive requires member states to deny deduction for input VAT on an "expenditure which is not strictly [a] business expenditure, such as that on luxuries, amusements or entertainment."[32] In the EU, a business that acquires an asset for use in taxable and other transactions can claim credit for tax on the proportion of the item used in taxable transactions.[33] For administrative reasons, credit for input VAT may be denied when

---

[30] See, for example, Value-Added Tax Act No. 89 of 1991, §17(2) (South Africa). South Africa proposed the removal from the disallowance rules vehicles used for certain game viewing. If enacted, VAT on game viewing vehicles designed or converted for the transport of seven or more passengers in game parks and similar areas would be deductible if the vehicles are used by registered persons in connection with making taxable supplies. Botes, "Game Viewing," *VAT Monitor*, Nov/Dec 2004, p. 456. See Value Added Tax Act, 2000, Act No. 1 of 2001, §20(2) (Botswana); and New Vatopia VAT, Appendix B, §28.

[31] Canadian GST, *supra* note 13, at §236. This 20 percent is recaptured by adding this amount to the registrant's net tax. *Id.*

[32] Sixth Directive, *supra* note 2, at Art. 17(6).

[33] VAT on the portion of a house purchased by a husband and wife and used in part to conduct economic activity is eligible for the input tax deduction in the EU if that portion of the home is allocated to the assets of the business. *Finanzamt Bergisch Gladbach v. Hans V. Hundt-Ewein*, Case C-25/03, [2005] ECR I-3123 (Judgment of the ECJ).

most of the use is unrelated to the making of taxable supplies. Other VATs deny any credit for input VAT unless the acquired asset is used principally in making taxable supplies.[34] In New Zealand, input tax on a purchase is creditable only if the tax is on "goods and services acquired for the principal purpose of making taxable supplies."[35] Thus, if an asset is devoted principally to personal use, no input credit is allowable, even if the asset may be used, for example, 20 percent in connection with taxable supplies. Some VATs deny credit for input VAT attributable to an asset used 90 percent or more for other than taxable supplies. In the EU, this denial requires a derogation granted by the European Commission. For example, Germany was authorized to deny deduction for input VAT on goods or services if they are used more than 90 percent for non-business purposes.[36]

Input credits are allowable for tax on purchases used in connection with the taxpayer's taxable activities. In fact, as discussed later, input VAT may be denied even if the acquisition is used in making taxable supplies (for automobiles) or when the acquisition is transferred as a business gift.[37] VAT statutes generally deny credits for tax on purchases used in making exempt supplies. In a departure from these general principles, Norway grants refunds outside the VAT system for some input VAT attributable to VAT-exempt activities of nonprofit organizations.[38]

Illustrated in the following two cases, purchases that may advance the taxpayer's personal rather than business interests are particularly suspect. In *Ian Flockton*, the issue was whether the purchase was in fact used in the taxpayer's business. *Edmond Michael Alexander* involves expenses that may contain both personal and business elements.

---

[34] The New Zealand GST relies on a principle purpose test; that is a credit is available only for tax on goods and services "acquired for the principal purpose of making taxable supplies." NZ GST, *supra* note 27, at §3A(1)(a). In *Wairakei Court Ltd v. Commissioner of Inland Revenue*, 19 NZTC 15, 202, at 15, 206 (High Ct. N.Z. 1999), the court attempted to define the elements of this test. In determining the principal purpose, it is "necessary to consider both subjective and objective indicators . . . [and] make an overall evaluation of all relevant purposes. While the evaluation needs to be made on the basis that the principal purpose is to be ascertained at the time the goods and services were acquired, this does not mean purposes which will not be fulfilled until some time in the future should be automatically ruled out. In some cases it may be possible to achieve the principal purpose within the taxation period under consideration while in other cases achievement of the principal purpose may be place at a later time." *Id.*

[35] NZ GST, *supra* note 27, at §2(1) definition of input tax.

[36] See COM (2004) 579 final of September 2, 2004, reported in *VAT Monitor*, Nov./Dec. 2004, p. 442. Austria also was authorized to deny input VAT on goods and services used more than 90 percent for nonbusiness purposes. Gurtner, "Austria: Deduction of input VAT," *VAT Monitor*, Jan./Feb. 2005, p. 39.

[37] For example, Belgium denies a deduction for input VAT on business gifts with a VAT-exclusive value exceeding 50 Euros. See Wille, Belgium: *Low-value business gifts*, VAT Monitor, Jan./Feb. 2003, p. 22.

[38] The VAT base was expanded. The refund is available for VAT on services previously exempt from VAT. See Gjems-Onstad, "Refund of Input VAT to Norweigan NPOs," *VAT Monitor*," July/Aug. 2004, p. 244.

Ian Flockton Developments Ltd v. Commissioners of Customs and Excise[39]

HEADNOTE. The taxpayer company was a manufacturing company of plastic mouldings and storage tanks and was registered for value added tax. The taxpayer company's customers were project engineers in chemical factories. The taxpayer company's orders were not sought by advertising but by personal contact and recommendation. At the material time the taxpayer company was anxious to find new customers and conceived the idea that the purchase and running of a racehorse would in some way advance the taxpayer company's business. The question arose whether for the purpose of value added tax the expenses relating to the purchase and upkeep of the racehorse were incurred wholly for the purposes of the business carried on by the taxpayer company. [The tribunal disallowed the input tax credits and the taxpayer appealed.]

Held – (1) The test to be applied in determining whether goods or services which were supplied to the taxpayer were used or to be used for the purpose of any business carried on by him was a subjective test. That meant that the fact-finding tribunal had to consider what was in the taxpayer's mind, and where the taxpayer was a company what was in the minds of the persons who controlled the company, at the relevant time in order to discover their object.

(2) Where there was no obvious and clear association between the taxpayer company's business and the expenditure concerned, the tribunal should approach any assertion that it was for the taxpayer company's business with circumspection and care and should bear in mind that it was for the taxpayer company to establish its case. It was both permissible and essential to test such evidence against the standards and thinking of the ordinary businessman in the position of the taxpayer company and, if the tribunal considered that no ordinary businessman would have incurred such expenditure for business purposes, that might be grounds for rejecting the taxpayer company's evidence. However, that should not be substituted as the test but only treated as a guide or factor to be taken into account when considering the credibility of the witness.

(3) The tribunal had found as a fact that the taxpayer company's object was to use the racehorse for the purposes of its business and accordingly the expenditure in question was incurred for the supplies of goods and services used or to be used for the purposes of its business.

DISPOSITION. Appeal allowed with costs.

---

[39] [1987] STC 394 (Q.B. 1987) (United Kingdom). [Edited by the authors.]

Edmond Michael Alexander v. The Commissioners of Customs and Excise[40]

Shortly after...registration Mr Alexander submitted to the Commissioners...a claim for relief in respect of tax which he alleged he had paid on 'clothes and ancillary items' required for his practice at the Bar. Subsequently on production of invoices the Commissioners conceded that Mr Alexander could deduct as input tax the amounts of tax charged to him on some items (including a gown, four collars, two bands and two shirts purchased from William Northam) and Mr Alexander withdrew his claim in respect of other items (including a wig purchased from another member of the Bar not registered as a taxable person). The foregoing leaves some 17 items still in dispute for us to consider on this appeal.

In evidence Mr Alexander stated that, as a manager before he entered Chambers as a pupil, he always wore a two-piece light coloured suit, that is to say, a jacket and trousers without a waistcoat. But it is a requirement of the Bar Council, the body which lays down the rule of etiquette which have to be observed by practising barristers, that members of the Bar appearing in court must wear a suit of a dark colour with a waistcoat. Accordingly, in order to meet such requirement he purchased...a dark navy-blue three-piece suit and...a black three-piece suit, for wearing in court. And, in order to wear such suits he bought the braces....Next, it is also a requirement of the Bar Council that male members of the Bar in court should wear white shirts, butterfly collars and bands, necessitating the wearing of shirts with detachable collars. Accordingly, in order to meet such requirements he purchased...a white tunic shirt without a collar,...one dozen stiff white naval collars,...two more white tunic shirts without collars, and...front and back studs. Then, it was another such requirement that shoes worn by members of the Bar in court should be black. Previously, Mr Alexander stated, he had only worn brown shoes and so, in order to meet this requirement, he purchased two pairs of black shoes,...dark socks to wear with such shoes, [and] a suitcase which he had bought for the purpose of transporting his wig, gown, collars, bands, briefs and books to and from court in the course of his practice. Finally,...[he purchased] stationery, such as a folder, writing cards, book pads and ruled pads for use in Chambers and in court.

The provisions of the Act relating to input tax...permits the deduction as input tax of 'tax on the supply to a taxable person of any goods or services for the purpose of a business carried on or to be carried on by him'. This is of no assistance to Mr Alexander as he was not a taxable person at the time when the foregoing supplies of goods were made

---

[40] [1976] VATTR 107 (London 1976) (United Kingdom). [Edited by the authors.]

to him. [Under the Regulations, if a taxable person, after registration, claims deductions for tax paid on purchases made before registration], supported by such evidence as the Commissioners may require, they may authorise him to deduct, as if it were input tax, tax on the supply of goods to him before that date . . . for the purpose of a business which either was carried on or was to be carried on by him at the time of such supply.

In the present case Mr Alexander submitted his claim on the requisite form.

At the time of the supplies Mr Alexander was not a taxable person and, as a result, was not entitled to require a supplier to give him a tax invoice for a supply. We consider that the till receipts and the oral evidence of Mr Alexander sufficiently establish to our satisfaction that he obtained such supplies . . . , and that all the suppliers, other than the Government Bookshop, were taxable persons.

So the foregoing involves two questions, first, whether the . . . items were supplies 'for the purposes of' Mr Alexander's profession as a barrister and, secondly, whether at the time they were supplied, such profession was then to be carried on by him'. On this second point Mr Alexander in his addresses to the tribunal assumed that, as the items were supplied after he had formed an intention to practise at the Bar and were so supplied either shortly before starting, or during, his pupillage, they must all have been supplied at a time when such profession was 'to be carried on by him'. No argument to the contrary was advanced by Miss Bolt and accordingly we assume that the Commissioners accept that, in this case, the supplies were obtained by Mr Alexander at a time when the profession was 'to be carried on by him'.

On this appeal, in relation to the words in . . . the General Regulations, 'for the purpose of a business' Mr Alexander submitted that his claim should be allowed because the items supplied were necessary for the purposes of his intended profession. It was, he argued, necessary for him to buy the suits and other clothing and the shoes in order to practice at the Bar and appear in court properly dressed, and it was necessary for him to buy the suitcase for travelling to and from court. Miss Bolt contended that the test to be applied . . . [is] whether the clothing was of a specialised nature bought specifically for the purposes of the business, trade or profession. She argued that this covered such clothing as protective or working overalls for a doctor or surgeon and a wig and gown for a barrister, but not clothing of the type supplied to Mr Alexander in this case.

[The] test to apply is whether or not the . . . items were obtained by Mr Alexander for the purpose of enabling him to carry on his intended profession. This suggests to us that the test is a subjective one. Miss Bolt in this regard submitted that the proper test should be an objective, and not a subjective one. On this point we consider that the proper test should be a subjective one unless there is some provision of the Act or the General Regulations which provides or indicates to the contrary. In our view the use of the word 'purpose', in an Act of Parliament prima facie requires the application of a subjective test.

A supply may, of course, be obtained for more than one purpose or reason.... Thus, in the present ease it could perhaps be argued that a main reason for Mr Alexander purchasing the clothing items was to clothe himself decently, and his intention to practise at the Bar only affected the type of suits, shirts and other clothing which he bought. On this aspect we consider that, to come within the foregoing statutory provisions, the purpose of the business must be a main purpose, but not necessarily the only purpose, of obtaining the supply. If Parliament had intended to limit the provisions to supplies exclusively for the purpose of the business, it would have so provided expressly or by necessary implication.

Having regard to the foregoing we consider that, on this appeal, we must consider... whether or not his main purpose, or one of his main purposes, in so doing was to enable him to carry on his intended profession as a barrister.... In the light thereof we are satisfied that, in relation to... three shirts, one dozen collars, one dark suit, a book pad and a ruled pad, Mr Alexander purchased the same for the purpose of his intended profession and that such purpose was his main purpose in obtaining such supplies.... But we are not satisfied in relation to the remaining ten items.

This appeal is accordingly allowed as to part and dismissed as to part.

DISPOSITION. Appeal allowed in part.

Until the EU establishes uniform rules, the EU member states must maintain their domestic rules disallowing input credits that were in effect when the Sixth Directive became effective.[41] Based on these rules, according to the ECJ, France violated its obligations under the input tax deduction rules by totally denying deduction for input VAT on diesel fuel used in vehicles that were denied input VAT deduction on acquisition.[42] France also denied input credits on hotel and restaurant expenses, entertainment and housing expenses, and taxpayers continued to challenge France's authority to expand these disallowance rules.[43] The French reason for the disallowance

---

[41] Sixth Directive, *supra* note 2, at art. 17(6).

[42] *Commission of the European Communities v French Republic*, Case C-40/00, [2001] ECR I-4539 (ECJ Judgment).

[43] See Not & Pichard, "Three French Tax Courts Ask ECJ to Rule on Deduction of VAT Invoiced on Hotel and Restaurant Expenses," 20 *Tax Notes Intl.* 584 (Feb. 7, 2000).

was that these expenses benefitted individual recipients rather than the business. Domestic French courts drew a distinction between housing expenses and hotel bills that were never eligible for the input VAT deduction, and entertainment and restaurant expenses that might have been deductible if incurred in furtherance of business, with the latter deductible even in light of the ECJ decisions.[44]

The following British case involves input credits relating to the cost of an accounting firm's dinner dance.

KPMG Peat Marwick McLintock v The Commissioners of Customs and Excise[45]

KPMG Peat Marwick McLintock (hereinafter called 'the Appellants') carry on business as accountants. [The] Appellants had claimed input tax in respect of a business entertainment held annually in the New Year for members of their staff. The Commissioners decided that the claim for input tax in respect of these business entertainments should be disallowed.

[Although a taxable person may deduct input tax on "goods or services used or to be used for the purpose of any business carried on or to be carried on by him; . . ."[46] input tax on such expenditures generally is not deductible if it is attributable to business entertainment.]

Paragraph 2 of the 1981 Special Provisions Order [SI 1981 No. 1741] defines "business entertainment" as follows:

> In this Order – 'business entertainment' means entertainment (including hospitality of any kind) provided by a taxable person in connection with a business carried on by him, but does not include the provision of anything for persons employed by the taxable person unless its provision for them is incidental to its provision for others.

The question at issue in this appeal has centred around the presence at the annual firm's dinner dance of not only employees (who by common consent come within the term 'persons employed by the taxable person') in respect of whom the expenditure on the provision of goods or services would normally be an allowable input tax deduction, but also their spouses or partners who are not partnership employees and who, it is argued, by their presence at the dinner dance, are receiving hospitality from the firm and thereby constitute the function 'business entertainment' resulting in no deduction of input tax.

---

[44] See Moisand, VAT Recoverable on Entertainment Expenses, Restaurant Bills, French Court Says, 2002 WTD 112–4 (Tax Analysts June 11,2002), citing *CAA Paris*, 14 Feb. 2002, 97-2492, and *Conseil d'Etat*, 27 May 2002, 229133.

[45] [1993] VATTR 118 (United Kingdom). [Edited by the authors.]

[46] A comparable rule is provided under VATA 1994, *supra* note 29, at §24(1). [Added by authors.]

The Appellants are a firm of accountants providing a whole range of financial services to its clients. Because of the very nature of the business this often means that staff have to work unsociable hours and the success of the firm depends upon the commitment of the staff. In return for dedicated commitment the firm feels that it should show its appreciation by organising an annual staff dinner dance. The purpose of this event is to thank employees in a tangible way for their hard work throughout the year and to foster in them a feeling of belonging to an organisation as a whole. Many of the individual members of the firm have to work away from the office in outlying districts auditing company accounts and so forth. The purpose of the dinner dance is to bring them all under one roof once a year for social purposes and to encourage as many employees as possible to attend. Invitations are sent out only to employees but each one is given the opportunity of bringing a guest of his or her choosing – in many cases this will be the employee's spouse.

[The Appellants claimed that it] was a purpose of their business to care for their own staff, to encourage a good morale and to reward hard work and commitment. Thus, any expenditure laid out to achieve that purpose by means of the provision of hospitality was for the purpose of business. The provision here of goods and services (hospitality) was not for commercial or business reasons and was not provided to business customers or clients or other non-employees. It was provided to the staff or . . . to "persons employed by the taxable person". In practice, of course, there may be occasions when hospitality is provided by a trader for customers or clients and upon which the trader's own employees are also present. In one sense the hospitality is provided to both employees and non-employees. The legislation involves a predominance test, as Counsel for the Appellants submitted. What was the paramount purpose of the entertainment or hospitality? If the paramount purpose is business entertainment then it matters not how the numbers are made up at the function. Even if "person employed" greatly outnumber customers or clients, input tax deduction is not allowed. Conversely, if the paramount purpose is provision for "persons employed" by the taxable person it matters not that there are others who are not employed, input tax is deductible.

In the instant case the Tribunal has found as a fact that the use to which the Appellants put the goods or services which they provided was for the entertainment of their employees; that was not a use for the purpose of business entertainment as defined in the section.The presence of wives, husbands, partners or guests of employees at the dinner dance appears to the Tribunal to be purely incidental and wholly ancillary to the main purpose of the function – to have employees present with their permitted guests so that their participation in the entertainment provided might be directly facilitated. . . .

For the foregoing reasons the Tribunal allows the appeal and holds that entertainment provided was not "business entertainment." The input tax in dispute is therefore deductible.

There are several methods used to allocate input VAT between taxable and other activities. The EU rules on the allocation of allowable input VAT on taxable supplies go beyond a formulary allocation based on taxable to total supplies. For example in appropriate cases, taxpayers may allocate input VAT on the basis of the amount of floor space used in making taxable supplies.

Canada has elaborate rules that not only limit credits on individual purchases to the percentage of the asset used in commercial (taxable) activities. Canada disallows a portion or the entire credit on purchases that may contain business and personal consumption elements.[47] Tax credits are also limited on vehicles and aircraft, on club memberships, and on certain food or entertainment.[48] In a case favorable to the taxpayer, a passenger ferry was exempt on transport charges and taxable on sales of food and other items on board the ferry. The court held that the taxpayer's method of allocating input VAT on the basis of the square footage of the vessel used by passengers to access taxable items (25 percent) rather than on the percentage of taxable to total supplies (1.2 percent) was fair and reasonable, even if another method may have provided a better result.[49]

Japan has less complicated rules to allocate credits between taxable and other activities. It allows registered businesses making taxable and other sales to calculate creditable input tax under the itemized or proportional method.[50]

Under the itemized method, the business must segregate its taxable purchases into three groups: purchases directly attributable to taxable sales, purchases directly attributable to exempt sales, and purchases attributable both to taxable and exempt sales. The deductible input tax equals the sum of (1) the tax on purchases directly attributable to taxable sales, and (2) the tax on purchases attributable both to taxable and exempt sales multiplied by a fraction, the numerator of which is *taxable* sales for the period and the denominator of which is *total* sales for such period. For example, assume that a business in a taxable period has taxable sales of 100 million yen (assuming 100 : I exchange rate – US$1 million) and exempt sales of 25 million yen ($250,000). The business has tax on purchases directly attributable to taxable sales of two million yen ($20,000), and tax on purchases attributable both to taxable and exempt sales of one million yen ($10,000). Under the itemized method, the seller is entitled to an input tax deduction of 2.8 million yen ($28,000), computed as follows:

---

[47] See, generally, Canadian GST, *supra* note 13, at §169.

[48] See, for example, *id.* at §§170(1), and 202(2) and (4). For leases of certain vehicles or purchases of food, beverages, or entertainment, the registered person may be required to make year-end adjustments to recapture a portion of the claimed credits. *Id.* at §§235 and 236.

[49] *Bay Ferries Ltd. v. The Queen*, 2004 TCC 663 (Tax Ct. Canada). The court in this case supported the use of alternative methods such as square footage over the percentage of taxable to total supplies. See *id.* at ¶55.

[50] Japan – National Consumption Tax Law: An English Translation (1989) [hereinafter Japan CT Law], Art. 30(2).

Input tax directly attributable to taxable sales	2.0 million

Input tax attributable both to
  taxable and tax-exempt sales
  one million of purchases × taxable
  sales/total sales = 1,000,000 × 100/125 =
	.8 million

Total deductible input tax	2.8 million

Instead of the above allocation formula based on the ratio of taxable sales to total sales (one million × 100/125), a business using the itemized method can allocate the total one million yen of input tax not directly attributable to taxable sales on the basis of a predetermined percentage. This percentage, to be approved by the head of the local tax office before the end of the tax period in which it is to be used, can be based on the number of employees, floor space, and similar factors.[51]

The CT proportional method of computing deductible input tax is based on input tax deemed paid on allowable purchases multiplied by a fraction, the numerator of which is taxable sales for the period and the denominator of which is total sales for such period.[52] Using the above example, the deductible input tax calculated under the proportional method is $2.4 million yen (US$24,000), computed as follows:

Input tax on allowable purchases × taxable sales/total sales
Three million ×100 million/125 million, or 2.4 million yen.[53]

B. Impact of Subsidies on Allowable Input Credits

When a registered person making taxable and other supplies receives a subsidy, what is the effect of the subsidy on the calculation of allowable credits for input VAT? If the subsidy is directly linked to supplies, it may be treated as part of the taxable amount or consideration for the supply.[54] If not, it may be included in the allocation formula that determines the creditable portion of input VAT attributable to taxable supplies.[55] The initial problem in

---

[51] Ishimura introduction to *id.* at *xx*.

[52] *Id.* at Art. 30(2).

[53] Schenk, "Japanese Consumption Tax After Six Years: A Unique VAT Matures," 69 *Tax Notes* 899, 906–907 (Nov. 13, 1995) [hereinafter Schenk, Japanese CT].

[54] See Sixth Directive, *supra* note 2, at Arts. 11A(1)(a) and 26b(B)(3).

[55] According to the ECJ, for a subsidy to be included as part of the taxable amount of a supply, it must be paid "specifically to the subsidized body to enable it to provide particular goods or services." Arias and Barba, "The Impact of Subsidies on the Right to Deduct Input VAT: The Spanish Experience," *VAT Monitor*, Jan./Feb. 2004, p. 13, 15 [hereinafter Spanish Experience with Subsidies], discussing the judgment in *ASBL Office des Produits Wallons v. Belgium State*, Case C-184/00, [2001] ECR I-9155. The authors suggest that four categories of payments in the nature of subsidies should not be treated as subsidies for VAT purposes. They are:

1. "Subsidies granted in exchange of taxable supplies . . . (w)hen a contractual relationship exists between a subsidy grantor and the taxable entity receiving it, that amount is the consideration for the taxable supply, even where it is paid under the heading of a subsidy." (footnotes omitted)

2. "What are know as 'private subsidies', i.e. grants by private enitities, even where such grants are conditional . . ."

the EU is that the term "subsidy" is not defined in the Sixth Directive. An Advocate General defined a subsidy in her Opinion as "a sum paid from public funds, usually in the general interest."[56] The European Commission challenged Spain's practice of limiting deductions for input VAT, even when the subsidy was not linked to the price of supplies.[57]

The Sixth Directive gives member states the option to include subsidies in the denominator of the fraction used to calculate allowable deductions for input VAT for registered persons making taxable and exempt supplies.[58] The European Commission disagrees with France's practice of restricting input VAT on acquisitions of capital goods financed in part with subsidies.[59]

C. Pre-opening Expenses and Posteconomic Activity

A general VAT principle is that a registered person making taxable supplies is entitled to claim credit for input VAT on acquisitions used in making those taxable supplies. Consistent with that principle, a registered person entering business should be entitled to claim credit for input VAT on acquisitions used in connection with economic activity that directly relates to taxable supplies to be made in the future. Thus, tax on store fixtures, electrical services, painting, and other purchases made before a retail store opens for business should be creditable if the sales to be made in the future are taxable. The opportunity for abuse in this area prompts many countries to restrict or impose conditions on the credit for input VAT attributable to acquisitions before the acquiring person starts making taxable supplies. A person may claim refunds for input VAT on purchases during the start-up phase of a business, and the person may never open its doors or make taxable sales. On the other hand, if input VAT during the preopeninig phase is not eligible for credit, the VAT will

3. "Payments made as compensation, to indemnify the taxable entity for a loss..." (such as a subsidy to discontinue milk production).
4. "Budget transfers between public institutions... without the obligation to do something in return and are not subject to conditions, for example, subsidies granted to cover the operating deficits..." (*Id.* at 14.)

[56] *Keeping Newcastle Warm Ltd v Commissioners of Customs & Excise*, Case C-353/00 [2002] ECR I-5419, Opinion of February 5, 2002, cited in Spanish Experience with Subsidies, *supra* note 55, at 13. In the Judgment of June 13, 2002, the ECJ held that the sum paid by the public authority to an economic operator such as Keeping Newcastle Warm (KNW) in connection with energy advice supplied by KNW to certain households was consideration for services supplied and therefore was part of the taxable amount of the supply of services. See Case C-204/03, *Commission of the European Communities v. Kingdom of Spain*, [2005] ECR I-8389 (Judgment of the ECJ 2005), the court ruled that limiting the input tax deduction on the purchase of goods and services used to conduct only taxable transactions when those acquisitions were subsidized by the government violates Articles 17(2) and (5) and 19 of Sixth Directive. In that case, the supplier received capital subsidies but made only taxable supplies.

[57] In New Zealand, a grant or subsidy by a public authority to a registered peson is part of the consideration for a supply to the public authority. See Pallot & White, "New Zealand: Public authorities," *VAT Monitor*, May/June 2004, p. 208.

[58] See Sixth Directive, *supra* note 2, at Art. 19(1).

[59] See *VAT Monitor*, Jan./Feb. 2003, p. 45, citing IP/03/57 of January 16, 2003.

not be economically neutral, and new businesses will be at a competitive disadvantage, and will bear VAT on these costs.

A similar issue arises for persons who purchase goods and services in anticipation of registering for VAT purposes. Should this person be entitled to claim credits for input VAT paid before registering and engaging in taxable activities?

The EU attempted to balance these concerns in favor of granting deductions for input VAT on preopening costs. In *Rompelman*,[60] the ECJ treated the registered person as being engaged in business when the person acquired a right to a portion of a building to be constructed and leased. To avoid abuse, the court acknowledged the tax administration's right to demand proof that the property was suitable for commercial rental.

In the *Inzo* case,[61] the ECJ went further. In that case, a company organized to turn sea water into drinking water commissioned a feasibility study, and conducted other preliminary activities, incurred input VAT on purchases attributable to this phase of its operations, and later decided to abandon the project and liquidate before ever making taxable supplies. The ECJ held that once the tax authority accepted that the company intended to engage in economic activity and registered the person, except for cases of fraud or abuse, the authority could not retroactively remove that status and deny credits for input VAT, even if the company did not proceed from the study phase to the operational phase making taxable supplies. Consistently, where a company that made improvements to land in preparation for making taxable supplies and the city then forced the company to exchange that improved land for other land so that the intended supplies were never made, the company was entitled to claim credit for input VAT on those improvements to the transferred property.[62] In fact, although EU member states can impose reasonable conditions to prevent fraud or abuse, they cannot establish a blanket denial of input VAT until a registered person commences economic or business activities.[63] The *Gabalfrisa* case[64] involved input VAT paid by entrepreneurs and professional practitioners before they started making taxable supplies. The Spanish VAT allowed this input VAT as a credit only when the individuals commenced those taxable activities. Under the Spanish VAT, the input VAT was creditable before the entrepreneurs or professional practitioners commenced taxable activities only for purchases other than land and then only if

---

[60] *Rompelman v Minister van Financin*, Case C-268/83, [1985] ECR 655, discussed at Ch. 4(III)(A).

[61] *Intercommunale voor zeewaterontzilting (INZO) v Belgium State*, Case C-110/94, [1996] ECR I-857 (ECJ 1996).

[62] *Belgium v Ghent Coal Terminal NV*, Case C-37/95, [1998] All ER 223 (Judgment of ECJ 1998).

[63] See Serrano, "VAT Deduction in Spain: The ECJ against the Spanish Regime for Deduction of Input VAT Related to Transactions Prior to Carrying Out an Economic Activity," *VAT Monitor*, July/Aug. 2000, p. 157, discussing *Gabalfrisa SL and Others v Agencia Estatel de Administracin Tributaria*, joined cases C-110/98 to C-147/98, [2000] ECR I-01577 [hereinafter *Gabalfrisa*].

[64] *Gabalfrisa, supra* note 63.

they met certain requirements. The conditions included the submission of a declaration of intent to commence business or professional activities before the input tax on purchases to be claimed as credit becomes due. The ECJ held that the Spanish legislation could not so restrict the right to deduct input VAT under Article 17 of the Sixth Directive.

Singapore has a procedure for an unregistered person who purchases taxable goods and services before registering and engaging in taxable activities. The Inland Revenue Authority of Singapore (IRAS) provides a checklist in a downloadable form[65] for a person to determine whether he is eligible for a preregistration input tax claim that can be made in the person's first GST return. To qualify, goods or services must have been purchased to make taxable supplies and must not be consumed or be related to goods consumed before the effective date of registration. For services, they must have been acquired not more than six months before registration and must not have been used in connection with services to customers before registration. Records must be maintained.

There are issues at the other end of the life of a business. Can a registered person claim deduction for input VAT paid after the person ceases to make taxable supplies? For example, are deductions available if a person ceases to conduct a restaurant business but is obliged to pay rent on the restaurant premises after the business closes, as required under a non-termination clause in the lease? The ECJ held that the input VAT was deductible until the lease expired.[66] The deductions would not be available if the leased property were converted to a private purpose.

D. DE MINIMIS RULE

To simplify the calculation of allowable input tax credits, Japan has a *de minimis* rule. If the taxable sales of a business account for 95 percent or more of its total sales, the business can claim credit for tax on purchases attributable to all sales.[67]

E. TRANSACTIONS INVOLVING SHARES AND DEBT

In EU countries, there has been litigation involving input tax attributable to transactions in stock. The *KapHag* case involved the admission of a partner to

---

[65] The form is entitled "Pre-Registration Input Tax: Checklist for Self-review of Eligibility of Claim."

[66] Case C-32/03, *I/S Fini H v Skatteministeriet (Danish Ministry of Taxation)*, [2005] ECR I-1599. The ECJ ruled that "a person who has ceased an economic activity but who, because the lease contains a non-termination clause, continues to pay the rent and charges on the premises used for that activity is to be regarded as a taxable person within the meaning of that article and is entitled to deduct the VAT on the amounts thus paid, provided that there is a direct and immediate link between the payments made and the commercial activity and that the absence of any fraudulent or abusive intent has been established." *Id*. at ruling.

[67] Japan CT Law, *supra* note 50, at Art. 30(2). A similar rule is included in New Vatopia VAT, Appendix B, §28(4).

a partnership for a cash contribution. The partnership paid VAT on an invoice for legal services related to the formation of the partnership and deducted the input VAT. If the admission of the partnership were a supply of services, it would have been an exempt transaction.[68] The ECJ held that the entry of a new partner into a partnership for cash is not an economic activity within the Sixth Directive and does not constitute a supply of services; the input VAT was not disallowed.[69]

The ECJ continues to consider cases involving input tax attributable to the issuance of ownership interests. The following *Kretztechnik* case is significant.

Kretztechnik AG v. Finanzamt Linz[70]

The questions were raised in proceedings between Kretztechnik AG (Kretztechnik) and the Finanzamt Linz (Linz District Tax Office) concerning the latter's refusal to allow that company to deduct value added tax (VAT) paid by it on supplies relating to the issue of shares for the purposes of its admission to the Frankfurt Stock Exchange (Germany).

Article 13B(d)(5) of the Sixth Directive provides that the Member States are to exempt from VAT transactions, including negotiation, excluding management and safekeeping, in shares, interests in companies or associations, debentures and other securities....
Article 17(2) of the Sixth Directive provides:

In so far as the goods and services are used for the purposes of his taxable transactions, the taxable person shall be entitled to deduct from the tax which he is liable to pay:

(a) VAT due or paid in respect of goods or services supplied or to be supplied to him by another taxable person;...

The Sixth Directive was transposed into Austrian domestic law....
Kretztechnik is a company limited by shares established in Austria whose objects are the development and distribution of medical equipment. By resolution of its general meeting of shareholders of 18 January 2000, its capital was increased from EUR 10 million to EUR 12.5 million. With a view to raising the capital needed for that increase, it applied for admission to the Frankfurt Stock Exchange.

Kretztechnik was listed on that stock exchange in March 2000. Its capital was increased by the issue of bearer shares.

---

[68] Sixth Directive, *supra* note 2, at Art. 13B(d)(5) exempts transactions in shares, interests in companies or associations, debentures and other securities. As a result, the input VAT attributable to that transaction would not have been deductible.

[69] *KapHag Renditefonds 35 Spreecenter Berlin-Hellersdorf 3. Tranche GbR v Finanzamt Charlottenburg*, Case C-442/01, [2003] ECR I-06851 (Judgment of the ECJ).

[70] Case C-465/03. [2005] ECR I- 4357; [2005] ECJ CELEX LEXIS 187 (Judgment of the ECJ). [Edited by the authors.]

[The Finanzamt Linz claimed that issuing shares was exempt from VAT and therefore disallowed the input tax deduction for VAT paid by Kretztechnik on the supplies linked with its admission to the stock exchange.]

Kretztechnik challenged that tax assessment [and the court sought] ... a preliminary ruling from the Court of Justice. ...

THE FIRST QUESTION. [Kretztechnik claims that the issuance of new shares was to finance its business activities, not as a commercial activity of dealing in shares, and therefore] was not a supply for consideration within the meaning of Article 2(1) of the Sixth Directive. ...

[The Finanzamt Linz maintains that] ... the issue of shares by a taxable person in order to increase its capital with a view to carrying on its economic activity constitutes a taxable transaction within the meaning of Article 2(1) of the Sixth Directive.

It is settled caselaw that the mere acquisition and holding of shares is not to be regarded as an economic activity within the meaning of the Sixth Directive. ... If, therefore, the acquisition of financial holdings in other undertakings does not in itself constitute an economic activity within the meaning of that directive, the same must be true of activities consisting in the sale of such holdings. ...

On the other hand, transactions that consist in obtaining income on a continuing basis from activities which go beyond the compass of the simple acquisition and sale of securities, such as transactions carried out in the course of a business trading in securities, do fall within the scope of the Sixth Directive but are exempted from VAT under Article 13B(d)(5) of that directive. ...

[The VAT consequences do not depend on whether a company's issuance of shares occurs] ... in connection with its admission to a stock exchange or by a company not quoted on a stock exchange.

[U]nder Article 5(1) of the Sixth Directive, a supply of goods involves the transfer of the right to dispose of tangible property as owner. The issue of new shares – which are securities representing intangible property – cannot therefore be regarded as a supply of goods for consideration within the meaning of Article 2(1) of that directive.

The taxability of a share issue therefore depends on whether that transaction constitutes a supply of services for consideration within the meaning of Article 2(1) of the Sixth Directive.

In that connection the Court has already held that a partnership which admits a partner in consideration of payment of a contribution in cash does not effect to that partner a supply of services for consideration within the meaning of Article 2(1) of the Sixth Directive. ...

The same conclusion must be drawn regarding the issue of shares for the purpose of raising capital.

As the Advocate General rightly observes ... , a company that issues new shares is increasing its assets by acquiring additional capital, whilst granting the new shareholders a right of ownership of part of the capital thus increased. From the issuing company's point of view, the aim is to raise capital and not to provide services. As far as the shareholder is concerned, payment of the sums necessary for the increase of capital is not a payment of consideration but an investment or an employment of capital.

It follows that a share issue does not constitute a supply of goods or of services for consideration within the meaning of Article 2(1) of the Sixth Directive. Therefore, such a transaction, whether or not carried out in connection with admission of the company concerned to a stock exchange, does not fall within the scope of that directive.

The answer to the first question must therefore be that a new share issue does not constitute a transaction falling within the scope of Article 2(1) of the Sixth Directive.

THE THIRD QUESTION. [The third question is whether VAT on supplies attributable to a share issue is deductible under the Sixth Directive, Article 17(1) and (2).]

The Finanzamt Linz and the Austrian, Danish, German and Italian Governments maintain that, since a share issue associated with admission to a stock exchange does not constitute a taxable transaction within the meaning of Article 2(1) of the Sixth Directive, there is no right to deduct the VAT levied on the supplies acquired for consideration for the purposes of that share issue. In . . . the present case the inputs, which are subject to VAT, do not form an integral part of Kretztechnik's overall economic activity as a component of the price of the products that it markets. The expenses associated with those supplies are linked only to the admission of the company to a stock exchange and have no connection with its general business on which tax is paid.

Conversely, Kretztechnik, the United Kingdom Government and the Commission consider that, even if the inputs subject to VAT were connected not with specific taxable transactions but with expenses relating to the share issue, they could form part of the overheads of the company and constitute components of the price of the products marketed by it. In those circumstances, Kretztechnik has a right to deduct the input VAT on expenditure incurred in obtaining the supplies linked to the admission of that company to a stock exchange.

[A]ccording to settled case-law, the right of deduction provided for in Articles 17 to 20 of the Sixth Directive is an integral part of the VAT scheme and in principle may not be limited. . . .

It is clear . . . that, for VAT to be deductible, the input transactions must have a direct and immediate link with the output transactions giving rise to a right of deduction. Thus, the right to deduct VAT charged on the acquisition of input goods or services presupposes that the expenditure incurred in acquiring them was a component of the cost of the output transactions that gave rise to the right to deduct. . . .

> [The share issue was designed to increase capital for the benefit of its economic activity. VAT on the supplies associated with the share issuance is tax associated with its overhead and therefore constitutes] ... component parts of the price of its products. Those supplies have a direct and immediate link with the whole economic activity of the taxable person. ...
>
> It follows that, under Article 17(1) and (2) of the Sixth Directive, Kretztechnik is entitled to deduct all the VAT charged on the expenses incurred by that company for the various supplies which it acquired in the context of the share issue carried out by it, provided, however, that all the transactions carried out by that company in the context of its economic activity constitute taxed transactions.
>
> The answer to the third question must therefore be that Article 17(1) and (2) of the Sixth Directive confer the right to deduct in its entirety the VAT charged on the expenses incurred by a taxable person for the various supplies acquired by him in connection with a share issue, provided that all the transactions undertaken by the taxable person in the context of his economic activity constitute taxed transactions.

An earlier ECJ judgment in the *Polysar Investments* case[71] involved the claim of input VAT by a holding company whose only activities related to holding shares in subsidiary companies. The court held that the holding company was not a taxable person and therefore it could not claim input VATs unless it was involved directly or indirectly in the management of the subsidiaries.[72]

In the Netherlands, a company (the taxpayer) that held 50 percent of the stock in a subsidiary also rendered services to that subsidiary. When that company and the other 50 percent shareholder sold the subsidiary, a bank charged the taxpayer a fee plus VAT on services related to that sale and the company claimed a deduction for that input VAT. The Dutch Supreme Court held that holding and selling shares in another company is not economic activity within VAT unless the shareholder is a professional dealer in securities or the shares (in a subsidiary) are held in connection with the shareholder's direct or indirect involvement in the management of the subsidiary. In that case, the court found that there was a direct link between the bank's services and the overall business activities of the shareholder and therefore the input VAT was deductible in relation to the shareholder's taxable to total activities.[73]

---

[71] *Polysar Investments Netherlands BV v Inspecteur der Invverrechten en Accijnzen, Arnham,* Case C-60/90, [1991] ECR I-3111; [1993] STC 222.

[72] *Id.* at ¶19 of the Judgment.

[73] Case 38,253 (Hoge Road 14 March 2003)(Netherlands), discussed in *VAT Monitor,* May/June 2003, p. 266, and Bijl & Kerékgyárt, "Recovery of Input VAT Incurred on Costs Relating to the Sale of Shares," *VAT Monitor,* May/June 2003, p. 209.

For the purchaser of stock of a company engaged in commercial activities, Canada by statute allows the purchaser to claim credits for tax on services related to the stock acquisition.[74]

South Africa requires a direct link between a venture capital firm's services to find investors for a company's stock and the taxable business of the company issuing its stock. In one case, the Tax Court held that the connection was not close enough and denied the input VAT on the fee charged by the venture capital firm.[75]

F. Bad Debts

A seller who reports on the cash method generally reports sales as the sales price is collected.[76] If the purchaser defaults, no tax adjustment is necessary. Most VATs require most registered persons to report on the accrual or invoice method. Under those methods, the seller must report sales and remit VAT when the sale occurs or the invoice is issued, even if the VAT-inclusive price is paid later. "If the seller in a VAT regime serves as collection agent for the government (not the taxpayer that is to bear the VAT), and the buyer fails to pay the tax, the seller should recover the tax attributable to the bad debt."[77] Some countries follow this model and allow sellers to claim credit (or reduce output tax) for the tax attributable to the bad debt.[78] This rule provides some opportunity for tax abuse, especially if the tax administration is not equipped to verify the propriety of these claimed credits for bad debts. As a result, some countries (especially developing countries) in effect make the seller the guarantor of the buyer's payment of VAT on purchases – or force the seller to collect the tax on the sale up front – and deny any VAT adjustment for bad debts.[79]

---

[74] Canadian GST, *supra* note 13, at §186(2) and (3).

[75] Case No. VAT 91, 2002(6) JTLR 209(c), discussed in *VAT Monitor*, Sept./Oct. 2002, p. 452.

[76] If a cash basis seller must report the sale and remit tax before receiving payment, such as with installment sales, the seller may be eligible for an input credit if the installment purchaser defaults and the debt is written off. See NZ GST, *supra* note 27, at §26(1).

[77] ABA Model Act, *supra* note 16, at 97. If merchants include the cost of uncollectible accounts and the VAT thereon in their pricing structure, they would recover the bad debt plus VAT from their paying customers. The VAT attributable to a bad debt therefore should be recoverable, so that it does not enter the pricing structure and result in VAT being imposed on the uncollected VAT shifted to paying customers. *Id.*

[78] The Sixth Directive, *supra* note 2, at art. 20(1)(b) and 11(C)(1), authorizes member states to provide relief for bad debts. The United Kingdom provides bad debt relief. VATA 1994, *supra* note 29, at §36. To qualify, the seller must meet several conditions, including the requirement that the debt be written off in the seller's books and the debt be outstanding at least six months since the sale. *Id.* at §36(1). State retail sales taxes [in the United States] typically authorize the seller reporting tax on the accrual method to deduct bad debts. See J. Due & J. Mikesell, Sales Taxation: State And Local Structure And Administration 40–42 (1994).

[79] See Value Added Tax Statute, 1996, Statute No. 8, 1996, §§23 and 29 (Uganda).

In the United Kingdom now, the supplier is not required to notify the debtor of his intention to claim bad debt relief, and a debtor loses her right to an input tax credit once a debt is more than six months overdue.[80]

Singapore takes a pragmatic approach to the allowance of credits for bad debts.[81] To qualify, the taxable person must have supplied the goods and accounted for and paid GST on the supply. The credit can be claimed no earlier than when the debtor became insolvent or twelve months after the supply if the supplier wrote off the whole or a portion of the consideration in his accounts as a bad debt. Certain records must be created and maintained, the supplier agrees to report any recovery, and certain other conditions must be satisfied.

II. TREATMENT OF EXCESS INPUT CREDITS – CARRY FORWARD, OFFSET, OR REFUND

As was discussed earlier and will be discussed in detail in Chapter 7, most countries define the jurisdictional reach of their VATs under the destination principle. Applying the destination principle, exports are free of tax (zero-rated). As a result, exporters commonly report excess input VAT in their periodic VAT returns. In addition, even registered persons making sales taxable at a positive rate may experience occasional excess input VATs, such as when they make capital purchases generating substantial input credits or when they increase their inventory as part of an expansion of their businesses.

There is an implicit assumption in VAT systems that registered persons will recover input VAT used in making taxable sales so that the input VAT does not enter into the pricing structure for those sales. To accomplish that goal, a normative or well-structured VAT must grant registered persons the right to recover excess input VATs within a reasonable period of time after incurring the input tex.

Independent of the kind of rules discussed in this section, VATs may provide for quick refunds of tax on imports and domestic purchases, such as acquisitions by diplomats, or imports of goods by international organizations under a humanitarian or similar program.[82] These refunds may serve

---

[80] These changes became effective January 1, 2003. See VATA 1994, *supra* note 29, at §26A, as inserted by FA 2002, §22(1). An input tax claimed on a purchase must be repaid if the supplier is not paid within six months of the later of (a) the date of the supply or the date the debt became due. See SI 1995/2518, Value Added Tax Regs. 1995, reg. 172F, G & H, reported in *CCH British Value Added Tax Reporter* ¶18–917.

[81] It provides that a registered person that completes a downloadable form entitled "Bad Debt Relief: Checklist For Self-Review of Eligibility of Claim" and satisfies the conditions listed in that form, the supplier can claim credit for the GST element in the bad debt. The form does not appear to be numbered, and is dated January 2005.

[82] See New Vatopia VAT, Appendix B, §47(1). For an analysis of the range of refund regimes, see Harrison & Krelove, "VAT Refunds: A Review of Country Experience," IMF Working Paper WP/05/218 (Nov. 2005).

as an alternative to issuing exemption certificates to the eligible individuals or organizations because it is too difficult to control the appropriate use of such exemption certificates.

This section discusses some of the numerous variations employed for the recovery or the denial of recovery of excess input VATs. Although legislatures and tax authorities are reluctant to grant quick cash refunds for excess credits due to the risk of fraud and the negative cash flow associated with that approach, registered persons (and foreign businesses) are frustrated when they cannot predict when they will recover excess input VATs.[83]

Some countries resolve this conflict by requiring a refund of excess credits within a prescribed period of time, unless the tax authorities institute an audit, in which case the refund can be delayed until a specified period of time after the audit is completed.[84]

With innumerable variations, there are three basic methods by which VAT systems provide for the recovery of excess input VATs. They can be illustrated graphically as follows:

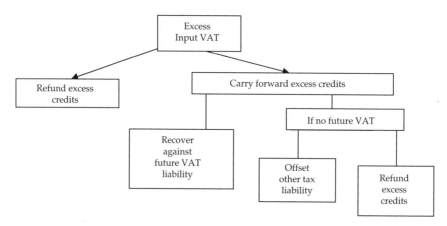

As the figure demonstrates, the excess input VATs can be recovered through an immediate refund procedure. This is quite unusual, except for input VAT attributable to exports and, in the European Union, refunds of input VAT claimed by non-EU businesses. Alternatively, the excess credits must be carried forward to a specified number of future periods ranging

---

[83] In Mexico, for example, customers purchasing some services are required to withhold and remit VAT chargeable on the services instead of paying the VAT to the supplier and claiming the VAT as an input credit. If VAT on these purchased services otherwise give rise to refundable excess credits, the withholding system permits the purchasers, in effect, to get the immediate benefit from the recovery of the input VAT. See Serrano Salas, "Focus on Mexico," *VAT Monitor*, Mar./Apr. 2003, p. 102.

[84] For example, Romania does not issue refunds without an audit for certain specified categories of taxpayers, including new companies, those involved with alcoholic beverages, and those with a record of economic offenses. Other taxpayers can obtain refunds without an audit, including those with a low risk. For a discussion of the formula for the analysis of risk, see Notingher, "New VAT refund procedure," *VAT Monitor*, Nov./Dec. 2004, p. 453.

from three to six periods, after which unused credits can either be used to offset the person's liability for other taxes or are refunded.[85]

"[A nation could] . . . consider giving businesses the option to apply excess credits to the business's payroll tax liability or withholding tax liability for income taxes instead of claiming a refund. If this option were granted, businesses could receive a more immediate benefit from excess credits. They would not be required to wait even a week or two until the Service processed a request for refund of excess credits."[86] The benefit apparently is not available under most VAT regimes. In New Zealand, the tax authority may set off an available refund against a registered person's unpaid liability under other taxes.[87]

The longer the time interval between the time the excess input credits are reportable on a VAT return and the time when the person receives the benefit from the credit, the less the benefit from the excess credits.[88]

As mentioned earlier, there are variations within these alternatives. For example, a registered exporter may claim a refund for excess credits attributable to exports when the exporter files his periodic VAT return reporting the exports, and he may be required to carry forward other excess credits (attributable to sales taxable at a positive rate) for three to six months, after which those excess credits are eligible for a refund.[89] Another alternative may permit exporters to apply for a refund for excess credits attributable to the exports or to apply the excess credits in payment for other taxes owed by the exporter. A third alternative gives taxpayers a prompt benefit from excess credits by allowing them to use these credits to pay VAT on their current taxable imports.[90] Some countries grant refunds of input VAT on capital goods not otherwise creditable in order to promote economic growth.[91]

Due to the revenue drain and the opportunity for fraud associated with the grant of refunds of excess credits, some countries restrict refunds. For example, in Hungary, cash refunds are not available unless the person requesting it paid the full price for the asset for which a refund claim is submitted.[92] As discussed above, other nations allow excess credits only to be carried forward and used to offset future VAT liability.[93]

---

[85] See Refunds of excess input tax, report on Bulgaria in *VAT Monitor*, Sept./Oct. 2002, p. 402.

[86] ABA Model Act, *supra* note 16, at 99.

[87] See NZ GST, *supra* note 27, at §46(6).

[88] For example, in Cyprus, registered persons may have to carry forward some excess credits for three years. See Tsangaris, "Refund of input VAT," *VAT Monitor*, Jan./Feb. 2004, p. 34.

[89] See Tzenova, "Bulgaria: Excess input tax," *VAT Monitor*, Jan./Feb. 2005, p. 43; see also "Slovak Republic, Refund of input tax," *VAT Monitor*, July/Aug. 2003, p. 343.

[90] See the Ukraine procedure discussed in Yumashev, "Ukraine: VAT promissory notes amended," *VAT Monitor*, Nov./Dec. 2004, p. 457.

[91] See, for example, the Argentina Law No. 25,954 (Official Gazette of 6 Sept. 2004), discussed by Calzetta, "Accelerated VAT refunds," *VAT Monitor*, Nov./Dec. 2004, p. 419.

[92] See Véghelyi, "Refund of VAT, report on Hungary," *VAT Monitor*, July/Aug. 2002, p. 331.

[93] For example, see Russian VAT, Letter of the Ministry of Taxes and Levies, No. BS-6-05/1150 @ of August 1, 2002, discussed in "Refund of excess input VAT," *VAT Monitor*, Nov./Dec. 2002, p. 521.

China has a unique system of granting refunds of input tax on exported goods that results in widely varying refunds. The refunds vary by product line.[94] Some refunds were issued by the central government and some by local government. Under a system effective in 2005, the central government will issue all rebates.[95]

In the EU, the Sixth Directive provides that if there are excess input tax deductions, "Member States may either make a refund or carry the excess forward to the following period according to conditions which they shall determine. For Member States, excess credits must be refunded after being carried forward six months.[96] However, Member States may refuse to refund or carry forward if the amount of the excess is insignificant."[97] As a result of the complexity and cost associated with the VAT refund process and the time it takes to obtain refunds, in some situations, over 50 percent of large firms in the EU do not apply for VAT refunds.[98]

A country's obligation to refund excess credits may not be satisfied by the issuance of government obligations to pay in the future. For example, the ECJ ruled that the issuance of government bonds by Italy does not satisfy Italy's obligation to make a refund "within a reasonable period of time by a payment in liquid funds or equivalent means. In any case, the method of refund adopted must not entail any financial risk for the taxable person."[99]

Taxable persons in one EU member state (A) that must pay VAT in another member state (B) are entitled to file for a refund of input VAT paid in member state (B) that is attributable to the person's taxable supplies.[100] According to

---

[94] See, for example, Zhang, "New tax refund rates for exported products," *VAT Monitor,* Sept/Oct 2004, p. 366. For example, the refund for agricultural products can be 13 percent or 17 percent; none for crude oil, timber, and 18 percent for some metals.

[95] Local government remains liable to pay the central government some base amount plus 7.5 percent of the rebates granted in excess of the base amount. Subler, "China Cabinet Clears Reforms To Export Tax Rebates System," *BNA Daily Tax Report,* Aug. 10, 2005, p. G-3.

[96] Eighth Council Directive, 79/1072/EEC of 6 December 1979, OJ 1979 L331 [hereinafter Eighth Directive], Art. 7(4). The European Commission brings action in the ECJ against Member States that fail to comply. See Case C-90/05, *Commission of the European Communities v Grand Duchy of Luxembourg.*

[97] Sixth Directive, *supra* note 2, at Art. 18(4).

[98] Commission of the European Union, "Commission Staff Working Paper: European Tax Survey," SEC (2004) 1128/2, Oct. 9, 2004, p. 6.

[99] Case C-78/00, *Commission of the European Communities v Italian Republic,* [2001] ECR I-8195, at ¶34 of the Judgment. A financial risk, for example, may entail a discount on the sale of the government bonds due to low interest payable on the bonds.

[100] Eighth Directive, *supra* note 96, at Art. 2. For a judgment finding that France violated this Directive, see Case C-429/97, *Commission of the European Communities v French Republic,* [2001]ECR I-0637, discussed in Leclerc, "VAT refund to Foreign Taxable Persons – Rules Applicable to the Waste Management Industry," *VAT Monitor,* May/June 2002, p. 180. The European Commission issued a proposal to allow traders to file a single electronic return and claim eligible refunds from other member states as well in that "one-stop shop" approach. See COM (2004) 728 final of 29 October 2004 and IP/04/1331 of 29 October 2004, discussed in Ainsworth, "The One-Stop Shop for VAT and RST: Common Approaches to EU-U.S. Consumption Tax Issues," *Tax Notes Int'l.,* Feb. 21, 2005, p. 693.

the ECJ, the refund is not available if it is attributable to exempt supplies made by the requesting person in the member state where he is established.[101]

Foreign persons not established in the EU also may be eligible to file for a refund of input VAT in a member state under a principle of reciprocity; that is, the refund is available if the country in which the foreign business is established does not impose a VAT-like tax or refunds VAT to businesses that are resident in the granting state. To be eligible, the foreign person must meet the conditions imposed in the Thirteenth Council Directive and by the granting state.[102] In addition, many countries provide for VAT rebates for foreign tourists where the country is satisfied that goods have been exported.[103] In Hungary, any excess credits not already refunded may be refunded when a registered business is liquidated.[104]

III. Impact of Change from Exempt to Taxable Status

"[I]f a person making exempt sales (such as a person exempt from tax on sales under a [small business exemption] . . .) purchases property and services, the VAT on such purchases is not eligible for the input credit. If the exempt seller becomes a taxable person, he then will charge VAT on all subsequent taxable sales and will be entitled to credit input tax on new purchases against this output tax liability. To the extent that the taxable person sells inventory that was on hand when he became taxable, he is selling property that already bore noncreditable input tax. He will be charging VAT on the cost of this

---

[101] See *Etienne Debouche v. Inspecteur der Invoerrechten en Accijnzen*, Case C-302/93, [1996] ECR I-4495, discussed in Swinkels, "Tax Neutrality and Cross-Border Services," *VAT Monitor*, Mar./Apr. 2005, p. 94. Swinkels refers to the Communication from the Commission to the Council and the European Parliament – A Strategy to Improve the Operation of the VAT System within the Context of the Internal Market, COM (2000) 348, June 7, 2000. This communication urges member states to harmonize restrictions on input tax credits and to allow taxable persons to deduct VAT incurred in other member states. See COM (98) 377 final, proposing the amendment to the Sixth Directive mentioned in COM (2000) 348.

[102] See Thirteenth Council Directive of 17 November 1986, 86/560/EEC. Based in part on *Commission of the European Communities v United Kingdom of Great Britain and Northern Ireland*, Case C-33/02, [2005] ECR I-1865, and on the Sixth, Eighth and Thirteenth Directive, the British Revenue & Customs has liberalized the procedure under which a non-EU business can claim a refund of input VAT. See Ostilly, "UK's U-Turn," *Int'l VAT Monitor*, Mar./Apr. 2006, p. 95. See also Swinkels, "VAT Refunds to Non-EU Banks," *VAT Monitor*, March/April 2005, p. 105, discussing a Dutch case granting refunds to an Australian bank without a fixed establishment in the Netherlands that rendered services exclusively to non-EU customers. For an overview of thresholds for refunds available in European countries to registered businesses, foreign traders that are not registered in the EU, and nonresident tourists, see "Practical Information on VAT," *VAT Monitor*, Jan./Feb. 2005, pp. 2–10. This information has been updated annually.

[103] See, for example, VATA 1994, *supra* note 29, at §30(6) on exported goods generally; and Sch. 9, zero-rating, Group 14, tax-free shops (United Kingdom); see also Canadian GST, *supra* note 13, at §252. Canada rebates the VAT on certain hotel accommodations for tourists as well. *Id.* at §252.1.

[104] See Hungarian VAT, discussed by Véghelyi, "Refund of excess input VAT," *VAT Monitor*, Mar./Apr. 2003, p. 137.

property a second time. If the taxable person were granted a credit for VAT attributable to the purchases of goods on hand when he switched to taxable status, he would be placed in the same tax position as if he acquired such property and services while he was a taxable person."[105]

To prevent a competitive disadvantage to a newly registered person, VAT systems may allow that person to claim credit in his first VAT return for tax on goods on hand that were purchased within a prescribed number of months before registration.[106]

To prevent a competitive advantage to a deregistering person, VAT systems may treat a deregistering person as having sold goods on hand immediately before the cancellation of registration becomes effective.[107]

IV. USED PROPERTY

A. BUSINESS-TO-BUSINESS SALES OF USED PROPERTY

A registered business making taxable sales claims credit for input VAT on assets (office furniture) acquired for use in making those taxable sales. The assets are held free of VAT. If the business sells this furniture after using it in his business for years, the sales are taxable, whether sold to a registered used-goods dealer or a private consumer. If the office furniture is purchased by a registered used-goods dealer for renovation and resale in a taxable transaction, the dealer claims credit for tax on the purchase and charges VAT on the resale price. The system works. The business purchasing the goods new held the goods free of VAT, but presumably included the value used up in the business (original cost less tax-exclusive selling price to the used-goods dealer) in the prices of its taxable sales, the used-goods dealer held the used goods free of VAT, and the used-goods dealer charged and the consumers of the refurbished used goods bear VAT only on the tax-exclusive prices of the used goods.

B. SALES OF USED PROPERTY IN NONTAXABLE TRANSACTIONS

A registered person may acquire goods in transactions not subject to tax. If the acquired goods are resold in taxable transactions and some noncreditable VAT is buried in the selling price, the VAT is imposed more than once, resulting in some cascading of VAT. For example, a consumer may sell a used refrigerator to a used appliance dealer in a transaction not subject to VAT. Cascading occurs in these sales of secondhand goods in consumer-to-registered business transactions.

"For example, assume that the first consumer bought a refrigerator for $1,000 plus $100 VAT (10 percent tax). After years of use, the consumer sells the

---

[105] ABA Model Act, *supra* note 16, at 100.

[106] See Canadian GST, *supra* note 13, at §171(1). The Canadian credit is not limited to goods or services purchased within a given period before registration becomes effective.

[107] See generally *id.* at §171(3)–(5).

used refrigerator to a dealer for $220, consisting of $200 plus the $20 VAT attributable to this portion of the original purchase price. The dealer resells it to a second consumer for $350, which includes the $20 VAT buried in the dealer's cost for the refrigerator. The only value added to this used property by the dealer is represented by the difference between this dealer's VAT-exclusive cost ($200) and VAT-exclusive selling price ($330), or $130. If the dealer charges $35 VAT on the [$350] selling price and does not obtain any VAT benefit from the $20 VAT element in the $220 purchase price, VAT will have been imposed a second time on the $200 VAT-exclusive cost of the used refrigerator (multiple tax), and VAT also will be imposed on the $20 VAT included in the dealer's $350 selling price (cascade effect). This multiple tax and cascade effect may further encourage the private sale of used refrigerators and similar products through newspaper advertisements or garage sales, thus creating a disadvantage for dealers in used consumer durable goods."[108]

The problem extends beyond these transactions. For example, in many countries, a registered business is denied credit for input VAT on automobiles because businesses may claim the automobile used by officers, owners, or their relatives is used in connection with taxable activities, and the tax authorities do not have the capacity to verify the accuracy of these claims. Because input VAT was not claimed on the acquisition of the automobile, many VATs treat a sale of the used automobile to a used car dealer as a transaction not subject to VAT, and in absence of a special rule, the tax-exclusive price charged by the used car dealer would include some element of VAT. The same effect can occur if an unregistered small business sells used property (such as office furniture) to a used office furniture dealer who resells those goods.

Many VAT systems include rules to reduce or eliminate the cascading of VAT on secondhand or used goods. The scope of the covered goods and the method of calculating the tax by the reseller of the used goods differ.

One possible approach to avoid this multiple tax effect is to calculate the taxable amount of the sale by the used goods dealer as the difference between the sales price and the dealer's cost for the used goods.

"In the above example, the used property dealer would calculate the taxable amount of the sale of the used refrigerator by reducing the $350 selling price by the $220 cost. The dealer would charge $13 VAT on the $130 taxable amount, the value added by the dealer. . . . [This approach] . . . removes appreciation in the value of used property from the tax base if the used property is sold by the first consumer to the dealer for more than the consumer's purchase price. . . .[109] Instead of providing a special rule to reduce the taxable

---

[108] ABA Model Act, *supra* note 16, at 103.

[109] For example, assume that the refrigerator was unique and that the consumer can sell it to the used property dealer for a VAT-exclusive price of $1,500. Because the dealer can reduce its tax base on sales by the full price paid for the refrigerator, if the market operates, the sales price should include all or most of the VAT that would be imposed if it were a taxable sale. The assumption here is that the selling price will increase to $1,650. The dealer resells it for a tax-exclusive price of $1,780. The price consists of the

amount of the resale of used property, the statute [could tax]... the used property dealer's sale on the basis of the selling price of the used property (the same as in any other taxable sale), and grant the dealer a constructive input credit for the amount of VAT that would have been imposed on its purchase of the used property if such used property had been acquired in a taxable transaction. . . .

This constructive credit approach limits the tax imposed on used property to the value added to the property after the sale by the first consumer to the dealer, but it presents problems resulting from the break in the credit chain. The dealer in used property obtains an input credit without a tax invoice, a central feature in the self-policing mechanism of an invoice method VAT. This break in the chain of tax invoices provides an opportunity for VAT evasion if the dealer improperly claims credits for purchases from other sellers that cannot issue tax invoices. While the opportunity for evasion or avoidance can be reduced by requiring used property dealers to obtain receipts from consumers that sell them used property, it would be difficult for the government to verify the authenticity of these receipts because these consumers would not be subject to VAT audits.

[This]... constructive credit technique may result in the complete removal of some of the value of used property from the tax base, if the first consumer sells the used property to the dealer for more than his cost. Many of the transactions that may give rise to tax avoidance will involve property that may have characteristics both of property acquired for investment and for consumption. The untaxed appreciation represents value added by external events that could be removed from a consumption tax base. On the other hand, new property of the same kind may be sold for the same price with the government collecting revenue on the basis of the full selling price."[110]

In the European Union, the Sixth Directive requires member states to tax only the profit margin on supplies by a taxable dealer of secondhand goods, works of art, collectors' items, and antiques acquired from a nontaxable person, acquired in certain exempt transactions, or acquired from another taxable dealer in a transaction reported under these rules.[111] The profit margin is the difference between the price charged for the goods and the cost.[112] The opportunity for tax evasion when the statute allows credits without tax invoices has prompted some countries to tax the full price of resales of used goods that are purchased from consumers.[113]

tax-inclusive $1,650 cost of the purchase plus $130 value added by the dealer. Because the reduction in the taxable amount of the sale is based on the dealer's entire purchase price, the government will never receive VAT on the $500 difference between the first consumer's $1,000 VAT-exclusive cost and his $1,500 tax-exclusive selling price.

[110] ABA Model Act, *supra* note 16, at 102–107.
[111] Sixth Directive, *supra* note 2, at Art. 26(a)(B)(1) and (2).
[112] VATA 1994, *supra* note 29, at §50A(4).
[113] See, for example, Value Added Tax Statute, 1996, Statute No. 8 1996, §§22 and 29(11) (Uganda).

Interpreting the scope of the term "secondhand goods,"[114] the ECJ held that a live animal (a horse in that case) purchased from a private individual, trained, and sold for a specific use (a riding horse) may be considered a secondhand good subject to the profit margin rules.[115]

The Canadian GST allows a deemed credit for the cost of used goods purchased from an unregistered person.[116] Subject to conditions, the Australian GST grants the registered purchaser an input tax credit on purchases of secondhand goods acquired for sale or exchange in the ordinary course of business.[117] This credit has given rise to some tax-avoidance motivated transactions. As a result, the Australian Tax Office issued a GST ruling to stop the abuses.[118]

V. POSTSALE PRICE ADJUSTMENTS AND REFUNDS

A. IN GENERAL

A rebate, return of merchandise, or adjustment of price may occur after a taxable sale has been completed and the tax invoice has been issued. These postsale adjustments take a number of different forms. In some countries, the person making the adjustment must issue a debit or credit note to give notice of the adjustment to the recipient, and provide an audit trail to verify that the adjustment has been properly accounted for by the parties.

B. RETURNS AND ALLOWANCES – CREDIT AND DEBIT NOTES

Under many VAT regimes, the registered person must issue a credit or debit note before it can make a VAT adjustment for a prior supply of goods or services. The New Zealand GST has rules representative of those in other countries. If a supplier accounted for an incorrect amount of output tax on a supply on a tax invoice and possibly in a previously filed tax return because the supply was canceled, the nature of the supply was fundamentally

---

[114] Secondhand goods are defined in the Sixth Directive, *supra* note 2, at Art. 26a(A) as "tangible movable property that is suitable for further use as it is or after repair, other than works of art, collectors' items or antiques and other than precious metals or precious stones as defined by the Member States."

[115] *Förvaltnings AB Stenholmen v. Riksskatteverket*, Case C-320/02, [2004] ECR I-3509.

[116] Canadian GST, *supra* note 13, at §176. There are rules to prevent excessive credits on certain used goods.

[117] A New Tax System (Goods and Services Tax) Act 1999, §66–40.

[118] For example, a member of a GST group may cancel its registration, and remove itself from the GST group. The cancellation triggers a clawback of some credits for equipment on hand on the date of cancellation. The deregistered firm then sells to a related company that equipment and assets acquired before the GST became effective. The purchaser claims input credit on the purchase of the secondhand goods, sells the equipment to a related entity and leases the equipment back. There are other variations. GSTR 2004/D4 finalized, Goods and services tax: arrangements of the kind described in Taxpayer Alert TA 2004/9 – Exploitation of the second hand goods provisions to obtain input tax credits, relies in part on the anti-avoidance rule in Div. 165 to disallow the input credit.

changed, the consideration was changed, or some or all of the goods or services were returned, the supplier can adjust its tax liability as a result of this cancellation, return, or change.[119] If the adjustment resulted in a previous overstatement of tax liability, the correction is made by claiming an input credit and by issuing a credit note to the recipient of the supply.[120] If the adjustment resulted in a previous understatement of tax liability, the correction is made by reporting additional output tax liability and issuing a debit note to the recipient of the supply.[121]

If the registered recipient of the supply receives a credit note as described earlier, and it previously claimed an excessive input credit as the result of the tax reported on that purchase, the recipient must report the tax adjustment as tax on a taxable supply.[122] If the registered recipient receives a debit note as described earlier and previously understated the allowable input credit as a result of the tax reported on that purchase, the recipient may claim an additional input credit to the extent listed on the debit note if that amount otherwise is creditable.[123]

C. Postsale Rebate by Pre-retail Registered Business to Final Consumer

A pre-retail registered producer may provide a cash rebate to a final consumer for various reasons, including a sales incentive or to obtain information about the retail sellers or customers of its products. For example, a manufacturer of a computer memory stick may offer retail customers cash rebates if they submit an invoice and a completed rebate form. When the manufacturer sells the memory sticks to wholesalers and the wholesalers sell to retailers, the VAT is charged on the sale and credited by the buyer on the purchase. The rebate does not alter the VAT imposed on the sales, including the retail sale to the consumer. The cash rebates reduce the consideration the producer receives on its sales of memory sticks and reduce the net consideration paid by the consumer. The VAT system should take account of that reduction in consideration paid for the memory stick. If the producer issues a consumer a cash rebate of $11.00 and the VAT rate is 10 percent on the tax-exclusive price, the producer should be entitled to claim an input credit (or reduction in output tax) of $1.00 (rebate × tax rate/100 + tax rate, or 11 × 10/110).

VI. Casual Sales by Consumers

Even if a casual seller were treated as selling in connection with taxable activities, the annual sales likely will not exceed the small business exemption

---

[119] NZ GST, *supra* note 27, at §25(1) and (2).
[120] *Id.* at §25(2)(b) and (3)(a).
[121] *Id.* at §25(2)(a) and (3)(b).
[122] *Id.* at §25(4).
[123] *Id.* at §25(5).

threshold in most countries. Most VAT statutes do not tax casual sales by consumers, even if the sale is of an item (such as a yacht) priced above the small business exemption threshold. Some countries make an exception for sales of real property.[124]

One alternative may be to tax sales by unregistered persons if the sale exceeds a certain threshold amount. The Model Act developed in the United States by the American Bar Association tax section committee on VAT taxes high-priced casual sales. It allows the casual seller to claim a deferred input credit for VAT paid on the asset sold in a taxable casual sale.[125]

Casual sales by consumers tend to be of used items. If they are taxed, the tax consequences should follow the rules on used goods discussed earlier. If the casual seller is taxed only on the margin – the spread between the sales price and the cost of the item sold – the seller should be required to substantiate the claimed cost with an invoice or other supporting document. To prevent possible abuse, if casual sales are taxed, the seller should not be eligible for a refund of any excess input credits.

VII. Japan's System to Calculate Input Credits

The calculation of creditable input tax under the Japanese Consumption Tax (CT) differs from most other VAT systems. First, in form, a person registered under the CT calculates creditable input tax from company records rather than from VAT invoices. This difference in form may not be substantively different from a European-style invoice VAT because the CT taxpayer still must substantiate its credits with "a bill, receipt, statement of delivery or other type of invoice that shows" the details of the transaction.[126] The CT taxpayer takes the total tax-inclusive cost of allowable purchases for the tax period and multiplies this total by the tax fraction, for a 5 percent CT – 5/105, to arrive at the allowable input credits for the period.

The second difference, an accommodation to the small business sector in Japan, is that credits are available for the tax fraction of the cost of purchases from CT-exempt small businesses. Credits also are available for the presumed CT element in "purchases of used goods from consumers, but do not include purchases treated as tax-exempt transactions.[127] The input tax

---

[124] A sale of a residential complex by an individual is taxable under the Canadian GST. See Canadian GST, *supra* note 13, at Sch. V, Part I, ¶9(d).

[125] ABA Model Act, *supra* note 16, at §§4000 and 4019.

[126] See Japanese CT, 1994 Amendment Act, at Art. 30 amendment. This change is effective for purchases on or after April 1, 1997. *Id.* at Appendix, Art. 7. See Beyer, Japan's Consumption Tax: Settled in to Stay, 2000 WTD 247–5, at 3 (Dec. 12, 2000).

[127] Japan CT Law, *supra* note 50, at Art. 30, and Art. 2(1)(9) definition of a "Transfer of Taxable Assets." For purchases of secondhand goods, the dealer in used goods can claim a credit based on the dealer's purchase price of the goods from the consumer. For example, if a consumer buys a Picasso painting for 130 million yen and later sells it to an art gallery for 150 million yen, the gallery can claim an input deduction based on the 150 million yen price.

credit, therefore, is available for presumed tax on purchases from a business that does not charge CT on its sales because its turnover is below the small business exemption threshold,[128] but the credit is not available on the purchase of insurance that is exempt from the CT."[129]

VIII. Calculation of Tax Liability and Special Schemes

Most countries with VATs rely on the credit-invoice method of calculating periodic tax liability. Japan is an exception, but has been moving to a method that relies increasingly on sales documents to verify output tax and input credits.

Registered businesses in most countries must report as output tax the tax on taxable sales taken from tax invoices. They claim as input credits the VAT charged on purchases used in making taxable sales. Businesses with turnover below the registration threshold are outside the VAT system. To ease the compliance burden on smaller businesses that are above the threshold but may not have sophisticated or computerized record keeping, the VAT, by law, regulations, or administrative practice, may authorize simplified schemes to minimize VAT record keeping and reporting obligations. For example, there are special schemes for retailers.[130] In addition, some countries rely on modified turnover tax regimes for businesses with turnover moderately above the registration threshold. For example, Belgium and the United Kingdom provide an election for registered businesses within a certain turnover range to report under a flat-rate scheme. Under the British scheme, electing traders are required to record only sales.[131] The VAT liability then is calculated on the basis of the markup for the trader's major business activity. For example, if a trader has turnover of £10,000 in a tax period and the mark-up is 10 percent, the person's tax base if £1,000, to which the 17.5 percent VAT rate is applied. The VAT for the period is £175. The U.K. system requires traders to calculate VAT liability on the basis of total turnover that may include exempt and zero-rated sales, not just sales taxable at a positive rate. In addition, the complex rules governing the conversion from the flat rate to the regular method of calculating VAT liability, when sales exceed the allowable limits, may deter some traders from electing the flat-rate scheme. There are restrictions on the use of this scheme. For example, it is not available to traders using the secondhand or cash accounting schemes.

For special methods to calculate the value of supplies for VAT purposes, see the margin schemes discussed in Chapter 8(II)(G).

---

[128] The 1950 Japanese VAT included a similar deduction for amounts paid on purchases from suppliers that were exempt from the Vat. Sullivan, The Tax on Value Added, pp. 134–135.

[129] Schenk, Japanese CT, *supra* note 53, at 905–906.

[130] See the U.K. Point of Sale and Direct Calculation Schemes.

[131] VATA 1994, *supra* note 29, at §23. This scheme is explained in VAT Notice 733. See Goodwin, "The flat-rate scheme for VAT – section 23," 2002 British Tax Rev. 253. Transactions involving capital goods must be accounted for outside this scheme. *Id.*

IX. Discussion Questions

1. One might think that a consumption type VAT system does not need any special treatment for input credits on capital goods. Explain why special treatment is provided by the Sixth Directive and how this treatment operates. What treatment is provided under the New Vatopia VAT?

2. What is the link between the tax credit mechanism and the concepts of self-supplies and self-services for business purposes under the Sixth Directive Art's. 5(7) and 6(3)? How are these concepts treated in the New Vatopia VAT?

3. In a VAT system, there are two ways to prevent private consumption from escaping tax when such consumption takes place in a business context: (a) deny the input tax credit, and (b) tax a deemed transaction between the taxpayer and himself or between the taxpayer and a third party. What use is made of these two models in the Sixth Directive? In the New Vatopia VAT?

4. Would you expect that problems and solutions for casual sales, used goods, and trade-ins to be the same under a retail sales tax and a VAT? For the theory and practice in the state RSTs in the United States, see Pomp & Oldman, "A Normative Inquiry into the Base of a Retail Sales Tax: Casual Sales, Used Goods, and Trade Ins," 43 *Nat'l Tax J.* 427 (1990).

7

Introduction to Cross-Border Aspects of VAT

I. Introduction to International Trade

For most countries with VATs, international trade is a significant component of their economies. A country with a VAT must define the jurisdictional reach of the tax; that is, the tax may be imposed on production within the country (an origin principle VAT), on domestic consumption (a destination principle VAT), or some combination of the two. Almost every country with a VAT relies on the destination principle to define the jurisdictional limits of the tax. Under a pure destination principle, imports are taxed and exports are completely free of tax (zero rated). With this system, it is important to identify the value of goods and services that are exported (and when they are exported) and identify the value of taxable imports and determine when they are taxable.

This chapter discusses the place of supply rules in the context of international trade, including the troublesome issues on cross-border transactions relating to the place where services are rendered.

The location or place of an international sale of services has become more significant with the advent of electronic commerce.[1] A significant problem with electronic commerce is to determine if the sale is of goods or services. For example, if computer software, music, and videos are transmitted by electronic signals rather than in compact disks or other physical form, is the transaction a sale of goods or a sale of services?[2] Before the EU change in the rules governing these services, the issue was confused because sales of

---

[1] See Progress Report and Draft Principles on the Application of Consumption Taxes to the International Trade in Services and Intangibles, OECD Committee on Fiscal Affairs (2005). The draft principles are that tax on services and intangibles should be imposed in the "jurisdiction of consumption," and "taxable businesses should not incur the tax as an economic cost on goods and services used in making taxable supplies." *Id.* at ¶19 and 20. This is a follow-up to the previous OECD report approved June 30, 2004. See "Report: The Application of Consumption Taxes to the Trade in International Services and Intangibles" (OECD). See also Lambert, "VAT and Electronic Commerce: European Union Insights Into the Challenges Ahead," 17 *Tax Notes Int'l* 1645 (Nov. 23, 1998) [hereinafter Lambert, VAT & E-Commerce].

[2] *Id.* at 1646.

standard packaged software typically were treated as sales of goods, but sales of customized software were sales of services.[3]

Before we get to these issues, the next two sections discuss the vocabulary of international aspects of VAT, and discuss the jurisdictional reach of a VAT under the origin and destination principles.

II. VOCABULARY OF INTERJURISDICTIONAL (CROSS-BORDER) ASPECTS OF VAT

The following terms are used in this chapter and throughout the book. They relate to various VAT aspects of cross-border trade in goods and services.

- International – between countries or outside of customs unions or trading blocks.
- Intrabloc – between member countries of a customs union or trading block (for example: the European Union (EU); North American Free Trade Agreement (NAFTA), Latin American Free Trade Association (LAFTA); Community of Andean Nations Agreement (CAN)).
- Intranational – between states or provinces within a country, for example, in federal countries such as the United States, Australia, Brazil, Canada, India, and Switzerland.
- Intrastate – between state and local units of government or between municipalities or within a state.
- Jurisdictional reach of a tax – destination and origin principles of defining the scope of a tax.
- Timing – when tax is imposed on imports and domestic supplies, when tax is deductible on acquisitions, and when excess deductions are recoverable.
- Location or place of supply – where a supply is treated as taking place for tax purposes.

III. TAXONOMY OF BROAD-BASED SALES TAXES ON INTERNATIONAL TRADE[4]

The next section discusses the details of the two major methods of defining the jurisdictional reach of a VAT – the origin and the destination principles. It is possible to combine various elements of these two principles in defining the jurisdictional reach of a VAT. Table 7.1 sets out the various options pertaining to the taxation of domestic transactions, exports, and imports, and indicates the extent to which they are used in national or sub-national sales or value added tax systems around the world.[5]

---

[3] *Id.*

[4] Adaptation by O. Oldman from 1979 lecture by C. S. Shoup.

[5] As has been discussed, if a supply is not taxed and the supplier is entitled to recover input VAT, in the common VAT lexicon, the supply is zero rated (under the EU Sixth Directive, it is exempt with a right to deduct, and in Australia, it is "GST-free"). If a supply is not

Table 7.1. Options for the Taxation of Domestic and International Trade

	Exports	Domestic Trans's	Imports	Comments
1	T	T	T	Rare, but see states of Brazil & 1981 proposal for Saipan
2	T	E	T	Argentina formerly
3	T	T	E	Origin principle
4	T	E	E	A general tax on exports only
5	E	T	T	Destination principle
6	E	E	T	Similar to Surrey's[6] proposed U.S. import surcharge
7	E	T	E	German turnover tax in the 1920s[7]
8	E	E	E	United States at the national level
9	Apportionment by formula			Michigan's state-level Single Business Tax

T = taxable transactions; E = exempt transactions

IV. Origin Versus Destination Principle

A. In General

As discussed earlier, a country can define its jurisdiction to tax international transactions under the origin or destination principles. Except for the remnants of the origin principle with respect to trade within the CIS countries[8] and the lack of complete zero-rating of exports by China,[9] all of the

taxed and the supplier is not entitled to recover input VAT, in the common VAT lexicon, the supply is exempt from VAT (under the EU Sixth Directive, it is exempt with no right to deduction input VAT, and in Australia, it is "input taxed"). If imports are exempt, they are completely free of VAT.

[6] Stanley Surrey was Professor of Law, Harvard Law School, and Assistant Secretary for Tax Policy in the U.S. Treasury Department from 1961 to 1969.

[7] See Sullivan, The Tax on Value Added 30 (1965).

[8] The Commonwealth of Independent States (CIS) countries are the Russian Federation and the former Soviet republics of Armenia, Azerbaijan, Belarus, Kazakhstan, Kyrgyzstan, Republic of Moldova, Tajikistan, Turkmenistan, Ukraine, and Uzbekistan. See, for example, Federal Law No. 102-FZ, dated August 18, 2004, providing for the zero rating of exports of goods to the Republic of Belarus and exports of oil and natural gas to all CIS members, reported in "Russia: Destination principle – Intra-CIS supplies of goods," *VAT Monitor*, Nov./Dec. 2004, p. 454.

[9] Except for certain industries in northeastern China, China does not allow input credits for VAT on capital goods. In addition, China imposes a business tax (BT), not VAT, on construction and the supply of real property, and the BT is not recoverable under the VAT system. China therefore has a mixed production-consumption VAT that does not completely zero rate exports of goods. See Ahmad, Lockwood, & Singh, "Financial Consequences of the Chinese VAT Reform," *VAT Monitor*, May/June 2005, p. 181. China is examining possible VAT reforms that will provide full input credits, including credits attributable to capital goods purchases.

major countries of the world rely on the destination principle to define the scope of the VAT with respect to international transactions involving goods. There is less consistency in the treatment of international trade in services.

Under the origin principle, VAT is imposed in the country of production, regardless of where the goods or services are consumed. Thus, imports are not taxed and exports bear tax on the value added within the taxing jurisdiction. As a result, there is no need for border tax adjustments. It is not essential that the tax authorities keep account of the imports and exports, but it is essential that the full value of exported goods bear domestic tax and a full credit be granted for the value of imports. The VAT becomes a tax on domestic production of goods and the domestic rendition of services. If a domestic firm sells hand-held music players, the VAT collected by the government will vary, depending on the amount of the value of the product manufactured domestically or imported. This is particularly important if other countries rely on the destination principle to define the jurisdictional reach of the VAT and this country relies on the origin principle. For example, little revenue would be raised if the entire product is imported and only the value added by the retailer is included in this country's VAT base.

Under a pure destination principle, VAT is imposed on imports and rebated on exports. For this kind of VAT, it is required that the country imposing VAT maintain "fiscal frontiers" (border tax adjustments). As implemented in most countries, under the destination principle, imports of most goods, imports of the value of services allocable to imported goods, and imports of some other services are taxed. The "other services" typically are services taxed under a "reverse charge" rule to a recipient who is not able to claim credit for tax on the import. For example, a university rendering exempt educational services that is denied credit for input VAT on purchases may be taxed on imports of architectural services in order to discourage the outsourcing of those services to avoid VAT.

On the export side with a destination principle VAT, exports of most goods, exports of services related to exported goods, and exports of only additional specified services are relieved of VAT (zero-rated). As a result, the full value of goods and services consumed within the taxing jurisdiction are taxed, even if some of the value is added outside the country and is imported. Continuing this example, the same amount of tax is collected on the domestic sale of the music player, whether the parts or the entire product is imported or is produced domestically. Services rendered domestically also are taxed in full.

The origin and destination principles are illustrated in the following chart. The example is limited to the tax consequences in the country where the exported goods are produced. It is assumed that the VAT rate is 10 percent. There are two illustrations of cross-border transactions. In the first, the manufacturer exports some of its output directly to a foreign distributor for sales abroad. In the second, a domestic distributor (an exporter) purchases the remainder of the manufacturer's output and after adding its margin exports to foreign customers.

Table 7.2. Example of Destination and Origin Principles (Example is for the country of production only; 10% rate)

	Price	Tax principle — destination	Tax principle — Origin.
Manufacturer's purchases from taxable supplier (taxable input)	4,000	+400*	+400*
Manufacturer's sales Direct exports to foreign distributors	5,000**	00	+500
Less input credit (a portion of the $400)		−150 −150	−150 350
Sales to exporter located in same country***	10,000	+1,000	+1,000
Less input credit (a portion of the $400)		−250 +750	−250 +750
Exporter's exports to foreign buyers	12,000**	00	+1,200
Less input credit for tax paid to mfr.		−1,000 −1,000	−1,000 +200
Total tax collected (the double underscored totals)		00	1,700

    * The $400 represents the tax paid by the manufacturer (input tax credit), assuming $150 attributable to direct export sales and $250 attributable to domestic sales to an exporter.

  ** The total of sales made outside the country is $17,000. Under the origin principle, these sales are taxable, resulting in $1,700 in VAT, consisting of:
$400 paid by the manufacturer's supplier
1,100 paid by the manufacturer
200 paid by the exporter

*** Some countries zero rate sales to exporters as well as direct exports.

B. Double Taxation of Consumer-to-Consumer Imports

The destination principle is designed to allocate tax jurisdiction to the country of consumption. The assumption and the typical result is that tax is not imposed more than once on the full value of final consumption. However, if a consumer in one country exports goods to a consumer in another country, and both countries rely on the destination principle, VAT may be imposed twice if the second country makes no allowance for the tax already paid to the first country and the first country fails to rebate any tax on the export by an unregistered consumer. The following case involves this issue under the EU Sixth Directive.

> ### *Staatssecretaris van Financïen v. Gaston Schul Douane-Expediteur BV*[10]
>
> [The dispute relates to the amount of VAT imposed by the Netherlands on the import of a secondhand pleasure and sports boat by a resident that was purchased in France from another private person. The Netherlands

---

[10] Case 47/84, [1985] ECR 1491, [1986] 1 CMLR 559 (ECJ 1985). [Edited by the authors.]

tax authorities imposed VAT at the normal Dutch 18 percent rate on the sale price of the boat. The boat was built in Monaco and taxed on import into France at 17.6 percent of its FF 269,571 value (FF 47,444.49).]

[T]he boat was sold to a Netherlands national residing in the Netherlands for FF 365 000, an amount which exceeded the price of the boat, including tax, at the time of its importation into France.

The [Dutch Regional Court of Appeal] ... took the view that ... the sum of the French VAT and the VAT payable on importation should not exceed the VAT charged in the Netherlands on a similar boat of equal value, net of tax, supplied to an individual on Netherlands territory. For that purpose the value on importation should be calculated by deducting the French VAT actually paid from the price on importation into the Netherlands; on that basis Netherlands VAT of 18 per cent should be calculated, and the French VAT paid should be deducted from the resulting amount.

[The Supreme Court of the Netherlands referred the following two questions to the ECJ for a preliminary ruling:]

'1. Where a Member State charges VAT on the importation, from another Member State, of a product which is supplied by a non-taxable (private) person, but does not charge VAT on the supply of similar products by a private person within its own territory, should that Member State, in order to prevent the tax from constituting internal taxation in excess of that imposed on similar domestic products as referred to in Article 95 of the Treaty,[11] take account of the amount of the VAT paid in the Member State of exportation that is still contained in the value of the product at the time of importation:

(a) in such a way that that amount is not included in the taxable amount for the purposes of VAT payable on importation and is in addition deducted from the VAT payable on importation, or else
(b) in such a way that that amount is deducted only from the VAT payable on importation?

2. In the case defined in the first question, how should the amount referred to therein be calculated?'

In its first question the Hoge Raad [Supreme Court] asks essentially whether the residual part of the tax with which the imported goods are still burdened in the event of a sale by one private person to another must be taken into account solely in the calculation of the VAT payable on importation or also in determining the taxable amount. The

---

[11] Treaty of Rome, as revised by the Treaty of Amsterdam, May, 1999, Art. 90 (ex Art. 95) provides: "No Member State shall impose, directly or indirectly, on the products of other Member States any internal taxation of any kind in excess of that imposed directly or indirectly on similar domestic products. Furthermore, no Member State shall impose on the products of other Member States any internal taxation of such a nature as to afford indirect protection to other products."

second question is designed to ascertain how that residual part should be calculated.

The Commission states that the practical problems to be solved are in particular the following: by what method should account be taken of the VAT paid in another Member State without depriving the Member State of importation of tax revenue; how should the residual amount of tax contained in the purchase price be calculated; how can the authorities in the Member State of importation ascertain the rates of VAT applicable at the time of the initial purchase in the country of exportation; how should the amount of the residual tax contained in the sale price be calculated where different transactions have taken place in three or four different Member States; what form of proof should be required; what rule should be applied where the price of the second-hand goods is higher than the price of the goods new; and, lastly, should an exemption be provided for?

[The Commission's view was that if the goods increased in value while owned by the exporting private person, the exporting state should not refund any VAT and the importing state should tax only the difference between the import value and the original cost of the goods to the exporting seller. In other cases (when the value declined while owned by the exporting seller), the Commission's view was that the exporting state should refund to the exporter the tax based on the current value and the importing state should impose VAT on the same value.]

Those solutions can only be achieved by legislative means, that is to say by the amendment of the national laws concerning VAT payable on imports on the basis of a new Council Directive.

[P]ending the adoption of a legislative solution, in charging VAT on imports account must be taken of the effect of Article 95 of the Treaty. It is therefore for the Court to lay down guidelines compatible with Article 95 of the Treaty, consistent with the general scheme of the Sixth Directive and sufficiently simple to be able to be applied in a uniform manner throughout the Member States.

The answer which must be given to the first question is therefore that where a Member State charges VAT on the importation, from another Member State, of goods supplied by a non-taxable person, but does not charge VAT on the supply by a private person of similar goods within its own territory, the VAT payable on importation must be calculated by taking into account the amount of VAT paid in the Member State of exportation which is still contained in the value of the product at the time of importation, in such a way that that amount is not included in the taxable amount and is in addition deducted from the VAT payable on importation.

The second question concerns the calculation of the residual part of the VAT paid in the Member State of exportation which is still contained in the value of the goods at the time of their importation.

The Netherlands and French Governments... suggest that a rule should be applied whereby the tax charged in the exporting State is written off. To write off the tax on the basis of the useful life of the imported goods would be too uncertain to be acceptable, in view of the different practices in the various Member States and sectors concerned; therefore, an approach should be adopted similar to the system laid down in Article 20(2) of the Sixth Directive for adjustment of deductions in the case of capital goods which have been sold after being used. Such a system would involve writing off the goods over five years and would thus mean that the residual part of the VAT contained in the value of the imported goods would correspond to the VAT actually charged in the Member State of exportation less one-fifth per calendar year or part of a calendar year which had elapsed since the date on which the VAT was charged.

Schul considers that the amortization of the tax charged in the country of exportation will, in the majority of cases, be reflected by a reduction in the value of the goods. For that reason the residual part should in its view be calculated on the basis of the VAT rate applied in the Member State of exportation, provided that the resulting amount does not exceed the amount actually paid in that State. Where the value of the goods has increased, the residual amount will thus correspond to the amount actually paid.

Eventually, at the hearing, the Commission adopted the same opinion.

Having considered the various arguments, the Court shares that view. Any standard method, such as that suggested by the Netherlands and French Governments, would have the disadvantage of diverging too far from the rules of the Sixth Directive to be developed by judicial interpretation. Irrespective of its intrinsic merits, the method adopted by the Gerechtshof stays close to those rules, whilst being practicable and observing the provisions of Article 95 of the Treaty.

The method is consistent with Article 95 of the Treaty and the provisions of the Sixth Directive. It can be applied by the tax authorities without giving rise to serious practical difficulties since, in cases in which the value of the goods has decreased, the residual part of the tax that is still contained in that value at the time of importation is calculated by reducing the amount of VAT actually paid in the Member State of exportation by a percentage representing the proportion by which the goods have depreciated, whereas in cases in which the value of the goods has increased, that residual part simply corresponds to the amount of tax actually charged.

In that connection it should be remembered that... the burden of proving facts which justify the taking into account of the tax paid in the Member State of exportation that is still contained in the value of the goods on importation falls on the importer.

On those grounds, [on the second question, the ECJ ruled:]

> The amount of VAT paid in the Member State of exportation that is still contained in the value of the goods at the time of importation is equal:
>
> > in cases in which the value of the goods has decreased between the date on which VAT was last charged in the Member State of exportation and the date of importation: to the amount of VAT actually paid in the Member State of exportation, less a percentage representing the proportion by which the goods have depreciated;
> >
> > in cases in which the value of the goods has increased over that same period: to the full amount of the VAT actually paid in the Member State of exportation.

V. Place of Supply Rules in International Trade

A. Basic Rules on the Place of a Supply of Goods and Services

Most VAT regimes (territorial taxes) rely on the destination principle for international transactions – exports are zero-rated and imports are taxed. To zero rate exports, exports are treated as taxable supplies within the exporting country and the exporter therefore can claim credit for input VAT attributable to the export sales. In contrast, under most VATs, foreign sales of goods located outside the taxing jurisdiction are beyond the scope of the tax.[12] VAT paid on purchases attributable to these foreign supplies generally do not qualify for the input credit. In addition, imports of goods and imports of some services are taxed. As a result, it is necessary to have rules to determine where a supply or import takes place – to classify a supply as domestic or foreign. A few countries, such as New Zealand, impose a GST with a global reach. The global versus territorial VAT is discussed later in this chapter.

Most countries with a territorial (in contrast to a global) VAT regime have detailed rules to identify the location of a supply. This location or place of supply approach also gives contracting parties some flexibility to establish the place where a supply takes place and therefore its VAT consequences. Supplies within the taxing country include supplies within the territorial boundaries of the country. Disputes may arise, for example, if a supply occurs in territorial waters that extend beyond the limits recognized by neighboring countries or by international law. Under the EU Sixth Directive, the location of a supply of goods depends in part on the terms of the supply since, if goods are to be delivered, the supply takes place where the goods are located when

---

[12] If a nonresident sells goods or services within the taxing jurisdiction, under some VAT regimes, the sale may be treated as a foreign sale unless the nonresident seller conducts business within the country, the seller is registered for VAT purposes in the country, or engages in activities for a short period of time and may otherwise avoid VAT liability. See Canadian Goods and Services tax, S.C. 1990, c. 45, §143(1). The last category covers nonresidents who charge admission to "a place of amusement, a seminar, an activity or an event." *Id*. at §143(1)(c).

the shipment begins.[13] The location therefore can be altered by altering the place where the goods reside when they are shipped to the buyer. The U.K. VAT, implementing the Sixth Directive principles, has a series of rules to determine the location of a supply. If goods are not exported or imported, they are supplied in the United Kingdom if the goods are physically in the United Kingdom.[14] If the seller must install or assemble the goods, the supply takes place where the goods are installed or assembled.[15]

Under the recast of the Sixth Directive, Article 44 (previously Article 9(1)), services take place "where the supplier has established his business or has a fixed establishment from which the service is supplied, or, in the absence of such a place of business or fixed establishment, the place where he has his permanent address or usually resides."[16]

> It is a feature of services that the location of supply or of consumption is often elusive or even meaningless. This is particularly important for international trade in services, where two problems arise. First, rules must be devised to define what actually constitutes an export or import of a service; defining the location of a service supply is a prerequisite for effective treatment of traded items. Second, the nontangibility of services makes it difficult to detect purchases of services by physical checks at border points or inland.[17]

The United Kingdom treats services as located where the supplier of the services belongs.[18] The U.K. VAT, nevertheless, assigns certain services to

---

[13] See Sixth Council Directive 77/388/EEC of 17 May 1977 on the harmonization of the laws of the Member States relating to turnover taxes – Common system of value added tax: uniform basis of assessment (OJ 1977 L 145 [hereinafter Sixth Directive], p. 1, as recast by Proposal for a Council Directive on the common system of value added tax (Recast), COM (2004) 246 final, 2004/0079 (CNS) April 15, 2004, and updated with a compromise text (FISC) presented by the Austrian Presidency 21 April 2006, 8547/06 [hereinafter Recast Sixth Directive], Art. 8(1)(a) in Sixth Directive and Art. 33 in Recast Sixth Directive. There are special rules, including those governing intra-Community supplies and supplies through distribution systems.

[14] Value Added Tax Act 1994, ch. 23 (United Kingdom) [hereinafter VATA 1994], §7(2). See Recast Sixth Directive, *supra* note 13, at Art. 37.

[15] VATA 1994, *supra* note 14, at §7(3). There are additional rules governing sales involving other EU member states. *Id*. at §7(4)–(6). If a sale of goods is not governed by other rules and the goods are removed to or from the United Kingdom, the sale is located in the United Kingdom if they are removed from the United Kingdom and had not previously entered the United Kingdom. *Id*. at §7(7).

[16] Recast Sixth Directive, *supra* note 13, at Art. 44 (Art. 9(1) in Sixth Directive before Recast). This rule does not apply to services by an intermediary. There are other exceptions. For a discussion of "fixed establishment" under the Sixth Directive, see Iavagnilio," Concepts of Permanent and Fixed Establishment under Italian Law – The Philip Morris Case," *VAT Monitor*, Nov/Dec. 2002, p. 470.

[17] Kay & Davis, The VAT and Services, ch. 6 of GILLIS, SHOUP & SICAT, VALUE ADDED TAXATION IN DEVELOPING COUNTRIES 70–82, at 77 (World Bank 1990).

[18] VATA 1994, *supra* note 14, at §7(10) (United Kingdom). The Russian VAT formerly included only this strict rule on location, even for consulting services and staff provision services, but required the user to pay VAT on these services under a "reverse charge" system. Russia changed its VAT to conform in large part to the U.K. approach discussed in the text. See Henry, "Proposed Amendments to Russian VAT Law Provide Needed Place of Supply Rules," 12 *Tax Notes Int'l* 2 (Jan. 1, 1996).

the place where the services are received. For example, advertising, legal, accounting, and data processing services take place where the services are received.[19] Certain other services, if not listed in Schedule 5 to the VAT Act, take place where they are received if the recipient is a registered VAT person.[20] The U.K. VAT also gives the government authority to issue orders varying the rules to determine the location of a supply of goods or services.[21] Recent amendments to the Sixth Directive reverse the basic place of supply rule governing some services. They treat electronic and other specified services as taking place where the customer is located.[22]

Some countries with territorial VAT systems, such as the member states of the EU, will continue to have place of supply disputes, even if they had clear rules on the allocation of tax jurisdiction among parties to a single transaction. For example, how should the place of supply be determined for the construction, repair, and renovation of a bridge that connects two countries? In a contract covering a bridge over the Rodebach between Germany and the Netherlands, the two countries involved asked the European Council for authority to depart from the rules of the Sixth Directive and treat the construction site and the bridge after its completion as being on German territory.[23]

Where does a broker involved in the sale of yachts render intermediation services involving a buyer and seller residing in different countries? In one case in the EU, the broker in the Netherlands arranged a transaction involving a yacht located in and owned by a person in France who sold it to a person in the Netherlands. The sale of the yacht took place in France, where the yacht was located when the transport of the yacht began. The ECJ held that the intermediation services took place where the transaction underlying the supply was carried out, not where the broker or customer resided.[24]

The complexity and lack of consistency in the EU in the treatment of the place of supply of services prompted the European Commission (EC) to issue a consultation paper on this topic that proposes, among other items, that the place of taxation of services is where the customer is established.[25]

The importance of the rules governing the location of services is illustrated by the following *Berkholz* case (governed by EU law) involving the provision of gaming machines aboard a ship traveling between Denmark and Germany.

---

[19] VATA 1994, *supra* note 14, at Sch. 5.

[20] *Id.* at Sch.5, &9.

[21] VATA 1994, *supra* note 14, at §7(11).

[22] See Recast Sixth Directive, *supra* note 13, at Art. 56 (Art. 9(2)(e) in Sixth Directive before Recast), and discussion of electronic and telecommunication services *infra* this chapter.

[23] See COM (2005) 109 final, discussed in IBFD – EVD ews: Terra/Kajus – 18 April 2005, p. 1.

[24] Case C-68/03, *Staatssecretaris van Financiën v. D. Lipjes* (ECJ Judgment 2004).

[25] Consultation Paper; Simplifying VAT obligations: The one-stop system, European Commission, TAXUD/C3/ . . . March 2004. This consultation is conducted in connection with the Communication on the VAT Strategy, COM (2003) 614. The VAT One-Stop-Shop project is IP/04/654.

Gunter Berkholz v. Finanzamt Hamburg-Mitte-Altstadt[26]

HEADNOTES. The territorial scope of the Sixth Directive . . . coincides, in the case of each member state, with the scope of its value-added-tax legislation. Hence, Article 9 of the directive, concerning the place where a service is deemed to be supplied, does not prevent the Member States from taxing services provided outside their territorial jurisdiction on board sea-going ships over which they have jurisdiction.

In order to determine the point of reference for tax purposes for the provision of services it is for each Member State to determine from the range of options set forth in [the Sixth] Directive . . . which point of reference is most appropriate from the point of view of tax. According to Article 9(1)[27] of the Directive, the place where the supplier has established his business is a primary point of reference inasmuch as regard is to be had to another establishment from which the services are supplied only if the reference to the place where the supplier has established his business does not lead to a rational result for tax purposes or creates a conflict with another member state.

JUDGMENT. [T]he activities of the applicant in the main proceedings, the undertaking Abe-Werbung-Afred Berkholz, whose registered office is in Hamburg, include the installation and operation of gaming machines, juke boxes and the like. It operates most of its machines in public houses in Schleswig-Holstein and Hamburg but has also installed some gaming machines on board two ferryboats owned by the Deutsche Bunderbahn (Federal German Railways) which ply between Puttgarden on the German island of Fehmarn and Rodbyhavn (Denmark). Those machines are maintained, repaired and replaced at regular intervals by employees of Abe-Werbung, who settle accounts with the Deutsche Bundesbahn in situ. Although those employees spend a proportion of their working hours in carrying out those operations, the applicant does not maintain a permanent staff on the ferryboats.

The German tax authorities consider that approximately 10% of the turnover generated by the gaming machines arises when the vessels are in the German port, 25% during the passage through German territorial waters and the remainder on the high seas, in Danish territorial waters or in the Danish port. The Finanzamt charged tax on the entire turnover generated in 1980 by Abe-Werbung on the two ferries, deeming it to have arisen at Abe-Werbung's place of business in Hamburg and hence in the German collection area in accordance with [the German VAT] introduced pursuant to Article 9(1) of the Sixth Directive.

---

[26] Case 168/84, 1985 ECJ CELEX LEXIS 2748, (Judgment of the ECJ july 4, 1985) [edited by the authors].

[27] Recast sixth Directive, *supra* note 13, at Art. 44 [added by the authors].

The applicant in the main proceedings considers that the services in question were provided from a 'fixed establishment' within the meaning of article 9(1) of the Sixth Directive, located on board the ferries. It therefore regards only 10%, or at the most a further 25%, of the turnover generated by the gaming machines on board the ships as chargeable to German turnover tax.

The Finanzgericht considers that article 9 of the Sixth Directive is designed to lay down a clear and straightforward basic principle for the determination of the state in which services subject to value-added tax are deemed to be supplied. It appears from the seventh recital in the preamble to the Sixth Directive that Article 9 is intended, through the harmonization of the relevant national legislation, to eliminate conflicts concerning jurisdiction as between Member States and make for a fairer distribution of the financial burdens between the Member States while, at the same time, taking account of the fact that a proportion of national value-added tax revenues constitutes an essential element of the communities' own resources.

[T]he Finanzericht referred the following . . . question to the court for a preliminary ruling:

[Does the Sixth Directive's] term 'fixed establishment' also cover facilities for conducting a business (such as, for example, the operation of gaming machines) on board a ship sailing on the high seas outside the national territory? If so, what are the relevant criteria for the existence of a 'fixed establishment'?

[The following observations were submitted to the court by Denmark, France, and the Commission.]

[According to the Danish government], it cannot be argued that a Member State may tax services supplied on board ship only in so far as the ship in question is within that state's territorial jurisdiction. As a result, it is for each Member State to determine the territorial application of its legislation in accordance with the rules of international law. The scope of the directive itself is coterminous with those limits. Hence there is nothing to prevent Member States from applying their tax legislation on ships flying the national flag which are outside their territorial jurisdiction. . . . In point of fact, difficulties have never arisen between Denmark and the Federal Republic of Germany in that regard; as far as the crossing in question is concerned, the Danish authorities assume jurisdiction over the Danish ferryboats and the German authorities over the German vessels.

The French government considers that a 'fixed establishment' within the meaning of article 9(1) of the Sixth Directive may cover any centre of activity where a person liable to value-added tax regularly carries out operations falling within the scope of that tax. It therefore considers that the installation on board vessels sailing the high seas of automatic gaming or other machines which are, inter alia, maintained, repaired and replaced in situ on a permanent basis by the operator's staff constitutes a fixed establishment within the meaning of the said article 9(1).

The Commission contends that, within article 9 of the Sixth Directive, the concept of a fixed establishment is placed on an equal footing with the place where the supplier has established his business. It considers that in view of the proliferation of automatic devices capable of providing services without the need for human operators to be present it ought, in principle, to be possible to view such machines as a fixed establishment within the meaning of article 9 of the Sixth Directive. [G]oods or services ought to be taxed in the state where they are consumed. The Commission argues that it follows that services provided by such machines – by the same token, moreover, as other services provided on the high seas by persons – should be exempt from all taxation.

Article 9 is designed to secure the rational delimitation of the respective areas covered by national value-added tax rules by determining in a uniform manner the place where services are deemed to be provided for tax purposes.

Article 9(1) reads as follows:

'The place where a service is supplied shall be deemed to be the place where the supplier has established his business or has a fixed establishment from which the service is supplied or, in the absence of such a place of business or fixed establishment, the place where he has his permanent address or usually resides.'

Since this case concerns services supplied on board sea-going ships, it is appropriate first of all to determine the territorial scope of the directive. [T]he territorial scope of the directive coincides, in the case of each Member State, with the scope of its value-added tax legislation. As the Danish government correctly contends, article 9 does not restrict the Member States' freedom to tax services provided outside their territorial jurisdiction on board sea-going ships over which they have jurisdiction. Contrary to the view of the applicant in the main proceedings, supported by the Commission, the Sixth Directive by no means requires services supplied on the high seas, or, more generally, outside the sovereign territory of the State having jurisdiction over the vessel, to be exempted from tax irrespective of the place where those services are deemed to be supplied – the place where the supplier has established his business or some other fixed establishment.

Equally, it is for the tax authorities in each Member State to determine from the range of options set forth in the Directive which point of reference is most appropriate to determine tax jurisdiction over a given service. According to article 9(1), the place where the supplier has established his business is a primary point of reference inasmuch as regard is to be had to another establishment from which the services are supplied only if the reference to the place where the supplier has established his business does not lead to a rational result for tax purposes or creates a conflict with another Member State.

It appears from the context of the concepts employed in article 9 and from its aim, as stated above, that services cannot be deemed to be supplied at an establishment other than the place where the supplier has established his business unless that establishment is of a certain minimum size and both the human and technical resources necessary for the provision of the services are permanently present. It does not appear that the installation on board a sea-going ship of gaming machines, which are maintained intermittently, is capable of constituting such an establishment, especially if tax may appropriately be charged at the place where the operator of the machines has his permanent business establishment.

The Finanzgericht's first question should therefore be answered as follows: Article 9(1) of the Sixth Council Directive . . . must be interpreted as meaning that an installation for carrying on a commercial activity, such as the operation of gaming machines, on board a ship sailing on the high seas outside the national territory may be regarded as a fixed establishment within the meaning of that provision only if the establishment entails the permanent presence of both the human and technical resources necessary for the provision of those services and it is not appropriate to deem those services to have been provided at the place where the supplier has established his business.

[According to the ECJ, the national court is to decide if the human and technical resources aboard the boat was sufficient to treat the boat as a permanent establishment.]

These place of supply issues continue to plague the ECJ and national courts within the EU. The *Antje Köhler* case[28] involved sales aboard a cruise ship that began and ended its journey within the EU but also stopped outside the EU. The ECJ ruled that sales made during the stops outside the EU were taxable in those non-EU countries, not in the EU. Although the place of supplies on board transport vehicles is based on the port of departure, this rule does not apply when there are stops outside the EU.[29]

In H.M. Revenue and Customs v. *Zurich Insurance Company*[30] Pricewater-houseCoopers AG in Switzerland (PwC) rendered consultancy services as part of the installation of SAP financial accounting software throughout the company that had its head office (HO) in Switzerland. The company's branch in the United Kingdom was a fixed establishment in the United Kingdom. The implementation of the software for the U.K. branch was conducted by the U.K. staff (60 percent) and by PwC staff in the United Kingdom (40 percent). The tribunal concluded that the supply took place at the company's home office in Switzerland, where the contract was entered into. On appeal, the

[28] Recast sixth Directive, *supra* note 13, at Art. 44 [added by the authors].
[29] See Sixth Directive, *supra* note 13, at Art. 8(1)(c).
[30] [2006] EWHC 593 (Chancery Div.).

court held that the services took place at the company's establishment in the U.K., where the actual services were performed. This conclusion "produces a rational result, which avoids non-taxation in a case where there might be taxation, and which avoids distortion of competition." The U.K. branch was not "a fixed establishment to which the service is supplied."[31]

B. Recent Developments in the EU on the Place of Supply

The place of supply rules in the EU remain unsettled. The EU recognizes that despite the required harmonization based on the Sixth Directive, the articles of the Sixth Directive have received varying interpretations in the member states. In an attempt to clarify and implement the Sixth Directive in a consistent fashion, the European Commission issued, among other pronouncements, a working paper,[32] a Council Directive,[33] and a Council Regulation that includes rules on the place of taxable transactions.[34] Thie Council Regulation contains articles on the place of taxable transactions, including rules governing electronically supplied services. These place of supply rules are covered in section VIII (B) of this chapter.

C. Territorial versus Global Reach of a VAT

An income tax may be imposed only on income earned within the territory of the taxing jurisdiction (a territorial tax) or imposed on income earned worldwide (a global tax such as the U.S. tax imposed on the worldwide income of its citizens and residents). The same is true of a transactional tax on consumption, such as a VAT. A VAT could be imposed on the worldwide supplies of registered persons domiciled or resident in the taxing country (global) or imposed only on supplies within the tax jurisdiction (territorial).

---

[31] *Id.* at ¶ The court concluded that the analysis based on the Sixth Directive produced the same result as under the reverse charge rule in the U.K. VAT Act.

[32] The working paper examines the criteria to determine a fixed establishment under Articles 9(1) and 9(2)(e).Value Added Tax Committee, Working Paper No. 498, TAXUD/ 1628/05, concerning the application of the Community VAT legislation (May 2, 2005).

[33] The Council Directive covers the place of supply of gas and electricity. The place of supply under this Directive depends on the recipient of the supply; that is, whether the recipient is a taxable dealer or another type of customer. Council Directive 2003/92/EC of October 7, 2003, amending Directive 77/388/EEC. There also is a proposal for a Council Directive on the place of supply of services, COM (2005) 334 final, proposing the replacement of the Sixth Directive, Articles 9 & 28b(C)–(F) with new Article 9 to 9j. See European Commission proposal to change the VAT rules on the place of supply of services, IBFD TNS Online, August 5, 2005.

[34] Regulation (EC) No. 1777/2005 of October 17, 2005, laying down implementing measures for Directive 77/388/EEC on the common system of value added tax. It generally takes effect July 1, 2006, except the provision governing card handling fees will take effect January 1, 2006 [hereinafter Regulation (EC) 1777/2005]. See generally Terra & Kajus, "The Council Regulation laying down implementing measures for the Sixth Directive," IBFD – EVD News Special, Nov. 7, 2005.

The Australian GST basically is a territorial VAT, but it has its unique set of place of supply rules.[35]

New Zealand, South Africa, and a few other countries basically start with a VAT with a global reach.[36] These countries tax registered residents on their worldwide supplies. They then narrow the tax base to treat internationally traded goods in a fashion similar to the destination principle used under a territorial VAT. South Africa zero rates exports and removes from the tax base supplies by branches or the head office outside the country if those foreign branches or head office can be separately identified and maintain an independent system of accounting for those foreign operations.[37] It generally is more difficult for a taxpayer, under a global approach, to structure a transaction to avoid VAT jurisdiction.

When a VAT is imposed on a global basis, the VAT typically does not contain detailed location or place of supply rules covering most supplies because the imposition of tax does not depend on the place where the supply occurs. In contrast, most VAT systems in use today are territorial taxes that rely on the destination principle. That is, the tax is imposed only on the supply of goods or the rendition of services to be consumed domestically. Those countries have the kind of place of supply rules that are discussed earlier.

New Zealand's global VAT imposes tax on the basis of the residence of the seller rather than the location of the sale.[38] Supplies by residents

---

[35] A New Tax System (Goods and Services Tax) Act 1999 [hereinafter Australian GST], §9–5. A supply of goods is connected with Australia if the goods are delivered or made available in Australia to the recipient of the supply, the goods are being removed from Australia, the goods are being imported or installed or assembled in Australia. A supply of real property is connected with Australia if the real property or its related land is in Australia. Any other supply is connected with Australia if the thing (like a service) is done in Australia or the supplier makes the supply through an enterprise conducted in Australia. *Id*. at §9–25. Although a business or other activity apparently does not have to be conducted in Australia to be an enterprise and therefore some supplies by a nonresident enterprise can be subject to the GST. See *id*. at §9–20 definition of an enterprise, which does not require that the business be conducted in Australia. Supplies of anything other than goods or real property that are not done in Australia are taxable only if the enterprise is carried on in Australia. *Id*. at §9–25(5). For this purpose, an enterprise is carried on in Australia if it is carried on through a permanent establishment (as defined in the Income Tax Act), or through a certain place that would be a permanent establishment if certain parts of the income tax definition of a permanent establishment did not apply. *Id*. at §9-25(6). Thus, supplies of services through a permanent establishment in Australia or services rendered in Australia appear to come within the scope of the GST, but most or all would be zero rated.

[36] See, for example, the New Zealand Goods and Services Tax Act 1985, 1985, No. 141 [hereinafter NZ GST], §8(2). Nonresidents are subject to the N.Z. GST if the goods supplied are located in New Zealand when the supply occurs, or the services are physically performed in N.Z. by a person who is in N.Z. when the services are performed. *Id*. at §8(3). There are special rules in section 8 governing imported services and telecommunication services.

[37] Value-Added Tax Act No. 89 of 1991 [hereinafter RSA VAT], §1 definition of "enterprise" (South Africa).

[38] Under an exception, sales made by nonresidents also may be treated as domestic sales subject to the Goods and Services Tax. NZ GST, *supra* note 36, at §8(2). If sales by nonresidents

occur, for GST purposes, in New Zealand. Supplies of goods by nonresidents occur in New Zealand if the goods are in New Zealand when supplied. Supplies of services by nonresidents occur in New Zealand if the services are rendered in New Zealand. Unless both parties to the transaction agree to the contrary, when a nonresident supplies goods to or render services for a registered person in New Zealand, the supply is treated as if it occurs outside New Zealand and therefore is not taxable.[39] Imports are taxed.

This global-territorial distinction may not be too significant in an island nation like New Zealand that can keep account of the international movement of goods. A similar approach, however, was adopted by the Republic of South Africa (RSA), whose businesses operate in contiguous and other neighboring countries.

The RSA imposes VAT not on supplies made in RSA but on supplies by a vendor in the course of an enterprise conducted within or partly within the RSA.[40] It also taxes imports into the RSA.[41] Although worldwide supplies (a global approach) by an RSA business could be taxed, the scope of the VAT is not that wide. Foreign supplies by an RSA enterprise are not subject to the RSA VAT if the supplies are made through an operation (such as a branch or main business) outside the RSA, but only if "the branch or main business can be separately identified, and an independent system of accounting is maintained by the concern in respect of the branch or main business."[42] For example, assume a business operating in the RSA has branches in Namibia and Swaziland. The Namibian branch engages in significant sales activity there and maintains separate accounting records. The Swaziland branch's supplies are too low to justify separate accounting. The Namibian supplies are not subject to the RSA VAT, but the Swaziland supplies are covered. If the Swaziland supplies qualify as RSA exports, they will be zero rated; otherwise, they are taxable.[43]

The following *Wilson & Horton Ltd.* case illustrates the difficulty under a New Zealand/RSA approach in determining it advertisements placed by foreign customers are subject to the VAT.

---

are deemed domestic source sales under this exception and the items are sold to registered persons to be used in connection with the latter's taxable activity, the sales are deemed foreign source unless the buyer and the seller agree that this rule shall not apply. This proviso permits the buyer to obtain a credit for input tax attributable to such purchase, so long as the seller treats the sales as a sale within New Zealand. A. SCHENK, VALUE ADDED TAX – A MODEL STATUTE AND COMMENTARY: A REPORT OF THE COMMITTEE ON VALUE ADDED TAX OF THE AMERICAN BAR ASSOCIATION SECTION OF TAXATION, p. 35. A supply may occur in NZ even if the supplier is not resident in NZ. This exception applies if the goods are in NZ when they are supplied or if services are physically performed in NZ by a person who is in NZ when the services are rendered. NZ GST, *supra* note 36, at §8(2)(a).

[39] See NZ GST, *supra* note 36, at §8.
[40] RSA VAT, *supra* note 37, at §7(1).
[41] *Id.*
[42] *Id.* at proviso (ii) of §1 definition of enterprise.
[43] See South Africa: Place-of-supply rules, *VAT Monitor*, Mar./Apr. 2005, p. 140.

Wilson & Horton Ltd. v. Commissioner of Inland Revenue[44]

HEADNOTE. Wilson & Horton Ltd (the objector) offered the service of publishing advertisements for its customers in its publications. This service was offered to people resident in New Zealand and overseas customers. In the case of advertisements placed by persons not resident in New Zealand, the advertisements were in five different categories, namely:

(Category 1)   Advertisements placed by overseas parties which refer to services offered by New Zealand residents.

(Category 2)   Advertisements placed by overseas parties which refer to goods situated outside of New Zealand which are offered by New Zealand residents.

(Category 3)   Advertisements placed by overseas parties which refer to goods situated inside New Zealand offered by persons not resident in New Zealand.

(Category 4)   Advertisements placed by overseas parties which refer to goods situated inside New Zealand which are offered by New Zealand residents.

(Category 5)   "Image" advertisements placed by overseas parties for the promotion of a brand name or brand product, where the goods or services referred to in the advertisement are sold in New Zealand.

The Commissioner...took the view that the objector had incorrectly zero-rated invoices sent to overseas customers. The Commissioner and the objector disagreed as to the proper treatment of invoices in the five categories referred to.

JUDGMENT: RICHARDSON J.[45] [Wilson & Horton publish advertisements for foreign clients in the New Zealand Herald. It consistently zero rated these advertisements. The question on appeal was whether the five categories of supplies listed earlier were taxable at the standard 12.5 percent rate or were zero rated under section 11(2)(e) of the Goods and Services Tax Act 1985.]

Section 11(2)(e) of the Act provides:

(2) Where, but for this section, a supply of services would be charged with tax under section 8 of this Act, any such supply shall be charged at the rate of zero per cent where –

(e) The services are supplied for and to a person who is not resident in New Zealand and who is outside New Zealand at the time the

---

[44] [1996] 1 NZLR 26 (Ct. App. Wellington). [Edited by the authors.]
[45] The opinions of the other members of the panel were omitted.

services are performed, not being services which are supplied directly in connection with –

(i) Land or any improvement thereto situated inside New Zealand; or
(ii) Moveable personal property … situated inside New Zealand at the time the services are performed;

and not being services which are the acceptance of an obligation to refrain from carrying on any taxable activity, to the extent that the conduct of that activity would have occurred within New Zealand.

Much of the evidence and argument in the High Court was directed to the question of who benefited from the advertisements and, in particular, the manner in which New Zealand retailers of goods and services advertised and other persons in New Zealand benefited compared with any benefit to the foreign client. It is sufficient to note four features or implications of any comparative benefit assessment.

First, many parties may benefit from an advertisement placed by a foreign client which advertises goods or services. For example:

(a) The foreign client which placed the advertisement (if the manufacturer or ultimate supplier of goods and services) will benefit from any increased sales to retailers;
(b) The retailers in New Zealand supplying the goods and services will also benefit from any increased sales arising from the advertisements;
(c) Wilson & Horton Ltd will receive a benefit from advertising revenue;
(d) Any advertising agency placing the advertisements on behalf of the non-resident client will receive a fee;
(e) Purchasers of the paper and members of the public reading the advertisements will benefit from an awareness of goods and services available in the market;
(f) Retailers and suppliers of related products may also benefit from cross-sales arising from the advertisements; and
(g) Investors in those businesses may benefit from increased sales arising from advertisements.

Second, there are obvious difficulties in measuring the benefits flowing to various parties from advertising activities.

Third, the newspaper office will neither know nor expect to be told what arrangements a foreign client has with its New Zealand franchisee or subsidiary whether for advertising of goods and services for supply in New Zealand or for image advertising of a brand, product or company, and for charging the franchisee or subsidiary for promotional activities.

Fourth, if New Zealand businesses benefit from the advertising by sales of advertised goods and services, those supplies are, of course, subject to GST.

Having regard to those considerations it is readily understandable why the benefit argument for the Commissioner in this Court was put on the basis that §11(2)(e) was not satisfied unless the foreign client was the exclusive beneficiary of the advertisement it placed in the Herald.

THE SCHEME OF THE LEGISLATION. Liability for goods and services tax arises on "the supply . . . in New Zealand of goods and services . . . by a registered person in the course or furtherance of a taxable activity carried on by that person, by reference to the value of that supply" (§8(1)). Taxable activity, as defined in §6(1)(a), is directed to "the supply of goods and services to any other person for a consideration"; supplier "in relation to any supply of goods and services, means the person making the supply" (§2); and the recipient is "the person receiving the supply" (§2).

Those provisions are directed to the contractual arrangements between the supplier and the recipient of the supply. In keeping with the general statutory scheme in that respect §11, providing for zero-rating of supply transactions where the stated overseas element is present, follows that same pattern. It follows that where, as in the presently material §11(2)(e), the provision refers to "services . . . supplied . . . to a person" the statutory dictionary applies and the phrase refers to the contractual position and so to the person who has provided the consideration. That is common ground between the parties, as it was in the High Court.

INTERPRETATION OF §11(2)(e). To qualify for zero-rating under §11(2)(e) the services supplied by Wilson & Horton in publishing advertisements in the Herald must satisfy two requirements.

First, the services must be supplied "for and to a person" who is not resident in New Zealand and who is not present in New Zealand when the services are performed. It is common ground that the latter elements, namely that the person concerned, the foreign client, was not resident in New Zealand and was not present in New Zealand when the advertisements were published in the Herald, were satisfied.

Second, the services must not be supplied directly in connection with land or moveable property situated in New Zealand. The statutory nexus expressed in the phrase "supplied directly in connection with" such advertised goods was not satisfied.

Interpretation of §11(2)(e): "for and to any person"

Reference to any standard dictionary brings home the wide variety of senses in which the preposition "for" may be employed.

In the context of §11(2)(e), services supplied "for" a person not resident in New Zealand may indicate several possible senses in which "for" may be intended. It may refer simply to the person to whom the services were supplied. It may be used in a representative sense, on behalf of or on account of a foreign client. In that meaning it contemplates that the person placing the order is acting on behalf of a third party. It may be used in the sense of purpose, for the purposes of the foreign client. It may connote benefit, for the benefit of the foreign client or in favour of the foreign client. Such a rubbery word has various shades of meaning. Frequently, too, it is deliberately employed to convey emphasis, as in the Gettysburg address, government of the people, by the people, for the people.

Section 11(2)(e) employs the composite expression "for and to a person".

While it is important to seek to give adequate meaning to all the words actually employed in the legislation, it is not realistic to expect that busy drafters or legislators will always ensure that each provision is tautly and precisely drawn without any surplusage. Also it is not uncommon for legislative drafting to convey emphasis through a combination of words. Some apparent repetition by the use of different or added words may be explicable for those reasons.

I am inclined to think that the framers of §11(2)(e) employed both expressions to convey emphasis and perhaps to bring out the intent that the contract must be genuine and so the services must be supplied under that contract to and for the other contracting party.

Further, if one may read a flavour of benefit to the foreign client into the composite expression, that is met if it is apparent that the foreign client will benefit from the advertising, whether or not anyone else does. The obvious commercial inference is that the contracting party paying the bill expects to benefit from the services supplied. Equally obviously, in some cases others may benefit from any resulting sales. Paragraph (e) would surely have been worded differently had it been intended to exclude its application unless the foreign client was the only person who could benefit from the services supplied. It would either have been totally recast or, at least, have been prefaced by an adjective so as to read "the services are supplied exclusively for and to ...".

The statutory focus under §11(2)(e) is on the contractual supply of services, not on non-contractual benefits. It is the foreign client to which the composite expression "for or to a person" relates. The statute is not in its terms concerned with whether, and if so, how the supply might affect other persons. Had Parliament intended to impose a separate benefit test calling for a comparative assessment of who might benefit from the content of particular advertisements, it could be expected to have said so explicitly rather than leaving it for implication. Had Parliament intended to exclude zero-rating wherever a New Zealand resident would benefit or might benefit from the advertisement (for example as a result of sales to readers of the newspapers) it would surely have said so. On a straightforward reading of §11(2)(e) it is sufficient if the services are supplied for and to an overseas person, whatever benefits might probably or might conceivably accrue subsequently to others.

RESULT. The Court being unanimous the appeal is allowed, the orders made in the High Court are quashed and the question posed in the case stated, namely whether the Commissioner acted incorrectly in excluding from zero-rated supplies in the amended assessment of 22 March 1990 advertising undertaken by Wilson & Horton for persons who were not resident in New Zealand at the time of supply, is answered in the affirmative.

VI. Imports

A. Imports of Goods

As discussed earlier in this chapter, most countries with VATs define the territorial reach of their VATs according to the destination principle. As a result, imports of goods and imports of some services are taxed. Except for imports exempt from VAT, imports of goods are taxable,[46] whether they are imported by registered persons or consumers. Goods generally are taxed when they "enter" the country for customs purposes. In practice, this means that the VAT is collected by Customs at the border or collected by the Post Office when they enter by post.[47] Services linked to the import of goods are taxed at the same time. Thus, insurance and freight are included in the value[48] of the goods that are subject to VAT.

Some countries provide for the deferral of VAT on imported goods until the importer files a VAT return for the tax period that includes the date of the import. The deferral privilege varies by country.[49] The Australian GST provides for deferral of tax on imports "in circumstances specified in the regulations, within such further time specified in the regulations, and at the place and in the manner specified in the regulations."[50] The regulations provide that a person may apply for approval to defer the payment of GST on taxable imports. Some countries restrict the deferral privilege to importers with a record of complying with the VAT. In Australia, the Commissioner may refuse the application in specified circumstances, including the case where the application is by a person convicted of a tax offense, or where the applicant has taxes due.[51] Persons approved under these Australian

---

[46] An import of money generally is not treated as an import of goods. See Australian GST, *supra* note 36, at §13–5(3).

[47] See, generally, *id.* at §33–15(1).

[48] The valuation rules are discussed in Chapter 8 *infra*.

[49] New Zealand has an optional deferred payment scheme that requires covered importers to pay duty within twenty-one working days after the end of the importer's billing cycle. Tax Information Bulletin Vol. 9, No. 11 (New Zealand).

[50] Australian GST, *supra* note 35, at §33–15(1)(b).

[51] A New Tax System (Goods and Services Tax) Regulations 1999, Reg. 33–15.04 (Australia).

regulations must pay GST on taxable imports "on or before the 21st day after the end of the month in which the liability for the GST arose."[52]

Consistent with the World Trade Organization rules that prohibit discrimination against imports from member WTO countries, items exempt or zero rated if supplied domestically typically are exempt if imported.[53] Thus, if the domestic sale of rice is zero rated, the import of rice is not taxed. Contrary to this practice, Peru taxes some imports that are not taxed if supplied domestically.[54]

Goods placed in a bonded warehouse or imported directly into a duty-free zone may not be treated as imported until withdrawn from the bonded warehouse or withdrawn from the duty-free zone for domestic consumption.[55] Goods manufactured in a duty-free zone that are exported are zero rated, but if those manufactured goods are sold to a domestic customer, they are treated the same as any domestic sale. They are taxed if a domestic sale of those goods are taxed.

B. Imports of Services

Some countries with VAT impose VAT on all imported services, but most countries tax only limited categories of imported services. At a minimum, VAT generally is imposed on services attributable to imported goods by including the value of those services as part of the value of the imported goods. For example, Australia defines the value of a taxable import as the customs value plus certain taxes and duties, plus, to the extent not included in customs value, the amount paid or payable for transportation to their place of consignment in Australia plus insurance.[56]

The place of supply rules developed in the EU (although in the process of change) and adopted by many countries outside the EU locate the supply of many services at the supplier's place of business. This rule encouraged businesses to provide services through a place of business outside the country or countries in which they rendered services, so that the services were zero-rated exports from the country of their seat and the services were not taxed in the country where the customers used the services. For example, when a South African company provided cable television services to subscribers in Uganda and the local related company provided some services to the South African parent, and the place of supply rule located the services where the services were rendered, the Uganda court held that the services supplied by

---

[52] *Id.* at Reg. 33–15.07.

[53] See Marrakesh Agreement Establishing the World Trade Organization, Apr. 15, 1994, 1867 U.N.T.S. 154.

[54] See Law 27, 614, effective December 30, 2001, discussed in *VAT Monitor*, May/June 2002, p. 226.

[55] See, for example, RSA VAT, *supra* note 37, at §13(1).

[56] Australian GST, *supra* note 35, at §13–20. A similar rule applies under the NZ GST, *supra* note 36, at §12(2).

the South African parent were provided outside Uganda and therefore were not taxable.[57]

Except for rules governing particular services, such as electronically provided services, in the EU, the basic place of supply rule governing services is as follows:

> Subject to . . . [exceptions], the place of supply of services, other than the supply of services by an intermediary, shall be deemed to be the place where the supplier has established his business or has a fixed establishment from which the service is supplied, or, in the absence of such a place of business or fixed establishment, the place where he has his permanent address or usually resides.[58]

The exceptions in article 9 of the Sixth Directive articles 46–59 of the recast of the Sixth Directive overwhelm the general rule, and provide that for many supplies of services, the services are located where the property on which the services are rendered are located, the place where the services are physically carried out, or the place where the customer is located. The EU continues to study the place of supply rules that should apply to services rendered by suppliers outside the EU to nontaxable persons within the EU.[59]

The failure to tax some imported services does not reduce the VAT base to the extent that the imported services are rendered to registered importers who could claim input credit for any tax on such imported services. Thus, if a registered person imports some accounting services that are attributable to the supply of taxable goods, if the import were taxed, the importer could claim credit for the tax on those services. The registered person is in the same VAT position, whether he purchased the accounting services domestically or imported them.

By contrast, the tax base is compromised and domestic suppliers of services are disadvantaged to the extent that imported services are rendered to consumers and others who are not able to recover the VAT on the acquisition of such services. As a result, many countries impose tax on services imported by consumers and others who are denied credit for input VAT on those services, and must rely on self-assessment to collect that tax. For example, the Sixth Directive authorizes member states to treat some services rendered by nonresidents to nontaxable persons to be treated as supplied within a member state if the effective use or enjoyment of the services takes place within the state.[60] The services are treated as domestically supplied and therefore taxable. The British VAT taxes some imported services under

---

[57] *Multi-Choice (U) Ltd. v. Uganda Revenue Authority*, Application No. TAT 1 of 2000 (Tax Appeals Tribunal Uganda). The Ugandan VAT law was amended after the tax year in question. See Finance Act 1999, §17(5) to provide that the supply takes place where the customer receives the signal or service.

[58] Recast Sixth Directive, *supra* note 13, at Art. 44 (Sixth Directive, *supra* note 13, at Art. 9(1)).

[59] See European Commission report TAXUD-2005-00843, Summary Report on the outcome of the public consultation from DG TAXUD [February–March 2005]: VAT – The Place of Supply of Services to Non-Taxable Persons (May 30, 2005).

[60] Recast Sixth Directive, *supra* note 13, at Art's. 56–58 (before the recast, it was Sixth Directive, *supra* note 13, at Art's. 9(2)(e) & (f), 9(3)).

a reverse charge rule.[61] New Zealand also relies on a reverse charge rule to tax recipients of some imported services.[62]

VII. EXPORTS

A. EXPORTS OF GOODS

Consistent with the destination principle, most countries zero rate the exports of goods and typically, but not universally, grant quick refunds of excess input credits attributable to the exported goods.[63] France has relaxed its rules relating to the proof required to zero rate exported goods. Exporters are permitted to prove that goods have been exported, even if they do not have copy 3 of the customs export statement provided by the customs authority when the goods leave France.[64]

Some countries extend the zero rating to the immediate prior stage on sales to exporters, although they may impose some restrictions in order to reduce the opportunities for fraud.[65]

B. EXPORTS OF SERVICES

While there is some consistency in the zero rating of exports of goods in countries with VAT, there is a lack of consistency with respect to exports of services. In Australia, supplies of many services to persons not established in Australia that are rendered for consumption outside Australia are zero rated (GST-free in the language of the Australian GST).[66] New Zealand zero

---

[61] VATA 1994, *supra* note 14, at 8(1) provides: Subject to ..., where relevant services are –
(a) supplied by a person who belongs in a country other than the United Kingdom, and
(b) received by a person ("the recipient") who belongs in the United Kingdom for the purposes of any business carried on by him, then all the same consequences shall follow under this Act (and particularly so much as charges VAT on a supply and entitles a taxable person to credit for input tax) as if the recipient had himself supplied the services in the United Kingdom in the course or furtherance of his business, and that supply were a taxable supply.

[62] The imported services are treated as supplied in New Zealand. NZ GST, *supra* note 36, at §§5B & 8(4B).

[63] Some countries require the excess credits, even if attributable to exported goods, to be carried forward to future periods and used to offset future output tax liability. China is one example of this approach.

[64] Decree 2004-468 of 25 May 2004, OJ No. 126 of 2 June 2004, reported in "France: Zero rate on export transactions," *VAT Monitor*, July/Aug. 2004, p. 283.

[65] See the practice in Italy and Turkey; 2005 Financial Bill Law No. 311 of 30 December 2004 (Italy), discussed by Anna Paola Deiana, "Italy: Zero-rated supplies preceding export," *VAT Monitor*, Mar./Apr. 2005, p. 136; Billur Yalti Soydan, "Simplifying Procedure for VAT Refunds in Turkey," *VAT Monitor*, Jan./Feb. 2002, p. 21.

[66] Australian GST, *supra* note 35, at §38–190. See GSTR 2003/7, Goods and Services Tax: what do the expressions 'directly connected with goods or real property' and 'a supply of work physically performed on goods' mean for the purposes of subsection 38–190 of the *A New Tax System(Goods and Services Tax) Act 1999*? (Australia ATO).

rates a list of exported services.[67], Singapore zero rates some categories of international services, but only if the services are not only provided to a person who belongs outside Singapore, but the services must directly benefit that person and not any person who belongs in Singapore.[68]

The opportunity for abuse exists with respect to exported services because it is so difficult to audit, months later, whether services were in fact exported.

The following Canadian Tax Court case illustrates the link in some cases between the classification of a supply as a supply of services or a supply of goods, and the treatment of the supply as a taxable domestic supply or a zero-rated export.

Robertson v. The Queen[69]

The Appellant [taxpayer]...resides in Yellowknife, Northwest Territories ("NWT"), [where he]...operated a taxidermy business under the name "Robertson's Taxidermy".

In his taxidermy business, the Appellant receives from a hunter a bird, pelt, hide, skin, head, antlers etc. (the "Wildlife Part"). The Appellant performs certain processes to preserve the Wildlife Part and, where the customer requests, proceeds to prepare the Wildlife Part for display as a life-size mount, a rug mount, shoulder mount or an antler or skull mount (the "Processed Wildlife Part").

Once the Hunter kills the animal,...he or she contacts the Appellant. The animal is then either shipped to or picked up by the Appellant.

Upon receipt of the animal and deposit, the Appellant fleshes out the animal skin and usually sends the hide to be tanned and processed by an unrelated, arm's length third party. Upon completion, the tanner returns the tanned head and hide to the Appellant and invoices the Appellant for the services rendered plus the applicable GST. The Appellant may also tan a hide himself if the animal is small.

The Appellant either creates or purchases the mannequins upon which the head and hide are mounted. Glass eyes, teeth, etc. are also utilized in the taxidermy process.

Once the Processed Wildlife Part is completed, it is then crated. For an "export sale", a U.S. transportation carrier is retained to ship the Processed Wildlife Part to the non-resident U.S. customer.

---

[67] The zero-rated services include services supplied directly in connection with (a) land outside New Zealand, (b) certain moveable personal property outside New Zealand when the services are performed, (c) goods supplied from outside New Zealand to a destination outside New Zealand, and (d) services supplied to a nonresident who is outside New Zealand when the services are performed, and (e) several others. N.Z. GST, *supra* note 36, at 11A(1).

[68] See Singapore Goods and Services Tax Act, Cap. 117A, 2001 ed., amended by GST (Amendment) Act No. 50 2004, at §21(3)(j).

[69] 2002 Can LII 910 (T.C.C.). [Edited by the authors.]

In order to export from the NWT the non-edible parts of a dead animal, the parts must meet the definition of a "manufactured product" under the *Wildlife Act*. The *Wildlife Act* defines a "manufactured product' as wildlife that is:

(a) prepared for use as or in an article to be sold as a garment, or
(b) preserved or prepared by a tanning or taxidermy process.

Counsel [for the Crown] submitted that at all material times, the Appellant did not supply tangible personal property to non-residents for export which would constitute a "zero-rated supply", by virtue of Schedule VI, Part V, section 7 of the *ETA* but rather provided a service related to tangible property located in Canada pursuant to section 7 of Part V of Schedule VI, particularly, subsections 7(a) and 7(e).

He was asked to describe the process that he uses with respect to the polar bear mount. He said that they receive the hide, they remove the meat, fat and flesh. They wash it two to three times. The hide is salted and this requires 50 to 100 pounds of salt. This cures the skin and removes moisture. When the skin is dried it is perfectly preserved. The hide is then sent to the tannery where it may stay for six months. After its return from the tannery they soak it again. This loosens up the fibres and it can be restretched to its natural size. The article is then placed into the freezer.

He researches for the proper supply company to obtain the mannequin. When it is received it has to be altered. It has to fit the skin perfectly. The teeth and eyes are put into the article. The skin is stretched over the mannequin. They use approximately 20 pounds of glue to affix it to the mannequin and put it in place. The skin is then sewed up and the mount is groomed. It takes two to three weeks to dry before the finishing work is done.

He referred to a typical invoice . . . [that] did not separate labour from the other items. The base and habitat are listed separately. The tanning is built into the price of the mount. Freight and crating are separate unless there is a flat rate agreed upon beforehand.

ANALYSIS AND DECISION. In the case at bar there is one main issue and there are several auxiliary issues. The main issue in this case is whether or not . . . the Appellant was supplying a service in his taxidermy business (a contract for services) or whether the contract was for the sale of goods. In essence, counsel for the Appellant said that the taxidermist entered into a contract for the sale of goods whereas counsel for the Respondent says that in essence the taxidermist provided his services and that was what he was paid for.

[T]he Court is satisfied that the hunters in the case at bar did not transfer ownership of the Wildlife Part to the Appellant. Rather, the Appellant assumed possession of that Wildlife Part on behalf of the hunter. There is no doubt that in accordance with subsection 49(3) of the *Wildlife Business*

Regulations, supra, the holder of a tanner or a taxidermist licence obtains a proprietory interest, akin to a lien, against the Wildlife Part and was entitled to recover his costs by selling the Wildlife Part, if it was not picked up for a period of one year. When the Appellant returns the Wildlife Part to the hunter, in its final form, he is not providing "property" within the meaning of subsection 123(1) of the *Act*, to the hunter, at least in respect of that part of the final product which is composed of the Wildlife Part.

As agreed to in the Statement of Facts, the total cost of basic supplies and materials accounted for approximately 15 to 25 per cent of the total cost of the processed Wildlife Part to the customer. The remainder of the consideration was in the labour required to create the finished article.

In the case at bar, property in the total cost of the basic supplies and materials was transferred to the hunter as an addition to the Wildlife Part.

[O]f use in the present case, is a quotation from [*Crown Tire Service Ltd. v. R.* (1983), [1984] 2 F.C. 219 (Fed. T.D.)] ... in reference to the text, *Benjamin's Sale of Goods (London, 1974)*, in considering the distinction between a contract for the sale of goods and a contract for work and materials, where it is stated:

> Where work is to be done on the land of the employer or on a chattel belonging to him, which involves the use or affixing of materials belonging to the person employed, the contract will ordinarily be one for work and materials, the property in the latter passing to the employer by accession and not under any contract of sale.

Again, the analogy to the present case, although the facts are different, is still an apt one. This Court is satisfied that the situation in the case at bar fits within the general principle as referred to in *Benjamin, supra*. There can be no doubt in the Court's mind that in the present case that the hunter retained ownership of the dead animal part throughout the process....

Counsel for the Respondent argued that ... [this case] dealt with the provision of services rather than a contract for the sale of goods. To that end he highlighted the high degree of talent possessed by the taxidermist in this case and the reputation that he enjoyed in the industry. Therefore, it was his position that customers hired the Appellant for his talent, skill and artistic ability, not for the materials that were incidentally provided during his service.

The [Crown argued that the] cost of the material that the Appellant affixed to the Wildlife Part was insignificant compared to the total cost that a hunter expends to obtain the final amount. The value of the trophy was derived principally from the Wildlife Part and not from the materials that the Appellant affixed to the part during the taxidermy process. Consequently, he argued, that the substance of the contract between the Appellant and the non-resident hunter was clearly one for services, not one for the sale of goods.

The Minister's administrative policy, with respect to section 7 of Part V of Schedule VI of the *Act*, provides that a service will be "in respect of" tangible personal property if the service is "physically performed on the tangible personal property" or if the service "enhances the value of the property". Again this interpretation is not binding on the Court, but it is indicative of the Minister's treatment of the matter.

[The]...Court is satisfied that the Appellant supplied a service to individuals who were in Canada at the time when the individual had contact with the Appellant in relation to the supplies of the taxidermy services and the contract was not one for the sale of goods as argued by counsel for the Appellant.

Further, the Court is satisfied that in accordance with subsection 7(*e*) of Part V of Schedule VI of the *Act*, during the appropriate period of time, the Appellant made a supply of a service to a non-resident person, which was, "a service in respect of tangible personal property that was situated in Canada at the time the service is performed" and consequently this subsection prevents the supply of that service from being zero-rated.

The appeal is therefore dismissed, with costs, and the Minister's assessments are confirmed.

VIII. Telecommunications, Electronically Supplied Services, and E-Commerce

A. Introduction

The international telecommunications[70] industry raises special problems in the international context. Electronic commerce, including electronically supplied services, conducted with the use of telecommunications and similar networks, raises related problems. They all can create competitive inequities, raise difficulties in identifying the place where the sale occurs, and the place where services, in particular, are consumed. In all three areas, tax administration and taxpayer compliance costs narrow the available choices. Restrictions on a nation's ability to collect tax from foreign sellers or to identify and collect tax from local consumers may require simple rules that foster voluntary compliance or rules requiring non-resident suppliers to register and remit tax on their sales to local nontaxable persons.

This portion of the chapter serves as a brief introduction to these diverse topics that have some common links.[71] It covers the problems raised by the

---

[70] For an interesting examination of the taxation of cable television, see note, "Taxation of Cable Television: first amendment limitations," 109 *Harv. L. Rev.* 440 (1995). Some countries, such as Singapore, zero rate international telecommunications services. See "Singapore: International telecommunications services," *VAT Monitor*, Jan./Feb. 2004, p. 58.

[71] See Lejeune & Cambrien, "Telecommunications Services – The New Regime As From 1 January 2000," 10 *VAT Monitor* 150 (July/Aug. 1999) [hereinafter Lejeune & Cambrien, Telecom]; Eriksen, "Telecoms – Norway and the EU Part I," 10 *VAT Monitor* 152

international movement of telecommunication and e-services (the ethereal international). Consider, as you read this chapter, the problems that arise when a tax system like VAT relies on business firms as the administrators and collectors of the tax, that is, as the operators of the system.

B. Place of Supply of Services Involving Telecommunications, Electronically Supplied Services, and E-Commerce

1. Telecommunications Services

Telecommunications involves a wide range of services provided by transmitting and receiving signals and other data by radio, optical, and electromagnetic means. Access to the Internet and other information networks is a telecommunication service. Although Internet access and electronic commerce involve telecommunications, the VAT issues related to telecommunications involving land line phones and mobile phone service are separated from the other telecom services.

Telephone and other telecommunication services can be provided without a central fixed location for the transmission and receipt of signals. For example, some services can be provided by satellite transmission. Services may be provided by a supplier that operates in or has working arrangements with companies in many countries. With the advent of mobile cellular phones, a customer of a telecommunications company in the United States can use his cellular phone in Europe or Asia. The phone customer controls the place where the service is used or enjoyed. A customer who purchases Internet access services in the EU may use that service to receive e-mail messages while on a business trip to South Africa through a local telephone access number in Cape Town, or may get those messages through a mobile phone.

These issues arise under state and local sales taxes in the United States. In 2000, Congress enacted the Mobile Telecommunications Sourcing Act.[72] This act allocates jurisdiction to tax mobile phone services. It provides that charges for mobile phones can be taxed "by the taxing jurisdiction whose territorial limits encompass the customer's place of primary use, regardless of where the mobile telecommunication services originate, terminate, or pass through, and no other taxing jurisdiction may impose taxes, charges, or fees on charges for such mobile telecommunications services."[73]

(July/Aug. 1999) Eriksen, "Telecoms – A Global Approach Part II," 10 *VAT Monitor* 266 (Nov./Dec. 1999); Report to Congress, Advisory Commission on Electronic Commerce, April, 2000, reproduced in *Tax Notes Today* Doc. 2000-10891, and available at http://www. ecommercecommission.org/ [hereinafter Commission Report to Congress on E-Commerce]; Jenkins, "VAT and Electronic Commerce: The Challenges and Opportunities," 10 *VAT Monitor* 3 (Jan./Feb. 1999) [hereinafter Jenkins, VAT & E-Commerce]; Lambert, VAT & E-Commerce, *supra* note 1.

[72] 106 P.L. 252, 114 Stat. 626 (July 28, 2000), adding §§116 to 126 to ch. 4 of title 4 of the U.S.C.

[73] *Id*. at §117(b).

Most VAT regimes have fixed rules on the place where a supply takes place. In many countries, these rules were not modified to take into account the explosion of new telecommunication services.

In the EU, before the 1999 amendments, the Sixth Directive[74] rules on the place of supply of services placed telecom companies operating in the EU at a disadvantage in areas where they competed with international providers of telecommunication services. Telecom services were not treated as supplied where the customer had the effective use or enjoyment of the service. In some cases, there was confusion over which place of supply rule applied to services that straddled the line between the provision of information and the transmission of information, such as between processing data in connection with its transmission and the mere transmission of data in its original form.[75]

For a VAT-registered telecom customer engaged in providing taxable services, the place of supply rules are not significant because any VAT paid on the telecom services rendered by a nonresident can be claimed as an input tax credit. Consumers and firms rendering exempt services cannot claim input credit for VAT charged on these telecom services. Banks, insurance companies, government entities, and nonprofit organizations generally fit in this group. These customers look for opportunities to purchase telecom services free of VAT.[76] Before the 1999 amendments, the Sixth Directive place of supply rules provided this opportunity.

Before the 1999 changes, a telecom company established in an EU country was at a competitive disadvantage in attracting customers outside the EU because the place of service was the place where the supplier established its business or had a fixed establishment. As a result, a vendor of telecom services established in the EU was required to charge VAT on services to customers outside the EU. Those customers could obtain telecom services from non-resident suppliers outside the EU free of VAT.[77]

To prevent abuse in the telecom service sector, the EC issued Council Directive 1999/59/EC of June 17, 1999,[78] amending the place of supply rules for telecom services. The following was added:

> Telecommunication services shall be deemed to be services relating to the transmission, emission or reception of signals, writing, images and sounds or information of any nature by wire, radio, optical or other electromagnetic systems, including the related transfer or assignment of the right to use

[74] Sixth Directive, *supra* note 13.

[75] Jenkins, "VAT and Telecommunications Within the European Union," 6 *VAT Monitor* 286 (Sept./Oct. 1995).

[76] Some countries zero rate telecommunications. Banks and other suppliers of exempt financial services have an incentive to obtain telecom services that are provided from those countries. In the past, reportedly, companies such as British Telecom have offered customers the option to designate the country in which they receive and pay for their virtual private network (VPN) telecommunications services. For example, by designating Austria, the customers are entitled to zero rating on their VPN services. See Data Communications, September 1995, p. 7.

[77] See Lejeune & Cambrien, Telecom, *supra* note 71, at 150.

[78] OJ L 162, June 17, 1999.

capacity for such transmission, emission or reception. Telecommunications services within the meaning of this provision shall also include provision of access to global information networks.

Under amended Article 9(2)(e) of the Sixth Directive, these services take place at the customer's (not the supplier's) place of business or fixed establishment if the customer is established in an EU country that is not the telecom supplier's country.[79] Consumers and unregistered EU public bodies do not have the opportunity to avoid VAT by purchasing telecom services from suppliers outside the EU. For these purchasers, telecom services take place where the effective use and enjoyment of the services occur.[80] The services therefore are taxed and the foreign supplier may be held jointly and severally liable for the payment of the tax.

2. Radio, Television, and Electronically Supplied Services

The following represents a thumbnail sketch of the development of the change in the place of supply rules governing radio, television, and certain electronically supplied services in the EU and by the OECD. A high level conference organized by the OECD Committee on Fiscal Affairs was held in Ottawa, Canada in October 1998. It was entitled "A Borderless World Releasing the Potential of Global Electronic Commerce." The conference participants identified problems related to electronic commerce and discussed possible solutions.

As a follow-up to this OECD conference, the OECD issued reports and draft principles, and the European Commission proposed[81] and later issued a directive covering radio and television broadcasting and certain electronically supplied services.

In a broader context, in 2005, the OECD issued draft principles governing the place of supply for the international trade in services and intangibles.[82]

---

[79] Lejeune & Cambrien, Telecom, *supra* note 71, at 151. For services covered by Art. 9(2)(e), the tax is payable by the recipient of the services. Sixth Directive, *supra* note 13, at Art. 21(1)(b), as amended by Council Directive 1999/59/EC of Jun 1999. According to amended Art. 21(1)(b): "taxable persons to whom services covered by Article 9(2)(e) are supplied or persons who are identified for value added tax purposes within the territory of the country to whom services covered by Article 28b(C), (D), (E) and (F) are supplied, if the services are carried out by a taxable person established abroad; however, Member States may require that the supplier of services shall be held jointly and severally liable for payment of the tax."

[80] Lejeune & Cambrien, Telecom, *supra* note 71, at 151. The vendor is responsible to pay the VAT. See Sixth Directive, *supra* note 13, at Art. 21(1)(b).

[81] See COM/98/0586, 1999 OJ C 030 (Feb. 5, 1999).

[82] See "The Application of Consumption Taxes to the International Trade in Services and Intangibles: Progress Report and Draft Principles" [hereinafter OECD Applying Consumption Taxes to International Trade in Services and Intangibles], Informal Working Group of Working Party 9 of the Committee of Fiscal Affairs (OECD Centre for Tax Policy and Administration 11 February 2005). For a list of other OECD reports on trade in international services and intangibles, see http://www.oecd.org/. On Feb. 23, 2006, the

According to this 2005 OECD report, consumption taxes should impose tax where goods or services are consumed, but for administrative reasons, countries may rely on proxies to determine where goods and services are consumed.[83] Internationally traded services and intangibles should also be taxed in the jurisdiction of consumption.[84] On the basis of the principle that final consumers should bear the economic costs of VAT, the report included the principle that taxable businesses should not bear, as an economic cost, the VAT on goods and services used in making taxable supplies.[85]

In the EU, the recast of the Sixth Directive, Article 44 (like the Sixth Directive, Article 9(1) before the recast) provides the general rule on the place where services are supplied:

> Subject to [articles 46 to 61 of the recast Sixth Directive], the place of supply of services, other than the supply of services by an intermediary, shall be deemed to be the place where the supplier has established his business or has a fixed establishment from which the service is supplied, or, in the absence of such a place of business or fixed establishment, the place where he has his permanent address, or usually resides.[86]

In addition, the recast Sixth Directive, Article 56(1)[87] contains a special rule that links the place of supply of some services to the place where the customer has his business, fixed establishment, permanent address or residence. It provides:

> The place of supply of the following services to customers established outside the Community, or to taxable persons established in the Community but not in the same country as the supplier, shall be the place where the customer has established his business or has a fixed establishment for which the service is supplied, or, in the absence of such a place, the place where he has his permanent address or usually resides.

The European Council adopted many of the earlier OECD draft principles in a 2002 Directive that obliged Member States to implement these principles in national law by July 1, 2003. This Council Directive amended (or temporarily amended) the Sixth Directive as it applies to radio and television broadcasting services and certain electronically supplied services.[88]

OECD launched a new project to provide guidance to governments in this area. IBFD Tax News Service, "OECD project on clarifying VAT/GST application in cross-border trade," Feb. 27, 2006.

[83] OECD Applying Consumption Taxes to International Trade in Services and Intangibles, *supra* note 82, at ¶¶17 and 18.

[84] *Id.* at ¶19.

[85] *Id.* at ¶20.

[86] See the Sixth Directive before the recast, *supra* note 13, at Art. 9(1).

[87] In the Sixth Directive before the recast, it was Art. 9(2)(e).

[88] Council Directive 2002/38/EC of 7 May 2002, OJ L128/41, effective 15 May 2002 [hereinafter Council Directive 2002/38/EC], amending and amending temporarily Directive 77/388/EEC as regards the value added tax arrangements applicable to radio and television broadcasting services and certain electronically supplied services. For a discussion

The Directive applied for an initial period of three years.[89] The Directive covers services rendered by persons not established or required to be identified for tax purposes within the EU, when they render covered services to nontaxable persons within the Community.

The place of supply for nontaxable persons receiving radio, TV, and "electronically supplied services" is where that person is established, has his permanent address, or usually resides within the Community. For this purpose, there is a list of services to be treated as electronically supplied services.[90] Instead of registering in each member state in which it renders services, a nonestablished taxable person may elect to use a special simplified online registration scheme for electronically supplied services. That person can elect to register and file one return electronically in a single member state, and report all EU sales within the EU in that single return. The nonresident receives an identifying number from that state, must file on a quarterly basis, and must list taxable supplies and VAT attributable to each member state. The nonresident business must charge its EU customers VAT at the rate in the customer's state. The VAT is to be paid into a bank account designated by the state of registration, but the nonestablished taxable person must recover any refundable input VAT from each state where it was paid.[91] The state of registration must allocate the revenue to the customers' states on the basis of information supplied by the non-resident business.[92] Records must be kept for ten years and must be available electronically.[93] The state of registration will audit the nonresident supplier. The United Kingdom has an excellent Web site explaining VAT imposed on e-Services (VOES).[94]

A Council regulation issued with the 2002 Council Directive required EU Member States, among other obligations, to exchange tax information about electronically supplied services, share identification numbers of

---

of the background and ultimate agreement in the EU on the taxation of electronically supplied services, see Joostens, Cambien, and Lejeune, "EU Agreement on Taxation of Electronically Supplied Services," *VAT Monitor*, May/June 2002, p. 154.

[89] Council Directive 2002/38/EC, *supra* note 88, at Art. 4. See IBFD Tax News Service 18 May 2006.

[90] They are:
Web site supply, Web hosting, distance maintenance of programmes and equipment.

1. Supply of software and updating thereof.
2. Supply of images, text and information, and making databases available.
3. Supply of music films and games, including games of chance and gambling games, and of political, cultural, artistic, sporting, scientific and entertainment broadcasts and events.
4. Supply of distance teaching.
When the supplier of a service and his customer communicates via electronic mail, this shall not of itself mean that the service performed is an electronic service within the meaning of the last indent of Article 9(2)(e). *Id.*

[91] *Id.* at Art. 1(3), adding Art. 26c to the Sixth Directive. In the Recast Sixth Directive, *supra* note 13, it is Art's. 352–361.

[92] See VAT on electronic commerce: Frequently Asked Questions – MEMO/03/142, at http//europa.eu.int/comm./taxation_customs/taxation/ecommerce/vat_en_faq.htm.

[93] Recast Sixth Directive, *supra* note 13, at Art. 362.

[94] Go to http://customs.hmrc.gov.uk and search VOES, and click VAT on e-Services (VOES).

persons under the special scheme and give notice if they are removed from the VAT roster, give information to the state of consumption of payments attributable to each filed return reporting electronically supplied services, and give each member state notice of VAT rate changes.[95] Some of the member states enacted domestic law to implement the Council Directive after the July 1, 2003, deadline.[96]

As a result of the 2002 Council Directive and Regulation, non-EU and EU suppliers are subject to the same VAT rules when they render electronic services to customers within the EU. Nonresident taxable persons who sell to VAT-registered business customers in the EU will not charge VAT on the services. The business customer is obliged to report the transaction under the self-assessment (reverse charge) mechanism. Sales by registered EU suppliers of electronic services covered by the Directive are zero rated when made to customers outside the EU.[97] For services covered by the Directive, in order to avoid double tax, avoidance of tax, or distortion of competition, member states may treat the place of supply where the effective use and enjoyment of the services takes place.[98]

> The downside for noncompliance [by non-established taxable persons] is penalties for not registering for VAT on time, and penalties for not accounting and paying for VAT to the relevant VAT authority in time. The real downside for noncompliance, should this come to light, is that the taxable person, that is, the provider, is held liable for any VAT due and if contracts or prices charged previously to customers are not agreed to on a VAT-exclusive basis, the cost of the VAT itself must be met by the provider. It is difficult, if not impossible sometimes, to obtain retroactive VAT payments from customers if these have not been agreed to up front.[99]

Sellers with the information on these sales are in the best position to collect the VAT. Attempts to collect the tax from consumers under a reverse charge rule have not proven effective.[100]

A Council Regulation issued in October 2005, and generally effective July 1, 2006, includes place of supply rules governing electronically supplied services covered by the Sixth Directive, Article 9(2)(e). For services to customers outside the EU or for taxable pesons established in another country within the EU, the services covered in the Regulation generally take place where the customer has established his business or has a fixed establishment

---

[95] Council Regulation (EC) No. 792/2002 of 7 May 2002 amending temporarily Regulation (EEC) No. 218/92 on administrative cooperation in the field of indirect taxation (VAT) as regards additional measures regarding electronic commerce, OJ L 128/1, 15.5.2002. The legal basis for this Regulation comes from Art. 95 of the Treaty of Rome, which provides for administrative cooperation among Member States.

[96] For example, Italy's enactment became effective October 4, 2003, instead of July 1, 2003. See Legislative Decree No. 273 of 1 August 2003, discussed at "Italy: E-Commerce," *VAT Monitor* Nov./Dec. 2003, p. 491.

[97] See Frequently Asked Questions, *supra* note 92.

[98] Recast Sixth Directive, *supra* note 13, at Art. 58(a) & (b) (Sixth Directive, *supra* note 13, at Art. 9(3) before the recast).

[99] Lambert, Vat and E–Commerce, *supra* note 1, at 1650–1653.

[100] *Id.*

to which the service is supplied or, in the absence of such a place, the place where he has his permanent address or where he usually resides. Article 11 of the Regulation covers services delivered over the Internet or over an electronic network, and include:

a. digitized products, including software (and changes and upgrades);
b. services supporting a Web site, Web page or other presence on an electronic network;
c. services automatically generated from a computer in response to data input by the recipient;
d. fee to put goods or services on sale on an Internet site operating as an online market (parties notified of sale by mail automatically generated from a computer);
e. Internet Service Packages (ISP) of information that go beyond Internet access and include content pages giving access to a variety of information;
f. services listed in Annex I to the regulations.[101]

3. Electronic Commerce

The following are excerpts from the Lambert article on electronic commerce.

> [The expansion of e-commerce] . . . is likely to be one of the great economic developments of the 21st century, leading to major structural changes in the economies of developed countries, and hastening the progress of globalization, encouraging the dismantling of trade barriers, and spurring growth and employment.
>
> At the same time, the potential growth of this form of trading causes major headaches for fiscal authorities, because of the difficulty in establishing audit trails and enforceable compliance requirements to bring it under adequate control.[102]
>
> International trade through electronic commerce can be conducted between parties situated anywhere in the world. The global village shop is truly with us and it is here to stay. Contracting parties may thus be less constrained by geography or the need for suitable business premises. The day when a travel agent sitting under a palm tree by his swimming pool in California, sipping a pina collada, sells a holiday package to Majorca through a Web site to a customer in rainy Leicester, England, cannot be that far away. The customer avoids getting wet going to his normal High Street travel agency, and the agent avoids the cost of setting up shop in Leicester. However, does this mean that the agent can avoid his EU VAT obligations in arranging the holiday package for his customer?
>
> New issues . . . arise if products traditionally sold as goods can be converted to electronic signals and transmitted online via modem and

---

[101] Council Regulation (EC) No. 1777/2005, *supra* note 34. Annex I includes a wide variety of electronically provided services, including Web site hosting, accessing and downloading a variety of products such as software (including antivirus software), pictorial images, book content, online news and other current information, music and sounds and films, and distance teaching (including workbooks) without human intervention.

[102] Lambert, VAT and E-Commerce, *supra* note 1, at 1645.

telecommunications links directly to customers' homes. Already, thanks to digital technology, taxation of virtual goods is firmly on the agenda. Customers can receive a wide range of products including perfect copies of computer software, CDs, and videos without the need for any physical transfer of goods in shrinkwrap form. With improvements in bandwidth capacity, and more secure electronic soundproof lines, the range of electronic products that can be delivered speedily, efficiently, and economically will increase. In this way, controlled movements of physical products are being replaced by uncontrolled and invisible electronic signals. In the United States, for example, some states require purchasers of virtual goods to self-account for sales tax in their state when buying from providers established in another state. This is policed on an honor basis. It would be interesting to establish the level of compliance and compare declared revenue take to actual revenue due to test this honor system. The rates of VAT in the European Union are higher than U.S. sales tax rates. The risks for the EU VAT authorities and the opportunities for businesses to gain a competitive edge are therefore greater in the context of EU VAT.[103]

As discussed earlier, an increasingly important aspect of the telecommunications services market is Internet access and the conduct of electronic commerce over the Internet. In 2001, an OECD working party issued guidelines on the consumption tax aspects of electronic commerce.[104] The report suggested that guidelines in this area should "define the place of consumption . . . by reference, for business-to-business (B2B) transactions, to the jurisdiction in which the recipient has located its business presence, and, for business-to-consumer (B2C) transactions, by reference to the recipient's usual jurisdiction of residence."[105] The report recommended that for B2B transactions, the tax should be collected through a reverse charge or self-assessment mechanism, and for B2C transactions, the tax should be collected through a registration-based mechanism.[106]

There have been some proposals to apply technological developments to the collection and enforcement of VAT, and the VAT aspects of electronic commerce in particular. Subhajit Basu recommended the involvement of "the very technology that made the Internet and e-commerce possible."[107] He relies on independent service providers (ISPs) to calculate, collect, and remit VAT.[108] Mr. Basu's proposal assumes that tax authorities (whether nations or subnational units of government) would enter contracts with the ISPs to administer the tax collection system.[109] To make the system work, the necessary tax information must be provided to the ISPs and retained and used

---

[103] *Id.* at 1645–1646.

[104] Consumption Tax Aspects of Electronic Commerce: A Report from Working Party No. 9 on Consumption Taxes to the Committee on Fiscal Affairs (OECD February 2001).

[105] *Id.* at ¶10.

[106] *Id.* at ¶11.

[107] Basu, *Implementing E-Commerce Tax Policy,* 2004 British Tax Rev., No. 1, 46, 68.

[108] *Id.* at 46.

[109] Mr. Basu assumes that the tax authorities would bear the cost of building the system. *Id.* at 49.

without disclosure of private information. The mechanism may be digital certificates.[110]

It is imperative under the Basu system that there be uniform definitions of products and services,[111] and adequate tax compliance software. The identification of the parties to a sale and the classification of the seller as a registered person (for VAT or sales tax purposes) and the buyer as a business or consumer are other necessary elements of his proposal. Mr. Basu's position is that governments must relinguish some of their authority as "largely autonomous agents of taxation" and accept "higher levels of international coordination in the field of taxation."[112]

With the explosion of commerce over the Internet and the concern about the multiple taxation of sales conducted via electronic commerce, the U.S. Congress enacted a moratorium on taxes on Internet access and on multiple or discriminatory taxes on e-commerce.

The challenge is to bring e-commerce within the VAT or sales tax net without placing domestic businesses at a disadvantage compared with foreign competitors. Many of the place of supply, place of consumption, and tax administration and compliance issues pertaining to telecom services discussed earlier apply to e-commerce supplies as well. It is not surprising that some of the proposed solutions for the taxation of e-commerce resemble the EU changes made in the taxation of telecommunications services under the VAT.

Electronic commerce, or e-commerce, has been defined "as business transactions taking place through the electronic transmission of data over communications networks such as the Internet."[113] The Advisory Commission on Electronic Commerce, established by an act of the U.S. Congress (Internet Tax Freedom Act),[114] reported its recommendations and proposals to Congress on April 20, 2000. It proposed to Congress that it (a) prohibit the taxation of digitized goods and products and their nondigitized counterparts, and

---

[110] "Digital certificates (also known as electronic credentials or digital IDs) are digital documents attesting to the binding of a public key to an individual or entity. They allow verification of the claim that a given public key does in fact belong to a given individual or entity. . . . Such technology is mainly used on 'commerce servers.' These server IDs allow websites to identify themselves to users and to encrypt transactions with their visitors. . . .

Digital certificates go hand in hand with digital signatures. Digital signature work on key pairs, one of which is public and the other private. The private key is used to encrypt a document while the public key is used to decipher it. . . . The digital certificate can be registered with a so-called 'trusted third party' such as a government agency or even a private company; the trusted third party can then act as a kind of bonding agency to ensure the veracity and accuracy of information given out by the digital certificates." *Id.* at 60–61.

[111] Basu suggests reliance "on the Harmonized Tariff Schedules proposed by the US International Trade Commission, the United Nations Product and Service Classification or any other suitable scheme." *Id.* at 48.

[112] *Id.* at 68.

[113] Jenkins, VAT and E-Commerce, *supra* note 71, at 3.

[114] Internet Tax Freedom Act, P.L. 105–277, 47 U.S.C. Sec. 151 [hereinafter Internet Tax Freedom Act], §1102 (1998).

(b) extend permanently the moratorium on transaction taxes on the sales of Internet access.[115] The commission supported "the formal, permanent extension of the World Trade Organizations's current moratorium on tariffs and duties for electronic transmissions, . . . [and recognized] the OECD's leadership role in coordinating international dialogue concerning the taxation of e-commerce. . . . "[116]

The Internet Tax Freedom Act's more expansive definition of e-commerce included "any transaction conducted over the Internet or through Internet access, comprising the sale, lease, license, offer, or delivery of property, goods, services, or information, whether or not for consideration, and includes the provision of Internet access."[117]

The U.S. Congress extended the moratorium on Internet access taxes and multiple or discriminatory taxes on electronic commerce through November 1, 2007.[118] States such as Wisconsin with existing Internet access taxes were exempt from the moratorium on taxes on such access.[119]

IX. INTERNATIONAL TRANSPORTATION SERVICES

International transportation involves the physical movement of goods and passengers across national boundaries. International transportation raises issues about the proper allocation of jurisdiction to impose VAT among countries with a connection to international freight and passenger travel by road, air, or water. The place where the services are rendered and the place where the services are consumed cause confusion if the tax belongs to the country of consumption, and the transportation services include travel in international waters or in the air that is beyond the tax jurisdiction of that country.

In some situations, international transportation services avoid VAT entirely. The country of origin typically zero rates these services as exports. They are zero rated in the EU.[120] A third country, whose borders are crossed, may not assert jurisdiction to tax the service provided within its borders. Passenger travel may be included in a tour package that escapes VAT because the destination country provides VAT relief to encourage tourism. By contrast,

---

[115] Commission Report to Congress on E-Commerce, *supra* note 7, at Executive Summary, &11.

[116] *Id.*

[117] Internet Tax Freedom Act, *supra* note 114, at §1004(3).

[118] P.L. No. 108–435, Internet Tax Non-Discrimination Act, 118 Stat. 2615,108th Cong., 2d Sess. This Act amended the Internet Tax Freedom Act, 47 U.S.C. 151 note. "'Internet access service' does not include telecommunications services, except to the extent such services are purchased, used, or sold by a provider of Internet access to provide Internet access." *Id.* at §2(3) of the Act. There are a few other exceptions, including one that does not prevent states from taxing charges for voice or other similar services that use Internet protocol or any successor protocol. *Id.* at §5 of the Act.

[119] *Id.* at §3 of the Act.

[120] See Recast Sixth Directive, *supra* note 13, at Art. 142(1)(e) [Art. 15(13) of Sixth Directive, *supra* note 13] and the Recast, Art. 164(b) [Art. 17(3) of the Sixth Directive].

for goods, the freight charges may be taxed by the importing country as part of the value of the imported goods.

In connection with the European Commission's principle that VAT should accrue to the country of consumption,[121] the Commission issued a consultation paper on the place of supply of services to nontaxable persons.[122] In that paper, the Commission suggested that the rule taxing intracommunity passenger transport according to the distance covered in each country was impractical and difficult to apply. Instead, the Commission offered an alternative that would treat the place of departure as the place of the supply of these transport services.[123] With respect to intracommunity transport of goods, the Commission suggested that the current rule continue; that is, the place of supply is the place of departure.[124]

Short-term leases of means of transport (cars, etc.) within the EU currently are treated as supplied where the supplier has established his business. This has created opportunities for abuse. As a result, the Commission suggests that these short-term hires be treated as supplied where the transport is put at the recipient's disposal.[125] Long-term leases of means of transport would continue to be treated as supplied where the supplier is located.[126]

X. Proposals to Fund Relief of Disaster Victims or Poverty with an International Tax

A. Introduction

The chapter ends with a proposal by Professor Hiroshi Kaneko to impose a consumption tax on international air travel and to dedicate the revenue to the relief of disaster victims. Other proposals in the EU and elsewhere rely on a levy on air travel or other subjects to fund efforts to fight AIDS or relieve poverty in the developing world.

B. Professor Kaneko's Proposal to Fund Disaster Relief with an International Humanitarian Tax[127]

"Although large-scale conflicts seem to have gone the way of the Cold War, violent regional disputes remain. Indeed, new religiously and ethnically based wars erupt regularly. These wars create huge numbers of refugees,

---

[121] COM (2000) 348 Final, 7 July 2000, "A strategy to improve the operation of the VAT system within the context of the internal market."

[122] "Consultation Paper: VAT – The Place of Supply of Services to Non-Taxable Persons, European Commission, D(2005). The purpose of the consultation paper is to provide input to the discussion of the issues presented.

[123] *Id.* at point 4.2.2.

[124] *Id.* at point 4.2.3.

[125] *Id.* at point 4.2.5.

[126] *Id.*

[127] The following is the proposal: Kaneko, "Proposal for International Humanitarian Tax – A Consumption Tax on International Air Travel," 17 *Tax Notes Int'l* 1911 (Dec. 14, 1998).

and with the refugees come famine, epidemics, and widespread mental and physical suffering – all in tragic proportions.

The economically advanced countries have not been indifferent to the plight of these victims. Both money and personnel have been contributed in substantial amounts. The governments of these countries have, however, targeted their aid in general to infrastructural development. Famine and medical relief have been left to groups like UNICEF and private relief organizations. In turn, these groups have faced chronic cash shortages.

To mitigate this shortage of relief funds, I propose a personal consumption tax on international airfare. The revenues raised would go into an international fund dedicated to the relief of disaster victims. Currently, countries with a consumption tax impose it only on domestic consumption items. Should a product subject to the tax leave the country, the government refunds any taxes already collected. That refund follows, of course, from the very nature of the consumption tax. As a corollary, almost all these governments tax domestic but not international airfare. Unfortunately, this policy violates tax neutrality by skewing consumer choice away from domestic travel or other consumption. Importantly, for our rapidly expanding internationalizing age, my proposal would reduce that tax non-neutrality. The writer thinks that there is no limitation on the tax jurisdiction of a sovereign country to impose a consumption tax on international air travel as long as the ticket is purchased in its jurisdiction.

A low tax rate would raise significant revenue. International air travel is a rapidly growing industry. Firms seem to add new routes monthly and new flights on existing routes daily. According to the statistics of the International Civil Aviation Organization (ICAO), total revenue from passengers of scheduled airlines of ICAO contracting states has been rapidly and drastically increasing and amounted to over US $200 billion in 1996. Though the revenue from personal passengers and that of business passengers are not distinguished in the statistics, it could be assumed that the former must also have been drastically increasing and has now reached a tremendously large amount. Therefore, as mentioned above, a modest tax on this base could also raise a correspondingly large amount of revenue. To use this revenue to help the victims of international disputes (perhaps for the removal of land mines as well) would be an important humanistic act. Most passengers would be glad to donate some money in the form of a consumption tax for people in misery.

Implementing this proposal raises a wide variety of difficulties. Countries will need to cooperate in adopting the necessary legislation and appropriate and efficient administrative arrangements.

Global humanitarian problems urgently require a new approach. Wars and famines show no sign of disappearing. Ethnic and religious divisions run deep, and the accompanying disputes touch long-held prejudices. In many ways, the famines in parts of Africa and Asia seem just as intractable.

Granted, this will not be an easy proposal to realize. The problems it addresses, however, cry out for an immediate humane response."

C. Proposals by President Chirac and Others to Fund Poverty Relief Efforts, the Fight against AIDS, or Development Projects with a Dedicated Tax

French President Jacques Chirac proposed a global tax on commercial aviation fuel to fund development in Africa.[128] Currently, under an international agreement, there is no tax on aviation fuel. After opposition from within the EU[129] and abroad, Chirac narrowed the scope of the tax to intra-EU travel,[130] and ultimately, with the support of other EU countries, proposed a voluntary tax on airline tickets covering travel within the EU. The revenue was to fund programs to alleviate poverty in African nations.[131] The other European proposals include a "Tobin tax" imposed on international currency exchanges.[132] The U.S. airline industry and the U.S. Chamber of Commerce oppose these taxes.[133]

At a conference in Paris in early 2006, a dozen countries agreed to implement a tax on airline tickets to finance health projects in poor countries. Other participants agreed to establish a committee to promote the airline ticket tax and other means to raise development financing. France and Brazil supported a voluntary "international solidarity tax" to help fight poverty and AIDS in the developing world.[134] The European Commission issued a study concluding that a tax on airline tickets in the EU could raise US$3.5 billion for development aid to the world's poorest countries. In a more tangible response, the French cabinet approved a proposal to impose an airline ticket tax. The proposed tax would range from 1–10 euros for economy, business, and first class within the EU, and from 4–40 euros for those classes for flights outside the EU. The tax is to fund antipoverty, AIDS, and health initiatives

---

[128] President Chirac favors a global tax system to fund development projects, which may include a tax on aviation and maritime shipping fuel, or a tax on the worldwide sale of airplane tickets. "International Taxes: European Airlines Mobilize to Fight EU Plans For Aviation Fuel Tax to Help Poorer Nations," *Daily Tax Report*, February 9, 2005, p. G-7.

[129] "Blair pours cold water on aviation tax idea," http://www.climateark.org/articles/print.asp?linkid, citing http://www.reuters.com/newsArticles.jhtml?storyID=7570162&type=businessNews (Feb. 8, 2005).

[130] See "EU Favors Aviation Tax to Fund African Aid," http://www.dw-world.de/dw/article/0,1564,1490644,00.html (Feb. 16, 2005).

[131] See "International Taxes: EU Ministers Stall on Air Ticket Tax But Give Final OK to Savings Tax Directive," *BNA Daily Tax Report*, June 8, 2005, p. G-3.

[132] This tax has the support of President Chirac and the European Parliament. Belgium imposed the "Tobin tax" on international currency exchanges to take effect only if all of the other EU countries adopt one. See "International Taxes: EU Finance Ministers to Consider Tax Measures for Fighting Poverty," *BNA Daily Tax Report*, February 15, 2005, p. G-3.

[133] Bennett, "Business Groups, Airline Industry Oppose Aviation Tax in G-8 African Aid Proposal," *BNA Daily Tax Report*, June 22, 2005, p. G-11.

[134] Speer, "Twelve Countries Agree to Implement Airline Tax for Development Financing," *BNA Daily Report*, Mar. 2, 2006, p. G-8.

in the developing world.[135] After initially opposing such a levy, the United Kingdom announced plans to devote a tax on airline tickets to fund development aid in Africa.[136]

XI. DISCUSSION QUESTIONS

1. How should public (government-owned) domestic and international transportation services be treated under a VAT?
2. If international competitive pressures force the zero rating of business to business international transportation services, will it be administratively feasible to apply VAT to consumer international transportation services? How?
3. Is it too far-fetched to envision a UNDP (United Nations Development Program) tax on value added in international air transportation (and perhaps other forms of transportation) that is now exempt or zero rated? The question reflects the growing importance (value) of personal consumption of international transportation and tourism services and their absence from the base of value added taxes. How would input taxes paid by business under national VATs be handled? How could such a world tax be administered? How does this proposal compare with the Kaneko proposal for a humanitarian tax on air travel?
4. When the U.S. Supreme Court in the *Itel* case upheld Tennessee's retail sales and use tax on containers leased in Tennessee for international transportation, that result implemented a tax on the export of container services. VATs generally tax only the value of container services included in imports. Do you see a problem here? A solution? If the United States adopts a national VAT, how should it deal with Tennessee's tax on containers at the state level of government? *Itel Containers Int'l Corp. v. Huddleston*, 113 S. Ct. 1095, 122 L. Ed. 421 (1993).

---

[135] See Speer, "French Cabinet Approves Plans for Airline Ticket Tax," *BNA Daily Tax Report*, Nov. 25, 2005, p. G-4.
[136] Kirwin, "U.K. Says It Will Join in Dedicating Airline Ticket Tax Revenue to Africa," *BNA Daily Tax Report*, Sept. 12, 2005, p. G-2.

8

Timing and Valuation Rules

The timing (or tax accounting) rules are used to identify the tax period in which a taxpayer must pay tax on imports, report taxable sales, and claim deductions or credits for tax paid on allowable imports and domestic purchases. When a VAT is introduced or the rate is changed, transition rules are needed to identify if sales and purchases are made before or after the effective date of the new or modified VAT.

VAT generally is imposed on the amount of money and the value of non-monetary consideration received for a taxable supply. Special valuation rules are provided for particular transactions. This chapter covers the timing, transition, and valuation rules.

I. The Timing Rules

A. Accrual, Invoice, and Cash Methods – in General

This section discusses the rules governing the basic methods of accounting for VAT. It does not discuss the innumerable varieties of special schemes for retailers that are available in many countries.

Some countries do not allow any person to use the cash method. Other countries permit registered persons who meet the statutory conditions (usually related to a lower level of taxable turnover) to report on the cash method.

The limits or prohibitions against the use of the cash method are imposed in order to prevent the mismatching that occurs if the seller can defer the payment of output tax to the government, yet the buyer can claim an immediate credit. The following excerpted *Ch'elle Properties* N.Z. case illustrates how one country relies on an antiabuse rule in order to prevent taxpayers from mismatching methods of accounting. In that case, the cash basis seller reported sales on the installment basis and the accrual method buyer used refunds of input credits on installment purchases to finance those purchases.

Ch'elle Properties (NZ) Ltd v. Commissioner of Inland Revenue[1]

HEADNOTES. One hundred and fourteen companies (the "A companies") were incorporated by Mr Ashby who was the sole director of the companies. Mr Ashby's idea was that each of the companies would purchase and on-sell a property with settlement deferred for a substantial period. The purchaser was a company named Ch'elle Properties (NZ) Ltd (Ch'elle), the taxpayer, registered for GST on an invoice basis whereas the A companies were registered for GST on a payments basis. As a result, the purchaser would become entitled to substantial tax credits but the liability of the A companies for output tax would be limited to what each received in cash. The contracts deferred settlement for between 10 and 20 years. The A companies each issued an invoice to Ch'elle. Ch'elle filed a tax return claiming some $9m in input payments. The Commissioner eventually disallowed this claim using the general anti-avoidance rule in §76 of the Goods and Services Tax Act 1985 (the GST Act) and Ch'elle entered a notice of opposition. The A companies were meanwhile unable to settle the contracts with the original vendor, which cancelled the contracts [for the land sold to Ch'elle.]

[Section 76 (1) & (4), the antiavoidance rule, provides as follows:]

(1) Notwithstanding anything in this Act, where the Commissioner is satisfied that an arrangement has been entered into between persons to defeat the intent and application of this Act, or of any provision of this Act, the Commissioner shall treat the arrangement as void for the purposes of this Act and shall adjust the amount of tax payable by any registered person (or refundable to that person by the Commissioner) who is affected by the arrangement, whether or not that registered person is a party to it, in such manner as the Commissioner considers appropriate so as to counteract any tax advantage obtained by that registered person from or under that arrangement.

(4) For the purposes of this section –
"Tax advantage" includes –

(a) Any reduction in the liability of any registered person to pay tax:
(b) Any increase in the entitlement of any registered person to a refund of tax:
(c) Any reduction in the total consideration payable by any person in respect of any supply of goods and services.

HELD. Section 76 of the GST Act required more than technical compliance with other provisions of the Act. The question was whether the arrangement entered into was one which, objectively, defeated the intent

---

[1] [2004] 3 NZLR 274; 2004 NZLR LEXIS 12 (High Court N.Z. 2004). [Edited by the authors.]

and application of the Act. This required the arrangement to be assessed by reference to the principles which underlay the Act. These included that an overall balance would be achieved between the inputs and outputs of a registered person and that there had to be some reasonable correspondence between the time at which outputs and inputs in relation to a particular supply were accounted for. Neither a tax advantage nor an intention to defeat the intent and application of the Act was required, the question of whether there had actually been a tax advantage was relevant only to the adjustment that was to be made once the determination had been made [that] the arrangement came within §76.

The use of a separate company for the purchase of each property led to the level of mismatch between invoice and cash payment bases for tax escalating to a level which Parliament had never intended. Although the scheme conformed to the letter of the Act, it departed from its fundamental objectives and therefore had the purpose and effect of defeating the intent and application of the Act.

The nature of the supply had been fundamentally altered by the cancellation of the contracts. In analysing the nature of supply, a careful consideration of the legal arrangements actually entered into and carried out should be made in the light of the factual background. At the time of the original supply the companies at least had a legal right to acquire the land they were selling and this right had been lost when the contracts were cancelled.

ORDER. Appeal dismissed.

1. Imports

Imports are subject to VAT under uniform rules that generally do not distinguish between cash and accrual basis importers. The timing rules on imports under the invoice method are discussed later in this section. In the EU, imports are taxable to the importer under the Sixth Directive when goods are imported.[2] If imports are subject to customs duties or other import levies, the VAT generally is imposed when those duties become chargeable.[3] VAT

---

[2] Sixth Council Directive 77/388/EEC of May 17, 1977, on the harmonization of the laws of the Member States relating to turnover taxes – Common system of value added tax: uniform basis of assessment (OJ 1977 L 145, p. 1 [hereinafter Sixth Directive], Art. 10(3). On the Sixth Directive, see Terra & Kajus, A GUIDE TO THE EUROPEAN VAT DIRECTIVES: COMMENTARY ON THE VALUE ADDED TAX OF THE EUROPEAN COMMUNITY (2005). The Sixth Directive was Recast, renumbering articles and rearranging them, but without any significant substantive changes. COM(2004) 246 final 2004/0079 (CNS) Proposal for a Council Directive on the common system of value added tax (Recast), April 15, 2004, as amended in the compromise text (FISC 14) presented by the Austrian Presidency (8547/06). [hereinafter Recast Sixth Directive], Art. 71(1).

[3] *Id.*

on imports of goods generally is payable to Customs or the Post Office, not reportable on periodic VAT returns. The rule is different for cross-border supplies of goods in the EU between registered persons. In those transactions, the goods are received free of VAT, and the VAT imposed on the imported goods is reportable in the VAT return covering the period in which the goods are imported.

In most countries, a VAT-registered importer claims credit for allowable VAT on imported goods in the period in which the goods are imported.[4] To claim the credit, the importer also must have possession of the import documentation listing the VAT imposed.

There is a cash-flow cost if the tax on imports is paid before the importer obtains the benefit from the input credit. But in countries such as New Zealand, the cash flow cost is avoided Customs issues a statement to importers that is the basis of an optional deferred payment arrangement. The importer must pay the duty and VAT within twenty-one working days after the importer's assigned billing cycle. The same statement serves as documentation to claim the offsetting input credits.[5]

The reporting rules on imports of services varies considerably by country because the taxation of imported services varies considerably.[6] The complexity increases where the classification of a supply as goods or services is ambiguous. Is computer software a good or a service?[7]

In some countries, imports of services are taxable under a reverse charge rule; that is, the importer treats the import of the service as a taxable supply by the importer to himself. In New Zealand, the import subject to the reverse charge rule is reportable at the earlier of the foreign supplier's issuance of the invoice or the importer's payment for the supply.[8]

2. Accrual Method

Under VAT systems in use today, most taxpayers must use the accrual or invoice method of accounting to report sales and claim input credits under a credit-invoice VAT (like the European VATs). Under the accrual method, taxpayers generally report taxable sales when goods are sold or when services

---

[4] See, for example, New Zealand Goods and Services Tax Act, No. 141, §12(1) [hereinafter NZ GST].

[5] See *Tax Information Bulletin*, Vol. 9, No. 11 (Nov. 1997)(N.Z.).

[6] See discussion of cross-border transactions involving services *supra* Chapter 7. Imports of services by registered persons generally are not taxed (see discussion *supra* Chapter 7 [Section VI]). As a result, there will not be any timing issue. If any imported services are taxed (e.g., the services supplied over the Internet by a foreign supplier – treated as a services rendered where used – are taxable and the supplier may be required to register in the EU and remit tax), the purchaser presumably can claim input credit under the timing rules governing domestic purchases.

[7] For example, in New Zealand, "shrink-wrapped" computer software is largely a service (intellectual property with respect to the contents). See the discussion in the text on the reverse charge rule applicable to some imports.

[8] NZ GST, *supra* note 4, at §§5B & 9(1). A special rule applies to supplies between associated (related) persons. *Id*. at §9(2).

are rendered (subject to acceleration rules), and they claim input credits when the business acquires the goods or services eligible for the input credits.[9] The timing rules governing imports were discussed above.

These VAT rules under the accrual method may or may not be consistent with the taxpayer's method of reporting sales and purchases for income or financial reporting purposes.

For most firms in Japan, the timing rules for the Consumption Tax (a VAT) and income tax are consistent. Most Japanese businesses use the accrual method,[10] and they can follow their method of accounting used for income tax purposes in accounting for the Consumption Tax.

Under the European Union's Sixth Directive, the tax is chargeable when the goods or services are supplied even though the time of payment may be deferred.[11] For businesses reporting on the accrual method, the chargeable event (when the conditions of the supply are fulfilled so that the tax is chargeable)[12] and the time the tax is chargeable coincide if goods are delivered or services are performed before payment is received and before an invoice is issued. However, the tax point (the date a taxable sale is reportable) is accelerated to a date before the chargeable event if payment is received before the goods are delivered or the services are performed.[13] For example, if a sale is completed and an invoice is issued on July 1, but the purchaser makes advance partial payment on June 28, the tax point is June 28.

The timing rules for the purchaser to claim an input credit on a domestic purchase generally are linked to the rules governing the date the *seller* reports the sale. Thus, in the EU, the input tax on domestic purchases is deductible to the purchaser when the seller must report the sale.[14]

Instead of a basic tax point linked to accrual that is accelerated only for early payment, Member States can require taxable sales to be reported on the earliest of the following three dates:

(a) no later than the time the invoice is issued;
(b) no later than the time the payment is received;

---

[9] See, for example, the VAT in the United Kingdom, Value Added Tax Act 1994, ch. 23 [hereinafter VATA 1994]. The U.K. rule provides that if goods are to be removed, the sale occurs on removal; otherwise, a sale occurs when goods are made available to the recipient. *Id.* at §6(2)(a) & (b). For a discussion of timing rules in the context of tax law design, see V. Thuronyi, editor, TAX LAW DESIGN AND DRAFTING, vol. 1, pp. 191–194 (IMF 1996).

[10] Special timing rules are provided in Japan for installment and deferred payment sales, and for long-term construction contracts. See Schenk, "Japanese Consumption Tax After Six Years: A Unique VAT Matures," 69 *Tax Notes* 899, 910 (Nov. 13, 1995).

[11] Sixth Directive, *supra* note 2, at Art. 10(1)(b); Recast Sixth Directive, *supra* note 2, at Art. 62(2).

[12] Sixth Directive, *supra* note 2, at Art. 10(1)(a); Recast Sixth Directive, *supra* note 2, at Art. 62(1) and (2).

[13] Sixth Directive, *supra* note 2, at Art. 10(2); Recast Sixth Directive, *supra* note 2, at Art. 65.

[14] Sixth Directive, *supra* note 2, at Art. 17(1); Recast Sixth Directive, *supra* note 2, at Art. 162.

(c) where an invoice is not issued, or is issued late, within a specified period from the date of the chargeable event.[15]

Under the VAT in the United Kingdom, a sale of goods generally is reportable when the goods are removed from the seller's possession. However, if goods are shipped on consignment, on approval, on sale or return or comparable terms, the sale may not be reportable until the sale is certain.[16]

The British VAT adopts the Sixth Directive's permissive three possible dates rule that a sale may be accelerated to a time before goods are delivered or services are performed (the accrual) if the seller issues a tax invoice or receives payment before that point.[17] The seller's receipt of payment accelerates the tax point for a sale if such payment discharges the buyer's liability (and the seller cannot sue for payment). See *C & E Commissioners v. Faith Construction Ltd*, (1989) 4 BVC 111. If the seller receives prepayment and therefore reports the amount received as part of taxable sales, but the sale never takes place, the seller is entitled to a refund.[18]

In the United Kingdom, the tax point for a sale is not accelerated by payment if the payment represents only a security deposit.[19] If, by contrast, the deposit represents part payment, the deposit is reportable at the time of receipt. The following case involves deposits on vacation accommodations. In this case, the deposits were refundable if the customer did not use the accommodation and the company was able to lease the property to another tenant, but not if the company was unsuccessful in releasing the property.

Customs & Excise Commissioners v. Moonrakers Guest House Ltd.[20]

Moonrakers Guest House Ltd (the company)... carries on business in the provision of holiday accommodation, and the premises where this takes place are in the Isles of Scilly.

The booking form and 'Conditions of Tenancy'... are in the form of a letter to Mr and Mrs Gregory asking them to reserve a flat for

---

[15] Recast Sixth Directive, *supra* note 2, at Art. 66. The prior version of the Sixth Directive, *supra* note 2, at Art. 10(2) provided that members can require taxable sales to be reported on the earliest of the date "no later than the issue of the invoice or of the document serving as invoice; or no later than receipt of the price; or where an invoice or document serving as invoice is not issued, or is issued late, within a specified period from the date of the chargeable event."

[16] To prevent lengthy deferrals of the tax point, some countries require these transfers to be reported not more than a fixed period after they are transferred by the seller. Goods sent on approval, on sale or return, or similar terms are subject to tax at the earlier of twelve months after removal or when it is certain that the sale occurred. VATA 1994, *supra* note 9, at §6(2)(c).

[17] *Id*. at §6(4).

[18] See VATA 1994, *supra* note 9, at §80 (United Kingdom); and discussion in Doran, "The Time of Supply Rules: How Far Do They Go?," 1998 *British Tax Rev*. 602.

[19] See Notice 700, The VAT guide, ¶14.2.3 (April 2002 ed.) [United Kingdom].

[20] [1992] STC 544 (Queen's Bench, U.K.). [Edited by the authors.]

a designated period at an identified rental. There then appears this passage:

'I enclose herewith Cheque/Cash by registered post/Postal Order/Money Order for £...(25% of total rent) balance payable on arrival, and agree to abide by the attached Conditions of Tenancy.'

The only relevant condition of tenancy is the last one.

'In the event of the cancellation of a booking, every effort will be made to re-let. However, if it is not possible to re-let the flat the full amount of rent exactly as if the accommodation had been occupied will be claimed.'

[T]he position thus is that a 25% deposit is paid at the time when a booking is made. If the booking is taken up, the balance of the rental is payable at the time when the occupation of the property starts. If the booking is not taken up, efforts are made to relet the property. If the property is relet, the deposit is repaid, but if the property is not relet the customer remains liable under his contract for the full rental and the deposit is retained as part-payment.

[T]he question at issue here relates to the timing of the liability. The commissioners contend, and contended before the tribunal, that the receipt of the deposit gives rise to a liability to value added tax at the time when the deposit is received. The tribunal rejected the commissioners' contention and it is submitted that the tribunal erred in law in reaching that decision.

The court must look at the facts as they are set out, particularly in the booking form to which I have already explicitly referred, in order to decide as a matter of law whether the money paid by way of deposit could conceivably be said to remain the property of the payer. In my judgment it could not. . . .

The statutory provisions governing the time of supply of service and thus the time when liability to value added tax arises are §§4 and 5 of the 1983 Act [now §6 of VATA 1994]. Section 4 reads as follows.

[A] supply of services shall be treated as taking place at the time when the services are performed.'[21]

Then §5(1) states:

'If, before the time applicable under . . . subsection (3) of section 4 above, the person making the supply issues a tax invoice in respect of it or if, before the time applicable under . . . subsection (3) of that section, he receives a payment in respect of it, the supply shall, to the extent covered by the invoice or payment, be treated as taking place at the time the invoice is issued or the payment is received.'[22]

---

[21] This provision now is in VATA 1994, *supra* note 9, at §6(3).
[22] This provision included *id.* at §6(4) is substantially the same as §5(1) quoted in the text.

The commissioners in this case rely first and foremost on the simple and straightforward wording of §5(1) of the 1983 Act. The deposit is a payment received in respect of the supply of services. Furthermore it is received before the time applicable under §4(3). Accordingly to the extent covered by that payment (that is to say, 25% of the value of the supply) the supply is to be treated as taking place at the time when the payment is received. That is the commissioners' interpretation of the statute and, in my judgment, it is palpably correct.

What happened factually in the instant case was that those moneys went into the company's general account. They were not earmarked in any way in a separate account. They were not kept separate. They represented, in accordance with the written contract, a 25% payment of the total rental. It is perfectly true that the money would have been repaid if the property was relet, but that situation arose probably from an implied contractual term and from nothing else.

I turn lastly to what might happen if tax had been paid and if the customer did not take the accommodation. What would happen then, if the property was relet, would be that the customer would receive back his deposit and the company would be able to bring into account the value added tax in a future period, so that the company would not be the loser in the long run. That seems to me to be common sense and it is, in my judgment, the law.

In all the circumstances therefore this appeal must by allowed and the decision of the commissioners, namely that tax is chargeable on the deposits at the time they were paid, is upheld.

The input credit rules for a taxpayer who must report on the accrual method generally provide that input VAT is creditable in the tax period in which the supply is made to him and he has a tax invoice for the purchase. Because most VATs require sellers to report taxable sales in the tax period in which an invoice is issued (even for a taxpayer reporting on the accrual method), the purchaser cannot claim input credits before the seller must report the sale. The following case resolves a dispute in the EU involving the time when an input tax deduction can be claimed, when services are received in one tax period and the invoice covering the services is received in a later period, and the law provides that a deduction cannot be taken until the purchaser has possession of the invoice.[23] The court was required to resolve differences between the German and the French and English language versions of the Sixth Directive.

---

[23] See discussion *supra* for a discussion of the conditions that must be satisfied before an input tax can be claimed with respect to imports.

Terra Baubedarf-Handel GmbH v. Finanzamt Osterholz.-Scharmbeck[24]

THE COURT (Fifth Chamber)

JUDGMENT-BY. von Bahr

Community legislation

The first sentence of the first subparagraph of Article 10(2) of the Sixth Directive[25] provides:

The chargeable event shall occur and the tax shall become chargeable when the goods are delivered or the services are performed.'

Article 17(1) and (2)(a) of the Sixth Directive[26] state:

1. The right to deduct shall arise at the time when the deductible tax becomes chargeable.
2. In so far as the goods and services are used for the purposes of his taxable transactions, the taxable person shall be entitled to deduct from the tax which he is liable to pay:
   (a) value added tax due or paid within the territory of the country in respect of goods or services supplied or to be supplied to him by another taxable person;'.

Article 18(1) and (2) of the Sixth Directive state:

1. To exercise his right to deduct, the taxable person must:
   (a) in respect of deductions under Article 17(2)(a), hold an invoice, drawn up in accordance with Article 22(3); . . . [27]
2. The taxable person shall effect the deduction by subtracting from the total amount of value added tax due for a given tax period the total amount of the tax in respect of which, during the same period, the right to deduct has arisen and can be exercised under the provisions of paragraph 1.[28]

Terra Baubedarf, a German company trading in building supplies, obtained supplies of services in 1999. However, the invoices relating to those services, although drawn up in December 1999, were not received by it until January 2000.

The [tax authorities] did not allow the deduction of the VAT paid by Terra Baubedarf for 1999 in respect of those services on the grounds that . . . the right to deduct could only be exercised in the case in point in respect of the year 2000, the year in which the relevant invoice was received.

---

[24] Case C-152/02, [2004] ECR I- 5583, *2004 ECJ CELEX LEXIS 151.*
[24] Recast Sixth Directive, *supra* note 2, at Art. 63.
[26] Sixth Directive, Article 17(1) is Recast Sixth Directive, *supra* note 2, at Art. 162.
[27] See Recast Sixth Directive, *supra* note 2, at Art. 217.
[28] *Id.* at Art. 178, when exercised in accordance with Art. 172.

Terra Baubedarf then brought an appeal [against an adverse decision by the tax office], claiming that a time- limit had been placed on its right to deduct the input VAT paid, in breach of the Sixth Directive.

The Bundesfinanzhof [the Federal Finance Court] observes that, according to the case-law of the Court, Terra Baubedarf's right to deduct arose in 1999 in accordance with Article 17 of the Sixth Directive, and that, in accordance with Article 18 of the Sixth Directive, that right could not be exercised until 2000, after receipt of the invoice.

[The question referred to the ECJ is whether a taxable person can] exercise his right to deduct input tax only in respect of the calendar year in which he holds an invoice pursuant to Article 18(1)(a) of Directive 77/388/EEC or must the right to deduct always be exercised (even if retrospectively) in respect of the calendar year in which the right to deduct pursuant to Article 17(1) of Directive 77/388/EEC arose?'

[The taxpayer claims that the German language version of VAT can be read as granting the deduction in the period in which goods or services are provided, and when a person receives the invoice for those items in a subsequent tax period, a literal reading of the VAT law requires the person to claim the deduction by amending the earlier return and claiming the deduction in that earlier period.] Technically, when the invoice is received after a tax period, immediate deduction can be guaranteed only through retroactive exercise of the right to deduct.

[The taxpayer claims] that, with regard to the rules governing the exercise of the right to deduct, that version does not establish clearly whether the period in respect of which the right to deduct may be claimed means the period in which the right to deduct arose or that in which the conditions referred to in the first paragraph of that article are satisfied in addition to the right to deduct. Other language versions enable that provision to be understood without ambiguity, however.

[The argument in response is that] a retroactive right to deduct would result in significant additional work for both taxable persons and the tax authorities. Through the retroactive deduction of input VAT, provisional returns filed for a tax period would in fact have to be adjusted, in certain circumstances even several times in the same tax period, and the tax authorities would have to draw up correction notices.

By contrast, the interpretation upheld by the German Government guarantees a VAT system that can be applied and checked effectively as regards the deduction of input VAT.

The Commission cites the Italian and Dutch versions besides the French and English versions. It appears from those that the period concerned is determined by the concurrent existence of the origin of the right to deduct and possession of the invoice.

Reply of the Court

It must be noted first that Article 18 of the Sixth Directive relates to the conditions governing the exercise of the right to deduct, whilst the existence of such a right is covered by Article 17 of that directive.

It follows from Article 17(1) of the Sixth Directive that the right to deduct arises at the time when the deductible tax becomes chargeable. In accordance with Article 10(2) of that directive, that is the case as soon as the goods are delivered or the services are performed.

On the other hand, it is apparent from Article 18(1)(a), read in conjunction with Article 22(3) of the Sixth Directive,[29] that the exercise of the right to deduct referred to in Article 17(2)(a) of that directive is normally dependent on possession of the original of the invoice or of the document which, under the criteria determined by the Member State in question, may be considered to serve as an invoice.

[T]he German version of the first subparagraph of Article 18(2) of the Sixth Directive does not establish clearly whether the period in respect of which the right to deduct may be claimed means the period in which the right to deduct arose or that in which the conditions of possession of the invoice and the right to deduct are satisfied.

However, although the German version of that provision is ambiguous on that point, it is apparent from the French and English versions of the Sixth Directive that the deduction referred to in Article 17(2) thereof must be made in respect of the tax period in which the two conditions required under the first subparagraph of Article 18(2) are satisfied. In other words, the goods must have been delivered or the services performed and the taxable person must be in possession of the invoice or the document which, under the criteria determined by the Member State in question, may be considered to serve as an invoice.

THE COURT (FIFTH CHAMBER). In answer to the question referred to it by the Bundesfinanzhof by order of 21 March 2002, hereby rules:

> [The input tax deduction referred to in the Sixth Directive, Article 17(2)(a) and provided under Article 18(2) means] that the right to deduct must be exercised in respect of the tax period in which the two conditions required by that provision are satisfied, namely that the goods have been delivered or the services performed and that the taxable person holds the invoice or the document which, under the criteria determined by the Member State in question, may be considered to serve as an invoice.

3. Invoice Method

Many countries require businesses to report VAT on the invoice method of accounting for VAT – not a pure accrual method. Countries such as New Zealand and the Republic of South Africa rely on the invoice method.

Under the invoice method, sales generally are reportable when the sales invoice is issued, but that tax point may be accelerated to the time consideration is received, if any consideration is received before the invoice is issued.[30]

---

[29] See *id*. at Art's. 209–216, and 243.

[30] See, for example, Value-Added Tax Act No. 89 of 1991, §9(1) (Republic of South Africa) [hereinafter RSA VAT], discussed in Chris Beneke, Editor, Deloitte & Touche VAT

Under the invoice method, input tax is deductible (the term used in South Africa) when the sale is made to the person claiming the deduction. Thus, the input tax generally is deductible when the supplier to the taxpayer issues the invoice or when the taxpayer makes a payment on the sale, whichever occurs earlier.[31]

Imports of goods generally are taxable when they "enter" the country for customs purposes,[32] regardless of the importer's method of accounting for VAT. When imports of services are reportable under a reverse charge rule, the import may be reportable and the offsetting credit claimed by the recipient in the person's taxable period in which the services are imported. In South Africa, imports of taxable services are reportable by the person subject to the tax in a separate return generally due within thirty days after the import.[33] In countries requiring nonresident suppliers of specified imported services to register and charge and remit VAT, the recipient generally will claim the credit under the timing rules governing domestic supplies.

4. Cash Method

"Taxable persons generally prefer to defer the tax point and payment obligation [on sales] as long as possible in order to invest and earn interest on VAT collected from customers. Since most sellers do not receive payment until after the sale is completed and income therefrom is properly accruable, taxable persons generally would prefer to base the timing rule (tax point) for sales on the cash rather than the accrual method."[34] If, under the credit-invoice VAT, a business reports on the cash method, it reports sales when it receives the consideration and it claims credits for input tax when it pays for its purchases. A seller receiving property instead of cash as consideration must report the property when received.[35]

Countries commonly require businesses to report on the accrual or invoice method. Many, however, permit specified businesses to report VAT on the cash (or payments) method of accounting. The option or election to use the cash method usually is limited to firms with taxable supplies below a statutory threshold. For example, under the British VAT, a business can elect to use the cash method if its annual taxable sales do not exceed £350,000.[36]

HANDBOOK 6th ed. 2003 [hereinafter RSA VAT Handbook]. Special timing rules apply to particular transactions, such as installment sales.

[31] RSA VAT, *supra* note 30, at §16(3)(a).

[32] See *id*. at §7(1)(b).

[33] *Id*. at §§7(1)(c); 14(1), (2).

[34] Excerpt from A. Schenk, reporter, VALUE ADDED TAX – A MODEL STATUTE AND COMMENTARY: A REPORT OF THE COMMITTEE ON VALUE ADDED TAX OF THE AMERICAN BAR ASSOCIATION SECTION OF TAXATION 136–138 (1989) [hereinafter ABA Model Act].

[35] In *A-Z Electrical v. The Commissioners of Customs & Excise* [1993] VATTR 389, the seller subject to the British VAT was required to report as taxable sales the shares and loan stock received as payment, even though the issuer subsequently liquidated.

[36] See Value Added Tax (Cash Accounting) Regulations 1987 (SI 1995/2518), issued under VATA 1994, *supra* note 9, at §58 and Sch. 11, ¶2(7).

Some countries, such as New Zealand and South Africa, require an eligible business to obtain advance approval to use the cash method.[37]

In Case J 69,[38] decided under the New Zealand GST, a business challenged the commissioners' decision to deny use of the cash (payments) method. The business operated a bakery that made sales both at wholesale and retail. About 60 percent of the value of its sales (and 85–90 percent of the number of sales) were cash sales, and the balance were sales on credit. Under the GST[39] in effect at the time, although taxpayers generally were required to use the invoice method, the Commissioner could allow taxpayers to use the payments method if the "Commissioner is satisfied that, due to the nature, volume, or value of taxable supplies made by that registered person and the nature of the accounting system employed by that person it would be appropriate for that person to furnish returns under this Act on a payments basis."[40] The court held that although accounting on the invoice method was not unduly burdensome, the taxpayer should be allowed to use the cash method.

B. Effects of Length of Taxable Period

The cost for the government to administer and for businesses to comply with a VAT depend, in part, on the length of each taxable period and on the number and complexity of the returns required to be filed each year.

1. Taxable Period – in General

For a newly registered person, a tax period starts on the date prescribed by statute (generally when registration becomes effective) or the date specified by the tax authorities. Whether a person's first tax period starts at the beginning or in the middle of a period, the person must report only taxable supplies made on and after the effective date of the person's registration.[41] In Canada, the first tax period of a newly registered person begins on the day the person becomes a registrant and ends on the last day of the reporting period.[42]

---

[37] NZ GST, *supra* note 4, at §19(2 (New Zealand)); RSA VAT, *supra* note 30, at §15(1) & (2). The cash (payments) method is available only for certain units of government and non-profit organizations and businesses with annual taxable sales not exceeding a threshold (2.5 million Rand in RSA). RSA also has an atypical rule requiring a business reporting on the payments method to report certain sales above 100,000 Rand on the invoice method, even if the business is authorized to use the payments method. RSA VAT, *supra* note 30, at §15(2A).

[38] (1987) 9 NZTC 1, 421.

[39] NZ GST, *supra* note 4, at §19(2)(c).

[40] The GST statute provides basically the same rule under NZ GST, *supra* note 4, at §§19(2) & 19A(1)(c).

[41] See the discussion of registration *supra* Chapter 4 (Section II). In Australia, where a person must apply for registration, registration generally takes effect on the date specified by the Commissioner. A New Tax System (Goods and Services Tax) Act 1999 [hereinafter Australia GST], §25–10.

[42] Excise Tax Act, R.S. 1985, Part IX Goods and Services Tax, S.C. 1990, c. 45 [hereinafter Canadian GST], §251(1)(b).

Under the Australian GST, the tax period starts at the beginning of a full reporting period, even if the person's registration takes effect within a reporting period.[43]

A tax period generally ends on the last day of a reporting period. If a person's reporting period is a calendar month, the tax period ends on the last day of each calendar month.[44] When a person ceases to be a registrant, in Canada, the person's last tax period as a registrant ends on the day before he ceases to be a registrant.[45] Australia has a special rule that terminates an individual or entity's tax period before the end of the reporting period. Under that rule, if an individual dies or becomes bankrupt, or an entity ceases to exist (such as on liquidation or being placed in receivership), the tax period ceases at the end of the day before death or other event.[46]

2. Variations in Length of Period

The length of a tax period varies considerably around the world, not only among countries but within a country. "The length of the regular tax period should be determined by balancing the government's cost of processing and auditing returns, its desire to receive tax revenue as soon as possible, taxable persons' cost of filing returns, and their desire to avoid adverse cash flow. Longer tax periods may reduce tax administration and compliance costs for small businesses."[47]

Most countries have standard tax periods of one, two, or three months. The shorter periods tend to be used in developing countries.[48] Countries with standard tax periods of two or three months generally grant registered persons the option to elect a one-month tax period, and grant the tax authorities power to require a registered person to file monthly. A registered person with substantial zero-rated supplies (e.g., exports of goods) may elect a one-month tax period in order to obtain quicker refunds of excess input credits.[49] The tax authorities may impose a one-month tax period on persons who have a history of failing to comply with the VAT rules.[50]

At the other end of the spectrum, a tax period may be as long as a year. For example, in Australia a person not required to register may elect to register

---

[43] See Australia GST, *supra* note 41, at §25–10 and Division 27.

[44] Some countries depart from this rule when the country's calendar departs from the Gregorian calendar. For example, in Ethiopia, the months of Nahase and Pagume are treated as one calendar month. See Value Added Tax Proclamation No. 285/2002, §2 definition of accounting period (Ethiopia).

[45] Canadian GST, *supra* note 42, at §251(2). For a person who becomes a bankrupt, there is a new tax period for activities as a bankrupt that begins the next day. *Id.* at §265(1)(g).

[46] Australia GST, *supra* note 41, at §27–40.

[47] ABA Model Act, *supra* note 34, at 136.

[48] See Value Added Tax Act 2000, No. 1 of 2001, §25 (Botswana).

[49] Australia provides for a mandatory one-month tax period for persons with annual turnover of $20 million or more. Australia GST, *supra* note 41, at §27–15(1)(a) & (3).

[50] *Id.* at §§27–10 and 27–15.

and adopt an annual tax period.[51] In the United Kingdom, a new business with annual taxable supplies of up to £150,000 can apply to file annually.[52] A business registered for at least twelve months with annual taxable supplies above the £150,000 threshold but not more than £600,000 can apply to file annually.[53] An annual filer in the United Kingdom must pay nine interim installments electronically.[54] In South Africa, a person engaged in farming activities can apply for a six-month tax period if the person's annual taxable supplies from farming do not exceed the statutory cap.[55]

Some countries specifically authorize persons to report on fiscal rather than calendar periods. Canada has elaborate rules providing for fiscal periods.[56]

To prevent abuse and the administrative cost for tax authorities, the VAT law may restrict a person's ability to change the length of the tax period frequently.[57]

3. Time to File Returns and Pay Tax

A VAT taxpayer generally pays its net tax liability at the time it files its periodic tax returns. The returns and payments generally must be submitted within a month after the end of the tax periods, although a longer delay such as two months may apply for persons with annual or other special accounting periods. If the tax period exceeds one month, taxable firms could be required to pay estimated tax liability between tax return due dates, with the interim payments credited against the tax liability for that tax period. This system designed to accelerate the payment of tax to the government has been used under federal excise and state retail sales taxes in the United States.[58]

4. Cash-Flow Effects

"A claimed advantage of a VAT over other sales or turnover taxes is that a VAT can be structured so that it does not influence the pre-tax pricing of taxable

---

[51] *Id.* at §151–5. To qualify for the annual tax period, the person must not have elected to pay GST in installments under §162–15. *Id.* at §151–5(b).

[52] Notice 732 Annual accounting (April 2003 ed.), ¶1.4 (United Kingdom).

[53] *Id.*

[54] Each installment is 10 percent of the expected annual liability. *Id.* at ¶6.1.

[55] RSA VAT, *supra* note 30, at §27(4). South Africa has a standard tax period of two months; a monthly tax period for large firms, electing persons, and those who repeatedly violated the VAT rules; and a twelve-month tax period for certain firms in the rental and management business. *Id.* at §27.

[56] Canadian GST, *supra* note 42, at §§243–250, as amended.

[57] For example, Australia prevents a person from withdrawing a one-month tax period election less than twelve months after the election took effect. Australia GST, *supra* note 41, at §27–20(2)(b).

[58] See J. Due & J. Mikesell, Sales Taxation: State and Local Structure and Administration 155–159 (1983). Although many of the federal excise taxes follow a common pattern for periodic deposits, the windfall profits tax provides a different payment schedule. See Internal Revenue Code of 1986, §4995(b) (United States).

property or services. To achieve this result, the timing rules governing the reporting and payment of VAT should not cause taxable persons to sustain a negative cash flow (negative float). . . .

A business that reports on the accrual basis and incurs net VAT liability for each tax period[59] will realize a cash benefit (float) if, on average, the business collects VAT from its customers before it must remit that tax to the government. . . . If on average a business reporting on the accrual method can claim credit for input tax on purchases before it must pay VAT on purchases, it also will realize a cash benefit and be able to invest the float. . . . On the other hand, a business reporting on the accrual method will experience negative float and therefore may have to borrow to pay VAT if on average the business must remit tax on sales before it collects that tax from its customers (for example, if on average the business must remit tax 35 days after the sale and the business collects tax 40 days after the sale), or if the business must pay VAT on its purchases before it can claim credit for input tax on purchases (for example, if on average the business pays VAT on purchases 20 days after purchase and it claims input credit 35 days after purchase).

If the cash method fixes the 'tax point' for output tax liability and input credits, a business must report output tax when it collects payments on sales, and claim input credits when it pays for purchases. A business reporting VAT on the cash method generally will enjoy float if it has net VAT liability, since it will receive payment on sales before it must remit the tax to the government.[60] . . . If an exporter or other business that reports VAT on the cash basis has more input credits than output tax liability, and therefore is entitled to VAT refunds, it will sustain negative float because it must pay VAT on purchases before it can recoup the input tax."[61]

C. Special Rules for Certain Sales

1. Installment or Deferred Payment Sales

VAT is imposed at the time taxable goods or services are sold, and generally is imposed on the price charged. For cash or credit sales, this timing and valuation rule does not present any special problems. Although, under the accrual method, there may be some negative cash float (if the sales price is not collected before the tax on sale must be remitted to the government), the impact is manageable. If, however, the sale is an installment or deferred payment sale, the time lag between the sale and the collection of the sales price may be substantial.

In essence, an installment or deferred payment sale consists of two transactions – a cash sale and a loan. Viewed in this fashion, under the accrual method, VAT should be imposed on the cash price at the time of sale, no

---

[59] By contrast, some taxable persons will report excess input tax credits and claim VAT refunds.

[60] This float will occur, even though the business must pay VAT on purchases before it can claim an input tax credit, as long as gross sales exceed gross purchases. Because it does not report output tax liability until it receives payments on sales, the seller does not bear VAT on bad debts.

[61] ABA Model Act, *supra* note 34, at 131–135. [Edited by the authors.]

matter how the sale is financed. The loan should follow the rules governing financial intermediation transactions (invariably exempt from tax).

Most VAT regimes adopt this approach and impose tax on the cash price at the time of sale.[62] Timing and valuation problems arise, however, if the legislature accedes to trade group demands and allows the tax on sale to be deferred until installment payments are received.

Assume that a seller sells goods for $1,000, payable over ten years with interest payable on the unpaid balance. The installment sale generally is reportable for VAT purposes when the sale is made or when the invoice is issued, even if payment is deferred.[63] With a 10 percent VAT, the seller thus must report the $100 tax on the sale when the sale occurs. Financial services (including finance or interest charges) usually are exempt from tax. Thus, separately stated finance charges on the installment sales are exempt from VAT. Under this scheme, the seller bears an interest cost whenever he must pay tax on the total installment sale price before the buyer pays the tax imposed on that installment sale; that is, the seller bears an interest cost if he must pay the $100 tax before collecting the entire tax from the buyer. If market conditions permit, the seller could avoid this interest cost if the purchaser on the installment plan were required to pay the full VAT imposed on the sale ($100 in this example) when the sale occurs.

If a government permits installment sellers to report installment sales as each installment is received,[64] the government can be compensated for the deferral of the tax on these sales by imposing an interest charge equal to the finance charge the seller imposes on the buyer. The seller, in this case, is taxed on the entire installment payment (interest and principal).[65] In this example, assuming the seller receives the first installment of $110 ($100 principal and $10 finance charge), the seller would report the entire $110 as taxable sales and remit tax of $11 ($110 × 10%) on the sale.

The Japanese Consumption Tax (CT) does not adopt either of these two possible methods of reporting installment sales. The CT permits an installment seller to use the income tax reporting rules to report installment sales for CT purposes. Under the income tax rules, the seller can report installment sales when each installment is received, rather than the total sales price

---

[62] Although installment sales are taxable when the contract is entered into, rental or lease agreements become subject to VAT on the earlier of receipt of payment or payment becoming due. NZ GST, *supra* note 4, at §§9(3)(a) & (b). This rule can be quite onerous in the case of high-priced real estate sales. See *Aukland Institute of Studies Ltd v. Commissioner of Inland Revenue*, 20 NZTC 17,685 (High Ct. N.Z.). There is an exception for progress payments covering the construction of a building or engineering work. See NZ GST, *supra* note 4, at §9(3)(aa)(ii).

[63] See VATA 1994, *supra* note 9, at §6.

[64] "The cash price for durable goods often is described by economists as equal to the discounted present value of the stream of consumption that takes place over the lifetime of the goods. The tax on the cash price, therefore, is assumed to be equal to the sum of the discounted value of the taxes imposed on the annual value of consumer durable goods over their lifetimes." Schenk & Oldman, principal draftsmen, Analysis of Tax Treatment of Financial Services under a Consumption-Style VAT: Report of the American Bar Association Section of Taxation Value Added Tax Committee, 44 *The Tax Law.* 181, 187.

[65] *Id.* at 188.

when the sale occurs. A seller who uses that installment method for income tax purposes therefore can also report installment sales for CT purposes as each installment is received. Financial services are exempt from CT. If the seller separately states the principal and interest charges on each installment of the installment sale, the seller reports only the principal portion of the installment for CT purposes. Applying the above example to the CT, when the seller receives the first $110 installment payment (with the $10 finance charge separately stated), the seller reports only $100 as taxable sales and remits $10 tax.[66] Thus, the CT rules permit installment sellers to defer their CT liability on installment sales without imposing an interest charge for the privilege of deferring the tax.

2. Goods Diverted to Personal Use

If an owner takes inventory off the shelf or uses other business property for personal use, the transaction may be treated as a taxable sale. When is such a transaction reportable? In the United Kingdom, a transaction like this – a self-supply – is treated as a taxable sale[67] reportable on the last day of the business's accounting period in which the goods are made available or used.[68]

3. Other Special Cases

It is common for a VAT Act to include different timing rules for specific kinds of transactions. For example, under consumer protection legislation, door-to-door sales[69] may be canceled by the buyer within a specified number of days after the sale. In some of those countries, a door-to-door sale may not be reportable until the cancellation period expires.[70]

Some countries have complex rules governing the time when a supply with the use of a voucher, a stored value card, or other payment instrument is reportable for VAT purposes.[71]

II. Transition Rules

A. Introduction

This section provides an overview of some of the issues that arise when a country makes the transition from a sales tax to a value added tax. It is not intended to provide a comprehensive review of the transition rules needed

---

[66] The CT rate is 5 percent (increased from 3 percent in 1997), not the 10 percent used in the example.

[67] VATA 1994, *supra* note 9, at Sch. 4, ¶5(4).

[68] S.I. 1995/2518, VAT Regulations 1995, Reg. 81 (United Kingdom)

[69] The value of supplies door-to-door are discussed *infra* this chapter.

[70] See NZ GST, *supra* note 4, at §9(2)(b), where the supply occurs a day after the cancellation period expires.

[71] See Goods and Services Tax Ruling 2003/12 (Australia).

when a VAT replaces a sales tax.[72] A more detailed analysis of transition rules is provided elsewhere.[73]

There are many transition problems that occur because an existing sales tax ends on the day before a new VAT becomes effective. Ideally, the transition rules should cover the reporting of output tax on supplies, VAT on imports, and input credits on acquisitions with respect to transactions occurring on or after the effective date of the new law.

In some cases, the transition rules serve as exceptions to the normal timing rules. In other cases, the transition rules allow registered persons to recover sales tax paid on acquisitions. Still others create "deemed" sales in order to tax supplies that otherwise would avoid both the sales tax and VAT.

The problems vary, depending on whether a person registered for sales tax also is registered for VAT, a person registered for sales tax is not registered for VAT, or a person not registered for sales tax is registered for VAT. Although a person's status may change because the threshold required for VAT registration may be higher than the threshold under the sales tax, the status also may change because a person with low taxable turnover not required to register for VAT may voluntarily register to gain some VAT benefits or to be eligible to issue VAT invoices to customers.

It is neither practical nor desirable to include in the VAT legislation all conceivable transactions that require transition rules. As a result, the VAT legislation should give the Minister or other appropriate official authority to issue regulations "for other transitional measures relating to the end of sales tax, the start of [value added tax] . . . , or the transition from sales tax to [value added tax]. . . . "[74]

This section is divided into several subsections. The first subsection covers some of the problems related to the repeal of the sales tax. The next subsection discusses rules that are used to prevent the double taxation or complete avoidance of sales tax and VAT on taxable sales. The following subsection covers contracts or agreements entered into before VAT becomes effective that govern supplies made after the VAT effective date but have not taken the new VAT into account.

B. Transition Rules Applicable to Repealed Sales Tax

In order to minimize double taxation resulting when both sales tax and VAT are imposed on a taxable supply that occurs during the transition to VAT, the statute can provide relief in one of two general forms. The person eligible for

---

[72] This section does not cover the rules needed when a VAT rate changes or when, for policy, revenue, or other reasons, some supplies or input credits must be phased in after a new VAT becomes effective. It also does not discuss bad debts and other adjustments to sales that were subject to the repealed sales tax but occur after the VAT becomes effective.

[73] See, for example, ch. 14 of A. Schenk & O. Oldman, Value Added Tax: A Comparative Approach with Materials and Cases, Transnational Publishers 2001. Most of the material in this section is taken from that source.

[74] A New Tax System (Goods and Services Tax Transition) Act 1999, No. 57 of 1999 [hereinafter Australian GST Transition Act], §25 (Australia).

the relief may be allowed to deduct qualifying sales tax as an input tax credit or deduction in one or more tax periods after the VAT becomes effective. Alternatively, the person eligible for the relief may be required to apply for a rebate of sales tax on a return prescribed for that purpose. Relief by filing for a rebate, rather than claiming the sales tax paid as an input credit, may be preferred to minimize opportunities for abuse. Even if the input credit option is selected, the claims for sales tax relief are easier to verify if they are reported on a separate schedule to the VAT return.

Some countries limit the sales tax credit to inventory or "trading stock" and then only if the person claiming the credit can satisfy the tax authorities that sales tax had in fact been paid on the stock.[75] It is not uncommon for sales tax to be buried in product prices. Where this occurs, the sales tax credit may be based on a percentage of the sales tax-inclusive price paid for the acquired stock.[76] As an audit tool, the VAT taxpayer may be required to take a physical inventory of goods eligible for sales tax relief and submit a copy of the inventory with the return claiming the rebate or input credit.

Some countries that authorize tax credits or rebates for sales tax paid on inventory narrowly define inventory to exclude items such as secondhand goods.[77] In addition, many countries deny input credits or rebates of sales tax paid on capital goods acquired before the effective date of VAT.[78]

Sales tax relief may have a significant effect on revenue when the VAT becomes effective, especially if relief is provided for sales tax paid on all goods purchased and on hand on the effective date. It therefore may be necessary to limit relief to sales tax paid on qualifying purchases made within a specified period of time (such as four months) before the effective date.

C. Timing Differences between Sales Tax and VAT and Supplies Straddling the VAT Effective Date

The transition from a single stage sales tax to a multistage VAT involves not only an expansion of the tax base but typically a modification of timing and other procedural rules as well. In many countries, sales tax on taxable sales is reportable in the tax period in which the goods are delivered or the services are rendered, but this tax point can be accelerated if full payment is made before delivery. The VAT timing rules typically require a taxable supply to be reported in the tax period in which the invoice is issued or *any* payment is received. As a result of these timing differences, a supply with elements that straddle the VAT effective date may be subject to the sales tax and the VAT or may be subject to neither.

Many supplies may be in process on the date that VAT replace the sales tax. Goods may be in the process of manufacture, structures in the process of

---

[75] NZ GST, *supra* note 4, at §83(3).
[76] *Id.*
[77] Australian GST Transition Act, *supra* note 74, at §16.
[78] RSA VAT, *supra* note 30, at §78(10).

construction, or services in the process of being rendered on the VAT effective date. Rules may be needed, so that these supplies are subject to the sales tax or VAT, not both or neither. Otherwise, for example, a seller may issue an invoice for the sale while the sales tax is effective (the issuance of an invoice may not require the sale to be reported), and deliver the goods when the VAT is effective (delivery does not trigger the reporting of the sale for VAT purposes), avoiding both taxes.[79]

If a person registered for VAT delivers goods before the VAT effective date (assume that sales tax is imposed at the point of delivery or when full payment made),[80] the sales should not attract VAT if the consideration for the supply is paid or becomes due (an invoice is issued) within a short period of time after effectiveness.[81] This is the approach under the Canadian GST. The rationale is that the sale occurred while the sales tax was in effect and it is not difficult to trace the proceeds received after the VAT effective date to the earlier sale. A short time may be four or five months. If, however, the sale is not invoiced or paid for within that grace period, it is more difficult to verify that the proceeds received by the supplier are not from a supply that took place after the VAT became effective. Thus, under the Canadian GST, if consideration attributable to a pre-VAT sale is not received or an invoice is not issued during that grace period, for administrative simplicity, VAT is payable on that pre-VAT sale.[82]

If a person registered for sales tax and VAT receives prepayment for a supply of goods while the sales tax is effective and delivers the goods when the VAT is effective, in the absence of a transition rule covering this supply, the supply may not be subject to the sales tax or VAT.

Under some sales taxes, services are subject to tax when the services are rendered or, under the cash basis, when the consideration is received. Services may be subject to VAT at the earlier of when the services are rendered or the tax invoice is issued, or at the earlier of when a tax invoice is issued or payment is received.[83] It therefore is difficult to generalize about transition rules needed for services.

If sales tax is imposed as hotel charges are entered on a hotel bill, and VAT is imposed as invoices are issued at the conclusion of a hotel stay or as payment is made (usually at the conclusion of the hotel stay), there is the opportunity for both taxes to be applied to the same hotel stay. With the differences in the timing rules, VAT also may be avoided completely if the

---

[79] The receipt of full consideration under the sales tax or any consideration under the VAT also may trigger the reporting of the supply, but it is not clear if VAT would apply to the full consideration for the supply if the invoice was issued and most of the consideration was received before VAT became effective.

[80] See, for example, RSA VAT Handbook], *supra* note 30, at ¶15.2.1.

[81] Canadian GST, *supra* note 42, at §337(1).

[82] *Id.* As an exception, if the proceeds received after this time period are from a sale pursuant to a written agreement, then the consideration received after that period is not subject to VAT See *id.* at §337(1.1).

[83] See, for example, RSA VAT, *supra* note 30, at §9(1).

hotel bill is prepaid before VAT becomes effective.[84] An antiavoidance rule can give the revenue authorities power to tax these services that escape sales and value added tax.[85]

A transition rule is needed to cover continuous supplies of goods or services over a period that straddles the effective date of a new VAT. For example, under the Australia GST, the supply is treated as occurring uniformly throughout the period.[86]

Under many sales tax systems, tax is imposed on some business inputs used in construction activities, but the supply of construction or civil engineering work is not subject to sales tax. Sales tax may be buried in construction costs and may be difficult to identify.

Australia made a reasonable compromise between the construction industry's concern that construction services rendered before VAT became effective should not be VAT-able and an overall policy of taxing construction work placed in service after the effective date. In Australia, the GST is imposed on construction, reconstruction, manufacture, or extension of a building or civil engineering work performed under a written agreement executed before the GST effective date if the property is made available to the recipient after that effective date.[87] The GST is imposed only on the value of the work performed after the effective date if the value on the effective date is determined in a manner approved by the Commissioner and is completed by the end of the supplier's first GST tax period (or a later date if authorized).[88]

There are transitional rules in countries that do not tax real property sales under the sales tax, but tax at least sales of commercial real property under the VAT. For example, the Australian GST transition rules tax real property supplied under an agreement executed before the effective date if the property is made available to the recipient on or after the GST effective date. The value of the work completed before the effective date may not be subject to GST if that value is determined in a timely way and in an approved manner.[89]

Transition problems exist if sales tax is not imposed on home sales, but VAT is imposed on sales of homes by registered persons – predominantly new home sales. As a result, transition rules are necessary to prevent registered sellers of homes from entering into contracts with buyers, issuing invoices, or encouraging prepayment before the VAT becomes effective, and delivering the property after the effective date.

---

[84] Similar transitional issues arise with prepayments of transportation, meals, and tours before VAT takes effect, especially to the extent that these services are not subject to sales tax.

[85] For example, see the Australian GST Transition Act, *supra* note 74, at §10.

[86] *Id.* at §12(2). This rule does not apply to a warranty that is included in the price of goods or services. This rule applies to contracts entered into after the GST Act received royal assent (July 8, 1999), but before GST became effective on July 1, 2000. See *id.* at §12(1).

[87] *Id.* at §19.

[88] See *id.* at §19(4).

[89] See *id.* at §19.

D. Pre-effective Date Contracts Not Specifying VAT

Businesses may enter into contracts for the supply of goods and services long before the goods are to be delivered or the services are to be rendered. These contracts may set consideration at an amount that does not take into account possible future tax changes. Thus, a contract executed before a VAT is proposed or enacted may not provide for the new tax for a number of reasons, including the fact that the current tax on consumption does not tax the goods or services to be provided, or the fact that the supplier is not registered under the existing tax.

Most new VATs allow a supplier to collect tax on a VAT-able sale, even if the tax is not contemplated or provided for in the contract. For example, the South African VAT gives the seller the right to recover the new VAT from the buyer, unless there is a specific provision in the agreement to the contrary.[90]

III. Valuation Rules

A. Taxable Amount or Value of a Supply – General Rule

The value of a taxable supply generally is the amount of money and the fair market value of the consideration received. VAT statutes contain special rules to calculate the value of particular transactions. In some cases, the valuation is linked to value under income or other taxes. For example, the value of taxable fringe benefits provided to employees may be based on the value of these benefits under the income tax rules.[91]

The EU Sixth VAT Directive defines the taxable amount or value of a supply as "everything which constitutes the consideration that has been or is to be obtained by the supplier from the purchaser, the customer or a third party for such supplies including subsidies directly linked to the price of such supplies."[92] For goods, this amount generally is the purchase price or cost; for services, the full cost of providing the services; and for other supplies under the Sixth Directive, Art. 6(3),[93] the open market value of services rendered.[94]

---

[90] RSA VAT, *supra* note 30, at §67(1).

[91] For example, see NZ GST, *supra* note 4, at §10(7).

[92] Sixth Directive, *supra* note 2, at Art. 11(A)(1)(a). Recast Sixth Directive, *supra* note 2, at Art. 72 contains only slightly language changes. It provides: "In respect of the supply of goods or services, other than as referred to in Articles 73 to 76, the taxable amount shall include everything which constitutes consideration obtained or to be obtained by the supplier, in return for the supply, from the customer or a third party, including subsidies directly linked to the price of the supply."

[93] See Recast Sixth Directive, *supra* note 2, at Art. 28.

[94] Sixth Directive, *supra* note 2, at Art. 11(A)(1)(b)–(d); Recast Sixth Directive, *supra* note 2, at Art's. 73, 74, and 76. The "open market value" for services is "the amount which a customer at the marketing stage at which the supply takes place would have to pay to a supplier at arm's length within the territory of the country at the time of the supply under conditions of fair competition to obtain the services in question." The Recast Sixth Directive, *supra* note 2, at Art. 76 definition of open market value is: "The 'open market value' of a service shall mean the full amount that, a customer at the marketing stage at

The taxable amount includes "(a) taxes, duties, levies and charges, excluding the value added tax itself; (b) incidental expenses such as commission, packing, transport and insurance costs charged by the supplier to the purchaser or customer. Expenses covered by a separate agreement may be considered to be incidental expenses by the Member States."[95]

There was a dispute in the EU as to whether a credit or debit card handling fee paid by a merchant and acknowledged by the retail customer was an exempt financial service that could be deducted from the taxable amount of the retail sale.[96] Although the U.K. court ruled that the taxable amount could not be reduced by the fee, merchants in other EU countries continued to remove the fee from the taxable amount of their sales. An EC Council Regulation specifies that such fees do not alter the taxable amount of the retail sale if the price the customer pays is not affected by how payment is accepted.[97]

In Singapore, grants received by a supplier generally are not treated as consideration for supplies made by the recipient. The grantor may be treated as making a supply if that person receives any value in return for the grant.[98] The dispute in the EU over the treatment of subsidies directly linked to the price of supplies as part of the value of a taxable supply was resolved in part by the ECJ in the following *Keeping Newcastle Warm* case.

Keeping Newcastle Warm Limited v. Commissioners of Customs and Excise[99]

Article 11A(1)(a) of the Sixth Directive provides [in part]:

The taxable amount shall be: . . . everything which constitutes the consideration which has been or is to be obtained by the supplier from the purchaser, the customer or a third party for such supplies including subsidies directly linked to the price of such supplies.

The Home Energy Efficiency Grants Regulations 1992 (hereinafter the Regulations) provide for the award of grants to improve energy efficiency in dwellings occupied by certain categories of persons.

which the supply takes place would have to pay, at the time of the supply and under conditions of fair competition, to a supplier at arm's length within the territory of the, Member State in which the supply of a service referred to in paragraph 1 is taxable, in order to obtain the service in question."

[95] Sixth Directive, *supra* note 2, at Art. 11(A)(2); Recast Sixth Directive, *supra* note 2, at Art. 77.

[96] *Debenhams Retail plc v Revenue and Customs Commissioners*, [2005] EWCA Civ 892, [2005] All ER (D) 233 (Ct. App. JULY 18, 2005)

[97] Council Regulation (EC) No. 1777/2005 of Oct. 17, 2005, laying down implementing measures for Directive 77/388/EEC on the common system of value added tax, Art. 13, effective Jan. 1, 2006.

[98] A grant to scientists engaged in research is not a supply by the grantor if the grantor does not receive any rights over the results of the research or other benefits. *CCH Singapore Goods and Services Tax Guide*, ¶3–180 (2005), citing IRAS e-Tax Guide No. 1994/GST/2.

[99] Case C-353/00, 2002 ECR I-5419, *2002 ECJ CELEX LEXIS 3571*. [Edited by the authors.]

In particular, Regulation 5 provides that a grant may be awarded for various kinds of work, including energy advice, which is defined as advice relating to thermal insulation or to the economic and efficient use of domestic appliances or of facilities for lighting, or for space or water heating.

KNW has for several years carried out work in the context of the grant scheme established by the Regulations, including the provision of energy advice. It has declared and paid VAT on the amounts paid to it by the EAGA [Energy Action Grants Agency] in the form of energy advice grants, in the amount of GBP 10 per piece of advice.

KNW brought proceedings before the VAT and Duties Tribunal for a refund of the VAT so paid by it between 1 April 1991 and 31 August 1996. KNW submitted that the grant for energy advice was not directly linked to the price of the supply, within the meaning of Article 11A(1)(a) of the Sixth Directive, and accordingly did not form part of the taxable amount for that supply. It claimed that the grant of GBP 10 was paid without reference to the price which would have been charged for the energy advice if it had not been provided to the consumer for free.

The Commissioners submitted that the amount of GBP 10 was not a standard sum but was linked to the amount properly charged for the energy advice and that in any event it constituted the consideration for the supply.

[T]he VAT and Duties Tribunal, Manchester, pursuant to an order of the High Court, referred the following questions to the Court:

> Is a payment made by the Energy Action Grants Agency to the Appellant, which receives it in respect of energy advice given to an eligible house- holder, a subsidy within the meaning of that word in Article 11A(1)(a) of the EC Sixth Council Directive?

KNW argues that the sum of GBP 10 awarded by the EAGA in respect of each piece of energy advice constitutes a subsidy, but one which is not directly linked to the price of the supply because the amount in practice always corresponds to the ceiling set for it. Furthermore, since the supply of energy advice to consumers is free, the grant is in fact in the nature of a flat-rate subsidy to the operating costs of KNW and is not directly linked to any cost. Accordingly, the grant does not form part of the consideration for the supply within the meaning of Article 11A(1)(a) of the Sixth Directive.

Relying inter alia on the Court's judgments in Cooperatieve Aardap- pelenbewaarplaats (Case 154/80 1981 ECR 445) and Tolsma (Case C- 16/93 1994 ECR I-743), the United Kingdom contends that the financial assistance at issue in the main proceedings constitutes consideration within the meaning of Article 11A(1)(a) of the Sixth Directive and that that concludes the dispute before the national court. In any event there is a direct link between the subsidy and the services supplied by KNW. The contract between KNW and the householder sets out the nature and cost of the work which KNW will carry out and deducts the amount of financial assistance available to the householder from the amount payable by the householder. But if for some reason the financial assistance is not forthcoming, the householder is obliged to pay KNW for the whole of the work.

The Commission submits that the purpose of Article 11A(1)(a) of the Sixth Directive is to ensure that the taxable basis includes the whole of the consideration paid in respect of the supply of goods or services, whether the consideration is paid by the recipient or by a third party, which may be a public authority. Accordingly, where a third party, including, as is the case in the main proceedings, a public authority, contributes a sum of money for a specific service provided to an individual, that sum is part of the taxable amount, irrespective of whether the payment constitutes a subsidy directly linked to the price of the supply. It does not follow from the fact that the sum paid systematically amounts to GBP 10 that the subsidy is not directly linked to the price.

It is clear that the sum paid by the EAGA to KNW is received by the latter in consideration for the service supplied by it to certain categories of recipient.

As consideration in respect of a supply, that sum forms part of the taxable amount within the meaning of Article 11A(1)(a) of the Sixth Directive.

Accordingly the answer to be given to the questions referred to the Court must be that Article 11A(1)(a) of the Sixth Directive is to be interpreted as meaning that a sum such as that paid in the case in the main proceedings constitutes part of the consideration for the supply of services and forms part of the taxable amount in respect of that supply for the purposes of VAT.

In some cases, it is not clear what amount is charged for the item sold. For example, is the amount for a service charge (or tip) on a restaurant bill includible as part of the taxable amount of the sale? In the United Kingdom, the service charge is part of the taxable consideration if it is automatically included in the bill and the customer must pay it[100] but not taxable if the service charge is added to the bill but is optional with the customer.[101]

In some financial transactions, the taxable amount may equal the spread between the bid and ask prices set by the trader.[102]

Sales of telephone cards, rail or bus passes, or other vouchers generally are not taxable if consideration of a stated value is indicated on the voucher.[103]

---

[100] See *Potters Lodge Restaurant Ltd v. The Commissioners of Customs & Excise*, LON/79/286.

[101] See *NDP Co. Ltd. v. The Commissioners of Customs & Excise*, [1988] VATTR 40 (London). According to Customs & Excise in Canada, a tip added to a restaurant bill as a mandatory or suggested gratuity is subject to the Canadian GST. Revenue Canada, Customs & Excise, Information for the Food Services Industry (1990).

[102] *Customs and Excise Commissioners v First National Bank of Chicago*, Case C-172/96, [1998], [1998] All ER (EC) 744, STC 850 (ECJ)

[103] See, for example, NZ GST, *supra* note 4, at §10(16).

The sale is taxable when the voucher or pass is used to pay for the service generally in the amount deducted from the voucher or pass for the service. However, tokens, stamps, or vouchers issued without a stated consideration may be taxed on issuance for the consideration paid if the voucher is exchangeable for a particular item, such as milk.[104] In that case, on redemption of this milk or other voucher, the value of the supply is treated as zero.[105]

In one case, a retailer sold its goods listed in a catalogue at its more than three hundred showrooms. It sold vouchers (for its merchandise) to other businesses at a discount. The purchasers of the vouchers used them as incentives, but the persons who used the vouchers were not aware of the fact that they were originally issued at a discount. In a judgment issued by the European Court of Justice, the court in *Argos Distributors Ltd v Customs and Excise Commissioners*[106] ruled that the retailer must treat only the amount received on sale of the vouchers, not the face amount, as consideration for the supply:

> Article 11(A)(1)(a) of the Sixth Directive must be interpreted as meaning that, when a supplier has sold a voucher to a buyer at a discount and promised subsequently to accept that voucher at its face value in full or part payment of the price of goods purchased by a customer who was not the buyer of the voucher, and who does not normally know the actual price at which the voucher was sold by the supplier, the consideration represented by the voucher is the sum actually received by the supplier upon the sale of the voucher.

Abuses in the use of "face value vouchers" prompted the United Kingdom to amend its VAT Act in 2003. It now provides that the issuance of a "face value voucher"[107] generally is a supply for VAT purposes and therefore is taxable upon issuance or subsequent supply.[108] In contrast, the supply of a "credit voucher"[109] generally is disregarded, "except to the extent (if any) that it exceeds the face value of the voucher.[110] If a face-value voucher (other

---

[104] *Id.* at §10(17).

[105] *Id.*

[106] Case C-288/94, [1996] ECR I-5311, 1996 ECJ CELEX LEXIS 10813.

[107] VATA 1994, *supra* note 9, at Sch. 10A, ¶1(1) defines a "face-value voucher" as "a token, stamp or voucher (whether in physical or electronic form) that represents a right to receive goods or services to the value of an amount stated on it or recorded in it."

[108] *Id.* at ¶2.

[109] *Id.* at ¶3(1) defines a "credit voucher" as "a face-value voucher issued by a person who – (a) is not a person from whom goods or services may be obtained by the use of the voucher, and (b) undertakes to give complete or partial reimbursement to any such person from whom goods or services are so obtained."

[110] *Id.* at ¶3(2). There is an exception if the person from whom the goods or services are obtained fails to account for VAT on the supply to the person using the voucher to obtain them. *Id.* at ¶3(3). Similar treatment is provided for the issuance of "retail vouchers." *Id.* at ¶4(1)–(4). The consideration received for the supply of a face-value voucher that is a postage stamp is disregarded, except to the extent that it exceeds the face value of the stamp. *Id.* at ¶5. Supplies of other face-value vouchers generally are supplies for VAT purposes. *Id.* at ¶6(1)-(5).

than a postage stamp) is supplied in a composite transaction with other goods or services, and "the total consideration for the supplies is no different, or not significantly different, from what it would be if the voucher were not supplied," the supply of the voucher is deemed made for no consideration.[111]

What if a purchaser fails to pay the purchase price for a supply when due and, in litigation, the purchaser is required to pay an addition amount in the nature of interest? Does the taxable amount include the interest added to the consideration that the purchaser owes the seller? In *BAZ Bausystem AG v. Finanzamt Munchen fur Korperschaften*,[112] the European Court of Justice held that as the interest had no connection with the services and did not represent part of the consideration in a commercial transaction, but merely represented compensation for the delay in payment, the interest was not part of the taxable amount within the meaning of Article 11A(a)(1) of the Sixth Directive.

B. Sales Free of Charge or for a Nominal Charge

A transfer of goods or services may be made for no charge or for less than fair market value for a number of reasons. The transfer may represent an arm's-length transaction undertaken for business reasons. For example, a company producing personal hygiene products may mail free samples of its toothpaste to consumers. Because VAT is imposed on sales for consideration and these transactions are not transfers for consideration, there is no taxable sale.[113] The company will factor the cost of these free samples into the sales price for its toothpaste. This cost will be taxed when the company sells its toothpaste. Of course, any related input tax is creditable.

If a seller receives services from his buyer as part of the consideration for the seller's sale, the value of the services received is included in the taxable amount of the sale, but only if there is a sufficient connection between the services received and the supply. In *Naturally Yours Cosmetics Ltd v. Customs and Excise*,[114] a wholesaler of cosmetic products marketed its products through independent contractors (exempt retailers selling through living room or hostess parties). The wholesaler sold its "retailers" "a pot of cream" for about 10 percent of its wholesale price as a "dating gift." In that case, the ECJ ruled that under the valuation rule in Article 11(A)(1)(a) of the Sixth Directive:[115]

> where a supplier ('the wholesaler') supplies goods ('the inducement') to another ('the retailer') for a monetary consideration (namely a sum of money)

---

[111] *Id.* at ¶7(b).

[112] [1982] 3 CMLR 688 (ECJ) (Case 222/81). This case involved Council Directive No 67/228, Art. 8(2).

[113] See, for example, Canadian GST, *supra* note 42, at §165(1), imposing GST on the value of the consideration for a taxable supply.

[114] Case 230/87, [1988] STC 879 (ECJ Judgment).

[115] See Recast Sixth Directive, *supra* note 2, at Art. 72, quoted at note 69.

which is less than that at which he supplies identical goods to the retailer for resale to the public on an undertaking by the retailer to apply the inducement in procuring another person to arrange, or in rewarding another for arranging, a gathering at which further goods of the wholesaler can be sold by the retailer to the public for their mutual benefit, on the understanding that if no such gathering is held the inducement must be returned to the supplier or paid for at its wholesale price, the taxable amount is the sum of the monetary consideration and of the value of the service provided by the retailer which consists in applying the inducement to procure the services of another person or in rewarding that person for those services the value of that service must be regarded as being equal to the difference between the price actually paid for that product and its normal wholesale price.

In *Empire Stores Ltd v. Commissioners of Customs and Excise*,[116] a mail order business gave "free" gifts to individuals who provided personal information about credit-worthiness of themselves or other potential customers. The court held that if there is a direct link between the goods provided and the consideration received (the information about the customer), there is a taxable transaction with the taxable amount equal to the cost to the firm (not the retail value) of the goods provided in return for that information.

If a supply is made at below fair market value, the transaction generally is taxed at the price charged if it is made at arm's-length, but not if the transaction is between related parties.

C. Discounts, Rebates, and Price Allowances

Under the EU Sixth Directive, the taxable amount does not include "(a) price reductions by way of discount for early payment; (b) price discounts and rebates allowed to the customer and accounted for at the time of the supply; (c) the amounts received by a taxable person from his purchaser or customer as repayment for expenses paid out in the name and for the account of the latter and which are entered in his books in a suspense account...."[117]

The taxable value of a cash sale is the cash price charged.[118] If the invoiced price is subject to a prompt payment discount or penalty for late payment, trade or quantity discount or other price allowance or rebate available at the time of the sale, the value of the supply may not be so clear. In countries that exempt interest (financial intermediation services), the portion of the price representing interest should not be taxed.[119] This is the rule in the United Kingdom for unconditional prompt payment discounts. Unless the supply is an installment sale, the taxable amount is the invoice price less the

---

[116] Case 33/93, [1994] 3 All ER 90 (Judgment of the ECJ 1994).
[117] Sixth Directive, *supra* note 2, at Art. 11(A)(3); Recast Sixth Directive, *supra* note 2, at Art's. 78 and 84.
[118] Canadian GST, *supra* note 42, at §153(1)(a).
[119] "Modern billing procedures provide two amounts – the full price and the VAT, and the discounted price and the discounted VAT." Tait, *Value Added Tax: International Practice and Problems* [hereinafter Tait, VAT], p. 374.

discount, even if the discount is not taken.[120] Conditional discounts are treated differently.[121]

> Many businesses, both retail and other, indulge in promotional schemes to induce customers to trade with them. These are common in both developed and developing countries and, while understandable from a commercial point of view, they are an annoyance to the tax administrator. The basic point is clear; the VAT is liable on the price actually paid by the customer.[122]

What if a shop sells its products to customers with zero percent financing? If the shop makes an arrangement with the finance company under which the finance company makes a loan to the shop's customer at the retail price and then pays the shop a discounted amount that represents the finance charges on the loan, must the shop report the retail price or the amount received from the finance company as the consideration for the supply? In *Customs and Excise Commissioners v. Primback Ltd*,[123] the ECJ ruled that the taxable amount of the sale is the full amount payable by the purchaser, not the net amount received by the shop from the finance company.

If a customer obtains a coupon from a newspaper or other advertising source or a customer receives a coupon on a package that entitles the customer to a discount on future purchases, must the seller include the face amount of the coupon in determining the taxable consideration for the sale of the merchandise sold at a price less the coupon discount? See *The Boots Company plc v. Commissioners of Customs & Excise*,[124] decided under Sixth VAT directive, Art. 11A.3(b), in which the court held that certain price discounts and rebates allowed at the time of a supply are not includible as part of the consideration for a supply. They cover "the difference between the normal retail selling price of the goods supplied and the sum of money actually received by the retailer for those goods where the retailer accepts from the

---

[120] VATA 1994, *supra* note 9, at Sch. 6, ¶¶4(1) and 4(2).

[121] If the discount is conditional, such as conditioned on the purchase of a certain quantity of the seller's goods, the United Kingdom ignores the discount. If the condition is satisfied, the seller can issue a credit note that includes a reduction in VAT. See Notice 700, The VAT guide, ¶7.3.2(c) (April 2002 ed.) (United Kingdom). "Credit, or a contingent discount, can permit a purchaser to reclaim all the tax on the supply as an input tax. The scheme can operate in two ways. Both seller and purchaser can agree that the credit need not affect the original VAT (usually because the credit is going to be used in the near future and is not permitted to be used for a good with a different rate; that is, the credit will be used for a similar good to that originally purchased). Alternatively, the credit can be held for some time and allowed to be used for the purchase of some other good liable to a completely different VAT rate. In the latter case, both purchaser and seller should adjust the original VAT charge and a credit note should be issued to the purchaser with, of course, the seller keeping a copy. The credit note shows the details of registration numbers and addresses, but also must show the total amount credited excluding the VAT and the rate and amount of VAT credited. When the purchaser receives a credit note which includes VAT, then he must reduce his input tax by the amount shown in the tax period when he receives the credit note." Tait, VAT, *supra* note 119, at 375.

[122] Tait, VAT, *supra* note 119, at 384.

[123] Case C-34/99, [2001] 1 WLR 1693, [2001] All ER (EC) 714 (Judgment ECJ).

[124] Case C-126/88, [1990] ECR I-1235, [1990] STC 387 (Judgment of the ECJ 1990).

customer a coupon which he gave to the customer upon a previous purchase made at the normal retail selling price."[125]

D. Pledged Goods and Repossessions

"When a consumer borrows money from a pawn shop and gives property as collateral for the loan, the transaction is a loan with no VAT consequences. If the pawned article is redeemed, the repayment of the loan also has no VAT consequences, other than the tax on the intermediation services provided by the lender, the pawn shop [if intermediation services are taxed]. If, on the other hand, within the prescribed time period (such as six months), the article is not redeemed or interest is not paid on the loan, the pawn shop generally acquires legal ownership and the right to sell the pawned article. When the pawn shop acquires the right to sell the property, the shop . . . [should be] treated as having purchased the pawned article. . . . When the pawn shop sells the article, VAT is imposed on the price charged."[126] To avoid the double tax, the pawn shop should receive treatment similar to that available to used goods dealers who buy goods from consumers for resale. One option is to grant the pawn shop a deemed or constructive credit for the VAT implicit in the shop's cost for the pawned item.[127] An alternative is to define the taxable amount of the sale as the difference between the sales price and the loan amount on the pawned item.[128]

E. Postsale Adjustments

"A seller may make a refund, rebate, or price adjustment after output tax on the sale is reportable. These post-sale adjustments should reduce the seller's output tax and the buyer's input credit. [One option is to grant the seller] . . . a credit for VAT deemed attributable to these post-sale adjustments, but only if the seller issues proof of the adjustment (a credit invoice). . . . A rebate like an automobile manufacturer's rebate to the retail purchaser of a car . . . [may be] treated as a post-sale price adjustment. . . . The manufacturer sold the car to a dealer and charged VAT on the selling price. When the manufacturer later issues a check to a retail customer, it is not reducing the sales price to the dealer. Nevertheless, the net effect is to reduce the consideration the manufacturer received for the car and the retail customer paid for the car. The manufacturer therefore should rebate some VAT to the customer and should reduce its VAT liability. Assume VAT is imposed at a 10 percent rate and that the manufacturer wants to rebate $550 ($500 plus $50 VAT)

---

[125] ABA model Act., *supra* note 34, at 49.

[126] *Id.*

[127] See Canadian GST, *supra* note 42, at §176. See also NZ GST, *supra* note 4, at §2(1) definition of input tax and §20(3)(a)(ia).

[128] See Sixth Directive, *supra* note 2, at Art. 26a(B); Recast Sixth Directive, *supra* note 2, at Art's. 304(a), 305–307, 310–312, covering taxable dealers in secondhand goods and other items typically purchased from unregistered persons.

to the retail customer.... [The manufacturer should be able to] claim a $50 credit."[129,130]

What are the VAT consequences of year-end rebates to members of a cooperative? Are they price discounts that reduce VAT liability or are they returns on the members' ownership interest in the coop that do not affect VAT liability? Under the Canadian GST, a patronage dividend is treated as a price adjustment, and a cooperative can elect one of several methods to calculate the GST reduction and to issue tax refunds to its members.[131] The following U.K. case represents a different approach.

Co-operative Retail Services Ltd v. Commissioners of Customs and Excise[132]

HEADNOTE. The Appellant, Co-operative Retail Services Ltd, owned and operated a substantial number of retail stores throughout the UK, selling a wide range of merchandise including food and also a travel agency. It was a member of the Co-operative Movement and was run on co-operative principles.

The Appellant was incorporated under the Industrial and Provident Societies Acts, its share capital being variable, depending on the amount invested with it by its members. A person became a member by investing money with it to a maximum of £10,000. Members received or were credited with interest on that capital and, in the case of qualifying members, with what the Appellant called a 'dividend'. Such dividend was calculated as a percentage of the aggregate amount of the members' respective purchases during a prescribed period, irrespective of any profit or loss the Appellant might make.

Under the Appellant's Shareholder Card Scheme, a [Visa] Shareholder Card was issued to qualifying members by the Co-operative Bank plc (an associated company). To obtain a card, a member with an investment of £50 or more must make application for a card and be subject to certain financial checks. In addition, a shareholder who retained the minimum investment of £50 for one year and remained a card holder, received a 'dividend' on his purchases (except food) of 5 per cent and on travel a dividend of 2.5 per cent. Every two months he received a statement showing how his purchases had qualified for a dividend. Once a year his total dividend was transferred to his Shareholders account where it earned interest.

---

[129] The credit is equal to the amount rebated multiplied by the tax rate at the time of sale/ 100 plus the same tax rate. In the example in the text, the credit would be $550 × 10/110, or $50.

[130] ABA Model Act, *supra* note 34, at 49–50.

[131] Canadian GST, *supra* note 42, at §233. The GST deduction is taken during the period the dividend is paid. *Id.* at §233(2).

[132] [1992] VATTR 60 (Manchester VAT Tribunal). [Edited by the authors.]

The dividend was paid only at the end of January in each year and not at the point of sale, save in the case of travel agency business where the 2.5 per cent dividend was immediately deducted from the cost of the travel arrangements. The average amount of dividend paid in one year was between £70 and £90.

The 'dividend' was so called partly for historical reasons and partly because the Appellant considered that it would appear more attractive to potential shareholders than if it were called a 'discount' which many retailers offered.

The Commissioners contend that those payments, known as 'dividends', are properly so called and represent distributions of profit.

The Appellant, on the other hand, contends that the dividends are in reality discounts, representing not a distribution of profit but a reduction in the price of the merchandise; and that the value of its outputs is to be calculated after deduction from the gross value of those outputs of the aggregate amount of the dividends paid to the relevant customers. The Commissioners acknowledge that if the Appellant's contentions are correct the assessment must be discharged.

[W]e have found nothing to identify the dividends as distributions of profit and have come to the conclusion that they are correctly to be regarded as rebates. We have found the decisive factor to be the contractual obligation upon the Appellant to make the payments regardless of the level of its profit – indeed, whether or not it makes a profit or a loss, and without any reference to the magnitude of that profit or loss. Such an obligation, we consider, is inconsistent with the payments' being distributions of profit.

Accordingly we allow the appeal.

F. Related Party Transactions

If a taxable person transfers property or services to an unrelated purchaser for less than market value, the tax generally is imposed on the price charged. What about sales to related persons or to employees at below fair market value? "While the 'price charged' rule may facilitate tax administration and may not result in any significant revenue loss if the related buyer or the employee is a taxable person eligible to credit any input tax on the purchase, the rule does not work well where the related buyer or the employee is not a taxable person or is a taxable person that is not entitled to input credit for VAT charged on the purchase. For example, employers may distribute or sell consumer goods or services to employees free of charge or at a below market price."[133] Below-market sales of goods or services by a corporation

---

[133] ABA Model Act, *supra* note 34, at 55. To the extent that these items are used for personal consumption by the recipients, the basic valuation rule would permit avoidance of VAT. In *Hotel Scandic Gasaback AB ('Scandic') v Riksskatteverket*, Case C-412/03, [2005] ECJ CELEX LEXIS 34, [2005] ECR I-743 (ECJ Judgment), the case involved the taxable amount of meals

to its shareholders may be undertaken to avoid VAT. "In these situations, the 'price charged' rule permits avoidance of VAT."[134]

To prevent this potential abuse in related party and similar transactions, the supplier may be required to value the sale at fair market value. For example, the Canadian GST uses the fair market value standard to value a sale to an unregistered person in a non-arm's-length transaction if the seller charges less than fair market value.[135]

G. Margin Schemes

There are a number of transactions that do not lend themselves to the credit-invoice method of calculating the taxable amount of a supply. The problem arises most frequently where the value of a supplier's service is represented by the margin or spread between the consideration received and payments made. The VAT treatment is complicated when some or all of the payments for business inputs are made to unregistered persons. Financial intermediation services, gambling, and other games of chance, and insurance are illustrative. These are discussed in detail in Chapters 10 and 11.

Sales of used goods, works of art, collectors' items, and antiques raise similar issues relating to the calculation of the taxable amount of a supply.[136] Many countries have adopted margin schemes to account for sales of these goods. Absent a special scheme, the entire price charged for these previously owned items would be taxed.

Travel agent services pose a special problem in the calculation of the taxable amount of a supply. A travel agent may serve as a principal in providing travel services (such as organizing a convention for a business) or serve as an agent. When the travel company serves as agent, it generally is compensated an amount represented by the spread between the price charged for the travel services and the company's cost in obtaining the services from hotel and other travel service providers. The ease with which travel or tour companies can supply these services offshore or over the Internet has created competitive inequalities that is prompting countries to modify their VAT rules governing travel agents and tour companies.

In the EU, the Sixth Directive provides a special margin scheme for travel agents,[137] if a travel agent deals with customers in his own name as principal

---

the company in the hotel and restaurant business provided in a company canteen at a fixed price to its staff. The price generally exceeds the company's cost, but a future price may be less than cost. The ECJ ruled that under Articles 2, 5(6) and 6(2)(b) of the Sixth Council Directive, a Member cannot adopt a rule "whereby transactions in respect of which an actual consideration is paid are regarded as an application of goods or services for private use, even where that consideration is less than the cost price of the goods or services supplied."

[134] ABA Model Act, *supra* note 34, at 55.

[135] Canadian GST, *supra* note 42, at §155(1). There are some exceptions. See *id*. at §155(2).

[136] See discussion of used goods *supra* Chapter 6 (Section IV).

[137] See Sixth Directive, *supra* note 2, at Art. 26, applicable when a travel agent deals with customers in his own name and uses supplies of other taxable persons in providing

and uses supplies of other taxable persons in providing the travel services. In contrast, when a travel agent acts as agent of his customer (acts as an intermediary) or when the agent supplies the travel services using his own facilities, the special scheme does not apply. When the agent acts as intermediary, the agent will bill his customers for the amount it paid to the suppliers of the travel services plus a commission, and charge VAT on the total amount. The agent then will claim credit for VAT imposed on the agent's purchase of the travel services on behalf of the customer. When the agent supplies travel services using its own facilities (such as when the agent owns the hotel providing the accommodations), under the normal VAT rules, the accommodation and other travel services are taxable where the service is provided (where the hotel is located).[138] The unequal treatment of travel agents operating within the EU and those operating outside the EU but providing services either for persons within the EU or on travel within the EU prompted the European Commission to propose a Directive changing the special scheme for travel agents.[139]

H. SALES TO DOOR-TO-DOOR SELLERS AND SIMILAR INDEPENDENT CONTRACTORS

"Some businesses sell their products through independent contractors who resell to ultimate consumers door-to-door and not through a regular place of business. For VAT purposes, the door-to-door sellers may be considered retailers. Alternatively, the supplier may be considered the retailer; and the door-to-door sellers may be treated as agents. The reason this difference is important is that if the VAT statute provides a de minimis exemption for small traders, many of these door-to-door sellers would come within the exemption. The establishment of a network of independent contractors instead of employees may enable a distributor to sell its products to ultimate consumers without VAT on the value added by the door-to-door sellers, thus obtaining an advantage over its competitors that market their products through company-owned stores or through employees selling door-to-door. This marketing arrangement is similar to franchise operations where the franchisee is selling only the franchiser's products or services. Arguably,

the travel services. The ECJ ruled that the margin scheme applies to a company that organized an international study and language trip for high school and college students. *Finanzamt Heidelberg v ISt internationale Sprach- und Studienreisen GmbH*, C-200/04, [2005] ECR I-8691.

[138] Dewilde, Eeckhout, & Boone, "The Margin Scheme for Travel Agents: The European Commission's Proposal to Simplify the European VAT Rules," *VAT Monitor*, Jan./Feb. 2003, p. 7.

[139] The proposal is part of a VAT strategy to improve the operation of the VAT system within the Internal Market (COM 2000) 348 final of June 7, 2000, discussed and cited in *id.* at p. 11. The proposal for the Council Directive was presented 8 February 2002. *Id.* To date, while there have been amendments by the European Parliament, the proposal has not become final. *Id.* at 13. The most recent action is a Proposal for a Regulation regarding supplies of travel services – COM (2003) 78 final/2 of March 24, 2003.

they should receive equivalent VAT treatment. There is, however, at least one significant difference. A franchisee typically sells to customers from a regular place of business."[140]

The potential abuse in this area can be minimized or eliminated if the small business exemption threshold is set at such a low level that these sellers (whether selling door-to-door or at living room parties) are caught in the VAT net. The problem with this approach, especially for developing countries without an adequate audit staff, is that it may substantially increase the number of tax returns that must be processed and may impose substantial compliance costs on small businesses that are not the target of the lower threshold, all without any significant increase in VAT revenue.

The alternative employed in some countries is to require the manufacturer or distributor who sells to these door-to-door sellers to report as the taxable amount of the sales the retail price of the items sold. The manufacturer and distributor know these prices because they generally set the recommended retail prices.

For example, in the European Union, it is common for member states to prevent loss of revenue by providing that sales by producers or wholesalers to unregistered persons for resale be valued at retail, not the price charged the unregistered retailers. In *Gold Star Publications Ltd v. Commissioners of Customs and Excise*, [1992] 3 CMLR 1 (Q.B. 1992), the taxpayer attempted to avoid this treatment under the U.K. VAT[141] by selling to unregistered intermediaries at catalogue prices less a 30 percent discount. The court held that the sales must be valued at the open market value, which in this case meant the value for a retail sale, not the value of the sale to the intermediaries.[142] In a similar case involving sales through unregistered agents, the court held that the Commissioners could order a mail order company to use the catalogue prices as reasonable estimates of open market value, even if the agents often resold the products at less than the full catalogue price. See *Fine Art Developments plc v. Customs and Excise Commissioners*, [1993] STC 29 (Q.B. 1993), in which the court stated, in part:

> Since it is impossible or excessively difficult to ascertain the actual prices at which these goods are sold to all the final consumers, the commissioners are entitled by Community law to use open market value as the basis for their assessments. What is the open market value in any case is a matter to be decided on the available evidence.

I. SELF-SUPPLY TRANSACTIONS

When business assets or services are diverted to personal use, the business generally must report that diversion as a taxable supply. Under the Sixth

---

[140] ABA Model Act, *supra* note 34, at 57.

[141] See VATA 1994, *supra* note 9, at Sch. 6, ¶2.

[142] By dictum, the court found that the 30 percent discount was not a discount as that term is meant in Sch. 6 of the U.K. VAT because the discount was the only compensation that the intermediary would receive for his or her efforts.

VAT Directive, Art. 11A(1)(b) and 11A(1)(c),[143] the taxable amount of this diversion of business assets or services to personal use generally is the purchase price of the goods or services, not the fair market value of such assets or services.

J. Taxable Amount – Imports

1. General Rule

Tax on imports generally is imposed on the customs value plus customs and other duties and taxes other than the VAT itself.[144] If insurance and freight are not included in customs value, they generally are added to the taxable value.[145] Some imports do not have a customs value or the customs value is not an accurate reflection of the value of the imports. The latter may occur if the invoice price is used as the customs value and the import comes from a related seller. In these situations, the taxable amount is the fair market value of the import. In the *Addidas* case,[146] the New Zealand court held that royalties paid by a N.Z. subsidiary to its foreign parent were includible in the VAT-able value of the goods imported by the subsidiary.

"Under United States customs law, dutiable value does not include any separately stated cost of transportation and insurance for the goods to the port of importation.[147] The European practice is to include these costs as part of the VAT-able value of imports."[148] In the United Kingdom, the value of imported goods from outside the EU includes, if not already included in customs value, the taxes, duties, and so on other than VAT; and incidental expenses like commissions, packaging, transport and insurance at least to the first destination in the United Kingdom.[149] New Zealand has a similar set of rules.[150]

---

[143] Recast Sixth Directive, *supra* note 2, at Art's. 73 & 74.

[144] See, for example, NZ GST, *supra* note 4, at §12(2). "[Historically, customs duties were]...imposed on imports to equalize foreign and domestic prices for goods, not primarily to raise revenue. It therefore would not be unreasonable to impose VAT on the customs duty-inclusive price of imports." ABA Model Act, *supra* note 34, at 47.

[145] See NZ GST, *supra* note 4, at §12(2)(c).

[146] *Addidas New Zealand Ltd v Collector of Customs*, 1 NZCC ¶55–001 (1999).

[147] 19 U.S.C.A. §1401a(b)(1)(West 1980) (United States), provides that the value of imported merchandise generally is the price payable for the merchandise when sold for exportation to the United States, increased only by the packaging costs incurred by the buyer, any selling commission incurred by the buyer, the value of any assist, any royalty or license fee that the buyer must pay as a result of the import, and the proceeds of any subsequent resale, disposal, or use of the import that accrue to the seller. Dutiable value therefore does not include the cost of transportation and insurance.

[148] ABA Model Act, *supra* note 34, at 52.

[149] VATA 1994, *supra* note 9, at §21(1) and (2). There are special rules covering prompt payment discounts, works or art, antiques and certain collectors' pieces. *Id.* at §21(3)–(6).

[150] NZ GST, *supra* note 4, at §12(2).

2. Imports Placed in a Bonded Warehouse

Imports generally are taxed when they "enter" the country of import. If imports are placed in a bonded warehouse in the importing country, they generally are not treated as imported until they are removed from the bonded warehouse for domestic use or consumption. The value of the import should be based on the value at the point that they are removed from the warehouse, which may be the price paid or some other amount.[151]

3. Imports of Previously Exported Articles

If a business sends goods to another business for repair, warranty work, assembly, manufacture, or other change and does not transfer ownership of the goods, the VAT consequences should be the same, whether the work is performed within or outside the . . . [country]. Normally, if goods are shipped abroad by a business, the transfer is zero rated. If the same goods are re-imported, VAT generally is imposed on the import on the basis of the customs value. . . . The importer may pay the import tax to Customs at the point of import and claim an input credit in the first return filed after the import. While the net result may be the same as having the work done . . . [domestically], the importer may suffer some cash flow cost. The cash flow problem could be avoided by [not zero rating the export and] taxing the re-import on the amount charged for the repair or other work abroad. . . . If the goods are repaired under warranty free of charge, the import tax is zero.[152] A non-taxable person would not have any VAT consequences associated with the export for repair and would be subject to VAT on the amount charged for the repair of the imported article.[153]

The United Kingdom taxes only the value of the work done abroad on goods exported for such work and then reimported, assuming ownership of the goods has not changed.[154]

4. Imports from Unregistered Persons

When imported goods are purchased from a foreign, VAT-registered supplier, the foreign supplier's export sale generally is zero rated (free of VAT) and the importer is subject to VAT on import. If the imported goods are purchased from an unregistered foreign person in a country with a VAT, the supplier likely was subject to VAT when he purchased the goods. The export by this unregistered person is not zero rated and therefore the price to the importer may include some embedded VAT. If the importing country taxes the full value or price charged for the goods, the goods will bear excessive

---

[151] See *id.* at §12. For a discussion of the British rules on fiscal warehousing, see VATA 1994, *supra* note 9, at §18A.

[152] Presumably, the buyer paid VAT on the value of the warranty that was included in the price of the product.

[153] ABA Model Act, *supra* note 34, at 53–54.

[154] Value Added Tax Regulations 1995 (SI 1995/2518), reg. 126 (United Kingdom).

VAT. In *Staatssecretaris van Financiën v Gaston Schul Douane-Expediteur BV*,[155] the ECJ interpreted the policies underlying the Treaty of Rome to reach a decision that prevented the imposition of VAT on the full value of the import if the import came from a consumer in another EU country.[156]

IV. Discussion Questions

1. How should VAT apply to credit sales and installment sales? Should the tax on the entire cash-equivalent sale price be collected by the seller at the time of the delivery of the goods or should the tax collection be based on each payment of part of the purchase price as received by the seller? Why? Compare the U.K. and the Japanese approachs (Section I(C)(1) of this chapter).
2. What are the advantages and disadvantages, to the government and to businesses subject to VAT, if businesses can use the same method of accounting for VAT purposes that they use for income tax purposes? What problems arise if a seller subject to VAT reports on the cash method and that seller's buyer subject to VAT reports on the accrual method, or vice versa?
3. Mr. Black is a furniture manufacturer. For his daughter's wedding, he gives her various furniture that he has manufactured. The cost of raw materials, supplies, and other items may be estimated at $1,000. The cost of labor may be estimated at $1,000. Mr. Black would sell this furniture to a wholesaler for $2,400 (including $400 profit). The wholesaler's price to the retailer would be $2,800, and the retailer's price to the consumer would be $3,300. Under the Sixth Directive or the New Vatopia VAT, is VAT chargeable on the gift made by Mr. Black? If you think that it is taxable, what is the taxable amount?

---

[155] Case 47/84, [1985] ECR 1491. See discussion of this case, *supra* Chapter 7 (Section IV(B)).
[156] In *Tulliasiamies and Antti Siilin*, Case C-101/00, [2002] ECR I-07487, [2002] ECJ CELEX LEXIS 3627, the ECJ reached a similar result with respect to the import of used cars from another member state.

9

Zero Rating and Exemptions and Government Entities and Nonprofit Organizations

I. Introduction

This chapter covers the use of exemptions and zero rating under a VAT. As discussed in more detail in Chapter 2, the exemption may be an "item" exemption limited to particular supplies or an "entity" exemption applicable to all or most supplies by a particular kind of entity. Zero rating generally is provided for exports of goods (regardless of the nature of the goods exported)[1] and exports of some services. An exemption may be provided for all supplies by a unit of government or nonprofit organization, the exemption may be provided based on the nature of the goods or services supplied, or may be provided for all supplies except those that compete with the private sector.

The next few parts of this chapter cover zero rating, exemptions, and mixed supplies, with attention focused on the complexity resulting from borderline cases involving "item" exemptions or "item" zero rating.

Part VI of this chapter discusses some of the special VAT problems associated with the nonprofit–governmental sectors and proposals to include certain services by these sectors in the VAT base.

II. Zero-Rated Sales

A. In General

A zero-rated sale is a taxable sale, subject to tax at a zero rate, and input tax on purchases attributable to that sale is creditable. The sale therefore is basically free of VAT.[2] If a sale at retail is zero rated, the consumer buys the item free of VAT. If the zero rate applied only at an intermediate (such as wholesale) stage, and the retail stage were taxable, the tax not collected at the intermediate

---

[1] For an exception, see Value Added tax Act 2005, Act No. 7 of 2005, Sch. II, ¶2(s), exemption for "an export of unprocessed agricultural products." (Commonwealth of Dominica)

[2] Purchases from an exempt small business and other exempt purchases may include the seller's noncreditable VAT paid on its costs (inputs). This VAT therefore is included in the price of zero-rated sales.

stage would be recovered on the retail sale. In the following chart,[3] this distinction is illustrated for a 10-percent VAT.

	Wholesale stage zero rating		Retail stage zero rating	
Manufacturer				
Sales $400,000	$40,000		$40,000	
No purchases	00		00	
Net VAT paid		$40,000		$40,000
Wholesaler				
Sales $1 million	$00		$100,000	
Purchases $400,000	(40,000)		(40,000)	
Net VAT pd (refund)		(40,000)		(60,000)
Retailer				
Sales $1.2 million	$120,000		$00	
Purchases $1 million	$00		(100,000)	
Net VAT pd (refund)		120,000		(100,000)
Total tax paid govt		$120,000		$00
Consumers pay		$1,320,000		$1,200,000

While most countries tend to limit zero rating to exports of goods and related services, the United Kingdom and Canada zero rate some food, and some countries zero rate other items considered necessities.

The tax advantage resulting from zero rating encourages businesses to test the limits of zero rating for particular goods or services. Litigation under the British VAT and Canadian GST is illustrative.

A U.K. VAT tribunal held that the zero rating granted for equipment and appliances designed solely for use by a handicapped person[4] was not available for a covered walkway constructed for the protection of students of a charity school providing training and education for disabled students.[5] The tribunal found that these walkways served as weather protection and were not designed solely for the use of handicapped students.

To tailor zero rating to particular food items, the United Kingdom zero rates food, then excepts some food items like confectionery, and then adds exceptions to these exceptions (so that some confectionery is zero rated). It thus is not surprising that courts in the United Kingdom are asked to make fine-line distinctions among various food items. For example, in *United Biscuits (UK) Ltd. v The Commissioners of Customs and Excise,*[6] the issue was

---

[3] See A. SCHENK, REPORTER, VALUE ADDED TAX – A MODEL STATUTE AND COMMENTARY: A REPORT OF THE COMMITTEE ON VALUE ADDED TAX OF THE AMERICAN BAR ASSOCIATION SECTION OF TAXATION [hereinafter ABA Model Act], p. 62.

[4] This zero rating now is included in Value Added Tax Act 1994, ch. 23 [hereinafter VATA 1994], Sch. 8, Group 12. If these items are purchased by a charity, they are zero rated under Groups 12 and 15.

[5] *Portland College v The Commissioners of Customs and Excise,* MAN/92/226 (1993).

[6] LON/91/160 (1991).

whether "Jaffa cakes" were zero-rated cakes or taxable biscuits. The tribunal held that the Jaffa cakes had characteristics of cakes and noncakes. On balance, the tribunal held that the Jaffa cakes had sufficient characteristics of cakes, were not biscuits, and therefore qualified for zero rating.

Although the United Kingdom zero rates food, it taxes the supply of food in the course of catering (such as restaurant meals). The catering exception applies to the supply of hot food for consumption off the premises on which it is supplied. One area of controversy was clarified in 2005.[7] It provides that in determining the temperature of the food, the temperature is to be determined at the time it is provided to the customer. Thus, if the customer receives the food after payment is made for it, the temperature is determined when it is received by the customer.

The following *Colour Offset Ltd* case is another example of the kind of line drawing problems that result from the grant of zero rating to particular goods or services.

Customs and Excise Commissioners v. Colour Offset Ltd[8]

HEADNOTE. The company [sold] ... diaries and address books the main purpose of which was to provide blank spaces to be written in. [T]he company contended that the supply fell to be zero rated as 'books' or 'booklets' within item 1 of Group 3 of Sch. 5 to the Value Added Tax Act 1983 [the same as Sch. 8, Group 3, item 1 of the VATA 1994]. The tribunal found that the diaries and address books were physically complete and held that they were 'booklets' within item 1. The commissioners [took the position that articles within item 1] were reading material conveying information and that as the main function of the diaries and address books in question was that they be written in.

JUDGMENT: MAY J. In my judgment, the English word 'book', although it always refers to an object whose necessary minimum characteristics are that it has a significant number of leaves, now usually of paper, held together front and back by covers usually more substantial than the leaves, is a word with a variety of possible more particular meanings. For any particular use of the word, its particular meaning will be derived from the circumstances in which it is used.

In the first instance, the only circumstance here is that the words 'books' and 'booklets' are used in the Schedule to a statute. They are accordingly relevantly devoid of context. Devoid of context, in my judgment the ordinary meaning of the word 'book' is limited to objects having

[7] The Value Added Tax (Food) Order, SI 2004 No. 3343, effective January 1, 2005.
[8] [1995] STC 85 (Q.B.Div.). [Edited by the authors.]

the minimum characteristics of a book which are to be read or looked at. (The same applies to 'booklet', which I think is a thin book perhaps with a rather flimsy cover. . . . If you ask of a particular object 'is this a book?', you immediately provide a context, which the words in the statute lack. You will get an answer which is affected by the context. If you ask instead what I regard as the right question here, i e 'what is the ordinary meaning of the word "book"?', you should get an answer which accords with the ordinary meaning to which I have referred. As Mr Richards submitted (although he accepted that these diaries and address books might be books or booklets within one possible meaning of those words), people generally think of books as things to be read rather than as blank pages bound together. A filled-in diary of historical or literary interest may be a book because it is retained to be read or looked at. But a blank diary is not a book in the ordinary sense of the word. Likewise a blank address book is not in the ordinary sense a book and it does not become one simply because its name includes the word 'book'. The tribunal reached a different conclusion which, in my judgment, was wrong in law. Accordingly this appeal is allowed.

The Canadian Tax Court held that "paan leaves" that are chewed to aid digestion and also used in Hindu religious ceremonies are not zero-rated "food for the purpose of human consumption."[9] Two Canadian Tax Court cases considered the difference between zero-rated "basic groceries" and taxable catering services. They involved prepared meals that required the customer to heat the food in an oven for thirty minutes or in a microwave for three minutes. The court held that the business supplied food, not catering.[10]

B. Zero-Rated Exports

Countries typically define the jurisdictional reach of their VATs under the destination principle; that is, goods and services are taxed in the country of consumption. Exports are zero rated and imports are taxed.[11] For

---

[9] See *Kandawala v The Queen*, [2004] GSTC 131 (Tax Ct. Canada), criticized in Sherman, Canada: Paan leaves are not "food" – But why exactly?, *VAT Monitor*, Mar./Apr. 2005, p. 147.

[10] See Sherman, "Canada," *VAT Monitor*, Sept./Oct. 2003, p. 441, criticizing the analysis but not the result in *Complete Cuisine & Fine Foods to Go (1988) Ltd. v. The Queen*, [2003] GSTC 81 (Tax Ct. Canada Informal Procedure); and *Chef on the Run Franchise Division Ltd. v. The Queen*, [2003] GSTC 82 (Tax Ct Canada Informal Procedure).

[11] To fully implement the destination principle, exports should be zero rated, even if the exporter comes within the de minimis exemption or otherwise is not a taxable person subject to VAT. C. Sullivan, The Tax on Value Added, p. 33. The United States Constitution does not require Congress to remove VAT from exports. The United States Constitution provides that "(n)o tax or duty shall be laid on articles exported from any State." U.S. Const., art. I, §9, cl. 5. If Congress enacted a VAT, it would not be required to zero rate exports of property and services in order to comply with this clause. According to *Turpin v. Burgess*, 117 U.S. 504, 507 (1886), a general tax can be imposed on all property, even if it

administrative reasons, most countries zero rate only defined categories of exported services (usually linked to exported goods). For the same reasons, most tax imported services (insurance and freight) as parts of the taxable value of imported goods, and typically tax, under a reverse charge rule, recipients of imported services who cannot claim input credits on the imports.[12]

Many countries encourage purchases by travelers by rebating VAT on goods that physically accompany departing tourists and that can be inspected by customs officials at the airport or border post.

C. Authority to Zero Rate Other Transactions

There are some business-to-business sales that may appropriately be granted zero rating if such treatment does not result in the loss of any net revenue and taxing such transactions may impose unnecessary cash and other burdens on the parties to the transactions. This applies in particular to sales of a going concern. EU countries typically zero rate those transactions.[13]

If a sale of a business is a zero-rated sale of a going concern, the purchaser is not eligible for any input credit (there is no tax on the purchase).[14] In New Zealand, there were several cases in which the seller claimed that the sale was zero rated and the buyer claimed that the same sale was taxable and therefore eligible for an input tax credit.[15] From the seller's perspective, the selling price did not include any GST. If the buyer was successful in claiming that the purchase was taxable (not zero rated), the buyer recovered the assumed VAT element in the sales price and thereby obtained the business at a lower tax-exclusive price. To prevent the parties from taking inconsistent VAT positions, a 1995 amendment conditioned zero rating on a written agreement signed by both the seller and the purchaser certifying that the transaction was considered a sale of a going concern.[16]

---

burdens exports, so long as the tax is "not levied on goods in course of exportation, nor because of their intended exportation...."

[12] See discussion in Chapter 7 *supra*.

[13] See, for example, VATA 1994, *supra* note 4, at §30(4) and Sch. 8.

[14] See Case N23 (1991) 13 NZTC 3,196 (Taxation Review Authority). The N.Z. Taxation Review Authority ruled that the sale of a going concern may be zero rated even if the purchaser does not operate the same business operated by the seller. Case M98 (1990) 12 NZTC 2,599 (Tax Review Authority).

[15] For example, in Case N46 (1991) 13 NZTC 3,382 (Taxation Review Authority), the sale of grazing land without livestock was held not to be a sale of a going business. In case P22 (1992) 14 NZTC 4,158 (Taxation Review Authority), the sale of land and building (used as a motel) to a purchaser was not a zero-rated sale of a going business, in part because the prior lessee of this property sold the assets used in the motel business to the same purchaser.

[16] New Zealand Goods and Services Tax Act, No. 141, §11(1)(c), as amended, 1995 No. 22, §6(1), effective April 10, 1995.

What is the real justification for the zero rating of the sale of a going concern? Does the same rationale apply to sales of other high-priced assets, such as the sale of aircraft and ships?

III. Exempt Sales

In exempt sales, the seller does not charge or list VAT on sales documents and, as a result, the buyers are denied input credits on those purchases. In addition, the seller is not able to claim input credits for VAT on any of its purchases attributable to the exempt sales. Although exemptions on retail sales may be expected to reduce prices to consumers and VAT revenue to the government, sales exemptions granted in the middle of the production-distribution chain that are followed by taxable sales by the purchasers of the exempt items actually increase consumer prices and VAT revenue over the amounts that would occur if those midstream sales were taxable. For example, with a 10 percent VAT:

> If a wholesaler makes purchases of $400,000 plus $40,000 VAT, and makes sales of $1,000,000 exempt from VAT, the seller probably will shift the $40,000 VAT into the prices for its products or services. Thus, if the selling prices in the absence of VAT would total $1,000,000, the seller would charge $1,040,000. The exemption in the middle of the production-distribution chain may result in a higher total tax burden on final consumers. Continuing the example, if a retailer made taxable sales of $1,240,000 ($1,200,000 plus $40,000 VAT built into the $1,040,000 cost of its purchases), the retailer will charge consumers $1,240,000 plus $124,000 VAT, or $1,364,000. The retailer does not receive any input credit because the wholesaler did not charge VAT on its sales.[17] If the wholesaler's sales were taxable, the retailer would have paid $60,000 more for its purchases ($1,100,000 VAT-inclusive price), but it could have claimed a $100,000 input credit and probably would have sold its goods to consumers for $1,200,000 plus $120,000 VAT, or $1,320,000 VAT-inclusive prices. The midstream exemption therefore increased the tax-inclusive prices to consumers by $44,000 over what they would have been if the sales were taxable at the wholesale stage, the $40,000 non-creditable VAT on the wholesaler's purchases and a $4,000 VAT at the retail level on this $40,000 cost buried in the retail prices.
>
> A retail stage exemption does not produce the punitive effect on consumers described above. The effect of an exemption from VAT on retail sales is to remove from the tax base the value added at the exempt retail stage. If, in the example, the wholesaler's sales were taxable and the retailer's sales were exempt, the retailer would charge customers $1,200,000 plus the non-creditable $100,000 VAT on its purchases, or $1,300,000. The $200,000 value added by the retailer would be exempt from the 10 percent ($20,000) VAT. These examples of exempt sales, expanded to cover sales to the wholesaler, are tabulated in the following chart.[18]

---

[17] If the wholesaler's sales were VAT-able, the wholesaler would have charged $1,000,000 plus $100,000 VAT on its sales and would have obtained an input credit for the $40,000 VAT on its purchases. The wholesaler would have remitted the $60,000 net to the government.

[18] ABA Model Act, *supra* note 3, at 62–64.

	Wholesale stage exemption		Retail stage exemption	
Manufacturer				
Sales $400,000	$40,000		$40,000	
No purchases	00		00	
Net VAT paid		$40,000		$40,000
Wholesaler				
Sales if exempt are $1,040,000	$00			
Sales of $1,000,000 if taxable	00		100,000	
Purchases $400,000		00	(40,000)	
Net VAT paid (refund)				60,000
Retailer				
Sales if wholesaler exempt =	124,000			
$1,240,000	00		00	
Sales if wholesaler taxable =				
$1,300,000			00	
Purchases if wholesaler				
exempt = $1,040,000		124,000		00
Purchases if wholesaler				
taxable = $1,000,000				
Net VAT paid				
Total tax to government		164,000		100,000
Consumers pay		$1,364,000		$1,300,000
Consumers would have paid if		$1,320,000		$1,320,000
sales at all stages taxable				

Businesses with low turnover may be exempt from VAT on all of their sales if they are covered by a small business exemption.[19] The exemption has effects comparable to the effects just described for item exemptions. The small business exemption is discussed in Chapter 4.

The difficult line-drawing problems for zero-rated items, discussed above, exist for exemptions for specific items as well. For example, the United Kingdom exempts the "disposal of the remains of the dead."[20] The exhumation and reinternment of human remains in order to clear the former cemetery for redevelopment was held not to qualify for exemption.[21]

A principle in the European Union is that member states must exempt imports that are exempt if supplied domestically. In *Commission of the European Communities v. Italian Republic*,[22] the court held that by imposing VAT on imports of free samples of low value, Italy violated the Sixth Directive because comparable domestic supplies of free samples were exempt from VAT.

The EU Sixth Directive defines activities that are eligible for exemption. There are two exemptions that cover medical and related care. The Recast

[19] *Id*. at 86–89.
[20] This service is exempt under VATA 1994, *supra* note 4, at Sch. 9, Group 8, item 1.
[21] *UFD Limited v. The Commissioners of Customs and Excise*, [1982] 1 CMLR 193. The tribunal held that the service was not supplied in the course of the service provider's business as an undertaker.
[22] [1990] 3 CMLR 718.

Sixth Directive, Article 129(1)(b) is identical to the Sixth Directive, Article 13A(1)(b). It exempts "hospital and medical care and closely related activities undertaken by bodies governed by public law or, under social conditions comparable to those applicable to bodies governed by public law, by hospitals, centres for medical treatment or diagnosis and other duly recognised establishments of a similar nature." The Recast Sixth Directive, Article 129(1)(c) is the same as the Sixth Directive, Article 13A(1)(c). Article 129(1)(c) exempts "the provision of medical care in the exercise of the medical and paramedical professions as defined by the Member State concerned." An earlier version of the Recast used the term "patient care" instead of medical care. Is the difference between patient care and medical care significant? Do these provisions cover care provided by veterinarians?

The following cases involving the exemption for medical care are based on the Sixth Directive before the Recast. The first two cases illustrate the differences in the analysis of a VAT case in the EU by the supranational European Court of Justice and by the national court in the United Kingdom. In the *Commission of the European Communities v. United Kingdom of Great Britain and Northern Ireland*, the European Court of Justice held that the United Kingdom violated the Sixth Directive by adopting an expansive definition of the exemption for medical care. In the *Yoga for Health Foundation* case, the Queen's Bench in the United Kingdom more liberally construed the "medical care" exemption under the Sixth Directive.

Commission of the European Communities v. United Kingdom of Great Britain and Northern Ireland[23]

FACTS. [Article 13A(1)(c) of the Sixth Directive exempts: "the provision of medical[24] care in the exercise of the medical and paramedical professions as defined by the Member State concerned." The U.K. VAT applies the exemption to the rendition of medical care by individuals in:]

(a) the register of medical practitioners or the register of medical practitioners with limited registration;

(b) the dentist's register;

(c) either of the registers of ophthalmic opticians or the register of dispensing opticians kept under the Opticians Act 1958 or either of the list kept under section 4 of that Act of bodies corporate carrying on business as ophthalmic opticians or as dispensing opticians.

Pursuant to that provision the supply of goods by members of the medical and paramedical professions is exempt from VAT when the goods

---

[23] Case 353/85, 1988 STC 257 (ECJ 1988). [Edited by the authors.]

[24] The Sixth Directive was Recast, renumbering articles and rearranging them, but without any significant substantive changes. COM(2004) 246 final 2004/0079 (CNS) Proposal for a Council Directive on the common system of value added tax (Recast), April 15, 2004, amended by Presidency compromise, FISC 2006-60, 8547/06, [hereinafter Recast Sixth Directive].

are supplied in connexion with the provision of services. That applies in particular to the supply of corrective spectacles by approved opticians after they have carried out eyesight tests.

[The U.K.] argued that the phrase "medical care" contained in Article 13(a) (1) (c) of the Sixth Directive indicated that the exemption covered not only services provided by way of medical care but also goods which are an integral part of medical treatment.... [The European Commission maintains] ... that the exemption under Article 13 A(1)(c) is limited to the supply of services and does not extent to the supply of goods "unless such goods are supplied as an integral part [thereto] and included in the price of the service."

DECISION. The United Kingdom maintains that the exemption for "Medical Care" provided in Article 13 A (1) (c) covers goods supplied in connexion with the services provided by certain recognized medical and paramedical professions. It therefore takes the view that even the supply of corrective spectacles, either by an ophthalmic optician or by a dispensing optician, is closely connected with the service provided.

Indent (b) provides that the Member States are to exempt from value added tax "hospital and medical care and closely related activities undertaken by bodies governed by public law or, under social conditions comparable to those applicable to bodies governed by public law, by hospitals, centres for medical treatment or diagnosis and other duly recognised establishments of a similar nature." The services involved therefore encompass a whole range of medical care normally provided on a non-profit making basis in establishments pursuing social purposes such as the protection of human health.

On the other hand, indent (c) provides that the Member States are to exempt from value added tax "the provision of medical care in the exercise of the medical and paramedical professions". It is clear from the positions of that indent, directly following the indent concerning hospital care, and from its context, that the services involved are provided outside hospitals and similar establishments and within the framework of a confidential relationship between the patient and the person providing the care, a relationship which is normally established in the consulting room of that person. In those circumstances, apart from minor provisions of goods which are strictly necessary at the time when the care is provided, the supply of medicines and other goods, such as corrective spectacles prescribed by a doctor or by other authorized persons, is physically and economically dissociable from the provision of the service.

It follows that the exemption from tax of goods supplied in connexion with the medical care referred to in indent (c) cannot be justified by indent (b), as the United Kingdom maintains.

It must therefore be held that, by exempting supplies of goods from the imposition of value added tax, ...the United Kingdom of Great Britain and Northern Ireland has failed to fulfil its obligations under ... [the Sixth Directive].

Yoga for Health Foundation v. Customs and Excise Commissioners[25]

HEADNOTE. The taxpayers, a charity, provided, for a consideration, residential accommodation for the study and practice of yoga to help people improve their mental and physical well-being. The Commissioners of Customs and Excise assessed the taxpayers to value added tax on the ground that the taxpayers were making taxable supplies of services in the course of a business carried on by them. The taxpayers [claimed]...the services supplied by them were closely linked to welfare and social security within art 13A(1)(g) of [the Sixth Directive] and, accordingly, were exempt from value added tax.

JUDGMENT: NOLAN J. The issue, so far as I am concerned, turns solely on the question whether the services supplied by the taxpayers come within the exempting provisions of art 13A and in particular para 1(g) of that article [of the Sixth Directive].

The taxpayers became a registered charity in 1976. Clause 3 of the trust deed, so far as material, reads as follows:

'The Trustees shall hold the capital and income of the Trust Fund upon trust for the purpose of research into the therapeutic benefits to be obtained by the practice of Yoga both mentally and physically and the promotion of such benefits by means of training therapists, publishing relevant material and setting up Centres both for training and for the practice of the principles of therapeutic Yoga and by any other means upon which the Trustees may decide (hereinafter called "the charitable purposes of the Foundation")'.

In 1977 the foundation launched an appeal to set up its own residential centre at which the study and the practice of yoga as preventive and remedial medicine could be carried on. The centre was duly opened at Ickwell...a large country house and stable block set in extensive grounds. It is the supply for a consideration of accommodation at Ickwell in respect of which value added tax is claimed.

[Ickwell's]...day-to-day management is in the hands of its life-director, Mr Howard Kent. He is not medically qualified and there is no resident doctor but a number of medical consultants are available. He has also a resident teaching staff of five, one of whom is a state registered nurse, a second of whom is Red Cross trained and a third is now a qualified osteopath. There are also administrative and house staff but much work is done by volunteers. Mr Kent gave evidence, which the

---

[25] [1984] STC 630, [1985] 1 CMLR 340 (Q.B.Div.). [Edited by the authors.]

tribunal accepted, that people who work at Ickwell do so for salaries which are below the normal rate. Considerable emphasis is placed by the foundation on assisting people suffering from multiple sclerosis, although people with other illnesses such as cancer, Huntington's chorea, rheumatoid and osteo-arthritis, asthma and varying forms of nervous depression have also benefited from staying at Ickwell.

It is not claimed that yoga cures illnesses but the tribunal accepted that many people get much better on account of their own activities and initiatives through yoga and peace of mind.

[According to the tribunal], 'a preponderant part of what the Foundation does is to help people to improve their mental and physical well being through therapeutic yoga, together with peace of mind and meditation'.

The centre is unlikely to break even (disregarding donations) on a full rate charge of £139dp50 per week. In addition, many of the people who come to the centre suffer from disabilities and it is the policy of the foundation not to refuse to assist any person who is at Ickwell on the grounds of ill-health on account of lack of money. Nevertheless, people are expected to contribute as much as they can.

[Article 13(A)(1)(g) of the Sixth Directive includes as exempt:] 'the supply of services and of goods closely linked to welfare and social security work, including those supplied by old people's homes, by bodies governed by public law or by other organisations recognised as charitable by the Member State concerned.'[26]

Finally sub-para (k) covers 'certain supplies of staff by religious or philosophical institutions for the purpose of sub-paragraphs (b), (g), (h) and (i) of this Article and with a view to spiritual welfare.'

I accept that I must do my best to adopt a European as distinct from a traditionally English approach to the question of construction, but by that I think little more is meant than that I should adopt what is often called a purposive or sometimes a teleological method of construction, which has been developed and increasingly applied in recent years by the courts of this country and in particular by the House of Lords.

My task, as I see it, is simply to give a fair meaning to the language in sub-para (g) and if I find that meaning obscure, to seek what help I

---

[26] The Recast Sixth Directive, *supra* note 24, at Art. 129(1)(g) is similar, but the last clause "by bodies governed by public law or other organisations recognised as charitable by the Member State concerned" was replaced by "by bodies governed by public law or by other bodies recognised by the Member State concerned as being devoted to social wellbeing."

can get from the other sub-paragraphs. What is the meaning of sub-para (g)? One tends, in England at least, to think of 'welfare' in the context of the 'welfare state' but it is clear – and counsel for the Crown accepted it at once – that as used in the sub-paragraph the term 'welfare' is not confined to state benefits.

[The term "welfare"] includes, generally, being well and thus includes the state of mental and physical well-being which, as the tribunal has found, the taxpayers seek to promote.

I think it significant, coming to the words of the article itself, that in sub-para (k) we find an express reference to 'spiritual welfare'. I find it hard to accept that the author of art 13 viewed the word 'welfare' as being limited to the provision of material benefits. In any event the language of the sub-paragraph itself seems to me to go beyond mere material benefit or improvements in the standard of living. I refer in particular to the express inclusion of old people's homes. Other types of service which counsel for the Crown helpfully volunteered as admittedly falling within the sub-paragraph are Salvation Army hostels and the provision of home-helps and meals-on-wheels.

Counsel for the taxpayers submitted – and I accept his argument – that in none of these cases is the service essentially concerned with the relief of poverty or the provision of purely material benefits. In old people's homes, in particular, the inhabitants may include well-to-do people. It is not impossible to visualise an old people's home for the relatively well-to-do operating on a means test basis and financed and run in the same manner as Ickwell. That would be expressly within the sub-paragraph. Further, in all of the cases which admittedly come within the sub-paragraph the provision of encouragement and moral support will be of great and may be of overriding importance in the context of the work of the charitable organisations to which, apart from bodies governed by public law, the sub-paragraph is confined. In every case they will be concerned to a greater or lesser extent with the physical, mental or (at least in the case of the Salvation Army) spiritual health of the recipients of the service. It seems to me, therefore, that the taxpayers do supply services closely linked to welfare work in a manner comparable to that of an old people's home which similarly serves those who need help. Thus sub-para (g) is not confined, in my judgment, to services tending to the relief of poverty, it is agreed not to be confined to state benefit and it cannot, in my judgment, be construed as excluding health care. If one asks whether the voluntary workers at Ickwell are engaged in welfare and social security work the answer, in my judgment, is 'yes', and the answer must be the same in relation to the work of the foundation as a whole.

For these reasons it seems to me that the appeal should be allowed.

Note on EU "Medical" and Other Exemptions

The medical exemption under the Sixth Directive also was tested in cases in which the medical professional did not render services for the purpose of diagnosis, treatment, or cure of a disease or health disorder.[27] In these cases, the ECJ strictly interpreted the exemption for "medical care:"[28]

Where a medical expert conducted biological tests at the request of an Austrian court to determine the "genetic affinity" of individuals, the ECJ ruled that the tests were not exempt from VAT under Article 13(A)(1)(c) because they were not done for the purpose of diagnosis, treatment, or cure of a disease or health disorder.[29]

The ECJ ruled consistently in two other cases. In the *Dr. Peter L. d'Ambrumenil* case,[30] doctors served as expert medical witnesses in legal cases involving medical negligence, personal injury, and disciplinary proceedings and claimed that some of their services were exempt from VAT. The ECJ found that the "purpose" of a medical service determines its qualification as an exempt medical service. A service is not exempt if the purpose is to "enable a third party to take a decision which has legal consequences for the person concerned or other persons."[31]

---

[27] See generally, Swinkels, "VAT Exemption for Medical Care," *VAT Monitor*, Jan./Feb. 2005, p. 14. In the EU, while a Member State has discretion to define paramedical professions exempt from VAT, it must ensure that it is treating comparable medical practitioners comparably; thus, psychotherapists providing treatments like those of psychiatrists, psychologists, and others must be treated comparably. *H. Solieveld and J.E. van den Hout-van Eijnsbergen v Staatssecretaris van Financiën,* Case 443/04 and C-444/04, [2005] ECR I- >>>>; OJ C 6, 8.1.2005.

[28] See Recast Sixth Directive, *supra* note 24, at Art. 129(1)(c).

[29] Case C-384/98, D v. W [2000] ECR I-6795. In contrast, medical tests (to observe and examine patients for prophylactic purposes) conducted by a laboratory governed by private law were exempt. Case C-106/05, L.u.P. GmbH v Finanzamt bochum-Mitte, [2006] ECR I->>>>.

[30] Case C-307/01, *Peter d'Ambrumenil and Dispute Resolution Services Ltd v. Commissioners of Customs & Excise,* [2003] ECR I-13989.

[31] *Id.* at ¶61. The ECJ ruled that some services may be taxable and some exempt medical care under Article 13(A)(1)(c). The following medical services are exempt:

- conducting medical examinations of individuals for employers or insurance companies,
- the taking of blood or other bodily samples to test for the presence of virus, infections or other diseases on behalf of employers or insurers, or
- certification of medical fitness, for example, as to fitness to travel,
- where those services are intended principally to protect the health of the person concerned."
- The following medical services were not exempt:
- "giving certificates as to a person's medical condition for purposes such as entitlement to a war pension;
- medical examinations conducted with a view to the preparation of an expert medical report regarding issues of liability and the quantification of damages for individuals contemplating personal injury litigation;

Consistently, in *Margarete Unterpertinger*,[32] the ECJ ruled that an expert medical report on the taxpayer's state of health to be used in litigation involving her claim for payment of a disability pension was not exempt from VAT.

Other exemptions under the EU's Sixth Directive have been the subject of extensive litigation. One is education. The Recast Sixth Directive, Article 129(1)(i) exempts "the provision of children's or young people's education, school or university education, vocational training or retraining, including the supply of services and of goods closely related thereto, by bodies governed by public law having such as their aim or by other organisations recognised by the Member State concerned as having similar objects."[33] In a case the European Commission filed against Germany, Germany exempted from VAT the research activities conducted for consideration by state universities. The issue was whether these research services were "closely related" to university education for purposes of Article 13(A)(1)(i) of the Sixth Directive. Strictly interpreting the exemptions as exceptions to the general principle that VAT is to be levied on all services supplied for consideration by a taxable person, the court held that the "closely related" concept was "designed to ensure that access to the benefits of such education is not hindered by the increased costs of providing it that would follow if it, or the supply of services and of goods closely related to it, were subject to VAT."[34] According to the court, the conduct of research projects for consideration, if subject to VAT, would not increase the cost of university education.[35] By exempting these services, Germany violated its obligations under the Sixth Directive.

In the following *Open University* case, the issue was whether the production and broadcasting of correspondence courses by the BBC to the university came within the exemption for university education.

- the preparation of medical reports following examinations referred to in the previous indent and medical reports based on medical notes without conducting a medical examination;
- medical examinations conducted with a view to the preparation of expert medical reports regarding professional medical negligence for individuals contemplating litigation;
- the preparation of medical reports following examinations referred to in the previous indent and medical reports based on medical notes without conducting a medical examination.

[32] Case C-212/01, *Margarete Unterpertinger v. Pensionsversicherungsanstalt der Arbeiter*, [2003] ECR I-13859.

[33] Sixth Council Directive 77/388/EEC of May 17, 1977, on the harmonization of the laws of the member states relating to turnover taxes – Common system of value added tax: uniform basis of assessment (OJ 1977 L 145, p. 1 [hereinafter Sixth Directive], Art. 13(A)(1)(i) is almost identical. Instead of having "the provision of" at the beginning of the paragraph, it is "provided by bodies governed by. . . ." Also, in place of the word "recognised" by the member state, it is "defined" by the member states.

[34] Case C-287/00, *Commission of the European Communities v Federal Republic of Germany*, [2002] ECR I-05811, at ¶47.

[35] *Id.*

Open University v. The Commissioners[36]

HEADNOTE. In 1966 a report to Parliament recommended the establishment of a university which would present its courses through television
and radio, programmed learning and audio-visual aids. [I]t was envisaged that such university would enter into 'an educations partnership'
with the British Broadcasting Corporation ('the BBC').

[T]he Open University ('the University') was founded by Royal Charter dated the 23rd April 1969 having as its main object the advancement
and dissemination of learning and knowledge by teaching and research
by a diversity of means such as broadcasting and technological devices
appropriate to higher education, by correspondence tuition, residential
courses and seminars and in other relevant ways.

Each University course includes a number of television programmes
which a student taking that course is expected to watch. At the beginning of a year the University sends to each student taking a course
a printed guide to that course which summarises the television programmes included therein and indicates the work which he is expected
to undertake during the year. At the same time it sends out printed and
other material for the course. Students are required periodically to complete and submit assignments for evaluation and each summer to attend
a six-day residential course. At the end of the year students must sit for
an examination in their subjects.

[Under the Agreement between the BBC and the University:]

(a) the BBC would at the request of the University prepare and produce
    programmes incorporating such material as the course teams (on
    which the BBC should be represented) should nominate or approve;
(b) the BBC would provide adequate and suitable studio facilities for
    the production of the University programmes for broadcasting by
    television and by radio;
(c) programmes would be broadcast up to an eventual limit of thirty
    hours each week for a basic schedule of thirty-six weeks of the year,
    together with such additional supporting programmes as might be
    mutually agreed; and
(d) the University would pay to the BBC the actual costs ... to meet
    the requirements of the University as agreed by the BBC and the
    University. ...

[The University claimed that the BBC services were exempt] as 'the
provision, otherwise than for profit, of education ... of a kind provided
by a university', ... [or] as 'the supply of any ... services incidental to the
provision of any education ... comprised in items 1 and 2', and were not
excluded from such item 4 by Note (5) to such Group because, under the

---

[36] [1982] VATTR 29 [edited by the authors].

'educational partnership' between the BBC and the University, the BBC provided the University education jointly with the University. Further, in the alternative the University contended that such services supplied by the BBC were exempt from tax under Article 13A1(i) of the Sixth [Directive, and the taxpayer could rely on it.] The Commissioners argued that the BBC merely supplied to the University the services and the facilities specified. They also argued that . . . the University alone provided the education to the students.

JUDGMENT BY: TRIBUNAL. In our opinion, in making such supplies the BBC is not itself providing education. Education is provided by the University to its students in consideration of their fees. [T]he BBC is providing, in our view, the basic services of preparing, producing, presenting and reproducing the University's programmes on radio and television. . . . It may be that members of the staff of the BBC are working on the course teams in the preparation of such programmes, but this does not result in the education, or any part thereof, being provided by the BBC, either alone or jointly with the University. However, in making such supplies the BBC is, in our opinion, supplying services 'incidental to the provision of any education' within item 4 of such Group 6. But, in our judgment, as the BBC is not itself providing the students with education, such services are excluded from the exemption contained in item 4 by Note (5) to the Group.

We now go on to consider Article 13A1(i) of the Sixth Council Directive (VAT). In our view, [the] . . . services and goods supplied by the BBC are, in the words of the subparagraph, 'closely related' to the supply of university education, but are not themselves university education. In our view the natural meaning to be given to the subparagraph, read as a whole, is that exemption is granted to supplies of services and of goods closely related thereto if made by the body governed by public law providing the education, vocational training or retraining.

[T]he relevant services supplied by the BBC to the University are chargeable to tax at the standard rate. . . . This appeal must be dismissed.

See New Vatopia, Schedule II, for the items exempt under some VATs in developing countries. In some countries, the domestic transport of passengers is exempt. This exemption generally is included in order to reduce the VAT burden on lower-income households, especially where buses or minivans are used as transportation to work. Should the transportation in tour buses be included within the exemption?[37]

---

[37] See Botes, "South Africa: Game viewing," *VAT Monitor*, Nov./Dec. 2004, p. 456, noting that South Africa was proposing to remove from the exemption (and therefore tax) charges to transport passengers in a game viewing vehicle, such as part of a safari tour.

IV. ALLOCATION OF A SINGLE PRICE BETWEEN SUPPLIES WITH DIFFERENT TAX CONSEQUENCES

In some situations, a sale for a single price may represent both taxable and zero-rated components or both taxable and exempt components. In these transactions, should the supply be classified as a single supply or should the single supply be broken down into its component parts for VAT purposes? For example, if a sale is predominantly exempt and includes only an incidental component that is taxable, for administrative reasons, it may be treated as fully exempt. In *International Bible Students Association v. Commissioners of Customs and Excise,*[38] the Jehovah's Witnesses charged for food served at its annual religious convention. The court held that the catering was closely linked to "spiritual welfare" services conducted at the convention and therefore came within the exemption for such services under the Sixth Directive.[39]

The distinction between a single or composite supply, or in Australia, between a mixed and composite supply, is discussed in detail in Chapter 5, Section IIE. The discussion here assumes that a supply for a single price is split into two supplies, and each is taxed differently. The consideration must be allocated, for example, between the taxable and zero-rated supplies, or between the taxable and exempt supplies. This problem is discussed in the *Rogers* case.

Rogers v. The Commissioners of Customs and Excise[40]

HEADNOTE. Appeal. The Appellant carried on business as a coach proprietor and tour operator. In the course thereof he sold and supplied package tours consisting of coach travel, hotel accommodation and meals at all-inclusive prices. For tax purposes supplies of transport are zero-rated whereas supplies of hotel accommodation and meals are standard-rated. [T]he Appellant accounted for the amounts paid for the package tours by valuing the standard-rated supplies of accommodation and meals provided by him at their cost prices as charged to him and attributing the balances of the amounts so paid to the zero-rated supplies of transport.

The Commissioners decided that some part of the Appellant's profit element should be attributed ... to the standard-rated supplies of hotel accommodation and meals provided by him in the package tours. The Appellant thereupon appealed to the tribunal on the grounds that he had adopted a perfectly proper method of costing his supplies.

[The example in the case assumes that the taxpayer sells a tour package for £276. The cost to the tour operator of taxable hotel and meals is

---

[38] [1988] 1 CMLR 491.
[39] See Sixth Directive, *supra* note 33, at Art. 13(1).
[40] [1984] VATTR 183 (Manchester). [Edited by the authors.]

£61, the cost for zero-rated transport is £183, and the tour operator's profit is £32. These three items total £276. The taxpayer assumed that all of the profit was attributable to the zero-rated transport, leaving only £61 taxable. The Commisssioners claimed that because hotels and meals account for 1/4 of the tour operator's cost for hotels, meals and transport, 1/4 of the £32 profit, or £8 should be attributed to hotels and meals, making the taxable supply, £69 (£61 + £8)].

Held that the amounts received by the Appellant as the consideration for his package tours should be apportioned for tax purposes between the standard-rated elements and the zero-rated elements in proportion to their respective cost prices to the Appellant (and so that the costs of overheads should be similarly apportioned and not wholly added to the cost prices of the standard-rated elements of the package tours).

V. A-B-C Transactions

If the sale from B to C is exempt or zero rated, can the sale from A to B receive the same treatment, especially if the goods actually are delivered by A to C? This issue was raised in the *Velker International Oil Company* case.

Staatssecretaris van Financïen v. Velker International Oil Company Ltd NV, Rotterdam[41]

FACTS AND PROCEDURE. In November 1983 Velker International Oil Company Ltd NV, Rotterdam, a company incorporated under Antilles law (hereinafter referred to as "Velker"), ["C" in the A-B-C-D chain of transactions] sold to Forsythe International BV, The Hague, (hereinafter referred to as "Forsythe") ["D" in the transactions] two consignments of bunker oil which it had previously acquired from Handelmaatschappij Verhoeven BV, Rotterdam, (hereinafter referred to as "Verhoeven") ["B" in the transactions]. Verhoeven had itself bought the first consignment of oil from Olie Verwerking Amsterdam BV (hereinafter referred to as "OVA") ["A" in the transactions]. The two consignments were supplied to Forsythe directly, the first by OVA on 5 November 1983 ["A" to "D"] and the second by Verhoeven on 11 November 1983 ["B" to "D"]. Forsythe ["D"] stored the consignments of oil in tanks rented from a storage firm and they were then loaded on to sea-going vessels engaged in economic activities other than inshore fishing; the first consignment was loaded on 6, 7 and 8 November 1983 and the second on 17 and 18 November 1983.

Such transactions, known as A-B-C transactions, are governed by Article 3(3) of the Wep op de Omzetbelasting, the Netherlands Law

---

[41] (Case 185/89) (ECJ 1990). [Edited by the authors.]

on Turnover Tax. Pursuant to that provision, where there is a chain of several persons undertaking to supply the same goods and in reality physical delivery takes place directly from the first person in the chain to the last, each person in the chain is deemed to have supplied the goods and thus to have effected a taxable transaction.

In this case each of the parties to the transactions applied a zero VAT rate... [as] the supply of goods for the fuelling and provisioning of sea-going vessels engaged in economic activities other than inshore fishing to be zero-rated.

However, the Netherlands tax authorities considered that the... [zero rating] was not justified in this case and issued an additional VAT assessment notice on Velker for 1983.

DECISION. Under the terms of Article 15 of the Sixth Directive:

> "Without prejudice to other Community provisions member states shall [zero rate] the following under conditions which they shall lay down for the purpose of ensuring the correct and straightforward application of such exemptions and of preventing any evasion, avoidance or abuse:
> 1. the supply of goods dispatched or transported to a destination outside the territory of the country as defined in Article 3 by or on behalf of the vendor;
> 4. the supply of goods for the fuelling and provisioning of vessels: (a) used for navigation on the high seas and carrying passengers for reward or used for the purpose of commercial, industrial or fishing activities".

[T]he national court is asking whether the [zero rating] laid down by those provisions applies solely to the supply of goods to a vessel operator who is going to use those goods for fuelling and provisioning or whether it also extends to supplies effected at previous stages in the commercial chain on condition that the goods are ultimately used for the fuelling and provisioning of vessels.

The term "supply of goods for the fuelling and provisioning of vessels" is capable of bearing several literal meanings. It could refer to the supply of goods which the recipient will use for the fuelling and provisioning of his vessels or the supply, at whatever stage it takes place, of goods which will subsequently be used for that purpose.

In order to interpret the term recourse must therefore be had to the context in which it occurs, bearing in mind the purpose and structure of the Sixth Directive.

The provisions in the directive which grant... [zero rating] must be interpreted strictly since they constitute exceptions to the general principle that turnover tax is levied on all goods or services supplied for consideration by a taxable person.

A strict interpretation is required in particular when the provisions in issue constitute exceptions to the rule that transactions taking place "within the territory of the country" are subject to the tax.

With regard to Article 15(4), it should be noted that the operations of fuelling and provisioning vessels mentioned therein are [zero rated] because they are equated with exports.

[The zero rating . . .] applies only to the supply of goods to a vessel operator who will use those goods for fuelling and provisioning and cannot therefore be extended to the supply of those goods effected at a previous stage in the commercial chain.

According to [a submission by] the German Government, the [zero rating] at issue is designed to allow administrative simplification, not to grant a fiscal benefit. In view of that objective, the [zero rating] should, in its view, be extended to all commercial stages.

That argument cannot be accepted. The extension of the [zero rating] to stages prior to the final supply of the goods to the vessel operator would require Member States to set up systems of supervision and control in order to satisfy themselves as to the ultimate use of the goods supplied free of tax.

[N]othing in the wording of the relevant provisions of Article 15(4), nor the context in which they appear, nor the objective which they pursue, justifies a construction of those provisions to the effect that storage of the goods after delivery and before the actual fuelling and provisioning operation causes the benefit of the exemption to be lost.

Article 15(4) of the Sixth Council Directive of 17 May 1977 must be construed to the effect that only supplies to a vessel operator of goods to be used by that operator for fuelling and provisioning are to be regarded as supplies of goods for the fuelling and provisioning of vessels, but there is no requirement that the goods should be actually loaded on board the vessels at the time of their supply to the operator.

VI. GOVERNMENTAL ENTITIES AND NONPROFIT ORGANIZATIONS

A. INTRODUCTION

Services rendered by government entities and nonprofit organizations generally represent a substantial portion of a nation's GDP. For example, in the United States, the federal, state and local government and the nonprofit institutions account for about 19 percent of GDP.[42] Units of government and nonprofit organizations provide some services that may compete with the private sector.[43] There is tension between the desire to impose VAT on all personal consumption expenditures and the desire to provide some relief

---

[42] See *Survey of Current Business*, U.S. Dept. of Commerce, Bureau of Economic Analysis, Table 1.1.10, Percentage share of Gross Domestic Product (July 2005), listing the percentage in 2004 as 18.6 percent.

[43] The converse also occurs. Thus, for example, neighborhood groups may hire private security guards and trash collection companies to supplement the police and sanitation services provided by government.

from the burden of VAT to very low-income households. The exemption for services of exempt organizations focused on poor consumers helps address the basic regressivity of a tax on consumption reasonably efficiently. In contrast, an exemption for food benefits high-income households (larger food purchases) more than low-income households.

Some countries grant special VAT treatment to "charitable" and other "nonprofit" organizations. Some define NPOs as organizations that supply humanitarian aid. "[T]he qualifying NPO might be formal, private, nonprofit distributing, self-governing and voluntary. The final criteria for qualifying for special treatment under the VAT legislation depends upon the country's legal traditions and organizational structure."[44] In this chapter, unless noted to the contrary, activities of "nonprofit" and "charitable" organizations are used interchangeably.[45]

The problems associated with the grant of an exemption from VAT to individual sales or to particular entities were discussed earlier in this chapter. The same problems apply in the nonprofit and governmental sectors of an economy. For a variety of reasons, most countries exempt or zero rate a range of activities conducted by government and nonprofit organizations. Exemptions for activities of nonprofit organizations sometimes are granted because these organizations are providing services commonly provided by government. The following paragraphs mention some of the issues that arise when special treatment is provided for these activities. Keep these issues and principles in mind as you consider the material in this part of the chapter.

As a policy matter, should any activities of nonprofit organizations and government entities be granted special treatment? If it is desirable to grant special treatment to the "nonprofit-governmental" sector, what activities should receive this special treatment, and should the special treatment take the form of exemption or zero rating? For example, if it is desirable to reduce or eliminate the tax on necessities (such as residential housing) that represent a large percentage of the budget of low-income households, should the residential housing be exempt or zero rated? Assuming exemption is selected, what residential housing should be exempt – sales of residential property or both sales and rentals? Should the exemption be limited to subsidized housing provided by a charitable organization or a unit of government, or should it be extended to market rate residential housing provided by anyone? If not all residential housing is exempt, should the accommodation portion

---

[44] Ole Gjems-Onstad, "VAT and NonProfit Organizations," *VAT Monitor*, March/April, 1994, 69, 73–74.

[45] Some countries draw a distinction between charities and nonprofit organizations. For example, under the Canadian GST, a "non-profit organization" includes certain government organizations at the federal or provincial level. Canadian Goods and Services Tax, Part IX of the Excise Tax Act, S.C. 1993, c. 27, as amended [hereinafter Candian GST], §259(1) definition of nonprofit organization. A charity under this legislation "includes a non-profit organization that operates, otherwise than for profit, a health care facility. See §259(1) definition of "charity." A qualifying nonprofit organization is a nonprofit organization that receives at least 40 percent of its funding from the government. *Id.* at §259(2).

of charges in hospitals and in university dormitories be exempt under this exemption, or only if it fits within an education or medical care exemption? If exempt services rendered by government entities and NPOs are sold at intermediate stages of production and distribution to taxable businesses (such as exempt tuition paid for employees), the supplies may produce the cascade effect described earlier in this chapter.[46] If the exempt items are sold to nontaxable purchasers (such as final consumers) and comparable items are sold by taxable businesses (if a public university's tuition is exempt and a for-profit university's tuition is taxable), the exemption may create some competitive inequities. The seller of exempt items (the government or nonprofit) cannot claim input credits for tax on its purchases attributable to the exempt sales. This effect may encourage nonprofits and government entities with exempt sales, for example, education or health services, to integrate vertically by, for example, hiring employees to clean and maintain buildings and equipment rather than paying a VAT-registered service company to provide these services.

A nonprofit organization may provide services that compete with private firms, but charge lower prices because the service is subsidized with donations to the nonprofit. Museums operated by NPOs, university-sponsored concerts, and university sporting events are illustrative. A unit of government may subsidize the operation of public transport or may issue discount cards to students and senior citizens. Should these differences in form affect the tax treatment of transportation? The "Ronald McDonald" houses operated by a nonprofit organization provide subsidized or free accommodations near children's hospitals to parents of hospitalized children. Should these hotel services be subject to tax? If so, what is the taxable amount of the service?

A unit of government may receive cash or property to be used for a specified purpose. For example, land may be donated to a city in order to build a library or park. A nonprofit organization may receive cash or property from a variety of sources (government, a business, other nonprofits, or individuals) to provide a particular service. The tax consequences may vary, depending on whether the receipt is or is not linked to the provision of any goods or services. If it is linked to the provision of particular goods or services, then the tax consequences may differ if the services, for example, are welfare or other charitable services, or are goods or services that are sold by and compete with private firms. A government may award a grant to a university to do medical research. Private pharmaceutical companies may be engaged in similar research. Should the government grant be taxable or exempt, if the educational and research activities of a university generally are exempt from VAT?

A public radio station receives funds from a publisher to support the station. Should the taxation of the receipt depend on whether the station (a) does not publicize the name of the donor, (b) mentions the donor during

---

[46] Because the exempt seller cannot issue a tax invoice listing VAT on the sale, the taxable purchaser cannot claim any input credit on the purchase. This cost (including any VAT embedded in the price) will be subject to VAT when the purchaser shifts this cost to its customers in the form of higher prices for its products or services.

a broadcast, or (c) mentions the donor and the name of one of its recently released books during a broadcast? Should the VAT consequences depend on whether the publisher receives an income tax deduction for the donation?

This chapter discusses some proposals to expand the taxation of services rendered by government entities and NPOs. It explores the treatment of these services in New Zealand and the EU, and includes a number of cases that illustrate the problems encountered with the EU approach. The chapter ends with a brief discussion of the VAT treatment of purchases by diplomats and international organizations.

B. Various Approaches to the Taxation of Governments and NPOs

Many countries exempt most sales of goods and services rendered by governments and NPOs, but may tax sales of specific goods and services. For example, in the EU, states, regional and local government authorities, and other bodies governed by public law are not subject to VAT if they engage in activities as public authorities. Other activities conducted by the same entities and bodies may be taxed. The EU approach and the cases that it has produced will be discussed later in the chapter. The state or a local unit of government that renders taxable services may be required to register and charge VAT on its taxable sales, regardless of the level of its taxable turnover. In other words, the threshold required to registration does not apply.[47]

For years, commentators have suggested that a VAT could cover a much broader range of goods and services provided by governments and NPOs.[48] "If governmental units make sales of goods or services, there is no general justification for exclusion from tax simply because the vendor is a governmental unit. Only if there is some specific justification for the exemption of the service, whether provided by government or the private sector, is there a case for exemption."[49]

As will be discussed in the next section, New Zealand led in taxing government services by taxing the property taxes that are used to fund these services.

The following excerpt from the ABA Model VAT Act provides a framework for the examination of the taxation of the activities of government and nonprofits.[50]

For supplies made by the nonprofit-governmental sectors that are exempt from tax,

> the government agency or exempt organization can be treated either as the ultimate consumer or an agent for the group that ultimately will consume

---

[47] See New Vatopia VAT, Appendix B, §20(6).
[48] See A. Tait, Value Added Tax: International Practice and Problems 77–78 [hereinafter, Tait, VAT]; J. Due, Indirect Taxation In Developing Economies, pp. 141–143. [hereinafter Due, Tax in Developing Economies].
[49] Due, Tax in Developing Economies, *supra* note 48, at 141.
[50] ABA Model Act, *supra* note 3, at 82–86. The footnote numbers are different and some footnotes have been omitted. [Edited by the authors.]

the goods or services.[51] Under either theory, the sales *to* these entities should be taxed. As consumers, the exempt organizations and government entities should not charge VAT on their sales nor be entitled to input credits for VAT on their purchases. With respect to items purchased for free distribution to beneficiaries, these entities may add little value. Where these entities hire employees to perform services that are dispensed without charge, however, the exempt organizations and government entities may add substantial value that would not be taxed under this scheme. Some commentators have suggested that to equalize the tax treatment for goods and services provided free of charge, VAT should be imposed on the salaries paid to employees of exempt organizations and units of government who perform services that are provided without charge.[52]

Government entities distribute to some citizens cash grants or vouchers to purchase food or rent housing. These subsidies are not VAT-able; but, when the recipients use the cash or vouchers to buy food or rent apartments, VAT will be imposed.

When a government entity or exempt organization buys goods and services for resale to consumers, the purchasing entity is not a consumer. The sales to these entities should be taxed, and the buyer should claim input credits.... The government agency or exempt organization should charge VAT on the sales price, even if the government subsidizes the sale and charges less than cost. For example, tax should be imposed on the tuition charged students, even if the state subsidizes education and the tuition does not cover the school's costs.

Because the entities providing exempt services cannot credit input tax attributable to the exempt services, these entities have an incentive to produce goods or render services in-house instead of buying them from taxable businesses. [This incentive to vertically integrate can be minimized by treating the entity as rendering the in-house services to itself in a taxable transaction.]

Educational services raise special problems under a VAT, especially if public and private education are to be taxed alike. Education can be viewed either as capital investment or as current consumption.[53] Even though professional or vocational education may be primarily business, there is a significant personal component in most education. To the extent that education is personal consumption, VAT should be imposed on educational services.

A report to the European Commission recommended substantial changes in the taxation of public sector bodies. It divided government activities into four groups:

(1) government transfer payments to redistribute income or wealth;
(2) the provision of goods and services that do not compete with private sector sales;

---

[51] Mcdaniel and Surrey, International Aspects of Tax Expenditure: A Comparative Study [hereinafter McDaniel & Surrey], p. 92.

[52] *Id*. at 93.

[53] For a discussion of the role of education in a normative VAT base, see McDaniel and Surrey, *supra* note 51, at 79.

(3) the provision of goods and services that compete with private sector sales but may not be priced at market rates; and

(4) the provision of goods and services that may compete with the private sector and may be priced at market rates.[54]

Although government transfer payments enable the recipients to consume, the money transfers themselves do not constitute the sale of goods or services and therefore should not be taxed. Government bodies, nevertheless, pay input taxes on purchases used in connection with this activity and if the activity is not taxable, the input credit generally is not available.[55] Activities in the second group, for which there is no direct link to individual users and therefore no consideration paid specifically for these services, generally are not taxable. They include the operation of the government, and the provision of defense and similar services.[56] The third group of services that may compete with private sector sales, but may be subsidized, include services such as health care and education.[57] The fourth group includes postal services, telecommunications, electricity, gas, water, and passenger transportation. The EU member states and some other nations tax many of the services in this group.

Poddar, Aujean, and Jenkins propose a "full taxation system" that treats public sector bodies (predominantly governments) as intermediaries for VAT purposes that make sales to others, rather than treating them as final consumers of the goods and services that they provide (the treatment under many if not most VAT systems in use today). Consistent with this treatment, the authors suggest that governments collect tax on their outputs and claim credits for tax on their business inputs.[58] Even with this proposed full taxation system, the calculation of the value of a supply is complicated because governments collect revenue to fund their activities from explicit fees, levies, taxes, subsidies, borrowings, and other sources.[59] According to the authors, explicit fees, subsidies, and grant payments should be included as part of taxable consideration subject to VAT. Fines, penalties, and "general taxes such as income taxes and 'labelled' levies not linked to a supply should not be included" as taxable consideration because the link to the service provided is too remote.[60]

The full taxation model taxes all services provided by the public sector (even if not for explicit charges), regardless of the source of funding.[61] The public bodies therefore can claim credit for input tax on purchases used to provide these services. The authors claim that this system is neutral because it

---

[54] See an article based on this study in Aujean, Jenkins, and Poddar, "A New Approach to Public Sector Bodies," 10 *VAT Monitor* 144 (July/Aug. 1999).

[55] *Id.* at 145.

[56] *Id.* at 144.

[57] *Id.*

[58] *Id.* at 146.

[59] *Id.*

[60] *Id.* at 147.

[61] *Id.*

imposes a uniform tax on the consideration paid for sales. If no consideration is paid, no tax should be charged. They also propose that goods and services funded through taxation should not be taxed, although they acknowledge that the inclusion of subsidies (even including local tax levies like in New Zealand) as taxable consideration may simplify the tax administration. The authors suggest that the full taxation model can be combined with zero or reduced tax rates for "merit services" such as "health, education, cultural activities and child care."[62] According to the authors, a reduced rate combined with allowable credits is roughly equivalent to an exemption of these services with the consequent disallowance of input credits.

The various approaches to the taxation of services rendered by NPOs are to tax (at the standard or higher or lower rate), exempt or zero rate the services, depending on the policies to be implemented. The following excerpt discusses the taxation of NPOs.[63]

> One characteristic trait of (parts of) the NPO sector, compared to the government and the for-profit sector, is that some of the services provided by the organization are performed by workers who do not receive compensation, i.e. volunteers. In Canada, supplies made by charities may be exempt from VAT if all functions of the NPO are performed exclusively (90% or more) by volunteers. It is an incentive for voluntary work and helps donations made in the form of unpaid work to remain untaxed.
>
> Many NPOs serve clients who suffer from poverty, stress, physical handicaps or psychological illness. . . . Canada exempts food sold at a food kitchen from GST under a "relief of poverty, suffering and disease" exemption. In addition, relief agencies may also have clients abroad. In the United Kingdom, used clothing and medical supplies imported for sorting and which are subsequently re-exported for free distribution abroad are exempt from VAT.
>
> Unconditional donations to an NPO should not raise any specific questions. If the "donation" in fact is a payment for services or goods, it should be treated as such. In New Zealand, the test devised to distinguish between "real" and "contractual" donations is whether the person making the payment, or an associated person, receives a direct identifiable valuable benefit in the form of a supply of goods and services.
>
> A donation in cash has to be distinguished from an ordinary sale. If the donation is made in kind, one has to decide whether the donor should be liable to output tax for the donation as a deemed supply.
>
> NPOs and especially charities make use of many special activities to raise money, for example fund-raising dinners, where donations and the supply of taxable goods are combined. Again, a practical solution has to be devised. One alternative may be to treat the whole amount as a donation if at least 75%–80% of the amount can be regarded as a donation. Another approach would be to tax only the sales value of the goods if the donative element is at least, for example, six times the cost price. A less schematic and perhaps more "correct" (but more demanding) approach is the rule that seems to have been

[62] *Id*. at 148.

[63] Ole Gjems-Onstad, "VAT and Non-Profit Organizations," *VAT Monitor*, March/April, 1994, pp. 69–80. [Edited by the authors.]

chosen in Canada for charities. Output VAT is charged on the actual portion of the price that relates to the taxable goods supplied.

The supply of advertising is normally taxable. It may be difficult to draw the line between taxable sales of advertising services and the tax-free receipts of donations. The meaning of the everyday term "sponsorship" is unclear. This work may include both donations and advertising. One rule may be that any payments for direct advertising are taxable, such as advertising in the NPOs' magazines.... In Canada a "50% rule" is applied. The supply of promotional services by an NPO is not taxable if the money paid to the organization is not primarily (more than 50%) for the advertising service.

If . . . services are provided to an NPO free of charge, should the provider be taxed for deemed supplies just as if the services had been sold for a consideration?

From a theoretical point of view, there may be no clear-cut answer to these questions. One may argue that the donating person consumes goods and services by giving them away. This is the point of view that will often be applied if a taxable person makes gifts. On the other hand, it may be said that donations to NPOs typically represent abstaining from one's own consumption for the advantage of a common good.

Sales of donated goods, such as second-hand clothing and household items, which are sold in opportunity shops and similar retail outlets, may be exempt from VAT if the shops are run by nonprofit bodies. As private individuals will be able to sell their second-hand goods tax free, as is commonly the case under VAT legislation, allowing such sales by NPOs to be tax free may seem like a natural corollary. The price distortions which could occur between the sales made by a nonprofit opportunity shop and an ordinary business engaged in selling used goods may not be significant if these businesses are able to claim a credit for a notional input tax when buying second-hand goods from individuals. Without such a credit, ordinary businesses may effectively be excluded from competition.

The next sections of this chapter consider the taxation of services rendered by government and nonprofit organizations under the New Zealand GST and the EU Sixth Directive. The chapter closes with a brief discussion of the VAT treatment of purchases by diplomats and international organizations.

C. Taxation in New Zealand

New Zealand can boast one of the broadest VAT base in use today. Many of the principles discussed earlier in the EU study of the taxation of public sector bodies are incorporated in the NZ approach. The broad NZ base extends to nonprofits and government entities. Under the New Zealand GST,

> government departments, local authorities and other public bodies are treated as suppliers of goods and services both to the private sector and to the public sector. The value of supplies to the private sector is measured by the revenue received in fees and charges; the value of supplies to the Crown is represented by the Parliament's apportionment of funds.
>
> Public-sector bodies in New Zealand levy VAT on all goods or services sold to the private sector or other public-sector bodies and can reclaim VAT

on all goods and services bought. For example, a New Zealand hospital will add VAT to the bill. Likewise the New Zealand police or armed forces can reclaim VAT on supplies bought from a private supplier or from other public-sector bodies. Local rates (a tax on real estate) are subject to VAT since they are not considered taxes but payments for local public services. And local authorities can reclaim VAT on their purchases.[64]

New Zealand still grants significant tax concessions for nonprofit bodies. It "effectively zero rate[s] such organizations to the extent that their activities are funded from donations.... A number of concessions have been given to nonprofit bodies in relation to registration thresholds, accounting basis to be used and the ability to separate into branches and divisions."[65] The concessions are pragmatic ones, resulting from poor record keeping and volunteer labor.

> There are four arguments in particular which supported the proposed method of taxing government departments and local authorities in New Zealand. These are administrative simplicity, accountability and transparency of government operations, comprehensiveness of GST coverage and sound economic management.[66]

D. Taxation in the European Union

The EU Recast Sixth Directive has rules governing supplies by states, subnational government authorities, and bodies governed by public laws. Under the Recast Directive, Article 14 (Article 4(5) of the Sixth Directive):[67]

> (1) States, regional and local government authorities and other bodies governed by public law shall not be regarded[68] as taxable persons in respect of the activities or transactions in which they engage as public authorities, even where they collect dues, fees, contributions or payments in connection with those[69] activities or transactions.
>
> However, when they engage in such activities or transactions, they shall be regarded as[70] taxable persons in respect of those[71] activities or transactions where their[72] treatment as nontaxable persons would cause[73] significant distortions of competition.

---

[64] Owens, *The Move to VAT*, 1996/2 Intertax 45, 50–51.

[65] Barrand, "The Taxation of Non-Profit Bodies and Government Entities Under the New Zealand GST," *VAT Monitor*, Jan. 1991, pp. 2–3.

[66] *Id.* at 3.

[67] See Sixth Directive, *supra* note 33.

[68] The words "regarded as" replaced "considered" in the Sixth Directive before Recast, Article 4(5).

[69] The word was "these" in the Sixth Directive before Recast, *supra* note 33, at Article 4(5).

[70] The words "regarded as" replaced "considered" in the Sixth Directive before Recast, *supra* note 33, at Article 4(5).

[71] The word was "these" in *id.* at Article 4(5).

[72] The word "their" was added in the Recast Sixth Directive, *supra* note 33.

[73] The word "cause" replaced the words "lead to" in the prior version of the Sixth Directive, *supra* note 33, at Article 4(5).

In any event, bodies governed by public law shall be regarded as taxable persons in respect of the activities listed in Annex I,[74] provided that those activities are not carried out on such a small scale as to be negligible.[75]

(2) Member states may regard activities, exempt under Articles 129, 132, 133 or 364, or Articles 367 to 383, engaged in by bodies governed by public law as activities in which those bodies engage as public authorities.[76]

According to the European Court of Justice:[77]

The first subparagraph of Article 4(5)...[means] that the activities engaged in by the authorities 'as public authorities'...are those carried on by bodies governed by public law under the legal system that is applicable to them, with the exception of the activities which they carry on under the same legal conditions as private traders. It is for the national court to classify the activities in question in the light of that criterion.

The second subparagraph of Article 4(5)...[means] that the member-states are under an obligation to treat bodies governed by public law as taxable persons in respect of the activities which they engage in as public authorities where those activities can also be carried on, in competition with them, by individuals, if their treatment as non-taxable persons is liable to give rise to significant distortions of competition, but that they are not under

---

[74] Annex I provides: "(1) telecommunications services; (2) supply of water, gas, electricity, and thermal energy; (3) transport of goods; (4) port and airport services; (5) passenger transport; (6) supply of new goods manufactured for sale; (7) transactions in respect of agricultural products, carried out by agricultural intervention agencies pursuant to Regulations on the common organization of the market in those products; (8) organization of trade fairs and exhibitions; (9) warehousing; (10) activities of commercial advertising agencies; (11) activities of travel agents; (12) running of staff shops, cooperatives, and industrial canteens and similar institutions; and (13) transactions of a commercial nature, carried out by radio and television bodies."

[75] The prior version of this paragraph was: In any case, these bodies shall be considered taxable persons in relation to the activities listed in Annex D, provided they are not carried out on such a small scale as to be negligible. ANNEX D: LIST OF ACTIVITIES REFERRED TO IN THE THIRD PARAGRAPH OF ARTICLE 4(5) provided: "(1) Telecommunications, (2) the supply of water, gas, electricity and steam, (3) the transport of goods, (4) port and airport services, (5) passenger transport, (6) supply of new goods manufactured for sale, (7) the transactions of agricultural intervention agencies in respect of agricultural products carried out pursuant to regulations on the common organization of the market in these products, (8) the running of trade fairs and exhibitions, (9) warehousing, (10) the activities of commercial publicity bodies, (11) the activities of travel agencies, (12) the running of staff shops, cooperatives and industrial canteens and similar institutions, and (13) transactions other than those specified in Article 13A(1)(q), of radio and television bodies."

[76] The Sixth Directive before Recast, *supra* note 33, at Article 4(5)(2) provided: member states may consider activities of these bodies which are exempt under Articles 13 or 28 as activities which they engage in as public authorities. Under *id.* at Art. 13, member states shall exempt specified activities in the public interest, such as certain postal services and certain hospital and medical care. Art. 28 has rules under which member states can continue to treat certain supplies inconsistent with the Sixth Directive for a transitional period.

[77] *Comune di (Municipality of) Carpaneto Piacentino and Others v Ufficio Provinciale Imposta Sul Valore Aggiunto di Piacenza (Provincial VAT Office, Piacenza)*, [1990] 1 ECR 1869, [1990] 3 CMLR 153.

an obligation to transpose those criteria literally into their national legislation or to specify the quantitative limits of such treatment.

The third subparagraph of Article 4(5) . . . [means] that it does not impose on the member-States an obligation to transpose into their tax legislation the criterion that, in order for the activities listed in Annex D [to the Sixth Directive] to be considered taxable, they must not be carried out on such a small scale as to be negligible.

The problem under the Sixth Directive "is to define the activities in which public bodies act as public authorities, especially if their activities compete with similar business in the private sector. In [Germany] . . . , for instance, land registry offices that, on occasions, acted as quantity surveyors, were not taxable because they were public authorities. [As a result of] . . . protests of professional associations . . . , the law was changed to make the services of the Government liable to VAT."[78]

Article 4(5) of the Sixth Directive [Article 14(1) of the Recast Sixth Directive] provides that government authorities may be treated as taxable persons if their status as nontaxable persons would cause significant distortions of competition. "While this may be clear, for instance, in the case of transport where state-owned buses compete with private buses, it is less clear if all the railways are state owned. In this instance, there would be no competition with any other railway, but there could be a significant tax advantage if privately owned buses and trucks were competing for passengers and freight and were taxed."[79]

In *Royal Academy of Music v The Commissioners of Customs and Excise*,[80] the Academy, a registered charity, claimed that the reconstruction work on its concert hall was zero rated as the construction of a building for a relevant charitable purpose, not "in the course or furtherance of a business."[81] The tribunal held that the Academy's charitable objective to promote music and provide music instruction did not prevent it from conducting economic activities. The provision of music education for tuition was the provision of services for consideration, the same as services provided by private businesses. Because the building therefore was used in part to conduct economic activities, the building was used in connection with business. The renovation was not entitled to zero rating.

Exemptions under the Sixth Directive include public postal services; certain medical care; the provision of human organs, blood, and milk; certain dental services and prostheses, certain welfare services, certain services rendered by bodies governed by public law, by charitable organizations to protect children, certain education, certain religious and similar services

---

[78] Tait, VAT, *supra* note 48, at 76. The changes were effective January 1, 1982.

[79] *Id.* at 77.

[80] [1994] VATTR 105, LON/92/2416.

[81] Zero rating was claimed under VAT Act 1983, Sch. 5, Group 8A. VATA 1994, *supra* note 4, at Sch. 8, Group 5, provides that construction of a building for a relevant charitable purpose is zero rated, but under note 6, a relevant charitable purpose means "otherwise than in the course or furtherance of a business."

for spiritual welfare, certain sports related services rendered by nonprofit-making organizations, certain cultural services provided by public bodies or recognized cultural bodies, certain transport of the ill or injured in special vehicles by duly authorized bodies, and noncommercial public radio and television.[82]

In *Lord Mayor and Citizens of the City of Westminster v Commissioners of Customs and Excise*,[83] the provision of housing for homeless men at a nominal cost, the rental of lockers to the men, the service of simple meals to them, and the sale of cigarettes and soft drinks through vending machines were held to be exempt as services closely linked to welfare services, consistent with the Sixth Directive. The tribunal noted that comparable services were not provided by the private sector.

Article 129(1)(n) of the Recast Sixth Directive (Sixth Directive, Article 13(A)(1)(n)) exempts "certain cultural services and goods closely linked thereto, by bodies governed by public law or by other cultural bodies recognized by the Member State concerned." Recast Article 130(b) (Sixth Directive Article 13(A)(2)(a)) gives member states the authority to subject some exemptions (including (n)) to certain conditions, including the condition that the body "must be managed and administered on an essentially voluntary basis by persons who have no direct or indirect interest, either themselves or through intermediaries, in the results of the activities concerned." Relying on that condition, the U.K. tax authorities challenged the Zoolological Society of London's claim for a refund of VAT paid on admission charges to its zoos. The Society consists of a governing body, the council, members, and honorary members. The council, consisting of a president, secretary, and treasurer, and nonoffice members who appoint the management boards are not compensated. The director-general, the director of finance, director of personnel, and other employees are paid. The ECJ decided that the persons who are prohibited from having a financial interest "refers only to persons directly associated with the management and administration of a body and not to all persons working for reward in one way or another in its administration."[84] It is up to "competent national authorities" to determine if a person comes within the condition and therefore must not have a financial interest. It also is up to the competent national authorities to determine, by

---

[82] Recast Sixth Directive, *supra* note 24, at Art. 129. The Recast Sixth Directive contains rules limiting the services of government and nonprofits that can be granted exemption by member states. Article 129 authorizes exemptions for activities "in the public interest." Except for bodies governed by public law, member states can, in certain circumstances, deny the exemptions discussed next. For example, the exemptions may be available only (1) if the body does not systematically aim to make a profit, (2) if the body is managed essentially on a volunteer basis by persons without a direct or indirect interest in the results of the body's activities, (3) if the body's prices are approved by public authorities or do not exceed approved prices, and (4) if the exemption does not distort competition with taxable commercial enterprises. See *id.* at Art. 129.

[83] Case LON/87/564, [1990] 2 CMLR 81.

[84] Case C-267/00, *Commissioners of Customs and Excise v Zoological Society of London*, [2002] ECR I-03353, at ¶19.

looking at the contribution of persons with a financial interest to the management of the body, if the essentially voluntary character of the management or administration of the body is met.

A significant dispute exists in the EU as to whether to the issuance of licenses for frequencies auctioned by the Austria Telecom Control Commission is an exempt supply by a public authority (no input tax credit deduction to purchasers) or is a taxable supply entitling the purchasers to input tax credits for the tax component in the prices paid.[85]

The rules under the Sixth Directive have spawned a number of cases involving a member state's power to limit or expand the exemptions authorized by the Directive. The following *Ayuntamiento de Sevilla v. Recaudadores de Tributos de la Zona Primera y Segunda* and *Re VAT on Postal Transport: EC Commission v. Germany* cases are illustrative.

Ayuntamiento de Sevilla v. Recaudadores de Tributos de la Zona Primera y Segunda[86]

[U]nder Spanish legislation the tax collectors for a zone are appointed by the local authority whose taxes they collect and must provide the security fixed by that local authority. In the performance of their functions they are directed by the local authority. They are entitled to remuneration in the form of a collection premium, which is a percentage of the sums recovered without constraint, and a proportion of the supplements added on in the event of enforced recovery. Finally, they set up their own offices and recruit their auxiliary staff themselves.

When calculating the collection premium, the tax collectors . . . added on value added tax (VAT). The Commune of Seville lodged a complaint [that was rejected by]. . . . the Tribunal Economico Administrativo Provincial de Sevilla.

Question 1

Article 4(1) of the Sixth Directive provides as follows: "'Taxable person' shall mean any person who independently carries out in any place any economic activity specified in paragraph 2, whatever the purpose or the results of that activity." The national court wishes to know what factors must be taken into account in order to decide whether an activity such as that of tax collectors is to be regarded as carried out independently within the meaning of that provision. In that regard, the first subparagraph of Article 4(4) states that: "The use of the word 'independently' in paragraph 1 shall exclude employed and other persons from the tax in so far as they are bound to an employer by a contract

---

[85] See Fraberger & Gerdes, *Input Tax Refund for UMTS Frequencies under European Law,* 33 Intertax 603 (2005).

[86] Case 202/90, [1994] 1 CMLR 424 (ECJ). [Edited by the authors.]

of employment or by any other legal ties creating the relationship of employer and employee as regards working conditions, remuneration and the employer's liability."

[T]ax collectors do not receive a salary and are not bound to the Commune by a contract of employment. It must therefore be considered whether their legal relationship with the Commune nevertheless creates the relationship of employer and employee referred to in Article 4(4) of the directive.

[T]here is no relationship of employer and employee since the tax collectors themselves procure and organize independently, within the limits laid down by the law, the staff and the equipment and materials necessary for them to carry out their activities.

That being so, the fact that in the performance of their functions tax collectors are tied to the local authority, which can give them instructions, and the fact that they are subject to disciplinary control by that authority are not decisive for the purpose of defining their legal relationship with the Commune for the purposes of Article 4(4) of the directive.

With regard, secondly, to remuneration, there is no relationship of employer and employee since tax collectors bear the economic risk entailed in their activity in so far as their profit depends not only on the amount of taxes collected but also on the expenses incurred on staff and equipment in connection with their activity.

With regard, finally, to employer's liability, the fact that the Commune can be held liable for the conduct of tax collectors when they act as representatives of the public authority is not sufficient to establish the existence of a relationship of employer and employee.

The decisive criterion for this purpose is the liability arising from the contractual relationships entered into by tax collectors in the course of their activity and their liability for any damage caused to third parties when they are not acting as representatives of the public authority.

The reply to the first question must therefore be that Article 4(1) and (4) of the Sixth Directive must be interpreted as meaning that an activity such as that of tax collectors must be regarded as being carried out independently.

Question 2

The second question concerns the interpretation of Article 4(5) of the Sixth Directive.

[T]wo conditions must be fulfilled in order for the exemption to apply: the activities must be carried out by a body governed by public law and they must be carried out by that body acting as a public authority.

Article 4(5) of the Sixth Directive . . . is not applicable if the activity of a public authority is not engaged in directly but is entrusted to an independent third party.

[The court held that the tax collection activity was subject to VAT as an activity conducted independently and not within the "public authority" exception.]

Re VAT on Postal Transport: EC Commission v. Germany[87]

[T]he commission of the European Communities brought an action . . . for a declaration that, by exempting from value added tax 'the services provided by transport undertakings for the Deutsche Bundespost by virtue of statutory provisions', the Federal Republic of Germany has failed to fulfil its obligations under the EEC Treaty.

In support of its application the Commission argues essentially that the list of exemptions in Article 13 of the directive [Article 129 of the Recast Sixth Directive] is exhaustive, that, according to the wording of 13A(1)(a) [129(1)(a) of the Recast directive], the exemption relates only to the supply of services [to] others by the public postal services, and not to the supply of services by others for the public postal services, and that the exemption is not justified by any other provision of Article 13.

[T]he German Government contends that provision is intended to grant a general exemption for certain activities carried out in the public interest in order to avoid an increase in the price of services provided in connection with those activities. It would be inconsistent with that aim to tax transport services provided on behalf of the Deutsche Bundespost when they are performed for the same purposes as the activities engaged in directly by the Bundespost.

The German Government observes that the directive is not intended to harmonise the legislation of the member-States concerning the postal system but leaves them free to determine the way in which that system is to be organised. The interpretation put forward by the Commission would lead either to de facto harmonisation or to unequal treatment of the member-States, depending on the manner in which their postal services were organised; that would be contrary to the directive's main objective, namely the establishment of a uniform basis of assessment and the collection of the Community's own resources on a comparable basis in all the member-States.

Although it is true that in some of the language versions the expression 'public postal services' may be understood, when considered in isolation, as referring to all postal activities, the syntax of the whole phrase clearly shows that the words in fact refer to the actual organisations which engage in the supply of the services to be exempted. In order to be covered by the wording of the provision the services must therefore be performed by a body which may be described as 'the public postal service' in the organic sense of that expression.

Faced with such a clear provision, it is not possible to apply the exemption laid down by it to activities which, whilst pursuing the same objectives, are undertaken by bodies which cannot be regarded as 'public postal services' in the organic sense, unless there are other conclusive

---

[87] Case 107/84, [1986] 2 CMLR 177 (ECJ). [Edited by the authors.]

factors demanding an interpretation which goes beyond the actual wording of the provision.

Although it is true that the exemptions are granted in favour of activities pursuing specific objectives, most of the provisions also define the bodies which are authorised to supply the exempted services. It is therefore incorrect to state that the services are defined by reference to purely material or functional criteria.

Moreover, the exemption provided for by Article 13 is still completely meaningful where a member-State assigns postal activities to an organisation which is not a body governed by public law. Postal activities are still exempted even if they are carried out by a licensed undertaking. The provision restricts the exemption solely to the supply of services by the postal authority, whether it is a body governed by public law or a licensed undertaking, to the exclusion of services provided for the postal authority by other undertakings.

It must therefore be held that, by exempting from value added tax the services provided, by virtue of statutory provisions, by transport undertakings for the Deutsche Bundespost, the Federal Republic of Germany has failed to fulfil its obligations under the.... Sixth Council Directive.

The dispute between the European Commission and Member States over the taxation of postal services continues. The Commission sent letters of formal notice that effectively is challenging the decision of the United Kingdom and Germany to exempt postal services rendered by their former postal monopolies. The Commission's position is that the exemption applies only to services that discharge a country's universal postal service obligation. When they operate like commercial firms, they should be taxed. On the other hand, the Commission is challenging Sweden's decision to tax postal services rendered by operators required to provide universal postal services.[88]

The Sixth Directive, Article 13(A)(1)(h) provides an exemption for certain "charitable activities."[89] Can an organization with a "social character" operated for profit qualify as charitable under the Sixth Directive? In the *Kingcrest* case,[90] the ECJ ruled that "charitable" was a concept with its independent meaning in Community law. The taxpayers in that case were registered

---

[88] IP/06/484, 10 April 2006, VAT/ Postal services – Commission launches infringement proceedings against Germany, the United Kingdom and Sweden.

[89] Recast Sixth Directive, *supra* note 24, at Article 129(h) provides as follows: "the supply of services and of goods closely linked to the protection of children and young persons by bodies governed by public law or by other organisations recognised as charitable organizations recognized by the Member State concerned as being devoted to social wellbeing." The Sixth Directive, Article 13(a)(1)(g) exempted welfare and social security work, etc. "by other organizations recognized as charitable by the Member States concerned." That language was changed in the Recast Sixth Directive to "recognized by the Member State concerned as being devoted to social wellbeing."

[90] Case C-498/03, *Kingcrest Associates Ltd, Montecello Ltd v. Commissioners of Customs & Excise*, [2005] ECR I-4427.

under the Care Standards Act 2000, the Registered Homes Act 1984, or the Children's Act 1989, but were not governed by public law. An "organization recognized as charitable by the Member State concerned" under Article 13(A)(1)(g) and (h) does not exclude private profit-making entities. The ECJ ruled that it is up to the national courts to determine (taking into account equal treatment, fiscal neutrality, and the content and purposes of the services) if such an entity that is not "charitable" under domestic law can be exempt under those paragraphs without the Member exceeding its discretion under the same paragraphs.

VII. Special Treatment for Diplomats, Embassies, and International Organizations

Nations vary in their treatment of sales to and imports by foreign diplomats. Special treatment may be provided for sales to foreign governments or international organizations (such as NATO or the World Bank) and their staffs that operate within the taxing nation. When special treatment is provided, it generally is granted under international agreements or domestic law other than the VAT statute. For example, exemption may be linked to special treatment provided under a country's Diplomatic Privileges and Immunities Act.

Under many sales taxes, the exemption for diplomats and others was provided with the use of exemption certificates issued to the qualified organizations or individuals. The opportunity to use this exemption certificate for nonqualified purchases or by nonqualified purchasers resulted in abuses. When some of these countries converted their sales taxes to VATs, they retained the exemption certificate procedure. Others require eligible organizations or individuals to pay VAT on their purchases and submit invoices with documentation to support their requests for VAT refunds. The refund procedure reduces the opportunity for abuse, but imposes the administrative burden on the agency to verify eligibility for refund and to issue the refunds.

Whether a nation relies on the exemption or refund system, it must identify the goods and services eligible for the special treatment. In the EU, the Sixth Directive requires member states to zero rate supplies "under diplomatic and consular arrangements," supplies connected with NATO forces and their civilian staffs, and many others.[91] Exemption also is provided for imports of goods under diplomatic and consular arrangements, imports by NATO and some other international organizations, and certain other imports.[92]

Developing countries that receive significant aid from donor countries and international organizations typically exempt (or provide a refund) of VAT on purchases directly linked to technical assistance or humanitarian assistance agreements.[93]

---

[91] See Sixth Directive, *supra* note 33, at Art's. 15(10) and 17(3)(b), comparable to Recast Sixth Directive, *supra* note 24, at Articles 147(2) and 164(b).

[92] *Id.* at Art. 14(1)(g), comparable to Recast Sixth Directive, *supra* note 24, at Article 140(f)–(i).

[93] See New Vatopia, Appendix B, §47.

New Zealand severely restricts diplomatic exemption. For example, New Zealand taxes goods or services acquired in New Zealand by diplomatic and consular staff.[94]

VIII. DISCUSSION QUESTIONS

1. What are the different factors that make it difficult (or even impossible) for a VAT to reach all consumption expenditures? Is a direct expenditure tax likely to be more comprehensive in this respect? Point out the problems related to the definition of the tax base, that is, final consumption, which are common to a VAT and to a direct expenditure tax.

2. In defining taxpayer, the Sixth Directive takes into account neither the profit-making purpose nor the public nature of the organization supplying the goods or rendering the services except for Art. 4(5). However, these two factors are many times made explicit conditions of the exemptions granted under Art. 13A of the Sixth Directive. Is this consistent with the theory of VAT as a general consumption tax? How does the New Vatopia VAT handle these same two factors?

3. What differences do you perceive between the exemptions enumerated under the Sixth Directive, Art. 13A (termed "exemptions for certain activities in the public interest") and the exemptions granted under Art. 13B (vaguely named "other exemptions")? Compare these exemptions with the treatment of exemptions under the New Vatopia VAT.

4. Suppose that you are drafting a VAT statute. Would you choose to tax or to exempt the following items:
   - legal services
   - medical care
   - foreign travels
   - education
   - leasing and letting of immovable goods (RE)
   - dues paid to nonprofit organizations (including museums, sporting and other private clubs, professional associations, trade associations, and so on)
   - drugs delivered on prescription
   - public transportation of persons
   - sales to governmental bodies
   - food
   - newspapers and books
   - insurance
   - highway tolls
   - veterinary surgery
   - betting and gambling
   - transportation of goods

---

[94] See *N.Z. Tax Information Bulletin*, Vol. 5, No. 11 (Apr. 1994).

5. Now that you understand the concept of a zero rate of VAT, can you imagine the use of a negative rate of VAT, that is, consumption subsidy (temporary or selective)? How would such a system operate?

6. Is there any reason for nonprofits and units of government to register and report taxable sales on all taxable sales, even if they do not meet the registration threshold required for other businesses rendering taxable services?

7. What is the definition of a nonprofit organization (NPO) in the New Vatopia VAT?

8. What is the VAT regime applicable to NPOs and governmental bodies in the Vatopia VAT and in New Zealand?

9. What is the justification for exempting NPOs from VAT? Evaluate this justification.

10. Would the use of an addition type VAT, rather than the credit method, be desirable with respect to NPOs? Explain how it might work.

11. What are the VAT consequences under the New Vatopia VAT and other VATs if an NPO exports goods or services?

12. If you have to choose among the approaches discussed to cover NPOs and governments under the VAT, which would you choose for the United States? For your own country?

10

Gambling and Financial Services (Other than Insurance)

I. General Introduction

There are a group of services that pose particular problems under a credit-invoice VAT like the EU VAT. They are gambling, transactions involving money and other financial products that are priced to include implicit fees, and insurance (a particular kind of financial service). In all three cases, the value added by the service provider should be subject to a broad-based VAT, at least to the extent that they represent personal consumption expenditures. In all three cases, more than with other consumer goods (other than used goods) and services, a significant portion of the business inputs are obtained from consumers who are not registered for VAT purposes. As a result, those nonregistered suppliers do not issue VAT invoices and the casino, bank, investment firm, or insurance company is not entitled to claim credit for any VAT component embedded in the price of those acquired goods or services. If VAT were imposed on the consideration for these services or products, the tax would apply to more than the value added by the service provider. Absent administrable rules to tax only the value added, it is not surprising that the default rule was to exempt these services. Recently, rules have been developed to bring more of these services within the VAT base, but problems remain. The chapter starts with an easy to understand example, gambling.

II. Gambling, Lotteries, and Other Games of Chance

In a typical transaction involving goods or services, a registered person remits to the government the difference between the tax on the price charged the customer and the tax on business inputs (such as inventory and supplies) used in making these sales. In a gambling transaction, whether a table game, a gaming machine, or a lottery, the gambler pays for the service (the chance to win) up front, and the value added, for example, by the casino cannot be calculated until after winners are determined and winnings are paid out. Most, if not all of the bets are placed and winnings are paid out to consumers who are not engaging in these transactions as VAT-registered persons.

Under most VAT systems, tax is imposed on the price charged for the service. If applied to gambling, the tax would amount to a turnover tax on gross receipts, not a value added tax imposed on the net value added by the casino.

New Zealand, for example, imposes VAT on lotteries calculated as the difference between the proceeds of ticket sales less winnings paid out.[1]

In the EU, a member state has discretion to tax or exempt gambling. Once a member decides to exempt gambling, it is not permissible to limit the exemption to certain suppliers of games of chance or gaming machines. Thus, Germany was precluded from exempting only gambling activities conducted in licensed public casinos.[2] In the following case, the taxpayer claimed that when Germany taxed the operation of gaming machines, it was required to tax only the difference between the gross bets and the amount paid as winnings.

Kommanditgesellschaft in Firma KG HJ Glawe Spiel-und Unterhaltungs-gerate Augstellungsges MbH & Co v. Finanzamt Hamburg-Barmbek-Uhlenhorst[3]

OPINION.[4] The plaintiff installs and operates gaming machines in bars and restaurants. The machines are activated by inserting one or more coins. Once they have been activated, the machines are available to be played for a certain period of time. During that period, coins may be paid out as winnings to successful players. The amount of winnings, if any, paid out in the course of an individual game depends upon the luck (and possibly the skill) of the player concerned.

The machines in question are equipped with two separate compartments, which I shall refer to as the 'cash box' and the 'reserve'. The reserve holds the stock of coins from which winnings are paid out. The cash box holds coins which the operator of the machine is able to remove from the machines and retain for his own benefit. The machines are designed to ensure that, when the reserve is full, any stakes inserted by players enter the cash box. If the reserve is not full, on the other hand, the stakes enter the reserve.

Under German law, the machines are required to pay out as winnings on average at least 60% of the stakes inserted. Some particular machines are required to pay out only 60% of the amounts inserted after deduction of the VAT payable on those amounts. The operator is required to fill the

---

[1] New Zealand Goods and Services Tax Act, No. 141, §12(1) [hereinafter NZ GST].§10(14). Under the British VAT, the taxable amount attributable to payments to play a game of chance with a gaming machine is the amount paid by those playing the game less the amount received during the tax period by persons who won. Value Added Tax Act 1994, ch. 23, §13.

[2] Case C-453/02, *Finanzamt Gladbeck v Edith Linneweber*; and Case C-462/02, *Finanzamt Herne-West v Savvas Akritidis*, 2005 ECR I-1131, 2005 ECJ CELEX LEXIS 1.

[3] Case 38/93, (ECJ 1994).

[4] The case was edited and some of the language was changed by the authors.

reserve when the machine is first put into service, and whenever opening the machine he is required to replenish the reserve so as to ensure that cash is available to be paid out as winnings.

The tax office took as the taxable amount, an estimate of the gross receipts of the machines; that is to say, an estimate of the total stakes inserted into the machines, less VAT, without any deduction in respect of sums paid out as winnings. Glawe argues that VAT should be imposed only on an operator's net receipts, that is to say on the net takings of the machines after deduction both of VAT and of the amounts paid out to successful players.

By Article 2 of the Sixth Directive:

The following shall be subject to value added tax:

(1) the supply of goods or services effected for consideration within the territory of the country by a taxable person acting as such; . . .

According to Article 11A:

Within the territory of the country

(1) The taxable amount shall be:

(a) . . . everything which constitutes the consideration which has been or is to be obtained by the supplier from the purchaser, the customer or a third party for such supplies;

Article 13B(f) of the Sixth Directive exempts from VAT:

betting, lotteries and other forms of gambling, subject to conditions and limitations laid down by each Member State.

Article 33 of the Sixth Directive . . . reads as follows:

> Without prejudice to other Community provisions, the provisions of this Directive shall not prevent a Member State from maintaining or introducing taxes on insurance contracts, taxes on betting and gambling, excise duties, stamp duties, and, more generally, any taxes, duties or charges which cannot be characterized as turnover taxes.

Article 13B(f) has been interpreted by the Member States and by the Commission as permitting, in particular, the imposition of VAT on the use of gaming machines.

Notwithstanding the discretion conferred by Article 13 B(f), if a Member State has decided to exercise its option of imposing VAT on the use of gaming machines, the tax thereby imposed must, as the Commission points out, conform to the Community rules applicable to VAT. In particular, the tax must conform to the rules governing the basis of assessment laid down by Article 11 of the Sixth Directive.

By its first question the national court asks whether the taxable amount for the purposes of Article 11A(1)(a) of the directive constitutes the total stakes inserted into the gaming machine by players.

In my view the consideration which the operator obtains for his services for the purposes of Article 11A(1)(a) is limited to the amounts which he empties from the machine. That is apparent from an analysis of the transactions in issue and of other forms of gambling.

The placing of the bets and collection of the winnings is simply part of the gambling transaction. The placing of the bets, although it involves the outlay of money, does not constitute the consumption of goods or services which is the taxable event under the VAT system.

From the foregoing analysis it follows that, in so far as it is appropriate to charge VAT on gaming machine transactions, the taxable amount should be limited to the operator's actual takings, ie his net receipts after payment of winnings to the players.

Conclusion

Article 11A(1)(a) of the Sixth VAT Directive must be interpreted as meaning that, where a Member State subjects to VAT supplies of services consisting in the making available of gaming machines offering the possibility of winning money, the taxable amount in respect of such supplies over a given period does not include that proportion of the total stakes inserted which corresponds to the winnings paid out to successful players during that period.

III. FINANCIAL SERVICES INVOLVING MONEY AND FINANCIAL PRODUCTS (OTHER THAN INSURANCE)

A. INTRODUCTION

The financial service sector accounts for about 25 percent of the GDP of most developed countries.[5] Although taking deposits and making loans is a significant portion of a bank's activities, fee income accounts for about 40 percent of the operating revenue of the twenty-five largest U.S. bank holding companies.[6]

Some commentators raise the theoretical question of whether the value of financial services should be subject to VAT. They claim that to the extent that users of financial services are trying to maximize their returns to savings, the value does not belong in a tax base measured by consumption.[7] There are persuasive arguments to the contrary. Financial services are used to purchase consumer goods and services.[8] There therefore is support for a tax at least as high as on consumer goods for financial services to consumers.[9]

---

[5] Zee, "A New Approach to Taxing Financial Intermediation Services Under a Value-Added Tax," 58 *Natl. Tax J.* 77, 78 (Mar. 2005) [hereinafter Zee, Modified Reverse Charge Approach].

[6] Radecki, "Banks' Payments-Driven Revenues," 5 *Econ. Policy Rev.* 53 (July, 1999).

[7] See Jack, "The Treatment of Financial Services under a Broad-Based Consumption Tax," 53 *Natl. Tax J.* 841(1999) (zero rate intermediation services and tax fixed fees on financial services); and Grubert & Mackie, "Must Financial Services be Taxed Under a Consumption Tax?" 53 *Natl. Tax J.* 23 (1999).

[8] Auerbach & Gordon, "Taxation of Financial Services under a VAT," 92 *Amer. Econ. Rev.* 411 (2002).

[9] Rousslang, "Should Financial Services be Taxed Under a Consumption Tax? Probably," 55 *Natl. Tax J.* 281 (June 2002).

Taking deposits and making loans are core bank services. In recent years, there has been an explosion in the number of different financial products offered by financial institutions and brokerage companies, some combining financial and nonfinancial products into a single product, or combining multiple financial products in a single product.

This section focuses on the taxation of transactions involving money and other financial products. It is beyond the scope of this book to discuss all or even a majority of the services and financial instruments and products that can reasonably be classified as financial services, such as securitization arrangements,[10] derivatives, forward interest contracts, and interest rate or equity swaps. Transactions involving these instruments can be classified as supplies for VAT purposes, and they raise questions, such as who is the supplier, when does the supply occur, and what is the consideration for the supply.[11]

This section is divided into several parts. Part C discusses the nature of financial intermediation and other financial services, explains why the early VATs exempted financial services, lists the exempt financial services under the EU Sixth Directive, and explores the problems resulting from that decision, including the difficult problem of allocating input credits between taxable and other supplies.

Since the early 1990s, there have been radical changes in the way countries treat financial services and products under a VAT. Part D highlights some country practices that depart significantly from the common "exemption" treatment. Part E discusses some proposals to tax financial intermediation services and provide input credits to VAT-registered business users of those services.

First, the following subsection is a noncomprehensive list of the kinds of services that may be included within the concept of "financial services."

B. VARIETY OF TRANSACTIONS INVOLVING FINANCIAL SERVICES

The following list of transactions involving money and financial products (other than insurance) may be taxed, zero rated, or granted exemption from tax.

---

[10] For a general discussion of securitization arrangements and the VAT treatment of these arrangements under the Australian GST, see GSTR 2004/4, Goods and Services Tax Ruling: Goods and services tax: assignment of payment streams including under a securitization arrangement (ATO 2004). The Ruling treats payment streams like these as financial services and therefore input-taxed (exempt from GST). In *Canada Trustco Mortgage Co. v. The Queen*, No. 2003–3554 (TCC 2004), the Tax Court held that in securitization transactions, the amounts attributable to the servicing of the mortgages and the mortgages themselves are treated as part of a single exempt financial services transaction.

[11] See Mason, "Solving the Issues of VAT and Financial Derivatives or It's VAT Jim, but Not As We Know It?" *Derivatives & Financial Instruments*, July/Aug. 2000, p. 190.

1. International financial services
   a. financial service component in international transport and export trade
   b. financial services rendered to foreigners
2. Domestic financial services
   a. services provided by financial institutions and other intermediaries as principals, agents, or brokers
      i. credit card services
      ii. underwriting and other issuance of debt or equity securities
      iii. loan transactions (including factoring)
      iv. savings and checking accounts
      v. financial advisory services (estate planning, financial advice, etc.)
      vi. letters of credit and other credit guarantees
      vii. services of brokers and agents in arranging financial transactions
      viii. financial or asset management services for individuals and businesses[12]
      ix. interbank services
      x. foreign exchange of currency, interest rate swaps, and contracts and options involving currency
      xi. issuance of travelers' checks, and certified or cashiers' checks
      xii. data processing services
      xiii. safety deposit box rentals
      xiv. "arranging for" financial services[13]
   b. services provided by merchants as part of their charges for merchandise or services
      i. favorable payment terms with no interest charges
      ii. gas station or other retailer – prices vary for cash and credit card sales
   c. no charge for merchandise provided to customers of financial services
      i. toaster given to new depositor who opens an account at the bank
      ii. credit card company gives customers credit toward the cost of merchandise charged to the card, and the credit is linked to the interest they pay on their unpaid credit card balances
   d. free services linked to purchases charged to credit cards, such as airline frequent flier programs

C. Financial Intermediation Services

The same financial institutions charge fees for safety deposit boxes, financial advice, returned checks, and other services. Other entities, such as finance departments of retail stores, provide financial services to their customers in the form of installment or hire-purchase sales. A corporation may decide

---

[12] Canada taxes asset management services and the EU exempts them.
[13] Singapore taxes them, and Australia has special rules.

to raise funds for its operations by issuing its own debentures through an underwriter instead of borrowing from a bank.

A normative VAT imposed on all consumer goods and services may tax both explicit fees and implicit intermediation services. A challenge in designing a VAT base is to craft an administrable rule to tax financial intermediation services rendered by financial institutions, and to give registered businesses, on a transaction-by-transaction basis, credits for input VAT attributable to the intermediation services.[14]

There is no universally accepted definition of financial services. For purposes of National accounting, the International Standard Industrial Classification of All Economic Activities (ISIC Rev 3), the financial sector contains:

– 65 Financial Intermediation, except Insurance and Pension Funding (this includes lending, deposit taking, etc);
– 66 Insurance and Pension Funding, except compulsory social security; and
– 67 Activities auxiliary to Financial Intermediation (for example, trustees, fund managers).[15]

Henderson describes the three main groups as:

banking (making loans and/or offering deposits), investment [including pension and mutual funds], and insurance.... Commercial banks account for about one-third of total assets. Many of the other intermediary institutions are traditional financial firms, but some–especially in the category of finance companies–are subsidiaries of nonfinancial corporations. Finally, these services are increasingly being provided by nonfinancial corporations directly.... So the dichotomy between the nonfinancial firm and the financial

---

[14] For detailed discussions of the taxation of financial services, see CONSUMPTION TAXATION AND FINANCIAL SERVICES, 57th Congress of the International Fiscal Association (Sydney 2003); Howell H. Zee, ed., Taxing the Financial Sector: Concepts, Issues, and Practices (IMF 2004); Schenk & Zee, "Treating Financial Services Under a Value-Added Tax: Conceptual Issues and Country Practices," 22 *Tax Notes Int'l* 3309 (June 25, 2001) [hereinafter Schenk & Zee, Financial Services Under a VAT]; *Indirect tax Treatment of Financial Services and Instruments*, Report of the OECD (Oct. 1998) [hereinafter OECD Report on Financial Services]; Poddar & English, "Taxation of Financial Services Under a Value-Added Tax: Applying the Cash-Flow Approach," 50 *Natl. Tax J.* 89 (Mar. 1997) [hereinafter Poddar & English, Taxation of Financial Services]; Schenk, "Taxation of Financial Services Under a Value Added Tax: A Critique of the Treatment Abroad and the Proposals in the United States," 9 *Tax Notes Intl.* 823 (1994) [hereinafter, Schenk, Taxation of Financial Services]. See also Neubig & Adrion, "Value Added Taxes and Other Consumption Taxes: Issues for Insurance Companies," 61 *Tax Notes* 1001 (1993); Schenk & Oldman, principal draftsmen, "Analysis of Tax Treatment of Financial Services Under a Consumption-Style VAT: Report of American Bar Association Section of Taxation, Value Added Tax Committee," 44 *Tax Law.* 181 (1990) [hereinafter Schenk & Oldman]; Henderson [Kodrzycki], "Financial Intermediaries under Value-Added Tax," *New Eng. Econ. Rev.*, July–Aug., 1988, p. 37 [hereinafter Henderson]; Barham, Poddar & Whalley, "The Tax Treatment of Insurance Under a Consumption Type, Destination Basis VAT," 40 *Natl Tax J.* 171 (1987) [hereinafter Barham, Poddar & Whalley]; Hoffman, Poddar & Whalley, "Taxation of Banking Services Under a Consumption Type, Destination VAT," 40 *Natl Tax J.* 547 (1987) [hereinafter Hoffman, Poddar & Whalley].

[15] OECD Report on Financial Services, *supra* note 14, at 5. Services generally recognized as being financial in nature by most OECD countries are listed in Appendix I to the report.

intermediary...is somewhat artificial. Designers of a VAT would have to decide where to draw the lines in determining what activity should be taxed under general rules and what activity should be categorized as financial intermediation.[16]

Banks and other depository institutions take deposits and make loans. In this way, "they provide an intermediation service to both depositors and borrowers by channeling funds of person with certain preferences regarding risk and liquidity to other persons with different preferences."[17]

The services provided by the bank include the keeping of records and accounting for the depositors and borrowers' transactions. The banks combine the fee for these and other services with a charge for the pure cost of funds to calculate the amount imposed on borrowers as "interest." The percentage fee the bank would otherwise pay depositors as the pure cost of funds is reduced by the amount the bank charges for the bank's services to the depositors.

If the pure cost of funds is 2 percent[18] and the charge to make the loan (including keeping records), take the risk of a default, and make a profit is equal to an interest rate of another 2 percent, the bank will impose a 4 percent finance charge on the loans. If the charge to handle deposits and make a profit is equal to an interest rate of 0.5 percent, the bank will pay depositors 1.5 percent on their deposits.[19] In this example, the 2 percent pure cost of funds represents the agreement by the depositor to defer consumption. It is not part of national income accounts and should not be in the VAT base.[20]

There is a wide range of approaches to the taxation of financial services. Some countries, such as Argentina (discussed later in this chapter), tax gross interest. Mexico taxes interest paid on credit cards and interest on loans used for nonbusiness purposes but exempts mortgage interest.[21]

---

[16] Henderson, Financial Intermediaries, *supra* note 14, at 47–48.

[17] *Id.* at 37.

[18] Poddar and English use the rate the government pays on short-term obligations as the pure rate of interest. Poddar & English, Taxation of Financial Services, *supra* note 14, at 93. [Added by authors.]

[19] For a detailed analysis of the components of interest paid on deposits and finance charges on loans, see *Id.* at 185–187.

[20] "This example does not separate out the increase in the borrower's finance charge that is attributable to the risk that the borrower will default on the loan. Assume that the bank imposes a finance charge of 10 percent rather than 9.75 percent to cover the default risk. Arguably, the charge attributable to the risk of default should not be subject to VAT. [See Poddar & English, Taxation of Financial Services, *supra* note 14. The authors suggest that the charge attributable to the risk of default is a form of wealth transfer or redistribution of funds among the borrowers.] It may not be feasible, administratively, to calculate the charge attributable to the default risk on each transaction. There is an alternative, however. The charge for the risk of default (assumed to be 0.25 percent) can be taxed as part of the value of the intermediation services, and the bank can be allowed to claim an input credit for the tax attributable to bad debts." Schenk, Taxation of Financial Services, *supra* note 14, at 831–832 [footnotes renumbered].

[21] See Hernandez-Pulido, *Alternatives for Taxing Finanancial Services Through a VAT in Mexico*, p. 28 (ITP/LL.M. paper at Harvard Law School May, 1995). In Mexico, sales of repossessed or used assets related to exempt services are taxed and the seller is not entitled to input credits with respect to those sales. *Id.* at 32.

Some countries link the value of intermediation services to the margin or spread between the interest charged on loans and the interest paid on deposits. But this margin or spread may not represent an accurate measurement of the value of the intermediation services because these services may be bundled with other services. In addition, the intermediation services are rendered both to depositors and borrowers. Although banks may claim that costs and value are split equally between services to depositors and borrowers, banks may "cross-subsidize services to depositors," such as '"free" checking services.'[22]

An explanation of the financial intermediation services provided to depositors and borrowers is provided in the following excerpt and table taken from the Henderson article on financial intermediaries.[23]

[C]onsider the case of financial intermediation [table 10.1]. The banking sector provides services to both depositors and borrowers, and . . . [we] assume that the charges for (and benefits of) this intermediation are divided equally between the two groups.[24] In this example, value added by financial intermediaries equals 4, and the total value added in the economy rises to 474. To keep the example simple, we initially assume that intermediaries combine deposits with labor to produce loans – they use no purchased goods such as computers, buildings, pens, or paper. We will first consider three cases: deposits from manufacturers used to make loans to retailers, deposits from households used to make loans to retailers, and deposits from households used to make loans to other households. In all three cases, we will assume that the financial sector is exempt from value-added taxation. The examples will indicate that a key determinant of the revenue and neutrality effects is the extent to which the intermediation involves businesses as opposed to households. Exemption of financial intermediaries causes revenue losses when these services are provided to household (or any other sector not covered by the VAT). When intermediation services are provided to businesses, the tax lost by not taxing intermediaries is made up by taxing their customers.

In the first case, which has just interbusiness transactions, the actual purchases of the manufacturing sector rise from 150 to 152, since they now include financial intermediation services equal to 2. Assuming that demand for manufactured goods is basically identical to that in the original example, sales of this sector would also rise by 2, to 352, reflecting the use of banking services. Retailers would buy 352 of manufactured goods plus 2 of intermediation services, and their sales would rise to 474 if demand for their products were unchanged. In terms of overall revenue collection, this case presents no problem even though no tax is collected from the financial sector and even though the VAT does not recognize the implicit service component embedded in interest rates. Under the subtraction method, the

---

[22] *Id* at 42.

[23] Henderson, Financial Intermediaries, *supra* note 14, at 43 & 45. This excerpt has been edited by the authors.

[24] If the observed interest spread also included the value of checking services, then depositors would tend to bear more of the cost (and receive more of the benefit) of banking services. The example here assumes that banks do not provide unpriced checking services.

VAT for manufacturers and retailers undervalues allowed purchases by 2 in each case. Similarly, under the credit method, the input tax credit is too low by 0.2 at each of these stages. But these mistakes exactly offset the nontaxation of the financial intermediary. The total tax collected is correct, since 47.4 is 10 percent of value added in the economy.

Next take transactions involving both households and businesses. The second panel of table [10.1] considers the case where deposits from households are used to fund loans to retailers. (The results would be substantially the same if retailers' deposits were used to make loans to households, or if households' deposits were used to make loans to any other business sector.) In this case, retailers are overcharged 0.2 of value-added tax, but this is not enough to offset the 0.4 undercharge of financial intermediaries, and leaves total tax collections at only 47.2.

Finally, if deposits from households are used to make loans to other households, then the entire value added by financial intermediaries escapes taxation. Tax collections are only 47.

The examples in the top three panels of table [10.1] assume that intermediaries make no purchases from other firms. In the last panel, financial intermediaries buy goods equal to 2 from the primary processing sector. Because intermediaries are exempt, these purchases are never subtracted (or the VAT paid on them is never credited), and overall taxes collected are too high by 0.2. A similar result can be illustrated for capital purchases by intermediaries. Therefore, exemption of intermediaries raises tax collections to the extent that intermediaries buy goods and services for use in production. This factor tends to offset the revenue losses from not taxing households on their purchase of intermediation services.

The examples in [table 10.1] also help to illustrate some efficiency effects of exempting financial intermediaries. First, as shown in panels I and II, when business firms purchase exempt financial services, they end up paying additional tax because their purchases for purposes of computing value-added tax are understated. This makes them less likely to use financial intermediation services. Households, on the other hand, pay no tax on the intermediation services they purchase (panel III). This makes intermediation services relatively less expensive compared to other goods and services. To the extent that intermediation services are used more heavily in association with certain consumption purchases than others, this introduces a distortion in households' spending patterns.

The EU exempts many financial intermediation services, even if provided for explicit fees. That practice spread to many other countries that adopted a VAT. In recent years, there have been either new adoptions or major changes in VATs in some countries that depart significantly from the EU lead. These new approaches to the taxation of financial services attempt to reduce the cascade effect of an exempt supply of financial services in business-to-business transactions by expanding the scope of creditable business inputs or, like South Africa, by taxing more fee-based financial services relating to deposit accounts, loans, and currency transactions.

Some banking associations and other providers of financial services have objected to the exempt status for these financial services and products. Banks may prefer to be taxable on their intermediation services, especially those

Table 10.1. Percent value added tax with financial intermediaries excluded from the tax base

| | | | Subtraction method | | | Credit method | |
		Value added	*Sales*	*Allowed purchases*	*Tax*	*Sales*	*Input tax credit*	*Net tax*
I.	Deposits from Mf'g Sector, Loans to Retailing Sector Financial Intermediaries (interest recd = 12, paid = 8)	4	—	—	0	—	—	0
	Nonfinancial Sectors Primary Processing (purchases = 0, sales = 150)	150	150	0	15	15	0	15
	Manufacturing (purchases = 152[a], sales = 352)	200	352	150	20.2	35.2	15	20.2
	Retailing (purchases = 354[a], sales = 474)	120	474	352	12.2	47.4	35.2	12.2
	TOTAL	474			47.4			47.4
II.	Deposits from Households, Loans to Retailing Sector Financial Intermediaries (interest recd = 12, paid = 8)	4	—	—	0	—	—	0
	Nonfin. Sector Prim. Processing (pur. = 0, sales = 150)	150	150	0	15	15	0	15
	Manufacturing (purchases = 150, sales = 350)	200	350	150	20	35	15	20
	Retailing (purchases = 352[b], sales = 472)	120	472	350	12.2	47.2	35	12.2
	TOTAL	472			47.2			47.2
III.	Deposits from Households, Loans to Households Financial Intermediaries (interest recd = 12, paid = 8)	4	—	—	0	—	—	0
	Nonfinancial Sectors Primary Processing (purchases = 0, sales = 150)	150	150	0	15	15	0	15
	Manufacturing (purchases = 150, sales = 350)	200	350	150	20	35	15	20
	Retailing (purchases = 350, sales = 470)	120	470	350	12	47	35	12
	TOTAL	474			47			47

(continued)

Table 10.1 (*continued*)

| | Value added | Subtraction method | | | Credit method | | |
		Sales	Allowed purchases	Tax	Sales	Input tax credit	Net tax
IV. Dep's from Mf'g Sector, Loans to RetailSector; Fin. Intermed. Pur. Output of Primary Processing Sector Fin. Intermed (int.recd = 14; paid = 8; purchases = 2)	4	—	—	0	—	—	0
Nonfinancial Sectors Primary Processing (purchases = 0, sales to mfg = 148, sales to fin. Intermed. = 2)	150	150	0	15	15	0	15
Manufacturing (purchases = 151 [b], sales = 351)	200	351	148	20.3	35.1	14.8	20.3
Retailing (purchases = 354 [b], sales = 474)	120	474	351	12.3	47.4	35.1	12.3
TOTAL	**474**			**47.6**			**47.6**

[a] Includes intermediation services of 2, equal to 1/2 the difference between int. paid and int. received.

[b] Includes intermediation services of 3, equal to 1/2 the difference between int. paid and int. received.

rendered to taxable businesses for explicit fees, because the banks can deduct input tax on purchases attributable to taxable services, and the business users of these services can deduct input tax charged on such services.

The disallowance of input tax to the provider of exempt financial services (sometimes referred to as "blocked input tax") produces a cascade effect when these services are rendered to taxable businesses unable to claim input credits on the cost of these services.[25] Some countries proposed the taxation of financial services when they introduced VAT, only to back off as the VAT proposal proceeded through the political and legislative process.[26]

[25] Some economists claim "that in an open economy financial institutions cannot pass undeductable VAT on to their customers." Owens, *The Move to VAT*, 1996/2 Intertax 45, 49. On the forward shifting of a broad-based VAT, see C. MCLURE, JR., THE VALUE-ADDED TAX: KEY TO DEFICIT REDUCTION?, pp. 30–32.

[26] When New Zealand and Canada issued their White Papers on tax reform before enacting their VATs (their VATs are called Goods and Services Taxes (GSTs)), the governments indicated their intent to tax financial services. New Zealand ultimately enacted a GST that taxed only insurance services other than life insurance, and Canada enacted a GST that exempted domestic financial services and zero rated the export of financial services.

The European Union has been examining possible alternative treatment for financial intermediation services.[27]

The most common approach is the exemption for financial intermediation services, exemplified by the EU exemption. This exemption is discussed, followed by several cases that examine the concept of an exempt financial service and the allocation of input tax credits between taxable and exempt activities of financial institutions.

D. Principles to Guide the Taxation of Financial Services

A normative VAT base for financial services, including financial intermediation services, should incorporate some basic principles. The following are a list of principles that could be used to develop a system of taxation of financial intermediation services.[28]

1. VAT should be imposed on the intermediation service component of finance charges on loans, and of interest payments on deposits, with appropriate value allocated to depositors and borrowers.
2. Subject to modifications justifiable for administrative or compliance reasons, the intermediation services rendered by financial institutions should be subject to the same tax treatment as other taxable goods or services, whether these financial services are imported, exported, or rendered for domestic consumption.
3. Businesses rendering taxable financial intermediation services should receive the same VAT treatment of their business inputs (input tax credits or deductions) on a transaction-by-transaction basis as other businesses making taxable sales.
4. Providers and users of financial intermediation services should enjoy the same cash-flow effects from the VAT that exist for providers and users of other taxable services.[29]
5. The value of financial intermediation services should be taxed only once – the cascading of VAT should be avoided. Business users of financial services should receive a tax benefit for the actual tax component in the cost of the intermediation services if they use these services in making taxable sales of goods or services, but not if they use these services in making exempt sales.

---

[27] See Bureau of National Affairs, *Daily Tax Report*, June 15, 1993, G-5. The European Commission intends to make legislative proposals to modernize the taxation of financial services and insurance transactions. See Commissioner Kovacs speech at a conference 11 May 2006, IBFD EVD News: Terra/Kajus, 15 May 2006.

[28] These principles are taken, with some modification, from Schenk, Taxation of Financial Services, *supra* note 14, at 832–833.

[29] Under a credit-invoice VAT, the VAT ideally should not enter the pre-VAT pricing structure of goods and services supplied by the providers or taxable business users of financial services.

6. If any financial intermediation services are exempt from tax, to the extent that it is administratively feasible, the provider of the exempt services should be subject to self-supply rules; that is, it should not have any incentive to vertically integrate its operations in order to reduce the non-creditable VAT on its purchases.
7. The VAT regime for financial intermediation services should be able to accommodate to changes in the VAT rate.

E. Interest Paid on Credit Sales to Consumers

Economists equate the cash price for durable goods with the discounted present value of the consumption of the durable goods that takes place over the lifetime of the goods. It therefore is reasonable to tax the cash price of durable goods at the time of purchase, whether the consumer pays the price out of personal savings, with a bank loan, or under an installment sales agreement. The finance charge on the bank loan or the interest portion of each installment under the installment sales agreement should follow the VAT treatment of interest.

If the VAT could be paid on installment sales as each installment is paid,

> then the base for the VAT must be the total of each installment payment including interest and related finance charges.[30] The tax on the interest component is the government's charge for its agreement to wait to receive the tax.[31] It is not a tax on the portion of the interest paid on the loan to cover the purchase price.[32]

F. Exemption for Financial Intermediation Services as Implemented in the EU[33]

1. Introduction

As discussed earlier, the prevailing practice is for countries to exempt charges for financial intermediation services, including finance or interest charges.

---

[30] This treatment results in the taxation of a sale and a lease alike, even in situations where it is difficult to distinguish a sale from a lease.

[31] The assumption is that the seller sets the rate on the basis of such factors as the market rate of interest and the buyer's financial condition. The government would ordinarily charge the same rate for the privilege of deferring tax on the cash price of the item purchased. This transaction is treated as if the government made a loan to the consumer equal to the VAT on the cash price, and the consumer repaid the loan plus pure interest on the unpaid balance. In some cases, sellers may be willing to make installment sales to financially risky customers at a lower interest rate than the customers' credit standing would dictate because these additional sales have low marginal costs or for other reasons. These exceptions are not significant enough to invalidate our assumptions.

[32] Schenk & Oldman, *supra* note 14, at 187–188 (some footnotes omitted or edited).

[33] For a detailed analysis and justification for the exemption for financial intermediation services, see Edgar, "Exempt Treatment of Financial Intermediation Services under a Value-Added Tax: Assessing the Significance of recent Challenges to an Imperfect Status Quo," 49 *Can. Tax J.* 1133 (2001).

Although exemption generally is justified on administrative grounds, exemption does not necessarily simplify the VAT.[34]

The two most difficult aspect of any attempt to tax intermediation services is the lack of a mechanism for banks (1) to apportion their input credits between taxable activities and exempt intermediation services, and (2) to allocate VAT on those intermediation services (if taxable) to business users on a transaction-by-transaction basis. Has the problem been overstated? See the following discussion and the proposals to tax intermediation services discussed later in this chapter.

Banks that currently render exempt domestic intermediation services, zero-rated exports of intermediation services, and taxable other financial services (such as investment advice) may battle the tax authorities over the proper allocation of input VAT between the exempt intermediation services, and the taxable and zero-rated financial services, but countries that rely on the EU exemption system seem to have a system that functions adequately. Business users can claim credits for VAT charged by the banks on the taxable domestic services.

2. Exemption for Financial Services in the EU Followed Elsewhere

The Sixth Directive defines the EU mandate for the exemption for financial services. Under Article 13B(d), member states must exempt the following services from VAT:

1. "The granting and the negotiation of credit and the management of credit by the person granting it;
2. The negotiation of or any dealings in credit guarantees or any other security for money and the management of credit guarantees by the person who is granting the credit;
3. transactions, including negotiation, concerning deposit and current accounts, payments, transfers, debts, cheques and other negotiable instruments, but excluding debt collection and factoring;[35]

---

[34] *See* Canada's proposed Goods and Services Tax, Bill C-62, 2d Sess., 34th Parliament, 38–39 Elizabeth II, 1989–1990, as passed by the House of Commons, April 10, 1990, that includes complex input credit and other rules to implement the decision to exempt financial services, especially where a firm renders both exempt financial services and taxable services.

[35] Although the ECJ held that the purchase of debts in payment of a commission is taxable "debt collection and factoring," the Italian tax authorities take the position that the transfer of debts to a factor is an exempt financial transaction because the factoring finances the transferor's portfolio of debts. See Notice No. 126747 of 5 August 2004, discussed by Deiana, "Italy: Factoring," *VAT Monitor*, Nov./Dec. 2004, p. 446. For an article criticizing the ECJ decision in *Finanzamt Groß-Gerau v. MKG-Kraftfahrzeuge-Factoring GmbH*, Case C-305/01, [2003] ECR I-06729, see van der Corput, "Who Makes What Supply? – The Inverted World of MKG," *VAT Monitor*, Nov./Dec. 2003, p. 465. The ECJ relies on basic principles of statutory interpretation in holding that exemptions should be narrowly construed and exceptions to the exemptions should be interpreted broadly, and that debt collection is an exception to the exemption in Art. 13B(d)(3). The author claims that it was error for the ECJ to interpret "debt collection" as covering "true factoring," "which is

4. transactions, including negotiation, concerning currency, bank notes and coins used as legal tender, with the exception of collector's items; (collector's items' shall be taken to mean gold, silver or other metal coins or bank notes which are not normally used as legal tender or coins of numismatic interest);

5. transactions, including negotiation, excluding management and safekeeping, in shares, interests in companies or associations, debentures and other securities, excluding:
   • documents establishing title to goods,
   • the rights or securities referred to in Article 5(3) [certain interests in immovable property];

6. management of special investment funds[36] as defined by Member states..."

Notwithstanding the above rules on exemption, Article 13C provides that member states can give taxpayers the option to be taxable on financial services described in Article 13B(d). Germany, France, and Belgium give taxpayers this option.[37] According to Cnossen,

> [b]etween Germany and France, the option may be used in respect of all financial institutions (Germany) or it may be restricted to specified financial institutions (France). The option may apply to individual transactions (Germany) or to all transactions (France).... The option may be restricted to financial services supplied to taxable businesses (Germany) or it may apply to financial services supplied to registered as well as non registered person (France). If the concern is with cascading, the German approach suffices. If the concern is with cascading as well as uniformity of tax-to-user price ratios, the French approach is preferable. Clearly, the German approach is the simplest to administer and comply with.[38]

Article 15 of the Sixth Directive ("exempting" exports), combined with Article 17(3)(b) and (c) granting input credits on exports, has the effect of zero rating financial services. Thus, exports of financial services that would be exempt if provided domestically are zero-rated if exported. As a result, financial institutions that export financial services must calculate the available input tax credits attributable to the exported financial services.

Countries outside the EU that exempt financial services generally provide detailed definitions of the concept of a financial service. Nevertheless, there has been litigation over the kinds of supplies that qualify as financial services. For example, in New Zealand, one corporation issued redeemable (for NZD 1 in 2073) preferred shares (membership shares) in a sister corporation that

---

actually not even a service, and for which the true factor has never invoiced its customer a commission." *Id.* at 469.

[36] For a discussion of this exemption, with covered funds varying widely in different EU countries, see Nevelsteen & Van Den Plas, "Undertakings of Collective Investment and VAT in the EU," *VAT Monitor*, Nov./Dec. 2003, p. 456.

[37] See Cnossen, *VAT Treatment of Financial Services*, in G. Lindencrona, S. Lodin, and B Wiman, Eds., International Studies in Taxation: Law and Economics – Liber Amicorum Mutén 91(Kluwer 1999).

[38] *Id.* at 99.

owned and operated a country club. The shares carried rights to use the country club facilities, but with limited exceptions, did not carry other rights to participate in corporate distributions. Shareholders also paid annual "subscriptions" to cover the cost of operating the country club. The court held that the supply of the shares was an exempt financial service.[39] The court disagreed with the Commissioner's claim that the supply was a taxable golf club membership, or both an equity security with a nominal value (exempt from the GST) and a taxable golf club membership.

3. Effects of Exemption at an Intermediate or Retail Stage

[E]xemption at the retail stage reduces the revenue to the government and the cost of financial services rendered directly to consumers and not indirectly through business firms. In contrast, if the exemption applies at an intermediate stage (the bank renders exempt services to a business firm and not to a consumer) and a subsequent stage, such as the retail stage, is taxable, . . . this midstream exemption actually increases the cost to the consumer and the revenue to the government over what it would have been if the intermediate stage sale had been taxable. This result occurs under most foreign VATs if financial services rendered to businesses are exempt and sales by the businesses acquiring these services are taxable.[40,41]

G. Vertical Integration and Outsourcing

A supplier of exempt services, such as a financial service supplier, is denied credit for input VAT on purchases attributable to the exempt financial services. The supplier therefore has an incentive to provide more services in-house (vertically integrate) and thereby reduce noncreditable input VAT. For example, "instead of purchasing bank forms and stationery from an outside printer for $100,000 plus $10,000 in noncreditable VAT, a bank can operate its own print shop and reduce its costs if it can provide the same forms and stationery for less than the $110,000 tax-inclusive cost charged by the outside printer."[42]

Vertical integration creates several problems, including discrimination against outside domestic suppliers of the services needed by these financial service suppliers and discrimination against smaller financial institutions that are not in a position to vertically integrate.

There are several methods available to offset this incentive for financial service suppliers to vertically integrate. The VAT law can include a rule that taxes such self-supplies. For example, if a bank establishes its own print shop to avoid noncreditable VAT on printing services purchased from outside suppliers, the bank can be treated as having supplied those printing services

---

[39] *Commissioner of Inland Revenue v. Gulf Harbour Development Ltd*, CA 135/03 (Ct. App. 2004).

[40] A typical case exists if a manufacturer of taxable clothing borrows money from a bank in order to operate its business. The financial services rendered by the bank to the manufacturer are exempt and the manufacturer's sales of its manufactured clothing are taxable.

[41] Schenk, Taxation of Financial Services, *supra* note 14, at 826–828. [Edited by the authors.]

[42] *Id*. at 830.

to itself in a taxable transaction. A second option, adopted by Australia, is to give financial service suppliers an input credit for a portion of services purchased from outside suppliers if those purchases are used in making exempt financial supplies.[43]

The classification of some services rendered *to* financial institutions as exempt financial services may give those institutions an incentive to out-source those services to providers outside the EU. If a bank or other financial institution obtains services within the EU that are exempt from VAT, the cost of those services may include some disallowed input VAT. If the same ser-vices are imported, they are completely free of VAT, especially if the foreign supplier operates in a country that zero-rates the export of those services.

In many cases, the incentive to outsource services to foreign suppliers is minimized because the import is reportable (under a reverse charge rule) as a taxable supply by the importer. However, if the imported services would be exempt if provided domestically in the EU, the import is not subject to the reverse charge rule. The *Datacenter* and *FDR* cases, included later, have expanded the scope of services that may be classified as exempt financial services in the EU and therefore may be imported free of the reverse charge rule. For these services, there is discrimination against domestic suppliers of the same services.

Typically, the disputes relating to vertical integration arise in situations where an outside firm renders services to a financial institution and claims that the services that they render qualify as financial services. If the services rendered by the domestic supplier to the bank is exempt, there is no reason to bring those services in-house. As to outsourcing to foreign suppliers, as just discussed, if the outsourced services constitute part of an exempt finan-cial function when done by a financial institution, it is an exempt import of a financial service that is not subject to the reverse charge rule if that ser-vice represents a complete function. The *Sparekassernes Datacenter* and *FDR* cases involve the exemption for services rendered by domestic suppliers (not financial institutions) to banks. These cases provide encouragement to EU banks to outsource some of their functions, especially to foreign suppliers.

Sparekassernes Datacenter (SDC) v. Skatteministeriet[44]

Article 13B(d)(3) and (5) of the Sixth Directive is worded as follows:
`Without prejudice to other Community provisions, Member States shall exempt the following under conditions which they shall lay down

---

[43] See the input credit available for 75 percent of the cost of "reduced credit acquisitions," discussed *infra* Section III(I)(4)(c), this chapter.

[44] Case C-2/95, [1997] ECR I-03017 (ECJ Judgment) (edited by the authors). An earlier British Value Added Tribunal held that cash collection and delivery, as well as credit checking services were services normally performed by the Bank integral to its banking operations and therefore were exempt from VAT. *Barclays Bank PLC v. The Commissioners,* 1988 VATTR 23.

for the purpose of ensuring the correct and straightforward application of the exemptions and of preventing any possible evasion, avoidance or abuse:

. . .

(d) the following transactions:

3. transactions, including negotiation, concerning deposit and current accounts, payments, transfers, debts, cheques and other negotiable instruments, but excluding debt collection and factoring;

5. transactions, including negotiation, excluding management and safekeeping, in shares, interests in companies or associations, debentures and other securities, excluding:

• documents establishing title to goods,
• the rights or securities referred to in Article 5(3);

In Denmark, [based on Article 13B(d) of the Sixth Directive, in 1978, the VAT] provided that the activities of banks and savings banks and financial transactions were to be exempt from VAT. [A 1989 amendment] made deposits and management of shares, debentures and other securities, the management of credit and credit guarantees by persons other than those who granted the credits and the renting of safe-deposit boxes subject to VAT as from 1 January 1991.

The main proceedings

SDC is an association which is registered for the purposes of VAT. Most of its members are savings banks. It provides to its members and to certain other customers who are connected to its data-handling network (hereinafter 'the banks') services relating to transfers, advice on, and trade in, securities, and management of deposits, purchase contracts and loans. SDC also offers services relating to its members' administrative affairs.

Before 1993 SDC provided the banks with services performed wholly or partly by electronic means. Those supplies of services were analogous to those which the biggest financial institutions carry out themselves using their own data-handling centres.

A typical SDC supply of service [consists] of a number of components which, added together, made up the service which a bank or its customers (hereinafter 'the customers') wished to have performed. SDC did not receive the remuneration for its supply of services from the customers but from the banks.

SDC performed services only at the request of a bank, a customer or other persons who were authorized, under a contract concluded with the customer, to require transactions such as payments to be effected. A customer could give information to SDC only after having been authorized to do so by a bank, in particular by the issue of a payment or credit card. SDC's name was not used.

[T]he VAT Tribunal decided that none of the services provided by SDC were covered by the exemption. The court referred the following questions to the Court for a preliminary ruling:

1. Should Article 13B(d) points 3 to 5 of the Sixth VAT Directive be interpreted as meaning that VAT exemption should be granted for [supplies of data-handling services to SDC members and to other financial institutions]? [Is the exemption] precluded where a transaction within the meaning of that provision is effected, wholly or in part, electronically?

2. The wording used in Article 13B(d) points 1 to 2 of the VAT Directive is "by the person granting [the credit]" and "by the person who is granting the credit". That description is not employed in Article 13B(d) points 3 to 5. Should any importance be attached to that difference in the interpretation of Article 13B(d) points 3 to 5?

3. A. Is it significant, as far as the application of Article 13B(d) points 3 to 5 is concerned, whether transactions are effected by financial institutions or by others?

B. Is it significant, as far as the application of Article 13B(d) points 3 to 5 is concerned, whether the entire financial service is performed by a financial institution which has a relationship with a customer?

C. If it is unnecessary for the application of Article 13B(d) points 3 to 5 that the financial institution itself should perform the entire service, can the financial institution purchase transactions wholly or in part from another person with the effect that the services performed by that other person are covered by Article 13B(d) points 3 to 5, or may particular requirements be made of that other person?

4. How is the wording used in Article 13B(d) points 3 and 4 "transactions...concerning" to be interpreted? [Are] the words "transactions...concerning" to be understood as meaning that VAT exemption should also be granted in cases where a person either performs only a part of the service or effects only some of the transactions within the meaning of the Directive that are necessary for the supply of the complete financial service?

5. In interpreting Article 13B(d) points 3 to 5 should significance be attached to the fact that the taxable person who requests tax exemption for transactions within the meaning of the provision effects those transactions on behalf of the financial institution in whose name the service is performed?

THE COURT rules:

1. Points 3 and 5 of Article 13B(d) of the Sixth Council Directive are to be interpreted as meaning that the exemption is not subject to the condition that the transactions be effected by a certain type of institution, by a certain type of legal person or wholly or partly by certain electronic means or manually.

2. The exemption provided for by points 3 and 5 of Article 13B(d) of the Sixth Directive is not subject to the condition that the service be provided by an institution which has a legal relationship with the end customer. The fact that a transaction covered by those provisions is effected by a third party but appears to the end customer to be a service provided by the bank does not preclude exemption for the transaction.

3. Point 3 of Article 13B(d) of the Sixth Directive is to be interpreted as meaning that transactions concerning transfers and payments and transactions in shares, interests in companies or associations, debentures and other securities include transactions carried out by a data-handling centre if those transactions are distinct in character and are specific to, and essential for, the exempt transactions.
4. Services consisting in making financial information available to banks and other users are not covered by points 3 and 5 of Article 13B(d) of the Sixth Directive.
5. The mere fact that transactions concerning the management of deposits, purchase contracts and loans are carried out by a data-handling centre does not prevent them from constituting services covered by points 13 and 15 of Annex F to the Sixth Directive. It is for the national court to determine whether, before 1 January 1991, those transactions were separate in character and specific to, and essential for, those services.

Assuming the service provided by the taxpayer is an essential element in the service the bank provides, that element still may not be an exempt service. It is up to the national court to make this determination.

According to the *Sparekassernes Datacenter* case, it is the responsibility of the national court to determine, from the facts of each case, whether the operations carried out by the supplier qualify as specific and essential operations, or mere technical supplies. The status of services as exempt or taxable depend on the nature of the services, not the supplier. It is not essential for the exemption that there is a legal relationship between the service provider and the end customer. Assuming the service provided by the taxpayer is an essential element in the service the bank provides, that element still may not be an exempt service. It is up to the national court to make this determination.

The following *FDR* case held that credit card services provided by an outside supplier to banks constitute exempt financial services.

Customs and Excise Commissioners v. FDR Ltd[45]

HEADNOTE. FDR Ltd supplied credit card services to banks. Its clients were either 'issuers' (banks who issued credit cards to cardholders), 'acquirers' (banks who paid merchants, normally retailers, in exchange for vouchers accepted by those merchants in payment for goods or services), or banks who acted in both capacities.

In a typical credit card transaction, not involving FDR, a cardholder would hand his credit card to the merchant who then recorded the transaction, either manually or electronically. Before the transaction was

---

[45] [2000] STC 672 (Ct. App. U.K.). [Edited by the authors.]

finalised, the merchant could be required to obtain the issuer's authorisation. The merchant would subsequently be paid by the acquirer, the acquirer would be paid by the issuer, and the issuer would be paid by the cardholder on presentation of a monthly account.

Some banks 'outsourced' their obligations in respect of such transactions to FDR. FDR maintained two accounts, the cardholder account and the merchant account. On being notified that a credit card transaction had occurred, FDR, after, if necessary, authorising the transaction, posted a credit to the merchant account and then made an entry on a magnetic tape which was supplied on a daily basis to BACS Ltd, an automated clearing house, instructing it to effect a credit in the merchant's own bank account and to create a corresponding debit in the acquirer's central accounts. FDR reconciled the accounts between issuers and acquirers on a daily basis by establishing the net position of each client bank and the net amount which needed to be transferred from or to that bank (the netting-off procedure). FDR made a payment out of its own funds to each client bank which was a net claimant and received (later the same day) a payment from each bank which was a net debtor. Those payments were made through the banking system using the CHAPS mechanism. FDR also posted a debit to the cardholder account (to which it also posted credit entries when the cardholder paid his or her monthly bill).

If the cardholder had arranged to pay his bill by direct debit, FDR also provided for BACS to debit the cardholder's ordinary bank account, and credit the issuer's account, with the relevant sum. For some of its clients, FDR also provided connected services which consisted of arranging for the credit card to be embossed with the cardholder's name and account number, preparing and sending to the cardholder periodic statements of his indebtedness to the issuer, and enclosing with the mailing any promotional leaflets or circulars required to be included by the issuer. FDR also calculated at the end of each month the aggregate fee which the merchant owed to the acquirer by way of commission on transactions, and sent a statement of the merchant account to the merchant. It would then make an appropriate entry on the BACS tape effecting a debit to the merchant's bank account in favour of the acquirer.

The commissioners considered that FDR's services were taxable at the standard rate. FDR appealed contending that the services were supplies falling within art 13B(d)(3) of EC Council Directive 77/388 which exempted from VAT 'transactions, including negotiation, concerning deposit and current accounts, payments, transfers, debts, cheques and other negotiable instruments'. The tribunal allowed the appeal. It held, inter alia, that the daily netting-off procedure, the issue of instructions by FDR to BACS, and the maintenance and operation of the cardholder and merchant accounts were exempt supplies because in each of them FDR effected transfers within art 13B(d)(3).

The commissioners appealed direct to the Court of Appeal.

JUDGMENT BY-1: LAWS LJ. FDR's case is that the supplies made by them in the course of their business, at any rate what has been called the 'core' or 'principal' supply, are exempt by force of art 13B(d)(3).

THE ISSUES. [On the facts, does] FDR make 'transfers' within art 13B(d)3)? [S]hould at least some of those activities be treated as a 'core' or 'principal' supply, and thus a single supply (so as to attract a unitary tax treatment for the purposes of VAT even though the same activities, if treated individually, would or might attract differing tax treatments), and, if so, how should the core supply be described? [I]f there is a core supply, what should its tax treatment be – taxable or exempt?

[W]e find that the principal service provided by FDR consists of processing all their card transactions and settling their liabilities and claims under these transactions in accordance with the obligations of the Issuers and Acquirers.

It is plain that ordinary accountancy services are not exempt from VAT, and that the exemptions granted by the provisions contained in art 13B(d) are much more narrowly confined. It is well recognised that commercial transactions whose essence involves the movement of money are in many cases, for conceptual reasons, ill-suited for the application of the VAT regime, and it seems likely that this is what lies behind the art 13B(d) exemptions.

[The court tests FDR's services against the reasoning in the *Datacenter* case in three areas], (a) transfers and BACS, (b) transfers and netting-off, and (c) transfers and the cardholder/merchant accounts.

[I]t is in my judgment of the first importance to recognise that BACS for its own part exercises no judgment or discretion whatever. Once the relevant tape is prepared (and that is admittedly done by FDR) and delivered to BACS, the process is, as I have said, automatic. Moreover the inevitable outcome is a redistribution of the rights and obligations of payor and payee – a 'change in the legal and financial situation' – the very circumstances which in my judgment constitute a transfer of funds for the purposes of art 13B(d)(3). [I]t is a conclusion which conforms to the letter and spirit of art 13B(d) as it was explained in [the *Datacenter*] case.

The reality is that the netting-off process achieves precisely the same result as would be attained – unspeakably more laboriously – if, as between all the acquirers, issuers and payment systems, each debt owed by any one to any other were the subject of individual credit and debit entries in the bank accounts of the two of them. It cannot be right that the most inefficient way of doing X constitutes an exempt supply, but the most efficient way of doing it constitutes a taxable supply. On this issue the tribunal was in my judgment entirely right.

The truth is that to the extent that FDR indeed [effects] transfers of money, [it does so] by the CHAPS and BACS transactions. The former are admittedly transfers, and the latter I have found to be so.

[W]here the transaction in question comprises a bundle of features and acts, regard must first be had to all the circumstances in which that transaction takes place.

There is a single supply in particular in cases where one or more elements are to be regarded as constituting the principal service, whilst one or more elements are to be regarded, by contrast, as ancillary services which share the tax treatment of the principal service. A service must be regarded as ancillary to a principal service if it does not constitute for customers an aim in itself, but a means of better enjoying the principal service supplied.

In my judgment the tribunal's conclusions (a) that there was here a single or core supply, and (b) that [the principal service provided by FDR consists of processing all their card transactions and settling their liabilities and claims under these transactions in accordance with the obligations of the Issuers and Acquirers], are well established.

If my conclusions upon issues (1) and (2) are correct, they provide the answer to this last question.

I would have categorised the essential commercial activity here in very simple terms. It consists in the movement of money between cardholder, merchant, issuer and acquirer, for the convenience of the cardholder and the profit of the other three parties. Under the contractual arrangements which the tribunal examined at great length, that activity is essentially (with variations) 'outsourced' – a word not to be used without quotation marks – to FDR. So regarded, the supplies which FDR makes plainly fall within art 13B(d)(3).

H. Input Tax Credits and the Allocation of the Credits Between Taxable and Exempt Activities

1. Introduction

If financial intermediation services are exempt from VAT, banks must absorb the noncreditable input VAT. It is predictable that some or all of this added cost will prompt the banks to reduce the interest rate paid on deposits and increase the interest rate charged on loans. Retaining the exemption for intermediation services, the banking industry or the tax authorities could estimate the disallowed credits as a percentage of interest on deposits and loans, and the VAT law could grant credits to business users based on this estimate.[46] Henderson suggests another alternative:

> ... a system of granting credits on the basis of "the size of the financial asset or liability – that is, the firm's deposit or loan as a fraction of each bank's overall assets and liabilities.[47] Checkable deposits might be treated with an extra weight to reflect the value of free checking services in addition to the value

---

[46] For a more detailed discussion of this approach, see Schenk & Oldman, *supra* note 14, at 192–194.

[47] Henderson, *supra* note 14, at 47.

of intermediation."[48] Henderson recognizes that her system does not permit the financial intermediary, such as a bank, to notify the business customer of the size of the credit at the time of the transaction. After the bank determines its own VAT liability, the bank must determine the fraction of the overall business that is attributable to VAT-registered customers. The bank would then apportion the eligible credits to those customers and notify them of the creditable amounts.[49] A year or two of experience would give banks and their customers a good idea of the magnitude of the VAT and its associated credits and their relative importance in doing business.[50]

2. Methods of Allocating Disallowed Credits

One of the most vexing problems facing financial institutions rendering services exempt from the VAT is the allocation of the input tax on purchases between their taxable and exempt activities. As discussed earlier, the tax attributable to the exempt activities is not creditable against output tax liability on taxable sales.

The general principles applicable to the allocation of input VAT between taxable and other supplies are discussed in Chapter 6. A common approach is to allow full input credit for input VAT attributable to taxable (including zero-rated) supplies, to allow no input credit for input VAT attributable to exempt supplies, and to require an allocation between taxable and exempt supplies of input VAT attributable to mixed purpose supplies (or where the acquisition cannot be specifically allocated to either taxable or exempt supplies).

The discussion here focuses on the special problems in allocating input VAT for a registered person rendering financial services that may be taxable, exempt, and zero rated.

Australia attempts to address this allocation issue in a ruling. An Australian GST ruling includes an elaborate discussion of the issues involved and the various methods by which financial service providers may allocate input VAT under that GST.[51] The explanation that follows is taken in large part from this ruling.

Financial service providers first must allocate inputs that can be directly attributable to either taxable or other supplies. Under the direct attribution rules, tax on inputs directly attributable to taxable supplies are fully creditable. Those directly attributable to exempt supplies are not creditable. "Where financial supply providers are unable to match individual costs with individual revenue streams, other apportionment methodologies may need

---

[48] *Id.* at 46.

[49] *Id.*

[50] Schenk & Oldman, *supra* note 14, at 192–193.

[51] GSTR 2000/22, – Goods and Services Tax: determining the extent of creditable purpose for providers of financial supplies (Australia 18 December 2002) [hereinafter GSTR 2000/22]. See also the French tax administration Guideline 3 A-1-06, ignoring incidental exempt financial transactions, and treating transactions as such if, in general, they are distinguishable from a taxable person's principal activity, and not more than 10 percent of the taxable acquisitions are used in conducting the exempt financial transactions. See IBFD TNS Online, 24 Feb. 2006.

to be used."[52] In Australia, if the direct method is not available or does not allocate all costs, then for financial service providers, the general formula for the indirect method is revenue/total revenue, where revenue includes taxable and zero-rated (GST-free) supplies and total revenue includes exempt supplies as well. In this formula, "revenue" is net revenue for financial supplies (such as the net of interest received and interest paid), and gross revenue for nonfinancial supplies (such as fees charged). Other acceptable indirect formulas include the number of transactions, floor space, profit, or hours spent on each activity.[53]

Mexico tried to abolish the kind of direct method available in Australia in order to reduce abuses in this area. Until 1999, Mexico found that reliance on the traditional method that permitted financial institutions to deduct fully input VAT directly attributable to taxable activities gave creative tax planners the opportunity to claim excessive credits by classifying mixed purpose supplies as attributable to taxable activities.[54] Contrary to this practice and despite the fact that exempt activities represented about 80 percent of total activity, the banks did not try to allocate specific inputs to exempt activities.[55] Starting in fiscal year 1999, Mexico abolished direct attribution for input credits and, in most cases, required pro rata allocation to taxed and exempt activities on the basis of gross income (not net interest for financial institutions).[56] The banks challenged the law. The court struck down the denial of direct attribution on the grounds that taxpayers making only taxable sales should not be denied the right to attribute all of their input VAT to those transactions. In response, the Mexican Ministry of Finance administratively allowed full input credit for a list of items if they were "unequivocally" attributable to taxable activities but denied the use of net income in the pro rata allocation formula.

An amendment of the Mexican VAT in 2000 again allowed direct attribution to taxable and exempt activities, but only with respect to tangible goods, not services. Other than direct attribution for finance leasing and collection of loan collateral, a bank must apply annually for a ruling to obtain permission to use direct attribution. That ruling to a particular bank also addresses the method required to be used to apportion mixed purpose inputs.[57] The Mexican Ministry believed that abuses continued.[58] In 2001,

---

[52] GSTR 2000/22, *supra* note 51, at ¶58.

[53] *Id*. at ¶¶68–79.

[54] See Schatan, "VAT on Banking Services: Mexico's Experience," *VAT Monitor*, July/Aug. 2003, p. 287. "[T]he larger institutions invested substantial resources in reorganizing their cost centres in order to impute generous proportions of expenses to taxed activities. . . ." *Id*. at 289.

[55] *Id*. at 289. The author discusses other aggressive techniques used by the larger financial institutions to minimize or wipe out any VAT liability.

[56] "Net" was allowed for repossessions and transactions in stocks by financial institutions. *Id*. at 291.

[57] *Id*. at 292.

[58] In some cases, the Ministry takes a more conservative position than in other countries. For example, contrary to the South African decision to allows banks to claim full credit for input VAT on ATM machines, discussed *infra*, the Mexican Ministry reportedly takes

the Mexican Banking Association proposed the taxation of all loans made by banks.

The allocation of input credits attributable to financial services arises for banks exporting financial services. See *Commissioners of Customs and Excise v. First National Bank of Chicago.*[59]

3. Credit Denied for VAT on Purchases by Consumers: Credit When Purchase Is Made for Investment

"Consumers and other bank customers not registered under the VAT should not receive credit for the VAT component in the services that the bank rendered to them. To the extent that these non-registered customers use borrowed funds to purchase investments that do not belong in a consumption tax base (such as securities), they should receive a pass through of a credit for the VAT component in the purchased intermediation services. The net effect of this regime would be to tax only the value of intermediation services attributable to personal consumption.

VAT imposed on purchases of investment assets placed in an investment custody account (similar in principle to an individual retirement account) should be refundable.[60] The trustee of the investment custody account should be treated as though he were engaged in a taxable business. The trustee then could file a VAT return and claim a refund for the tax paid on the purchased investment assets.

The investment custody account concept may be used to pass through a credit to unregistered bank customers for the VAT component of intermediation services on loans used to purchase investments placed in an investment custody account. For reasons of administrative convenience, the legislature may deny refundable credits to consumers who borrow to purchase investments. The legislature may, however, grant credits to trustees of investment custody accounts on properly substantiated requests by the trustees."[61]

I. Departures from EU in the Taxation of Financial Services

1. Introduction

As discussed earlier in this chapter, member states of the European Union must exempt domestic financial services and zero rate exported financial services, but they may give domestic businesses the option to treat financial

---

the position that only "commissions paid by banks for cash withdrawals by their clients through ATMs that are operated by other banks can directly be attributed to taxed activities. The Ministry apparently takes the position that ATM services are not 'independent of the banks' efforts to obtain deposits from the public." *Id.* at 293.

[59] Case C-172/96, 1998 ECJ CELEX LEXIS 5819 (ECJ 1998).

[60] Special treatment could be provided "for investment assets placed in an investment custody account if the investor's interest in the assets is limited to an intangible right to an investment return and the investor cannot obtain possession of the property." A. Schenk, Reporter, Value Added Tax: A Model Statute and Commentary, A Report of The Committee on Value Added Tax of the American Bar Association Section of Taxation, p. 182 (1989); see *id.* at 183–185 (proposed §4020).

[61] Schenk & Oldman, *supra* note 14, at 193–194, as edited.

services as taxable. France, Germany, and Belgium grant that option. Most non-EU countries with VATs follow the EU practice and exempt financial intermediation and some other financial services.[62]

There now are an increasing number of countries that depart from the EU's Sixth Directive, some of which either overtax consumers or reduce cascading by granting some input credits on acquisitions used in rendering exempt financial services. This section discusses several of those different approaches. First, Israel[63] and Argentina tax more than the value of intermediation services, overtaxing many of the financial services. Second, South Africa taxes all fee-based financial services and grants business users credits for tax paid on those explicit fees. Third, Singapore effectively zero rates some domestic financial services rendered to taxable (registered) persons. Fourth, New Zealand zero rates financial services rendered to certain registered persons, and grants a large percentage of input tax credits attributable to outsourced financial services rendered to financial institutions. Fifth, Australia has complex rules to reduce the cascading of VAT on exempt financial services rendered by financial institutions to registered persons. Finally, Italy's subnational IRAP is discussed. Under the IRAP (challenged in the EU as violative of Italy's obligations under the Sixth Directive), financial services are taxable under a subtraction method, income form of VAT.

2. Israel and Argentina

Israel uses a modified addition method VAT to tax financial services, including financial intermediation services rendered by banks and similar depository institutions.[64] "First, banks pay and cannot recover VAT on their purchases of supplies, computers, energy, and other inputs that are used to provide their lending services.[65] Second, Israel requires banks to pay [tax] computed by the addition method on the total of their wages and profit."[66] In this way, Israel collects VAT on the bank's business inputs and collects tax on the value added by the banks. Combined, Israel taxes intermediation services rendered to businesses and consumers, overtaxing business users that cannot claim credit for any VAT embedded in the implicit charges for financial intermediation services.

> The only justification for the Israeli approach is that Israel intends to tax not only intermediation services but consumer interest as well. Consumer interest cannot be taxed directly in any administratively satisfactory manner, but it

---

[62] See Schenk, Taxation of Financial Services, *supra* note 14, at 833 [footnotes omitted].

[63] Taiwan imposed similar taxation until it decided to try to become a financial center. Taiwan then joined the majority of countries with VATs in exempting financial intermediation services.

[64] In Israel, this tax on financial institutions and insurance companies is administered by the Income Tax Authority, whereas all other VAT is administered by the VAT Administration. See Gliksberg, "Israel's Value Added Tax Law," *VAT Monitor,* July 1992, p. 2.

[65] All countries that exempt financial services from the VAT deny banks input credits for VAT paid on their purchases used in the rendition of these services. Like Israel, these countries collect and keep VAT paid by banks on their taxable purchases.

[66] Schenk & Oldman, *supra* note 14, at 191.

arguably can be taxed indirectly, at least in part, by [overtaxing] business and expecting business to pass through the extra tax on sales to consumers.[67,68]

Imposed as a device to stifle consumer consumption in order to reduce inflationary pressures in the economy, Argentina taxes gross interest on loans at the regular 21 percent VAT rate or a reduced 16 percent or 18 percent rate on debit and credit card interest respectively. Interest on some business loans are taxed at a lower 10.5 percent, and the VAT on these loans to registered businesses is creditable. Argentina exempts some interest, including interest charged on home mortgage loans.[69]

3. South Africa

The South African VAT originally exempted financial services[70] but imposed VAT on services customarily taxed, such as safe deposit box rental and certain advisory services. Exports of financial services were zero rated.[71] South Africa then expanded the taxation of services rendered by financial institutions to cover most fee-based services.[72] Thus, currency exchange transactions, transactions involving cheques or letters of credit, transactions involving debt, equity, or participatory securities, and provisions of credit are not "financial services" and therefore are taxable "to the extent that the consideration payable in respect thereof is any fee, commission or similar charge, excluding discounting cost."[73] The South African approach was adopted by Namibia and Botswana.[74]

---

[67] Business may not be able to pass through this extra tax on its sales for export.

[68] Schenk & Oldman, *supra* note 14, at 191.

[69] See Schenk & Zee, Financial Services Under a VAT, *supra* note 14, at 3314. Argentina reduced the VAT on interest charged on debit and credit cards. The rate on purchases made with debit cards was reduced from 21 percent to 16 percent, and on credit cards from 21 percent to 18 percent, purportedly to boost consumption and increase the use of the banking system. See Resolution 203/2006 discussed in Haskel, "Argentina Extends VAT Rebate For Users of Debit, Credit Cards," BNA Daily Tax Report, April 4, 2006, p. G-3. The resolution is in Spanish at http://infoleg.mecon.gov.ar/infolegInternet/anexos/115000-119999/115060/norma.htm.

[70] Financial services are broadly defined to include long-term insurance (including life insurance), currency exchange transactions, transactions involving checks, letters of credit, debt and equity securities, and loans. *Id.* at sec. 2(1). Section 2 includes rules to prevent the use of entities or other devices that attempt to convert taxable transactions into exempt financial transactions. Thus, financial services do not include conversion of taxable transactions into transfers of rights to receive payment under a contract, or by transferring rights under a contract, both resembling financial transactions. Parties cannot avoid transfers of shares in a share block company (condominium apartments) by characterizing the transaction as an exempt sale of an equity security.

[71] Value-Added Tax Act No. 89 of 1991, effective September 30, 1991, sec. 12(a).

[72] The Canadian GST taxes an extensive list of fee-based financial services, but does not tax all such services. See Technical Information Bulletin B-060, *Listing of Taxable, Exempt and Zero-rated Products and Services of a Deposit-Taking Financial Institution* (August 1991).

[73] *Id.* at sec. 2(1) proviso. In contrast, the OECD countries exempt many if not most of the services rendered for explicit fees. See OECD Report on Financial Services, *supra* note 14, at 7–10 and subsequent explanations.

[74] Value-Added Tax: Banking Services Provided and Fees Which May be Charged in Connection With Such Services, as prepared by Banker Association of Namibia and approved

In South Africa, the banking industry and the tax authorities worked together to classify (as taxable, zero rated, or exempt) an extensive list of services rendered by banks. Banking services provided to nonresidents, any transactions involving the collection of foreign bills or relating to letters of credit on imports and exports, and foreign guarantees in favor of or on behalf of a nonresident are zero rated.[75]

Not intending to be exhaustive, the following list illustrates the expansiveness of the categories of fee-based services that have been taxable since October 1, 1996. They include most fee-based services on checking and savings accounts, on money transfers, on off-site or electronic banking, on credit and debit cards, on foreign exchange transactions rendered in RSA for residents, on mortgage loans, on rental agreements, on documentation and similar motor finance services, on brokerage and underwriting transactions, on registration of shares, on custody of securities, on investment advice, and on safety deposit boxes. As a result, "virtually all fee-based financial related services" are taxable[76] or zero rated. Exemption is limited to interest charges or discounts that serve as interest charges or interest penalties.

As the list of taxable banking services expanded, the banks operating in South Africa could claim credit for a larger percentage of input tax on purchases, and registered businesses using these fee-based services could claim credit for VAT charged on these services. For example, the South African Revenue Services (SARS) ruled that input VAT on ATM machines is fully creditable because the machines generate taxable fees. Should input VATs attributable to Internet Banking be creditable as well, in whole or in part?

The banking industry and the tax authorities also established a standardized method for the financial services industry to apportion input VAT between taxable and exempt supplies.[77] Under the apportionment formula, the percentage input tax recovery rate is $A/B \times 100/1$. In this formula, A is the total tax-exclusive value of standard and zero-rated supplies, and B is the total tax-exclusive value of all supplies. For purposes of this formula, some items previously the subject of disputes between the banks and

---

by the Ministry of Finance – Inland Revenue as Ruling 2/00 on 8 Nov. 2000, effective 27 Nov. 2000 (a similar document exists for the Botswana VAT); and Value-Added Tax: VAT Apportionment Method for Financial Services Industry, as prepared by Banker Association of Namibia and Approved by the Ministry of Finance – Inland Revenue as Ruling 3/00 on 8 Nov. 2000, effective 27 Nov. 2000.

[75] This information was gathered from the schedule listing the tax status of banking services prepared by the Council of South African Bankers and approved by the Commissioner for Inland Revenue. It is Value-Added Tax: Banking Services Provided and Fees Which May be Charged in Connection with Such Services, as prepared by COSAB and approved by the CIR on 15 Aug. 1996, effective October 1, 1996.

[76] See *Deloitte & Touche VAT Handbook*, ¶8.2.2 (Butterworths 2003).

[77] See Practice Note, "VAT Apportionment Method for Financial Services Industry" (2003).

the tax authorities are specifically included or specifically excluded from the numerator and/or denominator of the A/B fraction. For example, net interest,[78] gross profit or loss from dealing in financial assets, and insurance proceeds are included only in the denominator B;[79] defined gross rental receipts less interest payments, proceeds from the sale of repossessed goods, zero-rated supplies, and noninterest income are included in A and B. Specifically excluded from both A and B are the cash value of installment credit agreements, bad debts, the deemed value of fringe benefits supplied, dividends, imported services, and a few other items.

4. Singapore, New Zealand, and Australia

a. *Singapore's Zero Rating of Financial Services Rendered to Taxable Customers*

In order to reduce the cascading of VAT on financial services rendered to taxable businesses, the Singapore GST regulations include rules that effectively allow financial institutions to claim input credits for VAT attributable to certain exempt financial services.[80] For input VAT that is not directly attributable to taxable supplies or to exempt supplies, a financial service provider must allocate the input tax in proportion to the ratio of taxable supplies to total supplies.[81] The regulations authorize the Comptroller to approve a method of allocating input VAT that treats specified exempt financial services[82] supplied by a taxable person to another taxable person as taxable supplies.[83] As a result, otherwise exempt financial services rendered to taxable persons are effectively zero rated.

b. *New Zealand Zero Rates Some Financial Services Rendered by Financial Service Providers*

Effective January 1, 2005, New Zealand revised its treatment of financial intermediation services rendered to certain registered businesses and to other financial service providers.[84] The guidelines for the new elective

---

[78] For this purpose, interest receipts and interest paid excludes interest in respect of rental agreements.

[79] Any zero-rated portion of these items is included in A.

[80] For a claim that the generous input credit allocation rules reduce the administrative issues of the classification of currency exchange or forward contracts involving currency, see Vaughan, "Exchange of Currency," *VAT Monitor*, Sept./Oct. 2002, p. 363.

[81] Goods and Services Tax (General) Regulations, (Rg 1) Part V, Reg. 29(2)(d).

[82] *Id.* at Reg. 29(3), referring to exempt financial services under paragraph 1 of the Fourth Schedule to the GST.

[83] *Id.* at Reg. 33, subject to regulations 34 and 35.

[84] See NZ GST, *supra* note 1, at §§20(3)(h) & 20C, amended by (GST, Trans-Tasman Imputation and Miscellaneous Provisions) Act 2003. For a discussion of the government report leading up to these changes, see Pallot & White, "Improvements to the GST Treatment of Financial Services – The Proposed New Zealand Approach," *VAT Monitor*, Nov./Dec. 2002, p. 481.

zero-rating rules apply to businesses that supply financial services as part of their normal business activity.[85] The following explanation is taken from these guidelines.

If a financial service provider files the election, it may zero rate financial intermediation services (otherwise exempt from GST)[86] rendered to a registered customer, but only if the customer's level of taxable supplies is 75 percent or more of total supplies for the period.[87] Financial services rendered to unregistered persons remain exempt from VAT.

To obtain this treatment, the financial service provider must satisfy itself that the customer is registered and meets the 75 percent test. To satisfy itself that the customer meets the 75 percent threshold, the financial service provider must either rely on information that it has on the customer or can rely on the Australian and New Zealand Standard Industrial Classification (ANZSIC) codes.[88] Inland Revenue provides guidance on how to determine eligibility per transaction or per customer account.[89]

Although the financial service provider is obliged to satisfy these conditions on a transaction-by-transaction basis, the GST Act provides that an alternative method approved by Inland Revenue may be used to satisfy the conditions, if it "produces as fair and reasonable a result as identifying eligible customers on a transaction-by-transaction basis would."[90]

Under the New Zealand GST, if the principal purpose of a GST-registered person's acquisition of goods or services is to make taxable supplies, the input VAT on the acquisition is deductible in full.[91] For purposes of meeting

---

[85] See "GST guidelines for working with the new zero-rating rules," Inland Revenue Department, Oct. 2004 [hereinafter Guidelines to zero rate financial services].

[86] Zero-rating applies to paying or collecting interest, providing or brokering loans, issuing securities, providing credit, or exchanging currency. Zero-rating does not apply to "debt collection, equipment leasing, credit control, sales ledger and accounting services, investment guidance, fire and general insurance and the provision of advice."*Id.* at ¶7.

[87] If the customer is part of a group, the services are zero-rated if the group meets the 75 percent threshold, even if the customer does not meet the threshold by itself. *Id.* at introduction. In calculating the 75 percent threshold, financial services that are zero-rated under these rules are omitted. In addition, imported services taxable under the reverse charge rule are excluded as well. *Id.* at ¶31.

[88] Reliance on the codes satisfies the 75 percent threshold requirement. *Id.* at ¶¶40–51. The codes identify groupings of businesses that conduct similar economic activities. Some industry or business classifications (Tables A and B) are either denied zero-rating, or may be denied zero-rating unless there is proof that the 75 percent test is satisfied. See *id.* at ¶¶41 & 51. The list of codes is on the Statistics New Zealand Web site: http://www.stats.govt.nz/domino/external/web/carsweb.nsf/94772cd591085044c25-67e6007eec2c/5b3e1b99a0d86615cc256cec007e6b14?OpenDocument. *Id.* at ¶36.

[89] *Id.* at ¶¶37–39.

[90] *Id.* at ¶10.

[91] See NZ GST, *supra* note 1, at §20(3)(a) and (b). An adjustment in the allowable input tax deduction is required to the extent that the registrant makes nontaxable supplies. *Id.* at §21.

the principal purpose test, the zero-rated financial services are counted as taxable supplies.[92]

Financial services rendered by a financial service provider to other financial institutions are not zero rated because the customer will not meet the 75 percent test. As an alternative, an electing financial service provider can claim an input tax deduction attributable to financial services supplied to another financial service provider (direct supplier) who supplies financial services to businesses that would qualify for zero-rate treatment. The formula is provided in the guidelines.[93] The information necessary to calculate this deduction must be obtained from the direct supplier. This deduction is in addition to input tax otherwise deductible, "relates only to exempt supplies of financial services made to the direct supplier, and is limited to the extent that the direct supplier makes taxable supplies, including supplies of zero-rated financial services, to business customers that meet the 75 percent taxable supplies threshold."[94]

Although New Zealand's new system effectively eliminates GST on registered business-to-registered business transactions, it appears to leave untouched the undertaxation of intermediation services rendered to final consumers.

c. *Australia's Treatment of Financial Services*

Australia's GST exempts ("input taxed" in the GST terminology) transactions treated as financial supplies under the regulations.[95] The regulations designate supplies that are financial supplies (or incidental financial supplies treated as financial supplies) and those that are not financial supplies.[96]

---

[92] See Guidelines to zero rate financial services, *supra* note 85, at ¶¶56–58. Special rules are provided to calculate the input tax deduction recovery ratio for financial service providers. *Id.* at ¶¶59–77.

[93] The formula is a x b/c × d/e, where a is the amount of input VAT deductible and nondeductible under §20(3) of the Act (other than 20(3)(h), if all financial services were taxable supplies; b is the total value of exempt financial services made to the other financial service supplier (direct supplier) for the period; c is the total value of supplies for the period; d is the total value of taxable supplies by the direct supplier determined under §20D of the Act; and e is the total value of supplies made by the direct supplier for the period under §20D of the Act. *Id.* at ¶78.

[94] *Id.*

[95] A New Tax System (Goods and Services Tax) Act 1999 [hereinafter Australia GST], §40–5.

[96] A New Tax System (Goods and Services Tax) Regulations 1999 [hereinafter GST regulations], Reg. 40–5.09 to 40.5.13. Schedule 7 to the regulations provides extensive examples of financial supplies and Schedule 8 to the regulations provide extensive examples of supplies that are not financial supplies. There remain questions of the classification of some supplies as financial supplies or not financial supplies. For example, see the controversy over guarantees in Stacey, "Guarantees: Multiple Supplies, Different GST Treatments," *VAT Monitor*, Nov./Dec. 2004, p. 398. On the GST status of securitization transactions, see Joseph, "Securitization – The Position of SPVs under Australian GST," *VAT Monitor*, Mar./Apr. 2005, p. 109. Australia treats the acquisition of securities (debt or shares) as the making of a financial supply in order to deny credits for costs incurred in making the acquisition. See R. Krever, GST Legislation Plus 2005 [hereinafter Krever, Australian GST], annotation to GST regulation 40–5.09.

Some financial services rendered for a fee are taxable, whereas others (below AUD1,000) are treated as exempt financial supplies.[97]

A registered person who makes some exempt financial services is entitled to claim full input credits for tax on purchases related to the exempt supplies if the person does not exceed the "financial acquisitions threshold."[98] The ruling provides that the inputs attributable to exempt financial services are not treated as attributable to exempt financial services if the supplier does not exceed that threshold, so long as the inputs relate to the person carrying on its enterprise. The financial acquisition threshold is exceeded if the input credits related to the making of financial services exceed AUD50,000,[99] or 10 percent of the input tax credits otherwise available in the current (or anticipated for the following) year.[100] If the registered person exceeds the financial acquisition threshold, the person may be able to claim credits for inputs attributable to exempt financial services under the "reduced credit acquisitions" discussed below.

A financial institution has an incentive to self-supply services instead of outsourcing them. A financial service provider rendering exempt financial services generally would prefer to provide services in-house in order to avoid noncreditable GST on purchases of the same services from outside vendors. With self-supply, the financial service provider would avoid GST on the labor and profit component of the service supplied to itself. For example, assume that a financial service provider purchased supplies for AUD25,000 plus an assumed 10 percent tax of AUD 2,500, hired labor, and printed forms and stationery in-house for a total cost of AUD102,500. If the same printing services would cost AUD100,000 plus tax of AUD10,000 from an outside vendor, the financial service provider would save the extra AUD7,500 tax that the outside vendor would charge. Because any input tax paid to the outside vendor generally would not be deductible for GST purposes, there exists a bias in favor of bringing the printing function in-house.

To offset this bias against self-supply, the Australian GST grants the financial service provider with an input credit of 75 percent of the tax on "reduced credit acquisitions."[101] In the above example, if the financial service provider purchased its forms and stationery from the outside supplier, it could claim an input credit of AUD7,500 (75 percent of the AUD10,000 tax on the purchase). In the example, the credit exactly offsets any benefit the financial service provider would obtain from providing its printing needs in-house.[102]

---

[97] See GST regulations, *supra* note 96, at Reg. 40–5.09(4).

[98] Goods and Services Tax Ruling 2002/2, Goods and services tax: GST treatment of financial supplies and related supplies and acquisitions, ¶3.

[99] The regulations can provide for a different amount. *Id.* at ¶14.

[100] *Id.*, based on Australian GST, *supra* note 95, at §§189–5 and 189–10. If the threshold is exceeded in the current or future period, the right to full credit is denied.

[101] GST regulations, *supra* note 96 at Reg. 70–5.03. The regulations list acquisitions that are reduced credit acquisitions (Reg. 70–5.02). They include domestic purchases and certain offshore supplies (Reg. 70–5.02A)

[102] See the example in "The Application of Goods and Services Tax to Financial Services: Consultation Document," Honourable Peter Costello, M.P., Treasurer of the Commonwealth of Australia, Aug. 1999, Appendix A, p. 13.

5. Italy's Subtraction-Method IRAP Imposed at the Subnational Level

In 1997, Italy replaced a local income tax, a wealth tax, and social security taxes that financed national health with the *imposta regionale sulle attivit-producttive*, or IRAP. The IRAP is imposed at 4.25 percent (or a rate that may vary by one percentage point, as set by the regional authorities) on the net value of production in each Italian region. The compatability of IRAP with the Sixth Directive is discussed in Chapter 12. The focus here is on the calculation of the IRAP for the financial sector. The IRAP is a subtraction method, origin principle VAT.

The IRAP applies to the gross margin for the financial sector. It includes explicit fees and commissions, and interest charges. The financial institution reduces this tax base by interest paid, the cost of intermediate goods and services, and depreciation on capital goods. As a result, the IRAP is an income form of VAT.

IV. Proposals to Tax Financial Intermediation Services

A. Introduction

This section discusses various proposals to tax financial intermediation services under a VAT. The first two, in Canada and the United States, were included in a Canadian White Paper and in two VAT bills introduced in the U.S. Congress, respectively. The third is Satya Poddar and Morley English's proposal for a cash-flow approach (modified by a TCA method) that was under consideration by the EU and has been pilot-tested. The fourth is Howell Zee's modified reverse-charge approach to the taxation of financial intermediation services on a transaction-by-transaction basis.

B. Canadian Flirtation with Taxation of Intermediation Services

The Canadian White Paper on Sales Tax Reform[103] discussed a few forms for a possible national VAT. One ultimately became the Goods and Services Tax. The White Paper recommended that financial intermediation services be taxed with the value of the taxable service calculated under a subtraction method. The tax base for intermediation services would be the spread between specific financial receipts and the cost of funds.[104] A flaw in the White Paper approach was that no input credit was provided for business

---

[103] Tax Reform 1987: Sales Tax Reform 126–31 (June 18, 1987).

[104] *Id.* at 130. the receipts are interest on bank loans, dividends on stock, foreign exchange gains, and other income from financial products. The cost of funds include interest paid to depositors and others, and a return to the bank's shareholders. The return to investors "could be either in the form of a deduction for dividends paid or a prescribed allowance on equity." *Id.* For a discussion of the Canadian White Paper approach to the *taxation of financial services*, see Poddar and Greene's paper, Taxation of Financial Services, presented at the International Institute of Public Finance, 44th Cong., Istanbul, August 1988.

users of the intermediation services.[105] In the final government proposal for the GST, financial intermediation services were exempt.[106]

C. Proposals in the United States

An adaptation of a cash-flow approach to the taxation of financial services was included as part of a sales-subtraction VAT proposed but never seriously debated in the U.S. Congress.

> Senators Danforth and Boren's proposed [Business Activities Tax] BAT taxes "financial intermediation services" that include insurance, allows the financial intermediaries to deduct business purchases allocable to these taxable services, and treats purchases of these services as deductible purchases to the customers who use these services in connection with their taxable business activity.[107] The problem is that the BAT does not solve the most difficult problem. It does not include rules to explain how financial intermediaries should allocate the cost of implicit "financial intermediation services" rendered to businesses, so that they can deduct the cost if the services are used in connection with their taxable business activity.[108]

---

[105] Henderson suggests a mechanism to grant input credits to business users for the VAT component in purchased financial services. See *supra* note 14.

[106] "The Canadian government decided to exempt financial intermediation services for three basic reasons. First, the government claims that in practice it is extremely difficult to identify the price of intermediation services. Second, the government noted that there were technical problems translating the earlier White Paper proposal into an operational tax structure. Third, no country has successfully applied sales tax to financial intermediation services. See 1989 Federal Budget: Sales and Excise Tax Changes (Canada) April 27, 1989, *reproduced* in Can. Sales Tax Rep., Special Report No. 25, Extra Edition, at 47. The third point is questionable because Israel taxes intermediation services. The government statement may be implying that the Israeli approach is not successful because it does not provide credit for VAT paid by business on these services, but it does not so state. No doubt, the Canadian government had some concern about the effect of taxing financial services on the competitiveness of Canadian banks in the international marketplace, but this concern was not expressed as part of the official reasons for exempting financial intermediation services." Schenk & Oldman, *supra* note 14, at 191, note 36.

[107] See The Comprehensive Tax Restructuring and Simplification Act of 1994, 140 Cong. Rec. S6527 [hereinafter Danforth-Boren BAT], §§10034 and 10015(a)(2)(B), (d). The provisions that refer specifically to these financial and insurance services occupy more than 15 percent of the pages of the proposed BAT legislation. This figure demonstrates that "financial intermediation services" raise complex issues under a VAT.

[108] Taxable financial intermediation services, under the BAT, include a broad range of financial and insurance services: lending and insurance services, market-making and dealer services, and a catch-all category of services rendered as an intermediary if the receipts come from "streams of income or expense, discounts, or other financial flows...." (*Id.* at §10034(e)).

The BAT uses a "cash-flow" or "flow-of-funds" approach to tax financial intermediation services rendered by financial intermediaries and insurance companies. [This approach resembles the Poddar and English cash-flow approach that is designed to produce the same results as if a VAT were charged on the taxable intermediation services and the business users of these services received deductions for the tax-inclusive cost of such purchased taxable services. See Poddar & English, Taxation of Financial Services, *supra* note 1.] The BAT base generally is equal to the difference between taxable gross receipts and deductible business purchases (which it should now be clear to the reader

To assure business users of taxable financial intermediation services that they can identify and deduct the cost of these services as business purchases, the BAT requires intermediaries to allocate and report fees for these services to business customers[109] within 45 days after the end of the taxable period in which the services are rendered.[110] The statute requires persons rendering these services to allocate these fees on a reasonable and consistent basis, but it does not provide any guidance on how the calculation is to be made.[111,112]

An elaborate proposal to tax financial intermediation services under the subtraction method was included in another proposal for a United States VAT.[113]

D. The Poddar–English Proposal

One proposal to tax financial intermediation services under a European credit-invoice VAT is the flow-of-funds system advocated earlier, and refined in a 1997 article by Satya Poddar and Morley English. It is the "truncated cash-flow method with tax calculation account [TCA]...that is designed to operationalize the cash flow method."[114] A basic cash flow system taxes cash receipts and gives credits for cash outflows from intermediation services. The earlier proposal imposed tax on financial intermediation services under a pure cash-flow approach. Under that system:

> Cash inflows from financial transactions are treated as taxable sales (e.g., a bank would remit tax on a deposit), and cash outflows are treated as

are in turn merely the supplier's taxable gross receipts). [Danforth-Boren BAT, *supra* note 107, at '10034(a)(2)]. For financial intermediation services, the statute substitutes financial receipts for gross receipts and adjusted business purchases for business purchases. Financial receipts are broadly defined to include all receipts attributable to these intermediation services, other than contributions to capital. The definition of adjusted business purchases is more elaborate. In addition to business purchases, as defined for other business activity, an intermediary can deduct principal and interest payments attributable to the firm's business activity, the costs and payments made under financial instruments (except for its own equity interests), payments of claims and cash surrender value in connection with insurance or reinsurance activity, and payments for reinsurance. [*Id.* at §10034(c)].

[109] See *id.* at §10034(d)(2), granting the Treasury authority to waive the notice requirement with respect to customers that are not receiving these services in connection with taxable business activity.

[110] *Id.* at §10034(d).

[111] *Id.* at §10034(d)(1)(A)(i).

[112] Oldman & Schenk, "The Business Activities Tax: Have Senators Danforth & Boren Created a Better Value Added Tax?" 10 *Tax Notes Int'l.* 55, 69–70 (Jan. 2, 1995).

[113] USA Tax Act of 1995, S.722, 104th Cong., 1st Sess., 141 CONG. REC. S5664 (1995). The Business Tax portion of the USA Tax attempts to tax all financial intermediation services. Assuming no loss carryover or transition basis deduction, gross profit of a financial intermediation business (an entity engaged in financial intermediation services for unrelated persons) is financial receipts less financial expenses. This calculation is designed to serve as a proxy to calculate the implicit charges for intermediation services. See Chapter 14 for a reference to a slightly revised USA tax introduced in a subsequent Congress.

[114] See Poddar & English, Taxation of Financial Services, *supra* note 14, at 89. See also Barham, Poddar & Whalley, and Hoffman, Poddar & Whalley, *supra* note 14. According to Poddar, this TCA system was pilot tested at ten major financial institutions and found to be "conceptually robust."

purchases of taxable inputs (e.g., a bank could claim an input tax credit on a deposit withdrawn)....To zero rate financial services rendered to nonresidents, transactions with nonresidents are ignored....[A]ll input tax credits related to commercial activity are now claimable, not just those related to nonfinancial supplies....[T]he results are the same as they would be if the financial institution were able to identify the value-added in each transaction, charge tax on it, and provide the appropriate invoice to allow business customers to claim input tax credits.[115]

The pure cash-flow approach could not easily accommodate problems encountered at the time such a tax on these services was introduced or, after enactment, the tax rate applicable to the services was changed.[116]

The European Commission commissioned Ernst and Young to undertake a project involving the truncated Tax Calculation Account (TCA) System, a modified TCA system developed earlier by Poddar and English of Ernst and Young.[117] Ten pilot studies were conducted as part of the project. "Under the TCA system, the tax base for margin services would be computed over the term of the financial contract, whereas the tax base under the normal VAT system is the explicit price charged for the goods or services....[The] TCA allocates the total margin earned by the financial institution (being the difference between the interest rate charged on the loans and paid on the deposits) between the borrowers and depositors using the indexing rate as the benchmark. It is proposed that a short term inter-bank rate (either 1-month or 3-month rate) be used for the indexing rate."[118]

To understand this system, it is helpful to identify the financial flows in intermediation services rendered by banks. They include:

(1) the transfer of funds from depositors to borrowers,
(2) the pure interest charge for the depositor's agreement to defer consumption,
(3) the premium charged for the risk that the borrower will default on the loan, and
(4) the compensation to the bank to take deposits and make loans.[119]

Even if the margin in (4) can be calculated, it still is necessary to allocate the value of the services between the depositors and borrowers in order to notify the business users of the amount of their input credits attributable to the intermediation services that they purchase.

Poddar and English's approach does not tax the pure interest or the risk premium in (2) and (3), and it nets out the transfers of capital by the bank from depositors to borrowers.

---

[115] *Id*. at 92.

[116] *Id*. at 98–99.

[117] See http://europa.eu.int/comm/taxation_customs/publications/reports_studies/taxation/tca/TCA_system.htm.

[118] *Id*. at Executive Summary.

[119] See Poddar & English, Taxation of Financial Services, *supra* note 14, at 91–92.

Instead of taxing loan proceeds and giving credits for loan payments to borrowers, their truncated cash-flow method has the bank calculate and remit the net tax due on intermediation transactions. Although this modified system corrects for the problems under a pure cash-flow appoach, it imposes its own complicated compliance rules on financial institutions. The revised system includes a tax calculation account (TCA). "The TCA is a tax suspense account" that handles "cash inflows and outflows of a capital nature."[120] It "allows deferral of tax on cash inflows and of tax credits on cash outflows. However, these deferrals are subject to interest charges at the government borrowing rate."[121] "The TCAs in the books of a business borrower or a business depositor are the mirror images of the TCAs for a loan or a deposit in the books of the bank.... [T]he TCA system eliminates any cash-flow problems by deferring tax payments and credits on capital transfers."[122] There remain issues such as the indexing rate and the frequency of indexing adjustments that are not fully addressed in the Poddar and English proposal. The other details of this proposed system are beyond the scope of this book.

E. ZEE'S MODIFIED REVERSE-CHARGING APPROACH

Howell Zee proposed a "modified reverse-charging" approach to the taxation of financial intermediation services (deposit-taking and lending activities) under a VAT.[123] One obstacle in taxing these services is that many of the bank inputs (deposits) come from unregistered final consumers who cannot issue VAT invoices. As part of his analysis, Zee notes that the reverse charge mechanism:

> shifts the collection of the VAT on deposit interest from depositors to banks, in conjunction with the establishment of a franking mechanism managed by banks that effectively transfers the VAT so collected to borrowers as credits against the VAT on their loan interest on a transaction-to-transaction basis. The outcome ensures that the net VAT revenue to be remitted to the government by a bank is equal to the VAT rate on the bank's provision of intermediation services, while, at the same time, the VAT burden on such services is borne by final consumers either directly as bank borrowers or indirectly when they consume goods and services in which the intermediation services have been embedded.[124]

Zee acknowledges that a major issue in the development of a system to tax intermediation services is to provide a credit to business users on a

---

[120] *Id.* at 99.
[121] *Id.* The (1) "tax payments on cash inflows ... [are] debited to the TCA; (2) input tax credits on cash outflows ... [are] credited to the TCA; (3) net balance in the TCA [is] subject to an indexing adjustment ...; and (4) a balance in the TCA payable (or refundable ...) periodically, after subtracting a notional amount equal to the tax rate times the value of the financial instrument at the end of the period." *Id.*
[122] *Id.* at 100.
[123] Zee, Modified Reverse Charge Approach, *supra* note 5. Zee suggests that the same approach can be extended to cover brokerage services and other services rendered for implicit fees. *Id* at 82–83.
[124] *Id.* at 78.

transaction-by-transaction basis in order to integrate this system with the credit-invoice VATs used around the world. Under the proposed system, the bank will issue a VAT invoice to itself for its purchased inputs (from registered and unregistered depositors) and claim the same as an input credit against its output tax on interest collected from registered or unregistered borrowers. The business borrower can claim credit for VAT charged on the loan interest. Consistent with the destination principle, a reverse charge is applied to foreign deposits and interest charged to foreign borrowers are treated as zero-rated exports.

The problem with the above straight reverse-charge approach is that borrowers who are final consumers are overtaxed – they must bear VAT that exceeds the value of the intermediation services embedded in the loan. To correct this problem, Zee devised a system that uses the reverse charge on depositors indirectly (a franking mechanism) to reduce the VAT paid by borrowers on a transaction-by-transaction basis; thus, the name – the modified reverse-charging approach.[125] The complexity in this approach, is that the available credits are calculated after each deposit and loan in the franking account. Zee analogizes it to "a pooled account of depreciable assets under the declining-balance method" that must "maintain three running balances: (1) cumulated unlent deposits, (2) cumulated unclaimed reverse charges on the unlent deposits, and (3) unclaimed reverse charge per unit of unlent deposit. These balances are updated after each deposit or lending transaction, with the former giving rise to a credit entry and the latter to a debit entry."[126] The bank must issue a VAT invoice for the net VAT payable by the borrower.

In actual practice, deposits and loans are not closed out precisely at the end of each tax period. It therefore is necessary to treat all outstanding deposits as withdrawn and loans as fully paid at the end of each period, and then redeposited and relent at the beginning of the next period at the same interest rates.[127] The audit for the tax authorities may be challenging, but computerized data bases and other newer techniques may make such a system verifiable.

The described "modified reverse-charging approach" assumes that the intermediation services are consumed by borrowers and not depositors. Zee suggests that this approach can be extended to treat both depositors and borrowers as consuming a portion of the intermediation services rendered by the banks. It appears that the calculation of the value of the service rendered to depositors would be based on a presumed percentage. The VAT charged on deposits would be reported to depositors on their account statements and business depositors could claim this VAT as an input credit. The "net VAT paid by borrowers would be reduced by exactly the amount of the VAT paid by depositors."[128] Will a bank have an incentive to set the percentage

---

[125] *Id.* at 86.
[126] *Id.*
[127] *Id.* at 88.
[128] *Id.*

in order to maximize the input VAT attributable to customers that can claim input credits?[129]

Zee compared the modified reverse-charge approach with the Poddar-English cash-flow approach. According to Zee, because the cash-flow approach includes the principal amounts of loans in the tax base, there will be cash-flow problems for borrowers and practical problems if the VAT rate changes over the life of individual loans and deposits,[130] but he acknowledges that the use of suspense accounts, the TCA accounts, maintained by the banks will track deposit and loan transactions by customer. On balance, Zee suggests that the TCA device "is unnecessarily complex, because the tracking . . . of inflows and outflows of the principal amounts of deposits and loans is superfluous for taxing financial intermediation services under an invoice-credit VAT. . . ."[131] His position is that the "modified reverse-charging approach removes an entire layer of administrative complexity [ignoring principal amounts] associated with the cash-flow approach that represents no value-added to resolving the problems entailed by the exemption approach."[132]

V. DISCUSSION QUESTIONS

1. Assume that Consumer borrows $1,000 from a friend to pay a Master Card bill that was entirely for personal consumption items, namely, a new stereo music setup. In the current year, Consumer pays $100 interest on this loan. Should the interest collected by the friend be subject to VAT? If a Corporation raises funds for its operations by issuing bonds for $1,000,000 and pays $80,000 interest to holders of the bonds, should the interest received by the bond holders be subject to VAT?

2. Consumer purchases a car for $13,000, paying a $3,000 cash down payment and financing the other $10,000. In the first year, in addition to the down payment, Consumer pays $1,000 principal and $1,200 interest on the car loan. If the goal is to tax value added in a manner that promotes administrative simplicity, how should the car sale and loan be treated? If for political reasons, it is necessary to permit the sale to be reported as installment payments are received, how should the car sale and loan be treated?

3. Bank lends Consumer $1,000 and Business $10,000 from funds received from depositors. Bank collects $150 interest from Consumer and $1,000 interest from Business. Bank pays depositors $770 interest on deposits of $11,000. If the VAT is imposed on the value of financial intermediation

---

[129] The percentage merely determines the allocation of the VAT burden between depositors and borrowers. According to Zee, the allocation does not provide any inherent benefit to the banks, so setting the percentage could be left to the banks. *Id.* at 89.

[130] *Id.* at 90.

[131] *Id.* at 91.

[132] *Id.*

services rendered by Bank, what should Bank's VAT base be and how should it be calculated?

4. If the VAT is imposed on the value of financial intermediation services, should the purchaser of those services receive an input credit for the VAT? If so, how should this credit be calculated?

5. Assuming that credit is granted for business purchases of financial services, should credit also be provided for those consumer-investors who obtain financial services to finance the acquisition of paintings, corporate stock, and gold bullion? Consider discussion in this chapter at subsection III(H)(3).

6. Underwriter charges Corporation $100,000 for its services in marketing $1,000,000 of Corporation's bonds (or alternatively 1,000 shares of Corporation's stock). Should the underwriting fee be subject to VAT? Any special problems? How would you handle "bought deals" and "swaps" where underwriting costs are built into the transaction price?

7. Are there tax policy or economic reasons to exempt from VAT the value of financial intermediation services?

   a. If these services are exempt, how should the exemption be provided? How should financial institutions calculate their VAT liability?

   b. If financial services are exempt from VAT, financial institutions have an incentive to provide internally some services previously purchased from outside vendors. For example, suppose that before VAT is enacted, Bank purchased cleaning services from a maintenance firm for $100,000. With the adoption of VAT, the maintenance firm would add $5,000 VAT (assuming a 5 percent VAT) to the Bank's bill. Bank cannot claim credit for the $5,000 VAT. How can the VAT statute prevent this incentive toward vertical integration? What purchases should be covered by this rule?

8. If financial services are exempt from VAT, how should the statute treat financial services used in connection with zero-rated exports of goods? (This question raises the problem of exempting items that relate to zero-rated exports. It is difficult to zero rate financial services attributable to export sales under a regime that exempts financial services if the exporter cannot identify the VAT component in the exempt services.)

9. Bank takes deposits and makes loans. In addition, it provides checking accounts, safe deposit boxes, and estate and financial planning services to its customers. Assuming that financial intermediation services are exempt from VAT, how should the statute treat the provision of Bank's other financial services? If the value of checking account services is taxable, how should the value be calculated?

10. Should the existence of a competitive international market for financial intermediation services affect the decision to tax or exempt these services?

11

Insurance

I. Introduction

An insurance company is a financial intermediary whose main line of business is the sale of a particular type of contingent contract, called an insurance policy. Under this contract, [in return for the premium], the insurer promises to pay some amount to the policy-holder, or to some other beneficiary, following the occurrence of an insured event.[1]

For VAT purposes, most countries lump together insurance and financial services rendered by financial institutions. The typical pattern is to include insurance within the definition of exempt financial services. There are some exceptions.

Israel taxes insurance companies under a system administered by the income tax department.[2] The Israeli tax is calculated under an addition method that includes wages and profits but does not allow any deduction for VAT paid on business inputs.[3] New Zealand taxes insurance other than life insurance under its Goods and Services Tax (GST). South Africa and some other southern African countries follow the New Zealand pattern of taxing property and casualty insurance on the margin between premiums received and claims paid.[4] Australia also is taxing property and casualty insurance under its new GST but departs from the New Zealand approach with respect to input credits available to insurers on claims paid.[5]

---

[1] Bradford & Logue, ch. 2, *The Effects of Tax Law Changes on Property-Casualty Insurance Prices*, p. 29, in D. Bradford, Ed., the Economics of Property-Casualty Insurance.

[2] See Chapter 10 for coverage of the Israeli approach to taxing banks and insurance companies.

[3] Schenk, "Taxation of Financial Services Under a Value Added Tax: A Critique of the Treatment Abroad and the Proposals in the United States," 9 *Tax Notes Intl.* 823 (1994) [hereinafter Schenk, Taxation of Financial Services].

[4] See, for example, Value-Added Tax Act No. 89 of 1991, §§1 definition of insurance, 2, 8(8), and 16(3)(c) (Republic of South Africa).

[5] A New Tax System (Goods and Services Tax) Act 1999 [hereinafter Australian GST], §78 (Australia).

The following is a nonexclusive list of insurance-related transactions that may be taxed, zero rated, or granted exemption from tax.

A. INTERNATIONAL INSURANCE SERVICES

1. offshore insurance and reinsurance
2. insure foreign risks and foreign people

B. DOMESTIC INSURANCE SERVICES

1. insurance purchased as a separate policy from an insurance company
   a. whole life or term insurance
   b. risk or hazard (property-casualty) insurance – home, auto, personal injury, tour or travel cancellation, etc.
   c. health and accident – treatment linked to treatment of medical care
2. reinsurance
3. services of agents, brokers, and claim adjusters
4. insurance protection that is not provided directly by an insurance company
   a. credit card company protects purchases made with credit card against breakage for a period of time
   b. automobile, equipment, or other rental company that charges separately for insurance or includes protection against damage in rental fee
   c. insurance provided as part of a tour or travel package
5. warranties provided through an insurance policy

A premium for property, casualty, or similar insurance coverage includes various elements. Part of the premium represents the fee for intermediation services rendered by the insurance company, including attracting customers, writing policies, investing the pooled funds to earn additional income to operate the business and pay claims, and finally, paying claims to the insured suffering covered losses. If the excess of the premium over the value of the intermediation services represents "protection against the loss, damage to, or destruction of the insured property, then, like the value of a warranty included in the price of a product, this component of the premium should be included in the VAT base."[6,7]

In setting the premiums, the insurance provider considers the present value of the expected claims. For competitive reasons, it is likely that the insurance company will reduce its premiums by a portion of the investment income earned on the pooled funds (or more accurately the net of investment

---

[6] This portion of the premium may represent the present value of the right to acquire replacement property in the future or may represent the purchase of a service in the nature of a product warranty. As an example of the latter, assume a consumer purchased a one-year warranty for a television. The cost of the warranty represents consumption taxable in the period in which the warranty is purchased. When warranty work is performed in the future, the consumer will not be charged VAT on the value of that service. To be consistent, the company performing the warranty service should be entitled to claim input credit for purchases attributable to the warranty service.

[7] Schenk, Taxation of Financial Services, *supra* note 3, at 832.

income over investment expenses). To tax the value of intermediation services rendered by property or casualty insurance companies fully, the VAT base should include the net investment income. The value added tax base of a property or casualty insurance company therefore should be:

Gross premiums

+ net investment income

− claims paid

No country includes net investment income as part of the taxation of nonlife insurance.

"Permanent life insurance contains additional elements. Permanent life premiums include '(1) a transfer element for claims paid to insured persons who die that year; (2) a savings element for additions to the insured's savings; and (3) a service element for administration and risk-taking by the insurance company.'[8] Only the third element represents the intermediation service provided by the insurance company that should be included in the VAT base."[9] To date, with the exception of Israel, no country taxes the intermediation services rendered by firms providing life insurance.

This chapter discusses the VAT consequences of insurance coverage (other than life insurance), starting with the exemption provided almost universally in the European Union and elsewhere. Subsequent sections of this chapter discuss ways in which nonlife insurance coverage can be taxed, with the primary focus on the New Zealand approach that is being copied in other countries. The Australian system and a U.S. proposal are considered. First, the next section discusses the possible inclusion of net investment income in the tax base.

II. BROAD-BASED TAX ON CASUALTY INSURANCE

As discussed earlier, to tax intermediation services rendered by insurance companies fully, the tax base should include net investment income earned by the firms. This section explores this broader tax base.

The following pro forma profit statement prepared for VAT purposes (not for income tax purposes and not in accordance with generally accepted accounting principles) shows income and expenses, including the VAT, of a casualty insurance company. Figures taken from this statement can be used to prepare the VAT return. Net investment income is treated as part of the receipts subject to VAT. The amounts in this statement (other than the tax itself) are shown exclusive of VAT. The tax rate is 10 percent, applied to a tax-exclusive base.

The difficult problems relating to the inclusion of net investment income in the VAT base are to determine the amount of VAT to be included in the insurance premiums and the claims paid, and to decide what income and

---

[8] Neubig & Adrion, "Value Added Taxes and Other Consumption Taxes: Issues for Insurance Companies," 61 *Tax Notes* 1001, 1006.

[9] Schenk, Taxation of Financial Services, *supra* note 3, at 832.

expense items should be included in calculating net investment income for VAT purposes. They are not addressed here.

The tax liability for the period is calculated under a credit-invoice VAT as the difference between the tax imposed on both the premiums charged and the net investment income, and the input credit attributable to the claims paid and the VAT on other business inputs used in making taxable sales of insurance services. Note that the claims paid to the insured are assumed to include the VAT. Therefore, to calculate the credit, this grossed-up VAT is multiplied by 10/110.

III. Exemption for Insurance Other than Life Insurance

The European Union established the standard practice of including insurance within the definition of exempt financial services. The Sixth Directive, in Article 13B(a), provides that member states must exempt "insurance and reinsurance transactions, including related services performed by insurance brokers and insurance agents."[10]

The practice in many countries that exempt insurance is to impose a separate insurance premium tax (IPT). In the United Kingdom, an IPT was imposed at a rate much lower than the VAT. To take advantage of this rate differential, suppliers of major household appliances set up their own insurance companies to structure service contracts on the appliances as insurance contracts. In response, the United Kingdom raised the IPT to the VAT rate, but only on premiums for insurance coverage on domestic appliances, motor cars, and certain travel. In a challenge by affected insurance and other companies offering these service contracts, claiming that the IPT is another turnover tax contrary to the Sixth Directive and claiming that the IPT nullifies the exemption for insurance provided in the Sixth Directive, the ECJ ruled that the higher rate was compatible with the Sixth Directive. The higher rate, according to the court, was not intended to confer a benefit on insurance coverage taxed at the lower rate.[11]

The following case involves the United Kingdom's attempt to limit the exemption for insurance to firms authorized to conduct the insurance business. In *Card Protection Plan Ltd (CPP) v. Commissioner of Customs & Excise*,[12] the taxpayer provided loss and theft coverage for credit cards, car keys, passports, and insurance documents. To cover its potential liability under its contracts with its customers, CPP purchased, through an insurance broker, block cover from an insurance company. The block cover policy lists CPP's customers as the insured parties. In addition to the insurance coverage, CPP provides its customers with other services, including the maintenance of a

---

[10] COM (2004) 246 Final, 2004/0079 (CNS), Council Directive on the common system of value added tax (Recast), Presidency compromise FISC 60 (21 April 2006) Art. 132(1)(a) contains identical language.

[11] *GIL Insurance Ltd and Others v. Commissioner of Customs & Excise*, Case C-308/01, [2004] ECR I-04777.

[12] Case C-349/96, [1999] ECR I- 973; 1999 ECJ CELEX LEXIS 2179.

list of each customer's credit cards, a twenty-four-hour telephone line to report losses, and assistance in replacing credit cards. Under the U.K. VAT, exemption for insurance services is limited to insurance provided by firms permitted to conduct an insurance business under U.K. law.[13] The European Court of Justice (ECJ) held that CPP, although not an insurance company, performed an insurance transaction entitled to exemption under Article 13B(a) of the Sixth Directive. A member state, according to the court, cannot restrict the exemption to insurers authorized by national law to conduct the insurance business. According to the court, it is for the national court to determine if the exempt insurance supply and taxable card registration services were two independent supplies (so one was exempt and the other was taxable) or a single supply, with the VAT treatment linked to the consequences of the principal service rendered.

Cases in the EU clarified some of the rules on allowable input credits for tax on purchases by firms providing exempt insurance services. Chapter 10 discusses attempts by data processing firms and others to claim that their services provided to banks come within the exemption for financial services. The cases typically involve services that some banks provide in house. The exemption benefits not only the data processing firm but the bank as well because the bank wants to reduce its noncreditable input VAT on purchases used in making their exempt financial services. The same incentive exists for firms supplying services to insurance companies that insurance companies sometimes provide in house. The following cases are illustrative.

In *Staatssecretaris van Financiën v Arthur Andersen & Co. Accountants*,[14] an insurance company outsourced some back office services to the accounting firm, and the service provider was claiming that the services were exempt insurance services. The ECJ held that back office services rendered to an insurance company were not exempt services carried out by an insurance broker or insurance agency within the Sixth Directive, Article 13B(a).

The VAT consequences of outsourced services also was the issue in *Assurandor-Societet, acting on behalf of Taksatorringen v. Skatteministeriet*.[15] In that case, the taxpayer was a member association of small or medium-sized insurance companies. The taxpayer assesses damage to motor vehicles on behalf of its members. The taxpayer's services are allocated to members exactly in proportion to the member's share of joint expenses. The ECJ ruled that the services rendered by the taxpayer on behalf of its members are not exempt under the Sixth Directive, Article 13B(a) as insurance transactions or services related to those transactions by insurance brokers or insurance agents.[16]

---

[13] This case involved section 17 and Sch. 6, Group 2 of the Value Added Tax Act 1983, limiting exemption to insurance provided by permitted to carry on insurance business under the Insurance Companies Act 1982.

[14] Case C-472/03, [2005] ECR I-1719 (ECJ Judgment 2005).

[15] Case C-8/01, [2003] ECR I-13711 (ECJ Judgment 2005).

[16] Art. 13A(1)(f) exempts services otherwise meeting the VAT exemption (for insurance) if provided for members, "provided that such exemption is not likely to produce distortion of competition...." The ECJ ruled that the exemption "must be refused if there is a

The following cases involve the scope of the exemption for insurance in the EU and Canada. The Portuguese Administrative Supreme Court liberally construed the Article 13B(a) exemption for insurance services to cover sales by an insurance company of unfixable motor vehicles obtained by the company from an insured after it compensates the insured for the covered loss.[17]

The Canadian GST exempts financial services, including insurance.[18] In *The Maritime Life Assurance Company v. HM The Queen*,[19] the taxpayer sold a variety of insurance products, including annuity contracts to provide retirement income. The contracts in issue require the taxpayer to invest the premiums in segregated funds, with the proceeds on maturity to be used to provide the annuity payments. Some of the policies provide additional insurance features, including guaranteed minimum value on maturity, and guaranteed payment if the insured dies before maturity. The court found that the financial service features of the supply constituted more than 50 percent of the consideration for all of the services provided under the contracts; thus, the supply is an exempt financial service.

The Canadian GST specifically exempts "the service of investigating and recommending the compensation in satisfaction of a claim under an insurance policy," whether provided by the insurer or another person.[20] In *Mitchell Verification Services Group Inc. v HM The Queen*,[21] the court, in narrowly construing the exemption, held that the service of investigating insurance claims and advising the insurance company (a) that it should conduct further investigation, (b) that the claim submitted was excessive, or (c) that the claimant was malingering did not constitute the exempt service of investigating and recommending amounts for the settlement of claims.

IV. New Zealand Taxation of Insurance

New Zealand developed its statutory scheme to tax insurance in consultation with accountants and the insurance industry. It does not attempt to include net investment income in the tax base. The New Zealand pattern is used in countries that tax nonlife insurance except Australia and Israel.

Except for the fact that New Zealand does not include net investment income in the tax base, the New Zealand approach is consistent with the ideal discussed earlier in this chapter. New Zealand taxes the gross premiums

---

genuine risk that the exemption may by itself, immediately or in the future, give rise to distortions of competition. *Id.* at ¶76. It did not matter to the court that large insurance companies provided the same services in-house.

[17] See Núncio, "Portugal: Exemption of insurance services," *VAT Monitor*, July/Aug. 2003, p. 356.

[18] Part IX of the Excise Tax Act, S.C. 1990, c. 45, as amended [hereinafter Canadian GST], Sch. V, Part VII.

[19] 1999 Can. Tax Ct. LEXIS 23.

[20] Canadian GST, *supra* note 18, at paragraph (j) of section 123(1) definition.

[21] Can. Tax Ct. LEXIS 2275.

charged on the covered nonlife policies. It also and zero rates "exports" of insurance if the risk is located outside the country. New Zealand exempts life insurance[22] and creditor protection policies.[23]

Insurance providers can claim input credits for two categories of payments – input VAT on purchases attributable to taxable insurance and the "grossed-up" portion of claims paid.

The tax consequences to an insured under a taxable insurance policy are linked to the status of the insured as a GST-registered or unregistered person. An unregistered person must bear GST charged on a taxable premium and does not have any GST consequences on receipt of an indemnity payment for a covered loss. The indemnity payment by the insurer is grossed-up to include GST, so that the insured has the funds to pay the GST-inclusive cost to replace the lost property or repair the damaged property.

If the insured is GST-registered and the coverage pertains to the insured's taxable activity, the tax on the premium is creditable. When the registered insured sustains a covered loss and receives an indemnity payment, the insured must report the GST component in the claim received as output tax "to the extent that it relates to a loss incurred in the course or furtherance of the registered person's taxable activity."[24] Combining the input credit to the insurer with the output tax reportable by the registered insured, the government does not receive any net GST revenue on a claim paid to GST-registered business that is attributable to the insured's taxable activity.

As noted earlier, New Zealand taxes gross premiums received and grosses-up claims paid. Each insured covered under a taxable premium that cannot claim credit for the input tax bears GST on the gross premium, and not just on the value of the intermediation services rendered by the insurer. This treatment can be justified as follows.

> If the spread between the gross premium and the value of intermediation services rendered by the insurance company is viewed as a form of consumption similar to a warranty agreement, then New Zealand's taxation of this spread when the insurance invoice is issued is appropriate.
> If the taxation of the gross premium represents taxation of intermediation services and taxation of the present value of replacement property, then the tax regime still works even if the tax rate changes between the time that the premium is invoiced and the claims are paid.[25]

The New Zealand approach to the taxation of insurance departs from the basic invoice VAT principle that input tax credits are available only if

---

[22] Exempted life insurance includes insurance covering "the contingency of the termination or continuation of human life, or marriage, or the birth of a child." New Zealand Goods and Services Tax Act 1985, No. 141 [hereinafter NZ GST], section 3(2) definition of "life insurance contract."

[23] *Id.* at section 3(1).

[24] *Id.* at §5(13), as amended in 2000.

[25] Schenk, Taxation of Financial Services, *supra* note 3, at 834–836. Some footnotes omitted.

Table 11.1. Ideal Casualty Insurance Co. Pro Forma Profit
Statement for VAT Purposes for the Year Ending December 31,
2005

INCOME	
Insur. premiums (VAT-exclusive)	$10,900,000[26]
Investment income	400,000
	$11,300,000
EXPENSES	
Wages	250,000
Investment expenses	200,000
Claims paid (VAT-exclusive)	10,200,000
Business purchases, incl. capital goods (VAT-exclusive)	400,000
Net VAT liability	___[27]
Total expenses	11,050,000
PROFIT FOR VAT PURPOSES	250,000

supported by a tax invoice from a registered supplier.[28] An insurance company subject to GST on its casualty or other taxable insurance premiums can claim input credit for the VAT element in its claims paid (grossed-up to include GST), whether the claims are paid to registered businesses or to consumers. The credit is available only if the premium was taxable at a positive rate.

Table 11.3 is a pro forma income statement for New Zealand GST purposes, assuming that net investment income is not included in the GST base. In order to compare the two approaches, the following discussion, as in Tables 11.1 and 11.2, assumes that the GST rate is 10 percent, not New Zealand's actual rate of 12.5 percent. The pro forma profit statements of Tables 11.1 and 11.3 are identical.

Applying the New Zealand GST formula, the casualty company's $30,000 tax liability is calculated in Table 11.4. The $20,000 tax difference between the broad base in Table 11.2 and the N.Z. base in Table 11.4 represents 10 percent tax on the $200,000 net investment income that is included in the broad tax base.

In this illustration, it is assumed that the casualty company reduces the premiums it charges its customers by the net investment income. In practice, this may or may not occur. The company has added value of at least $500,000 (wages and profits), but part of it is not taxed because net investment income

---

[26] The premiums are priced to include $10,200,000 anticipated VAT-exclusive claims, $400,000 in VAT-exclusive cost of business inputs, $500,000 in value added by the business (wages and profits), less $200,000 in net investment income.

[27] The net VAT liability of $50,000, as calculated in Table 11.2, is not included in the data reported exclusive of VAT.

[28] This principle also is violated in a few other situations, such as where a VAT statute authorizes a dealer in used goods to claim a credit for a presumed VAT component in the purchase price of used goods acquired from a consumer.

Table 11.2. VAT Return Ideal Casualty Insurance Co. for the Year 2005

OUTPUT TAX	
Taxable premiums $10,900,000 × 10% Net	$1,090,000
investment income $200,000 × 10%	20,000
	$1,110,000
INPUT TAX CREDITS	
Claims paid (tax-incl.) 11,220,000 × 10/110	(1,020,000)[29]
Taxable bus. purchases $400,000 × 10%	(40,000)
Total input credits	1,060,000
Net VAT Liability	50,000

is not included in the tax base. The government receives less revenue from the insurance company, equal to the tax on the net investment income.

In the following two subsections, the elements of the New Zealand approach are explained in more detail.

A. APPLICATION OF THE N.Z. TAXATION OF CASUALTY INSURANCE TO POLICYHOLDERS IN BUSINESS

We can disaggregate the casualty insurance company's total figures and look at the GST consequences to a group of customers who buy casualty insurance and to one customer who sustains a covered loss. Assume that ten businesses subject to GST purchased casualty policies for total GST-exclusive premiums of $10,900 and one of them (paying a premium of $1,090) suffered a loss of $11,220 (inclusive of GST).[30] Under the GST, the tax consequences to the business purchasers of the casualty insurance policies and the one firm sustaining the covered loss are as follows:

To the casualty insurance company selling the policies:
Output Tax
Premiums 10,900 × 10% = $1,090

To the business policyholders purchasing the policies:
Input Tax Credit
Insurance premiums
$10,900 × 10% GST rate = ($1,090)

The government does not receive any net revenue as a result of the sale of policies to these ten businesses subject to GST – the output tax remitted by the casualty company is offset by the input credit claimed by the policyholders.

---

[29] If an insurance company can claim an input credit for the VAT component in the claims paid, it is expected that the insurance company will gross-up the claims paid.

[30] Assume that the claim is for $10,200 and, when it is grossed-up to include $1,020 of GST, the claim paid is $11,220.

Table 11.3. New Zealand Casualty Insurance Co. Pro
Forma Profit Statement for GST Purposes for the Year
Ending December 31, 2005

INCOME	
Insur. premiums (GST-excl.)	$10,900,00
Investment income	400,000
	$11,300,000
EXPENSES	
Wages	250,000
Investment expenses	200,000
Claims paid (GST-excl)	10,200,000
Business purchases, incl. capital goods (GST-excl)	400,000[31]
Net VAT liability	——[32]
Total expenses	11,050,000
Profit for GST Purposes	250,000

When the insurance company pays the covered claim, the GST consequences to the insurance company and the one loss-suffering policyholder
are as follows:

To the insurance company paying the claim:
Input Tax Credit
Claim paid
$11,220 × 10/110 = ($1,020)[33]

To the policyholder receiving the claim:
Output Tax
Claim received
$11,220 × 10/110 = $1,020[34]

Again, the government does not receive any net GST revenue because the
input credit claimed by the insurance company is offset by the output tax
reported by the policyholder.

When the policyholder replaces the destroyed property for $10,200, he
will pay GST to the seller of this property, with the following consequences:

To the seller of the replacement property:
Output Tax
Taxable sale $10,200 × 10% = $1,020

[31] The $40,000 GST paid on these business inputs is creditable against GST liability on
premiums. It therefore is not included in this statement.

[32] The GST liability is not included in this data that is GST-exclusive. The net GST liability
is $30,000, as calculated in Table 11.4.

[33] The insurance company will include the GST payable on the purchase of the replacement
property because the N.Z. GST allows the insurance company an input credit for the GST
component in that claim paid.

[34] The GST component in the claim received is reportable as output tax, the same as the
GST component in any taxable receipt from sales by the policyholder.

Table 11.4. GST Return New Zealand Casualty Co. for the Year 2005

OUTPUT TAX	
Taxable premiums	
$10,900,000 × 10%	$ 1,090,000
INPUT TAX CREDITS	
Claims paid (tax-incl.)	
11,220,000 × 10/110	(1,020,000)
Taxable bus. purchases	
$400,000 × 10%	(40,000)
Total input credits	1,060,000
NET GST LIABILITY	30,000

To the policyholder buying the replacement property:
Input Tax Credit
Taxable purchase
$10,200 × 10% = ($1,020)

In this final transaction, the government does not receive any net GST revenue. This is the correct result because in transactions between taxable businesses making only taxable sales, the government should not receive any GST revenue. Net revenue should be collected only on sales to final consumers, to exempt small businesses, or to businesses making sales exempt from tax.

B. APPLICATION OF THE N.Z. TAXATION OF CASUALTY INSURANCE TO POLICYHOLDERS WHO ARE CONSUMERS

If we change this example and assume that all ten policyholders are consumers[35] and that one of these consumers suffers the same covered loss assumed in that example, the N.Z. GST implications are as follows.

To the casualty insurance company selling the policies:
Output Tax
Premiums $10,900 × 10% = $1,090

To the ten consumers who purchase the policies:
Insurance premiums
$10,900 × 10% GST rate = $1,090– No GST refunds

The government receives $1,090 GST revenue on the gross premiums as a result of the sale of policies to these ten final consumers – the output tax remitted by the casualty company is not recoverable by the consumers.

When the insurance company pays the covered claim, the government should be returning some of the GST the insurer charged on the gross premiums, so that GST is collected only on the services rendered by the insurer

---

[35] The same treatment applies to insured persons who are exempt small businesses or firms making sales exempt from GST.

measured by gross premiums less claims paid. The GST consequences to the insurance company and the policyholder are as follows:

To the insurance company paying the claim:
Input Tax Credit
Claim paid
$11,220 \times 10/110 = (\$1,020)$[36]

To the policyholder receiving the claim:
Claim received
$11,220, including \$1,020 GST[37]

The government, at this point, returns some GST to the insured via the input credit provided to the insurer. The insurance company reimburses the insured for the GST that she will pay if she replaces the property for $10,200. The government has collected net revenue[38] roughly equal to the taxed services rendered by the casualty insurance company to the policyholders.

When the policyholder replaces the destroyed property for $10,200, she will pay GST to the seller of this property, with the following consequences:

To the seller of the replacement property:
Output Tax
Taxable sale $10,200 \times 10\% = \$1,020$

To the policyholder buying the replacement property:
Taxable purchase
$10,200 \times 10\% = \$1,020$

In this final transaction, the government receives $1,020 GST revenue on the sale of the replacement property to the consumer, like any taxable sale to a final consumer.

C. Are Warranties "Insurance" in New Zealand?

In the introduction to this chapter, there is a comparison between a warranty and the portion of an insurance premium that exceeds the value of the intermediation services rendered by the insurance company. The warranty analogy is used as justification for the inclusion of this excess in a VAT base. If a warranty is included in a VAT base, so should this excess.

---

[36] The insurance company will include the GST payable on the purchase of the replacement property because the N.Z. GST allows the insurance company an input credit for the GST component in that claim paid, even when paid to a final consumer.

[37] The GST component in the claim received is not taxable to the consumer.

[38] These figures ignore the fact that the government received the revenue when the policies were sold and the government returns part of this revenue when the insurance company claims credits attributable to the claims paid.

In *Suzuki New Zealand Ltd v. CIR*,[39] the foreign parent that manufactured vehicles gave warranties on the vehicles. The New Zealand distributor (the taxpayer) made the repairs covered by the warranties and was paid by the foreign manufacturer. The court held that the warranty payments made by the foreign parent to the taxpayer were taxable. The GST was amended to reverse that decision and zero rate such warranty payments made by a non-registered foreign warrantor.[40]

V. Australia's Taxation of Insurance[41]

In broad outline, both the New Zealand GST and the Australian GST tax premiums and provide, to some extent, input credits on claims paid. Nevertheless, the details and the tax base for taxable insurance in these two countries diverge significantly with respect to claims paid. The Australian GST taxes the premiums charged for general insurance (property and casualty) but not life insurance.[42] "Exports" of insurance on the international transport of goods and passengers, and health insurance premiums are zero rated.[43]

Generally, when a company in Australia pays a covered claim under a taxable insurance policy, the insurance provider is denied an input credit for any portion of the claim paid. A registered insured (unlike New Zealand) does not report the receipt of the claim as a taxable supply. Under an exception, the insurance company may be entitled to claim an input credit on the payment of a claim as provided under the Decreasing Adjustment Model in Division 78 of the Australian GST.[44] A credit is available to the extent that the insurer funds the GST component in the claim paid, as provided next.[45] If the insured can claim credit for GST on the premium, then the general rule applies and under Division 78, the insurer is denied a credit for the claim paid. In contrast, if the insured is denied credit on the insurance premium (e.g., a consumer), then on the payment of a claim to that insured person, the insurer is entitled to a credit equal to the GST component in the claim paid (1/11 in the case of the 10 percent Australian GST).[46] In between, if the insured

---

[39] 20 NZTC 17,096 (Ct. App. 2001).

[40] See NZ GST, *supra* note 22, at §2(1) definition of "warranty," and §§5(2), 5(21), and 11A(1)(ma).

[41] See G. Chiert, Gst: Insurance and Financial Services, 2d Ed.; Joseph, "Insurance Transactions under Australian GST" [hereinafter, Joseph, Insurance Transactions under Australian GST], *VAT Monitor*, May/June 2004, p. 176.

[42] An Australian company issuing life policies that are exempt from VAT are denied input credits for VAT on purchases attributable to the exempt insurance. However, like any provider of exempt financial services, the life insurance provider can claim some input credits for "reduced credit acquisitions." See also the discussion in Chapter 10.

[43] Australian GST, *supra* note 5, at §38–3 55, item 6. See GSTR 2000/33, Goods and services tax: international travel insurance.

[44] See, generally, GSTR 2000/36, Goods and services tax: Insurance settlements by making supplies of goods or services (Australia).

[45] Australian GST, *supra* note 5, at §78–10.

[46] *Id*. at §78–15.

can claim a partial credit for the GST on the premium, the insurer can claim a partial credit on the claim paid under a complex formula in Section 78-15 of the GST.

> To enable the insurer to determine the correct settlement payment, the insured is obliged to state the percentage of input tax that it can recover not later than the time of making the claim.... In effect, the insurer funds only the GST component of the repair cost that is not available to the insured as input tax.[47]

VI. A U.S. PROPOSAL – THE NUNN–DOMENICI USA TAX SYSTEM

The Nunn–Domenici USA Tax System,[48] a plan to change the federal tax system in the United States radically, provides for the taxation of insurance. The treatment of insurance is under the Business Tax (BT) portion of that proposal. It includes the following basic elements:

1. Business loss and other nonlife insurance includes property and casualty, workers' compensation, corporate director and officer's (D&O) liability coverage, malpractice, health, disability, and business interruption policies.
2. A nonlife company's tax base includes not only intermediation services, but the warranty or protection services that are measured by the difference between the premiums and the intermediation services.
3. The BT applies a flow of funds approach that calculates the tax on insurance services under the subtraction method. An insurance company includes receipts, including premiums (but not equity contributions), and deducts business purchases (including financial expenses and claims). The resulting inclusion of principal transactions raises transition problems.
4. There are special rules governing international transactions, including special rules on the location of a supply of insurance. Insurance is provided where the provider is located (the location linked to the place where premiums are paid may be altered by regulations).
5. The international rules are as follows:
   a. Insurance provided outside the United States covering U.S. risks is treated as an imported service subject to the import tax. Payments of benefits are not imports.
   b. Insurance provided in the U.S. covering a foreign risk is treated as an exported service not subject to the BT. Payments of benefits are not deductible.

VII. DISCUSSION QUESTIONS

1. What is the rationale of the New Zealand decision to tax property-casualty insurance but not life insurance?

---

[47] Joseph, Insurance Transactions under Australian GST, *supra* note 41, at 179.
[48] S. 722, USA Tax Act of 1995, 104th Cong., 1st Sess., 141 Cong. Rec. S.5664 (Apr. 24, 1995).

2. If a legislature decides to tax some or all insurance services, what difference does it make to a business that purchases a taxable insurance policy if the legislature adopts the New Zealand or Australian approach?
3. Should a company selling property or casualty insurance charge VAT on the value of its intermediation services or on the entire premium? What does the difference between the premium and the value of intermediation services represent?
4. Explain the difference for VAT purposes between a warranty of a product's performance and insurance covering the product's loss by fire or theft.

12

Interjurisdictional Aspects of VAT in Federal Countries and Common Markets

I. Introduction

Almost all national-level (central-government) VATs rely on the destination principle to tax international transactions, with tax imposed on imports and removed from exports. For example, under the destination-principle Japanese Consumption Tax (a form of credit-subtraction VAT), domestic sales and imports for consumption within Japan are taxable, but exports of goods to be consumed elsewhere are zero rated.[1]

The adoption at the subnational level of some form of value adding technique (see Table 2.7 for a review of the forms) is being debated or enacted in many countries.[2] There has been renewed interest in the problems of cross-border trade in the European Union (EU) and within federal systems, especially in Canada, India, Brazil, and the United States. In addition to the long-standing problems faced by the EU and federal countries with cross-border trade, some of the recent attention to these issues by the EU, academics, the International Monetary Fund, and others has been propelled by the explosion of trade over the Internet (electronic or e-commerce). Indeed, the United States Congress enacted a moratorium on state taxes on Internet access and on multiple or discriminatory taxes on e-commerce.[3]

Subnational units of government should control the revenue necessary to provide the services that they render. In any federal system, the fiscal authority and responsibility of subnational (referred to in this chapter also as regional) units of government must be established – what revenue sources are available to the region, who defines the bases and the rates, and who

---

[1] Japan is unique. It imposes a 5 percent CT, with 1 percent of the 5 percent dedicated as prefectural revenue. This revenue is apportioned to the prefectures on the basis of population. A portion of the remaining CT revenue goes to the prefectures as part of Japan's revenue-sharing program.

[2] See Bird, *Subnational VATs: Experience and Prospects,* Proceedings, 93rd Annual Conference on Taxation of the National Tax Association 223 (2001) [hereinafter Bird, Subnational VATs: Experience and Prospects]. See also Bird, *A Look at Local Business Taxes,* State Tax Notes 685 (May 30, 2005) [hereinafter Bird, Local Business Taxes.]

[3] See discussion in Chapter 7, Section (VIII)(B)(2) *supra.*

administers the tax.[4] Two general principles should guide the development of their tax systems. To possess ultimate fiscal autonomy, subnational units of government should have the authority to choose the tax to be levied, define their tax bases, set their tax rates, and administer the taxes they impose.[5]

A recent body of literature addresses the sharing of revenue from a VAT between the central and local units of government, where there is only a central VAT or both a central and local VATs.[6] One option is for the central government to assign revenue to subnational governments by granting them power to impose their own taxes as just described. Alternatively, the central government could establish a harmonized tax applicable throughout the country and administered by the regional governments, or the central government could add a surtax on a national tax that belongs to the regional governments. A central government could enact a tax to be a shared source of revenue, with the central and regional units of government to share in a preestablished proportion. Finally, the central government may impose its own tax and share the revenue with the regions (revenue sharing is not tax assignment).[7]

The delegation of legislative power may result in complicated tax regimes that create unintended effects on the national taxes. In Spain the Spanish Autonomous Communities provided that some of their subnational taxes were linked to the national VAT; that is, some transactions were subject to the regional tax only if the VAT did not apply and other transactions were subject to tax if the transaction was subject to the national VAT. For example, a regional tax did not apply if the transaction (involving real property) was subject to VAT. As a result, sellers could elect to treat a real property transaction as VAT-able, notwithstanding the exemption generally applicable to the transaction, in order to avoid the regional tax. Sellers generally made that election if the sale were to a registered buyer who could claim the input VAT as a credit.[8]

A significant administrative and political issue in designing an effective regional tax in a federal system or in a common market (or customs union)

---

[4] For an article covering the options and the effects of various forms of central and subnational sales and value added taxes, see McLure, Jr., "Tax Assignment and Subnational Fiscal Autonomy," 54 *Bulletin of the International Bureau of Fiscal Documentation* 626 (Dec. 2000) [hereinafter McLure, Tax Assignment and Subnational Fiscal Autonomy]. In this article, McLure examines each of the various options of imposing at one or more levels of government various sales and value added tax combinations, and tests each alternative against the principles of subnational fiscal autonomy.

[5] *Id.* at 627.

[6] See, generally, R. Boadway & A. Shah, Fiscal Federalism: Principles and Practices (World Bank forthcoming); Zee, *Aspects of Interjurisdictional Sharing of the Value-Added Tax*, upcoming 2006; McLure, Tax Assignment and Subnational Fiscal Autonomy, *supra* note 4. Zee discusses the range of possible sharing arrangements, depending in part on whether the base and rates are set by one unit or each has autonomy in setting rates and even bases.

[7] McLure, Tax Assignment and Subnational Fiscal Autonomy, *supra* note 4, at 627–628.

[8] See Ruiz Almendral, "Autonomous Communities Taking Advantage of the Mechanism to Ensure the Neutrality of VAT," *VAT Monitor*, Sept./Oct. 2003, p. 373.

relates to the taxation of cross-border trade involving interregion or intra-Union transactions.

There have been a series of proposals to address the issues pertaining to cross-border trade within a federal system or common market. Some were developed for a specific country or union but may have broader application. Some were not designed for a particular situation, but may or may not have general application.

The purpose of this chapter is to acquaint the reader with the problems and proposed solutions for subnational or intra-Union transactions, including the VAT in the EU. Intra-EU cross-border transactions resemble interstate transactions under subnational sales or value added taxes in federal systems such as Canada, Brazil, India, and the United States. Australia and Switzerland may face similar problems.

This chapter discusses the European Union's commitment to the free flow of goods within the Union without border tax adjustments and sets out some provisions of the Treaty Establishing the European Community that address that commitment. The limit on the power of member states to impose VAT-like taxes, even at a subnational level, is explored with a discussion of the IRAP (regional business tax) in Italy. The commitment to an origin-principle VAT within the EU, with its attendant requirements, has stalled. Proposals designed to permit implementation of the origin principle are discussed. They include:

1. the Keen and Smith VIVAT (variable integrated VAT) designed for intra-EU trade;
2. the Canadian array of federal and provincial sales and value added taxes are discussed, along with the Bird and Gendron dual VAT adapted from the federal GST-Quebec Sales Tax (QST) in use in Canada and suggested for use in countries with well-developed subnational tax administration; and
3. the highly praised Varsano "little boat model," as modified by the McLure CVAT (compensating VAT) devised as an alternative method of taxing interstate trade under a subnational VAT may be particularly useful in countries without well-developed subnational tax administration.

The Poddar-Hutton Prepaid VAT (PVAT) obligates the seller of an interstate sale in the state of origin to obtain proof from the buyer in the destination state that the tax has been paid to the destination state before zero rating the sale. In the absence of this proof, the interstate sale is taxed.[9]

---

[9] Poddar and Hutton, *Zero-Rating of Interstate Sales Under a Subnational VAT: A New Approach*, 94th Annual Conference on Taxation of the National Tax Association 200 (Nov. 2001) [hereinafter Poddar & Hutton PVAT]. Poddar and Hutton proposed a set of principles to use in evaluating alternative systems for taxing cross-border transactions under a credit-invoice, destination-principle subnational VAT system. They are:

  1. Economic neutrality – all goods to be consumed within a state should be taxed alike, regardless of their state of origin. Although generally accomplished with a destination-principle VAT, it is difficult to administer when borders are not controlled. Zero rating interstate sales distorts cash-flow neutrality because out-of-state purchases do not require out-of-pocket VAT payments and domestic purchases

This chapter closes with a section discussing various proposals to reform state RSTs in the United States.

II. EU's Commitment to Intra-Union Borderless Trade

A. Introduction

The European Union's problems in designing a system to tax intra-EU transactions are similar to the problems encountered in federal countries like Canada, Brazil, and the United States under subnational VATs or RSTs that allow for the free flow of goods without border controls.

The harmonized VAT in the EU began as a destination principle tax both for trade between member states and for trade outside the Community. The ultimate goal, announced in Community documents, was to work toward a system under which trade both within a member state and between member states would be based on the origin principle (the "definitive VAT regime" for the internal market), and trade with countries outside the Community would be governed by the destination principle. Under the origin principle generally, there are no border tax adjustments. Tax is imposed in the country where goods are produced and services are rendered, with no rebate of tax on sales outside that country and no tax on imports into that country.[10] In contrast, under the destination principle, tax is imposed in the country where goods and services are consumed, with a rebate of tax on export sales and the imposition of tax on imports. For subnational taxes, the origin principle allocates revenue to the jurisdiction of production of value added, rather than to the jurisdiction of consumption. This makes the origin-based tax a competitive force in cross-border trade.

As early as 1963, there were recommendations for the adoption of the origin principle on intra-Community trade.[11] In 1989, the Council of the European Communities announced the termination of border controls for

require VAT to be paid before the benefit is obtained from the claim of input credit on the purchases.

2. Fiscal autonomy – states should have the power to establish the base and rates for their VAT, and not be dependent on an allocation of tax revenue from a higher unit of government. States also should have adequate autonomy in tax administration.

3. Compliance symmetry – interstate and intrastate sales should be taxed symmetrically. Arguably, the destination principle is contrary because interstate sales must be treated differently in order to be taxed in the destination state. This may impose an obstacle to competition and trade between states.

4. Low administration costs and encourage compliance without excessive compliance costs – maintain audit trail between seller and buyer. Zero rating interstate sales with no border controls weakens audit trail.

[10] The problem with a pure origin-principle VAT is that products leave the taxing jurisdiction with tax, increasing their prices in the international marketplace. Poddar & Hutton PVAT, *supra* note 9, at 202.

[11] See *Report of the Fiscal and Financial Committee* (Neumark Report), in The EEC Reports on Tax Harmonization (IBFD, Amsterdam), cited in Bird and Gendron, "Dual VATs and Cross-Border Trade: Two Problems, One Solution?" 5 *Int'l Tax and Public Finance* 429 (1998) [hereinafter Bird & Gendron 1998].

VAT within the Community, effective in 1993. In January 1993, the first step toward the implementation of the origin principle on intra-EU trade was introduced. The interim system relies on the origin principle to tax sales to consumers and other unregistered persons, whether those purchasers reside within or outside the taxing country. A sale by a retailer in London either to a French tourist there or by mail to a consumer in France is taxed in London at the U.K. rate of 17.5 percent (the French rate is 18.6 percent),[12] with the revenue staying with the British Exchequer. During this "transition" period, the destination principle remains for sales to registered purchasers (taxable businesses) within the EU. A Spanish company shipping goods to a German company subject to VAT will zero rate the exported goods. The Spanish government will not receive any VAT revenue from this transaction. The goods are taxed in Germany. The EU or Community (both are used interchangeably) is working on a definitive VAT regime that will convert the VAT to an origin base for all sales within the Union. Recent reports from the EU raise serious questions about the viability of zero rating sales within the EU.[13] Most of the proposals to implement the origin principle within the Union on businesss-to-business transactions, such as the "clearing house" scheme, have met with significant criticism or opposition on the basis of practical considerations. In response to the lack of progress toward the definitive VAT regime, British authors Keen and Smith (and Keen individually) developed the "VIVAT" system that relies on the destination (not origin) principle for trade between registered persons within the Union.

The Bird-Gendron dual VAT, the McLure-Varsano CVAT, and the Poddar-Hutton PVAT proposals also may have relevance for the EU.

Before those proposals are discussed, the following material provides the background for the EU's commitment to move to a full origin principle for intra-EU trade. It includes relevant provisions from the "Treaty Establishing the European Community," the timetable (repeatedly delayed) for the change, and the required exchange of information among members in order to make the system work.

B. Selected Provisions of the Treaty Establishing the European Community[14]

Article 14 of the Consolidated Version of the Treaty Establishing the European Community provides for the establishment of the internal market by December 31, 1992, a date not met. Article 14(2) provides:

---

[12] *British Value Added Tax Reporter* (CCH Editions Ltd. 1999); Terra & Kajus, A Guide to The European Vat Directives, 5A VAT and sales tax rates around the world, IBFD (1994/1995).

[13] See Kok, "VAT Fraud Growing: A Call for Action," *Eur. Taxation*, April 2000, EC-9, citing VAT Fraud: Commission calls on Member States to improve controls, European Commission Press Release IP/00/15, 7 Feb. 2000.

[14] Consolidated Version of the Treaty Establishing the European Community (originally the Treaty of Rome), OJ of the European Communities, C 325/33 of 24 December 2002, http://europa.eu.int/eur-lex/lex/en/treaties/dat/12002E.

The internal market shall comprise an area without internal frontiers in which the free movement of goods, persons, services and capital is ensured in accordance with the provisions of this Treaty.

Article 90 imposes the nondiscrimination rule. No member can impose a higher tax on imports from another member than it imposes on domestic products, nor impose taxes on another member to protect its own products.

No member state shall impose, directly or indirectly, on the products of other member states any internal taxation of any kind in excess of that imposed directly or indirectly on similar domestic products.

Furthermore, no member state shall impose on the products of other member states any internal taxation of such a nature as to afford indirect protection to other products.

Article 91 prevents a member from subsidizing exports to another member by excessive refunds of internal taxes.

Where products are exported to the territory of any member state, any repayment of internal taxation shall not exceed the internal taxation imposed on them whether directly or indirectly.

Article 92 prevents a member state from imposing charges or rebates on exports or imposing countervailing charges on imports from member states unless the European Council approves such measures for a limited time.

In the case of charges other than turnover taxes, excise duties and other forms of indirect taxation, remissions and repayments in respect of exports to other member states may not be granted and countervailing charges in respect of imports from member states may not be imposed unless the measures contemplated have been previously approved for a limited period by the Council acting by a qualified majority on a proposal from the Commission.

Article 93 gives the Council, by unanimous action, authority to harmonize indirect taxes in order to establish the internal market by the time (now delayed) specified in Article 14.

The Council shall, acting unanimously on a proposal from the Commission and after consulting the European Parliament and the Economic and Social Committee, adopt provisions for the harmonisation of legislation concerning turnover taxes, excise duties and other forms of indirect taxation to the extent that such harmonisation is necessary to ensure the establishment and the functioning of the internal market within the time-limit laid down in Article 14.

Article 94 gives the Council, by unanimous action, authority to issue directives related to the establishment and functioning of the common market.

The Council shall, acting unanimously on a proposal from the Commission and after consulting the European Parliament and the Economic and Social Committee, issue directives for the approximation of such laws, regulations or administrative provisions of the member states as directly affect the establishment or functioning of the common market.

Notwithstanding Article 94 and to achieve the objectives in Article 14, except as otherwise provided in the Treaty, Article 95(1) gives the Council authority to adopt nonfiscal measures[15] (according to Article 25(1)) "for the approximation of the provisions laid down by law, regulation or administration action in Member States which have as their object the establishment and functioning of the internal market."[16] According to Article 95(6), the Commission has six months to approve or reject national provisions after determining if they arbitrarily discriminate or restrict trade between member states or provide an obstacle to the functioning of the internal market. If a member state is authorized to maintain or introduce a provision covered under Article 95(6) that deviates from a harmonization measure, the Commission shall immediately examine whether to propose that the harmonization measure be adapted.[17]

C. Timetable to Move Toward a Definitive VAT Regime[18]

The European Union has not implemented the "definitive VAT regime." Article 395 of the Recast Sixth Directive (Article 281 of the Sixth Directive before Recast) provides that the transitional arrangements in the Directive are to be replaced by definitive arrangements (the origin principle) for the taxation of supplies of goods or services within the Community. Article 398 of the Recast Sixth Directive requires the Commission, every four years, to "present a report to the European Parliament and to the Council on the operation of the common system of VAT in the Member States and, in particular, on the operation of the transitional arrangements for taxing trade between Member States. That report shall be accompanied, where appropriate, by proposals concerning the definitive arrangements."

D. EU Required Exchange of Tax Information

The Council of the European Communities considers the exchange of information within the Community as an essential part of the establishment of the internal market. A 2003 Council Regulation greatly expands the areas of administrative cooperation in the field of value added tax.[19] In 2004, the Council issued another Regulation with rules to implement the 2003 Regulation.[20] The 2003 Regulation requires the administrative and competent authorities of member states to cooperate with each other and exchange

---

[15] Article 95(2) provides that paragraph (1) does not apply to fiscal provisions.

[16] *Id*. at Art. 95, ¶6.

[17] *Id*. at Art. 95, ¶7.

[18] COM(2004) 246 final 2004/0079 (CNS) Proposal for a Council Directive on the common system of value added tax (Recast) as modified by Presidency compromise, FISC 60 of 21 April 2006.

[19] Council Regulation (EC) No. 1798/2003 of 7 October 2003 on administrative cooperation in the field of value added tax and repealing Regulation (EEC) No. 218/92 [hereinafter Council Regulation No. 1798/2003].

[20] Commission Regulation (EC) No. 1925/2004 of 29 October 2004 laying down detailed rules for implementing certain provisions of Council Regulation (EC) No. 1798/2003 concerning administrative cooperation in the field of value added tax.

information, respectively. Some information on intra-Community transactions, including services supplied electronically, must be provided by electronic means.[21]

III. EU Member States Limited to One VAT

The First VAT Directive established a common system of VAT that required member states to eliminate and replace all national cumulative multi-stage taxes. This principle was carried over in the Sixth Directive, Article 33. "Art. 33 of the Sixth Directive seeks to prevent the functioning of the common system of VAT from being jeopardized by fiscal measures of a member state levied on the movement of goods and services and charged on commercial transactions in a way comparable to VAT."[22] This article prohibits taxes with the essential characteristics of a VAT.

The Sixth Directive, Article 33 [Article 394 of the Recast Sixth Directive, modifying Article 33(1) in some respects] does not restrict a member state's right to impose a tax, duty, or charge, so long as it cannot be characterized as a turnover tax like the harmonized EU VAT, and it does not impose border formalities with respect to trade between member states. Thus, for example, although this article permits a member state to impose a separate tax on betting and gambling (even though it is exempt from VAT under the Sixth Directive), it prohibits such a tax if it can be characterized as a turnover tax like the VAT. A member state can have only one VAT, and that VAT must comply with the Sixth Directive.

In a judgment in the *Careda* case,[23] challenging a supplementary tax on gambling machines as part of the Spanish gambling tax, the ECJ discussed the characterization of a tax as a turnover tax under Article 33 that is relevant for subnational taxes in the EU. As part of its ruling, the ECJ ruled that it was for the national court to determine if the tax was capable of being charged on the movement of goods or services in a manner comparable to VAT and, for this purpose, discussed the characteristics of a VAT.

For purposes of Article 33, in order for a tax to be characterized as a turnover tax, the ECJ in the *Careda* case ruled:

1. "it is not necessary for the relevant national legislation expressly to provide that it may be passed on to the consumer."[24]

---

[21] Council Regulation No. 1798/2003, *supra* note 19, at Art. 1.
[22] Philippart, "Cumulative Multi-Stage Taxes under Community Law," *VAT Monitor*, Mar./Apr. 2003, p. 83, provides an excellent, in-depth discussion of the history of this rule, a discussion of the Article of the EC Treaty discussed next, and the ECJ case-law development in this area up to 2002. On the "subsidiarity" principle in the EU, see T. C. Hartley, The Foundations of European Community Law, 5th ed., Oxford U. Press (2003); Jeffcoat, *The Principle of Subsidiarity in European Community Law*, unpublished manuscript, University of Leicester School of Law, 1999.
[23] Consolidated Cases C-370/95, C-371/95, and C-372/95, (Careda SA) *Federacion nacional de operadores de maquinas recreativas y de azar, (Femara) and Asociacion Espanola de empresarios de maquinas recreativas, (Facomare) v. Administracion General del Estado.*
[24] *Id.* at ¶1 of ruling.

2. "it is not necessary for the passing on of the tax to the consumer to be recorded in an invoice or other document serving as invoice."[25]

According to the ECJ, it is for the national court to determine whether a tax exhibits the essential characteristics of VAT. A tax possesses those characteristics "if it is generally applicable, if it is proportional to the price of the services, if it is charged at each stage of the production and distribution process and if it is imposed on the added value of the services."[26]

There have been a number of challenges to taxes in member states as violative of Article 33, including subnational taxes. In 1998, Italy replaced a regional income tax, a tax on corporate dividend distributions, a net worth tax, and payroll dedicated to a national health program with the *Imposta Regionale sulle Attivita Produttive* (IRAP), a tax imposed in each region of Italy and collected by the central government.[27]

The IRAP has different rules for different business sectors. "For commercial and manufacturing enterprises, the tax base is the difference between the value of the production in the tax year (i.e. the gross proceeds plus any increase in inventory and work-in-progress) and the cost of production (i.e. the cost of raw and other materials and services, the depreciation of tangible and intangible assets, the reduction in the inventory of raw and other materials, provisions for risks, and miscellaneous costs)."[28] It is an origin principle tax at the subnational level that does not tax imports (imports are deductible) and tax attributable to exports is not rebated.

The IRAP has been challenged as violative of Article 33 of the Sixth Directive. It is the subject of the *Banca Popolare di Cremona v Agenzia Entrate Ufficio Cremona* case (the IRAP case involving a bank that is exempt under the Sixth Directive and taxed under the IRAP) before the European Court of Justice.[29] In March 2005, Advocate General Jacobs issued his Opinion that the IRAP was prohibited by Article 33(1). He opined that a tax imposed at each stage of production and distribution on the difference between the proceeds and the cost of taxable activity, and which burdens goods and services in proportion to the price charged is a turnover tax prohibited under that Article. The Italian government announced that it would revise the IRAP

---

[25] *Id.* at ¶1 of ruling.

[26] *Id.*

[27] Legislative Decree 446 of December 15, 1997. Apparently, there are similar taxes in France, Germany, Hungary, and Lithuania. See Lyman, "Regional Italian Governments May Be Liable to Pay Billions in Refunds for Corporate Tax," *BNA Daily Tax Report*, March 23, 2005, p. G-5.

[28] *Id.*

[29] Case C-475/03, *Banco Popolare di Cremona*. The decision was requested by the Court of First Instance of Cremona. The Advocate General Jacobs issued on March 17, 2005 an Opinion that the IRAP was prohibited by Article 33(1) of the Sixth Directive (Article 394 of the Recast Sixth Directive, modified Article 33(1) in some respects). The Advocate General opined that a tax imposed at each stage of production and distribution on the difference between the proceeds and the cost of taxable activity, and which burdens goods and services in proportion to the price charged is a turnover tax prohibited under that Article.

to conform with the EU rules.[30] Reportedly in part resulting from the letter below,[31] in an unusual move, the ECJ ordered the case reheard by an Advocate General (AG). Before this action was taken, several noted tax and public finance professors submitted the following letter critical of Advocate General Jacob's opinion. The second AG opinion is discussed after this letter.

LETTER TO THE PRESIDENT OF THE EUROPEAN COURT OF JUSTICE
CONCERNING THE ITALIAN IRAP AND THE EUROPEAN VAT

Genoa, 20th July 2005

Prof. Vassilios Skouris President of the European Court of Justice
Blvd. Konrad Adenauer
L-2925 Luxembourg
Via fax (352) 4303.2600 - (352) 433766

Dear President,

C-475/03 – the Italian IRAP and art. 33 of the Sixth directive on Vat

I have the pleasure of forwarding to you and to the Court the opinion of professors Oliver Oldman, Richard Bird and Sijbren Cnossen and Paolo de'Capitani di Vimercate relating to the case, currently under the examination of the Court, of the compatibility of the Italian regional tax on productive activities (IRAP) with the Treaty of Rome and art. 33 of the Sixth directive on Vat.

As you will notice, this opinion dissents from the opinion delivered by the Advocate General, Mr. Jacobs, according which the Irap is incompatible with EC law because it has features which are purportedly similar to those of the Vat.

Please accept the deepest sign of my respect,

(Victor Uckmar)

September 9, 2005

Professor Vassilios Skouris President of the European Court of Justice
Blvd. Konrad Adenauer
L-2925 Luxembourg

---

[30] According to incoming Italian Prime Minister Romano Prodi, "The IRAP was a tax created by combining seven older taxes and it was not in any way illegal when it was drafted." "During its existence, the EU rules changed, and so the IRAP must be changed as well. It's as simple as that." See interview with PM Prodi reported in *BNA Daily Tax Report*, "New Italian Prime Minister Outlines Business Tax Plans," May 1, 2006, p. G-1. See also Lyman, "Italy Plans Gradual Reduction In IRAP Regional Business Tax," *BNA Daily Tax Report*, July 7, 2005, p. G-5, citing the nonbinding economic document "Documento di Programmmazione." A subsequent case in the Italian courts awarded a taxpayer a refund of IRAP on the authority of the AG's opinion in this case. The case involved a professional surveyor who claimed that he was not liable for the IRAP. The Regional Tax Commission of Piemonte, without considering the taxpayer's claim on the merits, granted his request for refund on the theory that the IRAP was incompatible with the Sixth Directive. Decision No. 15 of May 27, 2005, reported as Italy: Court holds IRAP incompatible with EC Sixth Directive, in IBFD Tax News Service Headlines, June 13, 2005.

[31] See *Il Messaggero*, March 21, 2006, p. 16.

RE: C-475/03 – The Italian IRAP and the European VAT

Dear President of the European Court of Justice:

We write this letter to provide you with some additional interpretation on one of the most important decisions the Court will have to take in the next few months.

Indeed, the decision of the pending case C-475/03 on the application of the subsidiarity principle and the compatibility of the Italian IRAP with art. 33 of the Sixth directive on VAT will have a crucial impact on the tax systems of the Member States of the European Union. The IRAP is one of the best tools of local taxation and is therefore considered a model for regional tax assignment in the international literature (see, ex pluribus, Bird, A Look at Local Business Taxes, in State Tax Notes, May 30 2005, p. 685 and ff.).

Should the IRAP be declared incompatible with EU law, many other countries would be affected, both among those already levying a tax similar to the IRAP and among those planning to introduce it in order to support their federal organization.

Equally important, an adverse decision of the pending case C-475/03 would also contradict the spirit of the Treaty of Rome. Indeed, one of the pillars of the European Union is the principle of subsidiarity. According to art. 5 of the EC Treaty "The Community shall act within the limits of the powers conferred upon it by this Treaty and of the objectives assigned to it therein. In areas which do not fall within its exclusive competence, the Community shall take action, in accordance with the principle of subsidiarity, only if and in so far as the objectives of the proposed action cannot be sufficiently achieved by the Member States and can therefore, by reason of the scale or effects of the proposed action, be better achieved by the Community. Any action by the Community shall not go beyond what is necessary to achieve the objectives of this Treaty". Also, believing that the public authorities should in principle be as close to the citizens as they can be, the Union has always encouraged and favoured federalism at the level of the Member States. Art. 1 of the EU Treaty clearly takes this view when providing that "This Treaty marks a new stage in the process of creating an ever closer union among the peoples of Europe, in which decisions are taken as openly as possible and as closely as possible to the citizen". The European Court of Justice has stated that Community intervention is justified on the basis of the principle of subsidiarity when the target "could not be achieved by action taken by the Member States alone" (C-377/98, in Rec. 2001, I-7079). According to the Protocol for the application of the principles of subsidiarity and proportionality, the action of the Community shall not go beyond what is necessary for achieving the objectives of the Treaty. Also the directives on direct taxation are based on the principle of subsidiarity and they limit their material scope to cases where the independent action of the single Member States would not be effective (e.g. considerandum n. 10 of the directive 2003/48 on the taxation of savings income in the form of interest payments). It is clear from the above that on the basis of the principles enshrined in the Treaty, the Member States retain their full sovereignty to the extent Community intervention is not needed for the pursuance of the objectives of the Treaty.

With regard to taxation, this means that the Member States are free to establish whatever tax or levy as long as these do not interfere with the objectives of the Treaty. This is also the *ratio legis* underlying art. 33 of the sixth directive, which forbids the enactment of taxes that could interfere with the application of the VAT and thus frustrate the main objective of the Treaty with regard to indirect taxation: the creation of a common market where competition is not influenced by differences in indirect taxes applied by the Member States.

We should stress that the IRAP is meant to sustain the finances of Italian Regions and to support, among others, the provision of healthcare services to the citizens of each single Region. Its structure and its particular features allow Italian regions to adjust its application in accordance with their needs for revenue. The link thus created between revenue and expenditure at the regional level is what the best practice of public finance suggests for efficient public administration, because the citizens are so enabled to better check the quality of the public services they receive in exchange for the taxes they pay.

While the IRAP, as is true of all existing taxes, has some drawbacks and vices, the Italian Parliament has already been studying ways to solve these problems. None of these problems relates to the interaction of the IRAP with the VAT under article 33 of the Sixth Directive on VAT. In this respect, we underscore the following.

The principal features of the Sixth Directive's VAT, which is designed to implement the harmonization requirement of Article 93 of the Treaty of Rome, as revised by the Treaty of Maastricht, are:

1. The basis for the VAT is to tax the personal consumption which constitutes both (a) the base or subject of the tax and (b) the formula for distributing the tax revenue among the member countries and for distributing the burden of the tax among consumers;
2. The credit-invoice method of administration of the VAT tracks purchase and sale transactions and provides the information needed to calculate and verify each taxable firm's tax liabilities. VAT paid on inputs by the entrepreneur can be recovered through deductions. The credit invoice method embodies the principles of proportionality and generality by applying to prices of all transactions of all taxable firms.
3. The destination principle, which applies the tax to imports and removes the tax from exports, implements the system for directing the tax revenues to the country of consumption.

To the contrary the principal features of the IRAP are:

1. The base of the tax is the net production of income or output in an Italian Region;
2. The tax revenue accrues to the region of production whether or not consumption takes place there;
3. An accounts based system is used to administer and track tax-able purchases, inventories, depreciation, wages, and profits in order to determine each firm's net production, or value added. The tax due may then be determined and paid;
4. The origin principle, applying the tax to exports, but not to imports, implements securing the tax revenue to the Regions where production occurs, regardless of where consumption takes place.

The Sixth Directive VAT and the IRAP each use a different value adding technique for determining the tax base. Each tax differs from the other in principle, in objective, and in operation.

Before this letter turns to an enumeration of detailed examples demonstrating how the two taxes differ, it is of fundamental importance to emphasize again that the outcome of this case will have a major impact on the meaning and application of the subsidiarity principle embodied in Article 5 of the EC Treaty.

We now elaborate in more detail the differences between the IRAP and the European VAT.

1) The Italian IRAP is calculated by the subtraction method, using the accounts that the taxpayers already have to keep for civil law and income tax purposes and

is represented by the difference between gross receipts and the deductible costs. Basically, the tax base consists of the sum of the profits of the firm, interest expense and wages.

The profits are calculated taking into account the changes in inventory over the taxable year, rent expenses and depreciation of both tangibles and intangibles. On the other hand, investment income such as dividends, interest received and capital gains and losses are not taken into account. Because the IRAP is not a transaction-based tax, the taxpayer has neither the right nor the obligation to charge the tax with the price. Thus, there is no statutory pressure to assure that the IRAP is borne by the consumers, as there is under the VAT. The actual incidence of the IRAP will be dependent on varying market conditions. This feature was considered as conclusive in a precedent of the ECJ for denying the incompatibility of an Austrian regional tax with art. 33 of the Sixth Directive, because such a tax cannot be considered a tax which applies proportionally to the price of the goods and services (ECJ, June 8 1999, C-338/97, Pelzl and others, in Rec. 1999, I. 3319).

2) From a financial point of view the IRAP must be paid only at the end of the year. This means that while the taxpayer has to pay the tax embedded in the price of his overheads, she can try to shift it onto the customers when she resells her products and pay the tax only months later. Further, under the IRAP there are not serious problems with the refunds, as there are under the VAT. In Italy some enterprises have to wait for months for refunds. All these differences basically relate to the difference in the fundamental principles underlying the two taxes: while the VAT is a transaction based tax on consumption and is connected to the actual purchase of goods or services, the IRAP is a tax on production that needs to be calculated on the basis of the accounts of the taxpayer, regardless of the actual purchase of goods and services by the taxpayer. A further consequence of the different way to calculate the taxable base in the VAT (on the basis of each transaction) and in the IRAP (on the basis of yearly accounts) is that under the IRAP (unlike the VAT) it is not possible to assess the exact amount of tax embedded in the retail price paid by the consumers. This also leads to the conclusion that the IRAP is not a proportional tax and thus should not be declared incompatible with art. 33. This was the holding of the ECJ in the mentioned case C-338/97, Pelzl and others, where the court stated that "since the charges [. . .] are calculated [. . .] on the basis of an overall annual turnover, it is not possible to determine the precise amount of the charge passed on to the customer when each sale is effected or each service supplied, and the condition that this amount should be proportional to the price charged by the taxable person is not satisfied either". Indeed, it is possible that in some economic sectors the price of the same good or service will vary over the year depending on market peaks (e.g. in the business of tourism or other seasonal activities), so that a customer purchasing the goods in February could actually pay a price with no embedded IRAP at all, while a customer purchasing the same item in September could pay a much higher amount which will be partly used by the seller to pay the IRAP.

3) Under the VAT it is administratively less complicated to apply reduced rates and exemptions on certain goods and services while under the IRAP this would imply a separate accounting for each of the favored items and the exclusion of exempt goods.

4) Rates of tax under the European VAT are high (Italy's is 20%) because the applicable destination principle effectively prevents competition for cross-border trade by zero rating of exports. The opposite is true of the IRAP, which requires the inclusion of exports in the taxable output accounts. Therefore the rates of tax

for IRAP lead to competitive pressure among the Italian regions to keep the rate low. The 4.75% rate of the IRAP reflects the competitive pressure to keep the rate low. Also, while a tax applied on imports like the VAT constitutes a proportion of the price of the goods and services consumed in the country, the same is not true for an origin based tax like the IRAP.

5) Under the IRAP banking and insurance services are not exempt as under the VAT; in this respect we should stress that the financial sector accounts on average for 25% of the GDP in OECD countries. Also, non commercial organizations are subject to the IRAP but not the VAT.

6) The IRAP is a not a consumption type VAT but rather an income type VAT. Indeed, under the IRAP capital expenditures receive the same treatment as under the income tax; thus, they can be depreciated over their lifetime. Instead, under the VAT the cost of capital expenditures is immediately deducted. In terms of national income accounts, the economic base of the VAT is personal consumption. For the IRAP the economic base is the net national income. This means that the IRAP is a tax completely equivalent, in macroeconomic terms, to the income tax: the IRAP taxes upon the enterprise the income earned by workers, by the lenders and by the enterprise itself, with the only difference that unlike the income tax, which is collected on each of these constituencies, the IRAP is collected at source on the enterprise.

7) Increases in inventory from year to year constitute part of the taxable production under the IRAP. Under the VAT the input tax credits for inventory accumulation prevent inventory from becoming part of the tax base until sold. Further, the credit method allows VAT taxpayers to carry over their losses to subsequent taxable years, while such carry over is not allowed for IRAP purposes.

8) The tax rates of the IRAP can be independently modified by the Regions. This feature of the tax has allowed Italian Regions to extensively maneuver with the tax rates: just for the sake of giving an example, Lombardia has applied a reduced rate to tour operators and travel agencies, exempted nonprofit organizations and applied an increased rate on banks and insurance companies, Piemonte exempted the agency for the organization of the Olympic winter games, Toscana applies a reduced rate to startup businesses and to businesses opened up by younger entrepreneurs and Abruzzo reduced the rate applicable to drugstores.

9) The VAT focuses attention on consumption as a reflection of ability to pay with a view towards providing revenue for all national government functions. The IRAP focuses attention on production as a reflection of ability to pay with a view towards providing revenue for local government functions related to servicing business activities. Each uses a different value added method identifying the tax due. Each has its own purposes, tax collection and computation techniques, and sphere of use in financing governmental expenditures. These differences distinguish this case from C-200/90, Dansk Denkavit, where the two taxes were closely similar, with the only difference from the VAT being that the Danish tax was not to be reported on the invoices.

10) While the VAT is a general tax, meaning that it applies equally to every kind of transaction entered into by a VAT taxpayer, the IRAP is calculated and administered in different ways depending on the nature of the taxpayer (e.g. banks or nonprofit organizations pay the tax on a taxable base different from the taxable base for industrial enterprises) and therefore cannot be considered a general tax like the VAT.

All the described features of the IRAP make it more similar to the income tax rather than the VAT: as an example, both the IRAP and the income tax are collected on origin and not on destination basis so that they both tax exports and not imports, they both tax the normal rate of return of capital, while the VAT only taxes inframarginal profits, they are both calculated on the accounts of the taxpayer and not on a transaction basis, they both tax increases in inventory, while such increases are irrelevant for VAT purposes.

In conclusion, upholding the IRAP would reinforce the process of fiscal federalism not only in Italy but also in other Member States. The repeal of the IRAP regional tax would contravene the principle of subsidiarity, as it would imply an undue interference in local tax policy in a case where no interest of the EU is affected with the consequence of an inefficient limitation of sovereignty of the Member States.

Respectfully yours,

Oliver Oldman[32]
Richard Bird[33]
Sijbren Cnossen[34]
Paolo de'Capitani di Vimercate[35]

The second opinion in the IRAP case was issued in March 2006. In it, Advocate General Stix-Hackl largely confirmed AG Jacob's opinion. She opined that the IRAP possessed "the four essential characteristics of VAT" and was prohibited by Article 33(1) of the Sixth Directive, "provided that, for a representative sample of businesses subject to both taxes, the ratio between the amounts paid in VAT and the amounts paid in the disputed tax [IRAP] is substantially constant."[36] She wrote that the Italian court should make that determination. AG Stix-Hackl judged the IRAP against the prohibition in Article 33 on the basis of what she described as the four essential characteristics of a VAT (presumably the EU-VAT):

- "it applies generally to transactions relating to goods or services;
- it is proportional to the price charged by the taxable person in return for the goods and services which he has supplied;
- it is charged at each stage of the production and distribution process, including that of retail sale, irrespective of the number of transactions which have previously taken place;
- the amounts paid during the preceding stages of the process are deducted from the tax payable by a taxable person, with the result that the tax

---

[32] Learned Hand Professor of Law, Emeritus at the Harvard Law School.

[33] Professor Richard M. Bird (Director of the International Tax Program at the University of Toronto in Canada) has read a copy of this letter and has authorized us to add his name in support of the letter.

[34] Professor of Economics, Faculty of Economics and Business Administration, University of Maastricht. Prof. Cnossen has read a copy of this letter and has authorized us to add his name in support of the letter.

[35] Attorney at Law in Milan; Harvard Law School International Tax Program; Attorney at Law in New York.

[36] Case C-475/03, *Banca Popolare di Cremona v Agenzia Entrate Ufficio Cremona*, Opinion of Advocate General Stix-Hackl, Mar. 14, 2006 [hereinafter IRAP case], point 128.

applies, at any given stage, only to the value added at that stage and the final burden of the tax rests ultimately on the consumer."[37]

When measured against these four essential characteristics of a VAT accepted by Ms. Stix-Hackl, accepting the fact that the IRAP does not tax the value of imports included in the price of taxable goods and services, and giving weight to the position taken in the above letter, it may be difficult to conclude that the IRAP is sufficiently similar to the EU-VAT contemplated by the Sixth Directive to be violative of Article 33 of that directive.

IV. EU Commitment to an Origin VAT: Its Problems and Proposals

1. In General and Early Proposals

The transition to an origin-based VAT within the European Union has raised many problems. Although the origin principle has been implemented for sales to individuals who purchase goods and services for personal use, little progress has been made in developing rules for intra-Community trade between related and unrelated businesses. During the transition, a VAT registered person has some incentive to purchase goods from a business in another member state rather than from a business in its home state. There is a cash flow advantage from intra-Community purchases, since intra-Community sales to registered persons are zero rated, and the buyer does not report any VAT on the imports until they are resold. In contrast, a domestic purchase carries VAT, which is recovered when the purchaser claims the input credit in the VAT return for the period in which the purchase is made.[38]

The literature contains several proposals that address the taxation of intra-EU transactions under a VAT system that allows the free flow of goods among member states without border posts.

One method proposed to handle the origin principle for intra-Community trade is the clearing system that taxes exports, allows input credit to the importer at the exporting country's VAT rate, and relies on consumption statistics or other data to allocate revenue on this trade between member states.[39]

Another proposal to implement the origin principle with little or no clearing system presupposes that (1) the Community will agree to impose

---

[37] IRAP case, *supra* note 36, at ¶ 22. According to footnote 33 of her opinion, the summary is based on paragraphs 20 and 21 of the *Pelzl* case. "The substance of the characteristics has remained constant, although there are slight differences in the precise formulation...." For an analysis that concludes that IRAP does not violate Article 33, in large part because it does not tax imports, see Schenk, *Italy's IRAP: An Analysis from Across the Atlantic*, VAT Monitor (upcoming August, 2006).

[38] See generally Vanistendael "A Proposal for a Definitive VAT System: Taxation in the Country of Origin at the Rate of the Country of Destination, Without Clearing," 1995 *EC Tax Review* No. 1, pp. 45–53.

[39] See Commission of the European Communities, A Common System of VAT: A Programme for the Single Market (Brussels 1996).

a uniform regular (18 percent) and reduced (6 percent) rate on all intra-Community transactions, and (2) the member states will interpret and apply the VAT rules in a uniform manner. With these preconditions, Vanistendael suggested that VAT be imposed in the country of origin and paid in that country directly to an agent of the destination country located in the origin country. For example, an Italian firm selling goods to a French firm would charge VAT and remit the tax to the French VAT agent in Italy. In that way, the revenue will go directly to the destination country without any clearing system. He acknowledges that there still may be some clearing required because the rates in the origin and destination country may deviate from the uniform rates.[40]

2. The Keen and Smith VIVAT for Intra-EU Trade

Although the European Commission, to date, seems committed to the origin principle for trade within the EU, some proposals rely on the destination principle. The Keen and Smith proposal retains the audit trail created with the invoice system and applies the destination principle for intra-Community transactions, but it requires a clearing system to allocate revenue from final sales to the consuming (or destination) jurisdiction.

In 2000, Keen expanded upon the proposal that he and Smith made in 1996[41] to address the EU stalemate over how to impose VAT on intra-EU trade.[42] In this article, Keen uses the term "province" to refer to member states (with respect to the EU), and to subnational states or provinces in federal systems. According to the Keen and Smith VIVAT (Variable Integrated VAT), the provinces must set a single tax rate on intra- or interprovincial sales to registered persons, but can impose the local rate set by the province on sales to unregistered persons (e.g., consumers). As with VATs in use worldwide, sales outside the EU or federation are zero rated, consistent with the destination principle. The VIVAT scheme therefore retains the audit trail through the use of tax invoices, relies on a clearing system to maintain the destination principle on interprovincial sales within the EU or federation. It relies on the clearing system to take the revenue received in the seller's state, give it to the destination state, and allow a credit to the registered buyer in the destination state.

The following example is adapted from the illustration in the 2000 Keen article: Assume that the tax rate on final consumption in the origin province is 8 percent, and in the destination province is 12 percent. The uniform rate on sales between registered persons, wherever located within the union, is 10 percent. A Corporation, a registered person, sells goods to B Corporation, a registered person in the same province for 100. For purposes of the example, assume that A does not have any inputs subject to VAT. B sells its entire output to C Corporation, located in another province, for 140, assuming that B does

---

[40] *Id.* at 51–53. The author discusses the need to adapt the place of supply rules so that the "origin" country can easily be identified.

[41] See also Keen & Smith, "The Future of the Value Added Tax in the European Union," 23 *Economic Policy* 375 (1996).

[42] Keen, "VIVAT, CVAT and All That," 48 *Can. Tax J.* 409 (2000).

not have any inputs other than the purchase from A. C Corporation sells all of the goods domestically for 200. C's only inputs are the purchases from B. All of the figures are exclusive of VAT. The table shows that the VIVAT system taxes final sales under the destination principle (the destination province receives the VAT revenue) even with respect to interprovincial sales.

A Corporation sale to domestic B Corporation

A's intraprovince sale 100 × 10% uniform rate =	10
A Corporation input tax	00
Net VAT paid to province	10

B Corporation export of goods from A

B's interprovince sale 140 × 10% uniform rate	14
B Corporation input tax (from A Corp)	(10)
Net VAT on interprovincial sales	4

C Corporation (importer) domestic sales

C's domestic sales 200 × 8% domestic rate	16
C Corporation input credit (from B Corp)	(14)
Net VAT paid to importing province	2
VAT collected by both provinces	16

(based on an 8 percent rate on sales of 200 in destination province)

According to Keen, the VIVAT is "equivalent to a common federal VAT levied at the intermediate [uniform] rate combined with a series of provincial retail sales taxes levied at rate[s] equal to the difference between the provincial VAT and the common intermediate rate."[43] VIVAT taxes inter- and intraprovincial sales to registered persons alike. A clearing system is needed to allocate the appropriate amount of revenue to the destination province. In the above example, the consuming province should receive revenue of 200 × the 8 percent provincial rate, or 16. It received only 2 on the sale by C Corporation, and is entitled to the 14 that the other province collected with A and B's VAT returns. Keen notes that this clearing function can be accomplished more easily if a single agency collects and refunds the tax on the business-to-business transactions.

VIVAT treats registered buyers the same, whether they are located in the seller's province or another province. Unlike most VAT systems that treat all buyers (registered or unregistered) the same, the VIVAT treats registered buyers differently than unregistered buyers. The VIVAT follows the usual rule of zero rating sales outside the federation (or EU). The seller therefore must separate sales into three categories: sales to registered persons within the federation, sales to unregistered persons within the federation, and sales for export outside the federation.

---

[43] *Id.* at 418.

There has been other significant scholarship that addresses subnational VATs in federal countries. The cross-border issues that confront national governments in the EU confront subnational governments in Canada that impose a national GST and provincial sales taxes or VATs, and in other federal systems, such as Brazil, Argentina, and India.

The dual VAT, discussed next, by Bird and Gendron has implications for the EU, but because it requires an understanding of the Canadian Goods and Services Tax and provincial sales or value added tax, the application of this alternative to the EU is deferred until after the following discussion of the variety of VAT systems in operation in Canada and the explanation of the Bird/Gendron dual VAT.

V. Canadian VATs and the Bird/Gendron Dual VAT

A. Introduction

In Canada, there is a VAT imposed at the federal level and sales or value added taxes at the subnational provincial level. In that federal system, the national VAT defines the jurisdictional reach of the tax on international transactions under the destination principle. The subnational sales or value added taxes also follow the destination principle on international transactions but may use the destination or a hybrid origin/destination principle on interstate transactions. Although it is relatively easy for provinces to zero rate exports to other countries, it is difficult to tax imports from abroad, especially if they do not enter the country directly into the importing province. Canadian authors Bird and Gendron (and Bird individually) expand on the federal GST-Quebec QST approach to the dual VAT problem in Canada, where the federal and provincial VATs rely on the destination principle, and suggest that the dual VAT model may be exportable to other federal systems or the EU. The next section discusses the array of federal-provincial variations of value added tax and provincial sales or value added tax.

B. Variety of Canadian Sales and Value Added Taxes

The taxation of interstate or interprovincial transactions (both referred to in this chapter as interstate) is more complicated if a country relies both on a national and subnational sales or value added tax, each imposed on different tax bases. For example, Canada has a federal VAT (called the Goods and Services Tax) and a variety of provincial level sales taxes or VATs. There is a Harmonized Sales Tax (HST) in effect with the Maritime Provinces, with the national government collecting both taxes and remitting the provincial portion of the tax to the appropriate provinces on the basis of a jointly developed formula using consumption patterns. The provinces have relinquished their power to set their own VAT rates – there is a uniform provincial rate of 8 percent. There is a provincial GST in effect in Quebec, with Quebec administering both taxes (at a tax-inclusive rate) and remitting the federal portion to the national government. In Prince Edward Island, the federal government administers the federal GST, and Price Edward Island administers the PST on a GST-exclusive base. In the majority of provinces, the GST operates alongside existing PSTs imposed on tax bases that differ by province. With this configuration, the federal government administers the GST and the provinces administer their own PSTs on GST-inclusive bases. In Alberta, there is only a federal GST, no provincial sales or value added tax.

The following excerpt discusses some basic elements of the Canadian Harmonized Sales Tax.[44]

In October 1996, the federal government entered an agreement with the three Atlantic provinces of Nova Scotia, New Brunswick, and Newfoundland for the harmonization of the provincial sales taxes with the new Harmonized Sales Tax (HST) that has a single base and single rate.[45] In the participating provinces, the HST, effective April 1, 1997,[46] is imposed at a single rate of 15 percent, with 7 percent to replace the GST and 8 percent to replace the provincial sales taxes.[47] There is a single administration of the HST and a "national approach to interprovincial sales...."[48] The federal government is providing adjustment assistance to the participating provinces that is designed to cover any excessive loss of provincial revenue resulting from the conversion to the HST.[49]

The HST incorporates the GST rules. "[B]usinesses that are registered for the GST [are]...required to collect and remit the tax at the HST rate

---

[44] The following material in this subsection is taken from Schenk, "A Federal Move to a Consumption-Based Tax: Implications for State and Local Taxation and Insights from the Canadian Experience," 3 *The State & Local Tax Law.* 89, 111–117 (1998) [hereinafter Schenk, Federal Move to Consumption Tax]. [Edited by the authors.]

[45] Dept. of Finance Canada News Release 96-075, Sales Tax Harmonization: Detailed Agreements Reached, Oct. 23, 1996 [hereinafter News Release 96-075].

[46] See S.C. 1997, c. 10, Part II, "Harmonized Sales Tax Amendments." The Agreement pertaining to Newfoundland applies to Labrador as well.

[47] Bill C-70, "An Act to amend the Excise Tax Act, the Federal-Provincial Fiscal Arrangements Act, the Income Tax Act, the Debt Servicing and Reduction Account Act and related Acts," S.C. 1997, c. 10. The 8 percent provincial rate is lower than the PST rates in some of the Maritime provinces. In Nova Scotia and New Brunswick, the effective sales tax rate will decline 3.77 percentage points. In Newfoundland and Labrador, the decrease will be 4.84 percentage points. "Technical Paper on Sales Tax Harmonization," Oct. 23, 1996, p. 7 [hereinafter Technical Paper on Harmonization]. Prior to the HST, "in these provinces, provincial retail sales taxes, where applicable, [were applied to]...the price of a purchase including GST. *Id.* at 9.

[48] News Release 96-075, *supra* note 45.

[49] According to S.C. 1996, c. 18, §64, the federal government may pay an amount "not exceeding nine hundred and sixty-one million dollars for payments to provinces as adjustment assistance for the purpose of facilitating their participation in an integrated value added tax system." Quebec claimed that it should have received adjustment assistance as a result of its harmonization of the Quebec sales tax with the GST. The federal government claims that it made a financial contribution to Quebec's harmonization and that adjustment assistance is not appropriate because the harmonization actually increased Quebec's sales tax revenue. See Dept. of Finance News Release No. 97-027, *Response to Allegations Regarding Sales Tax Harmonization*, Mar. 25, 1997. The provincial assistance is available if the provinces lose revenue exceeding 5 percent of their current sales tax revenue. See Dept. of Finance Canada News Release 96-039, GST Harmonization and Adjustment Assistance, May 21, 1996.

of 15 percent on any taxable (other than zero-rated) supplies they make in the participating provinces. Similarly, businesses engaged in commercial activities anywhere in Canada that purchase goods and services in participating provinces that are taxed at the harmonized rate will be entitled to recover tax payable at the HST rate."[50] Taxable businesses thus can claim input credits for the full HST on business inputs. This rule avoids the cascading of input tax when businesses in nonparticipating provinces purchase business inputs subject to the HST.[51]

The HST revenue will be shared between the federal and provincial governments on the basis of "final consumption data provided by Statistics Canada."[52]

A central feature of the HST is the grant of input credits for the entire HST paid on business inputs used in providing taxable goods and services.[53] The credit for HST on business inputs is expected to benefit exports from participating provinces by eliminating all federal and provincial sales tax from the prices of those exports.

The HST attempts to resolve the intractable cross-border shopping problem that exists under state RSTs; that is, the HST is imposed on mail order and other interprovincial sales by businesses in Canada. All Canadian businesses registered under the GST or HST must collect and remit the 15 percent HST "on goods or services sold into a participating province or shipped to a consumer in that province."[54]

C. Bird and Gendron Dual VAT Proposal

To handle the cross-border trade without border controls in a system consisting of a federal and subnational sales or value added taxes imposed at varying rates, Bird and Gendron advocate a two tier or dual VAT system. This dual VAT system is imposed on the destination principle with features of the Canadian federal Goods and Services Tax and provincial Quebec Sales Tax.[55] They suggest that the taxation of cross-border trade is alleviated if a nation has both a subnational and national VAT. Whereas, by zero rating interprovincial sales, the GST provides some opportunity for tax avoidance on mail order or e-commerce sales, the authors claim that the national VAT

---

[50] Dept. of Finance Canada News Release 97-003, *Governments Release Additional Guidelines for Tax-Inclusive Pricing Under Harmonized Sales Tax*, January 17, 1997.

[51] In fact, a business outside the participating provinces may have some incentive to buy from businesses in participating provinces in order to recover the full HST. The PST it pays on like purchases from suppliers in its nonparticipating province would not be creditable against its GST liability. The shipping costs incurred when supplies are purchased from another province may offset some of the incentive just described.

[52] Dept. of Finance Canada News Release 96-075, *Sales Tax Harmonization: Questions and Answers*, Oct. 23, 1997.

[53] Technical Paper on Harmonization, *supra* note 47, at 63–66.

[54] News Release 96-075, *supra* note 45, at An Overview.

[55] Bird and Gendron 1998, *supra* note 11. The authors emphasize in their 2000 article that the imposition of the subnational VAT on prices inclusive of the federal VAT provide the importing provinces with some incentive to apply the federal VAT properly. Bird and Gendron, "CVAT, VIVAT, and Dual VAT: Vertical 'Sharing' and Interstate Trade," 7 *Intl Trade and Public Finance* 753 (2000) [hereinafter Bird and Gendron 2000].

can be used to control or monitor interjurisdictional trade.[56] Indeed, they raise the possibility of using a "virtual VAT" in a place like the EU that does not have a central VAT.[57]

Bird and Gendron judge various alternatives for a dual federal–state VAT system by the following principles:

(1) harmonization should lead to simplification of the sales tax system, so that compliance and administration costs (and the related efficiency losses) are minimized;

(2) harmonization should respect provincial autonomy by allowing provinces to choose a sales tax rate that may differ from the federal sales tax rate; and

(3) there should only be one agency to administer and collect the sales tax.

On the basis of these principles, the authors concluded that the GST-QST combination is a good model. There is a single administration (at the provincial level), costs are reduced, and the province has autonomy in setting the tax rate (and, to some degree, even in granting exemptions).[58] Interprovincial sales are treated like sales outside Canada; that is, the sales are zero rated. Imports from another province are taxed at the next stage when the Quebec importer resells the imports. There is no clearing system required. A weak element in this approach is that unregistered persons must self-assess on purchases from Quebec.

To illustrate the dual VAT system, assume that the national GST rate is 20 percent, the QST rate is 8 percent,[59] and sales to other provinces are zero rated. Assuming that the interprovincial sale is to a province with a provincial sales tax (PST), not a VAT, it is assumed that the PST rate on sales to consumers is 8 percent. The GST-QST consequences (and the PST in the destination province) would be as follows:

A Corporation intraprovince sale to B Corporation

A's intraprovincial sale 100 × 28% GST-QST rate =	28
A Corporation input tax	00
Net VAT paid to Quebec (20 goes to nat'l gov't)	28

B Corporation interprovincial sale to C Corporation[60]

B's interprovincial sale 140 × 0% rate	00

---

[56] Bird and Gendron 2000, *supra* note 55, at 757 and 759.

[57] See *id*. at 754.

[58] Bird and Gendron 1998, *supra* note 11, at 436. Quebec does not tax books but accomplishes this exemption in an unusual way. Tax is imposed on books, and the purchaser receives an instant rebate of the tax. This procedure maintains the uniform VAT base at the federal and provincial levels. *Id*.

[59] The QST is imposed on a GST-inclusive base, so the effective combined rate is over 15 percent. The example assumes each tax is imposed on a tax-exclusive base, so the combined rate is 15 percent.

[60] Exports to buyers in other provinces or other countries are treated the same – both are zero rated.

B Corporation input tax (from A Corp)	$(28)^{61}$
Net VAT refund on interprovincial sales	(28)
C Corporation (importer) domestic sales	
C's domestic sales 200 × 20% GST rate	40
200 × 8% PST rate	16
C Corporation input credit (from B Corp)	00
Net VAT or sales tax paid to nat'l & provincial government	56
Tax collected by national & provincial gov't & paid by final consumers	56
Natl gov't 20% of 200 sales =	40
Provincial gov't 8% of 200 sales = 56	16

No revenue to the province of origin if all goods are exported to other provinces or countries.

The authors prefer the GST-QST dual VAT system over the Canadian Harmonized Sales Tax because the HST's uniform base and rates preclude any degree of fiscal autonomy for provinces to establish their independent rate or alter their tax bases without unanimous consent.

D. Application of Dual VAT Concept to the EU

Bird and Gendron suggest that if the EU values a system that permits members to set their own VAT rates and to maintain exemptions not shared by other members, it should consider changing the proposed transitional system, including improving administrative coordination among members, and removing the requirement for rate uniformity and even base. The authors leave open the question of whether there should continue to be national administration (analogizing to the QST) or administration by an EU agency.

In some respects, the HST is better than the GST/QST. For example, registered businesses across Canada must charge and remit the HST on all sales to buyers in an HST province, preventing a person in an HST province from avoiding HST by purchasing by mail order. The HST approach may be useful in the EU if an important principle is the reduction of administration and compliance costs.

Regardless of the approach chosen, the EU may need either a central VAT or a proxy for a central VAT. For example, the EU could adopt what the authors refer to as a EuroVAT – "some closely coordinated overarching administrative structure which would, for example, facilitate and insure information exchanges, development of agreed audit plans, and so on" that

---

[61] In fact, Quebec restricts the allowable input credits for the QST for some large registrants. It is done for revenue purposes. In this example, it is assumed that the entire input tax is creditable.

could "be administered by the member states."[62] This overarching structure or central VAT is needed to give each tax jurisdiction the capacity to monitor the cross-border transactions within the EU or, in the case of countries such as Brazil, the federal country.

VI. Brazil and the Varsano "Little Boat Model"

A. Brazil's Tax Structure in General

Brazil does what Bird suggests; subnational governments finance their programs with subnational taxes.[63] Brazil has a multiple rate federal VAT imposed up to the manufacturing stage (the IPI)[64] and a state VAT (state ICMS)[65] on agriculture, industry, and many services. The state ICMS (accounting for about 25 percent of total Brazilian taxes) is shared with municipalities. The national government establishes the main features of the ICMS, but within limits leaves the rate setting to the states. The services excluded from the ICMS are subject to the municipal tax, the ISS, imposed on the gross receipts (no input credits allowed) derived from a variety of industrial, commercial, and professional services.

In March 2005, the government and Congress reportedly reached an agreement to raise the minimum ICMS rate to 7 percent and to allow states to raise the rate up to 12 percent on up to four products. The reform also would reduce the number of ICMS tax brackets "from 44 to five with the same brackets for the same products throughout the country."[66]

In order to reduce the revenue disparity between producing and consuming states, and thus give more revenue to the less developed states, the state ICMS adopts a part origin–part destination principle with respect to interstate transactions. The central government sets the two low interstate

---

[62] Bird and Gendron 1998, *supra* note 11, at 439. In the United States, the Multistate Tax Commission provides a structure for the states to discuss and attempt to resolve problems under the wide variety of state and local tax bases.

[63] See *id.*, discussed in section V *infra*.

[64] "*Imposto sobre productos industrializados*" is imposed on the manufacturing sector "on raw materials, intermediary products, packaging materials and finished goods with set-off for the tax paid at the earlier stage...." Purohit, "Harmonizing Taxation of Interstate Trade under a Sub-National VAT – Lessons from International Experience," *VAT Monitor*, May/June 2002 [hereinafter Purohit, Harmonizing Tax under a Sub-National VAT], p. 169. Although generally there is no input credit on capital goods, an exception is made for "tax on machinery and equipment produced in Brazil forming part of fixed assets and used solely in the industrial process." *Id.* at 169.

[65] The ICMS is the *Imposto sobre operaços relatives à circulação de Mercadorias e services. Id.* ICMS is the Tax on Operations Related to the Circulation of Goods and on the Provision of Interstate and Intermunicipal Transportation Services and of Communication Services, described in Varsano, *Sub-National Taxation and Treatment of Interstate Trade in Brazil*, a paper presented to the Annual World Bank Conference on Development in Latin America and the Caribbean, Chile, 1999 [hereinafter Varsano, Sub-National Taxation].

[66] Taylor, "Agreement Reached With Brazil's States on Streamlining, Unification of State Taxes," *BNA Daily Tax Report*, Mar. 15, 2005, p. G-4.

rates (depending upon the economic position of the destination state),[67] so that the importing state can collect the difference between the interstate rate (applied on the origin principle) and the local rate in the consuming state. There are some notable consequences of the ICMS treatment of interstate transactions. Assume that a sale from a firm in state A to a firm in state B is taxed at a 7 percent interstate rate. The buyer in state B sells the goods to a buyer outside Brazil. Under the current regime, the buyer in state B can claim an input credit for the 7 percent VAT paid to the firm in state A and reports no tax (a zero-rated sale) on the export sale. State A has, in effect, received VAT revenue from this eventual export sale. State B loses revenue by granting an input credit to the exporting firm in its state. Ordinarily, a state foregoes revenue on international export sales as a consequence of the destination principle, but, in this case, state B not only foregoes revenue but suffers negative revenue because it did not receive any revenue from the import of the goods from state A.[68] This effect would not occur if the ICMS were imposed on the pure destination principle.

Brazilian states cannot tax international exports. They can tax domestic and interstate sales. Excess input credits resulting from exports can be transferred to other establishments of the same company in the same state, and any remaining excess apparently is transferable to other businesses in the same state.[69]

B. Varsano's "Little Boat Model"

Varsano developed another approach to the federal–state dual VAT dilemma that may be adaptable to the EU, Canada, and other federal systems. Varsano designed for his native Brazil the "little boat model," described by McLure as "ingenious and elegant," and that can have broad application elsewhere because it deals "with cross-border trade that is internal to a nation or to a group of nations that wish to form a single market without internal fiscal borders, such as the EU."[70] Bird added that Varsano's "little boat model" "may prove to be one of the key innovations in tax thought of the century."[71]

---

[67] The rates are prescribed by the National Public Finance Council (CONFAZ). Purohit, Harmonizing Tax under a Sub-National VAT, *supra* note 64, at 170. "The CONFAZ consists of all states' representatives with 27 councillors. Unanimity is required for any resolution to go through. The 1988 Constitution strengthened the legislative role of the CONFAZ." *Id.* at note 6.

[68] *Id.* at 16.

[69] See Marquez Roncaglia, "Brazil, Transfer of input ICMS," *VAT Monitor*, Jan./Feb. 2003, p. 66.

[70] McLure, "Implementing Sub-National Value Added Taxes on Internal Trade: The Compensating VAT (CVAT)," 7 *Int'l Tax and Public Finance* 732 (2000) [hereinafter McLure, CVAT]. For a current brief but comprehensive survey and principled analysis of subnational revenues including the important place and role of value added taxes, see Bird, *Sub-National Revenues: Realities and Prospects*, reprinted from S. J. Burki & G. Perry, Eds., Decentralization and Accountability of The Pubic Sector, Annual World Bank Conference on Development in Latin America and the Caribbean (The World Bank 2000), 319–336.

[71] Bird, *Rethinking Sub-National Taxes: A New Look at Tax Assignment*, IMF WP/99/165, December, 1999 [hereinafter Bird, Rethinking Sub-National Taxes]

McLure described his modification of the Varsano proposal as the Compensating VAT (or CVAT).

This subsection discusses the Varsano proposal. The following subsections explain McLure's modifications and his comparison of the CVAT and other proposals.

As discussed earlier, the Brazilian dual level VATs are complicated by a system that imposes differing rates on interstate sales, depending upon the origin and destination states.

The Varsano proposal was designed to replace Brazil's federal IPI, state ICMS, and municipal ISS with dual, consumption-style, destination-principle VATs. Brazil's origin-based state ICMS would be converted to a destination-based VAT.[72] To handle the tax avoidance or evasion resulting from zero rating interstate sales,[73] the Varsano proposal imposes, in essence, a second federal VAT that applies only to interstate transactions.[74]

The existing difference in ICMS rates on domestic and interstate sales has encouraged a tax scheme referred to as "invoice sightseeing."[75] The Varsano proposal assumes that the central government will set a standard ICMS tax rate that applies to interstate sales. The state ICMS rate, although fixed by each state, cannot vary from the standard rate, up or down, by more than 10 percent. If the standard rate were fixed at 20 percent, a state could set its ICMS rate within the range of 18 to 22 percent.

Varsano's proposal is for a tax imposed in each state on the origin principle to be converted to a destination principle tax when the revenue from interstate sales is allocated by the central government to the destination state. Varsano's proposal to tax interstate transactions, described as the "little boat model," uses the federal VAT to transport the state VAT across the border. The state VAT on cross-border transactions is reported on and paid with the federal VAT return and the importer will claim the input tax credit on the interstate purchase on the federal VAT return. This scheme does not require interstate clearance of input tax credits. The exporting state does not receive the revenue from the interstate sale, and the importing state does not lose revenue resulting from the allowance of the input tax credit on the federal return. Goods shipped interstate enter the importing state free of the

---

[72] See *id.* The services currently under the ISS would be brought into the VAT in order to reduce the cascade effect of this tax and the attendant incentive toward vertical integration to avoid the tax.

[73] According to Bird, with a destination principle state tax, unregistered persons may claim to be registered in order to avoid the state sales or VAT on interstate purchases. Bird, Rethinking Sub-National Taxes, *supra* note 71, at 30.

[74] The success of a Varsano-type approach may depend on extensive exchange of tax information between the federal and state administrations, and some uniformity in audits.

[75] For example, assume that the rate in state A on domestic sales is 17 percent and on interstate sales to state B is 7 percent. A seller in state A sells goods to a "buyer" (a wholesaler) in state B. The wholesaler in state B then resells the goods to a small business back in state A and applies the interstate rate of 7 percent. Only invoices are exchanged, the goods in fact are shipped from the seller in state A to the small business in state A, and the small business in state A saves 10 percent tax. This is tax advantageous if the small business is exempt from the ICMS and cannot recover tax on purchases.

exporting state's VAT, so that the importer's only input credits (from the federal and state VAT) will be claimed on the federal VAT return.

Interstate sales to unregistered importers or consumers are reported on the federal VAT return, and are subject to the federal and state VATs, like the business-to-business interstate sales described above. The central government now must allocate the state VAT revenue from this sale (no input credit allowed to the buyers) to the destination state. It is not clear how that revenue will be calculated and allocated to the appropriate state.

The Varsano dual VAT requires registered persons to separate sales into four categories. To illustrate, it is assumed that the federal rate is 5 percent, the state rate is 15 percent, and the VAT imposed only on interstate sales and reported on the federal VAT return (the tax carried by Varsano's "little boat") is imposed at a 15 percent rate:

1. Intrastate sales reportable on the federal VAT return taxed at the 5 percent federal rate and on the state VAT return at the 15 percent state rate.
2. Interstate sales to registered persons (except for small traders subject to a special scheme) are zero rated for state VAT purposes but reportable on the federal VAT return at a combined 20 percent federal and interstate VAT rate.
3. Interstate sales to unregistered persons, out-of-state households, and certain small businesses are zero rated on the state VAT return. They are reportable on the federal return and taxed at the combined 20 percent federal and interstate rates, but the interstate VAT is specially designated on the federal return (the explicit VAT), so that it can be allocated by the central government to the destination state.
4. Exports outside Brazil are zero rated. Federal VAT on business inputs creditable on the federal VAT return, and state VAT on business inputs creditable on the state VAT return.

Some interstate transactions require special treatment. For example, some interstate sales are made to registered persons who make both taxable and exempt sales. The seller cannot be expected to know the extent to which the buyer will use the purchased items in each activity. The buyer will be denied input credits for the portion of the combined federal–state VAT rates paid on purchases used in the exempt activity. There must be some mechanism for the buyer to notify the central government (presumably on the federal VAT return) of the extent of the disallowance of state VAT, so that this portion of the state VAT is allocated to the destination state.

C. McLure's CVAT Modification of Varsano Proposal

McLure modified Varsano's 1995 proposal for a subnational VAT that relies on an overriding federal VAT to handle interstate sales. Many of McLure's modifications were incorporated in Varsano's "little boat model" in his 1999 paper at the World Bank conference in Chile.

McLure named the modified Varsano proposal a compensating VAT (CVAT), even though CVAT is only part of the system.[76] He promotes the CVAT particularly for use in countries without sophisticated tax administration, especially at the state level, although it has application in the EU and in other federal systems with sophisticated tax administration at the state level. The McLure CVAT, consists of three separate taxes:

1. The federal VAT that relies on the destination principle for international trade.
2. The state VAT that taxes domestic sales, zero rates interstate and international exports, and does not tax imports until they are resold.
3. The CVAT, which is imposed at a uniform rate and is administered as a separate part of the federal VAT return, handles only interstate transactions; that is, every registered person engaged in interstate trade must charge CVAT on interstate sales and remit the tax as part of its federal VAT return, and every registered person who imports from another state and uses the import in a taxable activity can claim CVAT charged on the purchase as an input tax credit on the CVAT portion of that person's federal VAT return.

McLure makes a number of significant assumptions in designing his CVAT. For example, he assumes that the federal government will administer the state VAT, the federal VAT, and the CVAT. He assumes that the tax bases for the federal and state VATs will be harmonized and the administration of the taxes will be uniform. To accommodate the EU situation, McLure treats the CVAT and the federal VAT as separate levies.[77] He treats state autonomy to set domestic tax rates as an important value, even at the sacrifice of administrative simplicity.

McLure relies on the CVAT as a vehicle to handle "the digitized content over the internet," suggesting that, as it is so difficult to identify the location of the purchasers, these transactions could be covered by the CVAT. The Varsano-McLure CVAT represents a fresh, novel approach to the taxation of interstate transactions under a subnational VAT.

To make it consistent with the Bird/Gendron Dual VAT example, assume in the following example that the federal VAT rate is 20 percent, the origin state imposes an 8 percent rate, the destination state a 12 percent rate, and the CVAT rate is 10 percent.

A Corporation intrastate sale to B Corporation

A's intrastate sale 100 × 28% federal-state rate =	28
A Corporation input tax	00
Net VAT paid	28

---

[76] McLure, CVAT, *supra* note 70, at 724.
[77] McLure suggests that the federal VAT and CVAT could be combined for purposes of determining if the registered person is entitled to a refund.

On federal return: VAT of	20	
On state return: VAT of	8	

B Corporation interstate sale to C Corporation[78]

B's interstate sale 140 × 30%

(20% federal rate, 0% state, and 10% CVAT)   42

B Corporation input tax (invoice from A Corp)

(20 federal and 8 state)   (28)[79]

Net VAT payable		14
On federal return: VAT 28-20, or	8	
CVAT 10% of 140	14	
On state return: VAT 0-8, or	(8)	

C Corporation (interstate importer) domestic sales

C's domestic sales 200 × 32% federal-state rate		64
C Corporation input credit (from B Corp) (federal return)		42
Net VAT paid with federal and state returns		22
On federal return: VAT 40-28, or	12	
CVAT – federal refund	(14)	
On state return: net VAT liability	24	

VAT collected by gov't and paid by consumer (200 × 32%)

(Total of net paid by A, B, and C)   64

Like the Bird/Gendron dual VAT, under the destination principle CVAT, the state of origin does not receive any net VAT revenue when all goods are exported to other states or countries.

Registered persons subject to the state VAT must distinguish between sales to intrastate buyers and interstate buyers, regardless of the tax status of the buyers as registered or unregistered persons.[80]

Assuming that the system works as planned, the CVAT collected from interstate registered sellers is returned (via input credits) to interstate registered purchases, resulting in no net revenue to the federal and state governments.

---

[78] Exports to buyers in other provinces or other countries are treated the same – both are zero rated.

[79] In fact, Quebec restricts the allowable input credits for the QST for some large registrants. It is done for revenue purposes. In this example, it is assumed that the entire input tax is creditable.

[80] McLure claims that distinguishing between registered and unregistered buyers is not necessary because this difference does not have an impact on tax liabilities. *Id.* at 726. McLure acknowledges, however, that households and unregistered persons pay the CVAT, not the state VAT rate on interstate purchases. The incentive to engage in mail order shopping or e-commerce interstate depends on the disparity between the CVAT and destination state tax rates. The disparity also affects the number and dollar amount of CVAT refunds that would have to be paid. *Id.* at 729.

McLure pronounces the CVAT superior to the more complicated clearing system proposed for the EU by the European Commission. The clearing system requires interstate exporters to impose and remit tax on intra-EU transactions at the origin state rate to the origin state, requires the importing state to grant input credits for that tax, and finally requires the clearing house for the exporting state to reimburse the importing state for the credits given (the result under the destination principle for business-to-business sales).

McLure prefers the CVAT to the Keen-Smith VIVAT that is imposed at a uniform rate on interstate sales to registered persons and at the origin state rate on interstate sales to unregistered persons, with only registered persons who import goods interstate eligible to claim input credits for the VIVAT. McLure's disagreement is not only with VIVAT but also with the European Commission's commitment (on which VIVAT is based) to treat domestic and intra-EU transactions with registered persons alike. McLure thus does not support Keen and Smith's application of a uniform rate on all sales to registered persons within the EU (compliance symmetry), in part because the seller must distinguish between registered and unregistered buyers in the origin state. He finds it easier (except as noted on services) to treat all intrastate sales the same (whether the registered or unregistered persons) and subject interstate sales to the separate CVAT, not the origin state VAT.

McLure highlights the fact that the VIVAT weakens the audit trail of input credits on intrastate sales to registered persons (a point that Keen and Smith acknowledge) to the extent that the VIVAT rate is below the state VAT rate. McLure concedes that a similar problem may exist with CVAT, but with that system, the problem exists "only for interstate trade with registered traders in some states...."[81] McLure also criticizes the requirement under VIVAT that the destination state must allow credit for tax collected by the origin state, necessitating interstate clearance of credits.

McLure does not support a hybrid CVAT/VIVAT system that limits CVAT to interstate sales to registered persons. McLure's major criticism is that the CVAT then would not apply to interstate sales to buyers claiming to be registered, the case, according to McLure, where CVAT is most needed. Under VIVAT, revenue from sales to unregistered persons (including households) also would go to the wrong – the origin – state.

In a 2000 article, Bird and Gendron elaborate on the advantages of their dual VAT approach over the CVAT. The dual VAT patterned on the Canadian QST/GST provides states with more flexibility than CVAT to depart from the national tax base, including the possibility that they can set their own rules on major aspects of the tax, such as the allowable input tax credits.[82] The flexibility is built into the state structure that zero rates interstate sales. The Bird/Gendron dual VAT system relies on a single tax adminstration at the federal or state level, saving costs over the competing CVAT (two tax administrations).[83]

---

[81] *Id*. at 734.

[82] Bird and Gendron 2000, *supra* note 55, at 754. Quebec retained some restrictions on allowable input tax credits for large firms. Bird and Gendron 1998, *supra* note 11, at 434.

[83] Bird and Gendron 2000, *supra* note 55, at 757.

Bird and Gendron make an important practical point. The dual VAT, which accommodates the mixture of sales and value added taxes in Canadian provinces, may be more palatable politically than CVAT that requires all participating states to adopt a uniform tax base.

D. Comparison of the Features of the CVAT, VIVAT, and Dual VAT Proposals

None of the proposed systems is the best to handle interstate or intra-EU transactions in all countries or situations. The preference for one system, or a combination of the features of more than one system, depends on a country's ranking of features that are important to it, including an evaluation of which system will work with the level of its tax administration, especially subnational (referred to as state) tax administration.

Whichever system is selected, the system will be more likely to be successful if there is an extensive exchange of tax information among units of government, uniformity in audit procedures, uniform application of the VAT rules, and faith in the competence of the tax administration, especially at the state level. All commentators agree that it is preferable that the national and state level tax (in the EU, intra-EU transactions) should be administered by a single agency.

Dual VAT. The dual VAT, assumed to be administered by a single agency, gives fiscal autonomy to the states by allowing them to set their local tax rates (and maybe even some aspects of the tax base). It applies the destination principle to interstate sales, without the need for a clearing system. With a single agency administering the national and state tax, the dual VAT reduces administration and compliance costs. It allows the free flow of goods within the country without border tax adjustments. Interstate sales to registered and unregistered persons are zero rated. This zero rating of interstate sales provides the opportunity for tax avoidance or evasion, such as shopping by mail order or via electronic commerce.

The Bird/Gendron dual VAT zero rates interstate sales and taxes these goods, under the sales or value added tax in the buyer's state, when the buyer resells those goods (or incorporates them into goods or services subsequently sold). The tax treatment therefore is comparable to the deferral of tax on imports under a national VAT. This system may provide a cash flow advantage to a business that purchases goods interstate rather than domestically. The significance of the advantage, if any, depends upon a number of factors, such as the interest cost (relating to VAT) that is incurred if a registered person must pay VAT on a domestic purchase before the person can receive a VAT benefit by claiming an input credit on the first VAT return filed after the purchase. This cost may be higher if the business is in an "excess credit" position and the state does not refund excess credits, but it requires that they be carried forward to future tax periods.

The Bird/Gendron dual VAT also requires a firm exempt from VAT that imports taxable goods to file a VAT return and pay tax on the import at the importing state's tax rate (like businesses subject to a state use tax in the United States for goods imported into the state).

Bird and Gendron acknowledge that none of the three proposals adequately address the taxation of interstate sales to final consumers.[84] The scope of this trade may affect which of the three proposals is more desirable. In a nation with significant cross-border trade or mail order sales, or significant electronic commerce, the zero rating aspect of the dual VAT may rule it out.

VIVAT. The VIVAT was designed to handle intra-EU transactions under a system that taxes all sales to registered persons within the union alike. The VIVAT permits the free flow of goods within the union without border tax adjustments. It allows fiscal autonomy for member states to set their local VAT rates. The authors recommend a single agency to handle intra-EU trade; if adopted, the system would reduce administration and compliance costs. The taxation (at origin state rates) of sales to consumers may reduce cross-border shopping to reduce VAT to the extent the origin and destination states impose VAT at comparable rates. A significant disadvantage is that the destination state must grant input credits for VAT paid to the origin state on intra-EU sales, and the destination state recoups this credit under the clearance system. The VIVAT is designed with a single rate for sales to registered persons within the union. This will reduce the cost of clearing the tax among member states, but it requires clearance with its attendant costs. It requires a clearing system to handle business-to-business trade intra-EU. Assuming the VAT is designed to tax goods and services where consumed, the taxation, by the origin state, of sales of goods to persons from other EU states gives the revenue from these sales to the wrong state.

CVAT. The CVAT was designed for a developing country without a well-developed subnational tax administration to handle interstate sales in a way that minimizes opportunities for tax evasion. The CVAT permits the free flow of goods interstate without border tax adjustments. A significant advantage is that it can handle consumer transactions by mail order or electronic commerce, thereby reducing incentives to engage in tax avoidance schemes. No clearing system is required, other than the CVAT itself. The CVAT adds another layer of administration (incorporated into the federal VAT) that is not expected to increase administration and compliance costs; indeed, these costs may decline with the CVAT. States retain fiscal autonomy to set local VAT rates. The state level VAT applies the destination principle to interstate sales, so that the destination state receives the revenue from goods and services consumed there. CVAT requires sellers to distinguish between domestic purchasers and interstate purchasers, without regard to the status of the purchaser as a registered or unregistered person.

For unregistered importers of goods traveling interstate, McLure suggests that CVAT reported on these sales can be allocated to states "in proportion

---

[84] Except for automobiles and select other items, there is no attempt under the QST to collect provincial tax on consumer purchases from another province. See Bird, Rethinking Subnational Taxes, *supra* note 71, at 26.

to estimated intrastate sales to households and unregistered traders that are subject to VAT in each state."[85] This allocation presumably also could be used for services provided via electronic commerce.

All of the proposals discussed here must contain a formula to allocate the revenue from interstate sales to the appropriate state when the buyer is denied input credit because it either is not registered or it is registered but uses some of the imports in an exempt activity.

To illustrate the problem that occurs with the CVAT (as an example) if the purchaser of goods acquired from another state uses some of the goods in an exempt activity, assume that a bank in state B purchases computers for $1,000,000 from a firm in A and uses the computers 40 percent in rendering taxable services and 60 percent in exempt financial intermediation services.[86] Assume that the state rate in state A is 4 percent, in state B is 8 percent, and the CVAT rate is 6 percent. The seller will charge $60,000 CVAT on the sale of the computers and report the sale as part of its federal VAT return. The bank will claim an input credit for CVAT on its federal VAT return equal to tax on the computers used in taxable activity – 40 percent of the $60,000 CVAT, or $24,000. Assuming a destination principle state VAT, the federal tax administration should pay the remaining CVAT of $36,000 (60 percent of $60,000) to state B. To do so, the federal tax administration must be able to trace this transaction from the seller to the buyer and must identify the destination state, and ascertain the amount of disallowed CVAT credit. It may be important to identify these transactions if the remaining CVAT net revenue is allocated to the states on the basis of personal consumption statistics or a similar measure. In addition, it must be feasible for the destination state to impose the state VAT (at the difference between the CVAT and state VAT rates) on the portion of the computers used in the exempt activity (this step is not required if the state VAT rates are uniform and equal to the CVAT rate). These transactions may be too substantial to ignore if states exempt from VAT housing and services, such as education, financial intermediation, and medical care.

VII. Subnational VATs in India

A. Enacted State-Level VATs

In January 2005, the Empowered Committee of State Finance Ministers in India issued "A White Paper on State-Level Value Added Tax."[87] The White Paper reported on the consensus reach by state governments on the basic features of the state-level VAT. Remarkably, on April 1, 2005, twenty-one of

---

[85] McLure, CVAT, *supra* note 70, at 431.

[86] It is assumed that there is no threshold "primary use" test before even a percentage of the input VAT attributable to taxable activities is creditable.

[87] The Empowered Committee of State Finance Ministers, *A White Paper on State-Level Value Added Tax*, Constituted By the Ministry of Finance, Government of India On the Basis of Resolution Adopted in the Conference of the Chief Ministers on November 16, 1999 (New Delhi Jan. 17, 2005) [hereinafter White Paper on Indian State VAT].

the twenty-eight Indian states introduced a state-level VAT.[88] The twenty tax rates imposed by various states will be reduced to four rates.[89] The VAT will cover only goods, not services, and imports are not taxed.[90] The central (or union) government[91] will compensate the state governments for the anticipated loss of revenue resulting from the switch from the sales tax to VAT.[92] The revenue loss results in part from the reduction in the tax rates, especially by setting the standard rate at 12.5 percent.[93]

The state-level VAT has harmonized design features that include minimum rates, but it provides some flexibility for states to depart from each other within given parameters.[94] Although it is designed to be a broad-based VAT, some specific items are not covered by the VAT. Goods are taxed, but not services. "[L]iquor, lottery tickets, petrol, diesel, aviation turbine fuel and other motor spirit" will remain taxable under the Sales Tax Act or other state Acts.[95] There are forty-six commodities that cannot be taxed. Each state with the new VAT can choose to exempt up to ten other commodities.[96]

The state VATs apply to intrastate sales. The central government has the authority to tax interstate sales. In fact, it imposes an origin-principle Central Sales Tax on interstate sales in goods,[97] but the states administer that tax and retain the revenue.[98]

---

[88] Doshi, "India: Introduction of State VAT," *VAT Monitor*, May/June 2005, p. 204. According to Doshi, the states of Rajasthan, Madhya Pradesh, Gujarat, Jharkhand, and Chattisgarh announced that they will not introduce the VAT, and the states of Nadu and Uttar Pradesh announced that they will defer the introduction. The State of Haryana introduced its VAT previously. White Paper on Indian State VAT, *supra* note 87, at §1.7.

[89] The two basic rates are 4 percent and 12.5 percent. They will be imposed on more than five hundred products. Singh, "India VAT Faces Opposition but Ministry Says Early Problems Will Be Addressed," *BNA Daily Tax Report*, April 4, 2005: p. G-5. The 4 percent rate applies to products considered essential, like medicines and agricultural inputs. Gold and silver are taxed at 1 percent. *Id.*

[90] *Id.*

[91] The Constitution grants the central government power to impose excise duties on production or manufacture and power to tax interstate transactions, and the state governments can tax the sale of goods, but, in practice, the central government delegated some of its taxing power to the states. For example, the central government delegated power to tax interstate transactions to the states, and the states administer the tax imposed on an origin basis. Purohit, Harmonizing Tax under a Sub-National VAT, *supra* note 64, at 174.

[92] *Id.* The states are to be compensated for 100 percent of the lost revenue in the first year, 75 percent in the second year, and 50 percent in the third year. *Id.* at §4.2. The replaced sales taxes were "cumbersome to administer and costly to comply with. It contains several tax rate categories, numerous exemptions and concessions." Sebastian, "Implementation of VAT in India – The Tasks Ahead," *VAT Monitor*, Sept./Oct. 2002, p. 352.

[93] The reduced rates are 4 percent and 1 percent, and a higher rate, mainly for petroleum products, may range from 15 to 40 percent. White Paper on Indian State VAT, *supra* note 87, at §2.19.

[94] See *id* at §1.5.

[95] *Id.* at §2.18.

[96] *Id.* at §2.19.

[97] Central Sales Tax Act, 1956. The Central Sales Tax is going to be phased out. *Id.* at §4.3. The central government imposes the Central Value Added Tax that covers the manufacturing sector, including capital goods. Doshi, "India: Proposed Introduction of VAT at State Level," *VAT Monitor*, July/Aug. 2002, p. 309.

[98] Doshi, "India: State Level," *VAT Monitor*, Nov./Dec. 2004, p. 445.

Following are the basic design characteristics of the state-level VAT in India. It is basically an origin-principle VAT within India that taxes sales within the state, does not tax imports into the state, and does not zero-rate sales to other states. It requires dealers with turnover over the threshold to register,[99] and provides voluntary registration to those with turnover below the threshold.[100]

A registered manufacturer and trader can claim credits for input VAT on purchases, but the credit is limited. The input credit is available for sales made in state and out of state. Input credits are available for VAT paid on capital goods (except for a specified list of capital goods), but the input tax is creditable against tax on taxable sales over a period of thirty-six months.[101] If a registered person has excess input credits, those credits must be carried over to the remainder of the current financial year and to the end of the next year. If any excess remain after that time, it is eligible for refund.[102] As is common in other VAT systems, exports of goods outside the country are zero rated, and the exporter is entitled to a quick refund of input VAT attributable to the exported goods.[103]

B. Prepaid VAT Proposed for India by Poddar and Hutton

A prepaid VAT (PVAT) was proposed for India.[104] Under the PVAT, interstate sales are zero rated if the VAT on the sales is paid by the buyer to the destination state. The PVAT obligates the seller of an interstate sale in the state of origin to obtain proof from the buyer in the destination state that the tax has been paid to the destination state before zero rating the sale. The required proof is in the form of a copy of the receipt for the tax deposit. The authors analogize this system to the customs clearance procedure, under which goods are released by Customs when the importer submits proof that the customs duties and taxes were paid.[105] The seller must retain records of the shipment and the buyer's tax deposit receipt to substantiate the seller's treatment of the sale as zero rated. The registered buyers would claim credit for the tax paid.

---

[99] The threshold is annual turnover exceeding 500,000 rupees (US$11,468). Singh, India VAT Faces Opposition, *supra* note 89.

[100] White Paper on Indian State VAT, *supra* note 87, at §2.9. Dealers required to register (turnover above 500,000 rupees) but with turnover below 5,000,000 rupees, can elect to pay a lower rate turnover tax (without any input credits) in lieu of the VAT. *Id.*

[101] *Id.* at §2.4. States can reduce the number of months over which the input credit on capital goods must be allocated. There also is a transitional rule governing sales tax paid on goods purchased on or after April 1, 2004, that is in stock on April 1, 2005 – the effective date of the VAT for most states. Sales tax on these purchases is creditable over a six-month period. *Id.* at §2.7.

[102] *Id.* at §2.3.

[103] *Id.* at §2.5. The refund is to be made within three months.

[104] It was proposed by Satya Poddar, and discussed at a tax reform conference in India in 1994. Poddar, *Reform of Domestic Consumption Taxes in India: Issues and Options* (NIPFP, New Delhi 1994). He, along with Eric Hutton expanded on the proposal as part of a 2001 conference in the United States Poddar & Hutton PVAT, *supra* note 9.

[105] *Id.* at 204.

If the seller does not receive proof that VAT was paid to the state of destination, the seller will charge VAT at the domestic rate in the state of origin. This, in effect, gives foreign consumers a choice between paying the VAT rate in the state of origin or state of destination.

The compliance burden is on the buyer. Businesses that commonly purchase from out-of-state vendors could register and open "a special 'PVAT checking account' with an authorized financial institution.[106] This account would be used solely for making tax payments to the government on interstate purchases. The registered buyer could then submit a check drawn on this account to the vendor to satisfy the tax prepayment requirement. The vendor could deposit the check in the account of the destination state."[107] Alternatively, the buyer could mail the check to the destination state and provide a copy to the vendor.

The PVAT proponents suggest that the most significant feature of the PVAT may be that "it creates strong incentives for both the origin and the destination states to monitor compliance independently, as revenues of both are affected by the zero-rated sales declared by the vendor."[108] With the PVAT, the zero rating is the link between the origin and destination state. It has been suggested that the Indian Central Sales Tax (CST) could be converted to a PVAT by changing the CST to "a Central Purchase Tax, which would be collected and retained by the destination state."[109]

The PVAT conforms to the following desirable features of a good VAT:

- "Allows the tax to be levied on the basis of the destination in a neutral manner;
- Preserves the fiscal autonomy of state governments in tax design and administration;
- Does not require the existence of an overarching national body for the collection or administration of tax; and
- Satisfies the requirements of compliance symmetry (as reflected in the arrangements in the European Union)."[110]

It also does not provide any cash-flow advantage that occurs when interstate sales are zero rated.

VIII. Origin-Based Business Value Tax (BVT) to Finance Subnational Government

Independent of the above debate over how to craft an origin principle VAT to handle intra-EU trade and a destination principle VAT to handle interstate

---

[106] The advantage of registration is that the seller could accept documentary proof as valid. *Id.*

[107] *Id.* at 205.

[108] *Id.*

[109] *Id.*

[110] *Id.*

trade under subnational VATs in federal countries (both with consumption bases), Richard Bird urges subnational units of government to impose their own taxes to finance their programs. In a Working Paper of the International Monetary Fund, Bird recommends that subnational governments adopt subnational origin-based VATs imposed on income,[111] not consumption (what he calls a Business Value Tax [BVT]), to finance the services they provide.[112] The BVT is levied on income (profits and wages), not consumption; imposed on production, not consumption (tax exports but not imports); and calculated on the basis of annual accounts (subtraction or addition), not on transactions.[113]

Regional or local government needs fiscal autonomy to meet its fiscal responsibilities. As government functions become decentralized, revenue should be decentralized as well.[114] In many countries, either because of the tax base or the difficulty in administering the tax, the taxes assigned to subnational units of government, such as user fees and real property taxes, do not raise the level of revenue needed to finance the programs that are the responsibility of these local or regional governments. According to Bird, subnational governments should control their own revenue sources and tax rates.[115] They should not depend on revenue-sharing or other methods by which national governments distribute a portion of the national taxes to the subnational units.

A country could use a combination of a federal VAT for federal programs, a state VAT following the CVAT or other model for state programs, and a BVT instead of other levies on business to finance regional and local programs.

Bird claims that a subnational tax on business may be justified on a business benefit theory because businesses received valuable services from local government. Data from a study in the United States suggest that

---

[111] See discussion *supra*, Chapter 1, Section III. A key difference between an income and consumption base relates to the inclusion of capital goods in the tax base. Under an income base, the VAT on the acquisition of capital goods is recovered over the life of the goods, like depreciation under an income tax. Under a consumption base, the full VAT on the acquisition of capital goods is recovered immediately. See discussion in Chapter 1, Section X(E).

[112] Bird, Rethinking Sub-National Taxes, *supra* note 71. The concept of the BVT was discussed further in Bird, Subnational VATs: Experience and Prospects, *supra* note 2. See also Bird, Local Business Taxes, *supra* note 2, where the author considers the IRAP as the best example of an origin principle, accounts-based tax on value added by business firms by region, with the revenue retained by the region. For another analysis concluding that an origin principle, production VAT is a good replacement for the state corporate income tax and other business taxes, see Fox, Luna, and Murray, *Issues in the Design and Implementation of Production and Consumption VATs for the American States*, Proceedings, 94th Annual Conference on Taxation, Nat'l Tax Assn. 188 (2002).

[113] See Bird, Subnational VATs: Experience and Prospects, *supra* note 2.

[114] *Id.* at p. 16.

[115] See, for example, McLure, *The Tax Assignment Problem: Conceptual and Administrative Considerations in Achieving Sub-national Fiscal Autonomy*, paper presented at Seminar on Intergovernmental Fiscal Relations and Local Financial Management organized by the National Economic and Social Development Board of the Royal Thai Government and the World Bank, Thailand, 1999, referred to in Bird, Rethinking Sub-National Taxes, *supra* note 71.

businesses may receive benefits equal to over 10 percent of state and local expenditures.[116]

IX. Reform of Subnational Taxes in the United States

There are many reasons why there is a serious need to reform subnational sales taxes in the United States. There is a patchwork of retail sales taxes in effect in most of the states (and the District of Columbia). There are forty-six different RSTs, with complementary use taxes applicable to imports into the states. Businesses required to comply with many state and local sales taxes devote substantial resources to this task. The sales tax base is shrinking, in part as a result of the expansion of services (generally not taxed), including the growing area of electronic commerce. For constitutional and other reasons, these RSTs and use taxes do not effectively tax most cross-border and mail order shopping by consumers. As a result, there are structural budget deficits in many states.[117]

A recent development in the United States is the Streamlined Sales and Use Tax. A number of states have enacted legislation that would bring their sales and use taxes into compliance with the Streamlined Sales and Use Tax Agreement. In addition to the proposals discussed earlier that may be adaptable to the United States, Richard Ainsworth proposed a "digital VAT" that could be used to harmonize sales taxes among the states in the United States.

Most states in the United States impose retail sales taxes (RSTs) that generally do not apply to interstate sales, and impose use taxes on imports (but seldom collect them from consumers). The sales and use taxes are imposed on the destination principle. Consumers may avoid RSTs (of up to 8 percent or more in some locales) in both the state of sale and the state of destination by purchasing goods by mail order or on the Internet (electronic commerce).

The major revenue sources for state and local government in the United States are real property taxes, retail sales taxes (RSTs), and individual and corporate income taxes.

Some states in the United States have enacted or considered various forms of VAT or variations of VAT. Michigan has a Single Business Tax (SBT), an addition method VAT. New Hampshire has a Business Enterprise Tax that some commentators refer to as a form of VAT. West Virginia and Minnesota considered but did not enact VATs. Other states, including Texas and Louisiana, have looked at a VAT as a state tax. Texas enacted the Texas Margin Tax – a tax with some attributes of a VAT. Some of the subnational VATs proposed for other countries have been promoted as possible subnational VATs in the United States.[118]

---

[116] Bird, Subnational VATs: Experience and Prospects, *supra* note 2, at note 17, citing Oakland & Testa, "Community Development – Fiscal Interactions: Theory and Evidence from the Chicago Area," Working Paper Series, Federal Reserve Bank of Chicago (WP-1995/7).

[117] See Lav, McNichol, and Zahradnik, "Faulty Foundations: State Structural Budget Problems and How to Fix Them," Center on Budget and Policy Priorities, May, 2005, at http://www.cbpp.org/5-17-05sfp.pdf.

[118] See Keen, *States' Rights and the Value Added Tax: How a VIVAT Would Work in the United States*, Proceedings, 94 Annual Conference on Taxation, National Tax Association, 195

The literature in the United States has begun to address the anticipated problems that likely would occur if Congress were to adopt a federal VAT or other federal tax on consumption that would have to coexist with state RSTs. In states with taxes that resemble VATs, the problems of coordination with a federal VAT would be somewhat different. The alternatives must be judged by objective criteria. Charles McLure proposed five characteristics of a well-designed sales tax system for this purpose.[119] Three of the characteristics are economic, one is administrative, and one is political. They are:

(1) "essentially all sales to consumers in a given jurisdiction would be taxed at a single rate;
(2) essentially all sales to business would be exempt;
(3) sales would be taxed under the destination principle...;
(4) the first three objectives could be met without undue costs of compliance and administration; and
(5) each level of government would have the power – and the responsibility – to set its own tax rate. (Note that compliance with the first two characteristics would essentially eliminate the power of each level of government also to determine its sales tax base.)"[120]

According to McLure, it will be difficult to coordinate defective state and local retail sales taxes (as exist now) with even a federal VAT that meet his criteria for an ideal sales tax.[121] He and Richard Bird have come to the conclusion that the best way for two levels of government to "levy sales taxes at reasonable costs is by agreeing on a common tax base and letting one level of government collect the tax for both."[122]

Alice Rivlin proposed a uniform state level tax to replace part of the revenue from state RSTs and raise revenue needed to finance services the states are obliged to provide. She recommended that this tax be administered by a central administrative agency, a feature that better handles interstate transactions by mail order or electronic commerce. She did not limit the state level uniform tax proposal to some form of VAT. In part, she wrote:[123]

> (2002), in which the author suggests that the VIVAT can tax interstate sales to final consumers under the destination principle at the rate in the state of consumption (he omits any consideration of the U.S. Constitutional issues with out-of-state sales).

[119] His conclusions will be discussed *infra*, this chapter.

[120] McLure, Jr., "Coordinating State Sales Taxes with a Federal VAT: Opportunities, Risks, and Challenges," 36 *State Tax Notes* 907 (June 20, 2005) (footnotes omitted). In a footnote, he leaves "open the possibility of exempting some sales to consumers (for example, of prescription drugs) and taxing some sales to business (for example, of luxury automobiles ostensibly used in business)." He does not consider state use taxes. "Taxation that is economically equivalent to a use tax is inherent in a destination-based sales tax." *Id.*

[121] *Id.* at 918. McLure's principles of an ideal sales tax are listed *supra*, this chapter.

[122] *Id.* at 918, quoting from Bird, "Cost and Complexity of Canada's VAT: The GST in International Perspective," 8 *Tax Notes Int'l* 37 (Jan. 3, 1994).

[123] Extract from Rivlin, "Wanted: A New State-Level Tax to Prepare Us for the 21st Century," *Governing*, April, 1990, p. 74. [Edited by the authors.] Ms. Rivlin, at the time this article was written, had been an economist at the Brookings Institution, and then was appointed

The states should adopt a radical new approach to raising the revenues they urgently need. They should join forces to pass a new kind of tax, one that would be imposed by each state at a uniform rate. The money, which would be collected by some central agency, would then be distributed to each state on the basis of a formula, perhaps simply by population....[124]

[I]f the formula for sharing the common tax favored less affluent jurisdictions, it would reduce disparities among states in the quality of public services.

The increasing integration of the economy also makes a common tax attractive, both to states and to businesses. A rising share of business is now done by multistate and multinational corporations. Mail- and phone-order sales are exploding and largely escaping state sales taxes. The service sector, growing much faster than the goods-producing sector, is also becoming national and international, as legal, accounting, financial and advertising firms develop far-flung operations. Movement by the states to adopt common business taxes and share the proceeds could reduce the volume of business escaping taxation and cut the cost of administration for state governments and businesses alike.

The states that enacted a uniform common tax could either establish their own agency to collect and distribute it or, perhaps, let the Internal Revenue Service do the job under contract to them.

A radically different proposal was made in the U.S. Congress to impose a federal retail sales tax. For states that harmonized their state retail sales tax with the national tax, the states would administer the combined taxes. This proposal is discussed in Chapter 14. Some states have taken Ms. Rivlin's advice and have adopted legislation consistent with the Streamlined Sales and Use Tax Agreement, discussed later in this chapter.

A. Coexistence of Federal VAT and State Retail Sales Tax

There are several proposals to impose VAT or other sales taxes in the United States, both at the federal and subnational levels of government. "There have been a number of studies and commentaries suggesting that the states either move from their existing form of consumption tax (the state retail sales tax (RST)) to a broader-based consumption tax (the value-added tax)[125] or that the states shift from their state income tax and other taxes on business activity to a state VAT. States could follow Michigan's lead and replace their income and other taxes on business activity with an apportioned tax

director of the Congressional Budget Office. She subsequently served on President Clinton's Council of Economic Advisors and on the Federal Reserve Board.

[124] Japan allocates part of the Consumption Tax (a VAT) revenue dedicated for the prefectures on the basis of prefecture population in order to reduce the disparity in resources available to affluent and poorer prefectures. [Added by the authors.]

[125] See Due, "The Value-Added Tax: Possible State Use," 1 *State Tax Notes* 269 (1991), suggesting a possible origin-based state VAT. References in this article to state RSTs include local RSTs in those states that impose RSTs both at the state and local levels of government.

like the Michigan Single Business Tax,[126] an addition form of value-added tax."[127] Ironically, the Michigan SBT is scheduled for repeal.

Canadian consumers in Ontario and several other provinces experienced sticker-shock when the federal GST was imposed in addition to existing provincial retail sales tax at the cash register. If the United States adopted a federal VAT, a sales-subtraction VAT that is a period rather than a transactions tax and that is buried in product prices may be more compatible with existing state and local taxes than the European VAT.[128]

B. SUBNATIONAL VATs IN USE AND PROPOSED FOR THE UNITED STATES

Two states in the United States, Michigan and New Hampshire, impose imperfect state-level VATs. Several others, including West Virginia, considered their use.

Michigan imposed a state-level VAT, replaced it with income taxes, and then replaced the corporate income tax and several other taxes on business with a Single Business Tax (SBT), an addition-method VAT. New Hampshire imposed a tax with a base somewhat like VAT, called the Business Enterprise Tax. An overview of these developments is covered in the following article. It is followed by a discussion of the Michigan SBT, a broader-based SBT in the proposed West Virginia SBT, and the New Hampshire BET.

Will the Single Business Tax Catch On?[129]
[State value added taxes]...exist only in two states, Michigan and New Hampshire, but they have been proposed by study commissions in both West Virginia and the District of Columbia and are at different stages of consideration in Minnesota and Texas. While no tax is without problems of

---

[126] See Francis, "A Closer Look At A State Invoice-Credit VAT," Nat'l Tax. Assn Annual Meeting, Oct., 1992, published in 3 *State Tax Notes* 804 (Nov. 30, 1992). In his article, Mr. Francis, director of tax research at the Florida Department of Revenue, argues that an apportioned state-level addition method VAT is inferior to the EC-style invoice VAT. He suggests that an EC-style VAT at the state level will tax consumption and not production, whereas an apportioned VAT such as the Michigan SBT taxes only the portion of final consumption produced within the taxing jurisdiction. Mr. Francis notes that an addition method VAT could be structured to tax consumption (by using a sales only allocation formula), but that the Michigan SBT does not do so.

[127] In June 1994, the Standing Committee on Finance (the "Committee") issued its Ninth Report, entitled "Replacing the GST: Options for Canada." In this report, the Committee recommended that Canada replace its GST with a National VAT and that provincial sales taxes be integrated with this national tax. The proposed National Tax would be buried in prices, but vendors that made sales that currently require GST disclosure on invoices would be required to disclose on invoices both their registration numbers and either the VAT rate or the amount of VAT payable on the sale. Schenk, Federal Move to Consumption Tax, *supra* note 44.

[128] See Schenk, Federal Move to Consumption Tax, *supra* note 44.

[129] Steuerle, "Will the Single Business Tax Catch On?" 81 *Tax Notes* 1013 (Nov. 23, 1998). [Edited by the authors.]

defining the base or of enforcement, the potential for expansion of the single business tax [concept] is significant. . . .

One of the major reasons for considering single business taxes, therefore, is simply that they are a fairly stable source of revenue. While they don't have the type of bracket creep that makes individual tax rates rise over time, neither are they as cyclical or uncertain as taxes on corporate profits; and they don't decline over time in relative importance like most sales and excise taxes. In general, they tend to adopt a base that expands at roughly the same rate as the economy as a whole.

Even recessions do not tend to cause a large fall in single business tax collections, but rather a fall that is commensurate with declines in overall consumption and income. . . . A single business tax provides more flexibility and less need for reactive legislative action and less need for revenue changes that are so hurried that they proceed with inadequate consideration of long-term tax policy principles. . . .

Note that the issue is not necessarily the raising of revenues but of maintaining a broad enough base that rates can be kept low and stable over time. Contrast a single business tax with an equal yield sales tax on goods only. The latter continually raises fewer taxes relative to the size of the economy. That is one of the major reasons sales tax rates have tended to rise continually over the past few decades, increasing the tax on goods relative to services. The higher the rate differential, moreover, the more economists would argue that distortions in behavior arise. Such distortions result in too much consumption of services and too little consumption of goods, decreasing the well-being of consumers in general. Much of the momentum behind single business taxes comes from efforts to reduce or replace other taxes. . . .

In the case of West Virginia, its Commission on Fair Taxation bravely proposed reform that included the repeal of a wide range of distorting taxes that tended to "pick" on particular forms of activity or that simply were not worth the extra tax enforcement costs. These included the personal property tax that largely applied to business machinery, equipment, and inventory, the telecommunications tax, a health provider tax, an insurance premiums tax, an auto privilege tax, and a soft drink excise tax. The single business tax is also proposed to replace a business franchise tax, a corporate charter tax, a business registration tax, and a business and occupation tax. Many of these business taxes result in a double tax on different forms of income or consumption based mainly on organizational form or how many layers of business are involved in the final production. Such taxes are believed to be very distorting.

The District of Columbia's case is somewhat unique in that so many services, particularly those of lawyers and other professionals, are produced by residents outside the District who then pay little or no tax on the income they earn inside the District on the value of services they provide. A single business tax represents yet one more attempt to get at this issue.

None of this means that a single business tax is by any means some perfect form of taxation. None exists. Like many other areas of taxation that depend on geographical location, there are many border tensions as to whether income or consumption should be taxed by source or residence; even when one or another is chosen in theory, enforcement and implementation can be problems in practice. Transition problems can be significant.

Like so many other state taxes such as the income tax, apportioning the tax base across jurisdictions is not only difficult but is threatened by inconsistent rules in different states. These rules cause some consumption or income to be taxed twice in two different jurisdictions; others to be taxed not at all.

Whatever the future of the single business tax, it could unwind only over a long period of time. Any expansion is likely to go hand-in-hand with a reduced reliance on other taxes. It could give states more elastic and stable tax sources. At the same time, it would raise new issues of tension across state boundaries, and it could even affect the federal government's own choices with respect to income and various forms of consumption taxes.

1. Michigan Single Business Tax

Michigan adopted a state-level modified addition method VAT, its Single Business Tax (SBT), effective in 1975.[130] In broad outline, a business calculates its SBT base by adding to "business income" the compensation paid to employees (including contributions to retirement plans), depreciation taken for tax purposes, and several other adjustments. The business then can deduct:

(a) dividends, interest, and certain rent, royalty, and franchise fee receipts that are included in federal taxable income,
(b) capital losses not deductible for federal tax purposes, and
(c) a few other adjustments.

An apportionment formula then allocates a portion of the resulting tax base to Michigan.[131] The apportioned tax base then is adjusted by an investment tax credit that replaced, for years after 1999, a deduction for the apportioned cost of depreciable tangible assets physically located in Michigan and to be used in business activity in Michigan.[132] As an alternative to the special compensation deduction, a business can claim a deduction that in effect imposes tax on 50 percent of taxable gross receipts.[133] There is a variable annual exemption, and the legislature has granted several tax credits, including a small business credit, for businesses subject to the SBT. The tax rate for 2003

[130] For a detailed discussion of the SBT, see B. Schwendener, Jr., 1650 T.M., Michigan Single Business Tax (1994 and supplement) [hereinafter, Schwendener, SBT]. The SBT is the Single Business Tax Act, P.A. 1975, No. 228, MCL §208.1 et seq.

[131] For tax years before January 1, 1997, for businesses other than transportation, finance and insurance, the apportionment formula is 50 percent sales, 25 percent property, and 25 percent payroll. MCL §208.45. For tax years after 2005, the apportionment formula for these businesses will be 95 percent for sales, 2.5 percent for property, and 2.5 percent for payroll. 2005 Mi. P.A. 223, 2005 MI HB 4973, §45(a)(2). There is an option to allocate 100 percent on the basis of sales if the taxpayer does not own or rent real estate or tangible personal property associated with the taxpayer's business activities and gross sales in the state do not exceed $100,000. See MCLS §208.68(1).

[132] See M.C.L. §208.35a. The available credit is based on a percentage of creditable investment expenditures, based on a two-step process. The percentage varies, depending on the level of the taxpayer's adjusted gross receipts.

[133] Schwendener, SBT, *supra* note 130, at 1650-0012; MCL §208.22a.

was 1.9 percent.[134] The SBT rate is scheduled to be phased out as economic conditions warrant.[135]

2. West Virginia's Proposed Single Business Tax

A commission established by the West Virginia governor recommended the replacement of eleven taxes on business with a broad-based Single Business Tax (SBT) imposed on the privilege of doing business in West Virginia.

The SBT was recommended as a simple broad-based tax system with fewer taxes and limited tax preferences as part of a program to impose a limited number of broad-based general business taxes with limited exemptions. The following excerpt describes the proposed consumption-style VAT calculated under the addition method.[136]

Structure and Design
... [T]he SBT is measured by the "taxable economic value" of the business. Using the addition method, this base is the sum of "compensation," "rents," "interest," "dividends" and "depreciation payments" and "profit" made, less capital acquisitions. These elements represent, and, therefore, tax uniformly, a business enterprise's outlays for the use of labor and capital resources. There would be a small business exemption. [The following formula assumes that all sales are intrastate. The proposed SBT provides an immediate write-off for the cost of capital goods (and therefore an add back of any depreciation deducted in calculating profit).]
Compensation + Rents paid + Interest paid + Depreciation + Profits − Capital expenditures = SBT base
Single business tax base × SBT rate = Single business tax

i. Compensation
Compensation consists of three parts: (1) wages and benefits (2) equivalent compensation of pass through entities and (3) self-employment compensation....

ii. Rents
Rents are the amounts paid by the business enterprise during the taxable year for the rental of real property.

iii. Interest
... For these purposes, "interest" may be defined as "all amounts paid or accrued for the use or forbearance of money or property." Although the definition is broad, it is intended that the single business tax base include only the

---

[134] P.A. 1975, No. 228, Single Business Tax Act, §31(1), as amended, P.A. 1994, No. 247, §1. The rate reduction started with a reduction from 2.35 percent to 2.30 percent, effective after September 30, 1994.

[135] The rate is to be reduced by 0.1 percent in any year in which the comprehensive annual financial report of Michigan shows an ending balance of more than $250 million in the countercyclical budget and economic stabilization fund. The reduction occurs on January 1 following the end of the state fiscal year for which the report was issued. Mich. Stat. Ann. 7.558(31), §31(5).

[136] "West Virginia Governor's Commission Makes Reform Recommendations, Special Report," 15 *State Tax Notes* 541, 558–561 (Aug. 31, 1998).

amounts paid or accrued within a taxable period on indebtedness. . . . [Special rules are provided for insurance companies, voluntary employees' beneficiary associations, and financial institutions.]

iv. Profit

Profit is the sum of annual retained earnings plus dividend paid. . . . With respect to passthrough entities and sole proprietorships, . . . the SBT would utilize an "accumulated revenues and profits" account that would equal the total undistributed revenues of the enterprise from whatever source derived. If an amount is determined to have been paid out of this account to a shareholder in an S corporation, a partner, member or owner, then the amount would be treated as a dividend for SBT purposes. . . . [Distributions from family trusts are not considered dividends, and transactions treated as "deemed dividends" for federal income tax purposes are not dividends for SBT purposes.]

v. Capital Acquisition Deduction

The SBT would allow taxpayers a deduction from their West Virginia tax base for the cost of purchasing depreciable real property and depreciable personal property during the tax year in which the expense is incurred. The property must be located in this state.

Multi-Jurisdictional Issues

a. Constitutional Limitations

The ability of a state to impose a SBT on business enterprises that engage in activities in more than one jurisdiction is subject to limitations imposed under the U.S. Constitution. Under both the Due Process Clause and the Commerce Clause, a state may tax an entity only if the entity maintains a sufficient connection or "nexus" with the taxing state. Moreover, a state may not tax value earned outside its borders.

b. Nexus

The SBT would apply to business enterprises that engage in or carry on "business activity" in this state. The definition of business activity is extremely broad. Thus, it appears that any activity carried on in West Virginia by a "business enterprise" will create taxable nexus. Thus, the only limitations to the SBT's application are those provided by federal law and West Virginia law.

c. Apportionment

Businesses that are taxable in this state and also taxable in one or more other states must apportion their tax base among those jurisdictions. Traditionally, apportionment is based upon three factors: property, payroll and sales. Often, certain factors receive double weighting depending upon the activity, e.g., sales are double weighted in the general apportionment formula of the West Virginia business franchise and corporation net income taxes.

In order to meet constitutional standards, the SBT employs a unique apportionment method for multi-jurisdictional taxpayers. Unlike the traditional three-factor formula, the SBT applies a different apportionment factor to each of the three elements of the tax base. . . .

Under the three-tiered method, compensation is apportioned using only a payroll factor. The SBT calculates this factor by dividing compensation paid in West Virginia by total compensation paid to all employees of the business.

The interest element of the SBT base is apportioned in accordance with a single property factor. The factor is computed by dividing the value of an organization's West Virginia real and tangible personal property by the value of such property everywhere. This factor would not include the value of property a taxpayer rents from another.

The economic value measured by dividends – the use of equity capital – is based upon net income. . . .

The SBT permits taxpayers to apportion their tax base when they are subject to another state's jurisdiction to impose a business privilege tax measured by gross income or gross receipts, an income tax, a franchise tax measured by net income or net worth, capital stock tax on the value of the business or another tax similar to the SBT.[137]

3. New Hampshire Business Enterprise Tax

The New Hampshire Business Enterprise Tax (BET) is imposed at the rate of three-quarters of 1 percent of a business enterprise's taxable enterprise value tax base,[138] but only business enterprises with gross business receipts in excess of $150,000 or enterprise value tax base greater than $75,000 are required to file a return and pay tax.[139] The "taxable enterprise value tax base" is the "enterprise value tax base," as adjusted and apportioned to New Hampshire.[140] That base is calculated under the addition method as the sum of compensation, interest, and dividends paid.[141] The adjustments reduce the base to exclude such items as compensation that is retained for use in the business, and dividends received from an affiliated corporation that was included in the payor's BET base subject to tax.[142]

Is the New Hampshire BET a tax on value added when it includes only dividends paid or amounts treated as dividends paid in the tax base, rather than the enterprise's profits as commonly defined for VAT purposes?[143] The predominant factor in the BET is compensation. A business subject to the BET

---

[137] The proposal represents a well-documented, serious attempt to get a state VAT adopted after a long history of previous attempts. Capehart, "Proposing a State VAT: The Political Experience in West Virginia," *State Tax Today*, April 24, 2000.

[138] N.H. Rev. Stat. Ann §77-E:2 (2004). For additional discussions of the New Hampshire BET, see Kenyon, "A New State VAT: Lessons from NH," 49 *Nat'l Tax J.* 381 (1996); Berghaus and Ardinger, "The Policy and Structure of the Business Enterprise Tax," *N.H. Bar J.* (Dec. 1993).

[139] *Id.* at §77-E:5(I) (2004).

[140] *Id.* at §77-E:1(XV) (2004). The apportionment formula in §77-E:4, if applicable, is a three-factor formula that allocates compensation, interest, and dividends to New Hampshire. Dividends are apportioned on the basis of the average of the compensation, interest, and sales factors. If the apportionment "does not fairly represent the enterprise's business activity in this state," the enterprise can petition or the commissioner may require a different method of apportioning business activity to New Hampshire. *Id.* at § 77-E:4(II).

[141] *Id.* at § 77-E:1(IX).

[142] *Id.* at § 77-E:3.

[143] Profits of noncorporate enterprises are taxed as are dividends, but undistributed corporate profits retained for use in the business are not taxed. For a claim that the BET is not a true VAT, see Schenk, "New Hampshire: two views on the business activity tax (BET)," 5 *VAT Monitor* 234 (July/Aug. 1994).

is allowed to credit its BET liability against its liability under the separate New Hampshire business profits tax.

C. Streamlined Sales and Use Tax

Under current U.S. constitutional decisions, a seller cannot be required to collect sales taxes on interstate sales on behalf of the destination state unless the seller maintains a physical presence in the destination state.[144] In 2004, legislation was introduced in the U.S. Congress to give states that complied with the "Streamlined Sales and Use Tax Interstate Agreement" authority to require the out-of-state sellers to collect and remit sales tax on sales into that state.[145] To date, Congress has not enacted this or comparable legislation.

The Streamlined Sales and Use Tax Agreement[146] (different from the "Interstate Agreement" referred to above) creates a unified state RST system for participating states that does not depend on federal congressional action to be effective. This agreement imposes a series of requirements before a state can be certified as being in compliance.[147] The key features of this agreement emanating from the Streamlined Sales Tax Project are as follows. Each state that is a party to the agreement must establish a central state administration for all of its state and local sales and use taxes. Each participating state must adopt uniform definitions of key terms and a uniform base for its state and local sales and use taxes. A state can have only one general state sales and use tax rate (a different rate is permissible for food and drugs), and each substate jurisdiction can have only one tax rate per jurisdiction. States are required to maintain a database that will notify sellers of changes in rates or changes in the boundaries of tax jurisdictions within the state.[148] Although sellers must obtain information to support a purchaser's claimed exemption, the burden related to the validity of a purchaser's exemption under the state sales and use tax law is on the purchaser.[149] A sufficient number of states (at least ten) with adequate population (at least 20 percent of the total

---

[144] *Quill Corp. v. North Dakoda*, 504 U.S. 298 (1992); *National Bellas Hess, Inc. v. Department of Revenue of Illinois*, 386 U.S. 753 (1967).

[145] See S. 1736, "The Streamlined Sales and Use Tax Act," 108th Cong., 1st Sess (Oct. 14, 2003).

[146] See http://www.streamlinedsalestax.org.

[147] See Executive Summary, Streamlined Sales Tax Project, http://www.streamline-dsalestax.org (Apr. 2004). Sellers can use one of three technology models, including the use of a Certified Services Provider that is paid by the states. The Streamlined Sales Tax Project was established in March 2000, as a joint project of the National Conference of State Legislatures, the National Governors' Association, the Multistate Tax Commission, and the Federation of Tax Administrators. The project expects states to adopt the Uniform Sales and Use Tax Administration Act that allows the state to enter into an agreement with one or more other states, and the Streamlined Sales and Use Tax Agreement that brings the state's sales and use tax laws in compliance with the principles discussed in the text.

[148] See Streamlined Sales Tax Project: Rates and Boundary Databases Instructional Paper (May 2005), at http://www.streamlinedsalestax.org.

[149] Purchasers are liable for the tax, interest, and penalties if they claim incorrect exemptions. *Id.*

population of sales tax states) have been approved for membership, and the system became effective on October 1, 2005.[150]

A series of issues remains. For example, a central registration system must be established and authority to maintain the system must be granted to an organization or entity. Sellers without a physical presence in a participating state are not required to collect sales and use taxes unless Congress adopts a law such as the Streamlined Sales and Use Tax Interstate Agreement that could require out-of-state sellers to collect for and remit the tax to the destination state.

The governing board for the multistate compact is reviewing proposals from companies who are seeking contracts to collect and remit tax on behalf of registered retailers.[151]

D. AINSWORTH'S DIGITAL VAT

Richard Ainsworth proposed a "digital VAT" or "D-VAT" as a method for the United States to harmonize e-solutions among tax jurisdictions (federal and state, and among states) and make them more comprehensive within each jurisdiction.[152] This proposed broad-based credit-invoice VAT is a "technology-intensive" VAT that incorporates electronic and third-party tax collection aspects of EU Council Directives and the U.S. Streamlined Sales and Use Tax Agreement.[153]

Under the Ainsworth proposal, certified service providers (CSPs) serve as collection agents.[154] All VAT documents (including invoices, returns, and notices) must be electronic, except for those permitted to use paper documents. Uniform digital identification of goods and services, similar to the EU's CN8 codes or the UNCPC codes, are required.[155] Mr. Ainsworth supports reliance on electronic data, based on the fact that over 99 percent of data generated worldwide in 1999 were computer generated.[156]

---

[150] As of July 7, eighteen states were approved for membership and those sales represent over 28 percent of the population of states with sales taxes. Bennett, "Members of Streamlined Sales Tax System Make Up Almost 30 Percent of Population," *BNA Daily Tax Report*, July 11, 2005, p. H-1.

[151] See Gregory, "Five Years in Making, Streamlined Sales Tax System Begins Official Business Oct. 1 Although Collections Will Start Later," *BNA Daily Tax Report*, Sept. 30, 2005, p. J-1.

[152] Ainsworth, *Digital VAT: A Proposal for the President's Advisory Panel on Federal Tax Reform*, President's Advisory Panel on Federal Tax Reform (Apr. 30, 2005), at http://comments.taxreformpanel.gov; reprinted as "A Digital VAT (D-VAT for the U.S.?" 108 *Tax Notes* 938 (Aug. 22, 2005) [hereinafter Digital VAT]; Ainsworth, "Digital VAT and Development: D-VAT and Development," 39 *Tax Notes Int'l* 625 (August 15, 2005).

[153] Digital VAT, *supra* note 152, at 2.

[154] "Software variations of this theme, certified automated systems (CASs) and certified proprietary systems (CPSs) will further facilitate administration and compliance." Digital VAT, *supra* note 152, at 2. They all must be certified by the tax authorities. Based on the Streamlined Sales and Use Tax Agreement, §306, except for fraud, the users will be immunized "from liability for calculation or reporting errors." *Id*. at 4.

[155] The Combined Nomenclature in eight digits and the Central Product Classification, Version 1.0 are cited *id*. at 4.

[156] *Id*.

X. Discussion Questions

1. The main interjurisdictional issues in the context of federal countries are:
   a. dividing the VAT tax base among the jurisdictions while avoiding overlapping and underlapping.
   b. collecting the tax when transactions in goods and services cross borders.
   c. coordinating definitions, rates, and administration among states and between a tax at the national level and corresponding taxes at the state level.

   Is there a model solution for these issues for all federal countries? If so, what is it; if not, why not and what range of solutions exists? What other important interjurisdictional issues must federations face?

2. Are the issues in (1) the main issues for common markets? If not, what different problems do they pose?

3. Assume that in the United States the subnational units of government (states) are not willing to give up their power to define their tax base, their penalties, and so on, and that therefore the states retain their diverse single stage retail sales taxes. What are the differences between federal adoption of an EU-style VAT (a transaction tax) and an addition or sales-subtraction VAT? Consider the effect on the RST base, the ease of operation of the federal alongside the state taxes, and the state's receptivity or opposition to the federal levy.

4. States in the United States and provinces in Canada derive a significant portion of the RST revenue (ranging from 15 to 33 percent) from tax on business inputs. How will this fact affect the state and provincial governments' willingness to harmonize their RSTs with a European-style federal VAT?

5. If a single branch of government administers both a federal and state VAT, should the administrative function be given to the federal government, or the state governments, or divided between them?

6. What interstate competition problems are likely to arise if some but not all states in a federal system harmonize their RSTs with the federal VAT?

7. What are the administrative advantages and disadvantages associated with the imposition of a federal EU-style VAT alongside state RSTs?

8. If there is a federal–state integrated sales-subtraction VAT, with the states imposing varying tax rates, how can a business calculate its input credit for the state component of the combined VAT?

9. The Treaty of Rome in the EU [European Union, formerly the European Economic Community (EEC), and later the EC (European Community)] is analogous to the national "constitution" in federal countries, and the EU Sixth Directive is analogous to national legislation providing the rules of the game for VAT laws enacted by the members of the EU or the federation.
   a. With respect to VAT, which provisions or features of the U.S. Constitution are analogous to the provisions of the Treaty of Rome reproduced in this chapter?

b. Which provisions of the EU Sixth Directive would be appropriate for the U.S. Congress to enact by way of rules of the game for state retail sales taxes and VATs?

c. If your answer to (b) is "none," what federal legislative rules of the game would you regard as appropriate for state RSTs and VATs?

13

Real Property

I. Introduction

One of the most complicated problems in designing a VAT base involves the taxation of real (immovable) property. The tax base should consist of the personal consumption element in real property (for residential property, living quarters either owned or leased). In the United States, housing represents over 16 percent of total personal consumption expenditures.[1] The difficulty is to identify the personal consumption element, especially for real property that may be used for business or personal purposes.

There are a number of possible techniques for taxing real property under a VAT. They must consider valuation and other administrative issues in the context of business versus personal, investment versus consumption.

II. Array of VAT Treatment of Real (or Immovable) Property

A variety of approaches to the taxation of real property are available, even if they are based on the principles that a VAT is a tax on personal consumption, and the tax should not be imposed on the same value added to goods or services more than once.

Real property is a long-lived asset, even more so than other consumer durables. Ideally, the current use of consumer durables should be taxed each year. This approach raises significant administrative and practical problems. As a result, most consumer durables are taxed at the time of purchase (based on the consideration paid). This approach reflects a decision to tax the present discounted value of the stream of future personal consumption. The same approach could be used for real property.

Many sales of real property involve used property that turns over infrequently. Sales of other used consumer durables also raise difficult practical problems under VATs, with many countries opting to tax the full value of

---

[1] See Bureau of Economic Analysis, U.S. Dep't of Commerce, Survey of Current Business, National Data, Table 1.5.5 Gross Domestic Product, Expanded Detail (for 2004) (July, 2005).

previously taxed used goods resold by a taxable supplier.[2] This treatment results in the overtaxation of consumer durables. Resales of real property, especially by consumers, raise even more significant VAT problems.[3] The same piece of property may be sold more than once, and each subsequent sale may be at a higher price reflecting market appreciation. As a result, over the period of time that real property is held, the property may be consumed in part and appreciate in value as well; mixing the consumption and savings components of the property.

Real property may be sold or leased, held for investment or use, held for commercial use or as residential property, or held for a dual purpose. Focusing solely on the residential aspect of real property, a home or apartment may be owned or leased, may be leased without services or, like a hotel, may be provided with substantial services included in the daily, weekly, or monthly rate. Housing may be provided in a house boat.

There are a significant number of possible combinations of treatment for commercial and residential property leased or sold. All real property (even owner-occupied housing) can be taxed, exempt, or zero-rated. There can be a combination of these approaches for different kinds of real property, such as taxing commercial real property and exempting residential property, whether leased or sold,[4] or taxing new and exempting used residential property. In some countries, the construction of a multi-unit building for rental or for either current or future sale of individual units (condominiums) complicates the VAT consequences of the transactions involving this property, especially if, like in Australia, sales of new residential units are taxable and sales of used residential units are exempt from tax.

Canada has complex rules governing the taxation of real property transactions. In part, Canada taxes sales and leases of new or used commercial real property and sales of new residential property, taxes repairs and building material on commercial and residential property, and exempts leases of residential real property and sales of used residential property if the seller or lessor paid and did not claim credit for GST on that property.[5]

Australia also has a complex set of rules governing real property. Australia zero rates the grant of unimproved land by a unit of government (as a freehold or under a long-term lease).[6] It also zero rates certain grants

---

[2] See Chapter 6 (Section IV) *supra*.

[3] For a comprehensive discussion of the taxation of residential property in South Africa from the purchaser's perspective that has application to many countries with VAT, see Botes, "VAT Implications of Buying Residential Property in South Africa," *VAT Monitor*, Nov./Dec. 2003, p. 450.

[4] For example, Mexico exempts the supply of residential dwellings, except for hotels. See Serrano Salas, "Focus on Mexico," *VAT Monitor*, Mar./Apr. 2003, p. 102.

[5] The taxation of real property in Canada is more complex than suggested in the text. There is a tax rebate provided under section 256.1 of the GST to the landowner that leases land for residential purposes. See §§190–193, 206–211, Sch. IV, and Sch. V, part 1, and Sch. IX, part IV.

[6] A New Tax System (Goods and Services Tax) Act 1999 [hereinafter Australian GST], §38–445. The zero-rating covers a supply of a freehold or long-term lease by a unit of government, even if there was a prior zero-rated lease of the land and compliance with

by a government agency of a freehold interest or long-term lease of land as potential residential land or for a farming business, if the land is subdivided from land that was used for a farming business (or the land was a farming business) for at least five years.[7]

Australia exempts most real property used for residential purposes. A lease of residential premises (other than commercial residential premises) is exempt.[8] The exemption extends to a long-term lease of commercial residential accommodations, such as a long-term stay in a hotel.[9] A sale of residential premises is exempt if the property is to be used predominantly for residential accommodation.[10] The exemption on sale does not apply to sales of "commercial residential premises," or certain "new residential premises."[11] Long-term leases of residential premises are exempt, unless the lease is of property to be used by the lessee for sublease as commercial residential premises, or the lease covers certain new residential premises.[12] For example, the lease of a structure to be used by the lessee as a hotel is not exempt. Thus, except as noted earlier, sales of new residential premises and commercial residential premises (like a hotel) by a registered person are taxable. Property serving multiple purposes is considered a mixed supply that must be apportioned. For example, the sale of a used building by a registered person with retail and residential premises is taxable to the extent that it is attributable to the retail premises and exempt to the extent it is attributable to the residential premises.[13]

its terms entitled the recipient to this freehold or long-term lease. Leases preceding such zero-rated supplies of freeholds or long-term leases also may be zero-rated. *Id.* at §38–450. On the Australian GST, see R. Krever, GST Legislation Plus (2005).

[7] Australian GST, *supra* note 6, at §38–475.

[8] *Id.* at §40–35(1)(a). Residential premises is land or a building (including a floating home) occupied as a residence or intended to be, and capable of being occupied as a residence. *Id.* at §195–1 definition of residential premises. Commercial residential premises includes hotels and similar establishments, accommodations at a school, a ship used in connection with a ship rental business or for entertainment or transport, marinas leased to ships used as residences, a caravan park or camp ground, or similar to the above, but not premises used by students at an educational institution that is not a school. *Id.* at §195–1 definition of commercial residential premises.

[9] *Id.* at §40–35(1)(b).

[10] *Id.* at §40–65(1).

[11] *Id.* at §40–65(2). The exception does not apply to new residential premises that were used for residential accommodation before December 2, 1998. "Commercial residential premises" are discussed in note 8 *supra*. "New residential premises" is defined in §40–75 as residential premises not previously sold as residential premises and not previously the subject of a long-term lease. It also includes residential premises resulting from the substantial renovation of a building, or built or containing a building that was built to replace demolished premises on the same land. Premises are not new after a period of five years in the circumstances provided in §40–75(2). If premises, as described earlier, are considered "new residential premises" because of substantial renovation or built to replace demolished premises, the land that is a part of the premises is also considered "new."

[12] *Id.* at §40–70. The denial of the exemption does not apply to new residential premises used for residential accommodation before December 2, 1998. *Id.* at §40–70(2)(b).

[13] See Australian GSTR 2003/3, ¶8.

The following section discusses the EU approach to taxing real property.[14] It is followed by a section discussing a variety of proposals for the taxation of real property that depart from the EU model.

III. EU Approach to the Taxation of Real (or Immovable) Property

A. In General

The EU Sixth Directive has a series of provisions covering the taxation of land and buildings. A building is any structure fixed to or in the ground, and building land is unimproved or improved land that is defined as such by a member.[15]

The Sixth Directive, in principle, exempts leases and sales of residential and commercial real property. In contrast, new construction and repairs and maintenance of existing structures (as well as building material) are taxable.[16]

The Recast Sixth Directive, Article 132(2)(1)[17] exempts "the leasing or letting of immovable property."[18] This exemption does not apply to hotel and similar accommodations, holiday camps, camp sites, parking sites, leases of permanently installed machinery and equipment, and leases of safes.[19]

Subject to an exception described next, the supply of a building (or parts of a building) and the land on which it stands is exempt,[20] as is the supply of unimproved land.[21] This exemption does not apply in the limited case in which a person making an occasional supply of real property is treated as a taxable person with respect to that supply. Although VAT generally is imposed on taxable sales by taxable persons who conduct economic activity, members may treat a person as a taxable person even if that person engages in an occasional transaction involving land and new buildings.[22] A member state may treat as a taxable person a person making an occasional supply before a building (or part of a building) has been occupied for the first time.[23]

---

[14] For an analysis of the disparate taxation of real property in the EU, despite harmonization, and the authors call for a more restrictive exemption, see Amand, Schellmann, and Vermeulen, "Immovable Property and VAT – Lessons from Past Experience," *Int'l VAT Monitor,* Sept/Oct 2005, p. 325.

[15] Sixth Council Directive of May 17, 1977, On the Harmonization of the Laws of the Member States Relating to Turnover Taxes – Common System of Value Added Tax: Uniform Basis of Assessment, Official Journal No. L145 [hereinafter Sixth Directive], Art. 4(3)(a) and (b).

[16] Cnossen, "VAT Treatment of Immovable Property," 66 *Tax Notes* 2017 (Mar. 27, 1995).

[17] The Sixth Directive, before the recast, exempted the real property transactions under Art. 13B(b), (g) and (h). These provisions are discussed in the following excerpted cases.

[18] COM(2004) 246 final 2004/0079 (CNS) Proposal for a Council Directive on the common system of value added tax (Recast), April 15, 2004, as modified by the Presidency compromise, FISC 60, 8547/06, of 21 April 2006 [hereinafter Recast Sixth Directive], Art. 132(l)(1). Members can restrict the scope of this exemption.

[19] *Id.* at Art. 132(2).

[20] *Id.* at Art. 132(1)(j).

[21] *Id.* at Art. 132(1)(k).

[22] Sixth Directive, *supra* note 15, at Art. 4(3).

[23] *Id.* at Art. 4(3)(a). "Member States may determine the conditions of application of this criterion to transformations of buildings and the land on which they stand. Member

Supplies of goods used solely in the exempt activities described above (such as sales of property used solely in connection with exempt leasing) are exempt if input tax on those goods was not deductible.[24]

In some cases, members are required to follow the directive; in other cases, the member has the option to treat real property transactions differently. Member states can give taxpayers the option to treat as taxable the lease of immovable property and other exempt real property transactions[25] (and thereby claim input tax credits). The member state can impose restrictions on the scope and impose other conditions on the use of this option to treat real property transactions as taxable.[26] In practical effect, the exception in the Sixth Directive that gives member states the option to allow real property transactions to be taxable applies only to a person otherwise subject to VAT, not to a consumer.

The complexity of the rules governing real property predictably has generated substantial litigation. For example, in *Staatssecretaris van Financien (Secretary of State for Finance) v. Shipping and Forwarding Enterprise Safe BV (Safe Rekencentrum BV)*,[27] the European Court of Justice had to decide what kind of transfer of rights to property constituted a taxable supply. In that case (using letters to simplify the transaction), A gave B rights to property, including a power of attorney to transfer legal ownership of the property. Any change in the value of the property belonged to B. B[28] sold rights to the property to C, and A transferred title to the property directly to C. According to the court, a "supply of goods" in Article 5(1) of the Sixth Directive[29] includes the "transfer of the right to dispose of tangible property as owner, even if there is no transfer of legal ownership of the property.... It is for the national court to determine in each individual case, on the basis of the facts of the case, whether there is a transfer of the right to dispose of the property as owner within the meaning of Article 5(1) of the Sixth Directive."[30]

B. Exemption for Leasing and Terminating a Lease

1. What Is a "Lease" or "Letting" of Immovable Property?

The Sixth Directive Article 13B(b) exemption[31] covers the "letting of immovable property." It includes the rental of "both water-based mooring berths for

States may apply criteria other than that of first occupation, such as the period elapsing between the date of completion of the building and the date of first supply or the period elapsing between the date of first occupation and the date of subsequent supply, provided that these periods do not exceed five years and two years respectively." *Id.*

[24] Recast Sixth Directive, *supra* note 18, at Art. 133(a), previously Sixth Directive, Art. 13B(c).

[25] Sixth Directive, supra note 15, at Article 13B(d), (g) and (h).

[26] Recast Sixth Directive, *supra* note 18, at Art. 134(2); Sixth Directive before the recast, Art. 13C.

[27] (Case C-320/88), *Shipping and Forwarding Enterprise Safe BV*, [1990] ECR I-285, 1990 ECJ CELEX LEXIS 7163 (ECJ Judgment 1990) [hereinafter *Shipping & Forwarding*].

[28] It was the trustee in bankruptcy of B's assets that made the transfer.

[29] See Recast Sixth Directive, *supra* note 18, at Art. 15(1).

[30] *Shipping & Forwarding*, *supra* note 27, at ruling.

[31] Recast Sixth Directive, *supra* note 18, at Article 132(1)(l).

pleasure boats and land sites for storage of boats on port land."[32] The lease of a prefabricated building that is affixed to the land so that it cannot be easily dismantled or easily moved is the exempt lease of immovable property, even if the building is to be removed at the end of the lease and used at another site.[33]

In some cases, the issue is whether an agreement constitutes a lease of immovable (real) property for VAT purposes. The *Sinclair Collis* case involved an agreement by the siteholder to allow the taxpayer exclusive rights to sell cigarettes through cigarette machines located on its premises in return for a share of the profits from the operation of the machines. The machines were free-standing or affixed to a wall. The Queen's Bench held that the machine occupied land. As such, the supply was a license to occupy land exempt under the U.K. VAT.[34] The House of Lords referred the question to the ECJ for a ruling on the interpretation of the Sixth Directive, Article 13B(b). Sinclair Collis claimed that the use of space was not the lease of immovable property under the above-cited article of the Sixth Directive. To qualify for the exemption, the taxpayer claimed that the tenant had to obtain "a right to occupy a defined piece or area of property as one's own and to exclude or allow access to others."[35] The ECJ ruled that the grant of the right to install and operate the machines for two years was not an exempt lease of immovable property, in part as follows:

> [T]he fundamental characteristic of a letting of immovable property for the purposes of Article 13B(b) of the Sixth Directive lies in conferring on the person concerned, for an agreed period and for payment, the right to occupy property as if that person were the owner and to exclude any other person from enjoyment of such a right.
>
> According to the information supplied by the national court, the subject matter of the agreement is not the passive provision of an area or space, together with the grant to the other party of a right to occupy it as though he were the owner and to exclude all other persons from the enjoyment of that right.
>
> That finding is supported, first of all, by the fact that the agreement does not prescribe any precisely defined area or space for the installation of the vending machines at the premises. [U]nder the agreement there is nothing to prevent the machines from being moved about, to a degree, as the site owner wishes....
>
> Secondly, the agreement does not confer on SC the right to control or restrict access to the area where the machines are placed. Whilst it is true that under the agreement SC retains an exclusive right of access to the machines to maintain them, keep them stocked with cigarettes and remove the cash inside, that right concerns only access to the machine itself, in particular

---

[32] *Fonden Marselisborg Lystbadehavn v Skatteministeriet, and Skatteministeriet v Fonden Marselisborg Lystbadehavn*, 2005 ECJ LEXIS 74 (Judgment of the ECJ 2005).

[33] Case C-315/00, *Rudolf Maierhofer v Finanzamt Augsburg-Land*, [2003] ECR I-00563.

[34] [1998] STC 841 (Q.B. 1998).

[35] *Sinclair Collis Ltd v Commissioners of Customs and Excise*, Case C-275/01, ¶17, ECR I-5965 (Judgment of the ECJ 2003).

its inner mechanism, and not access to that part of the premises where the machine is situated. In any event, according to the information provided by SC at the hearing, the right is restricted to the opening hours of the commercial establishment and cannot be exercised without the site owner's consent.

[T]he reply to the question referred should be that, on a proper construction of Article 13B(b) of the Sixth Directive, the grant, by the owner of premises to an owner of a cigarette vending machine, of the right to install the machine, and to operate and maintain it in the premises for a period of two years, in a place nominated by the owner of the premises, in return for a percentage of the gross profits on the sales of cigarettes and other tobacco goods in the premises, but with no rights of possession or control being granted to the owner of the machine other than those expressly set out in the agreement between the parties, does not amount to a letting of immovable property within the meaning of that provision.[36]

In the following *Zinn* case, the British court considered whether fees paid for the right to occupy a particular seat in the Royal Albert Hall for 999 years was an exempt license to occupy land.

Customs and Excise Commissioners v. Zinn and Another[37]

HEADNOTE: In order to raise funds to build and maintain the Royal Albert Hall, the corporation of the hall was empowered in 1866 by Royal Charter to grant subscribers to the funds permanent seats within the hall for the whole term for which the site of the hall was leased to the corporation. The lease was for a term of 999 years from 1867. The names of seat holders were entered in a register of members. Registered holders were permitted to transfer their seats by the use of a prescribed form in consideration of payment to them of an unspecified sum of money. The instrument of transfer was to be executed by both transferor and transferee. The transferor was deemed to remain the holder of the seat until the name of the transferee was entered in the register. The ability to enjoy performances was merely consequential upon and not the subject of an assignment of a seat. A value added tax tribunal decided that what had been granted originally had been a licence to occupy land for 999 years and that accordingly the money obtained by the taxpayers from sales of their seats had been obtained as a result of an assignment of a right to occupy land and accordingly was exempt from liability to value added tax by virtue of the Value Added Tax Act 1983, Sch 6, Group 1, item 1 [Value Added Tax Act 1994, c. 23, Sch. 9, Group 1, item 1]. The commissioners appealed contending that having regard to the real

---

[36] *Id.* at ¶¶25, 27–31. [Edited by the authors.]
[37] [1988] STC 57 (Q.B. 1988). [Edited by authors.]

commercial purpose of the transaction, the sale of the seats was not a supply of a licence to occupy land but of a right to attend performances at the Albert Hall.

JUDGMENT. The taxpayers maintain...that the sale was an exempt supply by virtue of §17(1) and Item 1 of Group 1 of Sch 6 to the 1983 Act. Section 17(1)[38] reads:

'A supply of goods or services is an exempt supply if it is of a description for the time being specified in Schedule 6 to this Act.'

Schedule 6, Group 1, Item 1[39] reads:

'The grant, assignment or surrender of any interest in or right over land or of any licence to occupy land, other than ... [and there is then set out a list of transactions to which the exemption does not apply.]'

The question at issue is whether the sale of the seats was an assignment of a licence to occupy land for the purposes of this provision. Counsel for the Crown submits that ... [w]hat the purchaser was paying for was the right to attend performances, and such rights of occupation of land as he might acquire were purely incidental. I must begin by setting out what is involved in a sale or assignment of what are called permanent seats at the Albert Hall. To do so I must go back to the year 1866 when the Corporation of the Hall of Arts and Sciences was incorporated by Royal Charter. By the 4th article of the charter it was provided:

'With a view to raise the required funds for the building and maintenance of the Hall, the Corporation may receive Subscriptions or Donations from any persons or societies desirous of giving the same and,
subject to the rights reserved to Members of the Corporation by this
Our Charter, may grant to the persons or societies giving such Subscriptions or Donations, such interests in the Hall as the Corporation deem
expedient.'

The rights and obligations of subscribers and members were set out in the schedule referred to in the charter. The relevant paragraphs of the schedule are these:

'1. A register of Members shall be formed, and every person who has subscribed for, engaged to take, or is otherwise entitled to a permanent seat in the Hall, and whose name is entered on the register of Members, shall be a Member of the Corporation.... 5. Every person who has engaged to take a seat in the Hall before the granting of this Charter, shall, on the payment of the first instalment due from him, be entitled to

---

[38] Value Added Tax Act 1994, c. 23, §31(1) provides in part: "A supply of goods or services is an exempt supply if it is of a description for the time being specified in Schedule 9...."

[39] *Id*. at Sch. 9, Group 1, item 1 provides in part: "The grant of any interest in or right over land or of any licence to occupy land,...."

have his name inserted in the register of Members...7. The right of a Member to his seat shall continue for the whole term for which the site of the Hall is granted. 8. The interest of a Member in the Hall shall be personal estate, and not the nature of real estate...14. A certificate, under the Common Seal of the Corporation, specifying the seats belonging to any Member, shall be prima facie evidence of the title of the Member to such seats, and shall be given to any Member on payment of such sum, not exceeding 1s., as may be determined by the regulations of the Corporation for the time being in force...24. A permanent seat in the Hall may be transferred by the registered holder thereof, and the transferee shall be registered as a holder of such seat in the place of the transferor....

The forms of transfer or assignment giving rise to the money upon which value added tax is claimed are set out in the enclosures to the decision of the tribunal. They provide for the 'Seller' so-called 'in CONSIDERATION of the SUM of ', and then there follows the sum paid by the person referred to as the 'Buyer'. Then follow the words –

'...do hereby TRANSFER...stalls...of which I am registered as holder in the books of the "ROYAL ALBERT HALL" to hold unto the Buyer...subject to the several conditions on which I HELD THE SAME at the time of the execution hereof.'

By a supplemental Royal Charter of 1887 and by various Acts of Parliament the rights of members over their boxes or seats were restricted. For example, the 1887 supplemental charter allowed the corporation to let the hall for, amongst other things, private meetings and to exclude members from the hall on the occasion of such meetings.

Counsel for the Crown submits [as the question to be resolved]: looking at the substance and reality of the matter, was this a purchase of seats or a right to attend performances albeit seated. He submits that it is the latter. Counsel for the taxpayer submits that the ability to enjoy performances is consequential upon the assignment of the seats but not the subject of the assignment.

Counsel for the taxpayer further points out that in this case,...the vendor or supplier provided no services or facilities, nothing but the right to occupy the seat....Another difference in the present case is of course the very long term of years over which the seat licence extends. During that period it can, submits counsel for the taxpayer, like other items of property be exploited by its holder not merely for occupation and watching performances but also by sublicensing to others to whom the holder may sell tickets. The question at the end of the day is a short question, and answering it, I say at once that I prefer the arguments for the taxpayers. The agreement, and the only agreement, between the taxpayers and their assignees was that set out in the transfer document. Counsel for the Crown does not suggest that the transfer document is a sham. Yet he urges that it should be judged as if the consideration there set out was not the true or real consideration for the money paid.

The true consideration, he says, was the right to attend performances. But the taxpayers were under no obligation to provide the purchaser with performances, and no one suggests they could or would do so. Even the corporation is under no obligation to provide entertainment to its members, although no doubt it has a general obligation under the charter to make the Albert Hall available for performances. What is critical in my view is the nature of the consideration provided by the supplier. In law and in fact all that the taxpayers could and did supply in the present case was the licence to occupy [and therefore an exempt supply].

I would dismiss this appeal and hold that value added tax is not payable.

In one case, a taxable person tried to avoid the classification of a contract for the use of commercial space in a building as exempt "leasing or letting of immovable property." In *Belgium State v. Temco Europe SA*,[40] the taxable person (Temco) entered agreements with related companies that did not constitute rental contracts under Belgian law. Temco gave the transferees the right to conduct their operations in the property but without a fixed term or other usual attributes of a lease. Temco claimed input tax deductions for VAT paid on renovation work on the property. The ECJ ruled that the transactions with related companies constituted the exempt "leasing or letting of immovable property" under Article 13B(b) of the Sixth Directive;[41] that is –

> transactions by which one company, through a number of contracts, simultaneously grants associated companies a licence to occupy a single property in return for a payment set essentially on the basis of the area occupied and by which the contracts, as performed, have as their essential object the making available, in a passive manner, of premises or parts of buildings in return for a payment linked to the passage of time, are transactions comprising the letting of immovable property within the meaning of that provision and not the provision of a service capable of being categorised in a different way.[42]

2. Disposition or Transfer of a Lease

If rent received on the lease of real (or immovable) property is exempt, does this exemption extend to consideration received by a lessee for the surrender of its rights under a lease? In *Lubbock Fine & Co. v. Commissioner of Customs and Excise*,[43] the ECJ treated "transactions with similar economic consequences . . . the same regardless of their legal nature.[44] This economic equivalence approach was subsequently rejected by the ECJ, and replaced

---

[40] Case C-284/03, [2004] ECR I-11237 (Judgment of the ECJ) [hereinafter *Temco Europe SA*].
[41] Recast Sixth Directive, *supra* note 18, at Art. 132(l).
[42] Temco Europe SA, *Supra* note 40, at Operative part.
[43] Case C-63/92, 1993 ECJ CELEX LEXIS 3324 (Judgment of the ECJ). [Edited by the authors.]
[44] Teather, *Reverse Premiums and VAT – return to the beginning*, [2004] BTR 37.

by a more literal approach in the *Mirror Group* and *Cantor Fitzgerald*[45] joined cases. *Trinity Mirror* is excerpted next.

Mirror Group plc v. Commissioners of Customs & Excise[46]

JUDGMENT. By order of 15 October 1998, received at the Court on 17 November 1998, the High Court of Justice of England and Wales, Queen's Bench Division (Divisional Court), referred to the Court for a preliminary ruling on the interpretation of Article 13B(b) of the Sixth Council Directive.

Those questions were raised in proceedings between Mirror Group plc (Mirror Group) and the Commissioners of Customs & Excise (the Commissioners), who are responsible for the collection of value added tax (VAT) in the United Kingdom, concerning the liability to VAT of an undertaking given by Mirror Group agreeing in essence to become a tenant.

COMMUNITY LEGISLATION. Article 2 provides: The following shall be subject to value added tax:

1. the supply of goods or services effected for consideration within the territory of the country by a taxable person acting as such;

Article 5 – Supply of goods

1. Supply of goods shall mean the transfer of the right to dispose of tangible property as owner.

Article 6 – Supply of services

1. Supply of services shall mean any transaction which does not constitute a supply of goods within the meaning of Article 5.

Such transactions may include *inter alia*:

• obligations to refrain from an act or to tolerate an act or situation,

Article 13 of the Sixth Directive governs exemptions from VAT so far as transactions within the territory of the country are concerned. Article 13B provides, *inter alia*:

Without prejudice to other Community provisions, Member States shall exempt the following under conditions which they shall lay down for the purpose of ensuring the correct and straightforward application of the exemptions and of preventing any possible evasion, avoidance or abuse:
(b) the leasing or letting of immovable property....

---

[45] *Cantor Fitzgerald International v Commissioners of Customs & Excise,* [2001] ECR I-7257, [2001] STC 1453 [hereinafter *Cantor Fitzgerald*].
[46] Case C-409/98, [2001] ECR I-7175, [2001] STC 1453.

Background and the questions referred for a preliminary ruling

In 1993, Mirror Group, a company incorporated in the United Kingdom, was looking at various sites in London to which to move its newspaper publishing operations. According to the national court, it could expect favourable terms as an anchor tenant.

On 20 June 1993, Mirror Group entered into the following agreements with Olympia & York Canary Wharf Ltd (in administration) (O & Y):

- an agreement to lease floors 20 to 24 of One Canada Square, London (the building) (the principal agreement);
- the actual lease of those five floors;
- an option agreement giving Mirror Group an initial option, exercisable within six months, to take a lease or leases of up to four more floors of the building and - if that option was not exercised in respect of more than two floors during the six-month period – a second option, exercisable within 18 months thereafter, to take a lease or leases of one or two more floors (the option agreement).

The principal agreement stipulated that O & Y would pay Mirror Group a net inducement of £12 002 590, plus VAT, on or before 2 July 1993. That sum was described therein as consideration for the tenant entering into the agreement and as an inducement to it to take on the lease.

In accordance with the principal agreement, the following arrangements for payment were implemented:

- approximately £6.5 million (exclusive of VAT) relating to floors 20 to 24 of the building was paid into an escrow account and was released to Mirror Group in several instalments corresponding to when Mirror Group ceased to have a right to determine the leases and was thus obliged to take leases of those floors for the full 25-year period.
- approximately £5.5 million (exclusive of VAT) was paid to Mirror Group and was immediately placed by it, as it was required to do, in an escrow account by way of security. Mirror Group exercised its option only in respect of three further floors and thus retained only about £4.1 million.
- VAT of approximately £2.1 million was paid into an escrow account until 26 July 1993, on which date it was paid to the Commissioners.

It was stipulated that no rent was payable in respect of floors 20 to 24 of the building for the first five years. Starting with the sixth year and until the end of the lease, rent was payable and increased progressively, but at no time did it amount to a full market rent. Provision was made for the leases of the additional floors, in respect of which Mirror Group exercised its option, to include essentially the same provisions about rent.

Under the principal agreement, Mirror Group was required to complete the fitting out of floors 20 to 24 of the building. It actually spent about £7.2 million on fitting out floors 20 to 24 and about £1.4 million on fitting out the additional floors, 17 to 19, in respect of which it exercised its option.

According to the VAT and Duties Tribunal, London (United Kingdom), the inducement was not, however, paid by O & Y to Mirror Group as consideration for the latter fitting out the premises.

Mirror Group claimed repayment of VAT of £2.1 million on the £12 million inducement, which the Commissioners refused by decision of 1 January 1997. It then appealed against the decision to the London VAT and Duties Tribunal.

In the Tribunal's view, the acceptance by Mirror Group of the terms of the principal agreement and its execution of the lease and the option agreement constituted things done in return for the inducement of £12 million. Therefore the Tribunal held that Mirror Group had made a supply of services for consideration.

As to the question of whether that supply of services was exempt, the VAT and Duties Tribunal pointed out that that would be the case only if the supply amounted to the leasing or letting of immovable property for the purposes of Article 13B(b) of the Sixth Directive. According to the Tribunal, it follows from paragraph 9 of the judgment in Case C-63/92 *Lubbock Fine* [1993] ECR I-6665 that a supply made by a tenant who has surrendered an existing lease to a landlord in return for a capital sum is an exempt supply.

In those circumstances, there was no proper reason for excluding from Article 13B(b) of the Sixth Directive a transaction resulting in a lease where, in contrast to the standard situation, it was not the tenant who paid a sum to the landlord in order to enter into the lease but, as in the main proceedings, the landlord who agreed to pay consideration to the tenant to ensure that the latter entered into the lease and subsequently complied with its terms. As regards the £5.5 million, the Tribunal found that it was an inducement payment relating solely to the options and that therefore it was not exempt.

Both Mirror Group and the Commissioners appealed against that decision to the High Court of Justice of England and Wales, Queen's Bench Division (Divisional Court). [T]hat court decided to stay proceedings and to refer the following questions to the Court for a preliminary ruling:

1. Following the decision of the Court in Case C-63/92 (*Lubbock Fine & Co.* v *Commissioners of Customs and Excise*), does Article 13B(b) of Council Directive 77/388/EEC exempt from VAT a supply made by a person (the person) who does not initially have any interest in the immovable property, where that person enters into an agreement for lease of that immovable property with a landlord and/or accepts the

grant of a lease by the landlord in return for a sum of money paid by the landlord?

2. Following the decision of the Court in Case C-63/92 (*Lubbock Fine & Co. v Commissioners of Customs and Excise*), does Article 13B(b) of Council Directive 77/388/EEC exempt from VAT a supply made by a person (the person) who does not initially have any interest in the immovable property, where that person:

   a. enters into an option agreement in relation to leases of that immovable property in return for a sum of money being paid to the person, on terms that the money will remain in a special account as security for its obligations under the option agreement; and/or

   b. subsequently exercises the options under the option agreement and accepts the grant of leases of the immovable property in return for the release of the money in the special account to the person?

The first question

Mirror Group argues that the result of *Lubbock Fine* is that supplies of services which are directly linked to the creation, alteration, transfer or termination of a right to occupy immovable property fall within the scope of Article 13B(b) of the Sixth Directive. Further, the supply of services made by a tenant as a result of entry into an agreement concerning the letting of immovable property cannot be treated any differently from a supply made by the landlord, given the requirement for a coherent application of the Sixth Directive and respect for the principle of the neutrality of VAT.

The United Kingdom Government submits that the logic of the Court's reasoning in the judgment in *Lubbock Fine* was that payments for the renegotiation of a lease should be characterised in the same way for tax purposes as payments made for the lease as originally negotiated. That is not the situation in the case before the national court. Since Mirror Group had no title to the immovable property at the time of the transaction, it did not itself make a supply of leasing or letting services. However, the wording of Article 13B(b) of the Sixth Directive presupposes that there will be such a supply of services in order for that provision to apply.

According to the United Kingdom Government, the supply of services by Mirror Group consisted in entering into a lease or an agreement to enter into a lease. At the hearing, the Government pointed out that Mirror Group, by transferring its business to the building, attracted other tenants.

The German Government's analysis is, in essence, the same as that of the United Kingdom Government and it further takes the view that the supply of services made by Mirror Group should be likened to the supply made by an estate agent acting as broker for a lease to be entered into by the parties.

In its written observations, the Commission submits that Mirror Group made a supply of services for the purposes of Article 6(1) of the Sixth Directive consisting in entering into a lease or an agreement to enter into a lease. That supply falls within the scope of Article 13B(b) of the Sixth Directive, if the Court's ruling in the judgment in *Lubbock Fine* is followed.

At the hearing, the Commission accepted that where, in a new building, a person becomes an anchor tenant, whose presence might attract other tenants, that could constitute a taxable supply of services to the landlord. It could amount to a form of advertising. However, such a supply of services is difficult to define. If there were no separate identifiable supply of services, it would be preferable to treat the payment at issue as an assessment of the value of the lease and, therefore, as a payment inextricably linked to the lease.

Findings of the Court

It must be borne in mind that, under Article 2(1) of the Sixth Directive, a supply of goods or services effected for consideration within the territory of the country by a taxable person acting as such is subject to VAT.

It is not disputed that Mirror Group, when it entered into a contract relating to the lease of the building and agreed to take a lease of that building, acted as a taxable person but did not make a supply of goods. Therefore, it is necessary to consider whether Mirror Group, in acting thus, made a supply of services for consideration and, if it did, whether that supply falls within the leasing or letting of immovable property for the purposes of Article 13B(b) of the Sixth Directive.

As to whether a supply of services was made, it must be noted that a taxable person who only pays the consideration in cash due in respect of a supply of services, or who undertakes to do so, does not himself make a supply of services for the purposes of Article 2(1) of the Sixth Directive. It follows that a tenant who undertakes, even in return for payment from the landlord, solely to become a tenant and to pay the rent does not, so far as that action is concerned, make a supply of services to the landlord.

However, the future tenant would make a supply of services for consideration if the landlord, taking the view that the presence of an anchor tenant in the building containing the leased premises will attract other tenants, were to make a payment by way of consideration for the future tenant's undertaking to transfer its business to the building concerned. In those circumstances, the undertaking of such a tenant could be qualified, as the United Kingdom Government in essence submits, as a taxable supply of advertising services.

In that context, it is appropriate to point out that it is for the national court, in the light of the guidance given by the Court, to ascertain whether, in the case before it, Mirror Group made a supply of services for consideration to the landlord and, if it did, what that supply was.

However, an operation such as that carried out by Mirror Group, if it does actually amount to a supply of services, cannot be qualified as a supply of services covered by the term the leasing or letting of immovable property.

In that regard, it has consistently been held that the terms used to specify the exemptions provided for by Article 13 of the Sixth Directive are to be interpreted strictly, since they constitute exceptions to the general principle that VAT is to be levied on all services supplied for consideration by a taxable person.

The letting of immovable property for the purposes of Article 13B(b) of the Sixth Directive essentially involves the landlord of property assigning to the tenant, in return for rent and for an agreed period, the right to occupy his property and to exclude other persons from it.

It is thus the landlord who makes a taxable supply of services and the tenant who, in return for the supply, pays consideration. That is not the case in the proceedings before the national court.

It is true that the Court ruled in *Lubbock Fine* that the leasing or letting of immovable property for the purposes of Article 13B(b) of the Sixth Directive covers the case where a tenant surrenders his lease and returns the immovable property to his immediate landlord.

However, the Court must make clear that that judgment was given in respect of a tenant who had returned the immovable property leased to the landlord and who, consequently, for the purposes of taxation, had assigned his right to occupy the property back to the landlord by surrendering it. That is why the Court ruled . . . that the tenant's surrender of the supply of services made by the landlord, which involves a change in the contractual relationship, has to be exempt where the supply itself is exempt.

Those conditions are not met in the case before the national court. Mirror Group, as a prospective tenant, is not surrendering its right to occupy the property to the landlord.

Therefore, the answer to be given to the first question must be that a person who does not initially have any interest in the immovable property and who enters into an agreement for lease of that immovable property with a landlord and/or accepts the grant of a lease of the property in return for a sum of money paid by the landlord does not make a supply of services falling within Article 13B(b) of the Sixth Directive.

The second question

So far as the first part of the second question is concerned, the Commission rightly points out that a taxable person who merely enters into an option agreement of the kind at issue before the national court without a mutual exchange of supplies does not make a supply of services within the meaning of Article 2(1) of the Sixth Directive.

The second part of the second question raises the same issues as the first question referred by the national court. It is necessary to consider whether, on the exercise of the option and entry into the lease by the tenant in return for a sum of money paid by the landlord, the tenant merely entered into the lease or whether it made a specific supply to the landlord. In the first case, there is no supply of services within the meaning of Article 2(1) of the Sixth Directive. In the second case, nothing points to the tenant making a supply of services falling within Article 13B(b) of the Sixth Directive. Therefore, the answer to be given to the second question is that a person who does not initially have any interest in the immovable property and who enters into an option agreement such as the one before the national court in relation to leases of that immovable property in return for a sum of money paid by the landlord, on terms that the money will remain in a special account as security for its obligations under the option agreement, and who subsequently exercises the options under the option agreement and accepts the grant of leases of the immovable property in return for the release of the money in its special account, at no time makes a supply of services falling within Article 13B(b) of the Sixth Directive.

On those grounds,

THE COURT (Sixth Chamber),

in answer to the questions referred to it by the High Court of Justice of England and Wales, Queen's Bench Division (Divisional Court), by order of 15 October 1998, hereby rules:

1. A person who does not initially have any interest in the immovable property and who enters into an agreement for lease of that immovable property with a landlord and/or accepts the grant of a lease of the property in return for a sum of money paid by the landlord does not make a supply of services falling within Article 13B(b) of the Sixth Council Directive (77/388/EEC) of 17 May 1977 on the harmonisation of the laws of the Member States relating to turnover taxes – Common system of value added tax: uniform basis of assessment.

2. A person who does not initially have any interest in the immovable property and who enters into an option agreement such as the one before the national court in relation to leases of that immovable property in return for a sum of money paid by the landlord, on terms that the money will remain in a special account as security for its obligations under the option agreement, and who subsequently exercises the options under the option agreement and accepts the grant of leases of the immovable property in return for the release of the money in its special account, at no time makes a supply of services falling within Article 13B(b) of the Sixth Directive 77/388.

Cantor Fitzgerald International v Commissioners of Customs and Excise[47] involved payment by a lessee on the transfer of an unfavorable leasehold interest to a sublessee. There, the rent payable for the remaining term of an existing lease on immovable property was above the fair rental value of the

[47] *Cantor Fitzgerald, supra* note 45.

leased space. As a result, the taxpayer (sublessee) received from the lessee compensation to take over the lease, agreeing to be subject to all of the terms of the underlying lease. The lessee was not released of liability under the original lease. The Tribunal held that the receipt of this compensation was a supply exempt under Article 13B(b) of the Sixth Directive. It did not matter that the consideration moved from the assignor to assignee rather than from assignee to assignor. Consistent with the *Mirror Group* case, the ECJ ruled: "Article 13B(b) of the Sixth . . . Directive . . . does not exempt a supply of services which is made by a person who does not have any interest in the immovable property and which consists in the acceptance, for consideration, of an assignment of a lease of that property from the lessee".[48]

In Australia, the ATO issued an elaborate ruling covering the early termination of a lease.[49] The GST consequences depend in part on the reason for the termination. For example, a payment received by the lessor for an early termination of a lease that releases the lessee of its contractual obligations is a supply for consideration and if connected with Australia is a taxable supply.[50]

C. Mixed Business–Personal Use

The following *Armbrecht* case, decided by the European Court of Justice, involved the sale of a building used by the owner in part for business and in part as a private residence. He treated the residential portion as non-business property. As a result, he did not charge rent and did not claim credit for input VAT on that portion of the property.

Finanzamt Uelzen v. Armbrecht[51]

HEADNOTE. The taxpayer, a hotelier, owned a building comprising a guest house, a restaurant and premises used as a private dwelling which he sold in 1981 for DM 1715m. German law exempted such a transaction from value added tax (VAT) pursuant to art 13B(g)a of [the Sixth Directive], but also granted to taxable persons the right to opt for taxation on the transaction pursuant to art 13C(b) of the Sixth Directive where the transfer was made to another trader for the purposes of his business. The taxpayer opted for taxation on the transaction, but regarded only the sale of that part of the property which was used

---

[48] *Id., supra* note 45, at ruling.
[49] GSTR 2003/11 (Australia).
[50] *Id.* at ¶28.
[51] (Case C−291/92), ECR I-2775 (Judgment of the ECJ 1995) [hereinafter *Armbrecht*]. [Edited by the authors.]

for business purposes as subject to VAT and accordingly invoiced the purchaser for [13%] VAT only on that part. Following an inspection, the tax office [took the position]... that the taxpayer's property formed a single item in German civil law and should be treated as such for the application of the Sixth Directive. The taxpayer challenged that decision in proceedings before the finance court, Lower Saxony, which allowed his appeal. The tax office appealed to the Bundesfinanzhof (the federal finance court), which stayed the proceedings and referred to the [ECJ the question of]... whether the portion of an immovable property used for business purposes constituted a separate item of supply for the purposes of art 5(1)c of the Sixth Directive....

DECISION: ... Under art 2(1) of the Sixth Directive, the supply of goods or services effected for consideration within the territory by a taxable person acting as such is subject to VAT.

Article 5(1) provides: '"Supply of goods" shall mean the transfer of the right to dispose of tangible property as owner'.

Article 13B of the Sixth Directive sets up a series of exemptions for transactions in respect of immovable property, including:

'.... (g) the supply of buildings or parts thereof, and of the land on which they stand, other than as described in art 4(3)(a);

(h) the supply of land which has not been built on other than building land as described in art 4(3)(b).'

Article 13C adds the following proviso to those exemptions:

'Member States may allow taxpayers a right of option for taxation in cases of... (b) the transactions covered in B... (g) and (h) above. Member States may restrict the scope of this right of option and shall fix the details of its use.'

The German government stresses that the taxpayer's property forms a single item in German civil law and is entered as such in the land register. It should therefore be treated as a single item for the application of the Sixth Directive.

It is true that art 5(1) of the Sixth Directive does not define the extent of the property rights transferred, which must be determined in accordance with the applicable national law, but the court has held that the objective of the Sixth Directive, which is to base the common system of VAT on a uniform definition of taxable transactions, would be jeopardised if the preconditions for a supply of goods, which is one of the three taxable transactions, varied from one member state to another....

Consequently, the national law applicable in the main proceedings cannot provide the answer to the question raised, which concerns not the civil law applicable to supply but whether the transaction is subject to the tax.

The first question must therefore be understood as seeking to ascertain whether, where a taxable person sells property, part of which he had chosen to reserve for his private use, he acts with respect to the sale of that part as a taxable person within the meaning of art 2(1) of the Sixth Directive.

It is clear from the wording of art 2(1) of the Sixth Directive that a taxable person must act 'as such' for a transaction to be subject to VAT.

A taxable person performing a transaction in a private capacity does not act as a taxable person. A transaction performed by a taxable person in a private capacity is not, therefore, subject to VAT.

Nor is there any provision in the Sixth Directive which precludes a taxable person who wishes to retain part of an item of property amongst his private assets from excluding it from the VAT system.

This interpretation makes it possible for a taxable person to choose whether or not to integrate into his business, for the purposes of applying the Sixth Directive, part of an asset which is given over to his private use. That approach concurs with one of the basic principles of the Sixth Directive, namely that a taxable person must bear the burden of VAT only when it relates to goods or services which he uses for private consumption and not for his taxable business activities....

As Advocate General Jacobs pointed out..., apportionment between the part allocated to the taxable person's business activities and the part retained for private use must be based on the proportions of private and business use in the year of acquisition.....The taxable person must, moreover, throughout his period of ownership of the property in question, demonstrate an intention to retain part of it amongst his private assets....

The right of option provided for in art 13C, whilst making it possible to transform an exempted transaction into a taxable transaction and entitling the taxpayer to deduct input tax, does not enable a supply which does not fall within the scope of the tax as defined in the Sixth Directive to be transformed into a taxable supply.

The answer to the first question must therefore be that, where a taxable person sells property part of which he had chosen to reserve for his private use, he does not act with respect to the sale of that part as a taxable person within the meaning of art 2(1) of the Sixth Directive....[52]

[The taxpayer prevailed.]

Contrary to the facts in the *Armbrecht* case, a taxable business may construct a building and treat the entire building as a business asset, even though a portion of the building is used for private residential purposes. What are the VAT consequences on the sale of that building?

In the EU, a taxable person can treat capital goods used both for business and private purposes as business goods and claim deductions for input tax on the acquisition of those goods.[53] The private use of the goods by

---

[52] This decision is consistent with *Stirling v. H.M. Customs and Excise*, (1985) 2 BVC 205, excerpted in Chapter 3 *supra*.

[53] See *Armbrecht, supra* note 51.

the taxable person or his staff for non-business purposes then becomes a supply of services for consideration equal to the *cost* of providing the services.[54]

In *Wolfgang Seeling v Finanzamt Starnberg*,[55] the owner of a tree-surgery and horticultural business, constructed a building that he treated wholly as a business asset and used it partly as a private residence, deducted all input tax on the building, and treated the personal use as taxable. Germany denied input tax on the personal use portion of the building, claiming that it was used for exempt "leasing or letting of immovable property" under the Sixth Directive, Article 13B(b). According to the ECJ:

> The letting of immovable property for the purposes of Article 13B(b) of the Sixth Directive essentially involves the landlord of property assigning to the tenant, in return for rent and for an agreed period, the right to occupy his property and to exclude other persons from it.

> The private use by the taxable person of a dwelling in a building which he has treated as forming, in its entirety, part of the assets of his business does not satisfy those conditions.

> It is a feature of such use not only that no rent is paid but also that there is no genuine agreement on the duration of the right of enjoyment or the right of occupation of the dwelling, or to exclude third parties.

> It follows that the private use by the taxable person of a dwelling in a building which he has treated as forming, in its entirety, part of the assets of his business does not fall within Article 13B(b) of the Sixth Directive.

> Articles 6(2)(a) and 13B(b) ... must be interpreted as precluding national legislation which treats as an exempt supply of services, on the basis that it constitutes a leasing or letting of immovable property within the meaning of Article 13B(b), the private use by a taxable person of part of a building which is treated as forming, in its entirety, part of the assets of his business.[56]

D. Tax-Motivated Transactions

In order to claim credit for input tax on real property that is, in substance, used in making exempt supplies, a taxpayer may engage in tax-avoidance motivated transactions designed to convert the real property into an asset used in making taxable supplies. In one case, a British university leased newly-renovated university buildings and then leased them back, and opted to be taxable on the lease in order to claim credit for input tax on the renovations. In judgments by the European Court of Justice in the *University of Huddersfield* and *Halifax* cases,[57] the court ruled that for VAT purposes a

---

[54] See Sixth Directive, *supra* note 15, at Art's. 6(2)(a) & 11A(1)(c); Case C-97–90, *Lennartz*, [1991] ECR I-3795.

[55] Case C-269/00, [2003] ECR I-04101.

[56] *Id.* at ¶¶49–52, and Operative part (footnotes omitted).

[57] Case C-223/03, Opinion of April 7, 2005. [As of the cutoff date for the book, the ECJ had not issued a judgment in this case.]

person's transactions can be respected as supplies of goods or supplies of services and the person can be treated as being engaged in economic activity (and entitled to input tax credits), even if the transactions are carried out solely to obtain a tax advantage and not for any other economic objective. A taxable person is not entitled to deduct input VAT if the transactions constitute an abusive practice; in that case, the transactions can be restructured to eliminate the abuse practice.[58]

To be given vitality, the transaction must satisfy the objective criteria on which the concept of economic activity is based.[59]

IV. Proposals for the Taxation of Real Property

There have been a variety of approaches to the taxation of real property transactions in countries with VAT. The following represents only a sample of the proposals on how real property should be treated under a VAT.

Conrad proposed the stock value added tax (S-VAT). Only the essential elements of this proposal are discussed here. The tax is imposed on all sales of new and used real property, with taxable purchasers eligible to claim input credits for VAT paid on the purchase. Except for a possible small business exemption, real estate agents and construction firms are taxable. Durable goods (such as refrigerators) should be taxed when sold for home improvement or home construction. Rentals should be taxed when provided by a taxable person. The first nontaxable purchaser (such as a consumer) bears the tax, which serves as a prepayment of future taxes, whether the future use is for investment or consumption. On resale, the nontaxable seller is expected to recover from the purchaser any remaining balance of the prepaid taxes. Any resales back to a taxable person triggers a restart of the input credit system.[60]

The model act developed by the American Bar Association Section of Taxation Committee on Value Added Tax taxes a broad range of transactions involving real property.[61] For administrative reasons, the committee decided not to tax the imputed rental value of home ownership. The committee compromise was to require a taxable person to charge VAT on sales, leases, and resales of land and improvements. Indeed, a taxable person who sells or leases real property for residential or other nonbusiness purposes

---

[58] *Id.* at ¶101.

[59] *University of Huddersfield Higher Education Corporation v Customs and Excise Commissioners,* Case C-223/03, [2006] ECR I->>>>, [2006] All ER (d) 273 (Feb. 21, 2006); *Halifax plc and others v Customs and Excise Commissioners,* Case C-255/02, [2006] ECR I- >>>>, [2006] All ER (D) 283 (Feb. 21, 2006).

[60] See generally on VAT and real estate, Conrad, *The VAT and Real Estate,* from chapter 8, Gillis, Shoup, & Sicat, Value Added Taxation in Developing Countries (World Bank 1990), pp. 95–103. See especially his discussion of Stock Value Added Tax (S-VAT) at pp. 98–99.

[61] See A. Schenk, reporter, Value Added Tax: A Model Statute and Commentary, A report of the Committee on Value Added Tax of the American Bar Association Section of Taxation [hereinafter ABA Model Act], pp. 72–79.

must charge VAT on those transactions, and the buyer or tenant cannot claim input credit for tax paid on the purchase or rental payments. A taxable person who purchases commercial real property can claim credit for tax on the purchase, and must charge VAT on rentals. The model act includes an unusual provision that taxes casual sales by sellers who are not taxable persons, if the sales price exceeds the statutory threshold set for high-priced casual sales. To prevent the double tax of real property disposed of in a casual sale, the model act provides a deferred credit for the tax paid when the property was acquired.[62] The following chart summarizes the tax treatment of real property under the model act:[63]

	For business use (including rental)		For residential or other nonbusiness use	
	Output tax	Input credit	Output tax	Input credit
Sale of land	Yes	Yes	Yes	Deferral
Sale of improve's	Yes	Yes	Yes	Deferral
Rental – land or improvements	Yes	Yes	Yes	No

The commentary to the ABA Model Act makes a novel recommendation to classify property, such as raw land, as property acquired for investment and therefore eligible for input credits. According to the commentary, special treatment can be provided for "investment assets placed in an investment custody account (ICA) if the investor's interest in the assets is limited to an intangible right to an investment return and the investor cannot obtain possession of the property."[64] The ICA would resemble a trust similar to an individual retirement account, but subject to income tax. VAT-able sales to an ICA trustee would be treated like purchases by a taxable business in connection with taxable activity and therefore eligible for an input tax credit. For example, if the trustee leases real estate placed in an ICA, the rents would be taxable as sales made in connection with business and the input tax on the purchase of the property would be claimed as input credit. VAT would be imposed on any sale of the investment property or distribution of the property to the investor.

The Basic World Tax Code developed by the Harvard International Tax Program taxes a wide range of transactions involving immovable property within the VAT base.[65] All sales of immovable property are taxed, even if the sale is made by a consumer or the sale is not in the ordinary course of business. A taxable person is entitled to claim an input credit for tax on taxable

---

[62] *Id.* at 78.

[63] *Id.*

[64] ABA Model Act, *supra* note 61, at 182–184.

[65] See excerpts from the Value Added Tax Law and Commentary portion of the Basic World Tax Code, 1996 edition, pp. 123 and 289. The commentary criticizes the approach in some countries that exempt land and buildings, but impose "high, cascading transfer taxes" instead. *Id.* at 289.

purchases of immovable property if the property is used in connection with business. To prevent double taxation in the case of taxable sales of immovable property between nontaxable persons, the purchaser can claim a VAT refund to the extent he can establish the amount of tax previously paid on the sale to his seller. The World Tax Code follows the common practice of taxing business leases and exempting nonbusiness leases; thus, input credit is allowed for tax paid on business leases, but not for any VAT buried in the rent charged on nonbusiness leases.

Cnossen supports the approach that fully taxes real property, including the rental value of owner-occupied housing.[66] He acknowledges the practical problems associated with the taxation of owner-occupied housing, and notes that if the residential rentals are taxed and the rental value of owner-occupied housing is exempt, home ownership is favored over residential rentals. The difficulty in taxing small landlords led most countries to tax new construction and exempt residential rentals.[67] In an attempt to reduce the tax burden on housing occupied by low-income households, some countries exempt sales of small housing units.[68] For ease of administration, Cnossen suggests that all construction activity (including repairs and maintenance) should be taxed at a single rate.[69]

Cnossen's "second-best solution" includes the taxation of newly created houses, the exemption of residential rentals, and the exemption of housing services and sales of existing housing. Commercial sales and rentals of immovable property other than housing should be taxed. He opposes preferential rates because of the distortions and administrative complications that they cause. Sales and leases of the same kind of property by the same kind of seller should be taxed alike. Cnossen recommends the abolition of transfer taxes on immovable property in the countries employing them, and their replacement with VAT.

V. DISCUSSION QUESTIONS

1. Under the Basic World Tax Code or ABA Model approach to applying VAT to real estate, does every lessor (landlord) of rented property become a VAT taxpayer? Under the Sixth Directive, does every seller of real estate collect and pay over VAT? What exceptions and why? How does the New Vatopia VAT handle real property?

---

[66] Cnossen, *VAT Treatment of Immovable Property*, ch. 7 of V. THURONYI, ED., TAX LAW DESIGN AND DRAFTING (IMF 1996).

[67] *Id.* at 2018.

[68] Turkey "exempt units up to 150 square meters. Presumably, some families are then tempted to buy two units and subsequently connect them." *Id.* at 2019.

[69] *Id.* Some countries do not follow this practice. For example, Ireland imposes a low rate on concrete; Italy taxes materials for the construction industry and repairs on old buildings at a low rate. The U.K. rules are even more inconsistent. Construction is taxed, but sales of new residential property is zero rated, so allocation problems exist when renovation of a home is combined with the construction of a new adjoining structure. *Id.*

2. How should a VAT treat the investment component of residential property as distinguished from the consumption component?

3. Suppose that A, the buyer of a new home, is required to pay VAT on the full price of land and building at the time of purchase. Suppose, further, that after ten years A resells the home to B at a greater price than A paid. What VAT consequences follow under the ABA Model? Under Conrad's S-VAT? Under the Sixth Directive? What is the proper treatment in your view?

4. Many existing VATs around the world apply VAT to short-term rentals of living space, that is, hotels and other short-term lodging charges, but not to long-term residential rentals, that is, more than thirty days, or sixty days, or ninety days. Can this be justified on other than grounds of political or administrative expediency?

5. Does the purchase or rental of real estate by a business firm typically give rise to a VAT input credit? Even if the firm's output (or some of it) is exempt or zero rated?

6. Consider the following proposal in conjunction with the ABA's proposed Investment Custody Account that would allow consumers who purchase investments to transfer those investments into a trust or similar account and thereby become eligible to claim credit for the input tax on such purchases. Homeowners would be allowed to put newly purchased homes into investment custody accounts. The trustee could rent to the owner at a market rent. The trustee would get full input credit and refund after purchase, but would collect and pay over to the government the VAT on each rental payment. Is this proposal analytically sound? Is it workable?

14

Proposals for U.S. Tax on Consumption

I. INTRODUCTION

Thomas S. Adams, an American, was one of the first commentators to discuss the concept of a VAT.[1] Other than flirting with a possible federal sales tax as a source for revenue to finance World War II,[2] the U.S. Congress has not seriously debated a proposal for a federal tax on consumption.

Retail sales taxes account for a significant share of state and local revenue, and at least one state relies on a state-level value added tax.[3]

As discussed in Chapter 2, a consumption-based tax can take the form of an individualized consumption-based income tax (commonly referred to as a "consumed" or "cash-flow income tax) or the form of a consumption-based tax on sales of goods and services (single stage sales tax or multistage value added tax). This book has focused on the latter. Indeed, because most countries with consumption-based taxes rely on European-style VATs, this book concentrated on that kind of VAT.

On January 7, 2005, President Bush established a panel to recommend revenue-neutral options to reform the federal tax system to make it simpler, fairer, and more pro-growth to benefit all Americans. The panel issued its report on November 1, 2005. Although the panel received many submissions and discussed the possible introduction of a federal sales or value added tax,

---

[1] C. SULLIVAN, THE TAX ON VALUE ADDED 40–41, citing Adams, "Fundamental Problems of Federal Income Taxation," *Quarterly Journal of Economics*, XXV (1921), p. 553.

[2] The U.S. Department of the Treasury opposed the general sales tax proposed by Congress in 1942. See Considerations Respecting a Federal Retail Sales Tax, Mich. Tax Study Staff Papers 1104 (1958). There were other never-enacted congressional proposals for a general sales tax at the federal level, such as in 1862 as a revenue source to finance the Civil War, in 1918 to replace the excess profits tax, and in 1931 to finance the deficit caused by the Depression. See NATIONAL INDUS. CONFERENCE BD., INC., SALES TAXES: GENERAL, SELECTIVE, AND RETAIL 1–3 (1932), in Schenk, "A Federal Move to a Consumption-Based Tax: Implications for State and Local Taxation and Insights from the Canadian Experience," 3 *The State & Local Tax Law*. 89, 92 footnote 13.

[3] Michigan Single Business Tax Act, Mich. Comp. Laws §208.1 *et seq.*; Mich. Stat. Ann. 7.558(1) *et seq.* The New Hampshire Business Enterprise Tax, N.H. Rev. Stat. Ann. §77-E:2, discussed in Chapter 12 *supra*, is imposed on a business enterprise's taxable enterprise value tax base at the rate of three-quarters of 1 percent.

the panel did not include a transactional tax on consumption to supplement or replace any of the existing federal taxes on income, payroll, and wealth transfers. The next section discusses the panel's report.

Members of the U.S. Congress have introduced bills proposing European-style VATs but with broader bases. For example, Senator Hollings introduced a modified version of the Model VAT Act, a product of the VAT committee of the American Bar Association tax section.[4] Congressman Dingell periodically introduces the National Health Insurance Act[5] relying on a European-style VAT to finance a national health care program.

Several sales-subtraction VATs have been proposed in the United States. One proposal is to replace federal duties and the federal income, estate and gift, excise, and employment taxes with a revenue neutral system of two taxes on consumption, called the Helming National Consumption Tax Plan.[6] One part of this plan is a 15.2 percent destination principle VAT that applies to businesses conducted in all forms, nonprofit organizations, and federal, state, and local government agencies. The second is a 15.2 percent retail sales tax imposed on a broad base, but not on items such as housing, food for home consumption, prescribed medical purchases, school tuition, child care, and insurance. Mr. Helming suggests that his two-tiered plan could be adapted to replace all state and local taxes with about a 3.8 percent VAT and 3.8 percent retail sales tax in order to be revenue neutral.[7]

There have been proposals to use revenue from a VAT to take one hundred million taxpayers off the individual income tax rolls. Congressman Gibbons proposed the replacement of approximately 90 percent of federal taxes, including a portion of the federal individual income tax with a sales-subtraction VAT. The individual income tax would remain only for taxpayers with incomes above $75,000.[8] Professor Graetz proposed a similar replacement of the individual income tax on taxpayers with incomes below $75,000–$100,000, but he relies on a European-style, credit-invoice VAT.[9] Professor Graetz suggests that this reform would return the individual income tax to

---

[4] A. Schenk, reporter, Value Added Tax – A Model Statute and Commentary: A Report of the Committee on Value Added Tax of The American Bar Association Section of Taxation. In 1999, Senator Hollings introduced this bill as the Deficit and Debt Reduction and Social Security Solvency Act of 1999, S. 1376, 106th Cong., 1st Session (July 15, 1999). Several sections of the bill refer to the tax as a Business Activities Tax. See *id.* at §6318.

[5] H.R. 15, National Health Insurance Act 109th Cong., 1st Session (Jan. 4, 2005), was Congressman Dingell's most recent bill to finance national health with a European-style VAT.

[6] See Helming, Summary Discussion Outline of the Helming National Consumption Tax Plan, testimony before U.S. House of Representatives Committee on Ways and Means (April 13, 2000), reproduced at 2000 TNT73–33.

[7] *Id.* at Executive Summary, ¶ 15.

[8] See Revenue Restructuring Act of 1996, H.R. 4050, 104th Cong., 2d Sess., 142 Cong. Rec. E1572 (Sept. 11, 1996) (introductory statement by Mr. Gibbons [hereinafter Gibbons, VAT]). The Gibbons VAT would be used to replace the federal corporate income tax, most of the individual income taxes, and the Social Security and Medicare taxes.

[9] See Michael. Graetz, The Decline (and Fall?) of the Income Tax (1997) [hereinafter Graetz]; Michael. Graetz, The U.S. Income Tax: What It Is, How It Got That Way and Where Do We go From Here (1999) [hereinafter Graetz, Where Do We Go From

its pre–World War II status as a tax only on families with substantial incomes. These proposals are discussed after the panel's report.

An elaborate legislative proposal for radical tax reform was the USA Tax system that included a sales-subtraction VAT (the Business Tax) and a consumption-based tax on income of individuals (the Income Tax).[10] The successor, the Simplified USA Tax, will be discussed after the Gibbons/Graetz proposals.

Subsequent sections of this chapter discuss two different kinds of consumption-based taxes proposed in the United States – the "flat tax" and a national retail sales tax. The flat tax basically is imposed on a consumption base, except that the wage component of value added by business is reportable by and taxable to wage earners, subject to an exemption designed to bring some progressivity into the system. The Shelby and Hall-Rabushka flat tax proposals are discussed. There was another flat tax proposal (not discussed further in this chapter) designed to convert the federal income tax to what has been described as a progressive flat tax, with almost no deductions or tax credits.[11] The Gebhardt tax would be imposed at a 10 percent rate and apply to 75 percent of all taxpayers. Unlike the other flat taxes imposed on a consumption base, Gebhardt's tax is imposed on an income base. The Chambliss national retail sales tax also is discussed

An unusual proposal was made by Congressman Burgess.[12] His bill retains the existing individual and corporate income taxes. Under that bill, individuals may elect to be subject to a new flat rate income tax regime rather than the current individual income tax. Corporations and others engaged in business activity may elect to be subject to a flat rate business tax regime rather than the current income tax on business activity conducted in individual, partnership, corporate, or other form. An outline of this elective flat rate income tax proposal is included at the end of this chapter.

II. President Bush's Advisory Panel on Tax Reform

A. Introduction

In January 2005, President Bush appointed an advisory panel to recommend options "to make the tax code simpler, fairer, and more conducive to

---

Here]; Graetz, "Essay, 100 Million Unnecessary Returns: A Fresh Start for the U.S. Tax System," 112 *Yale L.J.* 263 (2004) [hereinafter Graetz Essay].

[10] A comparable tax was proposed in 2003. It is Congressman English's Simplified USA Tax that would replace the federal income tax and the estate and gift taxes. See also Senator Smith's Tax Simplification Act introduced in 2003. Smith's proposal would replace the current federal tax system with a flat rate individual income tax and a flat rate tax on business activities.

[11] See Congressman Gebhardt's tax plan discussed in *Gebhardt Release on 10 Percent Tax Plan*, 96 TNT 13–16 (Jan. 19, 1996). See also Godfrey, "A Progressive Flat Tax? Gebhardt Says Yes," 70 *Tax Notes* 337 (Jan. 22, 1996).

[12] H.R. 1040, Freedom Flat Tax Act, 109th Cong., 1st Sess. (Mar. 2, 2005).

economic growth."[13] The panel recommended only the options that obtained unanimous support on the panel. The directive from President Bush was that the proposals must be limited to the income taxes and must be revenue-neutral, assuming that the tax cuts enacted earlier in his administration would become permanent. As enacted, many of those Bush tax cuts are scheduled to terminate. The panel recommended two tax reform plans – the Simplified Income Tax Plan, and the Growth and Investment Tax Plan.

Although the panel could not reach consensus on recommending a trans-action form of sales or value added tax to replace some or all of the existing federal income taxes, the Growth and Investment Tax Plan would move the federal income tax on individuals and businesses closer to a consumption base. This section discusses both the panel's consideration of a transactional form of value added tax, the Partial Replacement VAT, and the Growth and Investment Tax Plan.[14]

B. Value Added Tax Considered

The panel considered a "Partial Replacement VAT" that would combine the introduction of a 15 percent VAT imposed on tax-inclusive prices with reduc-tions in the top individual and corporate tax rates to 15 percent.[15] It was esti-mated that the VAT would raise about 65 percent of the revenue currently raised by the income taxes. The panel could not reach consensus on this kind of VAT because some felt that the addition of a VAT to the federal tax arsenal would lead over time to a larger federal government, whereas others were supportive, claiming that the additional revenue source "could be used to solve the nation's long-term fiscal challenges, especially unfunded obliga-tions for Social Security, Medicare, and Medicaid programs."[16] The panel reported that the VAT considered would be economically efficient, would improve incentives for investment in the United Sates, but might increase administrative and compliance costs by adding another federal tax. Lower rates for income taxes made possible with the addition of a VAT may reduce the level of income tax noncompliance, but the panel acknowledges that a VAT introduces its own opportunities for tax evasion. A federal VAT may raise some serious coordination problems with state and local sales taxes, unless those sales taxes were harmonized with the VAT.[17] The panel thought that this option should receive further consideration.

---

[13] The President's Advisory Panel on Federal Tax Reform, Simple, Fair, and Pro-Growth: Proposals to Fix America's Tax System, November 2005 [hereinafter Advisory Panel on Tax Reform], Executive Summary, p. xi.

[14] For an evaluation of the panel's report, see Gale & Burman, *A Preliminary Evaluation of the Tax Reform Panel's Report*, Tax Analysts Tax Break, *Tax Notes*, Dec. 5, 2005, p. 1349. For the proposal on which part of the panel's recommendations were based, see D. Bradford, The X Tax in the World Economy: Going Global with a Simple, Progressive Tax [hereinafter Bradford X Tax].

[15] Advisory Panel on Tax Reform, *supra* note 13, at 192.

[16] *Id*. at 193.

[17] See *id*. at 200–203.

The panel considered a single positive rate, credit-invoice VAT imposed on the destination principle, so that imports were taxed and exports were free of VAT. The tax base was broad, removing only noncommercial government services, primary and secondary education, existing residential housing, and charitable and religious services. Special treatment was provided for the financial sector and for "other goods and services difficult to tax."[18]

The panel considered a VAT with a $100,000 small business threshold, but businesses with taxable gross receipts below $100,000 could voluntarily be subject to VAT. That small business exemption threshold was estimated to reduce businesses within the VAT system from twenty-four million to about nine million.[19]

C. The Growth and Investment Tax Plan

The panel's recommended Growth and Investment Tax Plan (GITP) was designed to shift the federal income tax system toward a consumption tax, but maintain progressivity in the system. The panel considered but could not reach a consensus on a consumption tax base with the Progressive Consumption Tax Plan (PCTP).[20] The PCTP differs from the GITP in some fundamental ways. Under the PCTP, there was no tax on capital income at the household level; that is, interest, dividends, and capital gain would not be taxed. As a result, there were no special savings accounts, since all saving was exempt. There would not be any record keeping required for investment accounts. However, for revenue neutrality, the top tax rate under the individual and business cash flow tax would increase to 35 percent, the tax benefits for employee-provided health coverage would be less, and the overall distribution of tax burdens would be less progressive.[21]

The recommended GITP combines "a progressive tax on labor income and a flat-rate tax on interest, dividends, and capital gains with a single-rate tax on business cash flow."[22] Although labor income is taxed at rates of 15, 25, and 30 percent, interest, dividends, and capital gains are taxed at 15 percent.[23]

Businesses are subject to a single 30 percent tax rate on "their cash flow, which is defined as their total sales, less their purchases of goods and services from other businesses, less wages and other compensation paid to their workers. Thus, businesses would be allowed an immediate deduction for the cost of all new investment."[24] Businesses, other than financial institutions, are not taxed on dividends and interest received and capital gain on the sale of financial assets, but are denied deductions for interest paid. According

---

[18] *Id.* at 198.

[19] *Id.* at 199.

[20] See discussion *id.* at 182–190.

[21] *Id.* at 184.

[22] *Id.* at 151.

[23] The Panel failed to achieve a consensus for a "Progressive Consumption Tax" that completely eliminated the tax on capital income.

[24] Advisory Panel on Tax Reform, *supra* note 13, at 152.

to the panel report, "the very substantial reduction in the tax burden on investment would stimulate capital formation, keep American capital that would have gone to other countries at home, and attract foreign capital to the United States."[25]

Many current deductions in the individual income tax are replaced by tax credits, so that all taxpayers receive the same tax benefit. Items like the personal exemption and standard deduction are replaced by a family credit.[26] The deduction for interest on home mortgages is converted to a credit of 15 percent of interest paid, but it is capped. Charitable contributions are deductible to the extent they exceed 1 percent of income. Health insurance can be purchased with pretax funds, but the benefit is capped at about $5,000 for an individual and $11,500 for a family. There also are some benefits for the cost of education and for savings for retirement, education, and health. Social security benefits are not taxed to lower-income households.[27]

The business portion of the Growth and Investment Tax Plan dramatically changes the tax base for business activity. According to the report, "all business investment can be expensed the year when it is made."[28] In addition to expensing rather than depreciating capital expenditures, the territorial reach of the tax changes. The current tax on business (whether under the corporate tax or the individual tax on business operated as a sole proprietorship or in partnership form) relies on a global approach; that is, tax is imposed on worldwide income and foreign tax credits are given for tax imposed on income earned abroad. The panel's GITP converts the tax to a territorial tax imposed on the destination basis. The tax is not imposed on exports and imports are in the tax base because they are not deductible.[29] Business operated outside the United States is not included in the tax base. For businesses operated as sole proprietorships, the owner will report the results of operations on the owner's tax return and will be taxed at the graduated individual tax rates of 15–30 percent.[30]

Although most losses must be carried forward rather than eligible for refund, loss carry-forwards will be grossed-up to include interest on the

---

[25] *Id.* at 158.

[26] The child tax credit is eliminated. The family credit for a married couple is $3,300 and $1,650 for a single person. A $1,500 credit is provided for each child (although an unmarried with a child is $2,800). *Id.* at 157.

[27] See generally the chart *id.* at 157.

[28] *Id.* at 164. The report acknowledges that the denial of a deduction for interest paid prevents a "net tax subsidy to new investment." *Id.* "The presence of expensing for new investment under the Growth and Investment Tax Plan would make the United States an attractive place to invest foreign capital." *Id.* at 170.

[29] The report notes that an origin-based system creates the opportunities for "transfer pricing" disputes. "The term transfer pricing refers to amounts charged (or not charged) for sales and transfers between related entities, often controlled by a single corporate parent." *Id.* at 169. These disputes occur under the current income tax system.

[30] See *id.* at 162.

delayed benefit.[31] An exception is provided for exporters. The tax element of the costs attributable to exports, including labor costs, is refundable, not subject to the carry-forward rule governing other business activity subject to the GITP.[32] The panel believes that the GITP is a border adjustable tax, consistent with the World Trade Organization (WTO) rules. This kind of tax has not received the scrutiny of the WTO or member nations. The report suggests that the GITP "is equivalent to a credit-method VAT at a 30 percent rate, coupled with a progressive system of wage subsidies and a separate single-rate tax on capital income."[33] The panel acknowledged the "uncertainty over whether border adjustments would be allowable under current trade rules, . . . [so] the panel chose not to include any revenue that would be raised through border adjustments in making the Growth and Investment Tax Plan revenue neutral."[34]

The panel recognized the significant transitional problems associated with a movement to a consumption-based system that allows expensing rather than depreciation of capital expenditures, that changes the taxation of interest receipts and payments, that changes the current tax incentives to use debt rather than equity, and that moves to a system with border tax adjustments. The panel recommends a five-year phase out period that, for example, allows continued depreciation of depreciable assets purchased before the effective date of the new system, and gives relief to others affected by border tax adjustments and other significant changes.[35]

The business tax portion of the GITP resembles some of the VAT proposals discussed later in this chapter. It has some of the features of the Business Tax portion of the USA Tax, except that the USA Tax requires reporting on the accrual method. It also has some of the features of the business tax portion of the Hall-Rabushka Flat Tax,[36] except that the Hall-Rabushka Flat Tax is an origin-, not destination-principle tax that includes exports in the tax base. The GITP differs from the Gibbons sales-subtraction VAT because it provides a deduction for wages and other compensation.[37]

The GITP provides special rules for the taxation of firms rendering financial services. The basic GITP rules do not work "because the cash flow tax base for these financial firms would not include the revenues that they generate from lending and investing at rates above their cost of funds, but it would

---

[31] Although "trading" losses with profitable companies may provide an immediate benefit from negative cash flows, the panel did not recommend this option. The panel presumes that rules similar to current rules would limit the use of losses by combining companies with losses and profits. *Id*. at 167.

[32] *Id*. at 171.

[33] *Id*. According to the report, "(m)any developed countries with border-adjustable VATs couple those VATs with a single-rate tax on capital income at the individual level. Some of these countries also have wage subsidies, progressive taxation of wages, or both." *Id*.

[34] *Id*. at 172.

[35] *Id*. at 172–175.

[36] See *infra* subsection V(A).

[37] See also Bradford X Tax, *supra* note 14.

allow a deduction for the cost of compensation for workers as well as other purchases."[38] The report provides only a broad outline of the possible taxation of these firms. The panel's recommendation is that "financial institutions would treat all principal and interest inflows as taxable and deduct all principal and interest outflows."[39]

III. Gibbons and Graetz VATs Replacing Most Income Tax[40]

Congressman Gibbons proposed a broad-based 20 percent sales-subtraction VAT in 1996. A unique feature of the Gibbons proposal is the progressivity it provides by granting a tax rebate to households with incomes up to $30,000, by subjecting households with incomes between $30,000–$75,000 to only the 20 percent VAT on all taxable goods and services, and by subjecting households with incomes above $75,000 to the VAT and a 17 percent income tax on incomes above $75,000.[41]

A Gibbons sales-subtraction VAT requires estimates of tax to be rebated on exports because, like the allowance under the Japanese CT, the Gibbons VAT allows input credits for a presumed tax embedded in purchases from exempt small businesses. A sales-subtraction form of VAT should not affect its compatibility with World Trade Organization rules on acceptable border tax adjustments. "If, however, Congress approaches [a sales-subtraction VAT] like an income tax and grants or denies deductions for economic, administrative, or political reasons, [Congress could] . . . change the nature of the tax so substantially that our trading partners may successfully claim that the tax no longer is an indirect tax that is border adjustable under GATT [WTO]."[42]

Professor Graetz proposed a European-style, credit-invoice, destination principle VAT to replace the individual income tax for those with incomes below $75,000 or $100,000. One option Graetz suggests is to adopt a 20 percent flat rate income tax on incomes above $75,000 or $100,000.[43]

In his 1999 book and 2004 essay,[44] Professor Graetz updates his earlier book, including the data. He suggests that a 10–15 percent VAT "could finance an exemption from income tax for families with $100,000 of income or less

---

[38] Advisory Panel on Tax Reform, *supra* note 13, at 165–166.

[39] *Id* at 166. "To prevent the over-taxation of business purchases of financial services, financial institutions would inform business customers of the amount of financial cash flows that are attributed to deductible financial intermediation services. This amount would be deductible as an expense" to the business user of these services. *Id*. The appendix to the report discusses other alternatives.

[40] For a discussion and comparison of these proposals, see Schenk, "Radical Tax Reform for the 21st Century: The Role for a Consumption Tax," 2 *Chapman L. Rev.* 133 (1999) [hereinafter Schenk, Role for Consumption Tax].

[41] See Gibbons, VAT, *supra* note 8, at proposed §§ 1601–1602 and 1611–1612.

[42] Schenk, Role for Consumption Tax, *supra* note 40, at 147–148, quoting from Oldman & Schenk, "The Business Activities Tax: Have Senators Danforth & Boren Created a Better Value Added Tax?," 10 *Tax Notes Intl.* 55, 62 (1995).

[43] Graetz, *supra* note 9, at 265.

[44] See Graetz, Where Do We Go From Here; Graetz Essay, *supra* note 9.

and would allow a vastly simpler income tax at a 25% rate to be applied to incomes over $100,000."[45] That change would eliminate 90 percent of all persons filing individual income tax returns.

If the Graetz-proposed VAT had a $25,000 small business exemption, one-half of the businesses would be taken off the VAT rolls.[46] Graetz proposes exemptions from VAT for education, religion, and most health care expenditures.[47] New residential construction is taxed but not resales of existing homes.[48]

Instead of exempting food and clothing, he suggests that low-income people receive cuts in their payroll tax withholdings.[49] Graetz concedes that "protecting low- and moderate-income workers from a tax increase or loss of the EITC [earned income tax credit] wage subsidy without requiring them to file tax returns is probably the most challenging task for the new tax system I am urging here."[50] One alternative is to provide "negative withholding" for individuals earning $20,000 or less.[51]

The Gibbons sales-subtraction VAT may be easier to administer alongside transparent state and local retail sales taxes than the Graetz European-style VAT if the Gibbons VAT is buried in product prices and the Graetz VAT is transparent. The Graetz VAT "could be buried in retail prices, but as a transaction-based tax, businesses still must comply with two transaction-based sales taxes imposed on different bases in states with state retail sales taxes. The compliance burden may be increased if a business makes sales both at retail and pre-retail stages."[52]

> Were it not for the operation of a federal VAT alongside state and local sales taxes, the Graetz European VAT proposal would be preferable. It would maintain the tradition in the United States of transparent sales taxes, which are separately stated on sales invoices.... Negative aspects of the Gibbons VAT include the fact that it is not transparent and it appears, in statutory form, more like a tax on business income. [Border tax adjustments, or BTAs]... may be imprecise because the tax is buried in product prices, and if Congress views the VAT as a tax on business, it may distort the tax with exemptions and deductions improper for a broad-based tax on consumption. It is possible to bury a European VAT in retail prices to prevent the sticker shock from two sales taxes being added at the cash register. However, the difference between a period tax (the sales-subtraction VAT) and a transaction tax (the European VAT) still remains.[53]

---

[45] Graetz Essay, *supra* note 9, at 284–285.
[46] There would be 12.5 million businesses on the tax rolls if the exemption is $25,000, and 5.5 million if the exemption is $100,000. *Id.* at 289–290.
[47] *Id.* at 290. Financial services should be in the base.
[48] *Id.*
[49] *Id.*
[50] *Id. at* 292.
[51] *Id.* at 293.
[52] Schenk, Role for Consumption Tax, *supra* note 40, at 149–150.
[53] *Id.* at 154–155.

IV. The USA Tax System: Coordinated Consumption-Based Individual and Business Taxes

A. Introduction

In 1992, U.S. Senators Nunn and Domenici cochaired the Strengthening of America Commission.[54] In its report, the commission recommended the replacement of the individual income tax "with a consumption-based income tax system that would exempt savings and investment from taxation."[55] The report discussed the broad principles for this tax, making it clear that it should be a progressive tax. With this tax, "income itself is only subject to tax if consumed, rather than saved."[56] Although the system is described as an income tax system, it is consumption-based.

Alliance USA issued a discussion paper[57] on the Unlimited Savings Allowance (USA) Tax System that, with some modifications to the Strengthening of America Commission's report, was introduced in legislative form by Senators Nunn and Domenici as the "USA Tax Act of 1995."[58]

The Simplified USA Tax, a modified USA Tax, was introduced a few times, including a bill by Representative English in 2003.[59] This section discusses the USA Tax and the identifies some of the differences between that initial proposal and the subsequent "Simplified" versions.

The USA Tax System would replace most of the income and payroll tax revenue with a sales-subtraction VAT collected by business (the Business Tax [BT]) and a cash-flow or consumption-based individualized income tax on individuals (the Income Tax [IT]). Tax under the USA Tax System is expected to be paid by individuals when they earn and not save income (the IT) and when they buy goods and services for consumption (the BT). An 11 percent tax also is imposed on imported goods and services, measured by the customs value of imports of property and services.[60]

---

[54] The CSIS Strengthening of America Commission: First Report (Center for Strategic and International Studies 1992).

[55] *Id*. at 20. They also recommend "a tax on business cash flow" – a form of value added tax. *Id*. at 21.

[56] *Id*. at 99.

[57] The paper was prepared by legal consultants Ernest S. Christian and George J. Schutzer, with advice from economic consultants Rudolph G. Penner and Barry K. Rogstad. See "Unlimited Savings Allowance (USA) Tax System," 66 *Tax Notes* 1481, 1485 (special supp.) (Mar. 10, 1995) [hereinafter USA Tax System Paper].

[58] S.722, USA Tax Act of 1995, 104th Cong., 1st Sess., 141 Cong. Rec. S.5664 (Apr. 24, 1995) [hereinafter USA Tax Act].

[59] H.R. 269, Simplified USA tax Act of 2003, 108th Cong., 1st Sess., Jan. 8, 2003 [hereinafter Simplified USA Tax]. The earlier versions were The Simplified USA Tax introduced as H.R. 4700, 105th Cong., 2d Sess. On Oct. 5, 1998; and reintroduced as H.R. 134, 106th Cong., 1st Sess. On Jan. 6, 1999.

[60] USA Tax Act, *supra* note 58, at §§286–288. The import tax does not apply to imports for personal consumption that are "duty free under subchapters I through VII of chapter 98 of the Tariff Schedules of the United States." *Id* at §286(d). Tax on services that are treated as imported under §§267 or 270 is reportable by the person receiving the imported services as if it were an addition to the BT. *Id*. at §287(b)–(d). The only credits available against

The BT portion of the USA Tax System is discussed next. It is followed by a brief review of the IT part of the USA Tax.

B. The Business Tax

The Business Tax (BT) is a sales-subtraction VAT that relies on the destination principle to define the jurisdictional reach of the tax. It is a consumption-style tax that differs substantially from the existing income tax on business because it allows business an immediate deduction for the cost of business inputs, including the cost of capital goods and the cost of inventory purchased for use in the business. The BT rate applies to prices inclusive of tax.

A business entity[61] is subject to tax equal to the business tax less the payroll tax credit.[62] The business tax is 11 percent of the gross profits for the year.[63] The payroll tax credit is a credit for the employers' share of the social security, railroad retirement, and hospital insurance taxes.[64]

As just discussed, the business tax is imposed on gross profits, defined by the USA Tax System as taxable receipts less deductible amounts for the tax year.[65] Taxable receipts include receipts from the sale or use of property and from the performance of services in the United States, receipts from games of chance, and receipts from exchanges in kind, but not separately stated federal, state or local taxes, and not financial receipts other than from taxable intermediation.[66] Capital contributed by owners and dividends reinvested in the business are not reportable as taxable receipts.

A business can deduct the cost of business purchases, any loss carryover, and the transition basis deduction.[67] For this purpose, business purchases include the acquisition of property or the use of property and services acquired for use in a business activity[68] in the United States,[69] such as

---

the import tax are "for prior overpayment or credits for deposits of the import tax. *Id.* at §288.

[61] A business entity is a "corporation, unincorporated association, partnership, limited liability company, proprietorship, independent contractor, individual, or any other person engaged in business activity in the United States." *Id.* at Title III, adding §206(a).

[62] *Id.* at §201. It is not clear that the U.S. trading partners will not challenge under World Trade Organization rules a VAT that replaces the payroll tax (or that is viewed as not imposed on wages).

[63] *Id.* at §201(b).

[64] *Id.* at §201(c). The credit is the *lesser* of the business tax for the year (before any payroll tax credit) or the sum of the current credit and credit carryovers to the current year. *Id.* at §281(a). The bill includes detailed rules to calculate the credit for FICA, railroad retirement, and self-employment taxes paid. *Id.* at §282.

[65] *Id.* at §202.

[66] *Id.* at §203. The taxation of financial intermediation is covered in §§235–246.

[67] *Id.* at §204(a). Businesses subject to tax on intermediation services obtain deductions under those provisions. *Id.* at §204(b).

[68] Business activity is broadly defined to include the sale, lease or development of property or services, but not casual or occasional sales of property used by an individual, such as an individual's sale of a personal vehicle. *Id.* at §206(b). Business activity also does not include services provided as an employee or domestic household services of an employee. *Id.* at §206(c).

[69] *Id.* at §205(a)(1).

purchases or rentals of real property, capital equipment, supplies, inventory, purchases from independent contractors, imports, and financial intermediation services.[70] Business purchases do not include payments for interest or dividends, life insurance premiums, the purchase of savings assets, property acquired or services performed outside the United States and not imported, taxes (other than product taxes), and most importantly, compensation paid to employees in cash or in kind.[71] A major component of the tax base therefore is the nondeductible labor costs. A loss[72] for a year may be carried forward for fifteen years.[73]

The BT is imposed on a broad base that excludes only some services rendered by units of government and nonprofit organizations that are provided without explicit charges. Trade associations, labor unions, cemetery corporations, and other income tax–exempt organizations are subject to the BT.[74] Churches and certain educational and charitable organizations are exempt, except on unrelated business activity.[75]

Although the Alliance USA discussion paper requires businesses to report on the cash method, the Nunn-Domenici USA Tax bill mandates the accrual method of accounting for reporting purposes.

In the international area, the BT has a territorial rather than a global reach. The BT base does not include exports, and it does not apply to business operated outside the United States. Imports of services are not subject to the import tax, but the value of these imported services are effectively taxed to importers subject to the BT by denying them deductions for the cost of such services. Imports of services by consumers and by entities exempt from the BT presumably escape tax. If a business has a negative tax base for the year, as may occur for an exporting company, the business does not receive a tax refund, but must carry forward the excess deductions to the following year. The BT therefore does not completely remove BT on exports by a business that reports excess deductions.[76]

The transition to the BT raises significant problems that include the treatment of the remaining unamortized cost of capital goods, inventory, and other items that were capitalized under existing income tax rules. The discussion paper suggests that the unrecovered tax basis for these assets is recoverable when the BT becomes effective. Business may lose the benefits

---

[70] *Id*. at §205(a)(2).

[71] *Id*. at §205(a)(3), (4).

[72] A loss equals the taxable receipts less the sum of deductible business purchases and any transition basis adjustment for the year. *Id*. at §207(c). Special rules apply to carryovers of acquired businesses and to businesses filing consolidated returns. *Id*. at §207(d).

[73] *Id*. at §207(b). The allowable loss carryover deduction is the *lesser* of the business's gross profit for the year (before the carryover) or the loss carryover to that year. *Id*. at §207(a). The loss carryover includes all losses from prior years that can be carried over to the current tax year. *Id*. at §207(b)(2).

[74] See USA Tax System Paper, *supra* note 57, at 1527–1528.

[75] *Id*. at 1528–1529.

[76] To take advantage of the excess deductions, an exporting company may become an attractive target for a company with substantial BT liability.

of carryovers (such as net operating losses and capital loss carryovers) existing when the BT becomes effective.

It is not clear how this dramatic change in the taxation of corporations will affect corporate policy, such as whether it will put pressure on corporations to distribute rather than reinvest their profits. Under the USA Tax System, there is no BT or IT on corporate distributions to shareholders that are reinvested by shareholders.

If the business community views the BT as a tax on business rather than a tax on consumption to be collected by business, certain segments of the business community (especially those that have substantial labor costs and that sustain operating losses during periods of economic downturn) are likely to oppose any switch from the corporate income tax to the BT. For example, assume that a professional baseball club has the following results of operations for a year:

Gross revenue	$80,000,000
Compensation	(70,000,000)
Other costs	(20,000,000)
(purchases from outside vendors)	
Operating loss	($10,000,000)

With a BT, the baseball club will incur a tax liability on the following $60 million tax base, even though it did not earn a profit under the current income tax.

Sales	$80,000,000
Purchases	20,000,000
BT base	$60,000,000

The Simplified USA Tax on Business follows the basic framework and includes a base similar to the USA Tax. It is imposed on taxable business activitiy, defined as the business tax, less the payroll tax credit.[77] The rates are different. The USA Tax has a single 11 percent tax rate for business. The Simplified USA Tax has two rates – 8 percent on the first $150,000 of gross profits, and 12 percent on gross profits exceeding $150,000.[78]

C. The Income Tax

The USA Income Tax (IT), designed to replace the existing individual income tax and much of the employee's share of the social security tax, is a progressive consumption-based tax imposed on the portion of an individual's income that is not saved and the portion of an individual's savings that is diverted to consumption.

---

[77] Simplified USA Tax, *supra* note 59, at §201(a) of the Act.
[78] *Id.* at §201(b) of the Act.

The IT is imposed, for citizens and resident aliens, on taxable income less the allowable USA tax credits.[79] Taxable income is calculated as follows:[80]

Gross income and deferred compensation
−Alimony, child support, and the savings deduction
Adjusted Gross Income
less

(a) the personal and dependency deductions,
(b) the family allowance, and
(c) the sum of the homeowner, education, charitable, and *transition basis deductions.*

Taxable Income

Gross income for IT purposes includes receipts from all sources, including compensation, alimony, and gain from the sale of nonfinancial assets,[81] but does not include gifts, bequests, proceeds of loans, and certain government transfers.[82] The IT portion of the USA Tax System retains many of the exclusions available under the existing income tax rules. For example, there are exclusions for military combat pay, parsonage allowances, some employment-related fringe benefits, certain meals and lodging associated with employment, food stamps, and rent and energy assistance to low-income households.[83] Income previously deferred is included in gross income when it is withdrawn from savings.[84] Salary provided by a deferred compensation agreement is not reportable as gross income while it is being deferred.

The IT provides only limited deductions. A number of deductions available under the existing income tax are not available for IT purposes. For example, no deduction is allowable for state and local taxes, for casualty or theft losses, for investor expenses, and for employee business expenses.[85] An individual, for example, receives deductions for net savings, for personal and family exemptions, for a family living allowance, and for certain expenditures for education,[86] for home ownership,[87] and charitable contributions.

---

[79] USA Tax Act, *supra* note 58, §201 adding ch. 1, the Unlimited Savings Allowance Tax for Individuals, at §§1 and 2. The tax does not apply to nonresident aliens. *Id.* at §2(b). Nonresidents are taxed on certain compensation income. See *id.* at §2(c).

[80] See *id.* at §1(b)–(e).

[81] Nonfinancial assets include personal residences, art, and other collectibles.

[82] USA Tax System Paper, *supra* note 57, at 1489.

[83] *Id.* at 1510–1511.

[84] *Id.* at 1505.

[85] *Id.* at 1523.

[86] See *id.* at 1522.

[87] An interest deduction is available on a mortgage covering a personal residence or a second residence, subject to a $1 million cap on acquisition indebtedness. See *id.* at 1523.

The deduction for net savings converts the tax to a consumption base. The deduction defers taxation of returns to capital until those returns are used for consumption.[88]

If an individual borrows (other than exempt borrowing) to buy a savings asset, the individual does not have any net savings. Exempt borrowing (that does not reduce savings) includes borrowing on a personal residence, loans of up to $25,000 per year to buy consumer durable goods such as furniture, appliances, or a car, and up to an additional $10,000 in loans for any purpose. Detailed rules are necessary to calculate the basis of assets, including the basis of assets acquired with borrowed funds or assets that do not increase net savings.[89]

An individual calculates his or her USA income tax on taxable income at progressive rates.[90] For example, for 1996, the proposed tax rates for married individuals filing joint returns were 19 percent on taxable income up to $5,400, 27 percent on taxable income between $5,400 and $24,000, and 40 percent on taxable income over $24,000.[91] The tax brackets are to be indexed for inflation.[92]

An individual can reduce his or her tax by allowable, refundable tax credits.[93] The tax credits include foreign tax credits,[94] payroll tax credits, earned income tax credits, and taxes-paid tax credits.

The payroll tax credit is available for the employee's share of the basic FICA or railroad retirement tax and one-half of the basic self-employment tax.[95]

The earned income tax credit, consisting of a complex set of rules, is a phased-out credit linked to earned income and the number of qualifying children.[96]

The taxes-paid tax credit includes the tax withheld from wages, the refundable excess social security tax paid, the overpayment of a prior year's tax, and any estimated tax paid for the year.[97]

---

[88] The allowable deduction is subject to a series of adjustments necessary to take borrowing and certain other sources of funds into account. Nonexempt borrowing reduces net savings. *Id.* at 1514. There is a broad antiabuse rule that denies a deduction if the allowance of a deduction would be contrary to the intended purpose of the savings deduction. *Id.* at 1519.

[89] *Id.* at 1517. Transitional rules are necessary to cover savings assets owned when the IT becomes effective. Individuals either must keep records of the tax basis in these savings assets or they may elect to amortize the bases of savings assets (if savings assets do not exceed $50,000) over a three-year period. See *id.* at 1515.

[90] USA Tax Act, *supra* note 58, at §1(a).

[91] *Id.* at §15(a)(1). Comparable rates for 1996 for an unmarried individual (who is not a head of household or a surviving spouse) are 19 percent up to $3,200, 27 percent between $3,200 and $14,400, and 40 percent over $14,400.

[92] *Id.* at §24.

[93] See *id.* at §20.

[94] The foreign tax credit is similar to the foreign tax credit rules under the Internal Revenue Code of 1986, except that the credit is limited to taxes on amounts included in the taxpayer's gross income. *Id.* at §20(a)(1).

[95] *Id.* at §21(a).

[96] *Id.* at §22. The earned income amounts are adjusted for inflation.

[97] *Id.* at §23.

The Simplified USA Tax for Individuals departs from the USA Income Tax on individuals in several ways. The tax is imposed on taxable income at progressive rates, less tax credits. The tax rates are lower. For married individuals filing jointly, the tax rates are 15 percent on the taxable income up to $40,000; 25 percent on taxable income over $40,000 and up to $80,000; and 30 percent on taxable income over $80,000.[98]

The Simplified USA Tax replaced the complex deduction for net savings with a dramatic expansion of the Roth IRA.[99] Although tax is imposed on wages, dividends, interest, and other financial income, when previously taxed income is placed in a Roth IRA, investment earnings on those funds are exempt from tax.[100] Income attributable to employer sponsored savings and retirement funds continue to be deferred.[101]

V. The Flat Tax

The concept of a consumption-based "flat tax" was introduced by Robert Hall and Alvin Rabushka in 1981, was published in 1985 and revised by the authors in their 1995 book entitled *The Flat Tax*. The flat tax was popularized in 1995 by House Majority Leader Richard Armey, introduced in the U.S. Senate in 1995 by Senator Shelby,[102] and represented the cornerstone of Steve Forbes's tax program in his 1996 unsuccessful bid for the Republican nomination for president. Indeed, the public perception of the flat tax was of a simplified income tax on individuals and businesses to replace the existing income taxes. In fact, they are consumption-based taxes. In 2003, Senator Specter introduced his flat tax proposal.[103]

This section will discuss both the Hall-Rabushka flat tax and Senator Shelby's flat tax bill.

---

[98] Simplified USA Tax, *supra* note 59, at Chapter 1 – Simplified USA Tax for Individuals [hereinafter Simplified IT], §15(a).

[99] With a Roth IRA, as currently structured, the taxpayer cannot deduct contributions into the IRA, earnings from the investments in the IRA are not taxed, and withdrawals are not taxed.

[100] Simplified IT, *supra* note 98, at §4(a)(1) (gross income does not include "returns or benefits from previously taxed income), and §30(d) (distributions from Roth IRAs are not includible in gross income). Contributions into Roth IRAs are capped at the taxpayer's adjusted gross income. *Id*. at §30(c)(2).

[101] See Simplified USA Tax, *supra* note 59, at §101(c)(3) of the Act.

[102] The concept of a Hall-Rabushka flat tax also was supported by Senator Specter. The Shelby bill, S.1040, Tax Simplification Act of 2003, 108th Cong., 1st Sess., (May 12, 2003) [hereinafter Shelby Flat Tax]. Congressman Smith introduced a bill like the Shelby flat tax, except that it proposed a 17 percent tax rate after 2004. See H.R. 3060, Tax Simplification Act of 2003, 108th Cong., 1st Sess., 2003 H.R. 3060 (Sept. 10, 2003).

[103] Senator Specter introduced his flat tax proposal most recently in 2003. S.907, Flat Tax Act, 108th Cong., 1st Sess., (Apr. 11 2003) [hereinafter Specter Flat Tax]. Some of the differences between the Shelby and Specter bills are noted.

A. Hall-Rabushka Flat Tax[104]

The Hall-Rabushka flat tax is an integrated two-part tax, with one portion collected by business and the other portion imposed on workers. According to the authors:

> Here is the logic of our system, stripped to basics: We want to tax consumption. The public does one of two things with its income – spends it or invests it. We can measure consumption as income minus investment. A really simple tax would just have each firm pay tax on the total amount of income generated by the firm less that firm's investment in plant and equipment. The value-added tax works just that way. But a value-added tax is unfair because it is not progressive. That's why we break the tax in two. The firm pays tax on all the income generated at the firm except the income paid to its workers. The workers pay tax on what they earn, and the tax they pay is progressive.

> To measure the total amount of income generated at a business, the best approach is to take the total receipts of the firm over the year and subtract the payment the firm has made to its workers and suppliers. This approach guarantees a comprehensive tax base. The successful value-added taxes in Europe work this way. The base for the business tax is the following:

> Total revenue from sales of goods and services
> *less*
> purchases of inputs from other firms
> *less*
> wages, salaries, and pensions paid to workers
> *less*
> purchases of plant and equipment

> The other piece is the wage tax. Each family pays 19 percent of its wage, salary, and pension income over a family allowance (the allowance makes the system progressive). The base for the compensation tax is total wages, salaries, and retirement benefits less the total amount of family allowances.[105]

It is apparent from the above description that the combined tax bases produce a tax on consumption. Businesses and individuals do not include returns to saving, such as interest, dividends, and capital gains, in their taxable receipts.

B. Shelby Flat Tax

The Shelby flat tax consists of two major parts – the individual income tax and the tax on business activities imposed on the origin principle. The 20 percent individual income tax is a wage tax that achieves some degree of progression with a generous standard deduction linked to the taxpayer's

---

[104] See R. Hall & A. Rabushka, The Flat Tax, 2d ed. (1995), pp. 55–64.
[105] *Id.* at 55–56.

filing status and the number of his or her dependents. The individual income tax is imposed on the taxable income of every individual.[106] Taxable income equals the excess of (a) cash wages, taxable retirement distributions,[107] and unemployment compensation over (b) the standard deduction.[108] The standard deduction consists of a basic standard deduction that depends on the taxpayer's filing status plus the additional standard deduction of $5,000 for each dependent.[109] Taxable income of dependent children under age 14 is reportable by the parents claiming the children as dependents.[110] Inflation adjustments are provided for the standard deduction.[111]

The second part of the Shelby flat tax is a tax on business activities. A 20 percent tax[112] is imposed on business taxable income of every person engaged in business activities (whether the business is operated as a corporation, a partnership, a proprietorship, or otherwise).[113]

Business taxable income equals gross active income less allowable deductions.[114] Gross active income is gross receipts[115] from the sale of property or services in the United States by a person and the export of property or services in connection with a business activity.[116] It thus is an origin-based tax that is not imposed on imports and is not rebated on exports. A special rule taxes a provider of financial intermediation services on the value of the intermediation services that it provides.[117] Business activity does not include activity of a governmental entity or a tax-exempt organization.[118] Thus, sales by governments and tax-exempt organizations are not subject to the flat tax, except to the extent that wages paid by these entities are subject to the individual income tax portion of the tax.[119] Finally, services provided by an employee to his or her employer do not constitute business activity subject to this portion of the flat tax.[120]

---

[106] Shelby Flat Tax, *supra* note 102, at §101.

[107] The proposal contains a broad definition of a retirement distribution. *Id.* at amendment to §63(c) of the 1986 Code.

[108] Specter's flat tax is imposed on the taxpayer's earned income for the year, less the sum of the standard deduction, cash charitable contributions, and the home acquisition indebtedness deduction. Specter Flat Tax, *supra* note 103, at §1(a).

[109] *Id.* at §101(b), amending §63(b)[now §63(c)] of the 1986 Code. 110. *Id.* at amendment to §63(e) of the 1986 Code.

[110] *Id.* at amendment to §63(e) of the 1986 Code.

[111] *Id.* at amendments to §63(e).

[112] The rate drops to 17 percent after an introductory period.

[113] Shelby Flat Tax, *supra* note 102, at §102(a), amending §11(a) of the 1986 Code.

[114] *Id.* at §102(a), adding §11(c)(1) to the 1986 Code.

[115] Gross receipts from an exchange equals the amount of money and the fair market value of the property or services received.

[116] Shelby Flat Tax, *supra* note 102, at §102(a), adding §11(c)(2) to the 1986 Code.

[117] Id. at §102(a), adding §11(e) to the 1986 Code. Otherwise, property does not include money or a financial instrument, and services do not include financial services. *Id.* at §102(a), adding §11(e) to the 1986 Code.

[118] Shelby Flat Tax, *supra* note 102, at §at §102(a), adding §11(c)(3).

[119] A 20 percent (17 percent after an introductory period) tax is imposed on the value of noncash compensation provided by certain governmental or tax-exempt employers to their employees. See *id.* at §102(b), amending §4977 of the 1986 Code.

[120] Shelby Flat Tax, *supra* note 102, at §102(a), adding §11(f).

A business subject to the tax on business activities can reduce its tax base by the cost of business inputs attributable to taxable business activity, cash wages paid to employees for services performed in the United States, and contributions to qualified retirement plans that make retirement distributions.[121] Business inputs include the amount paid (including separately stated federal, state, or local taxes) for property and services (other than services of employees) acquired or used in connection with a business activity.[122] By contrast, business inputs do not include wages and contributions to qualified retirement plans or items for personal use that are not used in connection with business activity.[123] If, for any tax year, a business has deductions exceeding gross active income, an amount is carried forward to the following year as additional deductions equal to the amount of the excess plus an interest factor equal to the excess multiplied by the three-month treasury rate for the last month of that tax year.[124]

The Shelby flat tax, and the flat taxes proposed by Representative Armey and by Hall and Rabushka, contain a tax base comparable to a VAT. The major difference is that the tax on the compensation portion of the VAT base is collected from wage earners rather than collected by the employer as part of the sales price of its taxable goods and services. In addition, the wage component in a traditional VAT is part of the selling price of the taxable goods and services. As a result of the standard deduction in the flat tax, the effective tax rate on the wage component of the base is reduced.

VI. NATIONAL RETAIL SALES TAX

A. INTRODUCTION

Single-stage retail sales taxes (RSTs) have been used extensively at subnational levels of government in the United States and Canada. The Canadian provinces, except for Alberta, impose either retail sales taxes or VATs harmonized with the federal Goods and Services Tax. In the United States, forty-five states and the District of Columbia impose retail sales taxes at the state and typically at the local level as well. Only Alaska, Delaware, Montana, New Hampshire, and Oregon do not have state level sales taxes imposed on taxable sales.[125]

The crazy quilt of state RST bases in the United States prompted some commentators[126] to suggest that state RSTs be harmonized. The harmonized state sales tax could be administered by state revenue departments, by regional tax authorities, or by a national administration (such as the Internal Revenue

---

[121] *Id.* at §102(a), adding §11(d).

[122] *Id.* at §102(a), adding §11(d)(2). Taxes do not include tax imposed by ch. 2 or 21.

[123] Shelby Flat Tax, *supra* note 102, at §11(d)(2)(B).

[124] *Id.*, adding §11(g).

[125] See Due & Mikesell, SALES TAXATION: STATE AND LOCAL STRUCTURE AND ADMINISTRATION (1983). Alaska has a fairly extensive local sales tax. See *id.* at 4.

[126] See Rivlin, "Wanted: A New State-level Tax to Prepare us for the 21st Century," *Governing*, April 1990, p. 74.

Service). In fact, an early stage of sales tax harmonization began in October 2005, with the implementation of a Streamlined Sales Tax.[127]

One of the proposals to radically change the federal tax system calls for the enactment of a national retail sales tax to replace a number of federal taxes. Representatives Linder and Peterson introduced the Fair Tax Act of 1999, which, if enacted, would impose a national sales tax to be administered by the states to replace a host of federal taxes.[128] Under Congressman Schaefer's bill, the "National Retail Sales Tax Act of 1996"[129] bill, the Internal Revenue Service would be abolished, and the administration of the tax would be entrusted primarily to the states. A comparable bill was introduced by Congressman Linder and Senator Chambliss as the Fair Tax Act of 2005.[130] They proposed a national sales tax to be administered by the states, to replace income, payroll, and estate and gift taxes. They also provide for a tax rebate to families with incomes up to the poverty level. This section describes the Chambliss bill.

B. The Chambliss Bill

1. Basic Framework and Scope of the Tax Base

The Chambliss bill imposes a 23 percent tax[131] generally to be collected by the seller of any taxable property or service for the use, consumption or enjoyment in the United States,[132] whether produced or rendered within or without the United States."[133] The seller must separately state the tax on sales invoices.[134] Imports are taxed.[135] The national RST thus is a destination principle tax that taxes imports and does not tax exports. Revenue is allocated

---

[127] See discussion *supra* Chapter 12.

[128] H.R. 2525, Fair Tax Act of 1999, 106th Cong., 1st Sess., 145 CONG. REC. H5571 (July 14, 1999). The bill would repeal the corporate and individual income taxes, the payroll taxes, and the estate and gift taxes. For an economic analysis of a federal retail sales tax, see Kotlikoff, *Rethinking A Federal Retail Sales Tax,* testimony to the Committee on Ways and Means of the U.S. House of Representatives, reprinted in 2000 STT 72–47 (Apr. 13, 2000).

[129] H.R. 3039, 104th Cong., 2d Sess, 141 CONG REC.H1775 (Mar. 6, 1996) [hereinafter Schaeffer National Retail Sales Tax]. This bill would repeal the individual and corporate income taxes, the estate and gift taxes, and a series of excise taxes.

[130] S. 25, The Fair Tax Act of 2005, 109th Cong., 1st Sess., 2005 S.25; 109 S.25, Jan. 24, 2005 [hereinafter Chambliss National Retail Sales Tax].

[131] *Id.* at §101(b). The Schaeffer sales tax is imposed at 15 percent.

[132] Taxable property or service is any tangible property (including leaseholds, but not used property) and any service (including financial intermediation services). Chambliss National Retail Sales Tax, *supra* note 130, at §2(a)(14)(A). Services include "any service performed by an employee for which the employee is paid wages or a salary by a taxable employer, and...shall not include any service performed by an employee for which the employee is paid wages or a salary...by an employer in the regular course of the employer's trade or business...[and other specified employers]." *Id.* at §2(a)(14)(B).

[133] *Id.* at §101(a).

[134] *Id.* at §501(a)(3).

[135] *Id.* at §101(c).

among administering states[136] on the basis of the destination of the taxable property or services.[137]

The tax does not apply to taxable property or services purchased for resale,[138] purchased to produce taxable items,[139] or exported.[140] These exemptions are not available for a purchase made by a person in connection with an activity not engaged in for profit (a hobby).[141] A seller therefore must obtain information from the buyer in order to ascertain the tax status of the sale.

Imports by persons not engaged in active trade or business are not taxed if the gross payments do not exceed $400 during the year.[142] This rule also raises administrative problems for customs if it is to be enforced at the border. Alternatively, it will require self-assessment by the importer.

Casual or isolated sales by persons not engaged in active business are not taxed if payments for all such sales for the year by such person do not exceed $1,200.[143] Presumably, this rule also will rely on self-assessment.

The tax is imposed on the person using or consuming taxable goods or services. That person is not liable for the tax if that person pays the tax to the person selling the taxable item, but only if that person (the person using or consuming the goods or services) receives a receipt from the supplier containing certain required information.[144] The tax is imposed on gambling.[145]

2. Special Treatment for Government Entities and Nonprofit Organizations

The Chambliss bill contains special rules for government entities and nonprofit organizations. Units of government generally are not exempt from tax "on any sale of taxable property or services."[146]

---

[136] See *id*. at §401(b).

[137] See *id*. at §405(h).

[138] A property or service is purchased for resale if it "is purchased by a person engaged in a trade or business and used in that trade or business for resale." *Id*. at §102(b).

[139] Property or service is purchased to produce taxable property or service if it is purchased by one engaged in a trade or business in order to employ or use such property or service to produce, provide, render, or sell taxable property or services. *Id*. at §102(b)(2).

[140] *Id*. at §102(a). For these exempt sales, if the seller is a wholesaler and has an exemption certificate from the purchaser, the seller is not required to collect and remit tax on that sale. Intra-firm sales between affiliated firms are not subject to these requirements. *Id*. at §103(g).

[141] *Id*. at §701(a). An activity is deemed to be engaged in for profit if the gross receipts from that activity exceed the sum of "taxable property and services purchased," "wages and salary paid," and "taxes paid, in two or more of the most recent three calendar years. *Id*. at §701(b).

[142] *Id*. at §901(b). The Schaeffer bill added an overall limitation. The exemption was capped at $2,000 per year. Schaeffer National Retail Sales Tax, *supra* note 129, at §2(b).

[143] Chambliss National Retail Sales Tax, *supra* note 130, at §901(c) The Schaeffer bill's cap was $5,000. Schaeffer National Retail Sales Tax, *supra* note 129, at §2(c).

[144] Chambliss National Retail Sales Tax, *supra* note 130, at §101(d), with the information specified under §510.

[145] The taxable amount of gaming services is the excess of gross gaming receipts over the sum of gaming payoffs and gambling specific taxes. *Id*. at §707(d)–(e).

[146] *Id*. at §704(a).

Dues, contributions,[147] and receipts of a not-for-profit organization are not taxable. Taxable purchases by nonprofits for resale or for use in producing taxable property or services are eligible for the resale or other exemptions.[148]

3. RST Credits

The national RST bill authorizes the following credits against tax liability:[149]

1. business use conversion credit,
2. intermediate and export sales credit,
3. administration credit,
4. bad debt credit,
5. insurance proceeds credit,
6. transitional inventory credit, and
7. refunds.

A seller can claim credit for some prior noncreditable tax paid on property if the seller converts its use and starts using such property "95 percent or more during the month" in the production of other taxable property or services.[150] Consistently, a seller must report tax if business property is converted to personal use.[151] The taxable amount is the fair market value of the converted property when it is converted to personal use.[152]

The credit for intermediate and export sales equals the sales tax paid for any taxable property or service purchased for a business purpose in a trade or business, or for export from the United States for use or consumption outside the United States.[153]

A taxpayer filing its monthly reports in a timely manner can claim a taxpayer administrative credit equal to the *greater* of \$200 or one-quarter of 1 percent of the tax remitted, subject to an overall cap of 20 percent of the tax due before this credit.[154]

---

[147] Property or personal services provided in connection with contributions or dues are treated as a purchase taxable at the fair market value of the property or personal services. *Id*. at §706(d).

[148] *Id*. at §706(e).

[149] See generally, *id*. at §201(a).

[150] *Id*. at §202(a),(b). For mixed use property, the credit is the product of "the mixed use property amount," "the business use ratio," and the RST rate. *Id*. at §22(f)(3). The mixed use property amount for each year varies, depending upon whether the property is real property, tangible personal property, a vehicle, or other taxable property or services. See *id*. at §22(f)(4). The business use ratio also varies by type of property or services. *Id*. at §22(f)(5). The business use conversion credit is the *lesser* of the prior tax paid on the converted property and the tax rate applied to the value of the property when the seller converts its use. *Id*. at §11(d)(2).

[151] *Id*. at §103(c).

[152] *Id*.

[153] *Id*. at §203.

[154] *Id*. at §204(a),(b).

A seller required to buy new equipment in order to issue required receipts to purchasers can claim a credit equal to 50 percent of the cost of the equipment.[155]

4. Rebate to Low-Income Households

To reduce the impact of the national RST on low-income households, a qualified family unit[156] is eligible for a sales tax rebate equal to the tax rate multiplied by the monthly poverty level.[157] The rebate generally is provided in the form of a check mailed to the qualified family unit.[158]

5. Taxation of Financial Intermediation Services

The national RST is imposed on explicitly and implicitly charged financial intermediation services. The bill adopts a method of calculating implicit charges for financial intermediation, that appears to be modeled somewhat after a system devised by Satya Poddar and Morley English of Ernst & Young in Canada. Implicit charges for financial intermediation include the gross imputed amount in relation to any underlying interest-bearing investment accounts or debts.[159] The gross imputed amount on an interest-bearing investment or account (such as a bank deposit) is the account balance multiplied by the excess of the applicable interest rate[160] over the rate paid on the investment.[161] The gross imputed amount on interest bearing debt (such as a bank loan) is the debt balance multiplied by the excess (if any) of the interest rate on the debt over the applicable interest rate.[162]

The Chambliss bill requires financial intermediaries to calculate and collect tax on financial intermediation services only when the financial institution issues statements on the investment account or debt, but at least quarterly.[163] Special place of supply rules are provided to determine if the financial intermediation services are provided within or without the United States.[164]

---

[155] *Id.* at §11(f).

[156] A qualified family unit is a family sharing a common residence. Family members sharing that residence are treated as part of one integrated family unit. *Id.* at §302(a).

[157] *Id.* at §301. The poverty level is linked to the poverty guidelines of the Department of Health and Human Services. *Id.* at §303(b). To determine the size of a family, family members generally include each spouse or the head of household, children, grandchildren, parents and grandparents. *Id.* at §301(b). There are other rules governing family members, such as rules pertaining to change in family circumstances. *Id.* at §305(c).

[158] *Id.*at §304(c). The Schaeffer bill provided for the rebate to be included in the paycheck of the qualified family unit. Schaeffer National Retail Sales Tax, *supra* note 129, at §15(d).

[159] Chambliss National Retail Sales Tax, *supra* note 130, at §801(3)(a).

[160] *Id.* at §512(a).

[161] *Id.* at §801(a)(3)(B)(i).

[162] *Id.* at §801(a)(3)(B)(ii).

[163] *Id.* at §803.

[164] Id. at §806(a). The services are deemed to be used or consumed in the United States if the person (or related party) purchasing the services is a resident of the United States. A related party is any affiliated firm (§205(e)). Such a firm exists when "1 firm owns

Special rules also are provided to separate the principal and interest components of a financing lease.[165]

6. Timing Rules

The seller generally must report taxable sales on the cash method of accounting – when payment is actually received.[166] If a purchaser returns taxable property or services, the seller receives a tax credit when the seller refunds the consideration to the person returning the property or services.[167] A seller can elect to report on the accrual method of accounting.[168]

7. State Authority to Collect Tax and Federal Support

A qualifying "administering state" will administer the tax, including the collection and remittance of the tax to the U.S. Treasury.[169] The Treasury will administer the tax in any jurisdiction that is not an administering state.[170]

A state is an administering state if it imposes a conforming sales tax (a sales tax that conformes to the federal tax)[171] and it enters a cooperative agreement with the Treasury Secretary.[172] An administering state must remit tax collected no more than five days after receipt,[173] but can retain as an administration fee of one-quarter of 1 percent of the otherwise remittable amount.[174] In certain limited circumstances, the Treasury can, on order of a federal district court, take over the administration of the tax in an administering state.[175]

A conforming state (a state that has a sales tax that conforms to the federal tax) can contract with another conforming state to administer its sales tax for a fee.[176] A conforming state can cooperate with audits of other conforming states but shall not conduct audits at facilities in other conforming states.[177]

---

50 percent or more of the voting shares in a corporation or the capital interests of a business that is not a corporation." *Id.* at §2(a)(1).

[165] *Id.* at §804(c).
[166] *Id.* at §503(a).
[167] *Id.* at §22(e)(4).
[168] *Id.* at §22(e)(2).
[169] *Id.* at §31(a).
[170] *Id.* at §404.
[171] *Id.* at §401(b)(1).
[172] *Id.* at §40(b)(2). §2(a)(11) provides that the "Secretary" is the Secretary of the Treasury.
[173] *Id.* at §401(d)(1).
[174] *Id.* at §401(d)(2).
[175] *Id.* at §401(e). The Treasury administration generally will occur only if the administering state fails to remit the tax in a timely manner or otherwise materially breaches the cooperative agreement. *Id.*
[176] *Id.* at §401(g).
[177] *Id.* at §401(h).

The Treasury shall facilitate information sharing among states, and may be a partner to a compact among states to facilitate the implementation of this tax.[178]

VII. ELECTIVE FLAT RATE INCOME TAXES

In 2005, Congressman Burgess introduced the Freedom Flat Tax Act.[179] Under this bill, individuals may make an irrevocable election to be subject to a flat tax instead of the progressive tax rate schedule and the alternative minimum tax.[180] The elective tax is imposed at the rate of 19 percent of income for the first two years, and thereafter at 17 percent.[181] For this purpose, taxable income includes only U.S. source income and does not include returns on investments such as interest, dividends, and capital gains.

Taxable income is the difference between the sum of (a) cash wages for services in the United States, (b) taxable retirement distributions, and (c) unemployment compensation, and the sum of the standard and additional standard deductions, as adjusted for inflation. The basic standard deduction varies, depending on a person's filing status. On a joint return, it is $25,580. The additional standard deduction is $5,510 for each dependent.

The Burgess Freedom Flat Tax Act also gives persons engaged in a business activity in any form an election to be subject to a flat tax on business taxable income.[182] The tax for a person on business activity conducted as a sole proprietor, partnership, corporation, or otherwise is 19 percent of business taxable income for the first two tax years, and 17 percent thereafter.[183] The tax base is the difference between gross active income and allowable deductions.[184] Domestic and export sales are included in gross active income, but not income from other sources. It thus is an origin-based tax. The activity of government entities and tax-exempt organizations is not considered business activity and therefore is not taxed. Businesses can deduct:

(a) business inputs (property and services) used in their business activity, including excise, customs, and other separately stated levies on those business inputs;
(b) cash wages paid to employees for services in the United States; and
(c) deductible retirement contributions for the benefit of employees.[185]

---

[178] *Id.* at §402(a)–(b).
[179] H.R. 1040, Freedom Flat Tax Act, 109th Cong., 1st Sess. (Mar. 2, 2005) [hereinafter H.R. 1040].
[180] The progressive rates and the alternative minimum tax are under the Internal Revenue Code of 1986 (IRC), §§1 and 55.
[181] H.R. 1040, *supra* note 179, adding IRC, §60A.
[182] *Id.*, adding IRC, §60B.
[183] There also is a tax at the same rate on certain noncash compensation paid to employees. *Id.*, adding IRC, §60C.
[184] *Id.*, adding IRC, §60B(c).
[185] The deductions for retirement contributions are those allowable under IRC, §404.

Excess deductions in any year are carried forward as a tax credit. The credit is the tax rate for the year multiplied by the sum of the excess deductions and interest.[186]

The Burgess bill repeals the estate and gift taxes, and requires a two-thirds supermajority in the House and Senate to approve an increase in the flat rates or a reduction in the standard deduction.[187]

VIII. Discussion Question

Do any of these proposals coordinate with or deal appropriately with the existence of and possible changes in state retail sales taxes?

---

[186] *Id.*, adding §60B(g)(2). The interest rate is the three-month Treasury rate for the last month of the tax year. See *id.* at §60B(g)(4).

[187] H.R. 1040, *supra* note 179, at §§3 and 4 of the bill.

Appendix A
VATs Worldwide[1]

No.	Country	Date VAT introduced	Standard rate
1	Albania	1996	20.0
2	Algeria	1992	21.0
3	Argentina	1975	21.0
4	Armenia	1992	20.0
5	Australia	2000	10.0
6	Austria	1973	20.0
7	Azerbaijan	1992	18.0
8	Bangladesh	1991	15.0
9	Barbados	1997	15.0
10	Belarus	1992	18.0
11	Belgium	1971	21.0
12	Benin	1991	18.0
13	Bolivia	1973	13.0
14	Botswana	2002	10.0
15	Brazil	1967	20.0 (avg IPI)
16	Bulgaria	1994	20.0
17	Burkina Faso	1993	18.0
18	Cambodia	1999	10.0
19	Cameroon	1999	19.25
20	Canada	1991	7.0
21	Cape Verde	2004	15.0
22	Central African Rebublic	2001	18.0
23	Chad	2000	18.0
24	Chile	1975	19.0
25	China	1994	17.0
26	Colombia	1975	16.0
27	Congo (Brazzaville)		18.00

(continued)

[1] VAT rates may change frequently. We cannot guarantee the accuracy of the information in this chart. We took the information from a number of sources written at different times. Our sources included the International Bureau of Fiscal Documentation, "The Value Added Tax Experiences and Issues: Background Paper prepared for the International Tax Dialogue Conference on VAT," Rome, March 15–16, 2005, and from Deloitte & Touche, Global Indirect Tax Rates, at http://www.deloitte.com/dtt.

No.	Country	Date VAT introduced	Standard rate
28	Congo Republic	1997	18.0
29	Costa Rica	1975	13.0
30	Côte d'Ivoire	1960	18.0
31	Croatia	1998	22.0
32	Cyprus	1992	15.0
33	Czech Republic	1993	19.0
34	Denmark	1967	25.0
35	Dominica	2006	15.0
36	Dominican Republic	1983	12.0
37	Ecuador	1970	12.0
38	Egypt	1991	10.0
39	El Salvador	1992	13.0
40	Estonia	1992	18.0
41	Ethiopia	2003	15.0
42	Faroe Islands		25.0
43	Fiji	1992	12.5
44	Finland	1994	22.0
45	France	1968 (or 1948)	19.6
46	French Polynesia		3.0
47	Gabon	1995	18.0
48	Georgia	1992	18.0
49	Germany	1968	16.0
50	Ghana	1998	12.5
51	Greece	1987	19.0
52	Guadeloupe and Martinique		8.5
53	Guatemala	1983	12.0
54	Guinea	1996	18.0
55	Guyana	Adopted, effective date to be announced	To be announced
56	Haiti	1982	10.0
57	Honduras	1976	12.0
58	Hungary	1988	25.0 (20% effective 1/1/06)
59	Iceland	1990	24.5
60	India	Some subnational VATs	
61	Indonesia	1985	10.0
62	Ireland	1972	21.0
63	Israel	1976	16.5
64	Italy	1973	20.0
65	Ivory Coast		18.0
66	Jamaica	1991	16.5
67	Japan	1989	5.0
68	Kazakhstan	1992	15.0
69	Kenya	1990	16.0
70	Korea	1977	10.0
71	Kyrgyz Republic	1992	20.0
72	Latvia	1992	18.0
73	Lebanon	2002	10.0
74	Lesotho	2003	14.0
75	Liechtenstein		7.6

No.	Country	Date VAT introduced	Standard rate
76	Lithuania	1992	18.0
77	Luxembourg	1970	15.0
78	Macedonia, FYR	2000	18.0
79	Madagascar	1994	20.0
80	Madeira		15.0
	Malawi	1989	17.5
81	Mali	1991	15.0
82	Malta	1995	18.0
83	Mauritania	1995	14.0
84	Mauritius	1998	10.0
85	Mexico	1980	15.0
86	Moldova	1992	20.0
87	Mongolia	1998	15.0
88	Morocco	1986	20.0
89	Mozambique	1999	17.0
90	Myanmar		
91	Namibia	2000	15.0
92	Nepal	1997	13.0
93	Netherlands	1969	19.0
94	Netherlands Antilles	1999	5.0 or 3.0
95	New Zealand	1986	12.5
96	Nicaragua	1975	15.0
97	Niger	1986	19.0
98	Nigeria	1994	5.0
99	Norway	1970	25.0
100	Pakistan	1990	15.0
101	Palestine Autonomous Areas	1976	17.0
102	Panama	1977	5.0
103	Papua New Guinea	1999	10.0
104	Paraguay	1993	10.0
105	Peru	1973	19.0
106	Philippines	1988	10.0
107	Poland	1993	22.0
108	Portugal	1986	21.0
109	Romania	1993	19.0
110	Russia	1992	18.0
111	Rwanda	2001	18.0
112	Samoa	1994	13.0
113	Senegal	1980	18.0
114	Serbia & Montenegro	S 2005	S 18.0
115		M 2003	M 17.0
116	Singapore	1994	5.0
117	Slovak Republic	1993	19.0
118	Slovenia	1999	20.0
119	South Africa	1991	14.0
120	Spain	1986	16.0
121	Sri Lanka	1998	15.0
122	Sudan	2000	10.0
123	Suriname	1999	10.0 goods

(continued)

No.	Country	Date VAT introduced	Standard rate
124			8.0 services
125	Sweden	1969	25.0
126	Switzerland	1995	7.6
127	Taiwan	1986	5.0
128	Tajikistan	1992	20.0
129	Tanzania	1998	20.0
130	Thailand	1992	7.0
131	Togo	1995	18.0
132	Trinidad and Tobago	1990	15.0
133	Tunisia	1988	18.0
134	Turkey	1985	18.0
135	Turkmenistan	1992	20.0
136	Uganda	1996	18.0
137	Ukraine	1992	20.0
138	United Kingdom	1973	17.5
139	Uruguay	1968	23.0
140	Uzbekistan	1992	20.0
141	Vanuatu	1998	12.5
142	Venezuela	1993	14.0
143	Vietnam	1999	10.0
144	Zambia	1995	17.5
145	Zimbabwe	2004	15.0

Appendix B

Commonwealth of New Vatopia Value Added Tax Act[1]

Arrangement of Sections

[1] This Act was prepared by Alan Schenk, relying on his experience serving as technical advisor for the International Monetary Fund Legal Department. This Act is on the IMF website: www.imf.org/external/np/leg. Go to Tax Law Drafting Samples: VAT.

Part V – Tax Period, Returns, and Calculation of Tax Payable

23. Tax period
24. Returns
25. Extension of time
26. Calculation of tax payable for tax period
27. Input tax deduction
28. Input tax deduction allocation and disallowance rules
29. Postsale adjustments
30. Bad debt
31. Interest on unpaid tax
32. Tax invoices and sales invoices
33. Tax credit and debit notes

Part VI – Payment, Collection and Recovery

34. Due date for payment of tax
35. Allocation of payments among tax, interest, and penalties
36. Recovery of tax as debt due
37. Recovery of tax from persons leaving Vatopia
38. Security
39. Preferential claim to assets
40. Seizure of goods and vehicles
41. Distress proceedings
42. Recovery of tax from recipient of supply
43. Recovery of tax from third parties
44. Duties of receivers

Part VII – Refund of Tax and Tax Relief

45. Carry forward of excess deductions and refund of tax
46. Interest on overpayment
47. Others eligible for tax refund

Part VIII – Assessments

48. Assessments
49. General provisions relating to assessments

Part IX – Objections and Appeals

50. Objections
51. Appeal to Commissioner of Appeals
52. Appeal to High Court
53. Burden of proof

Part X – Representatives and Special Cases of Taxable Persons

54. Persons acting in a representative capacity
55. Power to appoint representative
56. Branches
57. Bodies of persons (other than incorporated companies)
58. Death or insolvency of taxable person; mortgagee in possession
59. Trustee

Part XI – Records and Investigation Powers

Part XII – Offences and Penalties

Division I: Criminal Offences

Division II: Civil Penalties

Part XIII – Miscellaneous

Schedules

Schedule V   Registration Threshold, Interest Rates, and Other Amounts for Purposes of Various Sections of the Act

Schedule VI   Repeal of Laws and Interpretation for Purposes of Section 91

Bill for an act to provide for the imposition and collection of value added tax.

Be it enacted by the Parliament of Vatiopia as follows:

Part I – Preliminary

Short Title and Commencement

(1) This Act may be cited as the Value Added Tax Act and shall come into operation on the date that the Minister may by Order prescribe.

Interpretation

2. In this Act, unless the context requires otherwise –

"association not for gain" means an institution of religious worship; or a society, association, or organization, whether incorporated or not, which –
(a) is carried on otherwise than for the purposes of profit or gain to any proprietor, member, or shareholder; and
(b) is, in terms of its memorandum, articles of association, written rules, or other document constituting or governing its activities –
(i) required to utilise any assets or income solely in the furtherance of its aims and objects; and
(ii) prohibited from transferring any portion of its assets or income directly or indirectly so as to profit any person other than by way of (1) the provision of charitable assistance, or (2) the payment in good faith of reasonable remuneration to any of its officers or employees for any services actually rendered to it; and
(iii) upon its winding-up or liquidation, obliged to give or transfer its assets remaining after the satisfaction of its liabilities to another society, association or organization with similar objects;
"auctioneer" means a person engaged in a taxable activity that includes the supply of goods by auction as an auctioneer or agent for or on behalf of another person;
"business" means any profession, trade, venture or undertaking and includes the provision of personal services or technical and managerial skills and any adventure or concern in the nature of trade but does not include the provision of services as an employee;
"capital goods" means an asset, or a component of an asset, which is of a character subject to an allowance for depreciation or comparable deduction for income tax purposes, and which is used in the course or furtherance of a taxable activity;
"cash value", in relation to a supply of goods under a credit agreement, means–
(a) where the seller or lessor is a bank or other financial institution, an amount equal to the sum of –
(i) the consideration paid by the bank or other financial institution for the goods or the fair market value of the supply of the goods to the bank or other financial institution, whichever is the greater; and
(ii) any consideration for erection, construction, assembly, or installation of the goods borne by the bank or other financial institution; or

(b) where the seller or lessor is a dealer, an amount equal to the sum of
    (i) the consideration at which the goods are normally sold by the dealer for cash; and
    (ii) any consideration for erection, construction, assembly, or installation of the goods borne by the dealer;

"Commissioner" means the Commissioner of Value Added Tax;

"company" means an association or body corporate or unincorporate, whether created or recognised under a law in force in Vatopia or elsewhere, and whether created for profit or non-profit purposes, but does not include a partnership or trust;

"consideration", in relation to a supply or import of goods or services, means the total amount in money or kind paid or payable (including a deposit on a returnable container) for the supply or import by any person, directly or indirectly, including any duties, levies, fees, and charges (other than VAT) paid or payable on, or by reason of, the supply or import, reduced by any price discounts or rebates allowed and accounted for at the time of the supply or import, but does not include:
    (a) a cash payment made by any person as an unconditional gift to an association not for gain; or
    (b) a deposit (other than a deposit on a returnable container), whether refundable or not, given in connection with a supply of goods or services unless and until the supplier applies the deposit as consideration for the supply or such deposit is forfeited;

"credit agreement" means a hire-purchase agreement or a finance lease;

"exempt import" has the meaning in section 17;

"exempt supply" means a supply of goods or services to which section 16 applies;

"fair market value" has the meaning in section 3;

"finance lease", in relation to goods, means a lease of goods where –
    (a) the lease term exceeds seventy-five percent of the expected life of the goods; or
    (b) the lease provides for transfer of ownership at the end of the lease term or the lessee has an option to purchase the goods for a fixed or determinable price at the expiration of the lease; or
    (c) the estimated residual value of the goods to the lessor at the expiration of the lease term (including the period of any option to renew) is less than twenty percent of its fair market value at the commencement of the lease; or
    (d) the leased goods are custom-made for the lessee and at the end of the lease term will not be usable by anyone other than the lessee;

"game of chance" includes a raffle or lottery, or gaming by playing table games or gaming machines;

"goods" means all kinds of corporeal movable or immovable property,[2] thermal or electrical energy, heat, gas, refrigeration, air conditioning, and water, but does not include money;

"hire-purchase agreement" means an agreement that is a hire-purchase agreement for the purposes of the [Hire Purchase Act];[3]

---

[2] In some countries, corporeal movable or immovable property is referred to as real or tangible personal property.

[3] Alternatively, a hire-purchase agreement can be defined in the Act, such as the following: "hire-purchase agreement" means a transaction taking the form of a lease and intended to transfer ownership of goods at the end of a specified term under which

"immovable property" includes –

(a) any estate, right, interest, or servitude on or over any land, and things attached to land or permanently fastened to anything attached to land; or

(b) any real right in any such property;

"import" means –

(a) in the case of goods, to bring or cause to be brought into Vatopia; or

(b) in the case of services, a supply of services to a resident –

(i) by a non-resident; or

(ii) by a resident from a business carried on by the resident outside Vatopia, to the extent that such services are utilised or consumed in Vatopia, other than to make taxable supplies;

"import declaration" means the declaration documents required for the entry of goods into Vatopia:

"importer", in relation to an import of goods, includes the person who owns the goods, or any other person for the time being possessed of or beneficially interested in the goods;[4]

"input tax" means VAT paid or payable in respect of a taxable supply to, or an import of goods by, a taxable person;

"invoice" means a document notifying an obligation to make a payment;

"local authority" means [a political subdivision of government, including a city, a town, township, or a district and, where appropriate, a village and town council];

"Minister" means the Minister responsible for Finance;

"money" means –

(a) a coin or paper currency recognized in Vatopia as legal tender; or

(b) a coin or paper currency of a foreign country that is used or circulated as currency; or

(c) a bill of exchange, promissory note, bank draft, postal order, money order, or similar instrument,

other than an item of numismatic interest;

"non-resident" means a person who is not a resident and a person referred to in paragraph (d) of the definition of "resident" to the extent that the person is not a resident;

"output tax", in relation to a taxable person, means the tax charged under section 9(1)(a) on a taxable supply made by the person;

"person" includes the State, a local authority, board, natural person, trust, company, and partnership;

"promoter of public entertainment" means a person who arranges the staging of public entertainment, but does not include entertainment organized by:

(a) oved educational institution; or

(b) board of management or a parent teacher association of an approved educational institution; or

(c) a person who provides entertainment on a daily or weekly basis; or

(d) a church registered under [Act];

the periodic payments are credited against the purchase price, but the ownership of goods remains with the seller (or financial institution acting as seller) until the purchase price has been paid;

---

[4] Alternatively, the definition of importer under the Customs Act can be incorporated in the VAT Act.

"public entertainment" means any musical entertainment, sporting event, the-atrical performance, comedy show, dance performance, circus show, any show connected with a festival, or any similar show to which the public is invited;

"recipient", in relation to a supply or import, means the person to whom the supply or import is made or in the case of an import of goods, for whom the goods are intended;

"related persons" means –

(a) a natural person and a relative of that natural person; or

(b) a trust and a person who is or may be a beneficiary in respect of that trust or whose relative is or may be a beneficiary; or

(c) a partnership or company (other than a stock company) and a member thereof who, together with shares or other membership interests held by persons who are related to such member under another clause of this def-inition, owns 25 percent or more of the rights to income or capital of the partnership or company; or

(d) a shareholder in a stock company and the stock company if the shareholder, together with shares held by persons who are related to such shareholder under another clause of this definition –

(i) controls 25 percent or more of the voting power in the stock company; or

(ii) owns 25 percent or more of the rights to dividends or of the rights to capital; or

(e) two companies, if a person, either alone or together with a person or persons who are related to such person under another clause of this definition,

(i) controls 25 percent of more of the voting power in both companies; or

(ii) owns 25 percent or more of the rights to dividends or of the rights to capital in both companies;

(f) a taxable person and a branch or division of that taxable person which is separately registered under section 56(3) as a taxable person; or

(g) any branches or divisions of a taxable person which are separately registered under section 56(3) as taxable persons;

and, for purposes of clauses (c), (d), and (e) of this definition, a person is treated as owning, on a pro rata basis, shares or other membership interests which are owned or controlled by such person indirectly through one or more interposed persons;

"relative", in relation to a natural person, means –

(a) the spouse of the person; or

(b) an ancestor, lineal descendant of the person's grandparents, stepfather, step-mother, or stepchild; or,

(c) a spouse of a person referred to in paragraph (b),

and for the purposes of this definition, an adopted child is treated as a natural child of the adopter;

"rental agreement" means an agreement for the letting of goods other than a hire-purchase agreement or a finance lease;

"resident" means –

(a) the State or a local authority in Vatopia; or

(b) a natural person resident in Vatopia; or

(c) a company, partnership, board, or trust which is formed or created under the laws of Vatopia or which is managed and controlled in Vatopia; or

(d) any other person to the extent that such person carries on in Vatopia a taxable or other activity and has a fixed place in Vatopia relating to such activity;

"sale" means an agreement of purchase and sale, and any other transaction or act whereby ownership of goods passes or is to pass from one person to another;

"second-hand goods" means goods which were previously owned and used when acquired, including immovable property, but not including livestock.

"services" means anything that is not goods or money;

"State" means Vatopia or the Republic of Vatopia;

"supplier", in relation to a supply, means the person making the supply;

"supply" has the meaning assigned to it under section 4;

"tax" or "value added tax" (VAT) means the tax imposed under this Act, and includes any amount to the extent that it is treated as tax for the purposes of this Act;

"taxable activity" has the meaning assigned to it under section 5;

"taxable person" has the meaning assigned to it under section 6;

"taxable supply" means a supply of goods or services in Vatopia in the course or furtherance of a taxable activity, other than an exempt supply;

"taxation officer" means the Commissioner and any other person in the service of the Government who is appointed to an office in the [VAT Department], or is acting on behalf of the Commissioner;

"tax fraction" means the fraction calculated in accordance with the formula-

$$R/(1 + R)$$

where "R" is the rate of VAT (expressed as a percentage) applicable to the taxable supply;

"tax invoice" means a document provided as specified under section 32(1);

"tax period", has the meaning assigned to it under section 23;

"trust" means a relationship where property is under the control or management of a trustee;

"trustee" means a person appointed or constituted trustee by act of parties, by order or declaration of a court, or by operation of law, and includes a person having or taking upon himself the administration or control of property subject to a trust;

"value of an import" has the meaning assigned to it in section 14; and

"value of a supply" as the meaning assigned to it in section 13.

Meaning of "Fair Market Value"

3. (1) In this section –

"similar import", in relation to an import of goods or services, means any other import of goods or services that, in respect of the characteristics, quality, quantity, functional components, materials, and reputation of the first-mentioned goods or services, is the same as, or closely or substantially resembles, that import of goods or services; and

"similar supply", in relation to a supply of goods or services, means any other supply of goods or services that, in respect of the characteristics, quality, quantity, functional components, materials, and reputation of the first-mentioned goods or services, is the same as, or closely or substantially resembles, that supply of goods or services.

(2) For the purposes of this Act, the fair market value of a supply or import of goods or services at a given date is the consideration in money which the supply or import, as the case may be, would generally fetch if supplied or imported in similar circumstances at that date in Vatopia, being a supply or import freely offered and made between persons who are not related persons.

(3) Where the fair market value of a supply or import of goods or services at a given date cannot be determined under subsection (2), the fair market value is

the consideration in money which a similar supply or similar import, as the case may be, would generally fetch if supplied or imported in similar circumstances at that date in Vatopia, being a supply or import freely offered and made between persons who are not related persons.

(4) Where the fair market value of any supply or import of goods or services cannot be determined under subsection (2) or (3), the fair market value is determined in accordance with any method approved by the Commissioner which provides a sufficiently objective approximation of the consideration in money which could be obtained for that supply or import had the supply or import been freely offered and made between persons who are not related persons.

(5) The fair market value of a supply or import is determined at the time of the supply or import as determined under this Act.

Meaning of "Supply"

4. (1) Subject to this Act –
   (a) a supply of goods means –
       (i) a sale of goods; or
       (ii) a grant of the use or right to use goods, whether with or without a driver, pilot, crew, or operator, under a rental agreement, credit agreement, freight contract, agreement for charter, or other agreement under which such use or right to use is granted; or
       (iii) a transfer or provision of thermal or electrical energy, heat, gas, refrigeration, air conditioning, or water; and
   (b) a supply of services means anything done which is not a supply of goods or money, including –
       (i) the granting, assignment, cessation, or surrender of a right; or
       (ii) making available a facility or advantage; or
       (iii) refraining from or tolerating an activity.

   (2) The disposition of a taxable activity as a going concern, or a part of a taxable activity that is capable of separate operation, is a supply of goods made in the course or furtherance of such taxable activity.

   (3) For the purposes of subsection (2), a taxable activity or a part of a taxable activity capable of separate operation is disposed of as a going concern where
   (a) all the goods and services necessary for the continued operation of that taxable activity or that part of a taxable activity are supplied to the transferee; and
   (b) the transferor carries on, or is carrying on, that taxable activity or that part of a taxable activity up to the time of its transfer to the transferee.

   (4) A supply of goods for goods or services is a supply of goods.

   (5) A supply of services for goods or services is a supply of services.

   (6) Subject to subsections (17) and (21), the application by a taxable person of goods or services acquired for use in a taxable activity to a different use, including the provision of goods or services to an employee for personal use, is a supply of those goods or services by the taxable person in the course or furtherance of that taxable activity.

   (7) Where goods are repossessed under a credit agreement, the repossession is a supply of the goods by the debtor under the credit agreement to the person exercising the right of repossession, and where such debtor is a registered person the supply is made in the course or furtherance of the debtor's taxable activity unless such goods did not form part of the assets held or used by the debtor in connection with that activity.

(8) Where a lay-bye agreement is cancelled or terminates and the seller retains an amount paid by the purchaser or recovers an amount the purchaser owes under the agreement, the cancellation or termination is a supply of services by the seller in respect of the agreement.

(9) The placing of a bet by a person with another person operating a game of chance is a supply of services by the person operating the game of chance to the first-mentioned person.

(10) A supply of services incidental to a supply of goods is part of the supply of goods.

(11) A supply of goods incidental to a supply of services is part of the supply of services.

(12) A supply or import of services incidental to an import of goods is part of the import of goods.

(13) Regulations made under section 87 may provide that a supply of goods and services is a supply of goods or a supply of services.

(14) Where a supply consists both of a supply that is charged with tax at a positive rate and
   (a) a supply charged with tax at a zero rate; or
   (b) an exempt supply,
   each part of the supply is treated as a separate supply if reasonably capable of being supplied separately.

(15) A supply of services by an employee to an employer by reason of employment is not a supply.

(16) The provision of goods on consignment and the transfer of goods to a person acting in a representative capacity to the transferor is not a supply.

(17) Where a taxable person supplies goods or services and a deduction for input tax paid on the acquisition of such goods or services was denied, the supply by the taxable person is a supply of goods or services otherwise than in the course or furtherance of a taxable activity.

(18) Where a supply described in subsection (2) was charged with tax at the rate of zero percent in terms of paragraph 2 (o) of Schedule I, the acquisition of the taxable activity is a supply by the recipient in the course or further-ance of a tax-able activity carried on by the recipient to the extent that the goods and services comprising the taxable activity were acquired for a pur-pose other than consumption, use, or supply in the course of making taxable supplies, unless this purpose relates to less than 10 percent of the total taxable activity.

(19) Where a right to receive goods or services for a monetary value stated on a token, voucher, gift certificate, or stamp, other than a postage stamp autho-rized under [the Post Office Act], is granted for a consideration in money, the issue of such token, voucher, gift certificate, or stamp is not a supply, except to the extent (if any) that such consideration exceeds that monetary value.

(20) Subsection (19) does not apply to a phone card, prepayment on a cellu-lar phone, or a similar scheme of advance payment for the rendering of services.

(21) A person whose registration is cancelled under section 22 is deemed to have made a taxable supply in Vatopia of any goods or services on hand, at the date the registration is cancelled, but only if an input tax deduction was claimed with respect to the goods or services.

(22) Notwithstanding subsection (10), a supply of immovable property does not include the supply of services incidental to that supply.

(23) For a supply by an agent or at auction, see section 86.

Taxable Activity

5. (1) For the purposes of this Act, "taxable activity" means an activity which is carried on continuously or regularly by a person –
   (a) in Vatopia,
   (b) or partly in Vatopia,
   whether or not for profit, that involves or is intended to involve, in whole or in part, the supply of taxable goods or services to any other person for consideration.

   (2) Taxable activity[5] does not include –
   (a) an activity carried on by a natural person essentially as a private recreational pursuit or hobby or an activity carried on by a person other than a natural person which would, if carried on by a natural person, be carried on essentially as a private recreational pursuit or hobby; or
   (b) an activity to the extent that the activity involves the making of exempt supplies.

   (3) Anything done in connection with the commencement or termination of a taxable activity is treated as carried out in the course or furtherance of that taxable activity.

   (4) Subject to subsection (5), a supply is made for consideration if the supplier directly or indirectly receives a payment for the supply from the recipient or any other person, including a payment wholly or partly in money or kind.

   (5) A supply made for consideration includes
   (a) a supply made between related persons for no consideration; or
   (b) a supply of goods for use only as trade samples; or
   (c) a supply referred to in section 4(6) or (16).

   (6) Taxable activity includes a supply of public entertainment.

Meaning of "Taxable Person"

6. (1) A taxable person is a person who is registered or is required to register under section 20.

   (2) For purposes of subsection (1), a person is a taxable person
   (a) for a person required to register under section 20(1), 20(6), 20(7), or 20(8), from the date specified for that person under section 21(5)(a) and (b); and
   (b) for a person who applies for registration under section 20(5) and is registered under section 21(2), from the date specified under section 21(5)(c).

Part II – Administration

Powers and Duties of Commissioner

7. (1) The Commissioner has the responsibility for carrying out the provisions of this Act.

   (2) The powers conferred and the duties imposed upon the Commissioner by or under the provisions of this Act, may be exercised or performed by the Commissioner personally, or by a taxation officer engaged in carrying out the said provisions under the control, direction, or supervision of the Commissioner.

   (3) Subject to subsection (4), a decision made and a notice or communication issued or signed by an officer referred to in subsection (2) may be withdrawn or amended by the Commissioner or by the officer concerned, and for the purposes

---

[5] If not all activity conducted by the State or a local authority is considered a taxable activity, an additional paragraph can be added to exclude the activity of a State of local authority, except as specified in that paragraph.

of the said provisions, until it has been so withdrawn, is deemed to have been made, issued, or signed by the Commissioner.

(4) A written decision made by a taxation officer, other than the Commissioner, in the exercise of a discretionary power under the provisions of this Act shall not be withdrawn or amended after the expiration of [2 years] from the date of the written notification of such decision or of a notice of assessment giving effect thereto, if all the material facts were known to the officer when the decision was made.

(5) Subject to subsections (6) and (7), a decision made and a notice or communication issued or signed by the Commissioner or his delegate may be withdrawn or amended at any time.

(6) Where the Commissioner, knowing all the material facts at the time, makes a decision that a person is required or not required to register, and the person accepts the Commissioner's decision, and subsequently the Commissioner withdraws the decision, the Commissioner's decision governs the liability or non-liability of such person for payment of tax on any transaction concluded or event which occurred before the withdrawal of the decision.

(7) Where the Commissioner, knowing all the material facts at the time, makes a decision as to the nature of a transaction concluded by a person, and the person accepts the Commissioner's decision, and the Commissioner subsequently withdraws the decision, the Commissioner's decision governs the liability or non-liability of that person for payment of tax on any transaction concluded before the withdrawal of the decision.

Secrecy

8. (1) Subject to this section, a taxation officer carrying out the provisions of this Act must not –

(a) disclose to a person or that person's representative any matter in respect of any other person that may in the exercise of the officer's powers or the performance of the officer's duties under the said provisions come to the officer's knowledge; or

(b) permit any person to have access to any records in the possession or custody of the Commissioner, except in the exercise of the officer's powers or the performance of the officer's duties under this Act or by order of a court.

(2) Nothing in this section prevents the Commissioner from disclosing –

(a) any documents or information to –

(i) a person where the disclosure is necessary for the purposes of this Act or any other fiscal law;

(ii) a person authorised by any enactment to receive such information;

(iii) the competent authority of the government of another country with which Vatopia has entered into an agreement for the avoidance of double taxation or for the exchange of information, to the extent permitted under the agreement;

(iv) a law enforcement agency not described above where the Minister issues written authorization to make disclosures necessary for the enforcement of the laws under the agency's authority; or

(b) any information which does not identify a specific person to a person in the service of the State in a revenue or statistical department where such disclosure is necessary for the performance of the person's official duties.

(3) A person receiving documents and information under subsection (2) is required to keep them secret under the provisions of this section, except to the minimum extent necessary to achieve the purpose for which the disclosure was made.

(4) Documents or information obtained by the Commissioner in the performance of duties under this Act may be used by the Commissioner for the purposes of any other fiscal law administered by the Minister or Commissioner.

(5) If a person consents in writing, information concerning that person may be disclosed to another person.

(6) The Commissioner may disclose information concerning a taxpayer's affairs to a person claiming to be the taxpayer or the taxpayer's authorised representative only after obtaining reasonable assurance of the authenticity of the claim.

(7) A person who contravenes this section commits an offence and is liable on conviction to a fine not exceeding . . . [. . . vatiopians] or to imprisonment for a term not exceeding [2 years], or both.

Part III – Imposition of Tax

Imposition of Tax and Persons Liable

9. (1) Subject to the provisions of this Act, there must be levied and paid a tax, to be known as the value added tax, at the rate of [10] percent of the value of –
    (a) every taxable supply by a taxable person in Vatopia; and
    (b) every import of goods or import of services, other than an exempt import.
   (2) Except as otherwise provided in this Act, the tax payable under subsection (1) must –
    (a) in the case of a supply to which subsection (1)(a) applies, be accounted for by the taxable person making the supply; or
    (b) in the case of an import of goods, be paid by the importer; or
    (c) in the case of an import of services, be paid by the recipient of the services.
   (3) A transaction chargeable with tax under both subsections (1)(a) and (b) is treated as a supply chargeable under subsection (1)(a).

Time of Supply

10. (1) Subject to this Act, a supply of goods or services occurs on the earliest of the date on which
    (a) the goods are delivered or made available or the performance of services is completed;
    (b) an invoice for the supply is issued by the supplier; or
    (c) any consideration for the supply is received.
   (2) A supply of goods under a credit agreement occurs on the date of commencement of the agreement.
   (3) A supply of goods pursuant to a lay-bye agreement occurs when the goods are delivered to the purchaser.
   (4) A supply of goods or services under section 4(6) occurs when the goods or services are applied to a different use.
   (5) A supply of goods under section 4(7) occurs when the goods are repossessed, or where the debtor may under any law be reinstated in his rights and obligations under the credit agreement, the day after the last day of any period during which the debtor may under such law be so reinstated.
   (6) A supply of services under section 4(8) occurs when the seller obtains the right to retain any amount paid by the purchaser or when the seller recovers any amount owing by the purchaser under the agreement.
   (7) A supply for a consideration in money received by the supplier by means of a machine, meter, or other device operated by coin, note, or token occurs when the coin, note, or token is taken from that machine, meter, or other device by or on behalf of the supplier.

(8) Goods supplied under a rental agreement or services supplied under an agreement that provides for periodic payments are treated as successively supplied for successive parts of the period of the agreement, and each of the successive supplies occurs when a payment becomes due or is received, whichever is the earlier.

(9) Where

    (a) goods described under section 4(1)(a)(iii) are supplied; or

    (b) goods or services are supplied directly in the construction, major reconstruction, manufacture, or extension of a building or engineering work,

and the consideration becomes due and payable in instalments or periodically, the goods or services are treated as successively supplied for each period to which a payment for the goods or services relates and each successive supply occurs when payment in respect of the supply becomes due, or is received, or any invoice relating only to that payment is issued, whichever is the earliest.

(10) A supply under section 4(18) occurs when the supply under section 4(2), to which it relates, occurs.

(11) To the extent that the issuance of a token, voucher, gift certificate, or stamp is a supply under section 4(19), the supply occurs when the token, voucher, gift certificate, or stamp is issued.

(12) The forfeit of a deposit (other than a deposit on a returnable container) is a supply of services when the deposit is forfeited.

(13) A supply under subsection 4(21) occurs at the time the registration is cancelled.

Time of Import

11. (1) An import of goods occurs when the goods are entered for purposes of the [Customs Act].

    (2) An import of services occurs at the time determined by applying section 10 to the import on the basis that the import is a supply of services.

Place of Supply

12. (1) Subject to this Act, a supply of goods takes place where the goods are delivered or made available by the supplier or, if the delivery or making available involves the goods being transported, the place where the goods are when the transportation commences.

    (2) A supply of thermal or electrical energy, heating, gas, refrigeration, air conditioning, or water takes place where the supply is received.

    (3) Subject to this section, a supply of services takes place at the location of the supplier's place of business from which the services are supplied.

    (4) The supply of the following goods or services takes place where the recipient uses or obtains the advantage of the goods or services[6]

      (a) a transfer or assignment of a copyright, patent, license, trademark, or similar right;

      (b) the service of a consultant, engineer, lawyer, architect, or accountant, the processing of data or supplying information, or any similar service;

      (c) an advertising service;

      (d) the obligation to refrain from pursuing or exercising taxable activity, employment, or a right described in this subsection;

---

[6] The European Union added to this category some services supplied to non-taxable persons that take place where the recipient uses the services. Foreign service providers that supply services to be used in the EU are required to register in at least one EU country, and charge and remit VAT on those services. The services are listed as paragraphs (h) and (i). See Council Directive 2002/38/EC of 7 May 2002. OJ L 128/41, 15 May 2002.

    (e) the supply of personnel;
    (f) the service of an agent in procuring for the agent's principal a service described in this subsection;
    (g) the leasing of movable property (other than transport property);
    (h) radio and television broadcasting services; or
    (i) electronically-supplied services.[7]

(5) The supply of cultural, artistic, sporting, educational, or similar activities, or services connected with movable goods, takes place where the service is physically carried out, unless the service is described in subsection (4).

(6) The supply of services connected with immovable property takes place where the property is located, unless the service is described in subsection (4).

(7) A supply of services of, or incidental to, transport takes place where the transport occurs, unless the service is described in subsection (4).

(8) Services supplied from a place of business in Vatopia which would be treated as supplied outside Vatopia under subsections (4) – (7) are considered as supplied in Vatopia and are considered as exported from Vatopia for purposes of Schedule I.

Value of Supply

13. (1) Subject to this Act, the value of a supply of goods or services is the amount of the consideration for the supply.

(2) Where a portion of the price of a supply represents tax imposed by this Act that is not accounted for separately, the value of the supply is the price reduced by an amount equal to the tax fraction multiplied by that price.

(3) Where –
    (a) a supply is made by a taxable person for no consideration or for a consideration that is less than the fair market value of that supply; and
    (b) (i) the supplier and the recipient are related persons; or
        (ii) the recipient is a charitable organization, institution of religious worship, educational institution, old-age home, orphanage, children's home, or institution of a similar nature;
    the value of the supply is the fair market value of the supply.

(4) Where a taxable person makes a supply of goods or services referred to in section 4(6), the value of the supply is the lesser of –
    (a) the consideration paid or payable by the taxable person for those goods or services; or
    (b) the fair market value of the supply.

(5) The Minister may by regulation prescribe rules to determine the value of a supply governed by subsection (4) where the taxable person applies less than the entire goods or services to a different use.

---

[7] In the EU, the electronically-supplied services include the following services:

    1. Website supply, web-hosting, distance maintenance of programmes and equipment.
    2. Supply of software and updating thereof.
    3. supply of images, text and information, and making databases available.
    4. Supply of music films and games, including games of chance and gambling games, and of political, cultural, artistic, sporting, scientific and entertainment broadcasts and events.
    5. Supply of distance teaching.

Annex I to Council Directive 2002/38/EC. Communication between a supplier and a customer of services does not of itself constitute an electronically supplied service.

(6) The value of a supply of goods under a credit agreement is the cash value of the supply.

(7) Where a debtor makes a supply of goods as a result of the repossession of those goods from the debtor under a credit agreement, the value of the supply is an amount equal to the balance of the cash value of the supply of those goods to the debtor that has not been recovered at the time of the supply.

(8) For purposes of subsection (7), the balance of the cash value of the supply is the amount remaining after deducting from the cash value so much of the sum of the payments made by the debtor under the credit agreement as, on the basis of an apportionment in accordance with the rights and obligations of the parties to such agreement, may properly be regarded as having been made in respect of the cash value of the supply.

(9) The value of a supply of services under section 4(8) is an amount equal to the amount referred to in that subsection that is retained or recoverable.

(10) Where the grant of any right to receive goods or services for a monetary value stated on any token, voucher, gift certificate, or stamp is a supply under section 4(20), the value of the supply is an amount equal to the amount by which the consideration exceeds the monetary value of the token, voucher, gift certificate, or stamp.

(11) Where the holder of a token, voucher, gift certificate, or stamp issued by a taxable person (the issuer) for no consideration surrenders the token, voucher, gift certificate, or stamp to a supplier of goods or services (other than the issuer) in return for a price discount on a taxable supply, the supplier is required to include in the value of the supply of such goods or services the monetary value stated on the token, voucher, gift certificate, or stamp, less the tax fraction of the monetary value.

(12) For purposes of subsection (11), the monetary value is inclusive of tax.

(13) Where a taxable supply is not the only matter to which the consideration for the supply relates, the value of the supply is such part of the consideration as is properly attributable to it.

(14) Except as otherwise provided in this section, if a supply is made for no consideration the value of the supply is nil.

(15) The value of a supply of services under section 4(9) is the amount received in respect of the bet, reduced by an amount equal to the tax fraction multiplied by the amount received in respect of the bet.

(16) The value of a supply referred to in section 4(18) is the consideration for the acquisition of the taxable activity reduced by an amount which bears to the amount of such consideration the same ratio as the intended use or application of the taxable activity for making taxable supplies bears to the total intended use or application of the taxable activity.

(17) The value of a supply referred to in section 4(21) is equal to –

    (a) except as provided in (b), the fair market value of the goods or services deemed to be supplied; and

    (b) in the case of capital goods subject to the allowance for depreciation under the Income Tax Act, the undepreciated cost of the goods deemed to be supplied.

Value of Import

14. (1) The value of an import of goods shall be an amount equal to the sum of –

    (a) the value of the goods for the purposes of customs duty under the [Customs Law];

    (b) the cost of insurance and freight which is not included in the customs value under paragraph (a); and

(c) the amount of any customs duty, excise tax, or any other fiscal charge (other than VAT) payable on the importation of such goods.

(2) Subject to subsection (3), the value of an import of services is the amount of the consideration for the import.

(3) Where –
  (a) an import of services is made for no consideration or for a consideration that is less than the fair market value of that import; and
  (b) the supplier and the recipient are related persons, the value of the import is the fair market value of the import.

(4) Where a portion of the price of an import of services represents tax imposed by this Act that is not accounted for separately, the value of the import is the price reduced by an amount equal to the tax fraction multiplied by that price.

Zero Rating

15. (1) Where, but for this section, a supply of goods or services would be charged with tax under section 9(1)(a), the supply is charged with tax at the rate of zero percent if it is specified in paragraph 2 of Schedule I.

  (2) Where a taxable person has applied the rate of zero percent to a supply under this section, the taxable person is required to obtain and retain such documentary proof as is acceptable to the Commissioner substantiating the person's entitlement to apply the zero rate to the supply.

Exempt Supply

16. (1) Subject to subsection (2), a supply of goods or services is an exempt supply if it is specified in paragraph 2 of Schedule II.

  (2) A supply of goods or services is not an exempt supply if, in the absence of subsection (1), the supply would be charged with tax at the rate of zero percent under section 15.

Exempt Import

17. (1) An import of goods or services is an exempt import where –
  (a) the import is specified in Schedule III; or
  (b) the import would be a zero-rated supply under section 15 and paragraph 2 of Schedule I, or an exempt supply under section 16 and paragraph 2 of Schedule II if it were a supply of goods or services in Vatopia.

Import Declaration and Payment of Tax for Importation of Goods

18. (1) The Commissioner of Customs –
  (a) is required to collect, at the time of import and on behalf of the Commissioner of Value Added Tax, any tax due under this Act on an import of goods and, at that time, obtain the name and the VAT registration number, if any, of the importer, the import declaration, and the invoice values in respect of the import; and
  (b) may make arrangements with [Postal Services] to perform such functions on his behalf in respect of imports through the postal services.

  (2) Where tax is payable on an import of goods, the importer is required, upon such entry, to furnish the Commissioner with an import declaration and pay the tax due on the import in accordance with the arrangements referred to in subsection (5).

  (3) An import declaration under subsection (2) is required to –
  (a) be in the form prescribed by the Commissioner,

    (b) state the information necessary to calculate the tax payable in respect of the import, and

    (c) be furnished in the manner prescribed by the Commissioner.

(4) Except where the contrary intention appears, the provisions of the [Customs Act], relating to the import, transit, coastwise carriage, clearance of goods, and payment and recovery of duty apply, so far as relevant, to the tax charged under this Act on the import of goods, with such exceptions, modifications, and adaptions as the Minister may by regulation prescribe.

(5) The Commissioner of Customs may, by virtue of subsection (4), exercise any power conferred on the Commissioner of Customs by the customs legislation as if the reference to duty in that legislation included a reference to tax charged on imported goods under this Act.

(6) A person who fails to furnish any import declaration as required by this Act commits an offence and is liable on conviction to a fine not exceeding [. . .vatopians] or to imprisonment for a term not exceeding [1 year], or both.

(7) Where a person convicted of an offence under subsection (6) fails to furnish the import declaration within a further period specified by the Commissioner by notice in writing, that person commits an offence and is liable on conviction to a fine of [. . .vatopians] for each day during which the failure continues or to imprisonment for [3 months], or both.

(8) A person who fails to furnish any import declaration within the time required under this Act is liable for a penalty which is the greater of:

    (a) [. . . vatopians] per day for each day or part thereof that the import declaration remains outstanding; or

    (b) an amount equal to [10] percent of the tax payable for the period of such import declaration, for each month or part thereof that the import declaration remains outstanding.

(9) The penalty imposed under subsection (8) shall not exceed the amount of tax payable in respect of the import declaration.

(10) A person who fails to pay tax payable on an import in accordance with this section on or before the due date, is liable for a penalty which is the greater of:

    (a) [. . . vatopians] per day for each day or part thereof that the tax remains outstanding; or

    (b) an amount equal to [10] percent of the tax outstanding, for each month or part thereof that the tax remains outstanding.

(11) The penalty imposed under subsection (10) shall not exceed the amount of unpaid tax.

(12) A penalty paid by a person under subsection (10) shall be refunded to the person to the extent that the tax to which it relates is subsequently determined not to have been due and payable.

(13) A penalty imposed under subsection (10) is in addition to any interest payable under section 28.

Import Declaration and Payment of Tax for Importation of Services

19. (1) Where tax is payable on an import of services, other than where section 4(12) applies, the person liable for the tax under section 9(2)(c) is required to –

    (a) furnish the Commissioner with an import declaration, and

    (b) pay the tax due in respect of the import

        within [20] days after the tax period in which the services were imported.

(2) An import declaration under subsection (1) is required to –

    (a) be in the form prescribed by the Commissioner,

    (b) state the information necessary to calculate the tax payable in respect of the import, and

(c) be furnished in the manner prescribed by the Commissioner.

(3) A person who fails to furnish any import declaration as required by this Act commits an offence and is liable on conviction to a fine not exceeding [. . .vatopians] or to imprisonment for a term not exceeding [1 year], or both.

Part IV – Registration

Registration

20. (1) Subject to this Act, every person who carries on a taxable activity and is not registered, is required to apply for registration within 21 days of
    (a) the end of any period of 12 or fewer months where during that period the person made taxable supplies the total value of which exceeded the amount specified in paragraph 1 of Schedule V to the Act; or
    (b) the beginning of any period of 12 months where there are reasonable grounds to expect that the total value of taxable supplies to be made by the person during that period will exceed the amount specified in paragraph 1 of Schedule V to the Act.

(2) In determining whether a person is required to apply for registration under subsection (1), the Commissioner may have regard to the value of taxable supplies made by another person where both persons are related persons.

(3) For purposes of subsection (1), the value of a person's supplies is determined under section 13.

(4) A person is not required to apply for registration under subsection (1) where the Commissioner is satisfied that the value of taxable supplies exceeded the amount specified under subsection (1) solely as a consequence of –
    (a) the cessation, or substantial and permanent reduction in the size or scale, of a taxable activity carried on by the person; or
    (b) the replacement of capital goods used in the taxable activity carried on by that person.

(5) A person who makes, or intends to make taxable supplies, but is not required to apply for registration under subsection (1), may apply to the Commissioner for registration under this Act.

(6) Notwithstanding subsection (1), the State, an agency of the State, or a local authority that carries on a taxable activity is required to apply for registration from the date of commencement of that activity.

(7) Notwithstanding subsection (1), a person who is an auctioneer is required to apply for registration on the date on which the person becomes an auctioneer.

(8) Notwithstanding subsection (1), a promoter of public entertainment and a licensee and proprietor of a place of public entertainment are required to apply for registration at least [forty-eight hours] before they begin making supplies in connection with the first public entertainment promoted by them.

(9) A person who fails to apply for registration as required by subsection (1), (7), or (8) commits an offence and is liable on conviction –
    (a) where the failure was made knowingly or recklessly, to a fine not exceeding [. . .vatopians] or to imprisonment for a term not exceeding [2 years], or both; or
    (b) in any other case, to a fine not exceeding [. . .vatopians] or to imprisonment for a term not exceeding [1 year], or both.

(10) A person who fails to apply for registration as required by subsection (1), (7), or (8) is liable for a penalty equal to [double] the amount of output tax payable from the time the person is required to apply for registration until the person files an application for registration with the Commissioner.

Registration Procedure

21. (1) An application for registration under section 20 must be in the form approved by the Commissioner and the applicant must provide such further information as the Commissioner may require.

(2) The Commissioner must register a person who applies for registration within [10] days of receipt of the application, unless the Commissioner is satisfied that the person is not eligible to apply for registration under section 20.

(3) Notwithstanding subsection (2), where an application for registration is made under section 20(5), the decision to register is at the discretion of the Commissioner, except that no application under section 20(5) will be accepted where –

    (a) the person has no fixed place of abode or business; or

    (b) the Commissioner has reasonable grounds to believe that the person –

        (i) will not keep proper records; or

        (ii) will not submit regular and reliable tax returns, as required under this Act.

(4) Where a person required to register under this Act fails to apply for registration as required under section 20, the Commissioner may register the person from the date prescribed by the Commissioner.

(5) Registration takes effect, in the case of –

    (a) a person referred to in section 20(1)(a), from the beginning of the tax period immediately following the end of the 12 or fewer months;

    (b) a person referred to in section 20(1)(b), 20(6), or 20(7), or 20(8), from the beginning of the 12-month period, the commencement of the activities, the date the person becomes an auctioneer, or the date the promoter, licensee or proprietor begins making taxable supplies in connection with public entertainment, respectively; or

    (c) an application under section 20(5), from the beginning of the tax period immediately following the period in which the person applied for registration.

(6) The Commissioner, within [10] days of receipt of an application under subsection (2) or (3) must serve a notice in writing on an applicant for registration of the decision in respect of the application.

(7) An applicant dissatisfied with a decision referred to under subsection (6) may challenge the decision only under Part IX of this Act.

(8) The Commissioner must issue to each person registered a certificate of registration which states the name and other relevant details of the registered person, the date on which the registration takes effect, and the VAT registration number of the registered person.

(9) The Commissioner must establish and maintain a register containing the relevant details of all registered persons, and make publicly available the names of registered persons, their VAT registration numbers, and contact details.

(10) Every registrant must display the certificate of registration issued to him under subsection (8) in a conspicuous place at each location at which he engages in taxable activities.

(11) A taxable person must notify the Commissioner, in writing, within [21] days of –

    (a) any change in the name, address, place of business, constitution, or nature of the principal taxable activity or activities of the person; and

    (b) any change of address from which, or name in which, any taxable activity is carried on by the taxable person, or

    (c) any change in circumstances if the person ceases to operate or closes on a temporary basis in a situation not covered in section 22(1).

(12) Subject to subsection (2), where the Commissioner fails to serve a notice required by subsection (6), the Commissioner is deemed to have made a decision to register the applicant.

(13) A person who fails to notify the Commissioner of a change in circumstances as required by subsection (11) commits an offence and is liable on conviction –

    (a) where the failure was made knowingly or recklessly, to a fine not exceeding [. . .vatopians] or to imprisonment for a term not exceeding [2 years], or both; or

    (b) in any other case, to a fine not exceeding [. . . vatopians] or to imprisonment for a term not exceeding [1 year], or both.

(14) A person who fails to display the certificate of registration as required under subsection (10) is liable for a penalty of [. . .vatopians] per day for each day or portion thereof that the failure continues.

Cancellation of Registration

22. (1) Subject to subsection (2) and (14), a taxable person who ceases to carry on all taxable activities must notify the Commissioner of that fact within [21 days] of the date of such cessation, and the Commissioner must cancel the registration of that person with effect from the last day of the tax period during which all such taxable activities ceased, or from such other date as the Commissioner may determine.

    (2) The Commissioner is not required to cancel the registration of a taxable person under subsection (1) where the Commissioner has reasonable grounds to believe that the person will carry on any taxable activity at any time within 12 months from that date of cessation.

    (3) A notification pursuant to subsection (1) must be made in writing and to state the date upon which that person ceased to carry on all taxable activities, and whether or not that person intends to carry on any taxable activity within 12 months from that date.

    (4) Where the Commissioner is satisfied that a taxable person is not carrying on a taxable activity or is neither required nor entitled to apply for registration, the Commissioner may cancel that person's registration with effect from the last day of the tax period during which the Commissioner became so satisfied, or from such other date as the Commissioner may determine, and must notify that person in writing of the date on which the cancellation takes effect.

    (5) The Commissioner may cancel the registration of a person who is not required to apply for registration under section 20 if the person –

        (a) has no fixed place of abode or business; or

        (b) has not kept proper accounting records relating to any business activity carried on by that person; or

        (c) has not submitted regular and reliable tax returns as required by section 24.

    (6) A date determined by the Commissioner for the cancellation of registration under subsection (4) or (5) may be retrospective to a date not earlier than –

        (a) the last day of the tax period during which taxable activity carried on by the person ceased; or

        (b) the date on which the person was registered under this Act, if the Commissioner is satisfied that the person did not, from that date, carry on any taxable activity.

    (7) Subject to subsections (8) or (9), a taxable person may apply in writing to the Commissioner to have the person's registration cancelled where, at any time, the value of that person's taxable supplies –

(a) in the past 12 months has not been, or

(b) in the period of 12 months then beginning will not be more than the amount specified under section 20(1).

(8) A person –

    (a) required to register under section 20(1) who ceases to satisfy the criteria thereunder, or

    (b) registered as a result of an application under section 20(5), may apply for cancellation of the registration only after the expiration of 2 years from the date the registration took effect.

(9) Subsection (7) does not apply to the State, an agency of the State, or a local authority under section 20(6), to an auctioneer under section 20(7), or to a promoter of public entertainment under section 20(8).

(10) Where the Commissioner is satisfied that a taxable person who has made an application under subsection (7) or (8) is entitled to have a registration cancelled, the Commissioner is required to cancel the person's registration with effect from the end of the tax period in which the registration is cancelled unless the Commissioner orders the cancellation to take effect at an earlier date.

(11) Any obligation or liability under this Act, including the obligation to pay tax and file returns, of any person in respect of anything done or omitted to be done by that person while the person is a taxable person, is not affected by cancellation of the person's registration.

(12) Where the registration of a person is cancelled, the Commissioner is required to remove the person's name and details from the register described in section 21(9).

(13) A person dissatisfied with a decision of the Commissioner under this section to cancel or not to cancel the person's registration may challenge the decision only under Part IX of this Act.

(14) A taxable person who sells a going concern must notify the Commissioner of that fact at least three days before the earliest of the date –

    (a) the sale closes;

    (b) the purchaser acquires any legal interest in the assets to be acquired; and

    (c) some or all of the assets of the going concern are transferred.

(15) A person who fails to notify the Commissioner as required by subsection (1) commits an offence and is liable on conviction –

    (a) where the failure was made knowingly or recklessly, to a fine not exceeding [. . . vatopians] or to imprisonment for a term not exceeding [2 years], or both; or

    (b) in any other case, to a fine not exceeding [. . .vatopians] or to imprisonment for a term not exceeding [1 year], or both.

Part V – Tax Period, Returns, and Calculation of Tax Payable

Tax Period

23. (1) Subject to subsection (2), the tax period applicable to a taxable person under this Act is the calendar month.

(2) The Minister may, by regulations, authorise a different tax period for specific categories or classes of taxable persons.

Returns

24. (1) Every taxable person is required to file a tax return for each tax period with the Commissioner within [21] days after the end of the period, whether or not tax is payable in respect of that period.

(2) A tax return is required to –
   (a) be in the form prescribed by the Commissioner,
   (b) state the information necessary to calculate the tax payable in accordance with section 26 for the period, and
   (c) be filed in the manner prescribed by the Commissioner.
(3) In addition to or instead of any return required under this Act, the Commissioner may by notice in writing require a person, whether or not a taxable person, to file with the Commissioner, whether on that person's own behalf or as agent or trustee of another person, such fewer, additional, or other returns in the prescribed form as and when required by the Commissioner for the purposes of this Act.
(4) A person dissatisfied with a decision of the Commissioner under subsection (3) may challenge the decision only under Part IX of this Act.
(5) A person who fails to file a return as required by this Act commits an offence and is liable on conviction to a fine not exceeding [. . .vatopians] or to imprisonment for a term not exceeding [1 year], or both.
(6) Where a person convicted of an offence under subsection (5) fails to file the return within a further period specified by the Commissioner by notice in writing, that person commits an offence and is liable on conviction to a fine of [. . .vatopians] for each day during which the failure continues or to imprisonment for [three months], or both.
(7) A person who fails to file a return within the time required under this Act is liable for a penalty which is the greater of:
   (a) . . . vatopians] per day for each day or part thereof that the return remains outstanding; or
   (b) an amount equal to [ten] percent of the tax payable for the period of such return, for each month or part thereof that the return remains outstanding.
(8) The penalty imposed under subsection (7)(b) shall not exceed the amount of tax payable in respect of the return.

Extension of Time

25. (1) Upon application in writing by a person, the Commissioner may, where good cause is shown by the person, extend the period within which a return required under section 24 is to be filed.
   (2) The granting of an extension of time under subsection (1) does not alter the due date for payment of tax under section 34.
   (3) A person dissatisfied with a decision of the Commissioner under subsection (1) may challenge the decision only under Part IX of this Act.

Calculation of Tax Payable for Tax Period

26. (1) The tax payable by a taxable person for a tax period in respect of taxable supplies is the total amount of output tax payable by the person in respect of taxable supplies made by the person during the period, less the total input tax deduction allowed to the person under section 27 for the period.
   (2) Where the total amount of input tax deduction allowed to a taxable person for a tax period under subsection (1) exceeds the total amount of output tax payable by the person for that period, the amount of the excess is dealt with in accordance with section 45.

Input Tax Deduction

27. (1) Subject to this section, the total amount of input tax allowed as a deduction for purposes of section 26 is the sum of –

(a) the input tax payable in respect of taxable supplies made to the person during the tax period, and paid in respect of any import of goods by the person during the tax period, where the supply or import is for use in a taxable activity carried on by the person;

(b) any input tax deduction allowed under sections 29 and 30 for the tax period;

(c) any input tax to which subsection (4) applies for the tax period;

(d) an amount equal to the tax fraction of any amount paid during the tax period by the taxable person as a prize or winnings to the recipient of services under section 4(9);

(e) an amount equal to the tax fraction of any amount paid during the tax period by the taxable person to a supplier in respect of the redemption of a token, voucher, gift certificate, or stamp referred to in section 13(11) by the supplier;

(f) [8]subject to paragraphs (g) and (h), an amount equal to the tax fraction of the lesser of –

   (i) the amount paid for, or

   (ii) the fair market value, including tax, of second-hand goods acquired in Vatopia during the tax period by a taxable person from a person in a transaction not subject to tax if a supply of the goods is taxable at a positive rate under this Act and the goods are acquired for re-supply in a taxable transaction;

(g) an amount equal to the tax fraction of the lesser of –

   (i) the amount paid for, or

   (ii) the fair market value, including tax, of second-hand goods acquired in Vatopia during the tax period by a taxable person from a related person in a transaction not subject to tax if a supply of the goods is taxable at a positive rate under this Act and the goods are acquired for re-supply in a taxable transaction, but the deduction shall not exceed the tax imposed on the earlier supply of the goods to the related person;

(h) an amount equal to the tax fraction of the fair market value, including tax, of second-hand goods that are repossessed in Vatopia during the tax period by a creditor who is a taxable person from a defaulting debtor in a transaction not subject to tax if a supply of the goods is taxable at a positive rate under this Act and goods are acquired for re-supply in a taxable transaction, but the deduction shall not exceed the tax imposed on the earlier supply of the goods to the defaulting debtor;

(i) an amount carried forward under section 45(2).

(2) Subject to this section, no deduction of input tax is allowed in respect of a supply or import unless –

(a) a tax invoice, or tax debit or tax credit note, as the case may be, in relation to the supply, has been provided in accordance with sections 32 or 35 and is held by the taxable person taking the deduction at the time a return in respect of the supply is filed, other than when a tax invoice is not required to be provided;

(b) a bill of entry or validating bill of entry under the [Customs Act], or a document issued by [Customs] or the Commissioner evidencing payment of tax in relation to an import that has been delivered in accordance with

---

[8] An simplified alternative to subsections (1)(f)-(h) is to grant an input tax deduction based on a fixed percentage of the selling price: "an amount equal to [70] percent of the selling price of second-hand goods supplied in the taxable period in a supply taxable at a positive rate under this Act, if the goods were acquired in Vatopia in a transaction not subject to tax."

the [Customs Act] or this Act and is held by the taxable person taking the deduction at the time a return in respect of the import is filed; and

(c) for purposes of subsection (1)(f)–(h), with respect to the acquisition, the taxable person is in possession of documents required by the Commissioner.

(3) Where a taxable person does not have a tax invoice evidencing the input tax paid, the Commissioner may allow an input tax deduction in the tax period in which the deduction arises where the Commissioner is satisfied –

(a) that the taxable person took all reasonable steps to acquire a tax invoice; and

(b) that the failure to acquire a tax invoice was not the fault of the taxable person; and

(c) that the amount of input tax claimed by the taxable person is correct.

(4) Subject to subsection (5), a taxable person, in the first tax period in which the person is registered, is allowed a deduction for input tax paid or payable by the person in respect of –

(a) any taxable supplies of goods, including capital goods, made to the person; and

(b) any imports of goods, including capital goods, by the person, prior to becoming registered, to the extent that the goods are for use or re-supply in a taxable activity carried on by the person after registration.[9]

(5) Subsection (4) applies where –

(a) the supply or import occurred not more than [4 months] prior to the date the registration takes effect; and

(b) the goods are on hand at the date the registration takes effect.

(6) Subsections (1)(f)–(h) do not apply to a transaction covered by section 4(17).

Input Tax Deduction Allocation and Disallowance Rules

28. (1) In this section –

"entertainment" means the provision of food, beverages, tobacco, accommodation, amusement, recreation, or other hospitality by a taxable person whether directly or indirectly to any person; and "passenger vehicle" means a road vehicle, including a double cab vehicle, designed or adapted for the transport of nine or fewer seated persons;

(2) No amount may be deducted under section 27 by a taxable person for input tax paid or payable in respect of –

(a) a taxable supply to, or import by, the person of a passenger vehicle, unless the person is in the business of dealing in, or hiring of, such vehicles, and the vehicle was acquired for the purposes of such business;

(b) a taxable supply to, or import by, the person of goods or services acquired for the purposes of entertainment, unless –

(i) the person is in the business of providing entertainment and the taxable supply or import relates to the provision of taxable supplies of entertainment in the ordinary course of that business; or

(ii) the person is in the business of providing taxable supplies of transportation services and the entertainment is provided to passengers as part of the transportation service; or

[9] The amount of revenue lost and the ability of the tax authorities to verify the claimed deductions generally determines if a nation will include subsections (4) & (5) in the VAT Act.

   (c) any fees or subscriptions paid by the person in respect of membership of any person in a club, association, or society of a sporting, social, or recreational nature.

(3) Subject to subsection (4), where only a part of the supplies made by a taxable person during a tax period are taxable supplies, the amount of the input tax allowed as a deduction under section 27(1)(a) for that period is determined as follows-

   (a) in respect of a supply or import received which is directly allocable to the making of taxable supplies, the full amount of input tax payable in respect of the supply or import shall be allowed as a deduction;

   (b) in respect of a supply or import received which is directly allocable to the making of exempt supplies, no amount of input tax payable in respect of the supply or import shall be allowed as a deduction; or

   (c) in respect of a supply or import received which is used for the making of both taxable and exempt supplies, the amount calculated according to the following formula –

$$A \times B/C$$

where –

A is the total amount of input tax payable in respect of supplies and imports received during the period for which a deduction is allowed under section 27(1)(a), less the input tax accounted for under paragraph (a) and (b);

B is the total amount of taxable supplies made by the taxable person during the preceding financial year of the taxable person; and

C is the total amount of all supplies made by the taxable person during the preceding financial year of the taxable person.

For purposes of the fraction **B/C**, for the first financial year during which the person is a taxable person, the period referred to in **B** and **C** shall be the total number of tax periods, including the current tax period, during which the person has been a taxable person.

(4) Where the fraction B/C in subsection (3)(c) is more than 0.90, the taxable person may deduct the total amount of input tax on supplies and imports described in that paragraph.

(5) Notwithstanding subsection (3), where a taxable person makes both taxable and exempt supplies during a tax period, the Commissioner may determine the amount of input tax allowed for the tax period on such other basis as the Commissioner considers reasonable.

(6) A taxable person dissatisfied with a decision of the Commissioner under subsection (5) may challenge the decision only under Part IX of this Act.

Postsale Adjustments

29. (1) This section applies where, in relation to a supply by a registered person –

   (a) the supply is cancelled;

   (b) the taxation of the supply changes because the nature of the supply is fundamentally varied or altered;

   (c) the previously agreed consideration for the supply is altered, whether due to an offer of a discount or for any other reason; or

   (d) the goods or services or part thereof are returned to the supplier.

  (2) Subsection (1) applies only where the registered person making the supply has-

   (a) provided a tax invoice in relation to the supply and the amount shown on the invoice as the tax charged on the supply is incorrect as a result of the occurrence of one or more of the events described under subsection (1)(a)–(d); or

   (b) filed a return for the tax period in which the supply occurred and has accounted for an incorrect amount of output tax on that supply as a result of the occurrence of one or more of the events described under subsection (1)(a)–(d).

(3) Where subsection (1) applies, the registered person making the supply is required to make an adjustment as specified under subsection (4) or (6).

(4) Where the output tax properly chargeable in respect of the supply exceeds the output tax actually accounted for by the registered person (the supplier), the amount of the excess is deemed to be output tax charged by the supplier in relation to a taxable supply made in the tax period in which the event referred to in subsection (1) occurred.

(5) For purposes of section 26, where a registered person issues a tax debit note to rectify the output tax charged to a registered recipient in the circumstances specified under subsection (4), the additional tax specified in the tax debit note is deemed to be input tax payable by the registered recipient in the tax period in which the tax debit note is received.

(6) Subject to subsection (8), where the output tax actually accounted for by the registered person exceeds the output tax properly chargeable in relation to the supply, the registered person is allowed an input tax deduction under section 27 for the amount of the excess in the tax period in which the event referred to in subsection (1) occurred.

(7) Where a supplier issues a tax credit note to rectify the output tax charged to a recipient who is a registered person in the circumstances specified under subsection (6), the additional tax specified in the tax credit note is treated as output tax payable by the recipient in respect of a taxable supply made by the recipient in the tax period in which the tax credit note is received.

(8) Where the supply has been made to a person who is not a registered person, a deduction under subsection (6) is not allowed, unless the amount of the excess tax has been repaid to the recipient of the supply, whether in cash or as a credit against an amount owing to the registered person by the recipient.

Bad Debt

30. (1) Subject to subsections (5), (6), and (7), a taxable person is allowed an input tax deduction under section 27 for tax paid in respect of a taxable supply made by the taxable person where the whole or part of the consideration for the supply is subsequently treated as a bad debt.

   (2) The amount of the deduction allowed under subsection (1) is the amount of the tax paid in respect of the taxable supply which corresponds to the amount of the debt treated as bad.

   (3) The deduction under subsection (1) arises on the date on which the bad debt was written off in the accounts of the taxable person.

   (4) Where any amount in respect of which a deduction has been allowed in accordance with subsection (1) is at any time wholly or partly recovered by the taxable person, the taxable person is treated as having charged tax in respect of a taxable supply made during the tax period in which the bad debt is wholly or partly recovered, being an amount of tax calculated according to the following formula –

$$A \times B/C$$

     where –

A   is the amount allowed as a deduction under subsection (1);
B   is the amount of the bad debt recovered; and
C   is the amount of the bad debt previously written off.

(5) A deduction is allowed under subsection (1) only if –
   (a) the taxable supply was made to a person other than a registered person; or
   (b) the taxable supply was made to a registered person and the person claiming the deduction under subsection (1) issued a tax credit note to the registered purchaser listing the amount claimed under the formula in subsection (2).

(6) Where all or a portion of a bet referred to in section 4(9) and reported as part of tax payable by a taxable person operating a game of change is a bad debt under this section, the taxable person shall treat the amount of any bet written off as a prize or winnings for purposes of section 27(1)(d).

(7) Where an amount treated as a prize or winnings under subsection (6) is recovered in whole or in part, the taxable person operating a game of chance is treated as having made a supply under section 4(9) during the tax period in which the bad debt is wholly or partly recovered.

Interest on Unpaid Tax

31. (1) A person who fails to pay tax by the due date for payment under section 34 is liable for interest at the rate specified in paragraph 2 of Schedule V to the Act on the amount unpaid, calculated from the date on which the tax imposed was due until the date on which payment was made.

(2) Interest under subsection (1) is calculated as simple interest for each month, or part of a month, during which it remains unpaid.

(3) Interest paid by a person under subsection (1) must be refunded to the person to the extent that the tax to which it relates is subsequently determined not to have been due and payable.

(4) The provisions of this Act relating to the payment, collection and recovery of tax apply to any interest charged under this section as if the interest were tax due under this Act.

Tax Invoices and Sales Invoices

32. (1) Subject to subsection (2), a registered person, referred to as the "registered supplier", making a taxable supply to a person, referred to as the "recipient", is required to provide the recipient with an original tax invoice for the taxable supply containing such particulars as specified in paragraph 1 of Schedule IV.[10]

(2) A registered supplier making a taxable supply is authorized to issue a sales invoice in lieu of a tax invoice if the total consideration for the taxable supply is in cash and does not exceed the amount specified in paragraph 3 of Schedule V.

(3) A person is prohibited from providing a tax invoice in circumstances other than those specified under this section.

(4) Subject to subsection (6), a registered supplier must issue only one tax invoice for each taxable supply.

(5) Where, within 60 days after the date of a supply, a registered recipient who has not received a tax invoice as required by subsection (1) requests the registered supplier, in writing, to provide a tax invoice in respect of the taxable supply, the supplier is required to comply with the request within 14 days after receiving it.

---

[10] To reduce the opportunity for registered persons to obtain tax invoices from unregistered buyers and use them to claim unwarranted input tax deductions, the Act could authorise registered persons to issue tax invoices only to registered recipients.

(6) Where a registered recipient claims to have lost the original tax invoice for a taxable supply, the registered supplier may provide a copy clearly marked "copy."

(7) A registered person who fails to provide a tax invoice as required by this section commits an offence and is liable on conviction to a fine not exceeding [...vatopians] or to imprisonment for a term not exceeding [2] years, or both.

(8) A person who provides a tax invoice otherwise than as provided for in this section commits an offence and is liable on conviction –

   (a) where the failure was made knowingly or recklessly, to a fine not exceeding [...vatopians] or to imprisonment for a term not exceeding [2] years, or both; or

   (b) in any other case, to a fine not exceeding [...vatopians] or to imprisonment for a term not exceeding [1] year, or both.

Tax Credit and Debit Notes

33. (1) Where a tax invoice has been issued in the circumstances specified under section 29(2)(a) and the amount shown as tax charged in that tax invoice exceeds the tax properly chargeable in respect of the supply, the registered person making the supply is required to provide a registered recipient of the supply with a tax credit note containing the particulars specified in paragraph 2 of Schedule IV.

(2) A person must not provide a tax credit note in any circumstances other than those specified under subsection (1).

(3) Where a tax invoice has been issued in the circumstances specified under section 29(2)(a) and the tax properly chargeable in respect of the supply exceeds the amount shown as tax charged in that tax invoice, the registered person making the supply is required to provide a registered recipient of the supply with a tax debit note containing the particulars specified in paragraph 3 of Schedule IV.

(4) A person must not provide a tax debit note in any circumstances other than those specified under subsection (3).

(5) A registered person may issue only one tax credit note or tax debit note for the amount of the excess stated in subsection (1) or (3) respectively.

(6) Notwithstanding the provisions of this section, where a registered person claims to have lost the original tax credit note or tax debit note, the registered person who made the supply may provide a copy clearly marked "copy".

(7) A registered person who fails to provide a tax credit note or tax debit note as required by this section commits an offence and is liable on conviction to a fine not exceeding [...vatopians] or to imprisonment for a term not exceeding [2] years, or both.

(8) A person who provides a tax credit note or tax debit note otherwise than as provided for in this section commits an offence and is liable on conviction –

   (a) where the failure was made knowingly or recklessly, to a fine not exceeding [...vatopians] or to imprisonment for a term not exceeding [2] years, or both; or

   (b) in any other case, to a fine not exceeding [...vatopians] or to imprisonment for a term not exceeding [1] year, or both.

Part VI – Payment, Collection, and Recovery

Due Date for Payment of Tax

34. (1) Tax payable under this Act is due and payable –

   (a) by a taxable person for a tax period, by the due date for the return for the tax period;

   (b) by a person assessed under an assessment issued under this Act, on the date specified in the notice of assessment;

(c) by an importer of goods or a recipient of an import of services, by the due date specified under section 18 and 19 in respect of the import; or

(d) by any other person, by the date the taxable transaction occurs as determined under the Act.

(2) Subject to section 50(5), where an objection to, or a notice of appeal against, an assessment has been filed, the tax payable under the assessment is due and payable under subsection (1), and may be recovered, notwithstanding that objection or appeal.

(3) Upon application in writing by a person liable for tax, the Commissioner may, where good cause is shown, extend the time for payment of tax by the person beyond the date on which it is due and payable under this section, or make such other arrangements as appropriate to ensure the payment of the tax due, and any such extension does not alter the due date for purposes of section 31.

(4) A person dissatisfied with a decision of the Commissioner under subsection (3) may challenge the decision only under Part IX of this Act.

Allocation of Payments among Tax, Interest, and Penalties

35. Where, in addition to any amount of tax which is due and payable by a person under this Act, an amount of interest or penalty is payable, a payment made by the person in respect of such tax, interest, or penalty which is less than the total amount due is deemed to be made –

(a) first in respect of such penalty;

(b) to the extent that such payment exceeds the amount of such penalty, then in respect of such interest; and

(c) to the extent that such payment exceeds the sum of such penalty and interest, then in respect of such tax.

Recovery of Tax as Debt Due

36. (1) Tax that is due and payable under this Act is recoverable by the Commissioner as a debt due to the State from the person liable therefor in the manner provided in this section.

(2) Where a person fails to pay tax when it is due and payable, referred to as the "defaulter", the Commissioner may file, with the clerk or registrar of a court of competent jurisdiction, a statement certified by the Commissioner setting forth the amount of the tax due and payable by that person, and that statement has the effect of a civil judgment lawfully given in that court in favour of the Commissioner for a debt in the amount specified in the statement; and the court is required to issue a writ of execution in respect thereof against the defaulter.

(3) A writ of execution under subsection (2) shall not be issued until [14] days after service by the court on the defaulter of a notice informing the defaulter that a writ of execution will be issued by the court in respect of tax owed by the defaulter, and unpaid, unless before the expiration of that period of [14] days the defaulter produces proof of payment thereof satisfactory to the court.

(4) The Commissioner may, without prejudice to re-instituting proceedings under subsection (2), by notice in writing addressed to the clerk or registrar of the court, withdraw the statement referred to in subsection (2) and such statement shall thereupon cease to have any effect.

(5) Except where the contrary intention appears, the [customs legislation] on imported goods, with such exceptions, modifications, and adaptations as the Minister may be Order prescribe, applies (so far as relevant) in relation to any tax chargeable on the import of goods.

(6) The [Commissioner of Customs] may, by virtue of subsection (5), exercise any power conferred on the [Commissioner of Customs] by the [customs legislation] as if the reference to customs duty or excise tax in that law included a reference to tax charged on imported goods under this Act.

Recovery of Tax from Persons Leaving Vatopia

37. (1) Where the Commissioner has reasonable grounds to believe that a person may leave Vatopia without paying all tax due under this Act, the Commissioner may issue a certificate to the [Chief Immigration Officer] containing particulars of the tax due and request that the [Chief Immigration Officer] take the necessary steps to prevent the person from leaving Vatopia until the person makes –
    (a) payment in full; or
    (b) an arrangement satisfactory to the Commissioner for the payment of the tax.
(2) The Commissioner is required to issue a copy of the certificate issued under subsection (1) on the person named in the certificate if it is practicable to do so.
(3) If a certificate is issued under subsection (1), payment to a [customs or immigration officer] of the tax specified in the certificate or the production of the certificate signed by the Commissioner stating that the tax has been paid or satisfactory arrangements for payment have been made shall be sufficient authority for any immigration officer to allow the person to leave Vatopia.

Security

38. (1) Where it is reasonable to do so for the protection of the revenue or as provided for in this Act, the Commissioner, by notice in writing, may require a person to give security for the payment of tax that is or may become payable by the person under this Act.
(2) Security required under subsection (1), including security required from a promoter of public entertainment, shall be for such amount, in such form, and furnished within such period as the Commissioner may specify in the notice.
(3) Where security under subsection (1) is in cash and the Commissioner is satisfied that the security is no longer required, the Commissioner is required to apply the amount of the security as specified under section 45(4).
(4) A person dissatisfied with a decision of the Commissioner under subsection (1) may challenge the decision only under Part IX of this Act.
(5) A promoter of public entertainment must not allow the public entertainment to take place unless the promoter paid the amount required under subsection (2) and received the Commissioner's written approval.
(6) A person who fails to comply with subsection (5) commits an offence and is liable on conviction to a fine not exceeding [. . .vatopians] or to imprisonment for a term not exceeding [one] year, or both.

Preferential Claim to Assets

39. (1) From the date on which tax becomes due and payable under this Act and until the tax is paid, the Commissioner has a preferential claim as provided [in the Insolvency Act] upon the assets of the person liable to pay the tax.[11]

---

[11] The lien can be extended to cover "any asset of a related person if the Commissioner reasonably believes that the person liable for tax is the lawful owner of the asset transferred to the related person in order to avoid the payment of tax."

(2) Where a person is in default of paying tax, the Commissioner may, by notice in writing, inform that person of the Commissioner's intention to apply to the [Registrar of] to register a security interest in an asset, which is owned by that person, to cover any unpaid tax in default, together with any expense incurred in recovery proceedings.

(3) If the person on whom a notice has been served under subsection (2) fails to pay the amount specified in the notice within 30 days after the date of service of the notice, the Commissioner may, by notice in writing, direct the Registrar that the asset, to the extent of the defaulter's interest therein, shall be the subject of security for the total amount of unpaid tax.

(4) Where the Commissioner has served a notice on the Registrar under subsection (3), the Registrar is required to register the notice of security without fee, as if the notice were an instrument of mortgage over or charge on, as the case may be, such asset, and such registration operates while it subsists, subject to any prior mortgage or charge, in all respects as a legal mortgage over or charge on the asset to secure the amount due.

Seizure of Goods and Vehicles

40. (1) Where the Commissioner has reasonable grounds to believe that tax on a supply or import of goods has not been or will not be paid, the Commissioner may seize the goods.

(2) The Commissioner may seize a vehicle used in the removal or carriage of goods liable to be seized under subsection (1), unless it is shown that such vehicle was so used without the consent or knowledge of the owner of that vehicle or other person lawfully in possession or charge thereof; and at the discretion of the Commissioner, the vehicle may be sold by public auction or may be dealt with in such other manner as the Commissioner may direct.

(3) Goods seized under subsection (1) must be stored in a place approved by the Commissioner for the storage of such goods.

(4) Where goods are seized under subsection (1), the Commissioner is required to serve on the owner of the goods or the person who had custody or control of the goods immediately before seizure, a notice in writing as soon as practicable after the seizure –
   (a) identifying the goods;
   (b) stating that the goods have been seized under this section and the reason for seizure; and
   (c) setting out the terms of subsections (7), (8), and (9).

(5) The Commissioner is not required to serve notice under subsection (4) if, after making reasonable enquiries, the Commissioner does not have sufficient information to identify the person on whom the notice should be served.

(6) Where subsection (5) applies, the Commissioner may serve a notice under subsection (4) on a person claiming the goods, provided the person has given the Commissioner sufficient information to enable such a notice to be served.

(7) Subject to subsection (8), the Commissioner may authorise the delivery of goods seized under subsection (1) to the person on whom a notice under subsection (4) has been served, where that person pays or gives security, in accordance with section 35, for the payment of tax due and payable or that will become due and payable in respect of the supply or import of the goods.

(8) The Commissioner must detain the goods seized under subsection (1) –
   (a) in the case of perishable goods, only for such period as the Commissioner considers reasonable having regard to the condition of the goods; or
   (b) in any other case, until the later of –
      (i) …[10] working days after the seizure of the goods; or

(ii) ...[10] working days after the due date for payment of the tax on the supply or import of the goods.

(9) Where the detention period in subsection (8) has expired, the Commissioner may sell the goods in the manner specified under section 41(4) and apply the proceeds of sale as set out in section 41(5).

(10) Notwithstanding the provisions of this section, the Commissioner may proceed under section 36 with respect to any balance owed if the proceeds of sale are not sufficient to meet the costs thereof and the tax due.

Distress Proceedings

41. (1) The Commissioner may recover unpaid tax by distress proceedings against the movable property of the person liable to pay the tax, referred to as the "person liable", by issuing an order in writing, specifying the person liable, the location of the property, and the tax liability to which the proceedings relate.

(2) For the purposes of executing distress under subsection (1), the Commissioner may –
   (a) at any time enter any house or premises described in the order authorising the distress proceedings; and
   (b) require a police officer to be present while the distress is being executed.

(3) Property upon which a distress is levied under this section, other than perishable goods, shall be kept for [10] working days either at the premises where the distress was levied or at such other place as the Commissioner may consider appropriate, at the cost of the person liable.

(4) Where the person liable does not pay the tax due, together with the costs of the distress –
   (a) in the case of perishable goods, within such period as the Commissioner considers reasonable having regard to the condition of the goods; or
   (b) in any other case, within [10] working days after the [10]-day period referred to in subsection (3), the property distrained upon may be sold by public auction, or in such other manner as provided in regulations.

(5) The proceeds of a disposal under subsection (4) is required to be applied by the Commissioner first towards the cost of taking, keeping, and selling the property distrained upon, then towards the tax due and payable, and the remainder of the proceeds, if any, must restored to the person liable.

(6) Nothing in this section precludes the Commissioner from proceeding under section 36 with respect to any balance owed if the proceeds of the distress are not sufficient to meet the costs thereof and the tax due.

(7) All costs incurred by the Commissioner in respect of a distress may be recovered by the Commissioner from the person liable as tax due under this Act.

Recovery of Tax from Recipient of Supply

42. (1) Where, in respect of a taxable supply by a taxable person, the taxable person has, in consequence of a fraudulent action or misrepresentation by the recipient of the supply, incorrectly treated the supply as an exempt or zero-rated supply, the Commissioner may raise an assessment upon the recipient for the amount of unpaid tax in respect of the supply together with any interest or penalty that has become payable under sections 31 and 36.

(2) The Commissioner is required to serve notice of an assessment under subsection (1) on the recipient specifying –
   (a) the tax payable;
   (b) the date the tax is due and payable; and
   (c) the time, place, and manner of objecting to the assessment.

(3) An assessment raised under subsection (1) is treated as an assessment for all purposes of the Act.

(4) Subsection (1) does not preclude the Commissioner from recovering the tax, interest, or penalty from the taxable person making the supply.

(5) For purposes of subsection (4),

(a) any amount recovered from the recipient is to be credited against the liability of the taxable person; and

(b) any amount recovered from the taxable person is to be credited against the liability of the recipient.

(6) Where an amount of tax, interest, or penalty referred to in subsection (1) is paid by the taxable person, the taxable person may recover the amount paid from the recipient.

(7) An amount assessed under this section is treated, for all purposes of this Act, as tax charged under this Act.

Recovery of Tax from Third Parties

43. (1) Where a person liable to pay tax under this Act, referred to as the "person liable", fails to do so by the due date, the Commissioner may, by notice in writing, require any other person –

(a) owing or who may owe money to the person liable;

(b) holding or who may subsequently hold money for, or on account of, the person liable; or

(c) having authority from some other person to pay money to the person liable,[12] to pay the money to the Commissioner on the date set out in the notice, up to the amount of the tax due.

(2) The date specified in the notice under subsection (1) shall not be a date before the money becomes due to the person liable to pay tax, or held on the person's behalf.

(3) A copy of a notice issued under subsection (1) is required to be served on the person liable.

(4) A person making a payment pursuant to a notice under subsection (1) is deemed to have acted under the authority of the person liable and of all other persons concerned and is indemnified in respect of the payment.

(5) The provisions of this Act relating to the payment, collection and recovery of tax apply to any amount due under this section as if the amount were tax due under this Act.

(6) A person who fails to comply with a notice under this section commits an offence and is liable on conviction to a fine not exceeding [... vatopians] or to imprisonment for a term not exceeding [1] year, or both.

(7) Where a person is convicted of an offence under subsection (6), the Court may, in addition to imposing a fine or prison sentence, order the convicted person to pay to the Commissioner an amount not exceeding the amount which the person failed to pay as required under this section.

Duties of Receivers

44. (1) In this section, "receiver" means a person who, with respect to an asset in Vatopia is –

(a) a liquidator of a company;

---

[12] Subsection (1)(d) could be added to include the recovery of property in the hands of a third person that belongs to the person liable.

(b) a receiver appointed out of court or by a court;

(c) a trustee for a [bankrupt person];

(d) a mortgagee in possession;

(e) an executor of the estate of a deceased person; or

(f) any other person conducting business on behalf of a person legally incapacitated.

(2) A receiver is required to notify the Commissioner in writing within [14] days after being appointed to the position or taking possession of an asset in Vatopia of the person liable to tax, whichever first occurs.

(3) The Commissioner may in writing notify a receiver of the amount which appears to the Commissioner to be sufficient to provide for any tax which is or will become payable by the person whose assets are in the possession of the receiver.

(4) A receiver –

(a) is required to set aside, out of the proceeds of sale of an asset, the amount notified by the Commissioner under subsection (3), or such lesser amount as is subsequently agreed on by the Commissioner;

(b) is liable to the extent of the amount set aside for the tax of the person who owned the asset; and

(c) may pay any debt that has priority over the tax referred to in this section notwithstanding any provision of this section.

(5) A receiver is personally liable to the extent of any amount required to be set aside under subsection (4) for the tax referred to in subsection (3) if, and to the extent that, the receiver fails to comply with the requirements of this section.

(6) A person who fails to comply the requirements of subsection (4) commits an offence and is liable on conviction to a fine not exceeding [. . . vatopians] or to imprisonment for a term not exceeding [1] year, or both.

(7) Where a person is convicted of an offence under subsection (6) for failing to set aside an amount as required under subsection (4), the Court may, in addition to imposing a fine or prison sentence, order the convicted person to pay to the Commissioner an amount not exceeding the amount which the person failed to set aside as required under subsection (4).

Part VII – Refund of Tax and Tax Relief

Carry Forward of Excess Deductions and Refund of Tax

45. (1) Where –

(a) the total amount of input tax deductible by a taxable person under section 27 for a tax period exceeds the person's output tax for that period; or

(b) the amount of tax paid by a person, other than in circumstances specified under paragraph (a), exceeds the amount properly charged to tax under this Act,

(c) the amount of the excess is treated in the manner provided in this section.

(2) Except as provided in subsection (5), the excess described in subsection (1)(a) is carried forward to the next tax period and treated as input tax deductible in that period.

(3) Subject to this section, if any of the excess referred to in subsection (1)(a) for a tax period remains after being carried forward and used as an input tax deductible in [three] consecutive tax periods, the taxable person may file with the Commissioner a claim for refund for the amount remaining, in the form and with the documentation specified in regulations.

(4) By the end of the [second] calendar month following the date the claim for refund described in subsection (3) is filed or, where the Commissioner orders an audit of the claim for refund described in subsection (3), within 10 days after conclusion of the audit, if later, the Commissioner, to the extent satisfied that the taxpayer is entitled to the amount of the refund claimed–

    (a) may apply the amount of the refund claimed under subsection (3) in reduction of any tax, levy, interest, or penalty payable by the person in terms of this Act, other taxes collected by the Commissioner, and any unpaid amounts under the repealed [Sales Tax Act]; and

    (b) is required to refund any excess remaining to the taxable person.

(5) Where at least 50 percent of the amount of the taxable supplies of a taxable person for the taxable period is taxed at a zero rate, and the person reports an excess described in subsection (1)(a) for the taxable period, the person may file with the Commissioner a claim for refund for the excess deductions attributable to the zero-rated supplies in the form and with the documentation specified in regulations.

(6) By the end of the first calendar month following the date the claim for refund described in subsection (5) is filed or, where the Commissioner orders an audit of the claim for refund described in subsection (5), within 10 days after conclusion of the audit, if later, the Commissioner, to the extent satisfied that the taxpayer is entitled to the amount of the refund claimed–

    (a) may apply the amount of the refund claimed under subsection (5) in reduction of any tax, levy, interest, or penalty payable by the person in terms of this Act, other taxes collected by the Commissioner, and any unpaid amounts under the repealed [Sales Tax Act]; and

    (b) is required to refund any excess remaining to the taxable person.

(7) Notwithstanding subsections (4)(b) or (6)(b), if the amount of the excess to be refunded is not more than the amount specified in paragraph 4 of Schedule V, the excess must be carried forward to the next succeeding tax period and be accounted for as provided in section 27(1)(i).

(8) Where a person has overpaid tax in the circumstances specified under subsection (1)(b), the person may file with the Commissioner a claim for a refund of the excess, accompanied by documentary proof of payment of the excess amount.

(9) For purposes of subsection (8), if the claim for refund is filed by a taxable person,

    (a) the Commissioner is required to deal with the claim as if it were a claim under subsection (3); and

    (b) to the extent that any output tax claimed to be refundable is an amount borne by a recipient who is not a registered person, the output tax is refundable only to the extent that it will be repaid by the taxable person to that recipient, whether in cash or as a credit against an amount owing to the taxable person by the recipient.

(10) Where a taxable person has failed to file a return for any tax period as required under this Act, the Commissioner may withhold payment of any amount refundable under this section until the taxable person files such return as required.

(11) A claim for a refund specified in subsection (3), (5), or (8) must be made within 3 years after the date the person has the right to apply for the refund under this section.

(12) The Commissioner is required to serve on a person claiming a refund, a notice in writing of the decision in respect of the claim within [thirty] days of receiving the claim.

(13) A person claiming a refund under this section who is dissatisfied with a decision referred to in subsection (12) may challenge the decision only under Part IX of this Act.

(14) For purposes of subsection (3), the unused excess deductions carried forward from the earliest period are considered used before excess deductions carried forward from more recent tax periods.

(15) A person who improperly claims a refund under this section to that person or another person commits an offence and is liable on conviction to a fine not exceeding [... vatopians] or to imprisonment for a term not exceeding [3] years, or both.

Interest on Overpayment

46. (1) Where the Commissioner fails to pay a refund of tax relating to an excess under section 45 by the date specified under that section,[13] the Commissioner is required to pay the taxable person entitled to the refund an additional amount as interest at the rate specified in paragraph 5 of Schedule V to the Act, commencing from the date on which the refund was due and ending on the date the payment of the refund is made.

(2) Where the Commissioner is required to refund an amount of tax to a person as a result of –
   (a) an objection decision under section 50; or
   (b) a decision of the [Commissioner of Appeals] under section 51; or
   (c) a decision of the High Court under section 52, the Commissioner is required to pay interest at the rate specified in paragraph 5 of Schedule V to the Act on the amount of the refund for the period commencing from the date the person paid the tax refunded and ending on the date the refund is made.

Others Eligible for Tax Refund

47. (1) The Minister, in consultation with the [Minister of Foreign Affairs], may issue regulations that authorise the grant of a refund of tax paid or borne on a supply to or import by –
   (a) a person to the extent provided under the [Diplomatic Immunities and Privileges Act], an international convention having force of law in Vatopia, or the recognised principles of international law; or
   (b) a diplomatic or consular mission of a foreign country established in Vatopia, relating to transactions concluded for the official purposes of such mission; or
   (c) an organisation or government to the extent provided under a technical assistance or humanitarian assistance agreement entered into with the Government of Vatopia; or
   (d) a non-resident individual on goods specified in the regulations that are exported from Vatopia as accompanied baggage, but only if the total tax on such goods exceeds the amount specified in paragraph 6 of Schedule V to the Act.

(2) The refund provided for in subsection (1)(a) and (d) is not available to a citizen or a permanent resident of Vatopia as prescribed under [the Immigration Act].

(3) The Minister may authorise any relief under this section on such conditions and subject to such restrictions as the Minister may deem fit.

---

[13] Alternatively, this subsection can give the Commissioner an additional period, such as one month, to issue the refund before interest starts accruing.

(4) A claim for a refund of tax under this section is to be made in such form and at such time as the Minister may prescribe and shall be accompanied by proof of payment of tax.

(5) The Minister may by notice apply the terms of this section to a public international organisation and its officials and employees.

(6) For purposes of this section, a "technical assistance agreement" includes an agreement that provides assistance by grant, loan, direct payment by the Government, or a combination of funding options.

(7) A claim for refund under this section must be made within the time specified by the Minister after the date the person has the right to apply for the refund.

Part VIII – Assessments

Assessments

48. (1) Where –
   (a) a person fails to file a return as required by section 24 or fails to furnish an import declaration as required by section 18(2) or 19(1);
   (b) the Commissioner is not satisfied with a return or import declaration furnished by a person;
   (c) the Commissioner has reason to believe that a person will become liable for the payment of an amount of tax but is unlikely to pay such amount;
   (d) a person, other than a taxable person, supplies goods or services and represents that tax is charged on the supply;
   (e) a taxable person supplies goods or services and the supply is not a taxable supply or is a taxable supply charged with tax at the rate of zero percent and, in either case, the taxable person represents that a positive rate of tax is charged on the supply; or
   (f) the Commissioner has determined the liability of any person in terms of section 82(2),
   the Commissioner may make an assessment of the amount of tax payable by the person or of the amount of tax represented by the person as payable in respect of a supply.

   (2) The person assessed under subsection (1) –
   (a) in the case of an assessment under subsection (1)(d) or (e), is the person making the supply; or
   (b) in the case of an assessment under subsection (1)(f), is the person whose liability has been determined under section 82(2); or
   (c) in any other case, is the person required to account for the tax under this Act.

   (3) An assessment under subsection (1)(a), (c), (d), (e), or (f) may be made at any time.

   (4) An assessment under subsection (1)(b) –
   (a) where the default was due to fraud, or wilful neglect committed by, or on behalf of, the person who furnished the return or import declaration, may be made at any time; or
   (b) in any other case, may be made within [3] years after the date the return or import declaration was furnished.

   (5) The Commissioner may, based on the information available, estimate the tax payable by a person for the purposes of making an assessment under subsection (1).

(6) Where a taxable person is not satisfied with a return filed by that person under this Act, that person may apply to the Commissioner to make an addition or alteration to that return.

(7) An application under subsection (6) must be in writing and specify in detail the grounds upon which it is made and must be made within [3] years after the date the return was filed by the taxable person or, in the event an assessment is made by the Commissioner after such [3-year] period, may be made within [60] days after the date that notice of such assessment is served on the taxpayer.

(8) After considering an application under subsection (6), the Commissioner may make an assessment of the amount that, in the Commissioner's opinion, is the amount of tax payable under this Act.

(9) Where an assessment has been made under this section, the Commissioner is required to serve a notice of the assessment on the person assessed, which notice must state –
   (a) the tax payable;
   (b) the date the tax is due and payable; and
   (c) the time, place, and manner of objecting to the assessment.

(10) The Commissioner may, within [3] years after service of the notice of assessment, or in the case of assessments described in subsection (4), within the deadline specified therein, amend an assessment by making such alterations or additions to the assessment as the Commissioner considers necessary, in which case, the Commissioner is required to serve notice of the amended assessment on the person assessed.

(11) An amended assessment is treated in all respects as an assessment under this Act.

(12) An amount assessed under subsection (1)(d), (e) or (f) is treated, for all purposes of this Act, as tax charged under this Act.

General Provisions Relating to Assessments

49. (1) The original or a certified copy of a notice of assessment is receivable in any proceedings as conclusive evidence that the assessment has been duly made and, except in proceedings under Part VIII of this Act relating to the assessment, that the amount and all particulars of the assessment are correct.

(2) No assessment or other document purporting to be made, issued, or executed under this Act shall be –
   (a) quashed or deemed to be void or voidable for want of form; or
   (b) affected by reason of mistake, defect, or omission therein,
   if it is, in substance and effect, in conformity with this Act and the person assessed, or intended to be assessed or affected by the document is identified in it.

Part IX – Objections and Appeals

Objections

50. (1) For purposes of this section, an "appealable decision" means an assessment or a decision described in sections 21(7), 22(17), 24(4), 25(3), 28(6), 34(4), 38(4), 45(9), 50(8), 51(8), 55(2), and 76(4);

(2) A person dissatisfied with an appealable decision may file an objection to the decision with the Commissioner within [30] days after the service of the notice of the decision.

(3) Where the Commissioner is satisfied that owing to absence from Vatopia, sickness, or other reasonable cause, the person was prevented from lodging an objection within the time specified under subsection (2) and there has been no unreasonable delay by the person in lodging the objection, the Commissioner may accept an objection filed after the time specified under subsection (2).

(4) An objection to an appealable decision must be in writing and specify in detail the grounds upon which it is made.

(5) In the case of an objection to an assessment, the Commissioner may consider the objection only if –
   (a) the person assessed has paid the tax due under the assessment; or
   (b) the Commissioner is satisfied that the person objecting is unable to pay the full amount of tax due and has given sufficient security, to the extent in a position to do so, for the amount of tax unpaid and any penalty that may become payable.

(6) After considering the objection, the Commissioner may allow the objection in whole or part and amend the assessment or the decision objected to accordingly, or disallow the objection.

(7) The Commissioner is required to serve the person objecting with notice in writing of the decision on the objection.

(8) A person dissatisfied with a decision of the Commissioner under subsection (3) may challenge the decision only under Part IX of this Act.

Appeal to Commissioner of Appeals

51. (1) In this section – "Commissioner of Appeals" means the Commissioner of Appeals as appointed by the Minister pursuant to the [Finance Act] to hear and decide any matter in dispute between the Commissioner and any person in respect of the person's liability or assessment for tax.

(2) A person dissatisfied with an objection decision under section 50(6) may, within [30] days after being served with notice of the decision,
   (a) file a notice of appeal with the Commissioner of Appeals and, if filed;
   (b) must serve a copy of the notice of appeal on the Commissioner.

(3) Upon application in writing by a person dissatisfied with a decision under section 50(6), the Commissioner of Appeals may, where satisfied that owing to absence from Vatopia, sickness, or other reasonable cause, the person was prevented from lodging a notice of appeal within the time specified under subsection (2) and there has been no unreasonable delay by the person in lodging the notice, accept a notice of appeal filed after the time specified under subsection (2).

(4) In an appeal to the Commissioner of Appeals against an objection decision the Commissioner of Appeals may consider the objection only if the Comptroller certifies that
   (a) the person assessed has paid the full amount of the tax due under the assessment; or
   (b) the Comptroller is satisfied that the person objecting is unable to pay the full amount of tax due and has given sufficient security, for the amount of tax unpaid and any penalty and interest that may become payable.

(5) If the Commissioner has not made a decision on the objection, and [60] days have passed since the objection was filed, an appeal may be made under subsection (2) at any time, as if the Commissioner had made a decision to disallow the objection.

(6) In an appeal to the Commissioner of Appeals against a decision on the objection, the person is limited to the grounds set out in the person's objection,

unless the Commissioner of Appeals grants the person leave to add new grounds.

(7) In deciding an appeal, the Commissioner of Appeals may make an order –

    (a) affirming, reducing, increasing, or otherwise varying the assessment under appeal; or

    (b) remitting the assessment for reconsideration by the Commissioner in accordance with the directions of the Commissioner of Appeals.

(8) A person dissatisfied with a decision of the Commissioner of Appeals under subsection (3) may challenge the decision only under Part IX of this Act.

(9) The [Income Tax Act, sections . . .] apply to appeals under this Act to the extent not inconsistent with the provisions of this Act.

Appeal to High Court[14]

52. (1) A party who is dissatisfied with the decision of the Commissioner of Appeals may, within [30] days after being notified of the decision, file a notice of appeal with the [Registrar] of the High Court; and the party so appealing must serve a copy of the notice of appeal on the other party to the proceeding before the Commissioner of Appeals.

    (2) An appeal to the [High Court] may be made only on questions of law, including questions of mixed fact and law, and the notice of the appeal must state the questions of law that will be raised on the appeal.

    (3) On an appeal under this section, the High Court may –

        (a) confirm, increase or order the reduction of any assessment;

        (b) make such other order as it thinks fit; and

        (c) make such order as to costs as it thinks fit.

Burden of Proof

53. The burden of proving that an assessment is excessive or that a decision of the Commissioner is wrong is on the person objecting to the assessment or decision.

Part X – Special Cases

Persons Acting in a Representative Capacity

54. (1) In this section, "representative", in relation to a taxable person, means –

    (a) in the case of a company (other than a company in liquidation) –

        (i) in the case of a [corporation], the [treasurer or other designated officer or officers]; or

        (ii) in the case of an unincorporated association or body, any member of the committee of management; or

        (iii) in any other case, any person who is responsible for accounting for the receipt and payment of moneys or funds on behalf of the company;

    (b) in the case of a company in liquidation, the liquidator;

    (c) in the case of the State, any person responsible for accounting for the receipt and payment of money under the provisions of any law or for the receipt and payment of public funds or of funds voted by Parliament;

---

[14] If appeals beyond the trial court are included in the VAT Act, they should be inserted here.

(d) in the case of a local authority or board, any person who is responsible for accounting for the receipt and payment of money or funds on behalf of the local authority or board;

(e) in the case of a partnership, any partner in the partnership;

(f) in the case of a trust, any trustee; or

(g) in the case of a non-resident or a person referred to in paragraph (d) of the definition of "resident" in section 2, any person controlling the non-resident's affairs in Vatopia, including any manager of a taxable activity of the non-resident in Vatopia.

(2) Every representative of a taxable person is responsible for performing any duties, including the payment of tax, imposed by this Act on the taxable person.

(3) Every representative who in that capacity pays any tax payable under this Act by a taxable person is entitled to recover the amount so paid from the taxable person or to retain the amount so paid out of any money of the taxable person that is in the representative's possession or under the representative's control.

(4) Every representative is personally liable for the payment of any tax payable by the representative in his representative capacity if, while the amount remains unpaid, the representative –

(a) alienates, charges, or disposes of any money received or accrued in respect of which the tax is payable; or

(b) disposes of or parts with any fund or money belonging to the taxable person which is in the possession of the representative or which comes to the representative after the tax is payable if such tax could legally have been paid from or out of such fund or money.

(5) Nothing in this section shall be construed as relieving a taxable person from performing any duties imposed by this Act on the taxable person which the representative of the person has failed to perform.

Power to Appoint Representatives

55. (1) The Commissioner may, if the Commissioner considers it necessary to do so, declare a person to be a representative of the taxable person for the purposes of section 54.

(2) A person dissatisfied with a decision referred to in subsection (1) may challenge the decision only under Part IX of this Act.

Branches

56. (1) Where a taxable activity is conducted by a taxable person in branches or divisions, the taxable person is deemed to be a single person conducting the taxable activity for purposes of this Act.

(2) Subject to subsection (3), a taxable person who conducts a taxable activity in branches or divisions is required to register in the name of the taxable person and not also in the names of its branches and divisions.

(3) Upon application in writing, the Commissioner may authorise a taxable person to register one or more of its branches or divisions as separate taxable persons if the Commissioner is satisfied that the branch or division maintains an independent system of accounting and can be separately identified by the nature of its activities or its location.[15]

---

[15] An alternative is to deny registration by branch or division if the record-keeping and communication among branches or divisions is adequate to require a single registration.

(4) The registration of a branch or division under subsection (3) is subject to such conditions and restrictions as the Minister may deem fit.

Bodies of Persons (Other than Incorporated Companies)

57. (1) This Act applies to a partnership as if the partnership were a person separate from the partners of the partnership, except that –
    (a) obligations that would be imposed on the partnership are instead imposed on each partner, but may be discharged by any of the partners; and
    (b) the partners are jointly and severally liable to pay any amount due under this Act that would be payable by the partnership; and
    (c) any offence under this Act that would otherwise be committed by the partnership is taken to have been committed by each of the partners.

    (2) This Act applies to an unincorporated association or body as if it were a person separate from the members of the association or body, but the obligations that would be imposed on the association or body are instead imposed on each member of the committee of management of the association or body, but may be discharged by any of those members.

    (3) Where –
    (a) a partnership, or unincorporated association or body is dissolved, referred to as the "dissolved entity", in consequence of –
       (i) the retirement or withdrawal of one or more, but not all, of its partners or members; or
       (ii) the admission of a new partner or member;
    (b) a new partnership, or association or body comes into existence, referred to as the "new entity", consisting of the remaining members and one or more new members; and
    (c) the new entity continues to carry on the taxable activity of the dissolved entity as a going concern, the dissolved entity and the new entity, for the purposes of this Act, are deemed to be one and the same, unless the Commissioner, having regard to the circumstances of the case, otherwise directs.

Death or Insolvency of Taxable Person; Mortgagee in Possession

58. (1) Where, after the death of a taxable person or the sequestration of a taxable person's estate, any taxable activity previously carried on by the taxable person is carried on by or on behalf of the executor or trustee of the person's estate or anything is done in connection with the termination of the taxable activity, the estate of the taxable person, as represented by the executor or trustee, is deemed for the purposes of this Act to be the taxable person in respect of the taxable activity.

    (2) Where a mortgagee is in possession of any land or other property previously mortgaged by a mortgagor who is a taxable person, and the mortgagee carries on a taxable activity in relation to the land or other property, the mortgagee is deemed, from the date the mortgagee took possession of that land or property until such time as the mortgagee ceases to be in possession of the land or property, to be the taxable person carrying on the taxable activity.

Trustee

59. A person who is a trustee in more than one capacity is treated for the purposes of this Act as a separate person in relation to each of those capacities.

Part XI – Records and Investigation Powers

Meaning of "Records"

60. In this Part, "records" means accounting records, accounts, books, computer-stored information, or any other documents.

Record-keeping

61. (1) Every taxable person or any other person liable for tax under this Act is required to maintain in Vatopia –
    (a) original tax invoices, tax credit notes, and tax debit notes received by the person;
    (b) a copy of all tax invoices, tax credit notes, and tax debit notes issued by the person;
    (c) customs documentation relating to imports and exports by the person;
    (d) accounting records relating to taxable activities carried on in Vatopia; and
    (e) any other records as may be prescribed by regulations.
    (2) Records required to be maintained under subsection (1) are required to be retained for [6] years after the end of the tax period to which they relate.[16]
    (3) A person who fails to maintain proper records in accordance with this section commits an offence and is liable on conviction –
    (a) where the failure was made knowingly or recklessly, to a fine not exceeding [. . . vatopians] or to imprisonment for a term not exceeding [2 years], or both; or
    (b) in any other case, to a fine not exceeding [. . . vatopians] to imprisonment for a term not exceeding [1 year], or both.
    (4) A person who fails to maintain proper records in a tax period in accordance with the requirements of this section is liable for a penalty of [. . . vatopians] per day for each day or portion thereof that the failure continues.

Access to Records, Computers, Goods, and Vehicles

62. (1) For the purpose of the administration of this Act, a taxation officer who has been authorised by the Commissioner in writing may –
    (a) without prior notice and at any time,[17] enter any premises or place where records are kept and on such premises search for any records;
    (b) in carrying out a search referred to in paragraph (a) and in any manner, open or cause to be opened or removed and opened, any article in which the officer suspects that any records are kept;
    (c) seize any records which in the officer's opinion may afford evidence that may be material in determining the liability of any person for tax payable under this Act;
    (d) retain any records seized under paragraph (c) for as long as they may be required for determining a person's liability under this Act or for any proceeding under this Act;

---

[16] An alternative is to add the following: "A taxpayer may apply in writing to the Commissioner for permission to dispose of records required to be maintained under this Act prior to the expiration of the period up to which records are required to be kept and the Commissioner may grant permission in writing if satisfied that the records may not be required for any tax purposes."

[17] An alternative is to require a warrant from a magistrate or judge before a taxation officer is authorised to enter premises and open and remove items found there that are relevant for the tax inquiry.

(e) examine and make extracts from, and copies of, any records, and require from any person an explanation of any entry therein;

(f) where a hard copy or computer disk of computer-stored information is not provided, seize and retain the computer in which the information is stored for as long as is necessary to copy the information required; and

(g) stop and board a vehicle which the officer has reasonable cause to believe is importing goods into Vatopia, search any such vehicle or any person found in the vehicle and question the person with respect to any matter dealt with in this Act.

(2) A taxation officer who attempts to exercise a power under subsection (1) is not entitled to enter or remain on any premises or at any place if, upon being requested by the occupier of the premises or place, the officer does not produce an authorisation in writing from the Commissioner to the effect that the officer is authorised to exercise that power under this section.

(3) The owner, manager, or any other person lawfully on the premises or at the place entered or proposed to be entered under this section is required to provide all reasonable facilities and assistance for the effective exercise of power under this section.

(4) A person whose records or computer have been removed and retained under subsection (1) may examine them and make copies or extracts from them during regular office hours under such supervision as the Commissioner may determine.

(5) A taxation officer exercising a power under subsection (1) may request the assistance of a Customs officer or police officer as the taxation officer may consider reasonably necessary and any such Customs officer or police officer is required to render such assistance as may be required by the taxation officer.

(6) This section has effect notwithstanding any rule of law relating to privilege or the public interest in relation to the production of, or access to records.

(7) A person who fails to provide a taxation officer with reasonable facilities and assistance as required by subsection (3) commits an offence and is liable on conviction to a fine not exceeding [... vatopians] or to imprisonment for a term not exceeding [1 year], or both.

Records Not in Vatopian Language

63. Where a record referred to in section 61 or 62 is not in the Vatopian language, the Commissioner may, by notice in writing, require the person keeping the record to provide at that person's expense a translation into the Vatopian language by a translator approved by the Commissioner for this purpose.

Notice to Obtain Information or Evidence

64. (1) The Commissioner may, by notice in writing, require a person, whether or not liable for tax under this Act –

(a) to furnish such information concerning that person or any other person as may be required by the notice; or

(b) to attend at the time and place designated in the notice for the purpose of being examined on oath before the Commissioner or a taxation officer authorised by the Commissioner for this purpose concerning the tax affairs of that person or any other person, and for that purpose the Commissioner or the authorised officer may require the person examined to produce any record or computer in the control of the person.

(2) Where the notice requires the production of any record or computer, it is sufficient if such record or computer is described in the notice with reasonable certainty.

(3) A notice issued under this section is required to be served by or at the direction of the Commissioner by a signed copy delivered –
   (a) by registered post;
   (b) by hand to the person to whom it is directed; or
   (c) left at the person's last and usual place of abode, and the certificate of service signed by the person serving the notice is evidence of the facts stated therein.

(4) This section has effect notwithstanding any rule of law relating to privilege or the public interest in relation to the furnishing of information or the production of records or documents.

(5) A person who fails to comply with a notice issued under this section commits an offence and is liable on conviction to a fine not exceeding [... vatopians] or to imprisonment for a term not exceeding [1 year], or both.

Part XII – Offences and Penalties

Division I: Criminal Offences

Power to Bring Criminal Charges

65 (1) Subject to the powers of the [] under the Constitution no criminal proceedings in respect of any offence under this Act shall be commenced except where the Commissioner determines to bring charges and seek prosecution.

(2) Criminal proceedings under this Act shall be commenced in the name of the Commissioner.

(3) If the Commissioner resolves to bring charges or to seek prosecution under this Act, the matter shall be referred to the Attorney-General.

Time Limits for Proceedings to Be Taken

66. Proceedings under this Division may be commenced –
   (a) where the offence alleged has involved the doing of an act, within three years after the discovery of the act;
   (b) where the offence alleged has involved the failure to do an act, within three years after the Commissioner has become aware of such failure;
   (c) where the offence alleged has involved the non-disclosure or incorrect disclosure by a person of information relating to that person's liability to tax for a tax period, within one year after his correct liability to tax has become final for that tax period.

Tax Evasion

67. A person who wilfully evades, or attempts to evade the assessment, payment, or collection of tax commits an offence and is liable on conviction to a fine of up to [... vatopians], or to imprisonment for a term of [two] years, or both.

False or Misleading Statements

68. (1) A person who –
   (a) makes a statement to a taxation officer that is false or misleading in a material particular; or
   (b) omits from a statement made to a taxation officer any matter or thing without which the statement is misleading in a material particular,

Commits an offence and is liable on conviction

(c) where the statement or omission was made knowingly or recklessly, to a fine not exceeding [. . . vatopians] or to imprisonment for a term not exceeding [2 years], or both; or

(d) in any other case, a fine not exceeding [. . . vatopians] or to imprisonment for a term not exceeding [1 year], or both.

(2) A reference in this section to a statement made to a taxation officer is a reference to a statement made orally, in writing, or in any other form to that officer acting in the performance of the officer's duties under this Act, and includes a statement made –

(a) in an application, certificate, declaration, notification, return, objection, or other document made, prepared, given, filed, filed, or furnished under this Act;

(b) in any information required to be furnished under this Act;

(c) in a document furnished to a taxation officer otherwise than pursuant to this Act;

(d) in an answer to a question asked of a person by a taxation officer; or

(e) to another person with the knowledge or reasonable expectation that the statement would be conveyed to a taxation officer.

(3) It is a defence to a prosecution under subsection (1) that the person did not know and could not reasonably be expected to have known that the statement to which the prosecution relates was false or misleading.

Obstructing Taxation Officers

69. A person who obstructs a taxation officer in the performance of the officer's duties under this Act commits an offence and is liable on conviction to a fine not exceeding [. . . vatopians] or to imprisonment for a term not exceeding [2 years], or both.

Offences by Taxation Officers

70. A taxation officer in carrying out the provisions of this Act who –

(a) directly or indirectly asks for, or takes in connection with any of the officer's duties a payment or reward, whether pecuniary or otherwise, or any promise or security for any such payment or reward, not being a payment or reward which the officer was lawfully entitled to receive; or

(b) enters into or acquiesces in an agreement to do, abstain from doing, permit, conceal, or connive at an act or thing whereby the tax revenue is or may be defrauded or which is contrary to the provisions of this Act or to the proper execution of the officer's duty, commits an offence and is liable on conviction to a fine not exceeding [. . . vatopians] or to imprisonment for a term not exceeding [5 years], or both, and the Court may, in addition to imposing a fine, order the convicted person to pay to the Commissioner an amount of tax that has not been paid as a result of the officer's wrongdoing and which cannot be recovered from the person liable for the tax.

Offences by Companies, Aiders, and Abetters

71. (1) Where an offence under this Act has been committed by a company, every person who at the time of the commission of the offence –

(a) was a representative officer, director, general manager, secretary, or other similar officer of the company; or

(b) was acting or purporting to act in such capacity, is deemed to have committed the offence.

(2) Subsection (1) does not apply where –

(a) the offence was committed without such person's consent or knowledge; and

(b) the person exercised all such diligence to prevent the commission of the offence as ought to have been exercised having regard to the nature of the person's functions and all the circumstances.

(3) A person aiding and abetting the commission of an offence under this Act shall also be guilty of that offence and liable to the same penalties as the person committing the offence.

General Penalty

72. A person who commits an offence under this Act for which no penalty is prescribed is liable on conviction to a fine not exceeding [. . . vatopians], or to imprisonment for a term of [six] months, or both.

Compounding of Offences

73. (1) Where a person has committed an offence under this Act other than an offence under sections 8 or 70, the Commissioner may, with the approval of the Minister, at any time prior to the commencement of the court proceedings relating thereto, compound such offence and order the person to pay such sum of money as specified by the Commissioner, not exceeding the maximum amount of the fine prescribed for the offence.

(2) The Commissioner may compound an offence under this section only if the person concerned admits in writing that the person has committed the offence.[18]

(3) Where the Commissioner compounds an offence under this section, the order referred to in subsection (1) –

(a) must be in writing and shall have attached the written admission;

(b) must specify –

(i) the offence committed;

(ii) the sum of money to be paid; and

(iii) the due date for the payment;

(c) is required to be served on the person who committed the offence; and

(d) must be final and not subject to any appeal.

(4) When the Commissioner compounds an offence under this section, the person concerned shall not be liable for prosecution in respect of such offence or for penalty under section 20(10), 61(4), or 75.

(5) The amount ordered to be paid under subsection (1) is recoverable as if it were tax due and payable.

Division II: Civil Penalties

General Provisions

74. (1) No penalty is payable under this Division where, in respect of the same act or omission, the person has been convicted of an offence under Division I, or an offence has been compounded under section 73.

---

[18] An alternative is to require the person to request in writing that the Commissioner deal with the offence in this manner.

(2) If a penalty under this Division has been paid and the Commissioner institutes a prosecution proceeding under Division I in respect of the same act or omission,t he Commissioner must refund the amount of the penalty paid; and that penalty is not payable unless the prosecution is withdrawn.

(3) Where good cause is shown, in writing, by the person liable for a penalty, the Commissioner may mitigate in whole or in part any penalty payable.

Penalty for Making False or Misleading Statements

75. (1) Where a person knowingly or recklessly –
    (a) makes a statement to a taxation officer that is false or misleading in a material particular; or
    (b) omits from a statement made to a taxation officer any matter or thing without which the statement is misleading in a material particular,
    and the tax properly payable by the person exceeds the tax that would be payable if the person were assessed on the basis that the statement is true, the person is liable for a penalty equal to the greater of [. . . vatopians] and
    (a) in a case where an amount of tax payable by the person would be reduced if it were determined on the basis of the information provided in the statement, the amount by which that tax would have been so reduced; and
    (b) in a case where the amount of a refund that the person applied for would be increased if it were determined on the basis of the information provided in the statement, the amount by which that amount would have been so increased.

    (2) Section 68(2) applies in determining whether a person has made a statement to a taxation officer.

    (3) It is a defence to a prosecution under subsection (1) that the person did not know and could not reasonably be expected to have known that the statement to which the prosecution relates was false or misleading.

Recovery or Remission of Penalties

76. (1) Where good cause is shown, in writing, by the person liable for a penalty, the Commissioner may remit in whole or part any penalty payable.

    (2) Except as otherwise provided in this Act, the imposition of a penalty is in addition to any fine or prison sentence imposed as a result of a conviction for an offence under sections 8(7), 18(6) or (7), 20(9), 21(13), 22(15), 24(5) or (6), 32(7) or (8), 33(7) or (8), 43(6), 44(6), 45(14), 61(3), 62(7), 64(5), 78(2), or under Division I of Part XII of this Act.

    (3) Penalties may be assessed and collected as if the amount of penalty is tax due under this Act.

    (4) A person dissatisfied with a decision of the Commissioner under subsection (1) may challenge the decision only under Part IX of this Act.

Temporary Closure of Business Premises[19]

77. (1) Where a person repeatedly violates –
    (a) section 18 or 34 by failing to pay tax when due;

---

[19] In addition, the Act could provide that the Commissioner may publish the names of persons who repeatedly violate the Act in a newspaper of general circulation in the State or local community.

(b) section 24 by failing to file returns;

(c) section 32 in relation to tax invoices,

(d) section 33 in relation to tax debit notes or tax credit notes;

(e) section 45 by improperly claiming tax refunds; or

(f) section 69 by obstructing taxation officers;

after obtaining an order of a court having jurisidiction in respect of the person, the Commissioner may forcibly close one or more business premises of the person for a period of between [3 and 30 days].

(2) For purposes of subsection (1), the Commissioner may use reasonable force and police assistance necessary to close all or any premises of the person, barring access with locks, fencing, boarding, or other appropriate methods.

(3) For purposes of this section, a repeated violation means a violation that is committed within one year of receipt by the person of a written warning –

(a) that a violation of such kind has been committed more than once within the year preceding the year of the warning, and

(b) that repetition may result in closure under this section.

Part XIII – Miscellaneous

VAT Registration Number[20]

78. (1) The Commissioner may require a person to include the VAT registration number issued by the Commissioner to that person in any return, notice, or other document prescribed or used for the purposes of this Act.

(2) A person who knowingly uses a false VAT registration number, including the VAT registration number of another person, on a return, notice, or other document prescribed or used for the purposes of this Act commits an offence and is liable on conviction to a fine not exceeding [...] or to imprisonment for a term not exceeding [2 years], or both.

(3) Subsection (2) does not apply to a person who uses the VAT registration number of another person with the permission of that other person on a return, notice, or other document relating to the tax affairs of that other person.

Forms and Notices; Authentication of Documents

79. (1) Forms, notices, returns, and other documents prescribed or published by the Commissioner may be in such form as the Commissioner determines for the efficient administration of this Act, and publication of such documents in the [Gazette] is not required.

(2) The Commissioner is required to make the documents referred to in subsection (1) available to the public at the Vatopia [Revenue Authority] and any other locations, or by mail, as the Commissioner determines.

(3) A notice or other document issued, served, or given by the Commissioner under this Act is sufficiently authenticated if the name or title of the Commissioner, or authorised taxation officer, is printed, stamped, or written on the document.

---

[20] For tax administration reasons, it is desirable to issue each taxpayer a taxpayer identification number that must be used for all taxes collected (e.g., VAT, customs, income, and payroll taxes).

Service of Notices

80. (1) Unless otherwise provided in this Act, a notice required by this Act to be in writing must be served on the recipient of the notice.

(2) A notice described in subsection (1) is considered sufficiently served on a person if it is –

    (a) personally served on that person;

    (b) personally served on the representative of that person under section 54;

    (c) left at the person's usual or last known place of abode, office, or place of business in Vatopia; or

    (d) sent by registered post to such place of abode, office, or place of business, or to the person's usual or last known address in Vatopia.

Tax-Inclusive Pricing

81. (1) A price charged by a taxable person in respect of a taxable supply is deemed to include, for the purposes of this Act, the tax charged on the supply under section 9(1)(a), whether or not the taxable person has included tax in such price.

(2) Subject to subsection (3), a price advertised or quoted by a taxable person in respect of a taxable supply is required to include tax and this must be stated in the advertisement or quotation.

(3) A taxable person may advertise or quote a price in respect of a taxable supply as exclusive of tax provided –

    (a) the advertisement or quotation also states the amount of tax charged on the supply and the price inclusive of tax; and

    (b) the price inclusive of tax and the price exclusive of tax are advertised or quoted with equal prominence or impact.

(4) Subject to subsection (5), price tickets on goods supplied by a taxable person need not state that the price includes tax if this is stated by way of a notice prominently displayed at the premises in which the taxable person carries on a taxable activity, including the places in such premises where payments are effected.

(5) The Commissioner may in the case of a taxable person or class of taxable person approve any other method of displaying prices of goods or services by such persons.

Schemes for Obtaining Tax Benefits

82. (1) In this section – "scheme" includes an agreement, arrangement, promise, or undertaking whether express or implied and whether or not legally enforceable, and a plan, proposal, course of action, or course of conduct; and "tax benefit" includes –

    (a) a reduction in the liability of a person to pay value added tax;

    (b) an increase in the entitlement of a person to a deduction or refund;

    (c) a postponement of liability for the payment of value added tax;

    (d) an acceleration of entitlement to a deduction for input tax; or

    (e) any other avoidance or postponement of liability for the payment of value added tax.

(2) Notwithstanding anything in this Act, if the Commissioner is satisfied that a scheme has been entered into or carried out where –

    (a) a person has obtained a tax benefit in connection with the scheme in a manner that constitutes a misuse of the provisions of this Act; and

(b) having regard to the substance of the scheme, it would be concluded that the person, or one of the persons, who entered into or carried out the scheme did so for the sole or dominant purpose of enabling the person to obtain the tax benefit,

the Commissioner may determine the liability of the person who has obtained the tax benefit as if the scheme had not been entered into or carried out, or in such manner as in the circumstances the Commissioner considers appropriate for the prevention or reduction of the tax benefit.

Currency Conversion

83. (1) For the purposes of this Act, all amounts of money are to be expressed in Vatopians.
    (2) Where an amount is expressed in a currency other than vatopians –
        (a) in the case of imports, the amount must be converted at the exchange rate as determined in terms of the [Customs Act]; or
        (b) in all other cases, the amount must be converted at the exchange rate applying between the currency and the vatopian at the time the amount is taken into account under this Act.

International Agreements

84. (1) In this section, "international agreement" means an agreement between Vatopia and a foreign government or a public international organisation.
    (2) To the extent that the terms of a treaty or other international agreement to which Vatopia is a party are inconsistent with the provisions of this Act (apart from section 82), the terms of the treaty or international agreement prevail over the provisions of this Act.

Registration of Certain Goods Prohibited in Certain Circumstances

85. (1) For purposes of this section, "registering authority" means a person appointed under a law to issue a licence, permit, certificate, concession, or other authorization.
    (2) Where a form of registration is required under a law in respect of goods consisting of an aircraft, boat, fishing vessel, ship, yacht, motor cycle, motor vehicle, tractor, caravan, or trailer, hereinafter referred to as "registrable goods", no registering authority responsible for such registration under such law may effect such registration upon a change of ownership or importation into Vatopia of registrable goods unless the person applying for registration produces to such registering authority –
        (a) in the case of registrable goods –
            (i) which form the subject of any supply, or
            (ii) which are imported into Vatopia, a receipt or customs document issued by the [Commissioner of Customs] or a document issued by the Commissioner showing that tax which is payable under this Act has been paid in respect of such supply or importation into Vatopia, or a receipt or certificate showing that no tax is payable under the Act in respect of such supply or importation, as the case may be, of the registrable goods in consequence of which the registration is required;

    (b) a declaration, in such form as the Commissioner may prescribe, issued by a registered person who, in carrying on a taxable activity in the ordinary course of which registrable goods are dealt in, supplied such goods in consequence of which the registration is required, certifying that the tax payable under this Act has been, or will be, paid by such person; or

    (c) a certificate issued by the Commissioner, or other documentation acceptable to the Commissioner, to the effect that the supply or import of the registrable goods was an exempt supply or exempt import, as the case may be.

Auctioneer and Agent

86. (1) Subject to this section, a supply of goods or services
    (a) made by a person as agent for another person ("the principal") is a supply by the principal; or
    (b) made to a person as agent for a principal is a supply to the principal.

  (2) Subsection (1) does not apply to services supplied by an agent to the agent's principal.

  (3) Except for an exempt supply, a supply of goods by auction is treated as a supply of goods for consideration by the auctioneer as supplier made in the course or furtherance of a taxable activity carried on by the auctioneer.

  (4) Subsection (1) does not apply where the principal is a non-resident.

  (5) Where a taxable supply has been made in circumstances specified under subsection (1)(a), the agent may issue a tax invoice in accordance with this Act in relation to the supply as if the agent had made the supply, in which case the principal may not also issue a tax invoice in relation to the supply.

  (6) Where a taxable supply has been made in the circumstances specified under subsection (1)(b), at the request of the agent, a tax invoice in relation to the supply may be issued to the agent, in which case the supplier may not issue a tax invoice to the principal in relation to the supply.

  (7) Where tax is payable by an auctioneer in respect of the supply of goods specified under subsection (3), the auctioneer is required to charge the purchaser the amount of tax payable in respect of the sale by adding the tax to the amount of a successful bid or, in the case of sales out-of-hand, to the purchase price, and is required to recover that tax from the purchaser.

Regulations

87. (1) The Minister may make regulations for the better carrying into effect of the purposes of this Act, any for any matter which under this Act is to be prescribed by regulations, and without prejudice to the generality of the foregoing, such regulations may provide for –
    (a) provisions of a saving or transitional nature consequent on the coming into force of this Act;
    (b) specific offences and penalties for breach of the regulations; or
    (c) the application of terms used in this Act and ancillary rules that facilitate the application of provisions in the Act, including the determination of the value, time, and place of transactions for purposes of applying the Act to those transactions.

  (2) If the regulations so provide, they may take effect from the date on which this Act comes into effect or a later date, regardless of the date when they are published in the Gazette.

Variation of Consideration on a Change in Rate

88. (1) Where –
    (a) an agreement for a supply of goods or services by a registered person has
        been entered into; and
    (b) subsequent to entering into the agreement, tax is imposed on the supply or
        the rate of tax applicable to the supply is increased,
    the supplier, unless explicitly provided to the contrary in the agreement, may
    recover from the recipient, in addition to the amounts payable by the recipient,
    an amount equal to the amount of tax imposed or the amount by which tax was
    increased, as the case may be.
    (2) Where –
    (a) an agreement for a supply of goods or services by a registered person has
        been entered into; and
    (b) subsequent to entering into the agreement, tax on the supply is withdrawn
        or the rate of tax applicable to the supply is decreased,
    the supplier, unless explicitly provided to the contrary in the agreement, is
    required to reduce the amount payable by the recipient by an amount equal to
    the amount of tax withdrawn or the amount by which tax was decreased, as the
    case may be.
    (3) Subject to subsections (4) and (5), where subsection (1) or (2) applies in respect of
    a supply of goods or services subject to any fee, charge, or other amount, whether
    a fixed, maximum, or minimum fee, charge, or other amount, prescribed by, or
    determined pursuant to, any Act, regulation, or measure having force of law,
    that fee, charge, or other amount may be increased or must be decreased, as the
    case may be, by the amount of tax or additional tax chargeable, or the amount
    of tax no longer chargeable.
    (4) Subsection (3) does not apply where the fee, charge, or other amount has been
    altered in an Act, regulation, or measure having force of law to take account of
    an imposition, increase, decrease, or withdrawal of tax.
    (5) Nothing in subsection (3) shall be construed so as to permit any further increase
    or require any further decrease, as the case may be, in a fee, charge, or other
    amount where the fee, charge, or other amount is calculated as a percentage or
    fraction of another amount which represents the consideration in money for a
    taxable supply.

Application of Increased or Reduced Rate

89. (1) Where –
    (a) services are performed; or
    (b) goods are provided in respect of a successive supply contemplated in section
        10(8) or (9), during a period beginning before and ending on or after the date
        on which a change in the rate of tax levied under section 9(1)(a) becomes
        effective in respect of the supply of the goods or the date on which the tax is
        imposed or withdrawn in respect of the supply, and the supply is deemed
        under section 10 to have been made on or after the said date, the value of
        the supply shall, on the basis of a fair and reasonable apportionment, be
        deemed to consist of a part, referred to as the "first part", relating to the
        performance of services or provision of goods before the said date and a
        part, referred to as the "second part", relating to the performance of services
        or provision of goods on or after the said date.
    (2) For purposes of subsection (1), in the case of –
    (a) a change in the rate on the said date, the tax payable in respect of the first
        part shall be determined at the rate applicable before the said date and the

tax payable in respect of the second part shall be determined at the rate applicable on the said date;

    (b) the imposition of tax on the said date, the first part shall not be subject to tax; or

    (c) the withdrawal of the tax, the first part shall be subject to tax as if the tax had not been withdrawn.

(3) For the purposes of subsection (1), goods are deemed to be provided by the supplier of the goods when the goods are delivered to the recipient and goods supplied under a rental agreement are deemed to be provided to the recipient when the recipient takes possession or occupation of the goods.

Orders to Amend Schedules or Change Amounts or Tax Rate

90. (1) The Minister may by order published in the Gazette –

    (a) amend the Schedules to this Act; or

    (b) increase or decrease any monetary amount set out in this Act; or

    (c) increase or decrease a rate of tax under section 9(1).

(2) An order under subsection (1) must be approved by an affirmative resolution of Parliament.

Repeal of Laws and Interpretation

91. (1) The Acts specified in Schedule VI to this Act [and any regulations made thereunder] are hereby repealed.

(2) No reference to sales tax in any Act, other than this Act, shall be treated as a reference to tax under this Act.

Transitional

Subsections (1)–(11), (15)–(16), and (20) of this Section Depend Upon the Existence of a Sales Tax

[That will be Replaced by the Value Added Tax]

92. (1) In this section – "qualifying goods" means any stock held for sale in the ordinary course of business; "repealed legislation" means the legislation referred to in section 91(1); and "sales tax" means the tax imposed under the [Sales Tax Act].

(2) The repealed legislation, including the rules governing the levy, payment, assessment, reporting, and recovery of those taxes, continue to apply to a supply or import taking place prior to the date on which this Act comes into operation pursuant to section 1.

(3) All appointments made under the repealed legislation and subsisting at the date of commencement of this Act are treated as appointments made under this Act; and an oath of secrecy taken under the repealed legislation is treated as having been taken under this Act.

(4) All forms and documents used in relation to the repealed legislation may continue to be used under this Act, and all references in those forms and documents to provisions of and expressions appropriate to the repealed legislation are taken to refer to the corresponding provisions and expressions of this Act.

(5) Notwithstanding section 27(4), in calculating the amount of tax payable by a taxable person in respect of the first tax period after the tax becomes effective, the taxable person may claim as an amount deductible under section 27, an amount equal to the sales tax deduction calculated in accordance with subsection (6) and deductible as provided under subsection (7).

(6) For the purposes of subsection (5), where a taxable person held, at the end of the last business day prior to the beginning of the first tax period after the tax becomes effective, qualifying goods being goods acquired not more than [4 months] before the tax becomes effective, and the Commissioner is satisfied that sales tax has been paid on the acquisition or import of those goods, the amount of the sales tax deduction is the amount of such taxes paid on such goods, but with respect to each item qualifying for the deduction, the sales tax shall not exceed the amount of tax which would have been payable had the goods been subject to tax chargeable under this Act.

(7) If, in any tax period, a taxable person has sales tax deductible under subsection (5), the amount deductible is deemed to be input tax deductible under section 27.

(8) No deduction is allowed under subsection (5) for any sales tax paid in respect of the acquisition of any goods if VAT imposed on a supply in acquisition of those goods after the effective date of this Act would not qualify for the section 27 input tax deduction.

(9) A person wishing to claim a deduction under subsection (5) for sales tax paid on qualifying goods on hand on the date of the entry into operation of this Act is required to register as of such date.

(10) A person claiming a deduction under subsection (5) is required to submit with that return an inventory of all qualifying goods on hand at the beginning of the first day on which this Act comes into operation, supported by documentary evidence of the payment of sales tax.

(11) A disallowance of a deduction for sales tax imposed before the effective date of this Act shall not be treated as a disallowance for purposes of section 4(17).

(12) Where a contract was concluded between two or more parties before the entry into operation of this Act, and no provision relating to tax was made in the contract, the supplier may recover from the recipient tax due on any taxable supplies made under the contract after the date on which this Act came into operation.

(13) Where a contract concluded after the date on which this Act came into operation does not include a provision relating to tax, the contract price is deemed to include tax and the supplier under the contract is required to account for the tax due.

(14) Subject to subsection (16), if, in connection with a supply of goods or services,
  (a) title to goods passes, delivery of goods is made, or services are rendered after the date on which this Act came into operation, and
  (b) payment is received or an invoice is issued within [9 months] before that date,
  for purposes of determining the tax period in which the supply occurs or an input tax deduction is allowable, the payment is treated as having been made or the invoice is treated as having been issued on the date on which this Act comes into operation.

(15) If services subject to sales tax were rendered before the date on which this Act came into effect and payment is made within [4] months after this Act came into effect, VAT is not imposed on the supply of the services.

(16) If
  (a) successive supplies described in section 14(8) or (9) were provided, or
  (b) services subject to sales tax were rendered, during a period that began before this Act came into effect and ended after this Act came into effect, VAT is imposed on the consideration for the goods or services rendered after this Act came into effect, except that to the extent the consideration for the

goods or services rendered before this Act came into effect is paid more than [4] months after this Act came into effect, the consideration shall be treated as consideration for the supply of goods or services rendered on the day after the end of that [4-month] period.

(17) Notwithstanding the application of subsection 16(a) to supplies under section 16(b), if construction, reconstruction, manufacture or extension of a building or civil engineering work is performed under a written agreement executed before this Act came into effect and the property is made available to the recipient after that date, VAT is imposed only on the value of the work performed after that date if the value of the work on the day before this Act came into effect is determined in a manner approved by the Commissioner and is submitted to the Commissioner by the end of the supplier's first VAT period after VAT becomes effective.

(18) If immovable property is provided under a rental agreement for a period that commences before and ends after the effective date of this Act, the consideration for the rental shall not include the amount attributable to the portion of the period that ends before the effective date.

(19) For purposes of section 27(1)(d), an amount paid as a prize or winnings does not include an amount attributable to obligations or contingent obligations that exist immediately before this Act comes into effect.

(20) The Minister may issue regulations for other transitional measures relating to the end of sales tax, the start of value added tax, or the transition from sales tax to value added tax.

Schedule I   Zero-Rated Supplies for Purposes of Section 15

1. In this Schedule –

   "ancillary transport services" means stevedoring services, lashing and securing services, cargo inspection services, preparation of customs documentation, container handling services, and storage of transported goods or goods to be transported;

   "export country" means any country other than Vatopia and includes a place which is not situated in Vatopia, but does not include a specific country or territory that the President by proclamation in the Gazette designates as one that is not an export country;

   "exported from Vatopia", in relation to any movable goods supplied by a registered person under a sale or a credit agreement, means –

   (a) consigned or delivered by the registered person to the recipient at an address in an export country as evidenced by documentary proof acceptable to the Commissioner; or

   (b) delivered by the registered person to the owner or charterer of a foreign-going aircraft or foreign-going vessel when such aircraft or vessel is going to a destination in an export country and such goods are for use or consumption in such aircraft or vessel, as the case may be;

   "foreign-going aircraft" means an aircraft engaged in the transportation for reward of passengers or goods wholly or mainly on flights between airports in Vatopia and airports in export countries or between airports in export countries; "foreign-going vessel" means a vessel engaged in the transportation for reward of passengers or goods wholly or mainly on voyages between seaports in Vatopia and seaports in export countries or between seaports in export countries; "intellectual property rights" means a patent, design, trade mark, copyright, know-how, confidential information, trade secret, or similar rights;

   "international transport services" means –

(a) the services, other than ancillary transport services, of transporting passengers or goods by road, rail, water, or air –
(i) from a place outside Vatopia to another place outside Vatopia where the transport or part of the transport is across the territory of Vatopia;
(ii) from a place outside Vatopia to a place in Vatopia; or
(iii) from a place in Vatopia to a place outside Vatopia;
(b) the services of transporting passengers from a place in Vatopia to another place in Vatopia to the extent that transport is by aircraft and constitutes "international carriage" as defined in Article 3 of the Convention on International Civil Aviation;
(c) the services, including any ancillary transport services, of transporting goods from a place in Vatopia to another place in Vatopia to the extent that those services are supplied by the same supplier as part of the supply of services to which paragraph (a) applies; or
(d) the services of insuring or the arranging of the insurance or the arranging of the transport of passengers or goods to which paragraphs (a) to (c) applies.
2. Subject to paragraph 3, the following supplies are specified for the purposes of section 15[21] –
(a) a supply of goods where the supplier has entered the goods for export, pursuant to the [Customs Act], and the goods have been exported from Vatopia by the supplier;
(b) a supply of goods where the Commissioner is satisfied that the goods have been exported from Vatopia by the supplier;
(c) a supply of goods where the goods are not situated in Vatopia at the time of supply and are not to be entered into Vatopia for home consumption pursuant to the [Customs Act] by the supplier of the goods;
(d) a supply of goods under a rental agreement, charter party, or agreement for chartering, where the goods are used exclusively in an export country;
(e) a supply of goods in the course of repairing, renovating, modifying, or treating goods to which sub-paragraph (h)(ii) or (iv) applies and the goods supplied –
(i) are wrought into, affixed to, attached to, or otherwise form part of those other goods; or
(ii) being consumable goods, become unusable or worthless as a direct result of being used in that repair, renovation, modification, or treatment process;
(f) a supply of international transport services;
(g) a supply of services directly in connection with land, or any improvement thereto, situated outside Vatopia;
(h) a supply of services directly in respect of –
(i) movable property situated outside Vatopia at the time the services are rendered;
(ii) goods temporarily imported into Vatopia under [the exemptions in the Customs Act];
(iii) a supply of goods referred to in paragraphs (a) or (b) of the definition of "exported from Vatopia"; or
(iv) the repair, maintenance, cleaning, or reconditioning of a foreign-going aircraft;

---

[21] Alternatively, this paragraph can provide that the zero-rated items in this paragraph are zero-rated to the extent provided in regulations. Regulations then can define the scope of the zero-rated items. This alternative may be selected if the Ministry wants the flexibility to adjust the scope of the zero-rated items without going back to Parliament to amend the Act, especially if the Regulations must be put before Parliament.

(v) a supply of services directly to a non-resident who is not a taxable person, otherwise than through an agent or other person –

(i) comprising the handling, pilotage, salvage, or towage of a foreign-going aircraft while situated in Vatopia;

(ii) provided in connection with the operation or management of a foreign-going aircraft; or

(iii) comprising the storage, repair, maintenance, cleaning, management, or arranging the provision of a container temporarily imported under [. . . . of the Customs Act], or the arranging of such services;

(i) a supply of services to a non-resident who is not a taxable person comprising the arranging for the person of –

(i) a supply of goods referred to in paragraphs (a) and (b) of the definition of "exported from Vatopia";

(ii) a supply of services to which sub-paragraph (h)(iv) or (i) applies; or

(iii) the transport of goods, including ancillary transport services, within Vatopia;

(j) a supply of services comprising the repair, maintenance, cleaning, or reconditioning of a railway train operated by a non-resident who is not a taxable person;

(k) a supply of services physically rendered elsewhere than in Vatopia;

(l) a supply of services to a non-resident who is outside Vatopia at the time the services are supplied, other than a supply of services –

(i) directly in connection with immovable property situated in Vatopia;

(ii) directly in connection with movable property situated in Vatopia at the time the services are supplied unless the movable property is exported from Vatopia subsequent to the supply of services;

(iii) comprising the refraining from undertaking any taxable activity in Vatopia; or

(iv) comprising the tolerating of another person undertaking any taxable activity in Vatopia;

(m) a supply of services comprising –

(i) the filing, prosecution, granting, maintenance, transfer, assignment, licensing, or enforcement of any intellectual property rights for use outside Vatopia;

(ii) incidental services necessary for the supply of services referred to in sub-paragraph (i); or

(iii) the acceptance by a person of an obligation to refrain from pursuing or exercising in whole or part any intellectual property rights for use outside Vatopia; or

(n) a supply by a registered person to another registered person of a taxable activity, or part of a taxable activity, as a going concern, provided –

(i) sections 4(2) and 13(14) are satisfied; and

(ii) a notice in writing signed by the transferor and transferee is furnished to the Commissioner within [21] days after the supply takes place and such notice includes the details of the supply.

3. Paragraph 2 shall not apply in respect of any supply of goods which have been or will be re-imported into Vatopia by the supplier.

Schedule II Exempt Supplies for Purposes of Section 16

1. In this Schedule – "commercial rental establishment" means –

(a) accommodation in a hotel, motel, inn, boarding house, hostel, or similar establishment in which lodging is regularly or normally provided to five or more persons at a daily, weekly, monthly, or other periodic charge;

(b) accommodation in a house, flat, apartment, or room, other than accommodation in respect of which the provisions of paragraph (a) or (c) of this definition apply, which is regularly or systematically leased or held for lease as residential accommodation for continuous periods not exceeding [45] days in the case of each occupant of such house, flat, apartment, or room, if the total annual receipts and accruals from the lease thereof exceeded the amount specified in paragraph 7 of Schedule V to the Act or there are reasonable grounds for believing that such total annual receipts and accruals will exceed that amount;

(c) accommodation in a house, flat, apartment, room, caravan, houseboat, tent, or caravan or camping site which constitutes an asset, including a leased asset, of a business undertaking or a separately identifiable part of a business undertaking carried on by a person who –

(i) leases or holds for leasing as residential accommodation five or more houses, flats, apartments, rooms, caravans, houseboats, or caravan or camping sites in the course of such business undertaking;

(ii) derives total annual receipts and accruals from the leasing of all such houses, flats, apartments, rooms, caravans, houseboats, and caravan and camping sites which exceed the amount specified in paragraph 7 of Schedule V to the Act or there are reasonable grounds for believing that such total annual receipts and accruals will exceed that amount; and

(iii) regularly or normally leases or holds for lease as residential accommodation such houses, flats, apartments, rooms, caravans, houseboats, or caravan or camping sites for continuous periods not exceeding [45] days in the case of each occupant; or

(d) any other accommodation designated by the Minister by regulation to be a commercial rental establishment, but does not include, unless within paragraph (d) –

(e) accommodation in a boarding establishment or hostel operated by an employer solely or mainly for the benefit of the employees of such employer or of a related person of such employer or their dependents, provided such establishment or hostel is not operated for the purpose of making profits from such establishment or hostel for the employer or such related person;

(f) accommodation in a boarding establishment or hostel operated by a local authority otherwise than for the purpose of making profits from such establishment or hostel; or

(g) accommodation in a registered hospital, maternity home, nursing home, convalescent home, hospice, or clinic; "dwelling" means a building, premises, structure, or any other place, or any part thereof, used predominantly as a place of residence or abode of a natural person or which is intended for use as a place of residence or abode of a natural person, together with any appurtenances belonging thereto and enjoyed therewith, but does not include a commercial rental establishment; "education services" means education and hostel facilities for students and scholars provided by –

(i) a pre-primary, primary, or secondary school;

(ii) a technical college, community college, or university; or

(iii) an educational institution established for the promotion of adult education, vocational training, technical education, or the education or training of physically or mentally handicapped persons.

2. The following supplies are specified as exempt supplies for the purposes of section 16[22] –

---

[22] Alternatively, this paragraph can provide that the exempt items in this paragraph are exempt to the extent provided in regulations. Regulations then can define the scope of

(a) a supply of financial services to the extent provided in regulations issued by the Minister;[23]

(b) a supply of prescription drugs and medical services to the extent provided in regulations issued by the Minister;

(c) a supply of education services;

(d) a supply of –

   (i) accommodation in a dwelling –

      (a) under a lease or rental of the accommodation; or

      (b) where the supplier is the employer of the recipient, the recipient is entitled to occupy the accommodation as a benefit of his office or employment and his right thereto is limited to the period of his employment or the term of his or her office or a period agreed upon by the supplier and the recipient; or

   (ii) leasehold land by way of lease (not being a grant or sale of the lease of that land) to the extent that the subject land is used or is to be used for the principal purpose of accommodation in a dwelling erected or to be erected on that land;

(e) a supply of any goods or services by the State, a local authority, or an association not for gain where the consideration for the goods or services is nominal in amount or not intended to recover the cost of such goods or services.

Schedule III   Exempt Imports for Purposes of Section 17

1. An import of goods is an exempt import under section 17(a) if the goods are exempt from customs duty under the [Customs Act], unless the Minister provides otherwise by notice in the Gazette.

Schedule IV   Tax Invoices, Tax Credit Notes, and Tax Debit Notes for Purposes of Sections 32 and 33

(1) Except as the Commissioner may otherwise allow, a tax invoice as required by section 32(1) shall contain the following particulars –

(a) the words "tax invoice" in a prominent place;

(b) the name, address, and VAT registration number of the registered person making the supply;

(c) for a supply to a registered recipient, the name, address, and VAT registration number of the recipient of the supply;

(d) the individualised serial number and the date on which the tax invoice is issued;

(e) a description of the goods or services supplied;

(f) the quantity or volume of the goods or services supplied; and

(g) the total amount of the tax charged, the consideration for the supply, and the consideration including tax.

---

the exempt items. This alternative may be selected if the Ministry wants the flexibility to adjust the scope of the exempt items without going back to Parliament to amend the Act, especially if the Regulations must be put before Parliament.

[23] The scope of the exemption for financial services may vary widely. It may exempt a broad definition of financial intermediation services that includes credit card transactions, services to depositors and borrowers, services of brokers and dealers in securities, and life and casualty insurance, whether the services are provided for explicit or implicit fees. Alternatively, the exemption may be limited to financial intermediation services rendered for implicit fees, and tax all fee-based financial services (even if financial services are broadly defined). South Africa, Namibia, and Botswana tax all fee-based services. New Zealand was the pioneer in taxing casualty insurance.

(2) Except as the Commissioner may otherwise allow, a tax credit note as required by section 33(1) shall contain the following particulars –
   (a) the words "tax credit note" in a prominent place;
   (b) the name, address, and VAT registration number of the registered person making the supply;
   (c) the name, address, and VAT registration number of the recipient of the supply;
   (d) the date on which the tax credit note was issued;
   (e) the value of the supply shown on the tax invoice, the correct amount of the value of the supply, the difference between those two amounts, and the tax charged that relates to that difference;
   (f) a brief explanation of the circumstances giving rise to the issuing of the tax credit note; and
   (g) information sufficient to identify the taxable supply to which the tax credit note relates.

(3) Except as the Commissioner may otherwise allow, a tax debit note as required by section 33(3) shall contain the following particulars –
   (a) the words "tax debit note" in a prominent place;
   (b) the name, address, and VAT registration number of the registered person making the supply;
   (c) the name, address, and VAT registration number of the recipient of the supply;
   (d) the date on which the tax debit note was issued;
   (e) the value of the supply shown on the tax invoice, the correct amount of the value of the supply, the difference between those two amounts, and the tax that relates to that difference;
   (f) a brief explanation of the circumstances giving rise to the issuing of the tax debit note; and
   (g) information sufficient to identify the taxable supply to which the tax debit note relates.

Schedule V   Registration Threshold, Interest Rates, and Other Amounts for Purposes of Various Sections of the Act

1. For purposes of section 20(1)(a) and (b), the amount is [...] vatopians.
2. For purposes of section 31(1), the interest rate is [2 percent] per month or part thereof.
3. For purposes of section 32(2), the amount is [...] vatopians.
4. For purposes of section 45(7), the amount is [...] vatopians.
5. For purposes of section 46(1), the interest rate is [1 percent] simple interest per month or part thereof.
6. For purposes of section 47(1)(d), the amount of tax is [...] vatopians.
7. For purposes of Schedule II, sub-paragraphs (b) and (c)(ii) of the paragraph 1 definition of commercial rental establishment, the amount is [...] vatopians.

Schedule VI   Repeal of Laws and Interpretation for Purposes of Section 91

1. The [Sales Tax Act].

Index